Christi...

10 F

Hc

Moira

OF DIDCOT AND THE DEMON

OF DIDCOT AND THE DEMON

The Cricketing Times of Alan Gibson

Anthony Gibson

foreword by John Woodcock

FAIRFIELD BOOKS

Fairfield Books
17 George's Road, Bath BA1 6EY
Tel: 01225-335813

First published 2009

ISBN 978 0 9560702 5 8

Page design by Stephen Chalke
Jacket design by Rob Taylor

Printed and bound in Great Britain by
Midway Colour Print, Holt, Wiltshire

Contents

Each year consists of a two-page introduction by Anthony Gibson, followed by a selection of Alan Gibson's writing during that year.

Illustrations

We would like to thank the following for permission to reproduce photographs:

Alan Gibson's family, for all photographs of Alan Gibson.

Felicity Gibson, for The Star, High Littleton (page 283).

L.A. Summers, for Didcot Railway Station (page 283).

Ivan Ponting, for Tom Cartwright (page 91), Brian Close (two on page 199) and Colin Dredge (two on page 240).

Getty Images, for the photographs on pages 45, 123, 133, 161, 255, 285 and 313.

Popperfoto, for all remaining photographs except those on page 55 which appeared originally in *Playfair Cricket Monthly*.

Some of these Popperfoto photographs were taken by Bob Thomas, most by Bill Smith who worked for many years for *Playfair Cricket Monthly* and who died in 2006. The photograph on page 187, taken by Bob Thomas, features Bill Smith: the tall man second from the left in the front row.

We would especially like to thank Bob Thomas for the photographs he has contributed and for his help in working through the archive of Bill Smith's photographs to find so many good images for this book.

Note on Text

The articles and match reports were written mostly for *The Times* and *The Cricketer*.

Generally we have stuck to the text as reproduced in those publications, though a fair number of misprints and mis-transcriptions have had to be sorted out. Sometimes we have referred to Alan Gibson's notebooks for clarification.

Most mistakes were easy to spot: lines printed in the wrong order, 'differential' for 'deferential', 'High Middleton' for 'High Littleton' and so on.

But a mysterious description of an Essex batting performance, printed in *The Times* in 1978, almost survived undetected. 'They were captain Jack for a while,' Alan Gibson had apparently written of their batting. The question arose during proof-reading: 'Should captain take a capital C?' And this led to a second question: 'Who is Captain Jack, anyway?' It was only then that the penny dropped. Somebody in the office had misheard the sentence. They were not 'Captain Jack' but 'kept in check.'

The Observer once made a similar mistake with a report submitted from Lord's by Christopher Wordsworth. Middlesex and their opponents were due to play the following week in a one-day final, and he rang in the sentence: 'The two teams will appear next Saturday at the self-same arena.' This appeared in print as 'The two teams will appear next Saturday at the Selsey Marina.'

It is to be hoped that no such howlers have survived into the pages of this book.

Publisher's Introduction

I was in the Writing Room at Lord's, for the launch of John Barclay's book *Life Beyond The Airing Cupboard*, when I got into conversation with Marcus Williams of *The Times*. A collection of the writings of JM Kilburn, the one-time cricket correspondent of the *Yorkshire Post*, had just come out, and it had set me thinking.

"The book I'd really like to publish," I said above the din of the room, "is a collection of Alan Gibson's writing. His articles and match reports. They're the very best."

"It's funny you should say that," Marcus responded. "His son's just written to us, with exactly that idea."

"And what have you replied?" I asked anxiously. "Are you going ahead with it?"

"No, sadly we're not. But we did tell him we'd look out for a publisher for him."

It was not many days later that Anthony was sitting in our kitchen. I found that my idea of what the book should be accorded closely with his, but he proposed an added dimension: he would write some biographical passages about his father.

The book is a collection of the writings of Alan Gibson between 1967 and 1986, mostly for *The Times* but also for *The Cricketer* magazine. There are even a few unpublished gems recovered from his notebooks.

It is arranged chronologically, each year prefaced by a two-page introduction by Anthony, outlining the events of that year: both on the cricket field and in his father's life. So the book can be read at two levels: a portrait of English cricket as it evolved over twenty years, and an intimate study of a writer, who develops a wonderfully stylish and humorous voice all his own, then suffers a rapid and tragic decline. The two strands of the book make a fascinating combination, and Anthony's account of his father, loving but clear-eyed, has a poignant warmth that raises the book far above what I had in mind when I spoke to Marcus Williams.

We have had so much material from which to choose. We avoided drawing from his published books, concentrating instead on the day-to-day match reports, along with a sprinkling of longer magazine and newspaper articles. Often we have included whole matches, to capture the delightful rhythm of his reports, but we have also collected up pages of brief extracts, be they on the tail-end batting of Frome's Colin Dredge or the dreadfulness of the Basingstoke town centre.

There has been much hard labour in putting these pages together, but I have enjoyed myself immensely. Sometimes, as I have typed Alan's prose, I have been unable to go on for the tears of laughter in my eyes. Like all the best writers he creates his own imaginative universe, and the quirkiness of it all is counterpointed so beautifully by the formality of his sentences and the great breadth of literary and classical allusions.

Yes, of course, as I think he knew deep down, Alan Gibson wasted his great talent in writing about the mundane world of English county cricket – but oh! what joy he gave! How I wish today's sports editors would find space for a successor.

Anthony has done his father proud with this book. I hope you have as much pleasure reading it as I have had in preparing it for publication.

Stephen Chalke

Foreword by John Woodcock

Throughout the 20 years for which Alan Gibson wrote for *The Times*, I was their Cricket Correspondent and therefore, nominally, his senior partner. While I wrote about the cricket, Alan was usually elsewhere writing about a day *at* the cricket, which he did with a wit and learning enjoyed as much by the players as by his countless other readers. I can truthfully say that I basked in his reflected glory.

He saw cricketers (and barmaids, too, for that matter) not as technicians but as characters, picking out his favourites and making celebrities of them in his jocular way. So long as they were whole-hearted it didn't greatly matter how well they bowled or batted, though the barmaids, such as the exemplary GRIP (glorious red-headed imperturbable Pamela) from the Hammond Bar at Bristol, needed to pull their weight as it were.

Colin Dredge (the Demon of Frome) and Robin Jackman (the Shoreditch Sparrow) were two bowlers to be vested with an iconic, albeit ironic, status by Alan's adoption of them. As for the then station-master at Didcot, he can never have known what to expect from *The Times* of a summer's morning. Being where Alan changed trains and sometimes missed a connection on his way, say, to The Parks at Oxford, Didcot's station became as notorious as Crewe's. It was all a part of the drift of a Gibson piece.

To say that the Sports Editor of *The Times* was unwavering in his support of Alan would be wide of the mark. It hardly helped that Alan's copy was known to arrive late and didn't always tally with the scorecard: in a newspaper office readability without reliability, especially with an edition to catch, causes headaches. What is a good laugh for some can appear more as flippancy to others, and that, too, was a factor in the relationship, anyway until his first Sports Editor, the most estimable of professionals, went to spend a weekend with his son, then an exhibitioner at Oxford. As you may imagine, the unsolicited observation that "when Alan Gibson comes to cover a match in The Parks you have to queue to read *The Times* in the JCR next morning" had altogether favourable consequences.

Like Neville Cardus before him, Alan used the press box as much as a left-luggage office as a place of work. Neville would go off in search of an audience and Alan of a drink. Although the two of them never worked together or came to know each other well, Cardus's *Good Days* was described by Alan as his "most significant experience in cricket reading." That, and his eloquence and love of the pulpit, made him the natural choice to speak on behalf of the cricket world at Sir Neville's Memorial Service at St Paul's, Covent Garden which, in his Oxford hood and gown, he did beautifully. Wendy Hiller, with her reading of Francis Thompson's *At Lord's*, and Dame Flora Robson, who read *Shall I Compare Thee to a Summer's Day*, also played a part in a service "brimming with joyous music and amusing talk", as Michael Henderson put it.

But it was not so much in the style of Cardus that Alan "illuminated the craft of cricket writing" (his own Covent Garden tribute to Neville) as of Raymond Robertson-Glasgow, the much-loved 'Crusoe'. Alan and 'Crusoe' had a lightness of touch and generosity of spirit which entirely belied the depression with which they so cruelly and regularly wrestled. Another similarly afflicted was Alan Ross, 'Crusoe's' successor as Cricket Correspondent of *The Observer* and no less gifted as a writer on the game. But of the three of them only Alan was a broadcaster as well, and a brilliant one too – conversational, extraordinarily knowledgeable and with a scholar's recall.

The range of the programmes in which he took part – *Round Britain Quiz*, *Good Morning* (a distant forerunner of *Today* on Radio 4) and *Sunday Half Hour* among them – tells something of his virtuosity. As a cricket commentator, as distinct from a summariser, Alan alone has been in the class of John Arlott. For power of description, ingeniousness and the use of language, these two in the same *Test Match Special* team made a remarkable pair. They could have discoursed with humour and distinction on almost any subject under the sun. Alan may not have been indulged, I think, quite to the extent that John was when it came to having a glass of something in the commentary box, but that was an internal matter. He should have been more careful than he was in that direction and he knew it, and, sadly, it cost listeners to cricket many a diverting hour.

Much later, in the hope of keeping him going, I tried to persuade him to bring HS Altham and EW Swanton's *History of Cricket* up to date. Jim Swanton was keen on the idea and no one could possibly have done it better. Alan's book, on the captains of England, is wonderfully good, and Swanton's second volume of *The History of Cricket* had ended in 1961, leaving years to be covered which Alan would have remembered so well. But the will to work had gone, and desolation was setting in.

Alan had been the warmest of friends, the most loyal of colleagues and the jolliest of hosts when his second marriage, to Rosie, was still afloat. Many who knew little or nothing about cricket took *The Times* just to read his pieces, and to have a selection of them so well and affectionately assembled makes a serious and valuable addition to the literature of the game. Devotees, cricket historians and undergraduates alike have been done a favour, and I am fairly sure Alan himself, in whatever mood, would have been quietly delighted.

Before The Times

Alan, with his parents, at Ilkley

Alan Gibson was born in Sheffield on May 28, 1923. His father Norman was the Baptist Minister at Attercliffe and his mother Jenny was equally strong in her dissenting faith. Norman came from a working class family of Durham miners, the third of twelve children, having taken himself off to theological college after service in the First World War; Jenny was the youngest (and frailest) of the eight children produced by William Welch, a South Shields sea-farer sufficiently affluent to be able to employ a live-in servant, and his wife Elizabeth. The Gibsons lived frugally, but comfortably enough, and in strict compliance with nonconformist principles.

Both remained lifelong teetotallers. However, it was Alan's mother who was the stricter in her abhorrence of intemperance. It was undoubtedly her influence that persuaded the young Alan sometimes to run past any pub they encountered on their walks together holding his nose, so as not to be tempted by the sinful smell of drink. It was said that this was, at least in part, a reaction against his mother's experiences in her youth, surrounded by hard-drinking seamen. It may well be conjectured that the young Gibson's eventual enthusiasm for strong drink was similarly a reaction against his upbringing.

But that was far into the future. Alan's childhood was a happy one. Norman and Jenny may have been dry-as-dust Baptists, but they were loving parents, as devoted to their son as they were to each other. There was a little girl, Marjorie, but she was carried off by infant gastro-enteritis at the age of just nine months in 1930, so to all intents and purposes, Alan was an only child, and was doted on as such.

I have no personal memory of my father's father, for he died when I was only one, but he appears to have been a genuinely good man, deeply loved by his nonconformist flocks at Attercliffe, Ilkley, Leyton, Falmouth and, finally, Totnes. He seems to have responded to the many adversities that he encountered in life, from being sent down the mines at the age of 12, through being gassed in the first world war, to the cancer that carried him off at the age of just 59, not merely phlegmatically, but joyfully, as if they had been purposely sent by God to test him, in challenges which he delighted in facing. Of the two parents, it may have been the rather pious Jenny who appeared the more saintly, but it was unquestionably Norman who was the true saint, as Alan was to acknowledge, in his autobiography *A Mingled Yarn.*

History does not relate whether or with what success Norman Gibson played the game of cricket. It may well have been that his playing career was cut short by the after effects of his wartime gassing, which was to affect his eyesight and his general health for the rest of his life. But he was undoubtedly an enthusiastic follower of the game – of Yorkshire in particular – and his enthusiasm soon rubbed off on his young son. Alan liked to claim that his earliest memories of cricket were when the family had moved to Ilkley. In *Growing Up With Cricket*, he recalls – no doubt with a touch of poetic licence, given that he was probably less then five at the time – how 'at the end of morning service, as we gathered by the doors for a chat…my father's sermon was less discussed than how Yorkshire were doing. The biggest stir I can remember was when Herbert Sutcliffe came to play in a match there.'

Father and son

But it was when the family moved to Leyton, in 1930, that his interest both in cricket and in journalism was truly kindled. By great good fortune, the house in which they lived over-looked what was then the Essex County Cricket Ground. Over the next nine years, either from the balcony of the house or on the ground itself, the young Gibson was able to watch many of the great players of the day: men like Hobbs, Sandham, Hammond, Larwood and even George Gunn, who had made his debut as a first class player as far back as 1902.

However, the most vivid memory, which he was to recall in his writings and broadcasts on many an occasion in the future, was watching Sutcliffe and Holmes – Yorkshiremen like himself – compiling their record-breaking opening partnership of 555 in June 1932. He wrote about it in his 1985 book *Growing Up With Cricket*:

> At the end of the first day – I do not have to look this up – Yorkshire had scored 423 for no wicket. I remember the swift, silent running between the wickets (very different from modern Yorkshire practice) and the huge pull for six to mid-wicket with which Sutcliffe reached his 150.

> Next morning I raced back from school again. No wicket had fallen. It was about one o'clock that the 555 was reached (the previous record had been 554, made by two other Yorkshiremen, Brown and Tunnicliffe, in 1898). The cheering was rapturous, none more than mine. There was a big crowd by now, many Yorkshiremen having travelled south during the night. I saw Holmes and Sutcliffe stride down the pitch towards each other, majestically, and shake hands. Life, I felt, had not anything to show more fair, though I did not put it that way; and I am not sure that it has had.

Alan was something of an infant prodigy. He made his debut in journalism at the age of roughly nine, as editor of his class magazine at Farmer Road Elementary School, Leyton. The magazine was entitled – inevitably, I suppose – The Farmer Weekly, and the young Gibson took to the task of writing and producing it each week with boundless zeal and enthusiasm. It included, of course, "Our Sports Notes", written by Left Half, of which this report on the football matches of September 27th 1932 is the only surviving example:

> The twenty-sevenths matches were very successful. For the Green v Yellow match a draw was the fairest result, but an error by T. Davis, who headed through his own goal off Defries' corner, in the final minute, spoilt Yellow's chances. Apart from this Davis played a thoroughly sound game.
> Blue deserved to beat Red, although Pate showed up well in goal for the losers. Watts played a fine game at centre-forward. In the Final game a terrific fight ensued, Slee played well in goal for Blue, Watts was again brilliant. Once Watts was nearly through, but he was brought to a full stop by Eagle. It will be interesting to note that on Friday, Class Four go to Ive Farm with Mr Dreghorn, to play Football. We all hope it will be a fine day.

However, despite his obvious ability, Alan did not seem to be doing particularly well when he moved on to Sir George Monoux Grammar School in 1935, and his parents took what must have been the very difficult decision to send him away to public school. Taunton School was chosen, not least because it offered modestly reduced fees for the sons of nonconformist ministers. The decision was difficult on two counts: first, because it must have involved a huge financial sacrifice, for the Gibsons were far from well off; and second, because Alan hated the idea. So much did he hate it, in fact, that he tried to run away on no fewer than three occasions in his first year, and once even ran away from home, when the time came to go back to school.

He settled down eventually, and by the late 1930s his letters home were brimming with excitement and enthusiasm about almost every aspect of public school life, from the quality of the sermons to the performance of the school first XV. Those that survive certainly do not read as if they were written by a profoundly miserable, homesick young man, but then Alan always tended to put a brave face on his experiences, when relating them to a wider audience. There is plenty of rugby in the surviving letters, but I have been able to find only one account of a cricket match, in a letter dated May 30, 1939. Here it is, exactly as he wrote it:

Dear Mum and Dad,

Another terrific century from H.P. Fear – a hurricane 40 odd from Gerrard – a fighting 60 from Evans to pull the game round and force a draw – those were the salient features of the Old Boys Match yesterday. They had an overwhelmingly strong team, including Fear, who made 114 against us on Saturday, 'Doc' Marshall, R.A. Gerrard, M.A.L. Williams and P.M. Bennett. Batting first on a plum wicket, they simply slammed the college bowling. Fear made 119 not out and Gerrard 49. They declared at 237 for 3.

Henderson went for 6 and Pennington for 8 when the college batted. The outlook was gloomy. Hildreth and Evans held the fort. Hildreth, batting beautifully, was unlucky to be caught for 32. Robinson M.F. and Evans, who put on 97 against Taunton, now came together with a big stand to make us safe from defeat. Evans' 60 was a grand effort. Fuggel, back in the team instead of C.H.V. Robinson, and M. Robinson, played out time. 'Robbie' made 41 and Fuggel 20 odd. With the score 178 for 4, the college batting had turned up trumps, in spite of the undeniable weakness of the bowling.

Altogether, six elevens played six old boys elevens. To my surprise, I was picked for the sixth, and to my even greater surprise, was put in first. My runs were not legion – 0, to be precise – but as over half the side made exactly the same, I was not too deeply disgraced. We were beaten to a cocked hat, fielding all afternoon in a blazing sun, but I fielded keenly and was commended on my keenness at the end of the game. I had a bowl but didn't get a wicket, though I kept the score down at a time when we were being slammed all over the show. Afterwards, we had tea on the terrace. Our game was over by 4, so I saw a good bit of the first XI match.

I am back in House now as all the fellows have returned. There was down-town leave, so Pudner and I went and saw a couple of hours of the Somerset v Glo'ster match. I treated him, as it was near my birthday.

I have now received a white sweater from Auntie Ethel and cards from Mrs. H. and Miss Florie.

We have been cast into the heights of joy (some of us!) on hearing of Yorks' great win over Lancs. "La rose blanche" for ever!

I remain, your ever-loving son, Alan.

There writes the would-be sports reporter! The construction – with all the key details in the first paragraph – the phraseology and the delightful inclusion of almost every player's full set of initials speak of a boy who had made a thorough study, entirely off his own bat, as it were, of the art of sports writing. Those two terse sentences – 'The outlook was gloomy. Hildreth and Evans held the fort.' – perfectly capture not just the bare facts of the matter, but also what must have been the mood of the game at the time. And as a punchy summary of the key features of the match, the first paragraph could hardly be improved upon. It is the letter of a boy who had equipped himself to write about sport for a living, even if, at that stage, when he was still planning to follow his father into the church, such a career could have been was no more than an idle dream.

The letter may also serve as confirmation that Alan Gibson's ability in writing about cricket was never matched when it came to playing the game. I find it hard at this distance to assess his ability, as he gave up playing the game when I was only very young, but he never claimed to be anything more than an average club player, bowling gentle medium pace and batting halfway down the order. However, that particular duck obviously rankled. Almost 50 years later, in *Growing up with Cricket*, he was to describe his dismissal – LBW – as 'an appalling decision, given by a nervous schoolboy umpire at the behest of a very large, red-faced and loud-voiced Old Boy, who had not taken a wicket in many years.'

Alan's journalistic ability did not go unrecognised, for he became Editor of the school magazine, *The Tauntonian*, and wrote reports of school rugby and cricket matches, some of which were submitted to *The Times*, and at least one of which, on Taunton School XV's defeat by the Britannia Royal Naval College in November 1941, was printed. He also became the official scorer for the school first XI and spent a glorious final summer term, following and recording their progress across the West Country.

Then, in October 1942, it was up to The Queen's College Oxford, to read history. There was, of course, a war on, and Alan's university career was interrupted by two distinctly unheroic years in the army, before he was invalided out on account of a weak chest. Nonetheless, in his two spells of two years, he made a considerable mark, being elected President of the Oxford Union, President of the Oxford University Liberal Club, taking first class honours in modern history and being appointed cricket correspondent of the University magazine, *Isis*. His style had evolved since his schooldays, although judging by this extract from his report of how the great New Zealand left-hander, Martin Donnelly (who remained one of his greatest cricketing heroes) saved a match for the University against Lancashire, he was still capable of turning a cliché with the best of them:

> We watched with bated breath while Roberts wheeled up over after tempting over outside the off-stump. Donnelly was proof against his wiles. Oxford must not lose the match; and that meant, in effect, that he must not get out. Now and then, a loose ball – or one that could reasonably be pretended to be such – went to the boundary. The runs came along at a rate slightly faster than the normal scoring rate in first class cricket – that is to say, about half as fast as Donnelly usually makes them. It was a remarkable example of calculated restraint – the one attribute of batsmanship that we have sometimes thought he lacked. And it was never dull.

He also managed to play a fair amount of cricket, much of it for two casual sides, the Queen's Imperial Quondams, who played evening matches against some of the local village sides, and the Oxford Crocodiles, who went on boozy summer tours, which he recalled, many years later, in *The Times*:

It was during his second spell at Oxford that Alan Gibson met my mother, Olwen Thomas, who was reading English at Westfield College, part of the University of London, but whose undergraduates had been sent to Oxford to escape the blitz. They made a handsome couple: Alan the fiery intellectual – tall, slightly wild, with a shock of dark hair; Olwen the classic Welsh beauty – fair skinned, dark-eyed, black hair tumbling onto her shoulders.

At the Oxford Union

In 1948, when he finally came down from Oxford, he got a job with the University of Exeter as an extra-mural lecturer in the South Hams, and they married. I appeared about a year later, in May 1949. By this time, his parents had moved from Falmouth, where they had spent five happy years, to Totnes, and the extended family lived in the large and rather ugly Edwardian manse, overlooking the station.

It was not an entirely happy arrangement, by any means, for – much to his mother's disapproval – Alan had discovered beer at Oxford and had taken to it with relish, and mother and daughter-in-law weren't exactly soulmates, either. But the domestic tensions did not inhibit what was a blossoming career. From his schoolboy days, when he would provide running commentaries on the Test matches that he played out for days on the sitting room carpet, using his own improved variation of the cricketing game, Stumpz, Alan had dreamed of broadcasting on cricket. In 1948, he wrote to Frank Gillard, the controller of the BBC's then West Region, suggesting himself as a cricket commentator. He was given an audition when the Australian touring side played Somerset at Taunton, with John Arlott – already a Test match commentator – and Somerset's own inimitable Bill Andrews, sitting alongside. It must have been a nerve-racking experience, but he evidently did well enough, for he became a regular reporter for Sport in the West, every Saturday evening, and the following year was offered a job on the staff of the BBC, as a General Programme Assistant, based in Plymouth.

Alan, Olwen and a very young Anthony at Fleetwood House, Totnes, 1949

Despite the early death of his father, from cancer, in February 1950, there followed some of the happiest years of his life. He proved himself to be a natural broadcaster: fluent, vivid, erudite and often very funny. The many scripts which survive from those days cover a bewildering range of subjects, from the anniversaries of Devonshire sea-dogs, through celebrated local murder cases, to hymns and natural history. There was also a limited amount of sport, although as a producer, on the staff of the BBC, he was no longer able to provide commentaries or match reports, except on an occasional basis when there was no-one else available.

By 1955, he felt sufficiently confident of his abilities and prospects, not least as a cricket commentator, to take the plunge of leaving the BBC staff and going freelance. In those days, cricket commentary featured prominently in the BBC West of England Home Service's summer output, and with John Arlott being frequently away on Test Match duty, Alan found himself doing more and more commentary. Initially, this was confined to matches involving the region's three county sides – Somerset, Gloucestershire and Hampshire – but as he became better known, so invitations began to arrive from other BBC regions. In the winter, he commentated on rugby. Mostly, again, the county games, which were hugely important in the West Country in those days, although from 1959 onwards, he was also asked to cover internationals and other big occasions, like the Varsity Match.

He was now a broadcaster of many parts. The Saturday morning record request programme, *Good Morning*, that he co-presented with Derek Jones – Alan from Plymouth, Derek from Bristol – became a regional institution. Besides that, he was a regular on programmes like *Any Questions*, *Housewives Choice*, *Sunday Half Hour* and, as a testament to the depth of his all-round knowledge, *Round Britain Quiz*. Against that background, it was slightly surprising that it wasn't until 1962 that he received the invitation that he'd craved since boyhood, to become a member of the BBC's Test match commentary team, alongside the likes of John Arlott and Rex Alston, for the series against Pakistan.

The young BBC commentator

He was a success; his relaxed, almost conversational style blending well with Arlott's rough-hewn warmth, and Alston's rather clipped, old-fashioned approach. Fortune was on his side as well. The following year, for the Lord's Test against the West Indies, the luck of the rota dictated that it was Alan Gibson who had the microphone for the final frantic over of one of the greatest Tests ever played. Any one of four results was possible as Wes Hall walked back the 35 yards to his mark to bowl. England needed 8 to win, and West Indies two wickets, one of them that of Colin Cowdrey, his left wrist broken by a ball from Hall earlier in the innings. Two singles were scored off the first three balls; Shackleton was run out by Worrell off the fourth, leaving England's number 11, David Allen, to face the two final balls, with the injured Cowdrey mercifully at the non-striker's end.

In *I Was There*, a compilation of famous sporting moments, published in 1966, Alan recalled the excitement and tension of the moment:

> Twice more Hall thundered to the wicket and bowled. Twice Allen, his whole body seeming to shudder from the impact, brought down his bat, keeping the thunderbolt out from the stumps. Twice, great sighs of emotion came from the crowd. It was over. The match was drawn.

However, as so often in his life, professional success was counter-pointed by private turmoil. For all his apparent self-confidence, he was a highly strung man who lived on his nerves and, as he admitted in *A Mingled Yarn*, he found commentary an increasing strain:

> The tension builds up over the years; sleep is the first thing to go. This is when you begin to drink too much and reach for the barbiturates too often.

By the late 1950s, his drinking was becoming a real problem; not so much with his broadcasting – for he could remain lucid after imbibing volumes of alcohol that would have rendered lesser men speechless - as with his marriage. He became increasingly difficult to live with, often arriving home late, drunk and in a towering rage. He treated the drink-driving laws, such as they were, with a fine contempt, and twice contrived to drive his car into the bridge at Looe when completely blotto. On the first occasion, he somehow talked his way out of it. But from the second, in the autumn of 1963, there was no escape. He was prosecuted by the Police and banned from driving. His response was typical – to make a half-hearted attempt at suicide, not for the first or the last time. For that, he was sectioned, and he spent the Christmas of 1963, at the height of his fame, in Moorhaven Mental Hospital at Bittaford in South Devon. He wrote movingly, if not entirely honestly, of the experience in *A Mingled Yarn*. I remember very clearly the humiliation, for that is what it felt like, of visiting him with my mother and younger brother on Christmas Day. He seemed consumed with self-pity. Not many months later, the divorce came through and he moved to a flat in Clifton in Bristol, which was that much nearer the BBC's centre of gravity.

It would probably be fair to describe Alan Gibson as a mild schizophrenic, and he was undoubtedly manic depressive. Almost every aspect of his character had its exact opposite somewhere else in his psyche. He could be perfectly charming – and an utter bastard. He was an intensely sociable man – much given to condemning people whom he hardly new as 'bloody fools' on the flimsiest of evidence. He could moralise about the sins of the flesh with all the fervour of a dissenting preacher – and then go out drinking and womanising. He could be generous to a fault – and vicious to a degree. He was highly self-motivated – yet his problems were always someone else's fault. He was devoted to his wives and children – and frequently made their lives a misery.

What was not in doubt was the depth or strength of his intellect or his complete command of the English language. He was a true polymath, blessed with a remarkable memory. Not only was he a voracious reader, with tastes ranging from Billy Bunter, through science fiction, to the romantic poets, but he could remember details and plots, sometimes from even minor books, read decades previously. He claimed to have memorised the entirety of Milton's *Lycidas* whilst in the sixth form at school, and I don't doubt it for a moment. When he used quotations in his *Times* cricket reports he did so entirely from memory.

I suppose it could be argued that he was almost *too* blessed with intellectual gifts. By the age of 40, he was a multi-faceted broadcaster, a cricket and rugby reporter for the national press, a prominent Liberal politician, who had come second at Falmouth-Camborne in the 1959 general election, a scriptwriter, playwright, radio panellist, occasional television performer and a most impressive preacher. He could turn his hand to so many different subjects – be so many different people – dominate the conversation in so many different areas – that he never quite fixed on what his central purpose in life was and never really derived much satisfaction from his achievements, perhaps because he knew that they were only a small part of what he was capable of.

One of the many strings to his bow that really did provide satisfaction was writing scripts for the BBC Natural History unit, which was based, then as now, in Bristol, just down the road from where he was living in Clifton. Despite continuing health problems, which included acutely painful bouts of neuritis in his feet, work of all descriptions kept flowing in, and by 1966 he was working on a major radio adaptation of Malory's *Morte d'Arthur*. It was a daunting task – a challenge for even Alan's intellectual capacity and gift for words. It was certainly not the sort of the thing, as he no doubt reflected at the time, that you would find most 'ordinary' Test match commentators becoming involved in, with the possible exception of John Arlott, of course.

It was also at this time that he met the woman who was to become his second wife. Rosemary King, as she then was, worked in the BBC's Features Department. She was 28, fifteen years younger than Alan, and strikingly attractive, with big, dark, soulful eyes. Their wedding, in December 1966, was marked by a series of minor disasters: first, on the day before, Alan's trousers fell down on Waterloo station, as he was waving off his bride to be to stay with her parents at Croydon; then they left Rosie's case behind at Waterloo; and finally, when they arrived at Bournemouth, for the first stage of what was intended as a busman's honeymoon, following the Australian rugby tourists, Alan tripped over the carpet in their hotel room and broke his ankle!

It may not have been the most auspicious of starts to a marriage, and things may not eventually have turned out terribly happily, but getting married for a second time was unquestionably the saving of Alan Gibson. It gave him a new lease of life. A few months later, *The Times* was to give him what became almost a new career.

1967

1967 was a good year for Alan Gibson. He was happily re-married, I had saved him half of the school fees bill by, rather unexpectedly, winning an open exhibition to Queen's at Oxford so that I didn't have to stay on at Monkton Combe to re-take my exams, and he began reporting cricket regularly for *The Times*. He had contributed to national newspapers before, most often on rugby for the *Sunday Telegraph*, and he was, of course, an established Test match commentator for the BBC. But this was his first season as a regular on the county circuit and he undoubtedly enjoyed it.

His very first match report for *The Times* was of the third day of Derbyshire's nine wicket victory over Leicestershire at Derby on May 1, and he doesn't seem to have had much of an eye on posterity when he wrote in his opening paragraph: 'This may be remembered as Derbyshire's first championship win at their headquarters for five years. It will not be remembered for much else.' From Derby he travelled down to Oxford, for another third day, with the University holding out for a draw with Sussex. It evoked memories of the last time he had reported from the Parks, as the cricket correspondent of *Isis*.

1967 was a memorable year in many respects. Harold Wilson's 'technological revolution' was at full heat, Israel routed her opponents in the Six Day War, the Torrey Canyon disaster left Cornwall's coastline encrusted with crude oil. It was also, of course, 'the summer of love'. Not that that would have interested Alan in the slightest; when he wasn't oblivious to popular culture, he was loftily contemptuous of it. But one thing the year did not bring forth was a vintage cricket season.

The tourists were India and Pakistan, each with three Tests. Both showed tremendous potential: India with their spinners and Pakistan with fine stroke players like Mushtaq Mohammad and Asif Iqbal. But neither was strong enough overall to pose much of a threat to a powerful and experienced England side, pugnaciously captained by Brian Close. Alan did, of course, get to see a lot of both touring sides, but from the BBC commentary box rather than the press box. In those days, county matches against touring sides still counted for something, and were invariably covered for *The Times* by the cricket correspondent, John Woodcock.

A new points scoring system had been introduced for the county championship, with eight points for a win, plus four for a first innings lead and two for a draw. The incentive to settle for six points for a first innings lead in a drawn game was obvious, especially in May and early June, when the weather was atrocious.

Alan was at Taunton in early May for Somerset's match against Hampshire, one of very few in which the ageless Bill Alley failed to play a decisive part for Somerset. The 'astonishing' Alley, as he was described by *Wisden*, headed both the batting and the bowling averages for Somerset and played throughout the season with a zest and enthusiasm of a man half his age – whatever that was! He was profiled by Alan for *The Times* in May.

The championship quickly developed into a three-horse race involving the reigning champions, Yorkshire, an experienced Kent side and outsiders Leicestershire, who were inspired by Tony Lock's ebullient captaincy. Yorkshire, of course, were captained by Close, who sparked the controversy of the season – which was to cost him the captaincy for the winter tour to the West Indies – with the time-wasting tactics that denied Warwickshire a deserved win when the two sides met at Edgbaston in August. Mind you, the over-rate for which Close was roundly condemned – 24 in the last

Tests
England
beat India
3-0
England
beat Pakistan
2-0, with 1 draw

Championship
1 Yorkshire
2 Kent
3 Leicestershire
4 Surrey
5 Worcestershire
6 Derbyshire

Gillette Cup Final
Kent
beat Somerset

Most first-class runs
1 C.A. Milton
2 J.H. Edrich
3 K.F. Barrington

Most first-class wickets
1 T.W. Cartwright
2 D.L. Underwood
3 G.A.R. Lock

hour and forty minutes, or 14.7 per hour – would be regarded as positively sprightly by today's standards.

However, had there been an award for the most unlikely cricketing feat of the season it would undoubtedly have gone to Tony Lewis, for his performance in Glamorgan's match against Somerset at Neath on July 7. Alan missed the first day, but was there for the climax when, with Somerset seemingly holding out comfortably for a draw, Lewis – who was having a terrible season with the bat – put himself on to bowl his very occasional leg-breaks, and promptly took the last three wickets for 18 runs!

As one of the more junior the members of *The Times*' cricket-writing team, Alan spent a lot of the summer criss-crossing the country, reporting on bits and pieces of matches as the sports editor's whim and his other commitments dictated. Memorable days were relatively few and far between, although Roy Marshall's 160 against Northamptonshire was a real tour de force. The weather was fine for the second half of the season and, as the pitches got flatter and flatter, so more and more games turned into dour struggles for first innings points. At Worcester, reporting on the third day of a drawn game with Derbyshire, Alan observed that the approach of the Derbyshire openers did not suggest any match-winning intent. 'Why quarrel with six points? I have seen parts of four county matches in the past five days and every one of them has been dominated by those six points for a first-innings lead in a drawn match.'

Alan, Rosie and Adam at Queen's Court, Clifton, Christmas 1967

By August, only a handful of points separated Kent, Leicestershire and Yorkshire at the top of the table. Alan followed the three teams: to Lord's, Bradford, Cardiff, Dover and Leicester. 'If an award could be given to the side which has made the most of its talents this season,' he wrote, 'Leicestershire would win it by a street. The players would unite in giving the chief credit of this to Lock.'

Kent still had the chance of the double when they beat Somerset in a close, tense Gilllette Cup final on September 2 but it was, for the second successive year, to be Yorkshire's championship

For Alan Gibson, the end of the season meant a much-needed holiday, at his beloved Porthminster Hotel in St. Ives, with Rosie, who by now was six months pregnant. On November 30 she produced a fine baby boy, whom they called Adam, after the line in the hymn *Praise to the Holiest in the Height* which reads 'Adam to the fight and to the rescue came'. The new baby added to the financial pressures, and it was at this point that Alan's career nearly took a very different turn. Seeking the security of a regular salary, he applied for a job with the publisher Paul Hamlyn, and was offered it – but at a salary £200 less than the £2000 that he and Rosie had agreed was the minimum he should accept.. One can but wonder how different his life might have turned out to be, for better or for worse, had Hamlyn's been just slightly more generous. At any event, a momentous year was brought to an appropriately happy conclusion, with a Boxing Day match at Downend, in aid of the benefit year of David Smith, the Gloucestershire fast bowler.

MAY: Extracts from his first three days at cricket 1967

Derby on Monday

DERBY: Derbyshire v Leicestershire

This may be remembered as Derbyshire's first championship win at their headquarters for nearly five years. It will not be remembered for much else. From first to last the scoring rate was only a little above two runs an over.

... Black clouds piled up, and at a quarter to one the players disappeared into the pavilion in gloom, followed by a thick sleet near enough to snow to satisfy a journalist's conscience.

... Derbyshire needed 57 with more than two hours to go, but the threat of rain was always at their shoulder and they batted in a light against which in different circumstances there would certainly have been an appeal.

Oxford on Tuesday

OXFORD: Oxford University v Surrey

As one who began his connexions with journalism as cricket correspondent of "Isis", there can be no more delightful place than The Parks in May – provided that the weather is good and the University plays well. These *desiderata* were at least partially supplied.

The sun shone brightly, though there were clouds about and a sharp wind. The Oxford batting was of an equally fitful quality, but in the end proved sufficiently resolute to save the match.

Taunton on Wednesday

TAUNTON: Somerset v Hampshire

"Farmers rue unkindly May," says the ballad, but not so much as cricketers have had cause to do so far this year. There was some early, unconvincing sunshine which soon yielded to a cold south-wester, bringing with it increasingly heavy rain. There was play until luncheon, and two brief spells in the afternoon, but nothing after half-past-three. By six o'clock the captains, mercifully and sensibly, decided that no more could be done.

Nevertheless, such play as we had was lively and well contested. Marshall won the toss, decided to risk the early hazards which we associate with the Taunton pitch, and Hampshire lost two quick wickets. Reed was bowled off-stump in Rumsey's first over. Rumsey worked up a reasonable pace, although his fielding was a shade elephantine, and it was difficult to believe all those reliable reports that he has lost weight.

JULY: Hampshire v Northamptonshire at Portsmouth (first day)

Marshall's mastery

PORTSMOUTH: Hampshire have scored 352 for seven wickets in their first innings against Northamptonshire

Where does R.E. Marshall stand in the batting hierarchy of cricket? Because of his brief international career, because of his inability to resist a challenge, posterity may not rate him as highly as he deserves, which is surely among the best half-dozen of his era.

A few years ago the cricket correspondent of this newspaper suggested that if Marshall disciplined his exuberance a little, he might score 5,000 runs in a season. After yesterday the Northamptonshire side, muscles aching and palms stinging, would probably agree.

This, though a splendid innings, was for Marshall a relatively discreet one. In the morning he waited for quite long periods before finding the right ball to hit. In the afternoon he had bursts of violence, hitting Sully for four fours in an over and Scott for four and six off consecutive balls.

The field steadily retreated until there were six men on the off side in positions one would usually classify as deep. Marshall batted for 210 minutes, hit a six and 23 fours, and was out for 160 in the seventy-second over.

One must not forget Reed, who shared with Marshall in the second highest first-wicket stand in Hampshire history. If his was naturally a secondary role, he played it admirably. The contrast between the two added to the day's pleasures. Reed's bat was all solidity and might have been made of oak. Marshall's was light as a lath and seemed almost to bend as he stroked the ball away. One only realized the power there when one saw deep extra cover almost knocked over by it. Woolley's off-drives, a distant memory tells me, were like this. On the on side Marshall was more obviously robust, forcing the ball square off his body like Donnelly, or heaving it cheerfully down to long-on like Crapp.

All these comparisons are with left-handed batsmen. Perhaps it is part of Marshall's genius that he bats with more of the special graces of the left-hander than any other right-hander we have known.

Roy Marshall
'Among the best half dozen of his era'

Alley comes up from Somerset where his qualities still grow

According to *Wisden*, W.E. Alley was born on February 3, 1919, which would make him a few months over 48 years old. According to his former Somerset colleague and fellow-Australian, C.L. McCool, "if Bill Alley was born in 1919 he was playing Grade cricket in knickerbockers." Alley himself appears to regard the official date with some dubiety: "I'll tell you how old I am," he says to his friends, "– when I've stopped playing!"

For some years the senior first-class cricketer, he had always said he intended to play until he was 50. That is, until last year, when he was awarded a man of the match award in the Gillette Cup. He then blithely told Peter May (who was responsible for the presentation, and is a babe in arms in comparison), "Right. Now I've decided to play until I'm 60." He well could. Indeed, for all we really know, perhaps he has already.

The only clue, and a good one at that, is another man of the match award on Tuesday – for batting, bowling and catching! And this against the Gillette Cup holders.

Other great cricketers have played until they were 50 or thereabouts. Hobbs, Woolley, Rhodes, W.G. Quaife are examples. But what distinguishes these players? They all had a marvellously good technique. If the keenness of their eye faded they could play it by ear. Hobbs could have batted until he was 80 without making a clumsy or ill-considered stroke, except for fun. A picture of Rhodes, nearly blind, bowling in his seventies shows the same rounded, flawless action that he had in 1899.

Bill Alley is not, technically, in this class at all. He has carried on playing cricket, and playing it successfully, partly through the expertise acquired over many years, but chiefly because he loves playing, and what is more loves playing *well*. If he stopped making runs or taking wickets Bill Alley would not stick around. Certainly he plays for fun: but for him winning has always been an important part of the fun.

His expertise was well illustrated in the Gillette Cup match against Warwickshire. Barber was threatening to break Somerset into bits. He had scored 15 in half a dozen overs when Alley was brought on. Alley had let it be known that he believed Barber could be beaten with a fast yorker early in his innings. Barber came down the pitch to turn that yorker into a full toss. It was a fastish long hop.

Alley afterwards declared it had moved: I was in a good position to see, and I deny that it was anything but a straight ball. Barber was bowled, and it is not often that one has seen a batsman of such quality made to look such an ass.

But it needs more than tricks of the trade, more even than love for the game, to keep a man at the top for so long. Alley came to this country soon after the war, for one reason or another unhappy about his prospects in Australian cricket.

He went to the Leagues, and I met him first when he was professional for Blackpool. He held court in the bar when Lancashire was playing there, and I remember wondering who the dickens he thought he was to lay down the law so emphatically on every subject (including some far removed from cricket).

In the Leagues he learnt to bowl, because the professional was expected to – in Australia he had been almost exclusively a batsman. He came to Somerset after some hesitation on both sides. He was too old, it seemed, to play for more than a season or two: but Somerset needed players, and a good man for even a season or two would help. He duly obliged with 1,500 runs and 50-60 wickets, take it a bit up and down.

In 1960 McCool, then leaving Somerset, wrote (or allowed somebody to write for him) that Alley "is very nearly irreplaceable in the Somerset side, yet he is in his forties now and can't go on indefinitely." In that season, troubled by a calf muscle, Alley did no better than moderately.

Then came 1961. The extraordinary man scored 3,019 runs that season, among the 25 highest aggregates ever recorded, and by far the highest for Somerset. He made 11 centuries and averaged 57. He still hauled in a bagful of wickets.

Every year since then when he has struck a bad patch we have nodded wisely and said: "Well, it's catching up with the old man at last"; and every time we say it he confounds us with some new performance.

It was sad, and I think something of a lasting disappointment to him, that he was not made captain of Somerset. Nevertheless he has worked very happily with C.R.M Atkinson, and I believe the two men, though so different, have a real affection and respect for each other.

Alley has been known to be explosive in his views, and unguarded in his expression of them. But he has the great quality of not bearing grudges. He has made many friends in the game, and if he has made some enemies too, I think that is probably their fault and not his. He is always ready to wash away animosity in a pint.

Glamorgan are well placed

NEATH: Glamorgan, with all their second innings wickets in hand, lead Somerset by 106 runs

"Cricket's a lovely game, see?" said one cheerful visitor from the valleys, "so long as the sun's shining and there's a good bar." He had divided his day between sleep and beer, and was amiably disputing with his friends who, while not denigrating those occupations, had hoped to enjoy a little cricket as well.

It must be said that for most of the day the cricket was so unentertaining as to bore even the enthusiast, and, though Glamorgan are well placed for six points, it is doubtful whether – with an early finish today – they can get any more.

...

Not until the fifth over after the delayed tea interval was the last wicket stand broken, and when Glamorgan went in a second time they had only an hour and a quarter of the day left. They did their best to get a move on. A. Jones, especially, played a variety of handsome strokes and also made the most of them by his running between the wickets.

Lewis turns draw into victory

NEATH: Glamorgan (12 pts) beat Somerset by 54 runs

At 4.25 yesterday, this game seemed to be heading for a comfortable draw. The Somerset eighth-wicket pair, Clayton and Robinson, had been playing all the bowlers with such composure that it seemed doubtful whether Glamorgan would even bother to claim the extra half-hour.

Then Lewis, the Glamorgan captain, decided to bowl an over himself. Clayton obligingly pulled a ball into his stumps.

Ten minutes later Glamorgan were triumphantly celebrating victory, Lewis having finished off the innings. But although he was rapidly christened "Lewis the google" it must be said that the batsmen themselves collaborated in their downfall in a way which should have produced some severe words in the Somerset dressing-room.

Glamorgan's declaration had set Somerset to score 257 in 184 minutes. It was a stiff task on a wicket giving the spinners some help, and they never quite looked like doing it. However, they made a brave try, and did not give up until seven wickets had gone. Glamorgan played their part by bowling their overs at a good rate and giving long spells to Davis and Walker rather than the more accurate Shepherd.

When Glamorgan batted in the morning there were some more fine strokes from Alan Jones, who must in recent years have taken as many runs off the Somerset bowlers as anyone in the country. His off-drive was functioning famously, and even five men spread across the covers could not cut off the runs.

Lewis played a small tornado of an innings, scoring 26 out of 33 in a quarter of an hour. Rees improved as he went on, but the scoring rate dropped in the last half-hour of the innings, making it difficult for Lewis to declare as early as he must have hoped.

Both Langford and Robinson bowled steadily under pressure. Somerset held some good catches but also dropped two, due in each case to the wrong man going for the ball.

Virgin was caught at slip in the second over after luncheon, and in the one following so was Kitchen to a diving catch by Walker as good as even he has made for a long time.

The next over produced another slip chance, from Atkinson, which was not taken. Atkinson rode his luck, hit two sixes and five fours, and was dropped twice more before he was out to another fine catch.

All afternoon the Glamorgan fielding varied between the brilliant and the inept. Alley had also been going well, but even so when Atkinson was out 170 were still needed in the last two hours.

In the next twenty minutes Alley scored only three, apparently assuming the role of anchor while Burgess went for the runs. Then the old Adam asserted itself. Alley swung across the line at Walker and was bowled.

Langford came in to push things along and with 90 minutes left 134 were needed. Only an innings of exceptional quality from Burgess could win the match for Somerset now, and after a few powerful shots through the covers he mishit a skier to short leg.

Langford and Palmer were both out hitting, whereupon the Somerset tail settled down to trying to save the match. It looked as if they had done it, until Lewis made his remarkable appearance on the scene.

GLAMORGAN 275 (A. Jones 100, Palmer 5-72) & 217 for six declared (A. Jones 63, Rees 58*)
SOMERSET 236 (Burgess 65, I.J. Jones 4-48) & 202 (Davis 4-72, Lewis 3-18)

Marner steadies Leicestershire

LORD'S: Middlesex, with all first innings wickets in hand, are 217 runs behind Leicestershire

There is a certain ambivalence in the attitude of most cricketers towards Leicestershire's challenge for the championship. On the one hand there is a natural pleasure that a county traditionally among the Cinderellas should be making a claim to be queen of the summer ball. On the other hand the tactics sometimes employed by Leicestershire in the field have suggested that Cinderella is bringing into high society a trick or two from the scullery.

Nevertheless, at Lord's Leicestershire showed that they have one essential attribute of potential champions: resolution. They lost four wickets for 42 on a pitch which had some early dampness and in an atmosphere which seemed to help Price and Herman to swing the ball.

Marner and Dudleston not only checked the retreat, but were eager to move on to the counter attack. Marner scored most of his runs, as usual, with drives. Few contemporary batsmen hit the ball harder. Dudleston progresses more in the modern manner, with pushes and nudges, but he also showed us a stroke or two, including one hook off a short ball from Price that was worthy of Herbert Sutcliffe.

...

Marner was last out, having made 137 out of 223. Leicestershire scored at more than three runs an over, a creditable rate considering their disastrous start. On the other hand, Middlesex bowled fewer than 18 overs an hour, in spite of the fact that the spinners had a good share of the work.

Russell and Smith held the fort for Middlesex in the last hour; but Lock, from the nursery end, posed sufficient problems to suggest that this will not be a good wicket on which to bat last.

Inspiration of Lock plain to see

LORD'S: Leicestershire, with eight second innings wickets in hand, are 44 runs ahead of Middlesex

It was a hard-fought day's cricket at Lord's, and yet for the most part rather a dull one. For much of the time one was gloomily contemplating the new stand, still noisily in process of building, which M.C.C. have decreed shall replace that corner of their ground which was richest in beauty and tradition.

Utilitarian architecture, utilitarian cricket. Middlesex scored their runs at two and a half to the over. Leicestershire bowled their overs at 18 to the hour, only fractionally better than Middlesex the previous day. A holidaymaker from Middlesbrough confessed that the most interesting part of his day had been spent in the Lord's museum.

In the earlier play Middlesex got themselves into trouble, more through their own indiscretions than any venom in the wicket or the bowling. All the first four batsmen seemed to have taken the measure of the situation when they were out. Perspective was restored by a seventh wicket partnership of 58 between Radley and Latchman.

Latchman played sensibly, and was not afraid to hit the bad ball. Radley played an innings which went some way to justify those distinguished critics who foresaw for him, a year or two back, a brilliant future. He is a little cramped in his stance and defensive play, but will suddenly unfold into a lovely stroke, like a butterfly emerging from a chrysalis.

Latchman was well caught at slip, Herman was bowled with the new ball, and when Birkenshaw came back he had Radley out to a fine diving catch by Tolchard. At 248 for nine, Price and Stewart needed to score 15 for the first innings lead. They were seven short when Lock came on to have Stewart leg before. There was something a little odd about this decision, since Lock had stifled his appeal.

Leicestershire made few mistakes in their out-cricket. The inspiration of Lock was plain to see. He is justly earning an outstanding reputation as a captain, though he might perhaps have bowled more himself in the early stages.

Birkenshaw took four wickets. His success this season is the more remarkable in that last year he took only 15 wickets in the championship. He does not spin the ball much, but he has plenty of determination and the will to respond to a challenge. He was certainly faced with one when Lock decided to leave the main burden upon him yesterday.

In the Yorkshire chapels of my youth we used to sing a hymn every verse of which ended with the line "Give us strength to persevere". Birkenshaw, a Yorkshireman himself, has apparently taken the message to heart.

For 50 minutes Hallam batted elegantly and Norman placidly. Then Herman, for no obvious reason, took two wickets in an over. Birkenshaw came in as nightwatchman and it was appropriate that the day should end with his solid defensive prod.

Hardly like champions

LORD'S: Middlesex (2 pts) drew with Leicestershire (6 pts)

Lock's declaration, at five past three, left Middlesex to score 241 in 175 minutes. It would have been feasible to declare a quarter of an hour earlier, which would have reduced the target to 220 in 190 minutes.

The wicket was playing more easily than might have been expected, deadened by overnight rain. Yet Lock had two fast bowlers who can take a long time to bowl their overs, if the need arises. Even as it was, Leicestershire bowled only 16 overs in the first hour, four of them by spinners. At this rate, Middlesex needed to score at more than five an over to win.

Middlesex tried. Smith was run out seeking a sharp single, Russell was bowled attempting to drive. Radley again batted well and Murray hit a splendid six into the newly built stand, unfortunately without doing it any damage. But with five wickets down for 89, Middlesex decided they could not win the game and therefore must save it.

They were fortunate still to have Parfitt at one end, and he found a cool headed partner in Selwood. Lock changed his bowling repeatedly, gave Booth a spell, switched himself to the pavilion end and back, claimed the extra half hour, brought back Cotton. Middlesex appealed unsuccessfully against the light, but after a bumper from Cotton the umpires conferred again, and brought the players off.

Leicestershire played well in this match, but hardly like champions. They knew at an early stage that Yorkshire had won, and the situation demanded a more challenging declaration.

In the morning Leicestershire had progressed reasonably swiftly. Norman held an end firm while the others swung their bats. If Norman is nowadays something of a bread and butter batsman, Birkenshaw and Inman come in the category of fish and chips – plenty of body and flavour, even if they do not appeal to the palate of a connoisseur.

Marner, to pursue the gastronomical analogy, is a Lancashire hotpot; a rich and noble dish, which nevertheless sometimes contains unconventional elements. He drove as powerfully in the second innings as the first. This drive is very much his own stroke. He plays it off the back foot to a well pitched up ball, the upper part of his body leaning backwards to balance the fierce outward thrust of his forearm.

Marner scored 186 for once out in this match. He and Birkenshaw certainly have cause to remember it with satisfaction, as have Parfitt and Selwood for their brave defence at the end.

Middlesex v Leicestershire, Lord's, 9, 10 & 11 August 1967

Drawn

Leicestershire

M.R. Hallam	c Russell b Herman	15	c Radley b Herman	28
M.E. Norman	lbw b Price	20	b Latchman	31
B.J. Booth	c Murray b Price	6	b Parfitt	17
C.C. Inman	c Radley b Price	0	c Smith b Price	35
P.T. Marner	c Murray b Herman	137	*not out*	49
B. Dudleston	c Parfitt b Latchman	37	*not out*	9
J. Birkenshaw	b Latchman	1	c Latchman b Stewart	54
+ R.W. Tolchard	c Stewart b Latchman	2	b Herman	0
* G.A.R. Lock	st Murray b Latchman	41	c Smith b Price	5
J. Cotton	lbw b Stewart	0		
C.T. Spencer	*not out*	1		
	lb 1, w 1	2	b 2, lb 2, w 1	5
		262	(7 wkts, dec)	**233**

1/18, 2/39, 3/39, 4/42, 5/127, 6/135, 7/149, 8/243, 9/258, 10/262
1/35, 2/35, 3/103, 4/124, 5/134, 6/203, 7/224

Price	19	5	45	3	18	3	56	2
Herman	13.2	1	70	2	17	4	61	2
Stewart	16	2	59	1	3	1	6	1
Latchman	22	5	57	4	23	5	86	1
Parfitt	15	3	29	0	9	3	19	1

Middlesex

W.E. Russell	b Spencer	18	b Cotton	8
M.J. Smith	lbw b Birkenshaw	48	run out	13
P.H. Parfitt	b Birkenshaw	24	*not out*	43
*+ J.T. Murray	c Lock b Booth	28	c Cotton b Birkenshaw	17
C.T. Radley	c Tolchard b Birkenshaw	81	st Tolchard b Birkenshaw	20
D.G. Ottley	run out	0	c Dudleston b Lock	2
T. Selwood	b Birkenshaw	5	*not out*	15
H.C. Latchman	c Hallam b Cotton	17		
R.S. Herman	b Cotton	0		
J.S.E. Price	*not out*	13		
R.W. Stewart	lbw b Lock	2		
	b 16, lb 3	19	b 3, lb 4, nb 1	8
		255	(5 wkts)	**126**

1/63, 2/75, 3/96, 4/145, 5/145, 6/155, 7/213, 8/221, 9/248, 10/255
1/21, 2/23, 3/58, 4/86, 5/89

Cotton	21	1	60	2	8	1	27	1
Spencer	24	2	65	1	6	0	20	0
Birkenshaw	34	15	59	4	18	10	29	2
Lock	14.3	5	25	1	17	8	28	1
Booth	10	1	27	1	8	4	14	0

Umpires: R.S. Lay and W.E. Phillipson

Hard task ahead for Kent

DOVER: Warwickshire, with six second innings wickets in hand, are 87 runs ahead of Kent

Dover in the sunshine, all bright colours and gaiety, hardly an empty seat, several hundred spectators perched on the hills outside, enthusiasm and anxiety always fibrillating even when the pulse of the cricket was slow: here was a handsome climax to the season, and a fine place for Kent to win the championship this week – if they can.

They had a good day, though not so good as it might have been. Indeed, at one time in the evening Warwickshire were threatening to take command. The first innings arrears had been settled, and Barber was playing beautifully. A few minutes after tea he went to his second 50 of the match, scored out of 64 in 24 overs.

Then Graham suddenly bowled Barber. In came Mike Smith, to a fine farewell reception, if that is not a contradiction in terms. He was leg before first ball. With the next ball Graham beat Jameson. In the next over, Shepherd had Abberley caught at slip, and in the following over Jameson was dropped at short-leg.

Kent were poised for the breakthrough, but Jameson pulled himself together, and Richardson seemed cool and confident. They could hardly be expected to win back the initiative, but they did enough to ensure that today – with a 4.30 finish at the latest – Kent must work hard if they are to win.

Earlier in the day, Kent struggled for their lead. They were pinned down by Cartwright, with Bannister and Cook doing their part at the other end. An early mist may have helped the ball to swing in the air, and there was certainly the occasional sharp movement from the pitch, but few other bowlers than Cartwright could have turned these moderate advantages to such effect.

He took seven successive wickets, from the second to the eighth, and was never collared until Brown hit him for 18 in an over near the end of the innings.

Kent keep up title challenge

DOVER: Kent (12 pts) beat Warwickshire by three wickets

Kent won this match with five minutes to spare yesterday, maintaining their championship challenge and delighting their supporters, who turned out again in large numbers.

A glance at the score sheet in years to come may suggest it was a fairly comfortable win; but at times during the day it had seemed improbable. In the morning, when Warwickshire reached 180 for six, with Richardson still going well, we were beginning to wonder what Mike Smith would offer in his declaration. Then the Warwickshire tail drooped as it had done in the first innings, and again the man chiefly responsible was Shepherd. This young West Indian has learnt his trade quickly, and by next summer will surely be one of the best all-rounders in English cricket.

Kent had to score 155 to win in 152 minutes, which was not too difficult a proposition, especially as the wicket seemed to be playing more easily than at any time in the match (justifying Dixon's original decision to put Warwickshire in). Two runs came in four overs before lunch, and so the afternoon target was 153 in 140 minutes.

All went well until Cartwright came on, first change. He took the wickets of Nicholls and Wilson in his first over. Denness bravely responded by pulling Cook for four. Leary, who never looked happy, was out when he tried to drive Cook and did not get hold of the ball.

Kent needed 89 when the last hour began. Everything depended on Denness, or, from Warwickshire's point of view, on Cartwright. Shepherd was bowled by Cook, and Cartwright had Ealham leg-before. Denness did not take so much of the bowling as he might have done at this critical stage.

With Jones out, and the score 89 for six, Warwickshire looked like winning, Then Dixon had the happy inspiration of sending in Brown; Smith gave Cook one over too many before recalling Bannister; and Denness began to take a wider view of his duties. Brown's uninhibited hitting disorganized Warwickshire's careful planning. The partnership put on 42 in 18 minutes, and the game had taken its final turn. Of Denness one can only say that, in spite of his period of uncertainty, he had played the best innings of the match – a match which contained two 50s from Barber.

Towards the end some members of the crowd, desperate for the full points, made some uncomplimentary remarks about Mike Smith, of which a cry of "Come on, Yorkshire!" was probably the one that hurt him most. Warwickshire bowled almost 19 overs an hour for two hours, but only seven in the last 27 minutes. In other words, the over rate dropped sharply as the prospect of victory receded. But nobody seriously minded, as it was unobtrusively done, and Kent won anyway.

WARWICKSHIRE	171 (Barber 51, Shepherd 5-34) & 195 (Richardson 60, Barber 51, Shepherd 4-51)
KENT	212 (Denness 48, Cartwright 7-103) & 155 for seven (Denness 86*, Cartwright 3-60)

His last match: Leicestershire v Northamptonshire at Leicester 1967

FIRST DAY

They take their cricket quietly in the Shires. Here were Leicestershire, in the running for what would be their first championship, and the sun shining, at least for most of the day. Yet, as I remember on a similar occasion at Northampton two seasons ago, the ground was only half full, and there was scarcely one real cheer all day.

This was a long way from the bubbling enthusiasm of Dover, the fierce determination of Middlesbrough. However, in their undemonstrative, intent way, the crowd enjoyed their cricket, and their county gave them plenty to enjoy.

SECOND DAY

It was a disappointing day for Leicestershire, partly because Kent's rapid victory snuffed their championship hopes, and partly because they did not make such quick progress in their game as they must have wished. …

After 10 overs Lock came on. Immediately he made the ball bite and turn. … I envisaged Northamptonshire out twice in the day.

This reckoned without Milburn. His innings was not flawless, not even ebullient by his own standards, but he showed a maturity of judgment he has often lacked in the past. By the time he was fourth out, at 140, only 51 were needed to save the follow-on.

THIRD DAY

Leicestershire, winning comfortably, had the satisfaction of taking their total of points level with that of Kent and of being, at worst, third in the championship, a position they have only once previously reached.

Northamptonshire were set 277 to win in 248 minutes. … The fortunes of their batting depend a good deal upon Milburn. When he succeeds, as he did in the first innings, he will sometimes transmit his success to the others. Now, his downfall was followed by a dismal panic.

Two more wickets fell before lunch and in the afternoon, once Prideaux was gone, Northamptonshire seemed only anxious to get things over. This probably did not make much difference, as Lock was in a mood when he would have taken some stopping by anybody.

Leicestershire are not champions, but if an award could be given to the side which has made the most of its talents this season, they would win it by a street. The players would unite in giving the chief credit of this to Lock.

DECEMBER: Boxing Day cricket at Downend

Boxing Day cricket is always a hazardous business; but a lovelier day for the time of year could not have been imagined than was provided for the match at Downend, Bristol, in which David Smith's Gloucestershire XI tied with Alan Gibson's XI.

David Smith, the beneficiary, had most of the Gloucestershire side supporting him. The opposition had an interesting mixture of variety artists, Rugby and Association football players, broadcasters and journalists. The sun shone more warmly than on most days in summer, but the ground was too damp for fast bowling. But otherwise the cricket could be played straightforwardly enough. The final result, a tie, was entirely adventitious.

The Downend ground, only a few yards from the house where W.G. Grace was born, looked its best, and plenty of people turned up to see David Smith's benefit year off to a good start. The game began with a series of mighty if occasionally inelegant blows from David Green, who made an auspicious start to his playing association with Gloucestershire.

Progress was checked, however, by J.K. Graveney, who took four quick wickets: two bowled, one caught and bowled, and one well caught at the wicket by J.N. Blake, a former Bristol Rugby captain. After 15 overs – the allotted span – the score was 96 for five.

The opposition made a lively beginning with three big sixes from Peter Colston, another former Bristol Rugby captain. Then they fell into trouble for a while. A psychiatrist, who had been enlisted on the grounds that anyone playing cricket on Boxing Day must be in need of mental attention, was less effective in his treatment of the bat than with his off-field neurosis.

It was left to the church to put matters right: the Reverend Ronald Cowley (formerly captain of Dulwich Hamlet) scored a powerful 29, and this, taken into account with his triumphantly successful prayers for fine weather beforehand, caused him to be accorded the man of the match.

With three balls left Tony Fayne was bowled, and his old variety partner David Evans succeeded him; three wickets left, six needed to win. Evans, under captain's orders, scored a single (the theory being that he could not possibly hope to hit two consecutive balls) and John Brian brought glory to Hinton Charterhouse with a four from the last ball.

The best sight of the morning was a passing bus, glazed with the white faces of travellers who obviously felt they must have overdone it the night before. Everyone else was so happy that there were plans to make the match a regular event; but perhaps even W.G., who used to begin practice in the Orchard over the way every February, might feel that was pressing luck a bit far.

1968

Revolution was the theme of 1968. There were student riots in Paris, Alexander Dubcek's brave attempt to cast off the Russian yoke was snuffed out in Prague, huge demonstrations against the Vietnam war were staged in London, and there was a bottle-throwing riot at Sabina Park when Basil Butcher was given out caught down the leg side in the second Test of MCC's winter tour. I even got modestly into the act myself, being arrested and bound over to keep the peace, whilst demonstrating against Enoch Powell at Oxford. In a letter to my father, I described it as 'all very unfortunate and unspectacular; the policeman who arrested me wasn't even particularly brutal'!

Revolutionary would not be quite the word to describe the changes that had been made to county cricket since the previous season, but they represented significant progress, nonetheless. Counties were allowed to employ the services of one overseas player, not qualified by residence. Amongst others, Barry Richards went to Hampshire, a young Greg Chappell to Somerset, Mike Procter to Gloucestershire and Nottinghamshire's fortunes were transformed by the signing of the great Garfield Sobers as their captain.

Points for first innings lead were scrapped and replaced by a system of bonus points: one for every 25 runs over 150 scored in the first 85 overs to a maximum of five for the batting side and one for every two wickets, again in 85 overs, for the bowling side. It didn't take long for the county captains to appreciate that, batting first, with maximum batting points secured, they might as well declare with nine wickets down, to deny their opponents a fifth bowling point. On balance, however, the new points system was a success. Even Alan, who was always a traditionalist where the county game was concerned, was prepared to concede its merits, when Somerset played Yorkshire, giving him his first sight of Greg Chappell, on May 9.

1968 was an Ashes summer and, after the MCC's unexpected series win in the West Indies during the winter, was keenly anticipated. In the event, it was a thorough let down. The Australians were going through a period of transition. Bill Lawry, who rarely quickened the pulse, was their most prolific batsman and they fielded one of their weakest attacks of all time. One thing they did have on their side was luck. They owed their win in the first Test at Old Trafford largely to the toss of the coin, were saved by the weather at Lord's and Edgbaston and hung on grimly for a draw at Headingley. So even though Underwood managed to bowl England to victory in a dramatic last session at a saturated, sawdust-strewn Oval, the series was drawn and Australia had retained the Ashes.

Just as the weather spoiled the Test series, so it cast a damp pall over the entire season. 1968 was one of the most dismal summers of the century. It rained for most of May and June, and then again during August, when the county championship was reaching a climax. Yorkshire, the reigning champions, were the hot favourites despite (or Alan might possibly have argued because of) their spurning of the chance to hire an overseas star. They moved to the top in June and thereafter were never headed, despite a brave late run from an unfancied Glamorgan side, who won eight out of ten matches in July and August but then contrived to lose their last two games, against Derbyshire and finally Nottinghamshire. That last encounter, at St Helen's, Swansea, was given immortality by Sobers' six sixes off a Malcolm Nash over. Alan Gibson was there – but only for the second and third days. The first day,

Tests
England
drew with Australia
1-1, with three draws

Championship
1 Yorkshire
2 Kent
3 Glamorgan
4 Nottinghamshire
5 Hampshire
6 Lancashire

Gillette Cup Final
Warwickshire
beat Sussex

Most first-class runs
1 B.A. Richards
2 D.M. Green
3 J.H. Edrich

Most first-class wickets
1 R. Illingworth
2 R.M.H. Cottam
3 D.L. Underwood

when Sobers had made cricketing history, was a Saturday and, in those days, *The Times* didn't report Saturday cricket.

But there was plenty of good cricket that Alan did see. He always enjoyed his visits to the County Ground at Bristol, and was fortunate enough to be able to watch cricket on all three days there when Gloucestershire played Hampshire at the end of May. David Green, one of *Wisden*'s five Cricketers of the Year, and who was to become one of Alan's great friends, both as player and reporter, was in his first season for Gloucestershire, as was the young South African all-rounder, Mike Procter, whom Alan profiled for *The Times* in June.

A cricketer of a very different vintage was Hampshire's Derek Shackleton. Alan was always an admirer of his effortless action and relentless accuracy, which he described in a feature for *The Times* in August. Alan did not know it at the time, but this was to be Shackleton's last season. He retired when it ended, as did two other great bowlers, Statham and Trueman and – with rather more reluctance – Somerset's Bill Alley, who was rather churlishly only offered a contract for one day cricket for the following season. Still, Somerset's match against Kent in July at least gave Alan the chance to watch two Australian cricketers from entirely different generations – Alley at 49 and Greg Chappell at 19 – making a fascinating contrast as they played alongside each other at Clarence Park, Weston-super-Mare.

And there were the less exciting days, as well; often featuring, so it must have seemed, one PJK Gibbs of Derbyshire. His performance in a dull drawn game against Worcestershire at Kidderminster in June proved to be all too typical of an approach to batting that was to make him the villain of many an Alan Gibson cricket report over the seasons that were to follow.

But despite the weather, and some uninspiring matches, and the depredations of the *Times*' sub editors, Alan gives the impression of relishing the chance to write about cricket, five or even six days a week. In fact, on June 10th, he even managed to cover two matches in one day: reporting Nottinghamshire's lunchtime victory over Somerset, and then catching the train up to Bristol in time to watch the closing stages of Leicestershire's 30-run win over Gloucestershire. He must have been very keen – or possibly just very hard up!

The season ended for Alan in the best possible way – with ten days at the Scarborough Cricket Festival. His question about 'who will be President of the Festival 40 years on' has a distinctly poignant ring, although I'll bet he was the first cricket writer to give Boycott his honorary title of 'Sir Geoffrey'!

In the meantime, the D'Oliveira affair had been making headlines, not just on the back pages but on the front pages as well. I cannot now trace anything that Alan wrote on the subject, but I know precisely what his feelings would have been. He had been a ferocious opponent of apartheid all his adult life and believed firmly that sporting links with the racist Government of Dr Verwoerd should be severed. These were views that he, of course, shared with his great friend and brother in Liberal arms, John Arlott, who had been largely responsible for bringing Basil D'Oliveira to England in the first place. They both (and, to his eternal credit, Jim Swanton) made themselves thoroughly unpopular with the cricket establishment for broadcasting and writing as they did, but it was the sort of cause that Alan loved, and he never worried too much about upsetting people!

The Parks in April

OXFORD: Oxford University v Gloucestershire

For a few minutes yesterday, after play had started at 12 o'clock, the Parks looked as in Oxford memories they always do in the spring. The sun shone, the flannels gleamed, the flowers blossomed. Keble became a cardboard cutout from a Victorian children's book, and, bless us, there was a new, slimline David Green running round the third man boundary like a freshman.

But even then the clouds were banking over the city, and in a quarter of an hour the ideal had given way to the real, as it has an irritating habit of doing, even at Oxford. The sun put in a pale, brief reappearance during the afternoon, but the weather was always menacing, the drizzle recurring, the wind cold. The cricketers, wanting practice, stuck it out until a downpour shortly before six. The spectators mostly sought to further their education elsewhere.

An unlikely Notts victory

NOTTINGHAM: Nottinghamshire v Derbyshire

"How much", inquired a sinister poster on Nottingham station, "will there be in *The Times* tomorrow?" Not enough, I am afraid, to convey the full flavour of Nottinghamshire's win over Derbyshire, who lost for the first time this season. It is not that I am short of wordage, as the clumsy phrase goes, but short of words.

This Nottinghamshire side, shorn not only of Sobers but of Hill, Bolus and White, so pressed for players that a scoreboard operator was taken away to make up the second XI (or so I am told, and from the way the scoreboard was operated I can believe it) – this side gave Derbyshire a good hammering.

Gary Sobers at Trent Bridge

NOTTINGHAM: Nottinghamshire v Lancashire

There is no doubt who is the dominant figure at Trent Bridge just now. Even some Nottinghamshire supporters were wishing their own earlier batsmen out of the way, so that the great man might make his entry. It must be even more difficult to bat before Sobers than to play a curtain-raiser to Irving, since curtain raisers are at least determinate in duration.

Gillette Cup bowling tactics

BRISTOL: Gloucestershire v Kent

Milton did not bowl Allen, preferring Green as his fifth bowler. It is a strange situation where Green is considered a better bowler than Allen but who, in this tournament, dare say that Milton's decision is wrong? As Sir Neville Cardus wrote in another context, "a new game has been invented which employs the implements of cricket."

Alan Jones

CARDIFF: Glamorgan v Lancashire

I have seen little better all season than the innings of Alan Jones, who saw Glamorgan triumphantly through with a power and placing in his drives which repeatedly left a defensive field gasping in pursuit.

Perhaps I am prejudiced because I always seem to see him make runs, but surely he must be picked for England soon; unless, indeed, he prefers to wait until he can play for his native land.

Chesterfield in August

CHESTERFIELD: Derbyshire v Yorkshire

Although the weather was no better than all right, the pretty Chesterfield ground was full and had an air of carnival. There were family picnics, lost children repeatedly being reported by a harassed secretary upon the public address system, jovial groups round the beer tents, all of whom were old buddies of "Fred" and "George" – at least until Trueman dropped a sitter at mid-on and Pope gave a couple of Derbyshire men out.

Alan Oakman

HOVE: Sussex v Hampshire

Oakman began with an alarming snick and took some time to find his touch. He obviously enjoyed himself, banging assiduously at the wicket, taking little strolls around, chatting with the close fielders, and, when he called for a run, offering his partner a brief biography of the fieldsmen.

Ossie Wheatley at Cardiff

CARDIFF: Glamorgan v Derbyshire

His extraordinary success this season is due more to temperament than technical change. Now that he is not a full-timer, he has less at stake, is more relaxed, and therefore more confident. As he runs up, he waggles the ball in his hand as though it were a grenade, and the batsmen correspondingly tend to treat even the rare half-volley as explosive.

Close takes three quick wickets

TAUNTON: Somerset have scored 67 for three wickets against Yorkshire

Another aspect of the new scoring regulations, possibly not foreseen by the great and good men who made them, was revealed at Taunton. With no play possible until 10 minutes to three on the second day, and the weather so threatening that further interruptions seemed likely, Close, on winning the toss, put Somerset in. Clearly his best chance of gaining any first innings points was by taking Somerset wickets while he could. Had he batted, and then been halted by more rain, the only points going would have been Somerset's.

He may also have had some hopes of the wicket, but I doubt it. It was a little soggy, but not sticky – what we connoisseurs of Yorkshire pudding would describe as clarty.

Trueman made several balls move quite sharply from leg off the pitch, but that was because he was Trueman. Usually the batsmen had plenty of time for their strokes.

Virgin and Kitchen made a quiet but efficient start. Trueman soon gave way to Old at the river end, and then Old to Close. There seemed no particular reason why Close should put himself on at this stage, not did he at first seem to pose any problems. It was therefore entirely characteristic of him that he should take three wickets quickly, two of them in the last over before tea. Kitchen was stumped, Palmer caught at the wicket, and Barwell stumped on the left side, first ball: three for Binks as well as Close.

Soon after tea there was a stop because of the light, which was never good. When the players came out again, the lights of the members' bar had to be extinguished, as they were dazzling the batsmen. The members took this slightly amiss, maintaining that their proceedings were more interesting than those of the cricketers, and it was an arguable point. S.M.J. Woods and J. Daniell would scarcely have approved of this drastic step.

The sky grew steadily darker, and soon the lights were on again and the players off. These brief periods of play were notable for some good looking strokes by Chappell. One hook for four, from a short ball by Trueman, brought the only cheer of the day. Not that the players were to be blamed for the lack of interest. No one can play cricket standing on a sponge at the bottom of a chimney.

Innings closed after single ball

TAUNTON: Yorkshire (1 pt) drew with Somerset

Somerset and Yorkshire did their best to get a finish in this match, but the weather was too much for them. The brightest splashes of colour on a grey day were the towels used by the bowlers to dry the ball, brilliant orange and turquoise, piercing the gloom like Boycott's spectacles, Trueman's grin, and Alley's complexion.

Somerset declared before play started, and Yorkshire declared as soon as the single necessary ball was bowled – by Alley, with sardonic panoply.

Somerset then attempted to leave Yorkshire a goal which would give both sides a chance of winning, but with a short scheduled day, and rain about, it was a hopeless calculation. The fall of three quick wickets, raising the possibility that Yorkshire might win even without a declaration, complicated things further. Close must have been in a quandary: to continue attacking, or to give away some runs to tempt the declaration? Langford's position was equally difficult: tell his men to swing at the ball, and against this side they could have been all out in half an hour.

In the end he set Yorkshire 175 in 58 minutes plus 20 overs: hardly feasible, when Somerset had averaged only 2.3 an over in their second innings. More rain put an end to speculation.

Virgin battled well again, though he is unduly cautious for such a naturally fluent stroke player. "He bats for his wife and family," said an old Somerset cricketer. He did not say it unkindly, but it summed up the sociology of modern cricket.

There was another good innings from Chappell. He is one of the less heralded overseas players, but may turn out to be one of the most successful, judging by the way he adapted himself to the slow wicket. There was a good spell by Old, a player of infinite promise, and a superb catch by Binks, who seems in better form than ever. It is strange that he has never played against Australia, but if loss of form or injury should affect Knott, Binks is the obvious replacement.

His predecessor, Arthur Wood, he may be comforted to remember, first played against Australia in his fortieth year.

SOMERSET 67 for three declared & 107 for four declared
YORKSHIRE 0 for no wicket declared & 2 for no wicket

Defensive action turns into assault

BRISTOL: Hampshire, with nine first innings wickets in hand, are 244 runs behind Gloucestershire

Judging by the way Shackleton made the ball hop in the late afternoon, Gloucestershire have made a good score. It was one of the rebuilt Bristol pitches, less slow than that mattress of ancient grass cuttings used to be, but still unpredictable.

Gloucestershire's collapse in the morning, however, did not arise from any inequalities of the wicket, nor even from any exceptionally good bowling – though Shackleton, as usual, hardly bowled a bad ball, and White was much more impressive than I have so far seen him this season. There was also a marvellous catch, by Sainsbury at silly mid-on. Gloucestershire lost five wickets because they were so unaccustomed to the act of batting.

Procter and Bissex, to begin with, looked no better than the rest. But the catches did not go to hand, the appeals were turned down, and gradually what had begun as a rearguard action, turned into an assault.

Forty-nine for five – 198 for six: that sufficiently tells the story. Procter did not always bat elegantly, but he certainly batted efficiently. He rode his luck, kept his head, punished the bad balls, and sometimes punished the good ones too. He rounded off his day by getting Marshall out. He is a formidable cricketer.

Bissex batted well enough to suggest that he ought to go in at No. 3, surely his natural place in the order. He is a better stroke player than Procter, but so far lacks the confidence, not to say cocksureness, which characterizes most of our importations. Odd, this, considering that the British are the traditional imperial bullies. It seems that the ex-Empire can teach us a thing or two about the most successful approach to ball games.

Procter's century was warmly applauded by the 173 people in the public seats (a personal count), but once the partnership was broken, the innings drifted unexcitedly to the declaration. Thanks to Procter and Bissex, Gloucestershire took two batting points; one fewer than Hampshire for their bowling.

Timms and Hampshire dawdle

BRISTOL: Gloucestershire, with nine second innings wickets in hand, lead Hampshire by 57 runs

It will need some imaginative captaincy and challenging play if this match is to have any satisfying outcome. After an undistinguished day Gloucestershire are in the slightly better position and will presumably have to begin the bidding.

A substantial boost was given to the gate figures by the presence of a group of small boys in pink caps: a first XI, perhaps, on their annual outing. They were solemn and attentive, neophytes at an ancient rite, its full meaning doubtless only to be comprehended in maturity.

At the Orphanage end, now strictly the College of Technology end, older students came out at midday and kicked a red rubber ball about. They had a free view of the cricket, but only two out of a hundred or so bothered. I sought cheer in the Jessop Tavern, a handsome building from the outside: inside, litter all over the place, cracked windows, cold pies, two young men bemoaning the absence of a juke box. I fled to the members' bar, where a resonant snore announced that there was at least one happy man present.

For the cricket was as dull and dismal as the weather. It was also, for a long time, meaningless. Gloucestershire, finding no help in a pitch which seemed rapidly to be reverting to the traditional Bristol deadness, bowled tightly, Hampshire responded dourly. This in itself was natural enough, but what was baffling was the way Timms played.

A nightwatchman is entitled to a morning spree, but to bat for an hour and a half for 10 runs, and scarcely to increase the rate all day, simply made sure that Hampshire would earn no batting points. Reed played well – a fierce clubbed hook off Procter was a memorable stroke – but with the runs coming only at one end the scoring rate was rarely above one and a half an over.

Just before 1.30 a clatter and chirruping among the pink caps made me think that there was some merit in the play which I had missed, but it turned out that they were broaching the luncheon basket. A good spell by Mortimore in the afternoon (I could not fathom why he had not bowled more earlier) sent back Reed and Richards, who came in before Sainsbury, presumably in the hope of chasing the vanishing bonus.

By 3.45 I had nearly dropped off myself, but I was roused by a full-throated snore from my neighbour, a fitting accolade for Timms's 50. After 85 overs the score was 154 for three, and each side had taken three bonus points in the match. Mortimore had Sainsbury finely caught at square leg, an over too late to come into the equation. The rest of the Hampshire batsmen played as if they were slightly irritated with Timms. Turner, Gilliat and Shackleton were all out to impatient swings.

Easy task for Hampshire

BRISTOL: Hampshire (13 pts) beat Gloucestershire (3 pts) by five wickets

Outside the Grace Gates, at this ground, there was a battered sofa, guarded by two red lamps. "Someone must have put it there in the night," said the gateman. A number of less profound explanations were offered, mostly of a lascivious nature. My own view is that a disciple of Sartre offered it symbolically. For however much some of the players may have enjoyed it, this was for most of its course a secondhand and somnolent cricket match.

Hampshire won, quite comfortably in the end, in the sixteenth over of the last hour. The last day's play was better than what had gone before, which is not intended to be a lavish tribute.

When play began, Gloucestershire were 57 runs on, with nine wickets in hand. We were thinking in terms of a declaration at three o'clock or so, but doubting if, on a short day, anyone could win. For an hour Nicholls and Green carried sedately on. Then two boundaries from Green and one from Nicholls indicated acceleration.

Sainsbury bowled to Green with a wide, tempting space at midwicket. Green, who is one of those who believes that the best way of getting rid of temptation is to yield to it, went for the shot, and was well caught at mid-on. This was at a quarter-to-one, the score 76 for two.

Sixty-six playing minutes later, and hardly credibly, Gloucestershire were all out for 109, and Hampshire had about 170 minutes to score 140. I do not think it was a difficult wicket, though it became more and more slow, hazardous for making strokes.

Sainsbury was accurate, Cottam was able to move the ball from the off at an awkwardly quick speed. All the same, Gloucestershire batted badly, excessive boldness alternating with excessive caution.

Marshall put Hampshire on the right road, Gilliat came in at No. 3 and with some noble strokes, including a straight six, led them farther along it. There was a brief period of speculation when five wickets had fallen for 93, but Sainsbury and Turner thereafter played sensibly.

Quite the best feature of their partnership was the running between the wickets, a thing in which Gloucestershire had been deficient. In this way, without fuss or hurry, they reached journey's end. When we came out, the sofa was still there, but the red lamps had gone. A moral somewhere.

Gloucestershire v Hampshire, Bristol, 22, 23 & 24 May 1968

Hampshire won by five wickets

Gloucestershire

R.B. Nicholls	c Turner b Shackleton	6	b Sainsbury	42
* C.A. Milton	lbw b White	8	lbw b White	8
D.M. Green	c Timms b White	2	c Turner b Sainsbury	26
D. Shepherd	c Sainsbury b Cottam	15	c Marshall b Cottam	1
M.J. Procter	c Sainsbury b Shackleton	101	c White b Cottam	4
A.S. Brown	lbw b White	4	b Sainsbury	0
M. Bissex	c Richards b Shackleton	68	c Sainsbury b Cottam	12
D.A. Allen	*not out*	22	*not out*	6
J.B. Mortimore	b Cottam	6	c Sainsbury b Cottam	6
D.R. Smith	c Timms b White	14	c Turner b Cottam	0
+ B.J. Meyer			c Timms b Cottam	0
	b 2, lb 1, nb 2	5	lb 2, nb 2	4
	(9 wkts, dec)	**251**		**109**

1/11, 2/13, 3/23, 4/43, 5/49, 6/198, 7/209, 8/230, 9/251
1/10, 2/76, 3/80, 4/84, 5/84, 6/92, 7/97, 8/109, 9/109, 10/109

Shackleton	35	14	68	3	14	5	19	0
White	24	5	60	4	12	3	23	1
Cottam	22	6	52	2	19	5	35	6
Sainsbury	21	9	41	0	17	8	28	3
Wheatley	6	1	25	0				

Hampshire

* R.E. Marshall	lbw b Procter	4	lbw b Procter	16
B.L. Reed	b Mortimore	73	c Brown b Mortimore	14
+ B.S.V. Timms	*not out*	81		
B.A. Richards	b Mortimore	0	b Smith	14
P.J. Sainsbury	c Allen b Mortimore	25	*not out*	43
D.R. Turner	c Milton b Allen	8	*not out*	27
R.M.C. Gilliatt	lbw b Mortimore	0	c Smith b Mortimore	21
K.J. Wheatley	c Bissex b Mortimore	4		
D. Shackleton	c Milton b Allen	0		
D.W. White	run out	9	c Meyer b Procter	0
R.M.H. Cottam	c Brown b Procter	7		
	b 1, lb 6, nb 3	10	lb 4, nb 1	5
		221	(5 wkts)	**140**

1/4, 2/110, 3/112, 4/159, 5/178, 6/178, 7/182, 8/183, 9/202, 10/221
1/26, 2/38, 3/53, 4/92, 5/93

Procter	23.4	11	30	2	19	1	37	2
Smith	21	9	39	0	12	1	38	1
Brown	7	0	21	0				
Allen	25	11	37	2	4	0	24	0
Bissex	16	7	24	0	1.2	0	4	0
Mortimore	27	10	60	5	10	2	32	2

Umpires: C.S. Elliott and A. Jepson

Derbyshire's debt to two partnerships

KIDDERMINSTER: Worcestershire, with all their first innings wickets in hand, are 150 runs behind Derbyshire

Note: Senator Robert Kennedy was shot dead early that morning.

Only yesterday Geoffrey Green, from the hubbub of Florence, wrote a shade wistfully of cricket in peaceful Worcestershire. Well, here it was.

The trim little ground looked happy in the morning sunlight, the crowd was respectable in size, habit and demeanour, the opportunity ripe for a demonstration of our national oddity at its best. But I think I would have preferred Florence.

That it was a dreary day was not altogether the fault of the cricketers. It is the Spartan view that outside occurrences ought not to affect sporting events, but they do, and every now and then the crowd seemed to break into little clusters, round the newspaper men with their latest editions, or a transistor radio. We shall remember the day's cricket but not for the cricket. A pastoral loses credibility against the background of a battlefield.

This said, the play was still for the most part disappointing. Derbyshire scored 160 at less than two runs an over. If they win, which they yet might on a slow but awkward wicket, they will owe a lot to their resolute opening pair, who saw them through a difficult first hour, and to a partnership of 54 for the fourth wicket between Page and Morgan.

Morgan's was the best batting: the thoroughly competent professional, as always. Page played valuably and characteristically: dancing down the wicket like Trumper and then dabbing with a limp bat like Quaife out of form. When he starts following through with his strokes (and his thoughts) he will be a fine player.

Holder took most of the wickets. As against Lancashire last week, his second major spell was better than his first. He thrives on success which is a good fault, works up plenty of pace, and sometimes seems to make even an old ball curve in the air late. He looks a cricketer all over, except when he is fielding the ball on the ground, and even that he makes up for with a magnificent throw.

Gifford and Coldwell gave Holder good support, and so did Griffith, an off-spinner who can give the ball a real twist. His run-up is dragged in the middle, he had some difficulty in accommodating his line when the left and right-handers were in together, but he looks a useful cricketer.

Worcestershire took four points for bowling, and Derbyshire, rightly, none for batting. When Worcestershire went in we saw a stroke or two from Headley before it started raining. Rain had seemed improbable upon that sunlit morning, but so had much else.

Day of dull play at Kidderminster

KIDDERMINSTER: Derbyshire, with eight second innings wickets in hand, lead Worcestershire by 158 runs

Cricketers have to earn their living, I tell myself. The wicket was difficult. The weather prevented the batsmen from finding their proper form. I tell myself these things because I am paid for reporting first-class cricket, and do not like to admit that I am wasting my time.

The Kidderminster public, under no such compulsion, were drifting away long before the end of as dull a day's play as I can remember. For most of the time, the scoring rate was one an over. That it ultimately reached nearly one and a half of breathless glory, was because Derbyshire swung their bats just occasionally in the last hour, and because the Worcestershire tailenders, notably Brain, had been irresponsible enough to hit the ball. They did not realize, poor fellows, that 10 in 10 minutes is only one-sixth as valuable as 10 in an hour.

If the Worcestershire side had all batted as Brain did, and for that matter Coldwell, they could scarcely have scored less, and they would have been much more entertaining. If Derbyshire had capitalized their first innings advantage by going for the runs, it would have been tactically as well as morally correct. Incidentally, there is rain about, and a 5.30 finish tomorrow.

There were, however, some good things, as there always are in any cricket match. There was Edwin Smith's bowling: he is a much underestimated cricketer. Given a pitch such as this – it contrived to be both damp and dusty in the morning, though it dried and became easier later – there is hardly a better off-spinner in the business. He was helped by Rhodes, and by Swarbrook, only 17 years old slow left-arm, playing his first championship match. Fair, short but well-built, conquering his nerves, he did enough to suggest a distinguished future.

When Worcestershire fielded again, Coldwell had a fine opening spell, and Gifford made the ball hop dangerously from time to time. A little more luck for either of them, and Derbyshire might have been repenting their safety-first approach.

As for the batting, Fearnley played efficiently for Worcestershire, and so did Gibbs and Buxton for Derbyshire. I can put it no higher than that; but after all, cricketers must live. Yet, it seemed to me, as I trailed away in the wake of the crowd, must they? As Wilde once said in another context, I begin to doubt the necessity.

Lucky win for Derbyshire

KIDDERMINSTER: Derbyshire (15 pts) beat Worcestershire (4 pts) by 21 runs

The divinity that guards cricket shapes its ends, rough-hew them how we will. After a dreary match yesterday, there was some excitement in the last hour, a touch of tragedy, a touch of farce. Of course, these third-day scrambles are artificial, emphasizing the barrenness of what has gone before. Batsmen suddenly find they can score at four or five runs an over against the same bowlers and on the same wicket as had hopelessly tied them down the day before. But even artificial excitement is better than none at all.

Derbyshire hardly deserved to win, though Rhodes produced a fast, fierce spell at the crisis. Nor would they have won, but for one act of incredible folly by Worcestershire. In the twelfth over of the last 20, they needed only 29 with five wickets in hand. Turner had just been leg-before after an admirable innings, but Booth was still there, looking in command of the situation. He had come in at the fall of the fourth wicket, and reached 50 out of 63 in three-quarters of and hour. He usually employed the sweep, and was dropped once at square-leg, but generally he was middling the ball so well that Smith and Swarbrook hardly dared to bowl within his reach.

Holder came in when Turner was out, to hurry things on, though the necessity for that had largely gone. He hit the ball to deep mid-off. Booth set out for a run, which was there, and Holder did not move. He did not move even when Booth joined him in the crease. So when the bowler's wicket was put down, it was Booth who was out. It was Holder's call, but all the same he should have sacrificed himself. He presumably just did not think quickly enough.

Obviously distressed, Holder was out two overs later. Griffith was bowled first ball (a stump was splintered), and a few minutes later, Worcestershire had lost a match that had looked theirs for the taking.

Derbyshire had set them 230 to win in just under four hours, a fair declaration, but it was only when Booth came in that the goal began to appear attainable. Ormrod played carefully, but was often in difficulty against the spinners, who could turn the ball, although the wicket never became really difficult. Derbyshire's batting in the morning had been brisker than the day before, Buxton reminding us he has a stroke or two.

When Gibbs, however, was out for 40 scored in 223 minutes, he walked back to the pavilion in a silence which was eloquent and not, in the circumstances, churlish.

Worcestershire v Derbyshire, Kidderminster, 5, 6 & 7 June 1968

Derbyshire won by 21 runs

Derbyshire

P.J.K. Gibbs	lbw b Gifford	14	lbw b Coldwell	40
D.H.K. Smith	st Booth b Griffith	21	b Coldwell	4
M.H. Page	b Holder	45	c Brain b Holder	6
I.R. Buxton	c Ormrod b Holder	14	b Brain	78
* D.C. Morgan	b Brain	28		
J.F. Harvey	c Turner b Holder	10	*not out*	23
+ R.W. Taylor	c Booth b Holder	5	*not out*	8
P.E. Russell	b Coldwell	1		
E. Smith	b Holder	0		
F. Swarbrook	*not out*	4		
H.J. Rhodes	b Gifford	5		
	b 2, lb 6, w 2, nb 3	13	nb 4	4
		160	(4 wkts, dec)	**163**

1/33, 2/35, 3/65, 4/119, 5/139, 6/144, 7/145, 8/150, 9/153, 10/160
1/4, 2/14, 3/103, 4/145

Coldwell	15	7	19	1	25	7	51	2
Holder	18	7	21	5	16	4	40	1
Gifford	27.2	11	38	2	17	13	12	0
Griffith	14	0	39	1	8	0	20	0
Brain	16	5	30	1	15	3	36	1

Worcestershire

R.G.A. Headley	c Taylor b Smith(E)	7	c Swarbrook b Smith(E)	16
C.D. Fearnley	c Page b Smith(E)	23	c Harvey b Russell	16
J.A. Ormrod	c Harvey b Russell	6	c Buxton b Swarbrook	34
E.J.O. Hemsley	c Smith(E) b Swarbrook	10	c Smith(E) b Swarbrook	20
G.M. Turner	c Smith(D) b Swarbrook	17	lbw b Rhodes	48
*+ R. Booth	c Page b Smith(E)	0	run out	61
K. Griffith	*not out*	13	b Rhodes	0
V.A. Holder	c Taylor b Rhodes	1	lbw b Rhodes	1
N. Gifford	c Harvey b Smith(E)	1	*not out*	2
B.M. Brain	c Taylor b Rhodes	11	c sub b Buxton	3
L.J. Coldwell	b Smith(E)	5	b Rhodes	1
			b 1, lb 2, nb 3	6
		94		**208**

1/17, 2/36, 3/36, 4/59, 5/59, 6/63, 7/74, 8/77, 9/89, 10/94
1/19, 2/45, 3/71, 4/92, 5/201, 6/201, 7/203, 8/203, 9/206, 10/208

Buxton	6	4	5	0	8	4	12	1
Rhodes	12	2	32	2	14.3	3	33	4
Smith (E)	29.3	17	37	5	24	9	69	1
Russell	7	3	10	1	15	4	44	1
Swarbrook	10	6	10	2	20	8	44	2

Umpires: O.W. Herman and E. Petrie

Gloucestershire have not exactly set the Clifton Suspension Bridge on fire this season, but their play has had a welcome freshness and attack about it on most occasions, and on the Bristol ground – often a depressed place in recent years – a new hope is cautiously lifting its head. Perhaps the biggest single reason for this has been the arrival of M.J. Procter, from South Africa.

It is not his first acquaintance with the country, or the county. He toured with a South African schools side in 1963, and joined the Gloucestershire staff in 1965. He was then only 19 years old. While qualifying, he played for the second eleven in the match against the South African touring team of that year. But he was not certain that his future lay in county cricket, and returned home to Natal. There his game developed rapidly, and in the 1966-67 season he played in three Tests against Australia.

The relaxed qualification rule reopened the possibility of his playing over here, and he has signed a contract with Gloucestershire for three years, with the proviso that he should be released for the 1970 season if, as is obviously highly probable, he should be chosen for the visiting South African side in that year.

He will not commit himself to his future after that, saying sensibly that he will "see how things go". But there is no doubt that he has the ability to make cricket his career, if he has the inclination; and at present he is enjoying his cricket very much, and has settled down happily in a friendly side.

He has, however, a heavy burden to carry. He has been opening the bowling, usually with a long spell flat out, often switching to medium pace cutters later, to keep an end going. He has been batting at four or five in the order; if the previous batsmen fail (as they often did earlier in the season) he has had to hold the side together; if they succeed, he has had the responsibility of pushing things along.

I have wondered if he was not being asked to do too much, though it is understandable, since he generally looks more like taking wickets or making runs than anyone else. He himself will not hear of any suggestion that he is overworked – the more he has to do, the better he likes it.

He certainly has the right physique. I remember when McKenzie first came over here, a shrewd but taciturn Australian judge was asked his opinion of the newcomer. "He's a strong boy," he said succinctly, and if a little lacking in elaboration, it was the key fact about McKenzie. So it is, I think, with Procter. A strong boy: on the short side, broad, with great power in shoulders and wrists. The toughness of his body contrasts slightly oddly with his round, cherubic face, and straw coloured hair.

On the other hand, he must punish himself a good deal with his bowling action. "He bowls off the wrong foot from extra cover!" was the comment of one startled observer seeing him for the first time. His usual point of delivery is from the very edge of the crease. As for bowling "off the wrong foot", I am not sure that anyone has ever done this in the strictly accurate sense, and Procter's action is more rational when seen from square on than behind the arm. But if he cannot technically be said to bowl off the wrong foot, it would be hard to maintain that he bowls off the right one.

His batting style is quite different. There is no impression of hard labour at all. Even when the situation requires him to play quietly, he cloaks the utilitarian in grace. Attacking, he seems equally good on both sides of the wicket, and must be a very difficult man to whom to set a field.

As I write, he has scored centuries against Hampshire and Glamorgan, and nearly another against Somerset, which people who have seen them all rate his best innings yet. For myself, I ask nothing better for quality, if not for size, than the quick 26 last Sunday. Nottinghamshire were trying to keep the game tight, and had the bowlers to do it, but Procter simply would not let them. Among other memorable strokes there was that comparative rarity, the late cut, played as only the great batsmen can play it.

Yet this innings, like several other of his notable ones, was played on the Bristol wicket. For years we have been given to understand that the Bristol wicket is too slow for stroke play.

Jack Crapp maintains that the pitch is no different now from the time when Hammond used to play on it, and later Graveney, and that it is the attitude of the cricketers which has changed. Procter's performances lend some substance to this point of view. He had not had it drummed into him for years that strokes cannot be played at Bristol, and so he started making them before anyone could stop him.

Generally, he has not found it too difficult to adapt himself to English wickets. He has learnt how to check his stroke when the ball is moving. But he is not allowing, as some English batsmen do, the checked stroke to become the foundation of his game.

I hope I have not written too enthusiastically of this young man. His performance in first class cricket still does not amount to a great deal in terms of figures. He will doubtless find bowling, at least, more difficult as English players on the circuit "get to know him". But the potential is there, and I think the character. If he ultimately decides to settle in the county game it will be very much to the advantage of Gloucestershire, and indeed of cricket.

Mike Procter
'Every muscular inch a fast bowler in the high tradition'

Derek Shackleton 1968

When the future historian of cricket looks back on the period 1950-70, he may well see in Shackleton of Hampshire its most characteristic figure. For this has been the age (and I at least hope that by 1970 it will be passing) when first-class cricket in England has been dominated by seam bowling at fast-medium and medium pace.

There was a sudden flowering of fast bowlers in the 1950s, the heyday of Statham, Tyson and Trueman, but they left no immediate successors. There has been a handful of spin bowlers good enough to leave their mark on the game, even at a time when spin has usually been regarded as superfluous.

But the picture of a day's county cricket typical of this era has been that of a succession of seam bowlers, one following another to the bowling crease, wheeling up over after over at something above medium pace and letting the pitch take their wickets for them. Of this vast company Shackleton has been the most assiduous, accurate and successful.

This is not intended to be a disparagement. It is no disparagement of an infantryman to say that he cannot lead a tank charge. And though tanks may win dramatic battles, infantry are needed to win wars.

Shackleton has been the infantryman of his time par excellence. If all the other bowlers of his type had possessed his qualities, precious few batsmen would have reached 1,000 runs in a season, or a lifetime. To date he has taken 2,841 wickets at an average of 18.62. But this takes no account of the number of wickets he has taken "at the other end", when batsmen, driven to desperation by their inability to get the ball away, have taken unwise risks against lesser bowlers.

Shackleton seems to have been bowling for Hampshire for as long as I can remember. In recent years an early greyness in his hair has added to his venerable aspect. In fact he is not yet 43, and such is the strainless economy of his action that he can surely bowl for years more if he wishes. In 20 consecutive seasons he has taken more than 100 wickets.

Nobody else has done this. Wilfred Rhodes did it more often, in 23 seasons, but they were not consecutive.

His Test match career has not equalled his success with Hampshire. In 1950-51 he played for England against South Africa, the West Indies and India – once against each. He did not play again for England until 1963, which seems hardly conceivable when one thinks of some of those who did.

He was recalled for one of the most dramatic of all Tests, against the West Indies at Lord's, and no one who was there will forget his bowling on the first morning, skies grey and pitch green, a real Shackleton morning. He never bowled a bad ball, and he never took a wicket. Not until the end of the innings, when he took the last three wickets in four balls, were the figures made to do justice. He kept his place in the England side for the rest of the season.

A man who rarely shows emotion, he will admit to a certain nervousness after his recall at Lord's. "It were a bit grim, coming in for Brian (Statham had been dropped). I'd have hated to let lads down."

From which it may be gathered that Shackleton is a north countryman. He was born on the Yorkshire side of Todmorden. When he first came to Hampshire he brought with him something of the traditional northern dourness. Even in the great days of Eagar and Ingleby-Mackenzie, when Hampshire several times threatened to win the championship and once did, his comments were usually reserved ("Skipper's idea of bowling change is take me off at one end and put me on at t'other"). He has mellowed with the years: a grave, gentle person he is now, his character forged in the long, slow fires of 1,000 overs season after season.

Sir Neville Cardus some years ago denied that seam bowling had any tactical validity. He maintained that it cannot be explained logically, as spin bowling can be. Without getting involved in that argument, we may observe that Shackleton, though we think of him as the epitome of the seam bowler, has length, flight and line. In any phase of cricket's history these abilities would have made him an outstanding player.

A chance sneeze

CHESTERFIELD: Derbyshire (3 pts) drew with Yorkshire (6 pts)

The Devil (widely believed in these parts to be a Yorkshireman) once alighted on the pinnacle of a Chesterfield church for a breather on his way back to Sheffield, and by a chance sneeze left the town with its famous crooked spire.

Yesterday, however, Derbyshire showed that they are not to be sneezed at by any Yorkshireman, and at the end of an interesting, fluctuating day's cricket it was Yorkshire's championship prospects which had caught cold.

A Keith Fletcher hundred

SCARBOROUGH: England XI v England Under-25 XI

In the circumstances it seems harsh to criticise, yet I could not help feeling there was something lacking: not so much "personality", a vague and often over-stressed quality, as style. Styles change, of course, and what is considered elegant in one generation may be called clumsy in the next.

But on this evidence we are producing a new brood of Barringtons and Edriches, with never a sign of a Hutton or Compton, or for that matter a Richards or Graveney. There is no high backlift or generous follow through.

Fletcher's innings was highly efficient. He chose the right balls to hit, he hit them hard, he made few mistakes. Yet it could not have been called a beautiful innings, and if this is thought a precious comment, it is worth remembering that once the beauty vanishes from cricket there are lots of better games.

Not that anyone was seriously complaining among another large crowd on another sunny day. There were many things to enjoy one way and another, not least Rumsey's opening ball which nearly decapitated second slip.

Knott and limping Milburn stave off defeat

SCARBOROUGH: Yorkshire drew with M.C.C.

The cricket yesterday on the last day of another highly successful festival was not quite so good as most of what has gone before. This was not really anyone's fault – just the way things work out.

Prideaux, having batted on for a first innings lead of 123, had to try to bowl Yorkshire out; but Boycott and Hampshire looked so confident that soon (too soon, but his motives were understandable) he changed his policy, hoping to prompt a declaration in due course. With Yorkshire still behind, this necessitated a good deal of generosity. Hampshire, and to a lesser extent Boycott, batted well enough, but their hammers were usually hitting rubber anvils.

When the time came for considering a declaration, there was a further complication in that Boycott was gummed up in the 90s. I wondered yesterday whether he could bat like a domestic cat or a puma. He changed species and became a mule. Yet after a long dawdle he decided he would like his century after all (doubtless remembering it will come in useful when he has got the other 199), and Close humoured him to the extent of batting on for a quarter of an hour longer than he should have done.

M.C.C. were left to score 207 at 94 an hour. With Milburn unfit, and the pitch taking a little spin (though I wish most county matches were played on pitches as good as we have had here), it was not a reasonable proposition. Prideaux sportingly decided to try it, himself leading with some splendid strokes. He had some help from Fletcher, in a bright squib of an innings, and from that pleasing cricketer, Michael Buss. But the wickets inevitably tumbled, and by the last 45 minutes it was a question of whether M.C.C. could save the match.

This they just did, thanks chiefly to Knott, who mixed offence and defence in the right proportions. Milburn came in at No. 11, limping, and was carried part of the way from the pavilion by Trueman and Nicholson, staggering under the strain. This was a touch of rich and genuine comedy.

The best thing about the day was the bowling of Illingworth. When Trueman came on to bowl the band played "Old Man River", with actions by the hero. When Illingworth came on they played "For He's a Jolly Good Fellow". The crowd, taken by surprise, applauded hesitantly and then warmly. Illingworth stood quietly, head a little bowed. It was a moving moment. It made us remember, not what he might gain from leaving Yorkshire, but what he is giving up.

This festival will also be remembered for the happy presidency of Mr. Herbert Sutcliffe, who has come a long way since he first appeared here as Sutcliffe, H. It was the apotheosis of Sutcliffe, and it was interesting to see that he paid as much attention to the ordinary cricket follower as to the nobs; a great man moving among his own people.

Who, I wondered, will be president 40 years on? Mr. Close? The Rt. Hon. Frederick Trueman? Sir Geoffrey Boycott? It would be nice to think it could be Illingworth, R.

Farewell to the season, then, from Scarborough, which for 10 days has been, in more senses than one, an island of cricketing peace in a sea of storm.

YORKSHIRE	199 (Padgett 62, Hobbs 5-71) & 329 for four declared (Boycott 102*, Hampshire 97)
M.C.C.	322 for nine declared (Fletcher 113*, Prideaux 69, Milburn 56) & 158 for nine (Knott 62*, Illingworth 7-73)

1969

1969 was a curate's egg of a year. Neil Armstrong and Buzz Aldrin walked on the moon, Concorde made its first flight, colour television arrived in Britain and the Beatles released *Abbey Road.* On the other side of the coin, Richard Nixon was elected US President, the Battle of the Bogside triggered the start of The Troubles in Northern Ireland and the Beatles split up. In Alan Gibson's life, whilst he was now firmly established at *The Times*, the demise of BBC regional broadcasting represented a potentially serious blow to his earning capacity, as well as a considerable personal sadness.

The English summer could also be characterised as good in parts. After the usual dismal May, in which only five out of 24 championship matches were won or lost, the weather gradually improved, although the rain returned in August. As for the cricket, the county championship built steadily to an exciting climax, while the advent of the 40-over Sunday competition – known in its first season as the Players County League – drew in the crowds and provided a much-needed boost to county gate receipts. Alan was at Bristol to see Gloucestershire's first Sunday match, against Warwickshire, and, perhaps surprisingly, given his aversion to anything that smacked of modernity or populism, he seems quite to have enjoyed this 'instant cricket' as it was dubbed.

West Indies and New Zealand were the touring sides, each with three Tests. The West Indies, under Sobers, were in transition. In view of what was to come in the 70s and 80s, it seems extraordinary that they went into the First Test with a pace attack consisting of Vanburn Holder, the military medium John Shepherd and Sobers himself. They also had the worst of the weather, which ruined their first four matches against the counties. The fifth, against Gloucestershire at Bristol, was supposed to have marked my debut as a scorer for the BBC, and I duly travelled down from Oxford, armed with Bill Frindall's patent scoresheets, brimming with nervous anticipation and ready to provide the match commentators – who just happened to be my own father and Roy Lawrence from the West Indies – with all of the information they could possible require. Needless to say, it was raining steadily as I arrived, and never looked like easing. The commentators and their scorer duly repaired to the County Ground Hotel as soon as was decent, and remained there until closing time!

The county championship was also badly affected by the weather. However, by the middle of June, some pattern was beginning to emerge, with Gloucestershire out in front, thanks mainly to Procter's devastating fast bowling. At this stage of the season, few people would have tipped Glamorgan as potential champions. When they travelled to play Hampshire at Bournemouth on June 14, they were 11th in the table, with just one win and 27 points to show for their efforts. The match started on a Saturday, so *The Times* only carried reports on the second and third days, which turned out to include one of the most controversial incidents in the entire season.

The weather did provide the occasion for a classic Gibson report, which he devoted almost in its entirety to a description of that most famous of umpiring double acts – Syd Buller and Charlie Elliott – inspecting the pitch at Edgbaston. To their eternal credit, given the pressure on space, *The Times* printed it in full.

Meanwhile, Gloucestershire were marching on. From June 24, when their own spin twins, Mortimore and Allen, bowled out Hampshire in their second innings for just 63, they won six matches off the reel, all of them pretty comfortably. Alan watched the last three of those, against Worcestershire, Derbyshire and what seemed at the time to be the clincher, against Yorkshire, the reigning champions, at

Tests
England
beat West Indies
2-0, with one draw
England
beat New Zealand
2-0, with one draw

Championship
1 Glamorgan
2 Gloucestershire
3 Surrey
4 Warwickshire
5 Hampshire
6 Essex

Sunday League
1 Lancashire
2 Hampshire
3 Essex
4 Kent
5 Surrey
6 Gloucestershire

Gillette Cup Final
Yorkshire
beat Derbyshire

Most first-class runs
1 J.H. Edrich
2 B.W. Luckhurst
3 Mushtaq Mohammad

Most first-class wickets
1 R.M.H. Cottam
2 T.W. Cartwright
M.J. Procter

Gloucester. That win left Gloucestershire with 158 points, a full 50 points clear of second-placed Hampshire, with Glamorgan fourth on 89, a total which included the – subsequently rescinded – 10 points they had been awarded for their dubious 'victory' at Bournemouth. Under the circumstances, Alan's suggestion that 'Gloucestershire will take some stopping now' seems distinctly cautious.

But Nemesis was just around the corner. Gloucestershire's match against Glamorgan at Cardiff was the turning point of the season. Alan's assessment that the reverse would 'strengthen rather than blunt the team's resolution' proved not to be prescient. From that point on, they struggled, while Glamorgan, a happy side, who made the absolute utmost of their potential under the intelligent captaincy of Tony Lewis, moved cheerfully from strength to strength.

Yorkshire, county champions for the past two seasons, were having a disappointing time of it in the three-day game, although the Gillette Cup provided handsome consolation. On July 30, Alan was there to watch them defeat Nottinghamshire, Sobers and all, in the semi-final at Scarborough. Even without the injured Boycott, they proved to be too strong for Derbyshire in the final.

Alan saw relatively little of Somerset in 1969. Whilst their West Country neighbours flourished, they languished, winning only one championship match in the entire season and finishing comfortably bottom. They fared no better in the shorter form of the game: knocked out in the first round of the Gillette by Derbyshire, and second to bottom in the Sunday League. However, if this was a season that, overall, Somerset would rather forget, it did hold the promise of better things to come, not least in the shape of the county's two home-grown, blond-haired left-handers, Peter Denning and Brian Rose. The sight of them batting together against Warwickshire on a hot afternoon at Clarence Park in August is an abiding memory for me, and it is all of our good fortune that Alan was there as well.

Dressed for the beach, with Adam

After that, the season ended in anti-climax, for Alan Gibson as well as for Gloucestershire. For some reason, *The Times* could find room for only two county cricket reports a day in the run-in to the championship, despite it providing the closest and most exciting contest for years, and they mostly didn't include one from Alan. By the time he was sent to report the second and third days of Gloucestershire's penultimate match, against Somerset at Bristol, it was almost all over. Glamorgan were 12 points ahead, with three matches to play, as against Gloucestershire's two. So if they could get the better of Essex at Swansea they would be in an almost unassailable position. That is how it turned out, but only just. In front of an ecstatic crowd of 12,000, Glamorgan scraped home by one run, when John Lever was run out going for the second run that would have levelled the scores, in the final over. So even though Gloucestershire managed a win against their neighbours, they knew in their hearts it would be in vain.

With the championship now all over bar the shouting – of which there was a great deal, to the west of the Severn! – Alan was dispatched to Scarborough, for the Festival. And after that, it was back to the rugby, to his autobiography, to Rosie and Adam and to the ever-growing furore over sporting links with South Africa.

Ibadulla impresses

BRISTOL: Warwickshire (4pts) beat Gloucestershire by 59 runs

Sunday League cricket made a tolerably successful start in this match, which was seen by perhaps 2,000 people, which is more than Gloucestershire have had for most championship matches in recent years.

The cricket was of encouraging quality. With county pride at stake, quite apart from financial rewards, these matches are clearly going to be more than staged frolics.

On a more mundane level, this match suggested that 150 will be a good score in this competition (a very good one, on a wicket as slow as this) and that a sensible side will resist the temptation to rush things. In 12 overs, Warwickshire scored 13 runs, losing the wickets of Stewart and Barber while they were doing it. After 20 overs, they were only 46, with Amiss and M.J.K. Smith out. But they did not panic. Ibadulla and Jameson steadily pushed up the rate, without excessive risk. Ibadulla's cross-flat-batted bangs in the direction of mid-off certainly looked risky, but he chose the moments for them shrewdly.

Cartwright provided some genial thumps, and Gloucestershire, who had (we all thought) been doing so well, wanted just 150. The least effective of the Gloucestershire bowlers was Procter, who was clearly unhappy when deprived of his long, springing run.

Green and Nicholls set off full of confidence, and in 12 overs had more than doubled the equivalent Warwickshire score.

Warwickshire bowled and fielded diligently, and waited for the apples to fall, shaken from the tree by the wind of Gloucestershire's own anxiety. The remarkable individual performance was that of Ibadulla, who bowled his eight overs for 13 runs and took the first four wickets.

Gloucestershire v Warwickshire, Bristol, 27 April 1969

Warwickshire won by 59 runs

Warwickshire

R.W. Barber	c Meyer b Green	3
W.J. Stewart	lbw b Smith	6
D.L. Amiss	b Brown	16
M.J.K. Smith	b Green	11
J.A. Jameson	c Shepherd b Mortimore	33
K. Ibadulla	c Meyer b Brown	29
*+ A.C. Smith	c Meyer b Brown	3
T.W. Cartwright	b Mortimore	23
D.J. Brown	lbw b Mortimorre	1
W. Blenkiron	*not out*	4
L.R. Gibbs	*not out*	7
	b 4, lb 9	13
	(9 wkts, 40 overs)	**149**

1/10, 2/12, 3/38, 4/46, 5/93, 6/101, 7/115, 8/126, 9/137

Smith	8	3	24	1
Green	8	2	26	2
Brown	8	3	21	3
Procter	8	2	23	0
Mortimore	8	1	42	3

Gloucestershire

R.B. Nicholls	c Blenkiron b Ibadulla	14
D.M. Green	c Jameson b Ibadulla	13
M.J. Procter	b Ibadulla	7
C.A. Milton	lbw b Ibadulla	11
G. Pullar	run out	2
D. Shepherd	c Jameson b Blenkiron	12
* A.S. Brown	c Cartwright b Gibbs	11
M. Bissex	c & b Blenkiron	10
J.B. Mortimore	run out	6
D.R. Smith	b Gibbs	0
+ B.J. Meyer	not out	1
	lb 3	3
	(34.1 overs)	**90**

1/27, 2/30, 3/44, 4/47, 5/53, 6/62, 7/83, 8/83, 9/83, 10/90

Cartwright	8	3	16	0
Ibadulla	8	4	13	4
Blenkiron	8	1	30	2
Brown	5	1	14	0
Gibbs	5.1	1	14	2

Umpires: P.B. Wight and C.S. Elliott

Neighbours blamed

BATH: Somerset v Northamptonshire

It never seemed likely that there would be much play and sure enough, after a couple of preliminary showers which interrupted play, the clouds coming over from the hills to the south-east emptied themselves, and everything was drenched by lunchtime.

It was, a Somerset farmer explained, the fault of the neighbouring county. "We do never get this weather, not on our own. 'Tis Wiltshire sends it over to us."

Rain allows only ten overs

BIRMINGHAM: Somerset, with all their first innings wickets in hand, are 328 runs behind Warwickshire

There was one moment to cherish in yet another day conquered by rain. This was at 4.30 when the umpires, Buller and Elliott, stepped forth from the pavilion to determine whether further play was possible.

Not since the days of Hobbs and Sutcliffe have such noble entrances upon the field been made as by these two: "Elliott and Buller" the spectators murmured to themselves, just as they murmured "Hobbs and Sutcliffe" long ago. And this is not absurd since Buller and Elliott have become persons, almost in their cricketing right: more so, surely, than any other participant in this match.

Solemn their tread; stately their deportment. Elliott carries a huge green umbrella, upright as the back of Hobbs. Buller stumbles slightly in his attempts to keep under it, and we gasp as we did when Sutcliffe got an edge to Grimmett. The pitch is soaked, the rain has been pelting down for hours, and is going to do so for hours more, but Buller and Elliott examine the situation with infinite care. Elliott digs a delicate toe, Buller, robust Dalesman, presses with his thumb. They consult, shake their heads, return sedately to the pavilion, refusing to hurry as the rain whips their ankles and soddens the vast umbrella, with its poignant memories of roof gardens and ice cream, before our eyes.

Buller spoils the picture a little by an indication to the press box that all is off: but we hardened veterans of last week's Bournemouth campaign are having none of that and wait grimly for the formal announcement.

There were 10 overs of cricket before luncheon in spasms. Virgin and Clarkson scored 28 runs, and Warwickshire took no wicket.

The clouds always gave the proceedings a futile air. It took Elliott and Buller to remind me, and the hundred or so others present, that cricket is still not a joke.

Syd Buller and Charlie Elliott
'Solemn their tread; stately their deportment'

Majid and E Jones avert follow-on

BOURNEMOUTH: Glamorgan, with three first innings wickets in hand, are 81 runs behind Hampshire

Cricket at Bournemouth has lost a little of its charm for me, since I can no longer travel there by the Somerset and Dorset Railway. The perfect preliminary was to catch the Pines express, fighting for its dignity as it stopped and started at tiny stations with names like Evercreech Junction and Midsomer Norton, down through that blissful countryside.

Come to think of it, the day's cricket made rather a fitful, though quietly enjoyable journey. Much attention was directed to the wicket. It had obviously played well enough on Saturday, but yesterday morning the ball was lifting awkwardly, perhaps once or twice an over. This suggested trouble for Glamorgan, and when they had lost five batsmen for 73 – only Davis showing real promise of building an innings – we were thinking of an early finish.

As the afternoon wore on, the wicket was playing rather better. Perhaps the wet weather, which caused play to start 50 minutes late, had created under the covers slight moisture, which vanished in the afternoon sun. I cannot understand the physics of it, but this does seem to happen sometimes, especially on seaside grounds. Apart from this, though, the pitch showed signs of wear, and batting fourth will not be easy. Marshall might well not have enforced the follow-on.

However that may be, he was given no choice, thanks to a stand of 128 for the sixth wicket by Majid and E. Jones. They were in difficulties for a while, playing and missing and just dodging the fielders with some insecure lofted strokes, but they both have good temperaments for an awkward situation. They made a nice contrast: Majid glistened, elegant in the off drive and the glance, Jones (three sixes) squat and fierce on the leg side.

It was White who did the damage to the innings. He bowled at a fine pace and kept going for a long time, less the Pines express than the non-stop Bournemouth Belle. With a shade more luck he would have broken the Hampshire innings but he was short of support. Cottam did not seem able to find the right length for the wicket. Sainsbury provided accuracy, little more. Castell bowled leg breaks, frequently overpitching, and also seamers with the new ball. These were less interesting, but more effective. Majid was bowled when he attempted a drive with his head in the air. Jesty was off the field, unwell, a handicap to Hampshire which seemed more important after tea than at lunchtime.

Hampshire in all have taken seven bonus points against two, and are still well placed, though their cricket became a little untidy towards the end, with Jones still thumping away, and Cordle and Nash vigorously joining in.

Glamorgan have a one-sided victory

BOURNEMOUTH: Glamorgan (12 pts) beat Hampshire (7pts) by default

"When the umpire shall call 'play' the party refusing to play shall lose the match." This, referring both to the state of play, and to intervals (including the fall of a wicket) was set down in the Laws of Cricket as revised by the Marylebone Club in 1830. It has always been, and remains, the basic assumption of any match at cricket.

I suppose the result of this match should be recorded as: "Glamorgan won because Hampshire refused to play." Not that they refused in any deliberate sense. They had simply gone away under the impression that the match was over.

To set the scene: at the beginning of the day Glamorgan, faced with Hampshire's declared total of 337, had scored 256 for seven. A.R. Lewis, the Glamorgan captain, slightly surprisingly, decided to bat on. He was presumably hoping for a few more quick boundaries from E. Jones, who indeed got a couple of lusty ones. But when Jones was caught and bowled, after 20 minutes, Glamorgan declared, which was sad for Williams, who was just beginning to get his eye in.

The Hampshire second innings had not really begun to take shape when the rain started. It was slow, persistent, dismal rain. Lunch was taken early. The rain drizzled on. We longed for a storm to end the futility of hanging around. Duty, not hope, kept us miserably waiting.

The public, such of them as were present, was given no indication of what decisions might be taken about the future of play, and gradually drifted away. At four o'clock, sitting in the little pavilion and contemplating a cold, flat beer, I saw the Hampshire team leave, changed and off to the next engagement. I concluded that all was over, and ordered a taxi.

Perhaps five minutes later the Glamorgan team came out of their dressing room also changed, packed and ready to depart. A.R. Lewis spoke, casually but sensibly enough to the senior umpire, Wight. Lewis said: "I suppose it is all off?" Wight replied to this effect: "There are more than two hours to go, the rain is not heavy, the wicket will be playable almost as soon as it stops. It is far too early to abandon the match." Someone said: "Does Marshall know?" Wight replied: "I have not been asked."

In this decision, Wight was, in my view, unquestionably right, and his fellow umpire, Budd – a former Hampshire player – was strong in agreement with him.

So Glamorgan stayed on the ground. Efforts were unsuccessfully made to contact the scattered Hampshire team. At 5 o'clock the rain had almost stopped. The umpires made an inspection and ordered mopping up operations. Satisfied with these, they decreed a resumption of play at 5.30.

Glamorgan, unnecessarily, changed back into flannels (or thereabouts, Walker was partly revealing a fetching pink undergarment) and took their places on the field. Budd, the bowling umpire, called "Play". It was all quite properly done. There was no unseemly hurry. Cordle marked out his run.

And then, at 5.31 – believe me I do not exaggerate – the flimsy drizzle developed into serious rain. A batsman might have been justified in walking off, but there were no batsmen. Glamorgan stoicly stuck it out in the field (Walker had taken up an aggressive position within the return crease). Wight looked at his watch, measuring every agonizing second, and after the necessary two minutes turned back towards the pavilion.

Glamorgan had taken 10 points for a win, because the other party had refused to play. This gave them 12 points to Hampshire's seven, though I suppose it is arguable, and will be argued, whether a side failing to come up to the scratch is entitled to any points at all.

No criticism can be made of the umpires. The weather was good enough at 5.30 to resume play, and though it rained shortly thereafter both sides had played through heavier rain in the morning. The question why Marshall, the Hampshire captain, was so confident that the game was over, is more difficult. I was assured by the umpires that they had said nothing whatsoever to give him such an impression. My own guess is that it started from one of those well meaning busybodies who are sometimes found at cricket grounds. A glance at the foreboding sky, a wave of the hand, and "all off!" they knowingly say. And the rest of us, also liking to be busy and knowing, pass it on to our neighbours – "All off! All off!" – and it percolates to the dressing room. Still, it is a captain's job to make sure.

* *Editor's note: The umpires' decision was at first upheld by the MCC, and then reversed, on appeal. According to Roy Marshall's account, in his book 'Test Outcast', the 'misunderstanding' stemmed from a conversation between the two captains in which they (a) decided to call the match off but (b) agreed on an early tea. The umpires, not unreasonably, took it from the decision to take tea that the captains had not agreed on an abandonment. All one can say at this distance is that the final outcome was almost certainly the right one.*

JULY: J.G.W. Davies's XI v Cambridge University at Eastbourne

Jorden's good spell ends resistance

EASTBOURNE: Cambridge University beat J.G.W. Davies's XI by nine wickets

As a contest this match ended when Jorden took two wickets for one run almost as soon as play began. He kept himself on to take a third, and left the rest to the gentle spin of Ross and Pearman, which was sufficient for some undistinguished batting.

Haywood showed fight, and drove one noble six, but he had an air of impermanence. No one had both the skill and the resolution to organize a sustained counter attack. Cambridge needed only 21 when they went in again, and the match was over shortly after one o'clock.

This was a pity, except for those of us with journeys to make, and selfish thoughts of getting home for dinner, for it was a lovely day and the Saffrons is a fine place to watch cricket. Why, I wonder, is it called the Saffrons? No one seemed to know, not even Wilfred Wooller.

Mr Wooller has been groundsman for 50 years, following his father who put in a mere 40 or so at the job. He produces first-rate wickets, better than most county grounds. He is revered among cricketers in these parts. I asked if he was any relation to another man of the same name, and they said to me, "Who would that be?"

Shepherd century brings triumph in last over

WORCESTER: Gloucestershire (15 pts) beat Worcestershire (6 pts) by three wickets

Gloucesershire are keeping it up. They were asked to score 211 in 140 minutes yesterday, which had not at the time seemed a particularly generous invitation, and Allen hit the winning boundary from the first ball of the last over.

The last 20 overs took 85 minutes to bowl, half of them in pouring rain. When the rain was at its worst, both sides had a chance of winning and were obviously anxious to play on. There was general agreement that by doing so they made a fine, sporting finish. All the same, the rain was so severe that I doubt if the umpires were strictly justified in staying on the field.

In the morning Worcestershire scored 132 runs from 49 overs. It was hardly a match-winning rate, but the bowling was steady, and Worcestershire were handicapped when Graveney strained himself. The hamstring, as it is inelegantly called, is damaged, and Graveney is not expected to play again for about a fortnight.

After lunch D'Oliveira let the bat fly occasionally. The argument for the declaration was that on a wicket still playing easily, Worcestershire could only win if Gloucestershire took extravagant risks, and that in their present situation Gloucestershire would be bound to try for anything. Leading the championship is not all cherries.

This was more or less what happened. Gloucestershire lost two wickets to a good spell by Coldwell, and should have lost a third when Milton and Shepherd were again in an alarming mix-up between the wickets. Shepherd had no sort of form to begin with, and could have been out to his first two scoring strokes, each snicked for four off Brain.

Gifford, the acting Worcestershire captain, put on himself and Slade, which was the right sort of gesture. But had he given the fast bowlers another couple of overs at Shepherd, I cannot help wondering if the result might not have been different.

Shepherd began middling the ball, and had eight fours (five intended) and two sixes in his first 50. The quick bowlers returned but Gloucestershire had their teeth in: 102 runs were wanted when the 20 overs were called.

There was a minor collapse when Milton, who played admirably again, was bowled; and with six down for 166 Worcestershire glimpsed hope again. But then Shepherd began swinging once more, Mortimore and Allen lending valuable support; catches went down, overthrows occurred, 23 runs in three overs became three in one.

Mortimore and Allen in control

GLOUCESTER: Gloucestershire (18 pts) beat Derbyshire (2 pts) by an innings and 10 runs

The match ended at 3.35. Gloucestershire career onwards, with five wins on the trot or, more accurately, the gallop. Many of their supporters, feasting on success after years of a siege diet, are already saying grace after meat. This is premature. But they have a long lead, and are playing like giants. The Yorkshire match, which comes next should tell us a good deal about the long-term prospects.

It was another doleful day for Derbyshire. Their only comfort is that they are, as we all know, a much better side than such limp form suggests. Gloucestershire themselves were in a similar predicament two or three years ago.

The pitch yesterday took spin. Procter had a formal bowl, Smith a rather less formal one, several times beating the bat. Allen came on, then Mortimore. By 12.30 the scene was set. Here were the two great Gloucestershire spinners, the Goddard and Sinfield of their era. Their methods are very different, which is one of their strengths. Allen is most dangerous off the pitch, Mortimore in the air.

Allen has played in 39 Test matches, Mortimore in nine – a false ratio, since there has never been much between them in quality. Since Wilson and Illingworth parted company, there is no pair of spinners in the country so likely to bowl any side out quickly on a turning wicket.

Not, I must make clear, that it was a vicious pitch. It turned only a little more than a county wicket should on a third day. It needed to be allied with sensitive, skilled bowling to produce so crushing a result.

The batsman Smith was out sweeping, but for a while Gibbs and Hall tacked their responsibilities soundly. Hall played the spin with the face of the bat shutting, keeping it on the ground to thwart the two clutching short legs, but was caught there in the end. Gibbs played the line, head down, but Mortimore found the edge of his bat with a ball which, I would guess, went with the arm, and had him caught at slip. He then bowled one that, unusually, lifted steeply, and Buxton was gone.

Allen and Mortimore, taking turn and turn about, and holding each other's catches, wasted little time about the rest, until Rhodes and Swarbrook made a last-wicket stand. It is tempting to say that this showed the other batsmen what might have been done, but I doubt if that is true. It was simply that, with heaps of time to spare, the bowling had relaxed by then. Even Mortimore and Allen are human.

Gloucester make runs with time to spare

GLOUCESTER: Gloucestershire (15 pts) beat Yorkshire (4 pts) by five wickets

Gloucestershire had four overs to spare when they won, and indeed were always winning from the time they began their second innings, requiring 151 in 105 minutes. The crowd, a big one for a third day, cheered every run, and had few moments of anxiety.

Yet Gloucestershire only reached this position because of a declaration by Close which gave Yorkshire, with three fit bowlers and only one of them a spinner, the remotest of chances of victory. And this was the odder because Close himself had played an innings to stir any Yorkshire heart, in taking his side from imminent defeat to safety.

I can only suspect that he does not see Yorkshire as championship challengers this year, and felt friendly. Certainly this match was played in a friendly spirit: we even saw the Gloucestershire captain fielding as substitute when Yorkshire's collection of injuries had reduced them to 10 men in the neighbourhood.

But if it was a curious ending, it was another very good day of cricket. At one o'clock Yorkshire were 79 for five, Hutton just having played a stroke which might have prompted his father to dig a grave to turn in. Woodford had played well again, until he was caught at long leg, after unwisely but courageously engaging in a contest with Procter to see whether he could hook or not.

Binks and Johnson, who surely has a cricket career to look forward to, steadied Yorkshire but when Smith found a good one for Binks Yorkshire were only 70 on.

Then came forth Close, limping heavily, with runner. Some of the crowd cried "Old soldier", but that he was in real pain was obvious from all but the most obtuse angle. He battled on to tea, losing only Johnson on the way. He showed us defensive batting of the highest quality, against Mortimore and Allen – both of whom consistently tried to lure him into the area of pain; and also against Procter, who flung himself into action with both the old ball and the new.

At tea, the crowd now converted, warmly applauded Close back. It was "a captain's innings", as everyone was saying, and it had, we assumed, saved the match. Then he declared – only, to be sure, at the end of the tea interval, to knock ten minutes off Gloucestershire's time.

But Green and Nicholls, and then Procter, all of them bubbling with confidence, saw that Gloucestershire did not miss the opportunity.

Well, there. As we used to say in Ilkley, "nowt so queer as folk". Gloucestershire will take some stopping now.

Disasters that will fire the spirit of Gloucester

CARDIFF: Glamorgan (19 pts) beat Gloucestershire (3 pts) by 208 runs

"A great game of cricket," said the Cardiff announcer afterwards, "and we trust the return match at Cheltenham will be equally enjoyable." This produced a few wry Gloucestershire faces. They cannot have enjoyed themselves much.

They batted badly again in the second innings. They got themselves out before we had a chance to see whether the wicket would turn into a spinners' friend. Glamorgan's out-cricket was steady and keen, but no county side could have an adequate reason in such conditions for being bowled out before lunch, as Gloucestershire so nearly were.

They had lost nine wickets for 108 in the fiftieth over, before one o'clock, and it took a brave innings by Mortimore to take the game into the afternoon – by 11 balls. The damage occurred chiefly in four overs, from the twenty-fifth to the twenty-eighth, when Gloucestershire went from 59 for two to 62 for seven. Milton stopped in his stroke and was caught and bowled. Pullar was run out: a tight decision, but there had been hesitation on the run. If Gloucestershire do not win the championship, it will be due as much as anything to their lamentable running between the wickets. Shepherd was caught at mid-on from a lamentable stroke. Brown was smartly caught at backward short leg. Allen was bowled first ball from what, had it captured a less illustrious wicket, we would have called a half-volley.

Mortimore, who hardly ever looked in troubled, scored freely in the last wicket stand. I imagined he intended drawings things to an appropriate close in the last over before lunch, but he was batting too well, and hit two sixes instead. The clouds stayed high, no rain fell, and so Lewis, the Glamorgan captain, had no need of his fast car. Not to enforce the follow-on was still a perilous risk for him to take, but of course by the end he had no enemy in the world.

The match has been a useful corrective to the more exuberant Gloucestershire supporters, and the result will, I think, sharpen rather than blunt the team's resolution. At this moment, if compelled to choose, I would still favour Gloucestershire's chances over Glamorgan, because Glamorgan have no fast bowler – though they must be encouraged by the form of Williams, who bowls slightly above medium pace. But under the present points system, several other counties can yet have a good deal to say.

Palmer's good day

WESTON-SUPER-MARE: Somerset, with seven first innings wickets in hand, are 188 runs behind Warwickshire

The day was overcast, with a chill wind; a day on which Cartwright, when he won the toss, must have been tempted to bowl himself. He settled for the orthodox, and batted, whereupon Barber, Ibadulla, and Kanhai were out for 18. Their wickets fell to Roy Palmer, who has taken up succession to his brother, Kenneth, in Somerset's opening attack.

He has been on the edge of the side for some years, and at the end of this day's work found himself the richer by six wickets, and his county cap. He has an awkward, angular action, and his line is sometimes erratic, but he has plenty of vigour and can swing the ball about.

After their early losses, Warwickshire fell back on stern resistance. At luncheon 38 overs had been bowled, 67 runs scored, and another wicket lost, Jameson caught at mid-on from a poor shot.

Cartwright was out when Palmer returned; one was much the best batsman of the innings as the other was the best bowler. The rest swung their bats hopefully, but only with much heavy breathing did the run rate clamber above two an over.

Somerset had to face the Warwickshire fast bowlers for 40 minutes in poor light, and lost three wickets. This was the most interesting cricket of the day, partly because of the fine bowling, partly because of the batting of Chappell.

Two young men to the rescue

WESTON-SUPER-MARE: Somerset, with all second innings wickets in hand, need 205 runs to beat Warwickshire

All day the ball swung in the air and the pitch, with neither sun nor wind to dry it, made batting uncomfortable. Warwickshire's position at the end was the stronger, barring an unforeseen change in the weather.

Yet the cricket generally was better than the day before, both in its temper and tempo. The day began with an interesting contest between Chappell and Brown, who bowled really fast with eight men around the bat. Chappell hit him square on the off and wide on the on, both for four, and seemed to be winning the duel when he was out at the other end to a ball from Cartwright, which dipped under his diving bat.

It was the kind of situation which made it easy to predict five wickets for Cartwright (he has bowled Somerset out at Weston before) and, in fact, he finished with six. But he and Warwickshire were held up for a long while by two of Somerset's young men, Rose and Denning.

There are many similarities between these two. They are both fair-haired (the cut modern, but not extreme), and left-handed, and in their first season, and, most important of all, home-bred. Denning is from Chewton Mendip, where one hopes that great peal will one day ring in his honour. Rose is from Weston itself – he was warmly encouraged by some of those who only last year were his schoolmates. Both of them have style, and their stand suggested they may also have application. They put on 63 for the seventh wicket in 80 minutes and this, with a hearty blow or two from Langford, saved Somerset from ruin.

Somerset foiled

WESTON-SUPER-MARE: Warwickshire (15 pts) beat Somerset (2 pts) by 44 runs

Although Warwickshire won in the end with three-quarters of an hour as well as runs to spare yesterday, we had a day's cricket which will remind those who saw it to come again; a proper end to the Weston festival.

At 11.40 in the morning nothing seemed less likely. We had had just over half an hour's play in bad light, and the rain had begun with that quiet remorseless look which rain has when it does not intend stopping. Not that there was anything to cheer Somerset supporters if it did, because their county, setting out to score 211, had lost their first five wickets for 16 runs.

The collapse was caused chiefly by some searching, swinging bowling by Brown and, more particularly, by Blenkiron, who at one point took three wickets in five balls. They were assisted by some inept batting. Chappell and Kitchen both got out from airy heaves. I know that it is the readiness of such batsmen as these two to take chances which make them good to watch, but there is a difference, if you can swim a bit, between jumping in at the deep end and throwing yourself over the Clifton suspension bridge.

An hour and 40 minutes, in all, were lost to the rain. In a brief spell before lunch Rose and Denning, the youthful heroes of the first innings, if not exactly standing firm, at least kept their footing, and did so again for a while when another start was made, shortly before three. The score was 54 when Denning was caught at the wicket: at least, we said, an improvement. Rose decided to attack and had hit McVicker for 15 in an over when he was caught at slip: at least, we said, a brave gesture. But that was 81 for seven and all the batsmen gone.

Yet the stand which followed prospered so well that we began to think, incredulously, that Somerset might win. One cheerful gentleman went even further. A jolly, red-faced, tubby chap, he was all I suppose Somerset supporters ought to be. In the morning he had repeatedly declaimed, in reference to the early Somerset batting: "What a click!" But now his cry was: "We got un, boays!"

Robinson and Langford played extremely well. They settled in before they tried to go for their strokes. I do not remember seeing Langford bat better. At 147 for seven, 64 needed, with more than an hour to go, it was possible for a Somerset realist to be optimistic.

Then Cartwright bowled Robinson, and soon afterwards all was over. It would be Cartwright. It was Cartwright who had got Denning and Rose out. It was Cartwright who had twice saved the Warwickshire batting, and bowled Somerset out in the first innings. Yes, it *would* be Cartwright. "What a player that bloke is," said my Somerset supporter; at least, that was his meaning, if not precisely his phraseology.

Somerset v Warwickshire, Weston-super-Mare, 13, 14 & 15 August 1969

Warwickshire won by 44 runs

Warwickshire

R.W. Barber	lbw b Palmer	4	b Burgess	14
K. Ibadulla	lbw b Palmer	8	lbw b Palmer	1
R.B. Kanhai	c Carter b Palmer	6	c Carter b Chappell	45
J.A. Jameson	c Denning b Jameson	22	lbw b Chappell	11
D.L. Amiss	c & b Langford	60	c Carter b Chappell	0
* T.W. Cartwright	c Denning b Palmer	75	lbw b Burgess	25
+ J.I. McDowell	st Carter b Robinson	2	lbw b Chappell	7
D.J. Brown	b Palmer	15	b Chappell	3
N.M. McVicker	b Burgess	8	c Virgin b Robinson	10
W. Blenkiron	lbw b Palmer	18	*not out*	23
L.R. Gibbs	*not out*	0	b Robinson	0
	b 2, lb 4	6	b 4, lb 4, nb 2	10
		224		**149**

1/12, 2/13, 3/18, 4/53, 5/158, 6/167, 7/189, 8/202, 9/210, 10/224
1/15, 2/21, 3/71, 4/71, 5/80, 6/106, 7/110, 8/113, 9/149, 10/149

Palmer	22.3	5	49	6	8	1	41	1
Burgess	23	8	47	2	15	2	38	2
Langford	24	11	39	1	1	0	4	0
Chappell	11	1	34	0	18	6	33	5
Robinson	22	8	49	1	12	6	23	2

Somerset

R.T. Virgin	b Brown	14	c McDowell b Blenkiron	5
A. Clarkson	c McVicker b Brown	0	lbw b Brown	5
G.S. Chappell	b Cartwright	37	c McVicker b Blenkiron	3
M.J. Kitchen	lbw b Cartwright	1	c Jameson b Blenkiron	2
P.J. Robinson	b Brown	13	b Cartwright	33
P. Denning	*not out*	30	c McDowell b Cartwright	19
G. Burgess	b Cartwright	0	lbw b Blenkiron	0
B.C. Rose	c Blenkiron b Cartwright	42	c Amiss b Cartwright	40
* B.A. Langford	c Kanhai b Cartwright	22	*not out*	50
R. Palmer	b Cartwright	0	lbw b Brown	0
+ C.E.P. Carter	run out	0	c McDowell b Brown	0
	b 4	4	b 1, lb 4, nb 4	9
		163		**166**

1/3, 2/28, 3/29, 4/52, 5/66, 6/70, 7/133, 8/163, 9/163, 10/163
1/11, 2/11, 3/16, 4/16, 5/16, 6/54, 7/81, 8/147, 9/156, 10/166

Brown	17	0	72	3	11	5	29	3
Blenkiron	8	1	19	0	8	3	37	4
Cartwright	24	9	36	6	20	8	35	3
McVicker	5	0	20	0	6	1	28	0
Gibbs	12	6	12	0	8	4	7	0
Barber					6	2	21	0

Umpires: F. Jakeman and C.G. Pepper

The Wagon Works Ground, Gloucester

Clarence Park, Weston-super-Mare

Sharpe's batting wins award

SCARBOROUGH: Yorkshire beat Nottinghamshire by 68 runs

Even the return of Sobers to the Nottinghamshire side could not thwart a Yorkshire team determined to salvage something from what has been an unhappy summer for them. By reaching the Gillette Cup final for the second time Yorkshire have done far more than seemed likely at one stage of the season.

A bad start yesterday was redeemed by Sharpe, who earned the man of the match award. He dominated a more than useful stand with Padgett. Later the newcomers in the Yorkshire attack, Old and Stringer, both uncapped, proved too skilful and lively for some disappointing Nottinghamshire batting.

The Scarborough ground, which holds about 20,000, seemed to sway with the heat of the sun and the emotions of the packed crowd. Many more were there than paid to go in; whole processions of youngsters found weak spots in the outer defences when the gates were closed. Sheer physical pressure caused constant encroachment on the boundaries, and every time the screen was moved it was as if a volcano had erupted.

After all the rain the pitch was damp to begin with, the bowlers' feet cutting black marks on the pale green. Sobers put Yorkshire in and, when the first two wickets fell for three runs, it looked a good decision.

Stead had both Leadbeater and Boycott caught behind the wicket, and should also have had Padgett first ball. At the other end Sobers himself bowled eight overs, seven maidens, for two runs. But the supporting attack was less impressive, and the batting slowly grew in confidence. Sharpe was approaching his best form, especially in his cutting, when he too was caught at the wicket, in the 35th over, just before luncheon. The score then was 104 for three.

The later batsmen could not quite keep it up, though the wicket grew drier and the outfield faster. Hampshire looked an excellent prospect, but as so often, turned out to be no more than that. Padgett and Binks were both caught by Murray, who thus took five catches in all. Wilson hit one of the biggest sixes I have seen for a long time, but none of the bowlers was collared.

Bolus and Harris scored 40 for Nottinghamshire's first wicket at nearly three an over, quite sufficient for their purpose. They were assisted by nine byes in an over, with Binks rashly standing up to Nicholson. Bolus played on to Hutton (who bowled his 12 overs straight); White was bowled swinging at Wilson in the last over before tea; Smedley snicked Hutton to Binks and departed reluctantly. That was 52 for three, in the twenty-second over.

Harris had been coolly holding an end, and as Sobers came to join him a hush fell on the babbling multitude. Wilson bowled him two beautiful overs, both maidens.

The great man took his time to settle down. He hit the ball back to Hutton and a roar began to climb the sky as he walked away. But it was only his little joke, not universally appreciated.

The cricket was intensely keen at this stage, jerking the nerves. Sharpe dropped Harris at slip and the score moved steadily to 89, 33 overs gone. Then Old, who was fast and accurate, bowled Harris. In his next over what did look an especially good one found the edge of Sobers' bat, and this time the roar ascended unchecked, and revengeful. Old bowled Murray, who dragged the ball on to his stumps. Old was making the ball lift, more than anyone had done all day.

These three overs, with three wickets, cost him only seven runs. Wilson was an admirable foil, but when he had finished his spell we realized that Binks either had not got his sums right or had deliberately risked keeping on his best bowlers to break the batting. Stringer did not come on until the 42nd over, which meant that a sixth bowler would be needed for at least two overs should the innings go its full length.

Nottinghamshire's hopes now seemed to rest on Hassan, who made a businesslike beginning. The rate required was still reasonable – just over four to the over.

No sooner were such dubious thoughts harboured than they were banished and chiefly through the efforts of young Stringer himself. He took the last three wickets, including the vital one of Hassan, caught at the wicket by Binks, who more than made up for his disastrous over earlier.

YORKSHIRE	191 (59.4 overs, Sharpe 67, Padgett 46, Binks 22, Stead 3-46)
NOTTINGHAMSHIRE	123 (50.5 overs, Harris 31, Sobers 20, Old 3-32, Stringer 3-4)

Mortimore master

BRISTOL: Gloucestershire (14 pts) beat Somerset (3 pts) by 78 runs

It does not now seem likely (it never really did) that Gloucestershire will win the County Championship. The news from Swansea came through while Gloucestershire were still wrestling with the Somerset tail, which is long but enduring.

Gloucestershire won all right, in the 14th over of the last 20 (or, more probably, 25, so swiftly were the spinners getting through their work). It was a competent win, quietly received by the dismayed crowd. "The chances they've had," mourned a faithful, fretful Gloucestershire supporter. "No point in beating Somerset now. We can always beat Somerset." This is unhistorical but represented the mood. It will now take an unusual combination of the weather and the peculiar points system to give Gloucestershire the mastery. Still, it is still worthwhile uttering a few prayers beneath the yews of Painswick.

Gloucestershire scored 161 in the morning, batting well against opposition which naturally lacked its edge, as there would have to be a declaration. Brown's decision to declare at luncheon was sensible. He set Somerset 262 to get in 240 minutes, which would have been generous as these provincial contests are usually played – but, of course, Gloucestershire simply had to win this one.

The wicket took spin slowly, and just occasionally more than that. Mortimore and Allen would bowl Somerset out, no doubt. This was ultimately what happened, except that Allen did not bowl very well and Mortimore did. Indeed, I have not often seen Mortimore bowl better.

Pollock in a hurry

SCARBOROUGH: Barbados, with all first innings wickets in hand, are 297 runs behind International Cavaliers

Given so pleasant a day and so many distinguished names on the score card, the size of the Scarborough crowd was a little disappointing. Perhaps it is that Yorkshiremen are inclined to be suspicious of any suggestion of showmanship, even in festival cricket. Yet, as it turned out, they need have had no doubts. The day's play was keen and well contested and contained an innings which cannot have had many superiors even in the 82 previous festivals, which have seen so many great innings.

It was played by Pollock, who struck the ball to all parts of the field with every recognized stroke and a few more of his own. A veteran observer declared that he had never heard a cricket bat give out such a resounding ring as Pollock's did all afternoon. All the bowlers, it seemed, came to him alike, and his century, with 19 fours and a six in 52 minutes, was scored almost twice as quickly as any other century this season.

There was also a handsome contribution from Green, batting somewhere next his best again and tidy ones from Fredericks and the New South Welshman, Collins. Trueman had an appropriate spree with the bat, and bowled quite briskly, as did Hall. Yet there was as much anxiety as nostalgia in watching them in action again. The remarkable Evans made one beautiful diving save in the evening, which earned him a special round of applause.

Don Wilson

SCARBOROUGH: Yorkshire v M.C.C.

"This is more like Scarborough weather," said one veteran of the Festival resignedly, as the chilly south-westerly brought the clouds piling in. After the first hour the sun was scarcely seen, the light was always dim, and a piercing shower stopped play for half an hour in the afternoon. Yet what looked to me the largest crowd of the festival turned up, even if they did not all stay, proudly to cheer their Cup-winners.

They saw a traditional piece of attacking Yorkshire out-cricket planned round a slow left-arm bowler. When Wilson took the first wicket he reached his one-hundredth of the season and thousandth of his career. Cheered by this, and appetised by the thought of the next 1,000, he swept through the rest of the batting. He had some help from the pitch in the afternoon, but mostly it was just good bowling that got M.C.C. out so quickly.

What an excellent bowler Wilson is and how unlucky not to have played more for England! In some periods (say 1946-51) he would have been an automatic choice. During the afternoon I was watching the play from square leg, where you cannot hear the cinema organ, and it was interesting to see Wilson's subtle variations of length, pulling the batsman half forward, pushing him back a bit, bowling a quicker ball with a lower trajectory, and then a suddenly spinning half-volley. It was in this way that Verity bowled, stretching his technique by intelligence: height, long fingers, brain all working together.

Bristol

Scarborough

1970

The cricket season of 1970 was one of the most blessed of that era. The sun shone, especially, and most unusually, during the first part of the season; England and the Rest of the World fought out a series of Test matches which, whilst they might have been unofficial, provided some magnificent cricket from the greatest players of the age; and the county championship built to a thrilling climax, from which any one of half a dozen sides might have emerged victorious.

Yet nothing seemed less likely than such a happy outcome when the year began. 'The prospect of the cricket season must strike dismay into everyone who loves cricket,' wrote Alan Gibson in a letter to the Editor of *The Times*, printed on February 5.

He was referring, of course, to the impending cricket tour by South Africa, and the prospect of its disruption by the same demonstrators who, for most of the winter, had been dogging the progress of the Springbok rugby side around the country. With no MCC winter tour to serve as a distraction, the South African controversy just grew and grew.

As we have already noted, Alan was firmly against sporting ties with South Africa (although not to the extent of refusing to report their rugby matches). His letter to *The Times* called for the cricket tour to be scrapped, and replaced by a series of matches against a World XI, which would naturally include several leading South African players.

Alan's prescription was what came to pass, largely with the happy outcome that he had anticipated. But not before a great deal more blood had been spilt, much of it on the Committee Room floor at Lord's. Despite enormous political pressure, intensified by the prospect of a summer General Election, Billy Griffith, who was Secretary of the MCC, the Cricket Council and the Test and County Cricket Board, refused to cancel the tour. There were, they argued, no sporting grounds for doing so; indeed, sporting links with South Africa could well be seen as a force for good. As for the politics, that should be no concern of cricketers.

There were debates in Parliament, sermons from Episcopal pulpits, innumerable letters to *The Times* and an endless series of meetings at Lord's. Still, the MCC refused to buckle. On May 19, on the morning after a secret and agonised meeting of the Cricket Council lasting long into the night, the MCC issued what was intended to be its final word on the subject: the tour would go ahead. The Government had other ideas. On May 21, the Home Secretary, Jim Callaghan, summoned Billy Griffith and his Chairman MJC Allom to his office and "requested" that the tour be cancelled, on the grounds of public policy. It was as good as a directive. With an ill grace, the MCC surrendered.

By this time, the cricket season was well under way, under ironically cloudless skies. A bitter winter, in every sense, had been succeeded by a glorious spring, although it hadn't quite seemed like that when Alan had arrived at The Parks on April 29 for his first match. But it was his description of the Edgbaston outfield on May 6 which attracted critical attention – from the compilers of *Pseud's Corner*, in *Private Eye*::

> It was a hot, hazy, sometimes steamy day, the kind of day to win the toss. The Edgbaston field looked lovely, with its broad strips of dark and light green, rippling *crepe de chine* rather than velvet. The drab scar of the concrete wicket was unbearably poignant.

Tests
Rest of the World
beat England
4-1

Championship
1 Kent
2 Glamorgan
3 Lancashire
4 Yorkshire
5 Surrey
6 Worcestershire

Sunday League
1 Lancashire
2 Kent
3 Derbyshire
4 Essex
5 Warwickshire
6 Worcestershire

Gillette Cup Final
Lancashire
beat Sussex

Most first-class runs
1 G.M. Turner
2 R.T. Virgin
3 J.B. Bolus

Most first-class wickets
1 D.J. Shepherd
2 N. Gifford
F.J. Titmus

If memory serves, he was furious!

Glamorgan were the reigning county champions, and Alan saw a lot of them in May and June – including a brilliant win over Somerset at Swansea in early June.

There then followed something of a hiatus in Alan Gibson's travels for *The Times*. On June 9, England were knocked out in the quarter finals of football's World Cup by West Germany; whereupon the printing unions promptly called a strike, which took all of the national papers off the street for the best part of the week. Then came the General Election on June 18, in which Ted Heath defied the pollsters to win a surprise victory over Harold Wilson; an event straddled by the first Test against the Rest of the World at Lord's, which England lost by an innings against a side, be it noted, that contained only one Australian! Like the cricketing authorities, the BBC had decided to treat the matches as fully-fledged Tests, and accord them ball-by-ball coverage. Alan was part of the commentary team for all but the second Test of an uplifting series eventually won 4-1 by the Rest of the World.

The long hot summer days made for good wickets, ideal for the one-day competitions. The 40-over Sunday League had been re-branded as the John Player, but in every other respect it was the same successful mixture as before. That included, so it seemed, Lancashire's domination, in which the unlikely combination of the towering Clive Lloyd and the diminutive Harry Pilling was playing no small part. They were genuinely in mid-season form when Lancashire played Somerset in the JPL on July 12, an encounter that was followed closely by an exciting draw in the championship.

But when it came to the big one – the Gillette Cup semi-final at Taunton on July 18 – Lancashire were just too strong for a Somerset side which, since Greg Chappell's departure at the end of the previous season, lacked an overseas star. For them, and even more so for Gloucestershire, who plummeted from second in the championship in 1969 to bottom in 1970, it was a disappointing season. Lancashire, by contrast, would go on to beat Sussex in the Gillette final, retain their Sunday League title and finish third in the championship.

In a thrilling climax to the season Kent – bottom at the end of June – climbed the table to become county champions in their centenary year. Yet, as the crucial matches were played out, Alan Gibson was dispatched to Scarborough, to cover the entertaining, but frankly inconsequential, matches that made up the Cricket Festival. It seems distinctly odd, given that Alan was by now de facto number two to John Woodcock. Someone called Norman Creek, who sounds as if he ought to have been a racehorse, was deputed to cover Kent's momentous victory at Folkestone.

But Alan sounds as if he was pleased to be up there by the seaside in his home county, judging by his description of the band in his first-day report of the match between an England XI and Young England, and of the sea in his report of Yorkshire versus the MCC on September 10th. The MCC lost in the end, just as they had in their vastly more significant battle with the Government, earlier in the year. One likes to think, though, cliché as it is, that cricket was the winner on both occasions.

A World Eleven

Sir, - The prospect of the cricket season must strike dismay into everyone who loves cricket.

The situation could still be redeemed if, as has indeed been suggested in the press, the South African tour were to be abandoned, and its place taken by a tour of a World XI, which would naturally include some leading South African cricketers.

This would have the following advantages:

(1) Since the World XI would be chosen on an inter-racial basis, it would hardly be possible to demonstrate against on anti-racialist grounds.

(2) Those South African cricketers who were willing to play for the World XI would have made the clearest possible demonstration of their own views on race (and such South African cricketers as I know are liberally-minded on this subject). They would not only increase the esteem in which we hold them as individuals, but they would help to create an image of South African sport altogether more in keeping with the nature of its sportsmen.

(3) The counties, and cricket generally, could look forward to a pleasing financial bonus, instead of the possibility of bankruptcy.

(4) The public would be enabled to see most of the best cricketers in the world, at a high, competitive level. (I see no reason why England caps should not be awarded, and the matches treated as Tests for statistical purposes: this assumes a "World XI" of sufficient strength could be raised, but that is not impracticable.)

(5) We should all enjoy it so much.

This proposal irritates the extreme left-wing demonstrators, because they would have nothing left against which to demonstrate. It also irritates the extreme cricket-establishment people, some of whom seem to relish the thought of the tour, barbed wire and truncheons and all, to show that they are not going to be dictated to by the long-haired permissives. While both these attitudes are understandable, neither has anything to do with cricket.

The cricket council could reasonably and graciously withdraw the invitation to South Africa. There is no question of them having to "climb down". They could simply say that they regret the tour is not feasible, which is no more than the truth.

The Rugby tour has hardened extreme attitudes, often very unpleasantly. Cricket is a silly, precious, vulnerable game. I love it dearly, and so do countless others. Let us try to see it does not suffer the same miserable fate.

I think of the Nawab of Pataudi as the kind of man who could make a tremendous success of leading a tour such as this. How good it would be if we could look back on the season of 1970 as the beginning of a new and happy era in international cricket, and not as a stricken battlefield!

Yours sincerely,

ALAN GIBSON

8 Queen's Court, Clifton, Bristol 8

APRIL: Early season at The Parks

Encouraging for Oxford

OXFORD: Oxford University v Hampshire

I have never seen the trees in The Parks so black and bare for the time of year. There was a general feeling that this provided a parable of Oxford's prospects this season. Nor did it seem a happy omen when Hone, who bowled the first over, wore a light blue cap. Yet there were mildly encouraging signs, not apparent on the score sheet.

One is that Oxford should be a good fielding side. There are some faults. The deep fieldsmen take too long winding themselves up to throw in, and one or two players became a little ragged with weariness after such a day's chasing as they had not experienced before, and third man showed an inclination to chat to an admittedly fetching mini-skirt perched on the heavy roller. These things can be put right.

What is important is that on a cold, though fitfully sunny day, Oxford fielded with an enthusiasm and courage which it was heartening to see.

The Parks, Oxford
'There is nowhere I would rather have been than sitting in the sunshine at The Parks'

Basil D'Oliveira

WORCESTER: Worcestershire v Surrey

All Worcestershire's batsmen played well in their different ways, but it was D'Oliveira who captured the eye. This was his first century since the winter before last, but from the way he made it one would think it an everyday occurrence.

On Saturday he had been limping slightly and unable to bowl much. Yesterday he began diffidently, and was dropped at the wicket when he had made 14; but as his confidence grew, so did the power of his strokes. Perhaps "power" is not quite the word. He did not seem to bash the ball: he flicked his wrists, and mid-on started to turn and chase, and the distance between the ball and the fieldsman increased, giving the impression that the ball was picking up speed, until it came smack against the pavilion palings.

He scored many runs with this casually whipped on-drive. He cut Pocock square, the bowler's spin and the bat's angle causing the ball to fizz to the boundary in a semi-circle. He drove straight, allowing a suggestion of force to show itself, and it was with such a stroke that he reached his hundred. Unquestionably, he is a great player still.

Don Shepherd

CARDIFF: Glamorgan v Hampshire

The morning's cricket was saved from boredom by the batting of Richards and Marshall, and the bowling of Shepherd. After all, these are three of the cricketers of whom our grandchildren will enquire: "Ah, did you once see Shelley plain?" Not that Shepherd is a Shelley: more a Milton, justifying the ways of spin to men, and even groundsmen.

I estimated that Hampshire required to declare at about twenty past two, which would have set Glamorgan 225 at 90 an hour. While Richards was there, and again while Marshall was there, this seemed feasible.

Shepherd had them both out when they hovered on the edge of command. He also took the wickets of Reed ("I can always get him at square leg; he can't resist it") and Livingstone; made a catch in the deep, which was the end of Turner; and chased around the boundary like a sprinter.

Confronted with this display, and a turning ball, Hampshire faltered.

...

I must, however, fault the Glamorgan captain for not sending in Shepherd at number seven or, for that matter, at number one. The way things are going for the old warrior at present, I would not be surprised to see him take 30 in an over off Cottam, or Sainsbury, or any mere mortal.

Mike Procter

BIRMINGHAM: Warwickshire v Gloucestershire

Procter was bowling below his full pace. He had been unwell in the morning, and unable to field. Now, with the chance of a breakthrough, he made a great effort. His run grew longer, his pace extreme, and the light poorer. He thundered up to the wicket, reminding me of the deathless lines of a poet laureate on the Jameson raid: "They raced across the veldt as hard as they could pelt."

He made a fearsome sight as he walked back towards his mark, his fair hair tangled and flopping, his mouth moving, his brow dripping, every muscular inch a fast bowler in the high tradition. He must have made an even more alarming sight to the batsmen.

These were Amiss, who has been playing well this year, and the comparatively inexperienced Warner. They confronted Procter with courage, sense and luck. There were howls from the crowd, more of excitement than malice, when Procter bounced the ball short, and a series of edges and appeals. Suddenly Amiss hit him twice for four, bold, unconventional shots to extra cover with a horizontal bat and to third man with a vertical one. Then Jakeman, who as an umpire has a touch of Mr Harcourt about him, no-balled Procter twice. At the end of his eight-ball over Procter made a weary signal which I took to mean that he could manage two overs more.

Lloyd and Pilling ensure success

MANCHESTER: Lancashire (4 pts) beat Somerset by 100 runs

There was another big crowd at Old Trafford in spite of a grey afternoon. The John Player Sunday League may not be cricket as MacLaren knew it but this is the way they like it in Lancashire today, and well they might when their side plays it so well.

Yesterday's victory was another one for the Walrus and the Carpenter – the mighty Lloyd and the deft Pilling – and Somerset had little choice but to accept the role of oysters. It was a good pitch and Lancashire won the toss. Wood and Engineer were out with the score 42 in the 12th over and then the formidable and so strangely lopsided pair were together again.

Lloyd's first scoring strokes were 4, 4, 4, 2, 6 – all off Langford. Langford showed courage in keeping himself on. In fact two or three times in this early period Lloyd mistimed him slightly and might conceivably have been out. After that his hits carried unquestioned authority and compassed all a batsman's range. He was dropped once, at mid-off when 70, an awkward chance and that was the end of Somerset's hopes of a reasonable total at which to aim. Lloyd went on to 134, reaching his hundred in 74 balls, the third fastest span of the season.

Pilling must not be neglected; his strokes do not have Lloyd's high drama but the ball usually reaches the boundary just as quickly.

Burgess managed to bowl a maiden at Lloyd (one of only two in the innings) but paid dearly for it – though it was from his bowling that the catch was dropped. Langford, picking up two wickets in the fortieth over, raised his total to four. Though they were costly, his share in the day's spoils was deserved. To bowl against Lloyd in this mood must be like bowling against Woolley at his best. There is no good length.

When Somerset went in, Shuttleworth quickly had Virgin caught at the wicket and caught and bowled Clarkson. After such a start, Somerset could only score 17 in the first 10 overs. Kitchen and Robinson, and later Cartwright and Langford, could do no more than put a better face on defeat. Shuttleworth came back to cut off the tail. His figures speak of a highly efficient piece of bowling. But it was good to see the spinners in action and among the wickets. One more example of Lancashire's enlightened approach to this form of cricket. Of course with the Walrus and the Carpenter in the side, you can afford to be enlightened, at least in your approach to oysters.

Lancashire v Somerset, Old Trafford, 12 July 1970

Lancashire won by 100 runs

Lancashire

B. Wood	c Taylor b Palmer	2
+ F.M. Engineer	b Langford	23
H. Pilling	c Virgin b Langford	76
C.H. Lloyd	*not out*	134
J. Sullivan	c Palmer b Langford	13
F.C. Hayes	b Langford	0
* J.D. Bond		
D.P. Hughes		
J. Simmons		
P. Lever		
K. Shuttleworth		
	b 1, lb 5, nb 1	7
	(5 wkts, 40 overs)	**255**

1/9, 2/42, 3/224, 4/254, 5/255

Jones	8	0	35	0
Palmer	8	1	33	1
Langford	8	0	73	4
Cartwright	8	0	42	0
Burgess	8	1	65	0

Somerset

R.T. Virgin	c Engineer b Shuttleworth	3
A. Clarkson	c & b Shuttleworth	0
P.J. Robinson	c Hayes b Simmons	22
M.J. Kitchen	b Wood	34
G.I. Burgess	c Hughes b Simmons	12
T.W. Cartwright	c Lever b Shuttleworth	38
P. Denning	c Lloyd b Simmons	5
* B.A. Langford	c & b Hughes	23
R. Palmer	c Wood b Hughes	5
+ D.J.S. Taylor	*not out*	1
A.A. Jones	b Shuttleworth	2
	b 6, lb 4	10
	(35.4 overs)	**155**

1/3, 2/4, 3/56, 4/60, 5/79, 6/94, 7/147, 8/152, 9/152, 10/155

Lever	5	1	14	0
Shuttleworth	7.4	4	3	4
Wood	6	0	47	1
Simmons	8	1	27	3
Sullivan	4	0	34	0
Hughes	5	0	20	2

Umpires: D.J. Constant and C.G. Pepper

Somerset in late bid to raise rate

SWANSEA: Somerset have scored 264 runs in their first innings against Glamorgan

A warm, sunny day, with a gentle breeze off the Bristol Channel, made some tedious cricket bearable. The crowd, a good sized one, would have been hoarse with wrath if the weather had been colder. As it was, they contented themselves with a little cheerful raillery as they watched Somerset struggle painfully forward at a rate usually below two runs to the over.

The pitch played well enough, but Swansea pitches have often helped the bowlers before the end of a match, so in their present frail condition it was natural that Somerset, after winning the toss, should take care. Unfortunately, once Virgin was out, they allowed care to degenerate into anxiety and then into depression.

Four wickets fell before luncheon. Kitchen and Burgess, dourly, held the fifth for most of the afternoon. Kitchen has been out of touch, but his talents have always been aggressive. He did, at one point, hit Shepherd for two fours in an over, always a feat, but could not take command. One off drive from Burgess was only a tantalizing reminder of what an attractive stroke player he, too, can be. Both were out before tea. Their stand had restricted Glamorgan to two bowling points, but achieved none at all for batting.

Lewis kept his spinners on for a while after the 85 overs, but – maybe to give them a rest as much as anything – eventually took the new ball. This produced a relative rush of scoring from Cartwright and Taylor, and then from Langford. There were some edges and air shots, but the spirit was better, and Glamorgan's control wavered.

Taylor is a capital batsman, and though he must be given time to settle to his principal job of keeping wicket, I hope he will ultimately move up the order. His relaxed stance, quick but straight back lift, fluent forward drive and delicate late cuts all have the right look about them.

So Somerset finished in a better position than had seemed likely, and than they really deserved. Glamorgan tired a little near the end – six hours and a half make a long day in the heat. Their fielding was steady, if without all its usual snap; though the remarkable Walker took four more catches, including one of his best at short leg, and a diving caught-and-bowled which his length and anticipation made look simple.

So long as the wicket holds, Glamorgan's chief worry must be that only one innings has been completed, with so big a chunk of the match already gone.

Bygone days of windjammers

SWANSEA: Somerset, with eight second innings wickets in hand, are 16 runs ahead of Glamorgan

Lewis declared at 10 to 6 with a lead of 26, giving Somerset an hour to bat. This was a sensible attempt to put some life into the match, but the last 20 overs will be called at four o'clock today, which does not give much room for manoeuvre.

Glamorgan batted slightly better than Somerset had done, in rather more difficult conditions. There was a wind from the east, raising white crests in the channel. On such a day we would once have seen a multitude of white sails, as the tall ships took their brief chance of getting out to the Atlantic.

There are no more windjammers, but there is still Cartwright, sailing tirelessly up to the wicket, shrewd in making use of such a cross wind. He has the ability to bend the wind to his purposes, something which the old sea captains no doubt had, which certainly comes from experience, and which the other Somerset swing bowlers have not yet mastered. Cartwright had no luck but always looked a fine bowler.

As for the spinners: the pitch spitted sand-coloured dust, first in puffs and then in large gusts. This should have been encouraging for Langford and Robinson, but the ball only turned slowly, except now and then. The last hour did suggest it may present more problems today – but perhaps it was just that the Glamorgan spinners bowled the better.

Alan Jones added to his formidable total of runs this season, and would no doubt have got a move on after luncheon had he not been caught at the wicket from the last ball before it. Walker, who is in remarkable form in all departments, began to improve on the slow early run rate, but was bowled in a casual moment after reaching 50. Lewis took 20 minutes to score a run, hit two or three fine strokes, and was caught driving at Cartwright, as so many have been. Langford knew too much for Hill, and at a quarter to four, in the 71st over, Glamorgan were still 10 runs short of their first batting point.

Ultimately they managed three. Bryan Davis and Eiffion Jones provided the briskest batting of the match. In the 85th over Davis was run out, so Somerset scored a third point for bowling: this was one of the few occasions when they looked smart in the field. Another was when Jones dived to catch Nash off his own bowling, hurt himself and had to go off, conceivably with a cracked fibula.

Lewis shows purpose

SWANSEA: Glamorgan (15 pts) beat Somerset (3 pts) by three wickets

During the morning's play Somerset lost six wickets for 114 runs. Only Cartwright confronted Walker and Shepherd with much confidence. They were thus 130 on, with two wickets left, and 170 minutes left to play. Their fastest bowler was lame.

In these circumstances Langford presumably decided to save the match, since he could hardly win it – a legitimate decision. Somerset played some dismal cricket in this match, but in this instance they could not be blamed. It is not part of cricket to throw a match away.

Langford himself set about the saving, with assistance from Palmer and then from the limping Jones. Langford batted well. He was skilful in keeping the bowling away from his partners. In fact, he had the match as good as saved when, illogically, in view of his previous policy, he declared. I am afraid this gesture did nothing to endear him to the crowd, many of whom jeered him as he came in. Perhaps it was not tactful, either, to declare immediately after he had reached his own 50.

So Glamorgan had to score 188 in 45 minutes and 20 overs, stiff but not impossible since there was no chance of their being bowled out – the pitch never became difficult. The loss of Alan Jones in the fifth over was hardly a disaster, for though he has been scoring lots of runs he has not often been scoring them quickly. Lewis had gone in first with Jones, and Bryan Davis followed, first wicket down.

These two set about the job, and after a drab match it was good to see them. Lewis, whose tactical grasp has sometimes seemed uncertain – though much less so than Langford's – had a grim aspect to him.

All would be put right, he seemed to say, as he punched the ball through the covers and savaged it on the leg side, by the innings of a master. The opening bowling was untidy, and Robinson, inexplicably, was first change. When Cartwright at last came on, Davis hit him, first ball, for six. Cartwright was sure to have an answer to this, and Davis duly skied the ball to mid-off, who made such a lamentable attempt at it that I really think he had better be unnamed. The Somerset fielding deteriorated under pressure.

At 92 for two, 18 overs to go, Glamorgan were winning. Then Lewis was caught, at backward point off Cartwright, a ball that lifted. It looked interestingly like Cartwright v. Glamorgan. He had Walker caught at midwicket: 71 wanted in 14 overs. But it was only 24 in seven by the time Nash was out, after scoring 31 out of 47, including a huge six off Langford. Thereafter not even Cartwright could check the tide, and the winning hit came from Roger Davis (shrewdly held back, or foolishly not sent in earlier, take your pick) off the first ball of the last over.

Glamorgan v Somerset, Swansea, 3, 4 & 5 June 1970

Glamorgan won by three wickets

Somerset

R.T. Virgin	c EW Jones b Cordle	19	c EW Jones b Walker	30
A. Clarkson	c BA Davis b RC Davis	34	lbw b Walker	6
P.J. Robinson	c Walker b Shepherd	6	c EW Jones b RC Davis	34
M. Hill	c & b Walker	10	c Shepherd b Walker	16
M.J. Kitchen	c Lewis b Walker	38	c Walker b Shepherd	3
G.I. Burgess	c Walker b Shepherd	37	b Shepherd	16
T.W. Cartwright	c Lewis b Williams	32	c Walker b Shepherd	40
+ D.J.S. Taylor	*not out*	40	b Shepherd	1
R. Palmer	c & b Walker	8	c EW Jones b Walker	11
* B.A. Langford	c EW Jones b Walker	23	*not out*	50
A.A. Jones	c A Jones b Shepherd	0	*not out*	0
	b 7, lb 4, nb 6	17	b 4, lb 1, nb 1	6
		264	(9 wkts, dec)	**213**

1/24, 2/40, 3/70, 4/80, 5/146, 6/168, 7/199, 8/219, 9/258, 10/264
1/37, 2/42, 3/56, 4/78, 5/95, 6/109, 7/128, 8/156, 9/197

Nash	17	3	42	0	2	0	16	0
Williams	13	3	46	1	6.1	1	14	0
Cordle	15	6	32	1	4	0	8	0
Shepherd	31.2	17	33	3	29	10	65	4
Walker	37	13	78	4	32	14	58	4
R.C. Davis	9	5	16	1	23	10	46	1

Umpires: W.E. Alley and P.B. Wight

Glamorgan

A. Jones	c Taylor b Jones	56	c Taylor b Palmer	11
R.C. Davis	c Cartwright b Langford	25	*not out*	7
P.M. Walker	b Robinson	51	c Virgin b Cartwright	7
* A.R. Lewis	c Palmer b Cartwright	15	c Kitchen b Cartwright	43
B.A. Davis	run out	51	c Robinson b Cartwright	62
L.W. Hill	c Cartwright b Langford	9	*not out*	0
+ E.W. Jones	*not out*	35	run out	2
M.A. Nash	c & b Jones	22	c Robinson b Langford	31
A.E. Cordle	b Palmer	14	c Palmer b Langford	8
D.J. Shepherd				
D.L. Williams				
	b 5, lb 4, nb 3	12	b 9, lb 6, w 1, nb 1	17
	(8 wkts, dec)	**290**	(7 wkts)	**188**

1/65, 2/119, 3/143, 4/151, 5/165, 6/225, 7/262, 8/290
1/18, 2/92, 3/117, 4/164, 5/178, 6/179, 7/181

Jones	12.3	2	36	2				
Palmer	15.1	5	33	1	4	0	26	1
Burgess	15	3	42	0	4	0	17	0
Cartwright	24	7	64	1	13	0	58	3
Langford	19	5	62	2	10.1	0	54	2
Robinson	17	8	41	1	3	0	16	0

AUGUST: Derbyshire v Worcestershire at Chesterfield 1970

The master at his best

CHESTERFIELD: Derbyshire, with all second innings wickets in hand, lead Worcestershire by 12 runs

A good day's cricket was distinguished by Turner's eighth century of the season and ennobled by an innings from Graveney which must have been both a lesson and an inspiration to any young cricketer watching. Worcestershire took four points for batting, to Derbyshire's one for bowling, but may still find it hard to win the match on so placid a pitch.

Headley gave Worcestershire a lively start, aided by some erratic bowling by Eyre, and had scored 40 out of 62 when he was bowled by Russell, a painstaking performer in the medium-paced Derbyshire tradition (of course they have other traditions as well). Ormrod was soon caught at the wicket and Yardley came in to warm applause, created by the momentary impression that he was Graveney. Indeed he has acquired some of the mannerisms of the master, and even one or two of his strokes, so far as a left-hander can.

Yardley and Turner put on 105 for the third wicket before Yardley was caught, smartly, at mid-on. Graveney then came in, to slightly less warm applause. This indicated no disrespect, merely the discomfort of a Derbyshire crowd which sees a score of 180 for three against them and one of the best batsmen in the world coming in.

Almost at once Graveney hit a four to extra cover which made everything else in the game hitherto seem hackwork. He followed with a six to long-on, which alarmed the pleasure boats in the lake, and a four to fine-leg – not a glance but tucked away flat-batted, a remarkable stroke which he learned from D'Oliveira – or vice-versa. Perhaps they just worked it out together one day.

Graveney reached 50 at a run a minute, although he had much less than half the bowling. Taylor missed a difficult leg-side stumping chance, for which he should be thanked. As Graveney goes round the grounds, making his imperial farewells, there can be sensed the affection and admiration in which he is held. Past troubles are forgotten: beauty remains, for ever imprinted on the mind's eye.

I must not neglect the valiant Turner. What a shrewd move by Worcestershire when they signed him! His innings, as usual, followed the patterns of the silk-moth fighting its way out of the cocoon: the struggles are painful, but the end-product pretty, and the by-product valuable.

AUGUST: some brief extracts

Gloucestershire batsmen

BRISTOL: Gloucestershire v Yorkshire

Nicholls played gracefully, Milton neatly, Shepherd robustly, and Bissex fortunately. Bissex did play one noble stroke, a square off-drive with a touch of cut in it. It was the kind of stroke you see Bradman playing in the pictures. Bissex has played it often before, but usually some feet from the ball. This year he has begun to make contact now and then.

It is always a pleasure to watch Milton score runs, though perhaps one for the connoisseur rather than the small boy. I have no sooner written this sentence than I realise it is a piece of pomposity. Small boys are nearly always wiser than connoisseurs. You might almost say that, in county cricket, small boys *are* the connoisseurs. The man the small boys cheered yesterday was Shepherd, who is tubby and jolly, and hits the ball a terrible tonk. They had no doubt that his innings, with a six and five fours, all in front of the wicket, was the best thing of the day.

Bolus and Harris of Notts

NOTTINGHAM: Nottinghamshire v Lancashire

These two are both approaching their 2,000 runs for the season and they have carried the Nottinghamshire batting on their shoulders. Bolus we have long known as a resolute stylist: there is a touch of Sutcliffe about him, though the player of whom he most reminds me is Martin Young of Gloucestershire. They all had the same shining air of stepping out of cellophane wrapping.

Harris is more of a robust crate, the kind of thing in which they send the Cornish spring flowers up to town. He was born in St Just-in-Roseland, and although his Cornish cricketing associations are slight, there is something about him of a good second row forward from the west. His approach is orthodox, with few flourishes, but he hits the ball hard and is a great collector of runs so that his score keeps mounting, even though he may give an impression for a while of inactivity.

England XI v England Under-25

DAY TWO

Conservation Year can record one unqualified triumph; the band are back at Scarborough. The usurping cinema organ has gone, though it, or one of its brethren, could be heard from a neighbouring entertainment when the band stopped. The band were in their best form. Really, they played almost too well, because what is a band at a cricket festival without what the Irish call a bom note now and then?

DAY THREE

An innings by Boycott won this match satisfactorily, and almost nobly. It was as if he set out to demonstrate that England's bright young men, however well they had batted, have still something to learn. The England XI were set to score 274 in about three hours, and did it with 10 minutes to spare, Boycott scoring 147, even though he gave the others a glimpse of the bowling now and then, and never ran anybody out.

TN Pearce's XI v Rest of the World

The XI playing on behalf of the Rest of the World yesterday was less glamorous than the title suggests. Nevertheless, there was a big crowd at Scarborough which found plenty to enjoy. The cricket was cheerful, but keener than in the match last year when more famous names were more involved. The Scarborough watcher usually knows his cricket, and so does his wife, and by the time they were dwindling away for the third of the four knife-and-fork meals a day, which every self-respecting north-country boarding house provides, they had some nourishing play to digest as well.

Yorkshire v MCC

DAY ONE

It was a rough night at Scarborough (the weather I mean; I cannot answer for the festivities). Wind and rain thrashed the North Sea, making it look like the John Piper painting in the Sitwells' house in The Crescent (it was painted for Osbert's autobiography). Cricket in the morning seemed less an impossibility than a fantasy, the occupation of another world.

But the covers had been efficient, the storm eased, the cricketers were willing. Although the weather remained mostly unpleasant, we had nearly a full day, watched by a crowd of several thousand – another remarkable testimony to Scarborough's affection for cricket.

The best innings was played by Amiss, who reached the century he narrowly missed earlier in the festival, and again batted well in his bolder style, particularly strong in the drive. He was missed before he had scored, but was then hardly in trouble, until he was caught by Padgett, a remarkable diving effort at mid-off.

...

The stroke of the day was played by Hobbs, who hit Cope through the covers for four from a prone position after slipping. C.C.C. Case, of Somerset, is alleged to have played well while horizontal, but the most that was ever claimed for him, I think, was the forward defensive stroke.

DAY TWO

Yorkshire built a good position in a match they are always glad to win, declaring soon after 4 o'clock with a lead of 69. Boycott and Sharpe took their first wicket partnership to 82, Sharpe reaching a 50 which reminded us of happier days, before he was stumped off Hobbs. The youthful Dalton came in, trailing his bat nervously.

Hobbs brought up a threatening backward short leg and, with his second ball, produced a full toss which had Dalton caught in two minds and also by mid-on. It was a subtle piece of bowling, or perhaps the merest accident, for the wind, not consistent but gusty, what they call in Ireland a farrity wind – made laws of its own.

...

Padgett, Hutton and Close occupied the afternoon in their variously attractive ways. Nothing bettered the cover drive, off a long hop to be sure, with which Close announced his arrival. Hutton was inclined to hit the ball in the air against the wind, a policy which was bound to bring trouble sooner or later. Padgett played well, mixing the delicate and the fierce as few batsmen can. He looks so pink and earnest that he has no business to get out to the strokes of a roué, as he did again yesterday. He is none the less a considerable batsman.

1971

The world of English cricket was feeling pretty pleased with itself in the spring of 1971. Ray Illingworth's MCC team had regained the Ashes in an ill-tempered tour of Australia and New Zealand, thanks in large part to Boycott's batting, John Snow's fast bowling and Illingworth's own astute and assertive captaincy. With South Africa effectively out of the reckoning for the foreseeable future, England could justifiably claim to be the number one Test team in the world.

At home, the combination of overseas players, bonus points and a generally more attacking outlook had revitalised the county game after the doldrums of the 1960s. The pessimism as to the future of the first-class game expressed by Major Rowland Bowen in his magnum opus *Cricket: a History of its Growth and Development Throughout the World*, and to some extent echoed by Alan Gibson when he reviewed the book for *The Times*, was not generally shared.

> The so-called first-class game has lost most of its natural life. Like a diabetic, it lives on injections. It is still possible, however, to enjoy it, and to take pleasure in reporting it, provided it is seen as a ritual. Alternatively, it is possible to enjoy it in terms of arithmetic. Every cricket reporter today has to be either a ritualist or a statistician.

The thrills and spills of Illingworth's team apart, the big cricket news in the early part of the year was Brian Close's move to Somerset. But not as captain. The veteran off-spinner Brian Langford would continue as captain for one final season. Alan was not impressed:

> What an example it is of the time-honoured principle of the Somerset cricket authorities: do everything by halves.

The fact that there were no changes to the county championship points scoring system was testimony to the general air of content as to the way things were going. However, there was concern over slow pitches, and the rules on the covering of wickets were changed yet again, so that pitches had to be left uncovered overnight – a reversion to previous practice which was to have a significant impact as the season progressed.

The strongest county side in all forms of the game were probably Lancashire, who had completed the Gillette Cup/Sunday League double the previous year, and finished third in the championship.

Somerset enjoyed a significant revival in 1971. Close was having what *Wisden* was to describe as a 'triumphant season' with the bat, although I'm not sure what he would have made of Langford's lack of urgency in failing to finish off Essex inside two days at Bath in early June. Nonetheless, the arrangement whereby Langford was captain and Close effectively senior pro appeared to be working well enough, as Alan was happy to concede when he assessed the county's progress for a *Times* feature on June 12. Yorkshireman he may have been, but Alan always gave the impression of enjoying Somerset matches more than any others.

Both West Country sides were enjoying good seasons in one-day cricket. Somerset sat proudly on top of the Sunday League for several weeks in mid-season, before fading right at the end. Not just on the day, but for most of the rest of the season, the

Tests
England
beat Pakistan
1-0, with two draws
India
beat England
1-0, with two draws

Championship
1 Surrey
2 Warwickshire
3 Lancashire
4 Kent
5 Leicestershire
6 Middlesex

Sunday League
1 Worcestershire
2 Essex
3 Lancashire
4 Leicestershire
5 Somerset
6 Hampshire

Gillette Cup Final
Lancashire
beat Kent

Most first-class runs
1 G. Boycott
2 M.J. Harris
3 J.H. Edrich

Most first-class wickets
1 L.R. Gibbs
2 P.J. Sainsbury
3 T.W. Cartwright
Intikhab Alam
F.J. Titmus

confidence being displayed by the Bristolian supporter whom Alan encountered on his way to the match against Nottinghamshire on August 9 proved sadly misplaced.

But it was their neighbours and rivals Gloucestershire who were to feature in one of the most memorable one-day matches ever played, the famous Gillette Cup semi-final against Lancashire at Old Trafford on July 28, which went on until almost nine o'clock in the evening. Alan was there for the match itself, and reflected subsequently on the outcome. He may not have cared much for one-day cricket, but he did care for his friends in Gloucestershire CC, and the bitterness of the blow is there between every line. But the whimsy had returned by the time Gloucestershire played Northants at the Cheltenham Festival.

The race for the county championship was close throughout. Warwickshire, for whom Lance Gibbs took over 100 wickets during the first class season, were always there or thereabouts. Lancashire were well in the hunt as well, and Surrey came with a late burst, much as Kent had done the previous season. By the end of August, there was nothing in it.

Unlike previous seasons, when Alan had been dispatched to Scarborough for the closing rites, this time he was in at the championship death. First he watched Warwickshire strain every cricketing sinew to secure the win they so desperately needed against Yorkshire. Then it was down to Southampton to see if Surrey could claim the six bonus points that they needed to bring their total level with that of Warwickshire, and secure the title by virtue of winning two more matches. They could, but only just, and in the end it was a Hampshire victory that brought the curtain down.

If the county championship was close, the Sunday League was even closer, Worcestershire getting the better of Essex in the end thanks to a run rate that was 0.03 runs per over better over the entire course of the season. Happily for Alan, his BBC friend and colleague Bill Frindall was there with his calculator for what proved to be – when Lancashire lost the following week – the crucial encounter between Worcestershire and Warwickshire.

With Adam and the newly arrived Felicity, at Knill's Monument, St Ives

That was not entirely that, as far as Alan's cricket writing for *The Times* was concerned in 1971. By now he was writing regular features for them, and he clearly relished the opportunity to review John Arlott's *Fred: Portrait of a Fast Bowler*.

1971 had been a good year for Alan Gibson, as well as for cricket. He was now firmly established as *The Times*' number two cricket writer, with a large and loyal following, he was doing regular Test Match commentaries for the BBC, and his work was beginning to attract wider attention. Nothing in his entire cricket-writing career gave him greater pleasure than the award, in December 1971, of Cricket Writer of the Year by the Wombwell Cricket Society – not least because Wombwell folk, then as now, have a reputation of approaching their cricket with proper Yorkshire seriousness, and Alan, for all his lighter touches, did like to be taken seriously. The silver cup that he was presented with still has pride of place on my mantelpiece.

But there was to be an even greater joy in his and Rosie's life, when he at last became the father of a daughter, when Felicity Margaret Eve was born on September 23. It was the perfect end to a summer that must have been as happy and productive as any he ever spent in his adult lifetime.

Gordon Greenidge and a replacement ball

MANCHESTER: Lancashire v Hampshire

Greenidge will remember the day, for he made his highest championship score, and very likely would have got a hundred, had not the rain come. He is chiefly a backfoot player, a good puller and cutter, an uncertain but sometimes elegant leg glancer.

Greenidge hit a six to long leg which lost the ball. Lancashire were therefore provided with another of equal age, but naturally much drier. Shuttleworth seized upon it and bowled a dangerous over just before lunch. Ought balls in these circumstances to be dipped in water before use? And how often? And should the umpires supervise the dipping? Pepper scorned these deeply interesting nuances and, so far as I could see, just grabbed the first spare ball the 12th man brought out. They have no sensitivity for a fine point of law, these Australians.

Roy Marshall

PORTSMOUTH: Hampshire v Pakistanis

Marshall played the innings of the day, one that was a delight to see. Cricket in England since the war cannot have known half a dozen players better to watch when they are going well, and few from overseas have played spinners so well when the ball has been doing a bit.

Although he hardly ever employs the classical forward stroke – you do not see his left leg stretching down the pitch – Marshall is a handsome driver and the fact that he plays the ball late, together with his still quick reflexes, enables him to change his stroke composedly and often score runs when a spinning ball moves unexpectedly from the ground.

The end of a Peter Walker century

SWANSEA: Glamorgan v Lancashire

Walker was out to a fine, diving catch by Engineer. The ball had come off Walker's bat, pad, glove, or all three, and it was not clear whether it had been cleanly caught. Walker asked Engineer whether it was a catch, and on receiving his assurance that it was so, cheerfully departed. This is the kind of thing which continues to warm one's heart about cricket.

Kent and Derbyshire keep the brakes on

BLACKHEATH: Derbyshire v Kent

The second day of this match, like the first, resembled a train with engine trouble on the Metropolitan Line. There were occasional glimpses of light from above, but mostly we have been stuck in tunnels.

Derbyshire declared at 307, their Saturday score. At tea, Kent had made 161 for six after 83 overs, as flaccid a piece of cricket as I have seen for some time, even allowing for their absentees.

...

Taylor's wicket-keeping was a beguilement of the day's journey, like one of those attractive advertisements that beam at you across the compartment. It is fortunate for England that they have in him at once both a spur and a substitute for Knott.

Shepherd attacked hard a few times, and was out to impatience, in the circumstances a forgivable sin. Johnson hit a fine six to square leg, and with Leary put on 35 quite cheerful runs for the seventh wicket. Johnson was caught from a skier to short-leg, and Leary was last out, caught at deep square leg. By this time the run rate had increased to a little more than two to the over.

There were 50 minutes left when Derbyshire went in again, 104 ahead. The evening was enlivened by a characteristic innings from fireman Gibbs, who had scored one in half an hour when I stopped counting.*

Kent scored none for batting, Derbyshire three for bowling, so Derbyshire lead 5-4 in the first innings: a case of points jammed. Steam has vanished. The anonymous electric, and the drab diesel, reign.

** Gibbs was dismissed before the close for 2.*

P.J.K. Gibbs
'He had scored one in half an hour when I stopped counting'

Some competition for the cider tent

BATH: Somerset were all out for 279 in their first innings against Essex

The warmth of the sun, and the beauty of the setting, did more for the pleasure of quite a lot of people – perhaps 2,000 – than the quality of the cricket itself. There was also the satisfaction of seeing Somerset make a fair recovery from a poor start. Perhaps this accounted for the smiles in the evening, for Bath always provides a crowd cheerful but severely partisan.

The pitch was slow but never difficult. Somerset took only two points for batting, Essex taking the same for bowling. Kitchen was bowled by Lever in the second over. Close was caught at short leg, sweeping. The score was 56. Shortly before lunch Hobbs bowled Hill, and shortly afterwards Virgin was caught at short leg, off Acfield.

Virgin had looked like playing a big innings, and when he was out at 93 for four, Somerset hopes sank. "C'mon then boay, nice day, might's well have another. 'Tis the licensing, see, best thing 'bout cricket I do always say."

But Clarkson and Cartwright, in the afternoon, provided an alternative entertainment. Steadily, and then with touches of aggression, they restored Somerset to order. At tea, though the score was only 188, no further wicket had fallen. The 200 was up before Hobbs, who bowled with thought as well as spin, made the breakthrough he had deserved. Clarkson was splendidly caught at extra cover, and Cartwright bowled. Somerset then declined to 228 for eight, but there was still some spirited resistance to come.

The Essex fielding had been keen and tight for most of the day, but wavered a little under this unexpected onslaught. The spectators were equally keen, and possibly even equally tight. After 97 overs Essex took the new ball, a doubtfully wise decision, made to look no better as Boyce kept getting into trouble with his run up.

Taylor, a good batsman, enjoyed himself. Moseley and Jones, not good batsmen, enjoyed themselves even more. The scoring rate almost reached two and a half to the over, when Taylor swung so casually at Hobbs that he might have been hinting to his captain to declare. But there was not quite time for Essex to go in.

The last wicket had put on 26, and batsmen had so endeared themselves to the company by the cider tent that they were referred to, jocularly, of course, as Adge and Acker. This is the nearest thing cricketers can get to deification in this part of the world. But Acker and Adge could, I think, have kept the beat of the day moving more briskly.

Only rain can save Essex from defeat

BATH: Somerset, with all second innings wickets in hand, are three runs behind Essex

The relentless rules of cricket prevented a finish to this match yesterday, even though the extra half hour had been taken. It may rain again in the night, so that Somerset might be deprived of the four runs they need for victory. If so, Langford may remember in future that it is wise to send in batsmen to open the innings. As it was, against the Essex fast bowlers, Somerset finished absurdly short of the required total, after outplaying Essex all day.

Rain had come to Somerset like a benefactor in the night before, and one trusts it will not now change its favours. Perhaps as a result of the lengthy and noisy operations on the River Avon, which flows by the side of the ground, there was no flooding, the water drained away quickly, and play was possible from the scheduled start. But the pitch had been affected, and once sunshine came to dry it, Essex were in trouble.

The crux was whether they could save the follow-on, for which they needed 130. At luncheon they were 116 for five, and it seemed likely that Somerset would have to face the worst of the wicket in the afternoon, for blue skies suggested that a large score in the fourth innings might be feasible.

The half hour after luncheon was therefore of compelling interest, much more so than was usually possible in the middle of the second day, in the time of covered pitches. Essex lost their last five wickets for 11 runs, failing to save the follow-on by three. They ought not to have done so badly. They were assisted by two dropped catches, but Turner contrived to run himself out after playing the ball back to the bowler, a piece of cricket which was shamefully irresponsible if you came from Essex, but gave much mirth to the sturdy farmers of Mendip and Cotswold.

Langford had the best bowling figures in the first innings, and deserved them, but he owed much to the support of Cartwright and O'Keeffe – who, at the close, was awarded his county cap. Close, too, by his fielding and generally aggressive attitude, was a dominant figure as Somerset polished off the first innings in quite the old Yorkshire style. Boyce was the best Essex batsman first time round, in a determined and nearly successful attempt to break Somerset's grip by hitting.

In the Essex second innings, Fletcher played well: not in his top form, but showing us that he remembers what it can feel like. When he was out, at 115 for seven, we looked for an early finish, but Essex refused to be rushed. Cartwright, who came on in the fifth over, retired from the crease in the 69th, after as prolonged and valuable a couple of spells as even he has often achieved. O'Keeffe, a twisting bundle of arms and fingers, helped to strike out the main batting, but just before seven, Lever and Acfield made sure that Somerset would have to bat again.

THIRD DAY: Langford hit the seventh ball of the morning for four to give Somerset a ten-wicket victory

SOMERSET 279 (Cartwright 62, Clarkson 49, Virgin 44, Taylor 31*, Hobbs 4-62) & 8-0
ESSEX 127 (Langford 6-34) & 159 (Fletcher 44, Cartwright 5-43, O'Keeffe 5-60)

JUNE: Somerset cricket

A fair start in West Country ways

The Somerset cricket eleven has always been something of a League of Nations. Sam Woods was their captain at a time when Australians in county cricket were rare phenomena. In the twenties Somerset were graced by the batting of a New Zealander, P.R. Johnson (his qualification was that he was born in Wellington). There is a long tradition of making strangers welcome. Still, Brian Close was something new: a child of the storm if ever there was one. Indeed, I would call him a stormy petrel, except that the petrel hovers above the waves, and Close has frequently been plunged in them.

It was also intriguing that a former captain of England and Yorkshire, so successful in both jobs yet ultimately dismissed from both, should come to Somerset as a subordinate. Half the Somerset supporters seemed to want him chiefly for his captaincy, and the other half not to want him at all. When he was signed, but not as captain, neither party was exactly disgruntled. Somerset, it was said (in fact I was the fool who said it!), were back at their old game of doing everything by halves.

This is obviously no more than an interim report, and Close is a man who delights to cheat the prophets: so I will say no more than the experiment does seem to be working out. The clearest evidence of that is in Close's cricketing form. He has been scoring plenty of runs, on Sundays as well as weekdays, bowling usefully from time to time and is still holding hard catches near the wicket.

Sometimes, when the game is in a tense situation, as he crouches at short leg, he can be seen gesturing to fieldsmen to move a yard, this way or that, but this is instinctive habit, not usurpation. Indeed, I have no doubt that the hopeful development of this later stage in Close's career owes much to the cheerful understanding of his captain, Langford.

Langford has not abdicated, nor is he sycophantic towards the formidable cuckoo in his nest. He remains his own man, and Somerset's man, but does not spurn sound advice.

Off the field, Close has been quietly helping to build up the strength of cricket in the county. He is ready to speak at clubs and societies. He and Langford, with the county secretary, A.K. James, and young O'Keeffe, recently attended a public meeting at Crewkerne, where the public were invited to come and ask their questions, and nearly 100 did.

Langford will retire from the captaincy at the end of the season, and does not expect to be able to play more than occasionally thereafter. Although nothing has been formally decided, Close will presumably succeed him (the name of Virgin has been mentioned, and Roy Virgin has it in him to be an excellent captain, but he is eight years younger than Close, and his time will come).

Somerset under Close would be an interesting proposition. They have never won the championship. Indeed, they have never won anything, except friends, and they have a lot of those. Though they are still called a League of Nations, there is a stronger locally-born representation in the side than has often been the case in the past: Virgin, Kitchen and Burgess were all born in the county, and so were several useful reserves, not counting those, such as Langford, who have been there so long it is hard to tell the difference.

What remains unchanged, wherever the players may be born, is the Somerset style, the unpredictable style, the constant variations from the casual to the unspeakable to the brilliant. It will no doubt be a bit of a job for Close to adjust himself to the West Country ways. But he has certainly made a fair start, perhaps his very own unpredictability may turn out to be a sympathetic quality – and he has a Devon wife.

Amusement that makes the Gillette Cup a knockout

The second round of the Gillette Cup takes place tomorrow and, given good weather, there will be big crowds at all eight grounds. Oddly enough, there is no match north of Edgbaston, where Lincolnshire will endeavour to become the first minor county to beat one of their seniors, a task in which everyone but Warwickshire will wish them well.

When the Gillette Cup began in 1963 I was no enthusiast. I did not believe that county cricket could retain its proper quality on a limited-over, smash-and-grab basis. I did not think a knockout competition could be made to work in English summer weather.

I was wrong. When I look back on the cricket I have watched during the past eight years, some of the happiest memories are of Gillette Cup matches. I cannot say the same of the John Player Sunday League, apart from occasional exceptional individual performances: Majid working miracles in the twilight at Hove, Langford's eight maiden overs at Yeovil, Chappell's hundred at Brislington – these were virtuoso efforts, but the orchestration was freakish.

The Gillette Cup, once the players had accustomed themselves to it, has been real cricket. Is this just the difference between a match of 40 and 60 overs? Very likely – though there has also been a marked difference of style in sponsorship.

Sixty overs do give a chance of a serious match, even by county standards. Batsmen can build an innings, bowlers can work and plan for their wickets. If they have to set about these things with less margin of error than usual, it often does them no harm – witness the marvellous innings of Boycott in the 1965 final, the highest (146) yet played in the competition.

Forty overs would hardly do for a house match. Sixty can be a contest of skill, even at a high level.

The finest day's cricket I think I have seen in a Gillette Cup match was between Yorkshire and Nottinghamshire, in the semi-final of 1969, when the Scarborough ground was not so much brimful as running over.

Yorkshire won. They were put in, and they made 191, a score good enough to win most Gillette matches, but not conclusive, especially with Sobers to bat. The tension when he went in and began to settle, the heat, the roaring, and the agonized silences, racked the mind. Once he hit as bump-ball back to the bowler and turned dolefully towards the pavilion. There was a scream of joy, quickly checked by a laugh, less rueful than wrathful.

Yorkshiremen do not like having their legs pulled, and when Sobers was actually out, caught at the wicket a few minutes later, there was a revengeful quality in the applause that led him back to the pavilion.

If that was the most exciting match, the oddest I have seen was that between Somerset and Nottinghamshire at Taunton in 1964. In those early days we were not familiar with the refinements of the rules, and when this match ended, nobody (well, not the umpires, the captains, nor the radio commentators) was quite sure who had won it.

Nottinghamshire had been all out for 215 runs in the fifty-ninth over. When Wells was about to bowl to Langford the last ball of the sixtieth over, of the Somerset innings, and therefore in any case the last ball of the match, Somerset were one run behind, and had one wicket to fall.

Langford swung, and did not middle it, but the ball ran away backward of square leg, and they raced through for one. Stephenson, the Somerset captain, was leaning over the players' balcony, crying out to Langford to go again. The batsmen started for the second, but it was clearly not there, they scampered back to their creases, the game was over, the scores were level.

"I think that means you've won," said Millman, the Nottinghamshire captain, to Langford. "The rule is clear. In the event of a tie, the result will be decided in favour of the side losing the least number of wickets."

It is only if both sides have lost the same number of wickets, that the rate of scoring comes into account.

The match was therefore technically won by Somerset at the moment Langford and Hall completed their first run. But what if they had gone for that second run, as their captain and all the crowd were telling them to, and there had been a run-out? In that case Nottinghamshire would have won because the scores would have been level, both sides all out, and Nottinghamshire had scored their runs more quickly.

A match already won would have been, so to speak, posthumously lost. At least, I suppose that would have been the judgment. I doubt if any cricket match can have had a more extraordinary finish.

Perhaps the best of all Gillette days was at Trent Bridge in 1968, in the third round: Gloucestershire, 296 for eight, Nottinghamshire, 271. Green, who was made man-of-the-match from a fair company, scored 90; Milton, 67; Procter, 53; Smedley, 75; Sobers, 76.

I did not see this match, but I quote from Grahame Parker's account in the Gloucestershire Year Book: "At the end of the forty-eighth over of the Notts innings, the new Gloucestershire secretary, who should have known better, nudged his chairman: 'we've lost this game.' The chairman, who knew better, nudged back: 'one over can change all this.' We were sitting in the Nottinghamshire committee box – best view in English cricket – hemmed around by justifiably confident opponents: Sobers was hammering our bowling to all corners of Trent Bridge and had seemingly broken the grip we had held all day on this game."

The next over did indeed change it. White was run out after a collision with Meyer and Sobers was caught at cover next ball, a catch which caused Grahame Parker to write: "It was long enough in the air for Mike Procter to wish he had never left the veld."

But though I did not see that epic, I had seen Gloucestershire's second-round match that year, against Kent at Bristol, and this is stamped on my memory for different reasons.

No play had been possible on the Saturday, and on the Monday play was delayed until after noon. This meant that reporters were running late with the copy, and sub-editors were beginning to utter nine-letter words like deadlines.

However, the game appeared to offer no journalistic problems. Kent had been all out for 110, Gloucestershire were always in command, we thought, and by the time they had reached 109 for four, I had every word of my copy written and was poised near the gate, well placed for the telephone race. Five wickets then fell for no runs, before David Allen, the only calm man on the ground, made the winning hit.

I dreaded to think what my report, or come to that, my sub-editor, would look like in the morning.

Ships in the night and 'a propal hullaballool'

Jeremy Thorpe

TAUNTON: Somerset v Surrey

I knew it was going to be a good day when I passed Jeremy Thorpe at Taunton station. "So do great ships pass in the night," he said, a remark I hereby pass on to my grandchildren, with supplications to the compositor for no misprints. I might even have guessed that it would be a good day for Brian Close, another man who has been bludgeoned by fate but repeatedly emerged unbowed and unbloody, except in the strictly technical sense. Both, also, are not afraid to hit out at bowling of the slow left variety.

A Somerset supporter

TAUNTON: Somerset v Nottinghamshire (JPL)

I travelled down in the train with a Somerset supporter, a banner tucked under his arm. He came from that part of Somerset which is in Bristol, and his speech was splashed with the intrusive Bristol labials. "I can tell you," he said, "when Somerset do win today, "there'll be a propal ullaballool."

But Somerset did not win, rarely looked like winning, and the banner remained furled.

In need of substitutes

CARDIFF: Glamorgan v The Indians

Glamorgan were suffering various ailments. Lewis was unwell, and could only field intermittently. Llewellyn, a boy of 17, who bowls off-breaks, had a bang on the head in the morning, and had to retire in the afternoon.

As the second eleven were away, the provision of substitutes was difficult. Several senior members contemplated going home for their flannels, including an old friend of mine, appropriately named Hamlet. He was just about to volunteer, he explained, but his native hue of resolution was sicklied o'er with the pale cast of thought. Or words to that effect.

Showers in the afternoon

BIRMINGHAM: Warwickshire v Gloucestershire

The showers in the afternoon were heavy, really too heavy to play in, although they usually turned out to be brief. The players would retreat, turn round at the pavilion gate, return 10 paces, and then be driven in again by the torrent. On one occasion A.C. Smith, who likes a joke, remained in the middle taking guard while all the rest were running for shelter.

The ground staff moved in a state of limbo, for ever trundling their heavy covers to and from the boundaries, sometimes pausing helplessly halfway, uncertain where to go next. In their long black oilskins they looked like British trawlermen lost on the Russian steppes, dragging their boat along with them in the belief that sea power will tell in the end.

Tony Lewis
'Dignified but not stately, the Cambridge man at his best'

Boycott scores noisy 200

COLCHESTER: Yorkshire have scored 347 for one wicket in their first innings against Essex

An opening partnership of 240 and a double century by Boycott put Yorkshire in a strong position on a sunny day at the attractive, if not exactly pastoral, Garrison ground at Colchester. Boycott, who scored 200 here last year, must be considering joining the Army.

Yorkshire took only two points for batting, and at times were barracked for scoring slowly, but there were mitigating circumstances. The pitch was slow – Essex showed their opinion of it by resting Lever. It was hard to score runs quickly, especially in front of the wicket. East and Acfield were steady in length and direction – indeed there were few loose balls from anybody for most of the day – and the Essex fielding, so swift and accurate, must have knocked 10 runs an hour off Yorkshire's rate – helped, to be sure, by a slow outfield.

Boycott, until the latter part of his innings, scored mostly off the back foot. He cut and forced the ball to the offside, and sometimes hooked. After he had reached his hundred he began to let his drives go, and very handsome they were. Sharpe moved efficiently along, accepting a supporting part, never missing the chance of a nudge or two, occasionally cutting delicately and late.

The last time I saw a Yorkshire opening pair put on over 200 against Essex was in 1932, when Holmes and Sutcliffe scored the famous 555 at Leyton. The difference between that partnership and this that strikes me most concerns the noise. Holmes and Sutcliffe were not only quick between the wickets, they were quiet. They ran with only an occasional crisp call, often with a nod, a lifting of the finger, often with no mortal sign that could be detected, yet how rarely with a shade of misunderstanding.

The present Yorkshire system is for both batsmen to shout simultaneously, pause and then shout again. If, as happens about once an over, this has not cleared the situation up, it is considered wise to keep shouting. This is especially the policy of Boycott, whose progress down the pitch is often one long ululation.

It was to this sound of revelry that Sharpe departed, eight short of his hundred. Boycott thereafter gave his voice rather less work, and his bat rather more, surging in noble waves towards his second hundred, which he reached at 10 past six.

On only 45 occasions, I estimate, did Boycott give Essex the slightest hope. Just before lunch he played and missed at Boyce: at 84 he popped a ball which had checked just short of cover; there was one appeal for leg before which may not have been too far away, and on 42 occasions he might have been run out. He has reached his thousand runs for the season in 11 innings.

Late Essex stand cheers their supporters

COLCHESTER: Yorkshire lead Essex by 204 runs on first innings

Yorkshire batted on yesterday, adding 74 quick runs before the declaration. …. Boycott had scored only a few more when he was leg-before to Hobbs. Boycott had immediately set out for a run, and Sam Cook, the umpire, paused for reflection, finally lifting his finger only a yard or so in front of the victim's nose: a Tetbury handshake, we call it down West. ……

Ward and Francis had scored 43 without much trouble by luncheon. … At tea they were 117 for seven. …..

The Colchester crowd, and there was quite a lot of it, endured all this with Roman fortitude. They cheered up vastly when Taylor and East put on 67 for the ninth wicket, in the process snatching Essex a batting point and depriving Yorkshire of a fifth for bowling. Taylor we know to be a redoubtable fighter in such circumstances. East's play, at least to me, was a small revelation. He is lanky, with floppy hair, attributes which look elegant when he bowls but ungainly when he bats. He had luck with edges, and the ball dropping clear of fieldsmen, but he played with spirit, relishing every moment of it, and some of his strokes were good by anyone's standards.

Yorkshire did not show up too well under this unexpected assault. There was again a good deal of noise in the air, and when once the captain misfielded, and left the ball to a colleague to pick up, a cockney voice was heard: "Come on, Boycott, yer tellin' all the others." But after all captains have to learn by experience, and though they did not end the innings in time to send Essex in again, Yorkshire should still win.

Essex bat out time for a draw on the final day

Boycott captained Yorkshire with praiseworthy attention to detail, constantly switching his bowlers and field placings. He is not afraid of the unorthodox. …

But the long pauses for conferences and rearrangement did take up a lot of time, and it was time Yorkshire were short of in the end.

Cartwright's bowling too much for Warwickshire

GLASTONBURY: Somerset (16 pts) beat Warwickshire (4 pts) by an innings and 94 runs

Warwickshire began the day yesterday at 52 for no wicket, 206 behind the Somerset first innings score. They scored 43 more runs by lunch, while losing all their wickets. In the afternoon they followed on, and were bowled out for 69 by tea. Twenty wickets fell, therefore, at an average of 5½ runs apiece.

Before dealing with the burning question of the pitch, one which will keep the world of English cricket agog for a full day or less, let us salute those who played well. On this second day there were, for Somerset, principally Cartwright and Close. Perhaps Underwood might have been more dangerous on this pitch than Cartwright, or again perhaps not. I certainly cannot think of any other challenger. Warwickshire knew this only too well. So did Close, collecting the catches at short leg as a man ticks off the items on an account. Both Moseley and Burgess bowled well enough, but it was the compelling presence of Cartwright from the pavilion end, unchanged and unchangeable, which drew the batsmen into insupportable risks at the other end.

For Warwickshire, Mike Smith showed what might be done by a batsman of high skill and detached mind, and Ibadulla, who batted 90 minutes in his two innings for his 12 runs, and was not out in either, showed what might be done by obstinacy. Kanhai played a few splendid strokes, but it was like the condemned man gulping down the fried eggs and brandy on the fatal morning – strictly for taste, not nourishment.

At lunchtime on Saturday the umpires had asked Mr Bert Lock for an advisory opinion on his pitch, and yesterday he duly came down and had a look at it. By Saturday evening 310 runs had been scored on it for the loss of 10 wickets, at about the average rate of runs per over for a three-day match. It seemed then that the umpires had been precipitate, or at least unlucky, in that their opinions became so widely known; and it seemed yesterday that they had been triumphantly vindicated. The truth, as usual, lies somewhere between.

The pitch was not exceptionally difficult on Saturday. But even then it was dusty, and 36 hours of baking weather, plus a Sunday league match in which it was covered by inadequate matting, did make it a bad one yesterday. The top had become flaky and broken, the batsmen were ready to give up hope, and Cartwright was bowling with what in a more flamboyant character we might have suspected to be a knowing grin.

The Glastonbury pitch has usually provided plenty of runs; indeed Alan Jones of Glamorgan, who once scored two centuries in a match here, expressed to me last week the wish that he was accompanying me down to pick up a couple more. I think what happened on this occasion was that the long dry spell, on a ground perhaps short of watering facilities (which could easily be remedied), acting on a light grass which does not naturally root itself deep, caused the trouble. The reports will be made and argued.

I hope it is not forgotten that Mr Cecil Buttle, the head groundsman of Somerset, has for many years produced fine wickets, sometimes in improbable places; and that the Morland's company, whose ground it is, will certainly effect any improvements within their capacity. No one was more dismayed when the game ended so early. They have 200 people invited to lunch today, and will have to take them round the abbey ruins instead. No reference is intended to Cartwright or Close.

AUGUST: Nottinghamshire v Worcestershire at Newark

A Sunday century from Sobers

NEWARK: Nottinghamshire v Worcestershire (JPL)

The tidy pleasant ground, which provides a sound pitch and occupies part of a Civil War battlefield, saw an innings worthy of a Cromwellian cavalryman from Sobers. His century enabled Nottinghamshire to win with four balls to spare, and with rather more comfort than that statistic indicates. Since it was Cromwell who seriously began the British connexion with the West Indies, I could not help feeling it was a double triumph for that mighty and benevolent shade.

...

Worcestershire did not field so well as usual. Sobers was dropped at deep point when he had scored seven, and gave two more half-chances later. There were overthrows, and often the power of Sobers's driving on the ground burst through hands and legs.

He was rarely, in this innings, at his most majestic or sublime. He took what Worcestershire's faltering gods offered him. Yet at any point it was only necessary to look at him to recognize a dominant cricketer, a man of genius, warts and all.

Glastonbury

Taunton

30,000 see Lancashire reach final at 9 pm

MANCHESTER: Lancashire beat Gloucestershire by three wickets

At five minutes to nine on a fine Old Trafford night, with three overs and one ball to spare, Lancashire reached the final of the Gillette Cup. Rain had lost more than an hour after luncheon, but the weather became warm and sunny, and at half past seven the umpires decided to play to a finish.

They were within their rights, but at the time it seemed an imprudent decision, because once taken it could scarcely be reversed. Gloucestershire not unnaturally bowled their overs more and more slowly. They must have been very tired at the end, after four hours' fielding without a break, and in fact could not quite sustain their effort to the end. This handicap was fully counter-balanced by the increasingly bad light, but one way and another the contest had ceased to be one of true cricketing skills. It was, to be sure, exciting, and made a memorable day for nearly 30,000 people – the gates were closed in the morning. But it was really no way for so important a match to be settled.

Indeed, the decisive factor was a quick slog by Hughes in the fifty-sixth over. When that over began, Lancashire needed 25 to win. When it ended the scores were level, Hughes having hit Mortimore for two sixes, two fours and two twos. It was hard lines on Mortimore, who had previously bowled well and taken the crucial wicket of Clive Lloyd. Yet perhaps it was more than a kindly chance which saw Hughes through, since he has done this kind of thing before, and in fact has an average of 92 in the Gillette Cup, out only once in five innings. He was made man of the match, which in all the circumstances of this strange occasion was appropriate.

Until that point, the game had been evenly balanced all day. Gloucestershire's chances of putting up a good fight seemed to depend on the toss, a fair start, and a major innings from Procter. They got all three, and a total of 229 always gives a side a reasonable chance in this competition, even against Lancashire.

The score had reached 57 in the twenty-second over when the first wicket fell. Green was run out at the bowler's end, trying to take a single to Clive Lloyd. Nicholls continued to play coolly and precisely, and Knight was soon making his strokes. At lunch, the score was 83 for one after 33 overs: a sound foundation.

When the rain stopped, Nicholls was soon out, and Procter, with so much depending upon him, played watchfully. The Lancashire ground fielding and field placing had an important influence on the game at this stage. Clive Lloyd himself must have saved 20 runs, but although he took the eye and the cheers he was only one of 11. Procter was given a chance and a half, but that apart the batsmen had to fight for every run. The contrast when Gloucestershire were in the field was marked. It was not that they fielded badly, but they were not quite in the same class in either skill or tactics.

Procter's concentration slowly merged into confidence, and he began to beat the field with his drives on both sides of the wicket (54 of his 65 runs were scored in front of the wicket). He lost Knight, caught at square leg, at 113, and Shepherd – who looked in no sort of form – at 150. Bissex played a useful innings, but Milton would have been a great help – as he would, later, in the field. When Procter was caught at the wicket in the fifty-sixth over, he had kept Gloucestershire well in the game.

He made a further contribution with a fierce and accurate opening spell. His first three overs were maidens, but after that his bowling became rather disappointing, and he must have hoped to make more of the poor light. Furthermore, he wasted runs in pursuing a private duel with Clive Lloyd, which was highly entertaining but hardly to Gloucestershire's point.

David Lloyd and Wood had scored 61 together in the nineteenth over when Lloyd was out. For a while Lancashire stayed well up with requirements but Pilling was bowled at 105, and Wood run out, needlessly, at 136. Sullivan was splendidly caught by Procter on the square leg boundary, a catch which counted six (this season at any rate) because Procter went over the line in taking it.

However, Sullivan was out soon afterwards, and when Clive Lloyd followed, at 160 for five, it seemed that the game was going Gloucestershire's way. Engineer kicked his wicket down in making a drive three runs later. This was, as it turned out, the apex of Gloucestershire's success, for Simmons struck well around him, while the captain held an end, and when Simmons was bowled at 203 there came the decisive onslaught from Hughes.

Time limit less dramatic, but fairer and safer

REFLECTIONS TWO DAYS LATER

I shall never forget the last few overs. I was watching from high up at the Stretford end, and the lights were going on all over Manchester. The huge crowd – including members, it was probably about 29,000 – sat as if pinned to their seats. The special train to take home the Gloucestershire supporters, retimed from 8.10 to 8.30 (although there was no likelihood of a finish by then, once the decision to play on had been made) pulled into Warwick Road station and pulled away again, nearly empty, never to return.

The reason why cricket ought not to be played in bad light is as old as the game, once it had graduated to a hard ball. Someone might be killed. On this occasion nobody was, partly I think because Procter (he is really quite friendly) was inhibited from attacking as he might have done. His only bouncers were so short that the batsmen were put to no serious risk.

I think there is no doubt that the umpires were mistaken in playing on after 7.30. The only reason this can be done is if "a finish can be obtained" and they obtained their finish only by playing in conditions where the game became an absurdity. They were also mistaken in not coming off at 8.30, because the element of physical danger was then acute. Since they got their finish, and nobody was killed, they may congratulate themselves: on their luck, not their judgment.

I suppose they were scared of the reaction of the crowd had they called a halt. This might not have been too severe at 7.30, but could well have caused a bit of a riot an hour later. No doubt the county authorities were worried about reorganizing play on the next day. We come back to the rules. Would a fixed limit of 8 or even 8.30, in all circumstances, be better? It would have its problems. It would produce less drama. But it might produce fairer cricket.

Lancashire v Gloucestershire, Old Trafford, 28 July 1971

Lancashire won by three wickets

Gloucestershire

R.B. Nicholls	b Simmons	53
D.M. Green	run out	21
R.D.V. Knight	c Simmons b Hughes	31
M.J. Procter	c Engineer b Lever	65
D.R. Shepherd	lbw b Simmons	6
M. Bissex	*not out*	29
* A.S. Brown	c Engineer b Sullivan	6
H. Jarman	*not out*	0
J.B. Mortimore		
+ B.J. Meyer		
J. Davey		
	b 2, lb 14, w 1, nb 1	18
	(6 wkts, 60 overs)	**229**

1/57, 2/87, 3/113, 4/150, 5/201, 6/210

Lever	12	3	40	1
Shuttleworth	12	3	33	0
Wood	12	3	39	0
Hughes	11	0	68	1
Simmons	12	3	25	2
Sullivan	1	0	6	1

Lancashire

D. Lloyd	lbw b Brown	31
B. Wood	run out	50
H. Pilling	b Brown	21
C.H. Lloyd	b Mortimore	34
J. Sullivan	b Davey	10
+ F.M. Engineer	hit wkt b Mortimore	2
* J.D. Bond	*not out*	16
J. Simmons	b Mortimore	25
D.P. Hughes	*not out*	26
P. Lever		
K. Shuttleworth		
	b 1, lb 13, nb 1	15
	(7 wkts, 56.5 overs)	**230**

1/61, 2/105, 3/136, 4/156, 5/160, 6/163, 7/203

Procter	10.5	3	38	0
Davey	11	1	22	1
Knight	12	2	42	0
Mortimore	11	0	81	3
Brown	12	0	32	2

Umpires: H.D. Bird and A. Jepson

Prudence gives way to bolder batsmen

CHELTENHAM: Northamptonshire lead Gloucestershire by 129 runs, with six second innings wickets in hand

The gatemen at Cheltenham, where the cricket is played on the college ground, take their stations at battered old desks, scarred with the scratched and inky legends of generations. In the morning – for since it was raining there was nothing better to do – I inspected one, hoping to find a familiar name or two from the Cheltenham gallery. K.S. Duleepsinhji, perhaps? T.A. Higson? J.P.W. Mallalieu? But all I could decipher was the assertion NIGEL IS A FAIRY and a little lower down, even more boldly, the word PRUDENCE. Did this recall a divinity lesson or an assignation at the Ladies College?

Anyway, it was not prudence's day. For when play began properly in the afternoon (there were less than 10 minutes of it in the morning), it was the bolder batsmen who flourished: Shepherd, Brown and later Tait. The rain perhaps arrested the deterioration of the pitch for a while, but it was still one to make spin bowlers and close fieldsmen rub their hands.

Gloucestershire began at 36 for three, and were all out for 143. Of these 107 runs, 73 were scored by Brown and Shepherd, whose sixth wicket partnership put on 45. Brown hit the straighter, and looked in less trouble, but there is something very impressive about Shepherd when he gets a sight of the ball and his weight behind it. There is a lot of good cricket in that tubby frame, and I hope he shows us some more before the end of the season, for he would be a loss to the scene, and he will have to fight for his place when Zaheer and Sadiq arrive.

The Northamptonshire bowling and fielding was steady, with Swinburne, I thought, doing as well as any. Although born in Yorkshire, he used to play for Devon. And Shepherd, of course, is as Devon as a tiddy oggy, so it was a good day for the south-west.

The sky often looked black, the rain spat gently from time to time, like an old man in W.W. Jacobs ruminating outside his pub, but as the day went on there were quite long periods of warm sunshine. Now, we thought, when Northamptonshire went in again at ten to five, we shall see Mortimore and Allen bowl them out.

This did not quite happen. Tait took his chances before the spinners came on. I had not seen the boy before, and my impressions were of vigour rather than grace, but that was probably due to the demands of the situation. He was caught at slip off Allen, and Ackerman was caught at cover off Allen after making, with Steele, a dour resistance against the dangerous bowling.

Brown then brought on Bissex for Mortimore, and for the second time in the match Bissex justified him, with Steele caught and Mushtaq bowled – 54 for four. Cook and Watts hung on until the end, often in difficulty, especially against Allen. Gloucestershire will have to bat well to win this match, and if they are wise they will not make prudence their counsellor. They should, not to be misunderstood, scrub her off that desk.

SEPTEMBER: Scarborough Festival

SCARBOROUGH: TN Pearce's XI v The Indians

Hobbs, lobbing his leg breaks high into the strong wind, made me think he would emulate the feat J.M. Barrie claimed, and run after one of his balls and catch it.

...

In the bright sunshine there was a big crowd: a seat could scarcely be found on the popular side in the afternoon. There was a new festival flag, and I am inclined to think that the band played a new tune. If there is a touch of uneasiness at Scarborough in 1971, it is less concerned with the future of the festival than the state of Yorkshire cricket in general. "Inquest on Yorkshire," said the front pages. "Bill is an angry man" – an improbable reference to my old friend, Bill Bowes, with a picture of him at the top, looking even more than usually like a woolly baa lamb. But who could really be angry, let alone Bill, at Scarborough when the runs come and the sun shines?

...

It was appropriate that Gavaskar should be in the van of their victory. While he did not play a big innings in the Tests, he had always looked their most accomplished batsman. In years to come, it may be, we shall remember 1971 as the season when we first saw him.

77 + 51 = 128. 6 wkts.

CHELTENHAM:

~~&~~ The gatemen at Cheltenham, where the cricket is played on the college ground, take their stations at battered old desks, scarred with the scratched & inky legends of generations. In the morning – for since it was raining, there was nothing better to do – I inspected one, hoping to find a familiar name or two. K.S. Duleepsinhji, perhaps? T.A. Higson? V.P.W. Mallalieu? But all I could decipher was the assertion NIGEL IS A FAIRY, ~~–~~ a little lower down, even more boldly the word PRUDENCE.

~~A relic of moral adjuration recalling~~

Kanhai accelerates

BIRMINGHAM: Yorkshire, with six first innings wickets in hand, are 335 runs behind Warwickshire

Warwickshire, with nothing to lose, cast care aside yesterday, and have already taken ten points from the match, eight for batting and two for bowling. Yorkshire took four for bowling. Indeed, though their play lacked a sharp edge, Yorkshire did not bowl and field too badly. But in the evening they batted like demoralized men.

Warwickshire won the toss on a good pitch, perhaps a little quicker than is usual at Edgbaston, a pitch in favour of stroke play. At luncheon, after 34 overs, they had scored 137 for one, and when the news came through that Surrey were 68 for four, a whisper of hope rustled through the crowd (not a very large crowd, perhaps 2,000, though it is hard to judge the numbers scattered upon Edgbaston's far-flung terraces).

In the afternoon reports from The Oval were less encouraging, but the Warwickshire batting maintained its momentum.

...

Alan Smith declared at the end of the eighty-fifth over. Yorkshire had three-quarters of an hour to bat. McVicker and Rouse bowled with pace and optimism, and the batting could be called flaccid. Lumb, Sharpe and Hampshire were caught behind the wicket. Johnson, who in the circumstances ought not to have gone in, was bowled. Boycott and Hutton were together at the end. "Shake a bridle over a Yorkshireman's grave, and he will rise up and steal a horse." It is bridle-shaking time.

Boycott dominates the day's play

BIRMINGHAM: Warwickshire, with five first innings wickets in hand, are 246 runs ahead of Yorkshire

This was a day's cricket full of skill and competitive spirit, played in bright sunshine. Warwickshire took 13 points on the first innings, Yorkshire seven. It is even possible Yorkshire could win. At least they gave Warwickshire plenty to think about when they saved the follow-on. Warwickshire's response in the evening was to score, for a while, at five runs an over, with Kanhai making us wonder whether Boycott is the best batsman in the world.

Till then, it had been entirely Boycott's day. Yorkshire began at 19 for four, the captain 10. Hutton was leg before wicket, padding up; Bairstow was bowled between bat and pad; Nicholson, after a few vigorous swings, was finely caught at short leg. All three wickets fell to McVicker, the best of the bowlers. Boycott had been playing assuredly enough, but that was 79 for seven, and 125 more runs were needed to save the follow-on.

Now at last the bridle shook, not just for Boycott but for his partners in harness. With Old he put on 44, with Cope 62, and with Bore 47. These three all took their share of the drag. Old was a little unlucky to be run out, Cope's resistance was sensible and prolonged, and Bore, who scored an unaccustomedly bold 16, must already be thinking of emulating Rhodes, who also batted right and bowled left and who progressed from being Yorkshire's No 11 to England's No 2. I do not make this comparison seriously, though to be sure I shall recall it if anything of the kind happens.

Boycott carried his bat through the innings. He has scored more hundreds for Yorkshire this season than anyone since Herbert Sutcliffe, whom God preserve, in 1932. They have some resemblances, these two great players, though if Sutcliffe had ever captained Yorkshire – and it was a shame that he did not – they would never have finished in the bottom half of the championship table.

There are certain contradictions in Boycott's character. He did bat with the most remarkable control, sometimes majestic, sometimes almost impish. He edged two balls towards the wicket-keeper somewhere in the middle of his second 50, chances which Warwickshire may rue.

Otherwise, there was scarcely an error, even a mistiming. He acknowledged the applause for his century, doffed and beaming, with a graciousness which Sutcliffe could not have surpassed – in fact, which nobody could have surpassed, for the acknowledgements went on rather longer than the applause. He saved the follow-on with a six to midwicket, which he triumphantly signalled himself, before the umpire could. He ushered the valiant Bore off the field before him, a gesture at once touching and embarrassing. I am not sure why, but the lines come to my mind,

See the son of grief at cricket
Trying to be glad

It was a marvellous innings.

When Warwickshire went in, Whitehouse was caught in the gully second ball and Jameson caught at the wicket for five, a splendid catch down the leg side from the inside edge. Kanhai scored 50 of the first 58 runs, with 10 boundaries. Mike Smith supported him, and the score reached 89 for two in 19 overs. Then Smith was leg before, Kanhai caught at midwicket and the game had taken another turn, possibly not its last. Warwickshire ended cautiously. Boycott has scored three centuries against them this season, and has an innings to go.

Warwickshire hopes alive and twitching

BIRMINGHAM: Warwickshire (23 pts) beat Yorkshire (7 pts) by 22 runs

At two minutes to six, with the fifth ball of the twenty-second over of the last hour, Gibbs spun an off break across Bore, who could not quite keep his bat out of the way. The ball bobbed up over short square leg, and Ibadulla, with a leap and a backward stretch, caught it.

By this narrow margin did Warwickshire keep their championship hopes alive and even kicking, though it had been a case of twitches for most of the day, and especially in the last eight overs, when in steadily increasing darkness Bore and Cope held on for Yorkshire's last wicket.

A Yorkshireman present expressed his confidence in these two ("Now if it were Sharpe and Hampshire, 't game'd be oop"), and the crowd made noises like beasts in pain, such as must once have been heard in bear pits and bullrings; and Alan Smith spent more time off the ground than on it, so constant and enthusiastic were his appeals. But it could not quite be done.

Nearly all the really good games of cricket have been fluctuating, wayward games, and so it was in this one. When Warwickshire had scored 354 and Yorkshire were 25 for five, a finish in two days would not have been surprising. When Yorkshire needed only 150 to win, at little more than a run a minute, all wickets in hand and Boycott in a command that had scarcely been challenged, Warwickshire's hopes had almost vanished.

Perhaps two bowling changes won this match. In mid-afternoon Alan Smith brought on his still relatively inexperienced leg spinner, Tidy, from the city end. It was a brave thing to do. Boycott took quick runs from him, moving back to cut and hook. He looked in no possible trouble. Tidy pitched the ball further up, which was also brave, and suffered some severe drives. Then Boycott did not quite get to a ball, and Ibadulla took a running catch at long on.

By tea (177 for four) Tidy had taken three more wickets, with some help from batsmen who, the master gone, batted as if their knees were knitting. After tea Hutton and Johnson played more rationally, Tidy's length faltered, and Yorkshire were winning again at the beginning of the last hour: 67 wanted, only four wickets down.

The second important bowling change came when Gibbs was moved to the city end, and Jameson – an occasional off spinner – brought on at the pavilion end. Jameson seemed an improbable choice, for at this stage Yorkshire needed no tempting to chase runs, but was a triumphantly successful one. He had Johnson leg-before to a ball which kept low, Old bowled from a wild swing, then Nicholson leg before. In the meantime Gibbs had Bairstow caught, and then turned a ball sharply to beat Hutton: 255 for nine. That meant that Yorkshire could hardly win the match, but it was 20 palpitating minutes before we knew they could not save it.

Warwickshire v Yorkshire, Birmingham, 1, 2 & 3 September 1971

Warwickshire won by 22 runs

Warwickshire

J. Whitehouse	b Old	11	c Hampshire b Old	0
J.A. Jameson	c Bairstow b Old	95	c Bairstow b Nicholson	5
R.B. Kanhai	c Hampshire b Nicholson	135	c Johnson b Nicholson	62
M.J.K. Smith	c Bairstow b Bore	45	lbw b Nicholson	26
D.L. Amiss	run out	8	b Nicholson	23
K. Ibadulla	b Nicholson	19	lbw b Cope	1
N.M. McVicker	b Old	11	b Nicholson	37
*+ A.C. Smith	c Bairstow b Old	2	c Bairstow b Hutton	0
S.J. Rouse	*not out*	8	c Bairstow b Hutton	0
L.R. Gibbs	*not out*	6	*not out*	3
W.N. Tidy			run out	0
	lb 14	14	lb 2, w 1, nb 1	4
	(8 wkts, dec)	**354**		**161**

1/22, 2/162, 3/274, 4/302, 5/304, 6/321, 7/331, 8/345
1/0, 2/26, 3/89, 4/94, 5/96, 6/149, 7/156, 8/156, 9/160, 10/161

Old	23	3	112	4	5	0	40	1
Nicholson	24	4	72	2	20	4	48	5
Hutton	12	1	42	0	18	5	38	2
Cope	12	3	66	0	8	2	14	1
Bore	14	2	48	1	5	1	17	0

Yorkshire

* G. Boycott	*not out*	138	c Ibadulla b Tidy	84
R.G. Lumb	c AC Smith b Rouse	1	c Ibadulla b Tidy	65
P.J. Sharpe	c MJK Smith b McVicker	6	c AC Smith b Tidy	11
J.H. Hampshire	c AC Smith b Rouse	0	lbw b Tidy	6
C. Johnson	b McVicker	0	lbw b Jameson	34
R.A. Hutton	lbw b McVicker	4	b Gibbs	34
+ D.L. Bairstow	b McVicker	9	c Tidy b Gibbs	3
A.G. Nicholson	c MJK Smith b McVicker	23	lbw b Jameson	3
C.M. Old	run out	14	b Jameson	8
G.A. Cope	lbw b Gibbs	16	*not out*	0
M.K. Bore	lbw b Jameson	16	c Ibadulla b Gibbs	2
	lb 1, nb 4	5	lb 9, w 1, nb 1	11
		232		**261**

1/2, 2/11, 3/12, 4/13, 5/25, 6/45, 7/79, 8/123, 9/185, 10/232
1/134, 2/159, 3/167, 4/170, 5/223, 6/230, 7/249, 8/255, 9/255, 10/261

McVicker	19	4	54	5	9	1	29	0
Rouse	17	4	42	2	7	3	17	0
Ibadulla	5	0	15	0	17	5	29	0
Gibbs	23	8	50	1	37.5	13	78	3
Tidy	15	1	65	0	18	3	75	4
Jameson	1	0	1	1	12	3	22	3

Umpires: A. Jepson and J. Langridge

Surrey win championship for first time since 1958

SOUTHAMPTON: Surrey, with eight second innings wickets in hand, lead Hampshire by 49 runs

Surrey won the championship at ten to three yesterday when Intikhab had Gilliat caught by Long, the fourth Hampshire wicket to fall. It was the fifty-eighth over, so they had plenty of time to spare, yet their supporters suffered a twinge or two before the job was done. And although their sixth point ensured championship victory (for Surrey have won more often than Warwickshire, and therefore needed only to be level on points) it is far from certain that they will win this match. Take away the context, and Hampshire, especially Marshall, had much the better of the day's play.

When the Hampshire openers were out for 30 all was smiles for Surrey. The large crowd, many of whom had risked the hazards of the journey from Waterloo, basked in the sunshine, and the prospect of success. I met one enthusiast who had travelled from Stowmarket, another from Chipping Sodbury, and another (but this one was not a Surrey supporter) from Solihull.

A little anxiety crept in when Marshall and Turner settled to a third wicket partnership. They scored briskly, always ready to attack, especially against Intikhab and Pocock. My friend from Solihull – he had come in the hope of getting on television, he explained, since if Surrey failed he might be the only Warwickshire representative; at the least it ought to be worth a few beers – maintained the batsmen were taking too many risks. But taking risks is the only way Marshall plays cricket, and Turner, too, always looks a better player when he goes out for his strokes.

They had put on 101, these two, and it was only a few minutes to lunch, the 45th over, when Willis bowled Turner. Willis had been brought back for a special effort before the interval, and provided it.

Afterwards, Marshall continued to hit the ball about in his untroubled way. When Intikhab bowled from the city end, the leg boundary seemed scarcely a span distant, so swiftly did Marshall's hits travel to it. Gilliat's demeanour showed every intention of battling it out. There was still some tension. The crowd was quiet between balls. Gilliat was troubled by a wasp and swatted it angrily away. It buzzed at Stewart, at short leg, who swatted it back. "Drat these appledrains," said a voice nearby, suggesting that a Devonian was also among those present.

But soon the appledrains were routed, and all was rejoicing. The Surrey side embraced one another with what, in the permissive society, I suppose we must regard as reasonable decorum. Cameramen and champagne invaded the field. The Hampshire crowd applauded more than dutifully. If there was no real sense of climax, it is, after all, probably wiser not to seek success with dramatic sixes when nudges down the leg-side will do.

Yet for myself I would say that Surrey are the most convincing champions for some years, certainly since Close's Yorkshire side in 1968, and perhaps one could go even further back. We have known for a long time that Surrey had all the talent required, but it has not knitted together, under pressure, until these last couple of months.

Marshall was 75 when Gilliat was out. There was no obvious relaxation, but at tea, when the declaration was made, Marshall had scored 142. His innings gave almost as much pleasure to Hampshire supporters as the championship did to Surrey's. An outcast from Test cricket, as he has rather extravagantly described himself, I presume Marshall is planning to be selected for the Rest of the World in Australia, and upon my word they could do much worse.

Surrey have won the county cricket championship, and the county rugby championship, in the same season. This double success has only been achieved twice before: by Yorkshire in 1893 and in 1896. It would be good to think that the Surrey cricket and rugby sides were to share a joint celebration. It would most surely make for a jovial evening, quite apart from advancing international fellowship between Wales and Pakistan.

Greenidge and Richards bring Surrey to defeat

SOUTHAMPTON: Hampshire (20 pts) beat Surrey (6 pts) by four wickets

This was an entertaining day of cricket which drew the first class season to a close, and there cannot have been many better innings in the 1971 championship than that by Richards which saw Hampshire surely through. They needed to score 162 to win, and got them before tea, at a rate of more than four runs to the over.

Surrey had been bowled out for 187 after reaching 142 for two. Edrich nearly achieved another century, and did achieve his 2,000 runs for the season. The improbable "Sapper" of Surrey's collapse was Greenidge, who had not previously taken a first class wicket, but nevertheless led Hampshire from the field with a kind of bashful bravura which the young Trueman might have envied.

Surrey's defeat was not, I am sure, due to excessive celebrations overnight – their bowling was steady and their fielding at least earnest – but to a natural nervous relaxation.

This has affected previous champions, as Hampshire themselves will remember. One of the great Yorkshire sides of the 30s won the championship by the middle of August and then got into all kinds of trouble against unlikely customers during the rest of the season.

Nor should the fact that Surrey have only Warwickshire's total of points detract from the validity of their success. Their authority is much better indicated by the number of matches won and lost. They would have won, I am nearly sure, under any of the numerous systems for settling the county competition, except indeed for the first, before 1888, which would have made Leicestershire the champions of 1971. Under that system, Surrey would have been joint second with Gloucestershire, with Derbyshire and Lancashire joint fourth.

Hampshire lost the wicket of Greenidge in their two overs of batting before lunch. Turner, who again played handsomely, was second out at 38. Sainsbury, given the chance of completing the double, was sent in at No. 4, but was soon painfully hit on the inside of the thigh by Arnold. In the same over he narrowly survived a bouncer, and then was out, well short of his aim. All the same, he has had a memorably good season.

Richards and Marshall put on 70, and it was a fine sight to see them together. Marshall was caught at mid-off from a casual stroke, and in the same over Gilliat was caught from one rather worse than casual. Jesty came limping in with a runner, and he too was caught, at mid-wicket, Storey's third wicket in two overs.

There was a tremor of anxiety, but no more. Richards took charge of the situation, farming the bowling, and yet not striving unduly for his own century. It occurs to me that cricket will not do too badly, so long as it continues to produce batsmen so good as Richards or sides so good as Surrey, for whom Stewart, in a gesture which the crowd appreciated, bowled the last over.

Hampshire v Surrey, Southampton, 11, 13 & 14 September 1971

Hampshire won by four wickets

Surrey

J.H. Edrich	run out	113	b Greenidge	95
* M.J. Stewart	st Stephenson b Sainsbury	54	st Stephenson b Sainsbury	5
G.R.J. Roope	c Richards b Castell	40	c Richards b Worrell	12
Younis Ahmed	c Gilliat b Castell	0	c Sainsbury b Greenidge	10
S.J. Storey	b Cottam	25	c Sainsbury b Greenidge	0
Intikhab Alam	c Marshall b Cottam	0	b Greenidge	0
P.I. Pocock	c Worrell b Sainsbury	6	c sub b Sainsbury	16
D.R. Owen-Thomas	c Stephenson b Cottam	1	c Castell b Greenidge	22
+ A. Long	*not out*	10	lbw b Sainsbury	8
R.G.D. Willis	b Sainsbury	0	*not out*	4
G.G. Arnold	run out	9	st Stephenson b Sainsbury	1
	b 2, lb 9	11	b 9, lb 4, w 1	14
		269		**187**

1/109, 2/190, 3/190, 4/240, 5/242, 6/245, 7/249, 8/252, 9/253, 10/269
1/30, 2/59, 3/142, 4/156, 5/156, 6/156, 7/157, 8/177, 9/184, 10/187

Cottam	20	2	53	3	16	3	35	0
Castell	17	3	48	2	13	4	40	0
Jesty	14	2	48	0				
Sainsbury	24.1	3	67	3	14.3	5	28	4
Worrell	8	0	42	0	5	0	21	1
Greenidge					17	4	49	5

Hampshire

B.A. Richards	c Long b Arnold	14	*not out*	95
C.G. Greenidge	c Long b Willis	12	c Roope b Arnold	0
D.R. Turner	b Willis	48	c Long b Arnold	19
R.E. Marshall	*not out*	142	c Arnold b Storey	22
* R.M.C. Gilliat	c Long b Intikhab	10	c Willis b Storey	2
P.J. Sainsbury	*not out*	52	c Roope b Arnold	3
T.E. Jesty			c Edrich b Storey	1
A.T. Castell			*not out*	7
+ G.R. Stephenson				
L.R. Worrell				
R.M.H. Cottam				
	b 6, lb 6, w 1, nb 4	17	b 6, lb 5, w 2	13
	(4 wkts, dec)	**295**	(6 wkts)	**162**

1/30, 2/30, 3/131, 4/169
1/5, 2/38, 3/55, 4/125, 5/127, 6/129

Arnold	17	9	22	1	9	0	31	3
Willis	14	4	33	2	7	2	32	0
Storey	17	4	54	0	9	1	17	3
Intikhab	20	5	77	1	2	0	15	0
Pocock	12	0	72	0	4	0	16	0
Roope	6	0	20	0	5	0	34	0
Stewart					0.2	0	4	0

Umpires: W.E. Alley and C.S. Elliott

Topical reflections 1971

The editor of *The Cricketer* has honoured me by asking for a few thoughts on the current English cricketing scene, possibly because, though verging on the venerable, I am still a relative novice at cricket reporting, and certainly less predictable, than those of the youthful veterans who populate our press boxes amidst an increasing roar of decibels. Have press boxes always been like this? Even in my limited experience of them, I seem to notice a steadily increasing rate of noise, both in pace and volume, which sends a man scurrying to his transistor, seeking half an hour of the monastic peace of Radio One.

But that is by the way, and of course I love them all really, even the ones who tell you, as you creep guiltily back half an hour after lunch, that Boycott has just reached his century with his 27th boundary.

...

I wrote about cricket only sporadically for many years. In the last three years, owing to a series of unexpected events, I have found myself writing about it regularly. From watching maybe 30 days of cricket in a season, at most 40, I have been watching it five, six, and sometimes seven days a week all through the summer. And thus, as Artemus Ward said, the reason of this thusness. ... I find that cricket in such quantities changes my attitude to the game. I am not often bored. But I am, sometimes – well, it is hard to define, but perhaps the nearest word would be 'sceptical'.

...

A distinction is often made between those followers who actually watch the game, and those who hardly ever do, but demonstrate their interest by buying newspapers, listening to the radio, watching television, ringing up for the Test scores. They are often called the 'cricket-loving' public. It is on behalf of these millions, we are told, that the first-class – i.e. three-day – game must be kept going. Why this should be considered an obligation I cannot understand, but so it is. The three-day game must be kept going as a duty to the cricket-loving public. The cost may be spurious, contrived finishes which this cricket-loving public do not put themselves to the inconvenience of seeing; the cost may be dangerous tricks of sponsorship which ridicule the game, and benefit nobody but those warm-hearted human benefactors, the vendors of cigarettes and motor cars; the cost may be asking highly skilled professional sportsmen to perform at a basic wage of the value of two motor cars a year; all this must be accepted, with a stiff upper lip, because of the cricket-loving public.

Besides, it is argued, if we have no three-day cricket as a bridge, what will happen to Test matches? How could players suddenly shift from a one-day to a five-day tempo? Certainly this might create unexpected problems, such as strokes, or spectators, though for myself I would not be unduly worried, since I believe three days ought to be long enough for any game of cricket.

I enjoy three-day cricket, however, much more than the one-day stuff, though I sometimes enjoy that too. I should be very sorry if the three-day game stopped, and took my nice summer job with it. And yet we ought to recognize its unreality. Someone said to me the other day, not unkindly, that he feared cricket at the Oval was dying a natural death. It occurred to me that a natural death is to be preferred to an unnatural life.

Not all the gay pagans that breathe
Can with a dead body compare

– not perhaps Charles Wesley's most happily expressed lines: but a dead body is part of the natural order of things, and a dummy in suspended animation, giving only the appearance of life, totally dependent on injections and transfusions, is much deader than dead. In this respect I prefer the Oval to Edgbaston, that magnificent mausoleum with the kindest and most generous attendants – I do not wish to say anything to hurt them, but when I watch a few hundred scattered around Edgbaston on a fine summer afternoon (if all the bars were opened, you could have one apiece) I do not feel I am watching anything real. At best the proceedings are a pretty ritual, a relic of a bygone age and a bygone faith. At worst they can be seen simply as a monument to the popularity of football.

After all this, you will doubtless be bracing yourself for yet another remedy for cricket's ills, and this I shall not propound, for I have none. I will, however, offer an opinion and a hint. The opinion is that there is no need to worry about the future of cricket. People were playing cricket long before the county championship was invented; and will be doing so long after it has departed. To judge by the numbers of people playing the game, in this country and elsewhere, cricket is still very healthy – and that is the only sane test of any game that pretends to be a game.

The hint is that cricket suffers from too much love. That phrase, 'love of cricket', is used too often and too sloppily. It is made the excuse for every kind of absurdity and bigotry. Any kind of short-term measure, however illogical, not to say undignified, can be supported on the grounds that (a) it is for the welfare of the beloved, and (b) all's fair in love. There was a man who loved his wife so much that he sent her out on to the streets, because it was the only way he could find the money to preserve their home life inviolate. There was another man who never slept with his wife at all, though he loved her passionately, because he felt the mere act would age her untarnished beauty. Both these men were fools. What cricket needs, I suspect, is a great deal less undiscriminating love, and a great deal more civilized and affectionate respect.

Review of 'Fred: Portrait of a Fast Bowler' 1971

A cricketing biography is difficult to write: much more difficult than writing a full biography of a man who also played cricket, even if that man is known chiefly *because* of his cricket. Thus Bernard Darwin's life of W.G. Grace, a model biography, was a life not of the cricketer, but of the man. The long essay is probably the best form in which to deal with the lives of cricketers – especially if you are going to confine yourself to their cricket. What cricketer, if considered only as a cricketer, is worth a full-length book? Unless you have a taste for statistics it would be heavy eating.

Lives are not cheeses. To hack off a segment, even a large segment, prevents us from sensing the man in the round. Biographers of other professional men face the same problem. Not long ago I read a life of Norman Birkett which described in detail all his famous cases: and a gripping book it was; but at the end I did not feel I knew much about Birkett. Yet without some knowledge of the man himself, how can his professional career be judged? What stresses have impelled or restrained him? What religious beliefs drove him on or tempered him? What does he say, if only to himself, when the curtains are drawn?; what does he whisper when the lights are out?; what is it that causes those shivers of anguish when he wakes up at four in the morning?

No contemporary, not even a lover, can know these things, though it may be possible, 50 years later, for the calm discipline of history to deduce them.

In this sense, John Arlott's *Fred: Portrait of a Fast Bowler* (Eyre and Spottiswoode: £2) is no more than a document for the ultimate study of Fred Trueman, if ever anyone, other than God, should take the trouble to complete it. It is nonetheless, and I choose my words carefully, one of the best half dozen books concerned with cricket that I have ever read. When he was in the throes of it, Mr Arlott assured me it was the best thing he had ever written. I took no notice of this, because it is what any writer ought to feel whilst he is writing. Indeed Mr Arlott quotes a quizzical remark made by Richard Hutton to Trueman – Trueman happily describing how with masterful variety he had bowled a side out – "Tell me, Fred, would you say you were a modest man?" Dare I say that there is a touch of the kindred spirit here? Last spring, it was rumoured that Fred was travelling down to Hampshire to stay with his biographer, and have a look at the book. I am sure Trevor Bailey will not mind my quoting his comment on this majestic confrontation: "Which of them will stop talking first?"

They are both good talkers, all their lives they have talked, often together, and in their different ways they have talked a great deal of sense, and that sense, and pungency, and wit and indeed grace, is crystallized in the book. No cricketer of his time commanded such interest (a term which includes both love and hatred) as Trueman. No cricket writer of the same period commands such interest (the same inclusions) as Arlott. It is, no doubt, a fortunate match of biographer and subject, and though I cannot really say whether it is the best thing John Arlott has written (for he writes faster than I can read) I should be surprised if it were not.

"Mr Lely," Cromwell is supposed to have said, "I desire you would use all your skill to paint my picture truly like me, and not flatter me at all; but remark all these roughnesses, pimples, warts and everything as you see me." John Arlott does his best to meet this requirement. But warts are only superficial guides to the character; they can be charmed away, and Arlott charms away Fred's warts in the very act of pointing them out.

There are still, and I suppose there have to be, some gaps. Mrs Trueman, for instance, makes an appearance when she marries him, and then again when she tactfully subscribes to the testimonial for Vic Wilson, one of Fred's captains, and that is all we hear of her. Fred himself refused to subscribe for Wilson, because they had had a row. Mr Arlott's account of this row, when Fred was late on parade at Taunton, is long, tortuous, and in the end quite superbly uninformative. Such are the hazards of contemporary biography, once you leave the cricket field.

Yet we do learn enough about the non-cricketing Fred – the early chapters on his background and upbringing are especially interesting – to form provisional opinions. Fred Trueman is a typical Yorkshireman, but not at all typical in the sense that he tries to persuade himself he is. Yorkshiremen, nearly all Yorkshiremen I have met – and I am one – suffer from acute Latin American temperaments which they try desperately to disguise. I have sometimes lectured to Yorkshiremen to this effect, and their response usually demonstrates, dramatically, just how Latin American they are. "I'm a plain man, Mr Handley," said that ITMA character, Mr E Bagoom, "and I'm a bloont man." This is every Yorkshireman's desire; but the plain, bloont cushion on which we like to rest conceals a throne of bayonets. Yorkshiremen are deeply sensitive, and quick to take affront, just because they regard sensitivity as degenerate. They are usually warm-hearted, stiff-necked, broad-bottomed, and not more constant than an April day's weather. This is why Yorkshiremen are so good at an inconstant, fickle game like cricket. John Arlott has perceived this genius for cheerful inconstancy in Fred Trueman, and it is this which makes his book not only a good cricketing biography, but – as nearly as it can be done at this time – a real life of a real man.

1972

The summer of 1972 was anything but a vintage one. It was not only very wet through May and June, but also unseasonably cold, and although the sun came out fitfully in July, the rain returned in August. Of the 24 three-day matches that Alan Gibson covered for *The Times* that summer, only eight finished in a definite result and all but two of the 16 drawn games were ruined by the weather. Sunny prose was sometimes hard to conjure up against such a gloomy background.

But the cricket season was nonetheless a memorable one, thanks almost entirely to an exciting and closely contested Ashes series, which was heavily influenced by the weather – to Bob Massie and Australia's advantage at Lord's and to Derek Underwood and England's at Headingley – without being spoiled by it. It finished two apiece, leaving Ray Illingworth's slightly creaking side of seasoned veterans in possession of the urn. However, the emergence of the Chappell brothers – Ian, by now, as captain – and a certain Dennis Lillee suggested that after a period in the doldrums, Australia would soon once again be a force to be reckoned with.

The main change in county cricket in 1972 was the introduction of a third one-day competition – the 55-over-a-side Benson and Hedges Cup. The number of three-day matches played by each county was reduced from 24 to 20 to make room for the latest cuckoo in the nest. What with that, and the Scarborough Festival being given over almost entirely to the limited-overs game, including yet another one-day competition, the Fenner Trophy, it seemed that 'proper' cricket was fighting a losing battle against the 'instant' variety. Not for the last time, the editor of *Wisden* lamented the effect that the proliferation of one-day cricket was having on standards of English batsmanship.

Alan Gibson's first match of the season for *The Times* was a John Player League encounter between Middlesex and Gloucestershire at Lord's, and he wasted no time in saying what he thought about the surroundings! His itinerary for the rest of May consisted of rain-ruined championship matches, and unexceptional Sunday League games.

Miserable May was followed by joyless June. The opening paragraph of Alan's report of the second day of Warwickshire's match against Northamptonshire on June 1 summed up the general mood. However, by Saturday of that week, the weather had mercifully improved for the decisive encounter in the B&H western region qualifying round, between Somerset and Gloucestershire. It was a match completely dominated by Mike Procter.

If that was a setback for Somerset, who were having a decent season under their new captain, Brian Close, worse was to follow. On July 19, they travelled to Old Trafford to take on the Gillette Cup winners for the past two seasons, who were again in dominating one-day form. Alan saw Somerset fall just short, while Clive Lloyd's innings was a foretaste of the power and the glory that would eventually bring the trophy back to Lancashire for a third successive season.

The team to beat in all forms of cricket at this stage of the season were Leicestershire. They were leading the championship and the John Player and beat Yorkshire comfortably in the final of the B&H on July 22. As Alan remarked when he watched them beat Somerset by 83 runs a few days later, 'they are clearly still in the mood to win everything this season except the Golf Illustrated Gold Vase' – a reference which he added would be understood by 'senior readers' of *The Times*. But

Tests
England
drew with Australia
2-2, with 1 draw

Championship
1 Warwickshire
2 Kent
3 Gloucestershire
4 Northamptonshire
5 Essex
6 Leicestershire

Sunday League
1 Kent
2 Leicestershire
3 Essex
4 Yorkshire
5 Middlesex
6 Hampshire

Gillette Cup Final
Lancashire
beat Warwickshire

Benson & Hedges Final
Leicestershire
beat Yorkshire

Most first-class runs
1 Majid Khan
2 Mushtaq Mohammad
3 G.M. Turner

Most first-class wickets
1 T.W. Cartwright
B. Stead
3 J. Birkenshaw

two days later, the honest journeymen of Leicestershire were completely outclassed by two of the greatest opening batsmen of this or any other age, Richards and Greenidge, albeit only in a Sunday League game. It was to prove a costly defeat, as Leicestershire were eventually edged out by Kent. This was also the match, as far as I can ascertain, at which the philosopher Lecoq made his debut.

As the weather gradually improved, so the county championship began to take shape. Coming into August, Warwickshire were on top, two points clear of Gloucestershire, with Leicestershire third. Both the top two relied heavily on their overseas stars: Kanhai, Kallicharran and Gibbs for Warwickshire; Procter, Sadiq and, from August onwards, Zaheer for Gloucestershire. Procter in particular was having a tremendous season, bowling fast and batting beautifully. When the Cheltenham Festival arrived, with Derbyshire the visitors, all seemed set fair.

But that was to prove the zenith of Gloucestershire's season. Procter developed a heel injury, which first hampered his bowling and then prevented it altogether. He soldiered on gallantly with the bat but, without his wicket-taking threat, Gloucestershire were only half the side they had been. They played poorly in the second match of the Cheltenham Festival, to lose to Middlesex, leaving Alan to draw what comfort he could from a situation that was already evoking painful memories of three seasons previously.

By now he had been set to follow Gloucestershire through the run-in. Their next game was against the old enemy, Somerset, at Taunton. On the first day, on a dry pitch, Gloucestershire collapsed to 94 runs, and Close rubbed their noses in it with 158. Worse was to follow. Without Procter, Gloucestershire went down heavily against Notts at Bristol. With the match went any hopes of overhauling Warwickshire.

1972 marked the centenary of the births of two of cricket's all-time greats, as different from each other in character, temperament and background as could possibly be imagined, yet forever linked together as the very incarnation of cricket's golden age: CB Fry and KS Ranjitsinji. Alan Gibson paid eloquent tribute to them both in features for *The Times*. I came across a letter in Alan's papers from a Major Orpen, who had seen Ranji play for Cambridge in the Varsity Match of 1894 and who had also audited the accounts of the Great Central Hotel, where Ranji stayed when he was in London. Noticing that the great cricketer appeared to be considerably in the hotel's debt, Major Orpen asked the manager about it. He said: "Well, I am having a deal of difficulty in getting payment, but he is such a popular hero that I don't like to press him too much!"

In November 1972, EW Swanton's autobiography was published. Alan reviewed it – generously – for *The Times*, concluding with a quotation and a summation which was as apt in its way as anything he ever wrote:

> In all thy humours, whether grave or mellow,
> Thou'rt such a touchy, testy, pleasant fellow
> Has't so much wit, and mirth, and spleen about thee,
> There is no living with thee or without thee.

The lines were written by Addison. If Cardus is the Hazlitt of cricket writers, and Arlott the Cobbett, then surely Swanton is the Addison.

But who, I wonder, is Alan Gibson's literary counterpart?

Developments at Lord's

LORD'S: Middlesex v Gloucestershire

There has been some criticism of the large new advertisements at Lord's, for television sets, tea, chewing gum, cigarettes and other medicaments. For myself I think they harmonize well with the modern mood set by the recently-built stand, and if only the Post Office can be persuaded to move their tower, and put it on the Nursery ground, we should have a very striking ensemble.

A damp day at Worcester

WORCESTER: Worcestershire v Somerset

"The weather's a disgrace," said the lady behind the bar, as if she was intending to go across to the Cathedral and have a sharp word with God about it. Not that it was really too bad: warm enough but with a persistent drizzle which never quite went away.

John Snow

EDGBASTON: Warwickshire v Sussex

At the beginning of the eighth over, Snow took off his second sweater, revealing a third, and had Jameson leg-before-wicket with his next ball. Snow, while looking familiarly Byronic, did not run to the crease quite as the Assyrian came down like a wolf on the fold, but gave the batsmen plenty to feel sheepish about.

Two wet days at Bristol

BRISTOL: Gloucestershire v the Australians

DAY ONE

It was a miserably cold and wet day. Play was brought to a stop when rain grew heavy in mid-afternoon and was not resumed. The umpires, however, made hopeful excursions. The Gloucestershire secretary encouraged the dwindling band of spectators. He reminded them that they could have a bet on whether there would be any more play or not. The proposition struck me as cheerless as the weather.

DAY TWO

For nearly all the morning the sun shone, but it was a visionary gleam. I knew the weather would spoil the cricket when my small daughter roused me (it was my turn) in the middle of the night. It was then raining heavily; indeed the circumstances generally were wet. We have called her Felicity, but I sometimes think Cassandra would have been a better choice.

And yet more rain

EDGBASTON: Warwickshire v Northamptonshire

> The sixth month of the year
> In the month call it June

goes the madrigal

> When the weather's too hot to be borne
> The farmer doth say, as he goes on his way,
> Tomorrow my sheep shall be shorn.

And pretty silly those bell-wethers would have looked around half past one, while the thunder boomed and the hail bit into their untempered skins. Pretty silly the rest of us must have looked too, for we had spent the morning telling each other how warm it was, and what a nice change, as the young soprano said when the vicar put on his surplice.

But, as the elderly contralto reminded him, it was the same old Adam underneath. And sure enough it was not long before the rains descended and the floods came.

C.B. Fry

Fry's political career was handicapped by his faithfulness to the Liberal Party. He polled very well at Brighton, but was never elected. At the age of 70, he told the Oxford University Liberal Club: "I think I'll try again." There was loud applause, but he never did.

It was at Oxford, which he loved, that I mostly saw him. He was still magnificently built, and he retained his habit, of which many have written, of playing strokes with an umbrella. Indeed, in the buttery of the Queen's College, the umbrella momentarily mislaid, he seized an assegai from the wall in order to demonstrate how Ranjitsinhji played. It was a slightly alarming moment, as the buttery was not very large, and the assegai sharp: in consequence I failed to absorb important information, for never to this day have I been quite sure how Ranji played the famous leg glide.

...

Despite his politics, he was never a tribune of the people. On the other hand:

Omne tulit punctum qui miscuit utile dulci.
Lectorem delectando pariterque monendo.

This might be roughly translated: mingle profit and pleasure, delight your audience at the same time as you instruct them, and you will win all the votes. C.B. Fry did mingle profit and pleasure, did both delight and instruct, and he would get my vote every time.

Other entertainments on the longest day at Bath

BATH: Northamptonshire have scored 156 for six against Somerset

Another cold coming we had of it. In the morning, 36 overs were bowled by Somerset, 79 runs were scored by Northants, and five wickets fell. Northants decided to bat, which was sensible enough because complicated strategic plans can hardly be laid in such weather: you might as well get a few, and hope for the best.

Watts must nevertheless have wondered about his choice when his first five batsmen, himself included, were out for 53. The Somerset bowlers were competing to get to the crease, with the pitch damp and the cloud heavy. Burgess, who can cut the ball sharply in such conditions, was the most successful of them. None of the batsmen wore an air of content.

It rained at lunchtime, and when play started again, half an hour late, the batsmen took some easy runs. The ball was too wet for the bowlers to control, except Cartwright, who could, I suppose, control an oiled balloon. The flat rain, borne by the heavy wind, had actually made the outfield faster. Against this, the light was poor, and a neighbour observed that he hoped "they'd had plenty o' carrots for lunch."

Willey took the pros and cons of the situation in his stride, and batted very well. After eight more overs, 41 more runs had been scored. A poor score had been turned into a useful one. More than five minutes were lost when one of Willey's hits lost the ball, permanently so far as I know, underneath one of the temporary stands. I was in a good position to watch this episode, and can reveal that the difficulty was caused by three enthusiastic dog-owners, each of whom said "Fetch it, boy" simultaneously. They fetched it all right, but then engaged in their own match, as entertaining as anything all day, except for the Somerset secretary's personal competition with the scoreboard, which he valiantly operated for a couple of hours (the crew not turning up).

Nine more overs were bowled in the late afternoon. Every player by now must have been chilled to the marrow, but they stuck it until a quarter to six. In this period Willey was out, bowled Cartwright. He went to a ball well up to him, of which he did not in time pick up the flight. Well, it was the longest day, and my goodness, it felt like it.

Tom Cartwright
'He has the ability to bend the wind to his purposes'

Lloyd collars Cartwright

OLD TRAFFORD: Lancashire beat Somerset by nine runs

Lancashire scored 243 for nine on a day hot enough to make the slow over rate forgivable. There were about 15,000 people present, most of them desperate for a Lancashire success in a season when this competition seems to offer their only chance of winning something.

There was also a substantial contingent from Somerset – it is one of the pleasing aspects of the Gillette Cup, that it draws cricket supporters into one another's counties. A random survey suggested that the visitors did not think much of the cider, but there was warm approval for the pork pies.

Clive Lloyd was bound to get a lot of runs sometime soon, and when he began to collar Cartwright, which takes some doing, Somerset hearts sank. Two wickets had fallen for 30 in nine overs when Cartwright came on. In five overs only two runs were scored off him.

Lloyd then struck him for three fours, and after seven overs Cartwright was taken off. He bowled again later, but 29 of the 34 runs he conceded were scored by Lloyd, who made 54 of his 86 in boundaries. He was caught at midwicket when it looked as if his innings was reaching new heights of ferocity and splendour.

Thereafter Somerset contained Lancashire fairly successfully, though occasionally there was some untidy out-cricket, as 33 extras indicate. Moseley, erratic but lively, got four of the first seven batsmen out.

It was a plum pitch, Somerset's task difficult but not impossible, and Virgin and Kitchen made a sound start. It was 25 for no wicket in 11 overs at tea.

From the 19th to the 22nd over, three wickets fell: Virgin leg before, Close caught at long leg, Burgess finely at slip. That was 56 for 3 and Lancashire were winning.

Kitchen, however, in form but cautious for a long time, began to play his strokes, which are varied and powerful. He gave a hard chance when he was 13 and another much later; the ball just missed the edge of his bat a few times, and several lofted drives just missed fieldsmen, but it was an innings of high quality, which kept the game open.

Denning, another left hander, helped to put on 87 for the fourth wicket. The runs came at more than one a minute, but when Denning was out Somerset still needed 101 with only 15 overs left.

Ten overs left, 65 needed, Wilkinson nearly crippled Hughes by an accidental blow from his bat, and Hughes responded by bowling him.

All now depended on Kitchen, and bravely he set about it. He reached his century, lost two partners (nine wickets down), and in the 59th over hit Lever for six. In the same over, going for another, he was caught in the deep, Simmons hanging on to the ball at the third attempt amid a frantic collection of cheers and groans. There were eight balls left, and Somerset were 10 runs short. It was a capital match, and the holders had to battle all the way.

Lancashire v Somerset, Old Trafford, 19 July 1972

Lancashire won by nine runs

Lancashire

B. Wood	b Close	38
+ F.M. Engineer	c Close b Moseley	5
D. Lloyd	c Taylor b Jones	14
C.H. Lloyd	c Denning b Moseley	86
F.C. Hayes	c Cartwright b Close	1
J. Sullivan	c Cartwright b Moaseley	20
* J.D. Bond	c Cartwright b Moseley	15
D.P. Hughes	c Moseley b Burgess	26
J. Simmons	c Kitchen b Jones	4
P. Lever	*not out*	2
P. Lee		
	b 14, lb 13, w 4, nb 1	32
	(9 wkts, 60 overs)	**243**

1/15, 2/30, 3/119, 4/125, 5/179, 6/209, 7/216, 8/230, 9/243

Jones	12	2	36	2
Moseley	12	2	36	4
Cartwright	12	3	34	0
Burgess	11	1	52	1
O'Keeffe	5	0	22	0
Close	8	2	31	2

Somerset

R.T. Virgin	lbw b Hughes	19
M.J. Kitchen	c Simmons b Lever	116
* D.B. Close	c Lee b Hughes	11
G.I. Burgess	c Hayes b Wood	0
P.W. Denning	c Sullivan b Simmons	32
S.G. Wilkinson	b Hughes	5
T.W. Cartwright	c Wood b Hughes	6
H.R. Moseley	run out	15
K.J. O'Keeffe	b Lee	2
+ D.J.S. Taylor	c Wood b Lee	14
A.A. Jones	*not out*	1
	b 2, lb 8, nb 3	13
	(58.4 overs)	**234**

1/40, 2/56, 3/56, 4/143, 5/154, 6/179, 7/188, 8/202, 9/225, 10/234

Lever	11.4	3	39	1
Lee	9	0	52	2
Wood	12	2	30	1
Sullivan	2	1	3	0
Hughes	12	1	61	4
Simmons	12	1	36	1

Umpires: J.G. Langridge and H. Yarnold

Richards's century makes technicalities irrelevant

LEICESTER: Hampshire (4 pts) beat Leicestershire by 120 runs

A century by Richards, made with the casual power and grace of a cricketer born to authority, had this match won in less than an hour and a half. So it seemed, and so it proved, but the quirks of Sunday League regulations might possibly have reversed the result, and gave another big Leicester crowd enough to grip their attention, and tax their multiplication, almost to the end

Hampshire had scored their 248 in dry, warm weather. It grew increasingly overcast, and soon after tea it began to rain. The rain never quite stopped, its general tendency was to become heavier, and there were several occasions when, in a three-day match, the players would have left the field. A little more, and they would have had to come off yesterday, like it or not.

Now if this had happened at a time when the Leicestershire run rate was above 6.2 an over, Leicestershire would, barring a resumption – and once 10 overs had been bowled – have won the match. Indeed, it was their best chance of winning it, and they rightly took the most desperate risks, from the very start, to keep the run rate going. At times they were ahead. Indeed, according to my unreliable calculations, the lead changed four times in one over. No sooner had the Leicestershire umbrellas gone ostentatiously up, than the Hampshire ones were unfurled. Well, it was all good fun, but the wickets kept falling, and the right result was duly reached, in the 23rd over.

Apart from Richards, Hampshire owed much to a fine supporting innings by Greenidge, and the steadiness of Sainsbury's bowling under assault. Perhaps their quicker bowlers were helped by the heavier weather, but if so it was a mixed blessing, for Holder could hardly control his swing, and bowled a series of wides in between taking the early wickets.

Hampshire also fielded splendidly, saving many runs by their picking up and returns to the wicket from the deep. Leicestershire did not field badly although Richards was missed twice, but an occasional wavering was understandable. As the philosopher Lecocq observed, the hurricane is not a good time to pick the grapes.

Leicestershire v Hampshire, Leicester, 30 July 1972

Hampshire won by 120 runs

Hampshire

B.A. Richards	c Tolchard b McKenzie	105
C.G. Greenidge	*not out*	83
D.R. Turner	c Steele b Spencer	6
R.V. Lewis	lbw b Higgs	0
T.E. Jesty	c Haywood b McKenzie	33
* R.M.C. Gilliat	c Spencer b McKenzie	10
+ G.R. Stephenson	*not out*	1
P.J. Sainsbury		
J.M. Rice		
J.W. Holder		
R.S. Herman		
	b 1, lb 6, nb 3	10
	(5 wkts, 40 overs)	**248**

1/164, 2/176, 3/178, 4/229, 5/246

McKenzie	8	0	43	3
Higgs	8	0	37	1
Spencer	8	0	44	1
Illingworth	6	0	41	0
Steele	3	0	25	0
Davison	7	0	48	0

Leicestershire

B. Dudleston	c Stephenson b Holder	3
M.E. Norman	c Richards b Sainsbury	27
+ R.W. Tolchard	c Stephenson b Holder	4
B.F. Davison	b Holder	7
P.R. Haywood	b Sainsbury	37
J. Birkenshaw	run out	0
* R. Illingworth	c Stephenson b Herman	6
G.D. McKenzie	run out	5
J.F. Steele	c Holder b Sainsbury	13
C.T. Spencer	b Rice	15
K. Higgs	*not out*	0
	lb 5, w 6	11
	(22.2 overs)	**128**

1/9, 2/16, 3/28, 4/60, 5/60, 6/74, 7/86, 8/105, 9/126

Herman	8	0	41	1
Holder	4	0	23	3
Sainsbury	7	0	34	3
Rice	3.2	0	19	1

Umpires: J. Arnold and W.E. Phillipson

Back to traditional Cheltenham pitch

CHELTENHAM: Gloucestershire, with eight first innings wickets in hand, are 88 runs behind Derbyshire

Old Cheltenham hands tell me that the pitch for the first match of the festival was one of the best here, for batting, for many years, at least when the match began. Yesterday we were back on a traditional Cheltenham turner, for which the water was no doubt to blame. Although we suffered no interruption of play, there had been more storms overnight. Unless it rains again, which the sky suggests is possible, the match is likely to have an early finish.

Derbyshire scored their 176 in 84 overs. Thus they narrowly secured one point for batting and Gloucestershire, equally narrowly, took their fifth for bowling. Eager calculators round the ground were quick to point out that this, momentarily, brought Gloucestershire level with Warwickshire in the championship. There was an air of expectancy and tension about the play and a large crowd.

Derbyshire had 50 up with only Borrington out, but lost four wickets in three-quarters of an hour before lunch. The stand of 52 for the sixth wicket, between Buxton and Swarbrook, to some extent saved the innings. The runs came slowly, and both batsmen were often in difficulties, but they played with much determination. The batting point was won by Hendrick and Swindell, who put on 35 for the last wicket, swinging the bat. To say "It shows what the others could have done" is a routine remark about every tail-end swish, but I think Derbyshire might have done better with a slightly more vigorous approach.

No doubt the early fall of Wilkins discouraged the others. He was caught at backward point, having a dip at Graveney and getting a top edge. This was the first wicket of Graveney's first class career. His father, who once took all 10 wickets in an innings, and would have had a distinguished career but for an injury, bowled at fast medium. His uncle Tom, when inclined, bowled leg breaks. David Graveney maintains the individualist family customs by bowling slow left arm. He was steady, and made the ball turn, as well he might in such circumstances. He has an awkward kink in his run-up, almost stopping to balance himself just before delivery. He looks a good prospect, all the same.

Mortimore was of course Gloucestershire's principal asset. In the afternoon Brown gave Sadiq a long spell, with leg breaks. It was a good move, and got both Buxton and Swarbrook out.

Derbyshire were the less well equipped to bowl on this pitch, but there was a long and searching opening spell by Buxton himself. He cut the ball sharply, and hit the stumps of Milton and Zaheer. Knight and Nicholls, playing with increasing confidence, in the absence of telling spin, had put Gloucestershire in a promising position by the close. Nicholls played the best stroke of the day to the last ball, one of his most elegant square cuts. It was good to see him in form again.

Time for the relief of Gloucestershire

CHELTENHAM: Derbyshire, with seven second innings wickets in hand, are 15 runs behind Gloucestershire

There is an aura of history about the Cheltenham ground, nowhere more noticeable than in the gentlemen's lavatory tent, the equipment for which was, no doubt, captured intact by the Glorious Glosters after the relief of Ladysmith. Cheltenham is the place, it is always said, where Gloucestershire win or lose championships, and, as it is nearly 100 years since they won one, the second half of the statement can hardly be challenged.

However, they are quite well placed to win this match, though less so than they must have hoped in the early evening. In the morning Knight was soon out, but Nicholls played serenely on, and soon Procter's drives were echoing round the Cotswolds.

The fourth wicket partnership of 121 was made in not much more than an hour and a half. Procter scored 78 of the first 105, at which point he had overtaken Nicholls. Not that Nicholls was idle. He did not neglect chances of scoring, looking happy and relaxed. He seemed set for his first century of the season when he was caught at slip shortly before lunch.

In the afternoon Gloucestershire lost wickets trying to get a fourth batting point. They did not quite manage it, but eight first innings points in all (Derbyshire four) was satisfactory. Procter had scored 95 when at last he misfired and lobbed a catch to gully. Eighty-four of his runs came in boundaries, a proportion not often equalled, and most of them were manifest boundaries as soon as he had struck them.

Shepherd, and then Mortimore, played usefully, and the first innings lead was 127. Derbyshire were batting again soon after 4 o'clock, and the question was how the pitch would play. The sun shone nearly all day, though the weather is unsettled. The Gloucestershire batsmen had not faced many unexpected problems, but that is perhaps a comment on the bowling rather than the pitch.

Gibbs was soon leg before, but the pitch did not respond to Procter, though he tried more than one style. Mortimore did not come on until the fourteenth over, which suggested Brown was not optimistic about spin. Three overs later, Graveney came on, and bowled a length. Page played his third ball into his wicket. The field began to close in; puffs of dust arose from the pitch (or was it just that we had not noticed them before?). Borrington was leg before to Graveney, after an innings which indicated that he has been deeply influenced by Gibbs.

Graveney continued to bowl economically. Mortimore sometimes turned the ball sharply. Wilkins and Harvey played well forward, smothering the spin. After a cautious beginning Wilkins began to knock Mortimore around. Sadiq came on when Graveney rested, without making the much-needed breakthrough. Both batsmen had some luck, but all the same they played the best cricket Derbyshire have played to far in this match, and kept their side in the game.

Gloucestershire spin bowlers gain day

CHELTENHAM: Gloucestershire (18 pts) beat Derbyshire (4 pts) by five wickets

Gloucestershire made heavy weather of beating Derbyshire, though that is an inappropriate analogy as it was a beautiful day; blue sky and warm sun, not a cloud to be seen bigger than Shepherd's revised waistline. Still, the victory, if not quite in the manner of champions, keeps Gloucestershire in contention near the top of the county table.

All day the pitch helped the spin bowlers, though perhaps it had been most difficult on the first day. It is unusual to say, at Cheltenham, that any toss is an awkward one to win, but probably Derbyshire had slightly the worst of the pitch. Not that they were unlucky. They lost because Gloucestershire had better batsmen and better spin bowlers.

There was, however, a good century by Wilkins, arguably the best innings of the match. Derbyshire began 15 runs behind, with seven wickets left, and when Wilkins was seventh out they were 61 on, and Wilkins had scored 67 of the 76 runs. He came bravely down the pitch to the spin bowlers, even if it was only for a defensive stroke. Of his hits I remember particularly two drives, from successive balls off Graveney. The first whistled past Mortimore's right hand – he was standing deep at mid-on – and the second past his left. I was reminded of Hammond's remark to an anxious fielder: "Stand still, son, I shan't hit you."

Although Graveney took more wickets, it was Mortimore's bowling which sustained Gloucestershire. He took the first four wickets of the day. Harvey was caught at short leg, Buxton leg-before, Swarbrook caught at slip, and then Wilkins was bowled (he had not taken much of Mortimore's bowling). Mortimore might have had more wickets but for some slips by Swetman, but any wicketkeeper's first experience of a full Cheltenham Festival is liable to damage his reputation, and I ought to say that Swetman, of whom I was critical earlier in the season, has been keeping wicket well when I have seen him recently.

Gloucesteshire had to score 106, with plenty of time. Nicholls and Milton made a steady start. Nicholls was run out at 38, an unwise second run and good throw by Harvey. Milton took a sudden leap at Swindell and he was caught at mid-on. Zaheer, who might, I dare say, have signed on for another county if he had known about Cheltenham, was leg-before, to Russell.

Russell would have been Derbyshire's best bowler in this match, if he could bowl a little slower. That was 55 for three. Knight cheerfully hit Swindell against the spin. He had the right no-nonsense attitude, we said, but Procter, also trying to have no nonsense, was caught at deep mid-on, and then Swarbrook caught and bowled Knight. Ninety for five, anxiety creeping into the batting and the crowd - but Sadiq and Shepherd, rather nervously, saw Gloucestershire through. So we all went home with modified rejoicing, intensified in my case because I skilfully avoided a discussion on the price of beer with Fred Jakeman.

DERBYSHIRE	176 (Gibbs 34, Buxton 31, Swarbrook 31, Mortimore 4-51, Sadiq 4-51)
	232 (Wilkins 111, Graveney 5-63, Mortimore 4-73)
GLOUCESTERSHIRE	303 (Procter 95, Nicholls 82, Knight 32, Shepherd 29, Buxton 4-52)
	106 for five (Knight 28, Milton 22)

Gloucester look a better side in adversity

TAUNTON: Gloucestershire, with eight second innings wickets in hand, are 98 runs behind Somerset

A little breeze ruffled the heat of the sun. The Quantocks, green and gold – "the best wheat and barley in the west," Sam Woods said – smiled upon the scene. There was quite a large crowd, though fewer than in 1939, when first I saw this match. In those days it was always on a Bank Holiday, and there was Hammond. Looking back, the way querulous middle-aged men do, I feel I would have crawled over a mile of broken bottles to see Hammond. Still, I suppose that is the kind of thing football supporters have to do every week, and indeed you can get your knees cut trying to leave the university match at Twickenham (but that is middle-class glass, minimizing the risk of infection).

No doubt many Gloucestershire men did not come, because of the horrors of the A38, and because their county, needing to win the match, were so badly placed after Saturday's play. It is a Dickens of a job, a real Micawber job, getting back into a match after you have been bowled out for under a hundred on a good pitch in the first innings.

Gloucestershire tried hard enough. They may save this match, though it will be difficult to win it. They looked a better side in adversity than they sometimes do in success, though they were handicapped because Procter, who had strained a muscle, could not bowl.

Towards the end of the long Somerset innings several other Gloucestershire players were limping a bit, but this was a lack of youth, not a lack of effort. One stop by Mortimore was as good a piece of fielding as any all day.

Somerset scored 331, a lead of 237. Close took his score to 135. This, and his century against Warwickshire a fortnight ago, were innings as good as I have seen him play, for nine years or thereabouts. There was an echoing cheer when his captaincy of England was announced. "If they pick Tom Cartwright, we'll have a proper side," said (correctly) one of the cider contingent. It is curious how Somerset warms to foreigners. It would not happen in Cornwall.

There were some moments of comedy, something else traditionally associated with this fixture. During the change of innings a stray cricket ball was rolled into the pitch, without any apparently alarming subsequent effects. Jones, who puts much exertion into his bowling, split the seat of his trousers. He continued bowling for a while, the crowd behind him urging him on with cries of "extra!" or words to that effect.

Nicholls and Milton gave Gloucestershire a sound start to their second innings. When Milton was out soon after tea, Zaheer began to play confidently. Taunton is just the kind of pitch for him to make runs. I said as much immediately before his first innings, when he was bowled first ball. He did much better this time, but was caught from a casual-looking stroke, off Langford, shortly before a hideous row told us that Concorde was passing over. "Like a beautiful silver fish," said a lady who would clutch her skirts up in horror if she found a silver fish in her bath. Even the Quantocks seemed to shudder.

When Brown should have declared

TAUNTON: Somerset (9pts) drew with Gloucestershire (3 pts)

A.S. Brown, the Gloucestershire captain, is an exceptionally nice chap. I say this because he is one of the few first class cricketers I know fairly well. He is also an admirable all-rounder. He has been a good captain of Gloucestershire, but from time to time those bright blue eyes become opaque, fixed no doubt upon some inner or supernatural objective. This is a pompous way of saying that yesterday he should have declared.

Though it was improbable at any time that Gloucestershire could win: though Procter was not fit to bowl: though Close – cunning warrior he! – had shown no anxiety to press on with the game, taking a lot of time over his field settings even in the morning: though Gloucestershire never like, rightly, to be beaten by Somerset: despite these things, Gloucestershire had entered this match with a chance of the championship, compared to which the loss of the game was trivial. Yorkshire under Sellers would have had a go. So would Surrey under Surridge. So, for that matter, would Warwickshire under either of the Smiths. Championships are only won if you are prepared to challenge the odds in moments of crisis.

Well, and it seems a long time ago, in the morning Knight and Nicholls carried hopefully on for Gloucestershire, and when Knight was out, at 200, Procter struck about. He could not move with his usual speed or freedom, but when he hit the ball it travelled fast, and usually to the boundary. I was reminded a little of Von Cramm's match against Perry at Wimbledon in 1936, when he could not run, but collected several games by his service alone.

Nicholls played well. He has regained his touch, which was bound to happen with a player of such sound method (I hope that Virgin, who has been rested by Somerset, as Nicholls was by Gloucestershire earlier in the season, takes comfort from the example).

At a quarter to one, Gloucestershire drew level, three wickets down. With a 6 o'clock finish, they might have envisaged victory, the championship to play for. But the scoring rate slowed, and did not really get going again until after Procter and Nicholls were out – all to Cartwright (308 for 5, 71 on) – and Shepherd and Sadiq were joined in a fruitful partnership for the 6th wicket. By this time Somerset, without playing slackly, had reconciled themselves to the thought of a declaration.

The pitch was still playing well. O'Keeffe might perhaps – as we once knew him – have made it respond, but he has not got his bowling together this season. No doubt his omission from the Australian side disturbed him. He crouches too low as he bowls the ball. Grimmett, they say, did the same, but one cuckoo does not make the spring, as the philosopher Lecocq would often tell his old friend Delius.

Sadiq was out, after a good, gay innings, at 376, and nearly 4 o'clock. At tea Gloucestershire were 153 on. A declaration would have left Somerset to score at about six an over: hard, but in all the circumstances justifiable. Even if Somerset did not try, Brown would have made, and be seen to have made, an appropriate effort. That he did not, seemed to me perplexing and disappointing.

Somerset v Gloucestershire, Taunton, 19, 21 & 22 August 1972

Drawn

Gloucestershire

C.A. Milton	lbw b Moseley	6	c Close b Moseley	28
R.B. Nicholls	c Taylor b Jones	7	lbw b Cartwright	90
Zaheer Abbas	b Moseley	0	c Cartwright b Langford	59
R.D.V. Knight	b Jones	14	c Kitchen b Close	41
M.J. Procter	lbw b Moseley	2	c Rose b Cartwright	74
D.R. Shepherd	b Cartwright	7	b Rose	74
Sadiq Mohammad	b Cartwright	19	c O'Keeffe b Close	31
* A.S. Brown	lbw b Cartwright	0	*not out*	63
J.B. Mortimore	lbw b Jones	4	*not out*	8
+ R. Swetman	*not out*	25		
J. Davey	c Wilkinson b Jones	5		
	lb 1, w 1, nb 3	5	b 2, lb 8, w 6	16
		94	(7 wkts)	**484**

1/13, 2/13, 3/17, 4/21, 5/34, 6/38, 7/42, 8/55, 9/61. 10/94
1/40, 2/118, 3/200, 4/289, 5/308, 6/375, 7/459

Jones	14.5	3	31	4	15	4	38	0
Moseley	9	3	17	3	20	1	63	1
Cartwright	18	6	41	3	37	12	86	2
O'Keeffe					25	4	82	0
Langford					32	12	77	1
Close					21	7	84	2
Denning					3	0	15	0
Rose					2	0	5	1
Kitchen					3	2	9	0
Wilkinson					2	0	9	0

Somerset

M.J. Kitchen	b Procter	2
S.G. Wilkinson	c Milton b Davey	8
* D.B. Close	b Knight	135
B.C. Rose	b Mortimore	138
P.W. Denning	c Procter b Brown	24
T.W. Cartwright	c Brown b Mortimore	6
K.J. O'Keeffe	lbw b Davey	31
+ D.J.S. Taylor	b Davey	15
B.A. Langford	st Swetman b Sadiq	29
H.R. Moseley	*not out*	18
A.A. Jones	c Swetman b Sadiq	0
	b 3, lb 19, nb 3	25
		331

1/10, 2/29, 3/106, 4/163, 5/170, 6/249, 7/281, 8/286, 9/331, 10/331

Procter	8	1	34	1
Davey	30	4	93	3
Brown	21	4	65	1
Mortimore	33	10	68	2
Sadiq	11	0	31	2
Knight	8	3	15	1

Umpires: C.S. Elliott and A.G.T. Whitehead

Basingstoke

BASINGSTOKE: Hampshire v Essex

I have not watched cricket at Basingstoke before. It is now, I suppose, no longer a country town, but the ground is pleasant, surrounded by trees, and the public is enthusiastic.

Although the morning was grey and drizzly, more than 3,000 were present to fill the ground almost uncomfortably. I spent some time sitting alongside Mr Bill Shepheard, who was in charge of the public address apparatus. This is an essential part of Sunday League cricket. I was fascinated by the assortment of problems brought to him. When is the next bus to Reading? Would the owner of car number so-and-so care to know that the petrol is running out of his tank? Please can you direct us to the statue of John Arlott? (It might of course have been Jane Austen they had in mind.)

Wilf Wooller at Cardiff

CARDIFF: Glamorgan v Warwickshire

There were two disappointments for a large crowd on this sunny day. One was that we scarcely heard Wilfred Wooller, the Glamorgan secretary, on the loud-speaker. After all, it has long been one of the chief delights of this Welsh ground to discover what on earth he will say next, and I was only restrained from requesting my money back because I had not paid any.

Oxfordshire in the Gillette Cup

OXFORD: Oxfordshire v Durham

"Oh yes," said one GI to another, as they walked down The High during the war: "I've heard of Oxford. It's the English Detroit." And indeed yesterday the cricket was played far from the Latin Quarter of the city, at the Morris Motors ground in Cowley. There was quite a large crowd, more than you would get in the Parks, and it would have been easy to mistake many of the young engineers for undergraduates, except that they dressed with more flair and smelt much less unpleasingly.

I would like to see a minor county win the Gillette Cup much more than I would like to see England retain the Ashes, but I doubt if Durham will. They beat Oxfordshire comfortably enough in the end, thanks to some well-judged tactics and a fine innings by Burridge, but they will need to reach another dimension against Surrey, whom they meet at Chester-le-Street in the next round. The fielding could certainly be more tightly disciplined. Fieldsmen should not regard a spell in the deep as an opportunity for conversation with spectators.

Barry Richards in the slips

GLOUCESTER: Gloucestershire v Hampshire

Richards took five catches in the slips. The critical one got Procter out, making the score 98 for four, when a little earlier it had been 83 for one.

A senior Gloucestershire member told me that Richards in the slips reminded him irresistibly of Hammond – "Such a complete absence of fuss" – and when senior Gloucestershire members are prepared to admit comparisons with Hammond, you may be sure the subject of them has played pretty well.

Sixes from Hallam Moseley

TAUNTON: Somerset v Leicestershire

Moseley sometimes played and missed, but he did not give any chance that I saw, and in an hour he scored 67, his highest score, including six whacking sixes.

"'Tis another Arthur," the farmer said, referring not to the once and future king, but to one Wellard, still with us and far from mythical, the greatest hitter of sixes cricket has known. It was an extravagant comparison. Wellard, at Taunton, frequently hit his sixes into the river: that is to say, more or less straight. Moseley hits towards midwicket. Still, he scored 101 runs for once out in this match, and will have the farmers roaring many times yet.

Amiss, caught and bowled Mortimore

BIRMINGHAM: Warwickshire v Gloucestershire

When Mortimore came on, Amiss attacked him, and hit him for six over long on, but Mortimore caught and bowled him, falling to his left, a fine catch. George Emmett used to say: "John never catches them off his own bowling", so this must be an aspect of cricket which improves with increasing age; or maybe it is just that age brings increasing avarice.

A century by Majid Khan

BRISTOL: Gloucestershire v Glamorgan

It was Majid who took the eye. Once launched on his subject he was, to borrow Hazlitt's phrase about Coleridge, an eagle dallying with the wind. It occurred to me, as he was going through the gradations of his strokes towards long leg, not quite glances and not quite hooks, that Ranjitsinhji must have played much in this way.

Thoughts on the season 1972

Although the weather was so bad for so long and despite additional hazards such as railway and newspaper strikes, I enjoyed the cricket season. There were moments around the middle of June when I felt that almost any way of spending the summer must be preferable to reporting cricket, but the mood passed, as it always does. On several occasions I had the alarming experience of having to drive a car, something I do about as readily as riding a buffalo. At Pontypridd, I spent an hour and a half trying to find the ground. When I did get there, there was no play, and on departing I took a quite spectacularly wrong turn, and found myself some while later climbing a precipitous Welsh mountain. Some drivers rely on instinct, some on map-reading. I frenziedly alternate between them, and the results are often striking. The following day, after triumphantly driving from Bristol to Swansea and back, I took a wrong turning within a quarter of an hour's walk from home, and managed to cover another twenty miles before I arrived. The god in the machine is too strong for me.

However, the discomfort soon receded into material for a rueful anecdote – like watching a long innings by P.J.K. Gibbs – and by August both the trains and the cricket were more like their proper selves. I cannot comment usefully on the Australians, for on the few occasions I saw them in first-class matches it rained most of the time, but I watched a lot of good county championship cricket, and that is the form of the game I most enjoy.

All the same, the county championship has a problem; nor do I just mean the familiar problem of gate-paying support.

When the one-day competitions began – particularly the John Player League – it was widely felt, among players and such crusty addicts as I, that they were the price that had to be paid if the county championship was to carry on. The one-day competitions, especially the Gillette Cup, have turned out to have a real value of their own, but there was some substance in that original view. And at least the championship, if unsponsored, is still there.

The championship is a three-day competition. It always has been, apart from the one unsuccessful experiment in 1919. Three days is the best length for a two-innings game of cricket. Five days is far too long. If you are going to go beyond three days, it would be better to play the match out. I mourn the day when Test matches in England were allowed to go beyond three days. But since they are now played over five days, or even six, they have become a category as different from the three-day game as the three-day game is different from the one-day game. Since it is the five-day and one-day forms of the game which attract most public support, the three-day game exists as a limbo between them. The temptation is to regard it *either* as a proving ground for Tests, *or* as a mere extension of the one-day game. The first view lies behind the wish to extend county matches to four days. That would be deplorable, but the second view I find even more disturbing, and it is growing increasingly common.

...

Limited-over cricket *imposes* a finish, like unlimited Test matches. Someone has to win. This is not the case with the county championship, nor should it be. A drawn game has always been part of cricket. Some of the matches we remember as the best ended in draws (England v West Indies at Lord's in 1963 is one that immediately occurs to me.) Sam Woods said that 'drawers were only useful for bathing in', but all the same he led many a fierce fight for a draw when the match could not be won. The validity of the county championship depends on captains recognizing it as a three-day game, and not regarding close finishes as a *sine qua non*. If the result of a match invariably depends upon the luck of a slog in the last half hour, we might as well abolish the championship altogether.

...

If the championship is to be worth keeping, it must be played as a three-day game.

County captains have difficult jobs. I am reminded of my efforts at driving a car. Some take decisions by instinct, some by map-reading. It is when you mix the two that you end up on a barren mountain. Most captains would be well advised to stick to one method or the other. Of course now and then you have a captain of genius, one who knows when to welcome instinct and when to suppress it, which seems to me a better definition of genius than de Buffon's (perhaps I owe it to Lecocq). We have had no captain of genius in recent years, though the two Warwickshire Smiths put together come very near one.

Finally, let me express my thanks to Professor Herbert Dingle for the aptest quotation of the season. It occurred to him when poor Arnold had so many catches dropped from his bowling in the Tests. He writes: 'I couldn't help recalling wondering whether he recalled Uncle Matthew's sonnet, Anti-Desperation, and during his walk back for the next ball muttered to himself the lines:

Hath man no second life? Pitch this one high!

Alas! however he pitched it, the second life came.'

I do not get too depressed about the future of the championship, because however they pitch it, it has already shown itself to be a nine-lived kind of cat.

1973

The cricket season of 1973 was a good one for the county sides of the South and West of England. Hampshire won the county championship, Gloucestershire the Gillette Cup and Somerset made genuine progress under Brian Close and won seven of their 20 championship matches. And despite his protestations later in the year that he no longer much cared which side won or lost the cricket matches he was sent to cover, that also made it a good season for Alan Gibson. If the local teams were doing well, then he was much more likely to be asked to follow them and he vastly preferred pottering off down the road to the county ground at Bristol, or a cross-country train journey to Bournemouth, to the long trek to, say, Old Trafford or Grace Road. Besides, most of his cricketing favourites – men like Brian Close, Mike Procter, David Shepherd and Arthur Milton – played for the counties of the West. A day's cricket at Taunton was still a genuine pleasure, which was something that could not always be said of a trip to Northampton.

The weather also played its part in making the summer of 1973 a thoroughly enjoyable one. May was its usual fickle self, and heavy thunderstorms washed out or spoiled a good many matches in July, but June was mostly dry and August positively tropical. Alan spent as many column inches bemoaning a shortage of ice or the beer running out as he did the cold and the wet.

New Zealand and the West Indies were the touring sides, in that order, each with three Tests. Alan should have seen a lot of the New Zealanders in May, as they played Hampshire, Gloucestershire, Somerset and Glamorgan in quick succession. But rain was in the air, and the closing rituals at Taunton on May 14 – superbly evoked by the final paragraph of Alan's *Times* report – were all too typical of most of the tourists' early games.

But despite the damp wickets and frequent interruptions, Glenn Turner was piling up the runs. When he hit a brilliant 153 not out against the MCC on May 19, his aggregate reached 796, with a possible seven innings still to be played before the end of the month. Then it all became a bit of a struggle, and when Turner walked out to open the innings at Northampton on May 30, he was still 93 runs short. The cricketing world was on tenterhooks. Alan was there to see if he could accomplish something that hadn't been done since Don Bradman and Bill Edrich in 1938.

In the meantime, Alan had been reporting bits and pieces of games, in between the showers and his broadcasting commitments. The running joke about what the second J in the initials of Jack Davey, the Gloucestershire left arm fast bowler, might stand for – which would lead eventually to the formation of the JJ? Society – makes its first appearance in the report of Gloucestershire's win over Hampshire in two days on May 25, with a reference to Jumping Jack Davey. The next day he is Jovial Jack Davey; the following week he becomes Jesting Jack and Juggernaut Jack. But unquestionably the highlight of the early part of the season was the trip down to Taunton for the traditional bank holiday fixture with Gloucestershire – on his 50th birthday!

Mike Procter was always one of Alan's very favourite cricketers. He wrote about him with a special relish, and despite a series of injuries, this proved to be one of Procter's greatest seasons. He would top Gloucestershire's batting averages, play a crucial part in the Gillette Cup triumph, and if his 26 wickets represented a relatively meagre haul, that was far more a reflection of his injury problems than of any loss of

Tests
England
beat New Zealand
2-0, with one draw
West Indies
beat England
2-0, with one draw

Championship
1 Hampshire
2 Surrey
3 Northamptonshire
4 Kent
5 Gloucestershire
6 Worcestershire

Sunday League
1 Kent
2 Yorkshire
3 Hampshire
4 Lancashire
5 Leicestershire
6 Gloucestershire

Gillette Cup Final
Gloucestershire
beat Sussex

Benson & Hedges Final
Kent
beat Worcesterwshire

Most first-class runs
1 G.M. Turner
2 J.A. Jameson
3 M.J. Smith

Most first-class wickets
1 B.S. Bedi
2 P. Lee
3 R.D. Jackman
J.N. Shepherd

potency when he was fully fit. There was only one greater all-rounder at the time (and precious few before or since), and he was the incomparable Gary Sobers, captured in the evening of his county days for Nottinghamshire (for he had been injured and joined the West Indies touring party only for the Test matches), in a delightful cameo from their Benson and Hedges match against Worcestershire on June 13.

By mid-season, Hampshire and Northants were vying with each other at the top of the championship table, while Kent dominated one-day cricket. Under Mike Denness's thoughtful captaincy, they had reached the final of the B&H (and would win it, beating Worcestershire) and were running away with the Sunday League.

In early July, Alan went to Edgbaston to report Warwickshire against Essex. The previous issue of *The Spectator* had included a critique of sports writing. It was not to Alan's liking. And maybe just to demonstrate how a well-written sports report can rise above the clichéd and the mundane, I offer you the opening passage about Cutty Sark whisky from Hampshire against Middlesex on July 18.

The longer the season went on, the better Hampshire seemed to play. With that wonderful opening pair of Richards and Greenidge, an inspiring captain in Richard Gilliatt and no Test calls to worry about, they began to stretch their lead at the top of the championship. The win against Derbyshire on August 10 not only demonstrated their all-round strength, it also took them 44 points clear of their nearest challengers Northants, with just four games left. It proved to be a decisive lead. Alan was asked to cover Northants for the final few matches, and they never really looked like breaking their championship duck. The end came on August 30, with Hampshire on the way to a comfortable victory over Gloucestershire, and Northants in all sorts of trouble against Surrey on what sounds like a rather joyless day at Guildford. They would lose in the end by an innings, and with it – also to Surrey – their runners-up spot.

It was probably Hampshire's good fortune to play Gloucestershire when they did, for the minds of Tony Brown and his team must have been firmly fixed on their next match, which would be the Gillette Cup final against Sussex at Lord's. Alan had seen them beat Worcestershire in the semi-final, and in both games, it was Procter who made the difference, albeit with some substantial assistance in the final from Tony Brown, whose 77 at the death transformed the Gloucestershire total from respectable to daunting.

The cricket season over, Alan took Rosie and the two young children off to St Ives for a much-needed holiday, before reflecting on the season for *The Cricketer*. Later in the autumn, he wrote an affectionate tribute to the BBC's very first Test match commentator, Howard Marshall, which, with its equally illuminating follow-up, also revealed much about Alan's own attitudes to cricket commentary and reporting, as did his final piece for *The Times* that year when he looked back, not on the games he had seen, but the books he had read.

Cartwright finds a wicket to suit him

TAUNTON: Gloucestershire, with nine second innings wickets in hand, need 228 runs to avoid an innings defeat by Somerset

I reached my 50 yesterday, more than any of the batsmen did. A streaky innings it has been, badly dropped more than once, with much edging in the early 40s. But 50 is a comforting figure especially if you are a bad bat, or hat, and Taunton was a pleasantly appropriate place in which to be. It was from Taunton that I sent my first contribution to this newspaper (an unsolicited and unpaid account of a school match); from Taunton that I made my first broadcast, and at Taunton that I have seen much splendid cricket, not least when these two counties have been grappling on holiday weekends.

Gloucestershire are on the wrong end of this one. If the alternating rain and sun continue, the pitch can hardly get better. Somerset had scored 381 on Saturday. They went out to field at 2 o'clock – it was too wet to play before that – and immediately found that the ball would move from the pitch in unexpected directions.

Fifty years ago, in these conditions, it would have been a spinner's carnival, especially for a slow left-armer. J.C. White would have rubbed his hands, given his opening bowlers a perfunctory stretch, and then gone on himself, in full confidence of bowling Gloucestershire out twice before the close. Nowadays it is thought that seam and swing bowling are best for such occasions, and there is a case to be made for it, especially if you have such a bowler as Cartwright on your side.

Cartwright took six wickets, and Breakwell, slow left arm, bowled only briefly and not particularly well. Gloucestershire were all out at 5.50 for 148. Sadiq went quickly, bowled by Moseley. Knight was caught at short leg, something that seemed likely as soon as Cartwright came on. Milton brought all his experience to bear on the situation, but even his reflexes are slowing, and he did not seem to pick up the ball from Cartwright which bowled him.

Procter played some commanding strokes, trying hard to break the bowlers' control. He was caught from a mis-hit to mid-on, no doubt feeling it was better to take risks against Burgess than Cartwright. Shepherd was caught at cover off a slower ball from Burgess, following a less than nimble-footed heave. Cartwright had Brown and Swetman repeatedly baffled before dismissing both. When Cartwright bowled his first ball to Graveney, Close politely stepped forward from short leg and caught the ball as it dropped from the defensive bat.

Zaheer had been playing pretty well; he did more to suggest that he can come to terms with English pitches than he has done in many longer innings. Mortimore gave him some help, until Close came on and bowled him. Jesting Jack Davey emerged to loud cheers from the Gloucestershire addicts. "Kept the best wine to last," said one, in an unexpected scriptural allusion; and then, as Davey played his first ball from Cartwright: "Oh, well left alone, Jack." But it had hit the hero on his pads and he was leg-before-wicket.

Gloucestershire scored five runs in half an hour when they went in again, and lost Sadiq. Milton played well. I would love to see a long innings from him today, as a birthday present.

Procter personifies the batting art

TAUNTON: Somerset (20 pts) beat Gloucestershire (2 pts) by an innings and 38 runs

Somerset had bowled Gloucestershire out a second time by 3 o'clock. It was a predictable result, and one of those matches which Somerset men will remember with relish. But we still had more than three hours of compelling cricket because of Procter. I have seen Procter play a larger, longer, faster, more immaculate, more swaggering innings but never, given all the circumstances, a better one. The circumstances were a lifting, turning pitch; an almost hopeless position for his side; Tom Cartwright; and a strained back, which still prevents him from bowling and which, in the later part of his innings, was clearly causing him pain.

In the past I have said that it was more important (to Gloucestershire) that Procter should bowl than bat. After this innings, and the one against Hampshire at Bristol last week (though that was a much less testing occasion), I am almost inclined to hope that he never bowls again. His bowling is irrational or, at best, romantic. He is indeed very strong, but he will tear himself to bits with that action, sooner or later. His batting is classical, in the sense that Trumper and Hobbs and Hutton were classical. In a penetrating essay Sir Neville Cardus pointed out (it must have been about 1951) that from Hutton it would be possible to deduce the entire art and science of batting, if all other knowledge of it were to be wiped away; and that Hutton was the only batsman of his period of whom this could be said.

Today, I believe, this is true of Procter, and it is not quite true of Richards or Sobers, or even Boycott. This is not to say that Procter is the best batsman in the world, any more than it would have been true to say that Hutton was a better batsman than Bradman. But Procter is, I think, unique among current batsmen in the classical correctness of his strokes, whether attacking or defending. When he makes a cow-shot, which he sometimes does, you know that it was deliberately intended for the cattle. He banged Cartwright about in a way that can rarely have happened before, and you cannot bang Cartwright about for long without a classical technique.

Procter came in when Zaheer was out at 10, and scored 102, not out, of the 185 remaining runs. Cartwright was clearly the principal menace from the start, and I was sad when he had Milton caught at short leg. We did, however, see one beautifully characteristic off-drive from Milton, made as usual so late that the scorers had already put down a dot.

Knight never looked happy, but played a few good strokes; after he was out, wickets fell steadily, or unsteadily. We thought it would be over before lunch, when Cartwright, recalled at 1 o'clock, took two wickets in an over. Graveney, arriving at 119 for 7, with the prospect of a king pair, might have been run out from his first ball and caught at extra cover from his second, but survived to play a good innings. Indeed, although by now Procter was in increasing physical discomfort, Graveney did well to score half the runs of the eighth wicket partnership.

Possibilities of a draw? The occasional drop of rain fell, and soon after the game ended it was raining hard. Graveney was bowled by Cartwright. Mortimore, who certainly looked as if he intended to bat for a long time, was well caught at short leg by Wilkinson, off Close. Shortly afterwards Wilkinson took his fourth catch of the match, though the jocular Jack Davey had proudly avoided a king pair.

I have written so much about Procter that I have no space to write about Cartwright. No doubt his eleven wickets speak for themselves.

Somerset v Gloucestershire, Taunton, 26, 28 & 29 May 1973

Somerset won by an innings and 38 runs

Somerset

M.J. Kitchen	run out	19
S.G. Wilkinson	lbw b Brown	12
* D.B. Close	lbw b Knight	18
J.M. Parks	c Sadiq b Mortimore	68
G.I. Burgess	c Swetman b Davey	129
P.W. Denning	c Swetman b Knight	4
T.W. Cartwright	b Brown	54
D. Breakwell	b Davey	23
+ D.J.S. Taylor	*not out*	28
H.R. Moseley	*not out*	13
A.A. Jones		
	lb 10, nb 3	13
	(8 wkts, dec)	**381**

1/32, 2/44,3/57, 4/209, 5/213, 6/315, 7/315, 8/360

Davey	20	3	71	2
Brown	25	7	73	2
Knight	17	2	58	2
Mortimore	25	5	53	1
Graveney	19	5	66	0
Sadiq	11	1	47	0

Gloucestershire

Sadiq Mohammad	b Moseley	2	c Taylor b Jones	0
C.A. Milton	b Cartwright	19	c Close b Cartwright	7
R.D.V. Knight	c Wilkinson b Cartwright	10	c Cartwright b Burgess	21
M.J. Procter	c Wilkinson b Burgess	34	*not out*	102
Zaheer Abbas	*not out*	36	lbw b Jones	6
D.R. Shepherd	c Denning b Burgess	0	c Moseley b Breakwell	6
* A.S. Brown	lbw b Cartwright	11	c Burgess b Cartwright	10
+ R. Swetman	c Taylor b Cartwright	18	lbw b Cartwright	4
D.A. Graveney	c Close b Cartwright	0	b Cartwright	32
J.B. Mortimore	b Close	8	c Wilkinson b Close	2
J. Davey	lbw b Cartwright	0	c Wilkinson b Cartwright	0
	b 2, lb 2, nb 6	10	b 2, nb 3	5
		148		**195**

1/8, 2/26, 3/69, 4/70, 5/72, 6/87, 7/118, 8/118, 9/147, 10/148
1/0, 2/10, 3/18, 4/57, 5/92, 6/115, 7/119, 8/183, 9/194, 10/195

Jones	9	2	23	0	12	6	29	2
Moseley	11	3	21	1	14	4	32	0
Cartwright	26.5	11	41	6	26	6	68	5
Burgess	6	2	28	2	4	0	14	1
Breakwell	2	0	12	0	10	2	36	1
Close	10	5	13	1	5	0	11	1

Umpires: C. Cook and J. Langridge

The last day of a damp match

TAUNTON: Somerset v the New Zealanders

The last hour, with the New Zealanders quietly plodding it out, was dull so far as the cricket went. But there was some compensation in the sunshine; now warm, and the towers of Taunton etched against the blue sky, with the weathercocks swinging reassuringly to the south; and the gentle chime of the bells; and even the chip shots (I hope I have my golfing term right) which Close markedly played from short leg, both left-handed and right-handed.

Fredericks in the 90s

CARDIFF: Glamorgan v the New Zealanders

Fredericks seemed to be overcome by the imminence of his 100. He dawdled a long time in the 90s, and was ultimately out, caught in the covers where he had just given a hard chance, still short of it. No doubt he realized he had been dawdling and was trying to make sudden compensation. When you are approaching a hundred the evenness of mind, it is all, as the philosopher Lecocq likes to say in his old age, though I doubt if he was thinking of cricket.

Turner's 1,000 in May

NORTHAMPTON: Northamptonshire v the New Zealanders

The list of those who have scored 1,000 runs by the end of May is a distinguished one, and now another name, that of Glenn Maitland Turner, is added to it. Many great batsmen have never done it: Compton and Hutton, even though they recorded two of the four highest aggregates in a season, never achieved this particular feat. It is usually easy to score 1,000 runs in other months, when a batsman has had time to find form and the pitches are drier. A thousand in May can also be a bit of a waste, before the big matches. Bill Edrich, for instance, followed it with a disastrous Test season, but I doubt very much whether this will happen in the case of Turner.*

The list of the previous "thousands" is:

W.G. Grace (Glos), 1895.
T. Hayward (Surrey), 1900.
W.R. Hammond (Glos), 1927.
C. Hallows (Lancashire), 1928.
D.G. Bradman (Australia), 1930.
D.G. Bradman (Australia), 1938.
W.J. Edrich (Middlesex), 1938).

Turner scored the remaining 23 he needed cautiously, in an hour and 10 minutes. There were not many palpitations. Once, from the bowler's end, he set off for a run, and had to scamper back when Milburn made a good stop and return. Once he was beaten by a ball from Bedi which jumped, outside the off stump. Bedi tested him severely in a fine spell of bowling. Northamptonshire gave him nothing, not even a full toss when he wanted the last four, as Sam Woods gave WG in 1895.

I think this was the correct approach, in the best tradition of Macaulay. I mean Macaulay, the Yorkshire bowler, not the historian and poet, though now I have brought the other one in I might as well observe that it was an occasion when the ranks of Tuscany cheered loud and long.

The only 11 Northamptonshire men who wanted to prevent Turner getting the runs were on the field of play, and the players were warm in their congratulations to the hero when the magic score was reached. Appropriately, it was done with one of the strokes which he plays best, one of his own, backward of square on the off side, not a true cut but a controlled forcing of the ball with a vertical bat. The bowler was Bedi, and the ball went to the boundary.

I awoke during the night and heard it raining, and wondered if Turner heard it, too, but play started on time. It drizzled occasionally, but only once heavily enough to interrupt play, after Turner had gone on to his century, and then cheerfully got out. It occurs to me (though it would take some checking) that the other batsmen who scored 1,000 runs before the end of May (except perhaps Hayward) did so in better summers than this has been so far, and therefore suffered fewer interruptions from the weather than Turner has done. For instance, May was fine in 1938, when it was done, uniquely, by two people. With the present limited amount of three-day cricket it is only touring players who are likely to do it again – until one-day and three-day matches are given the same status, which is bound to happen sooner or later.

I saw Turner carry his bat through a routed New Zealand innings on his last tour here. That was a performance of great staunchness, but there were few indications that he would so swiftly mature into so good a player. He must be better than Hallows and Edrich already, and if his imagination keeps pace with his skills, he will not look an unfit companion for the mighty other names on the list.

** Contrary to Alan Gibson's forecast, Turner had a poor Test series, scoring only 116 runs in his five innings.*

"Over four thousand persons visited Lord's Ground yesterday to witness one of the most remarkable spectacles that has occurred at this place for a long time past .... The Colonials beat the greatest and most powerful club in the world by nine wickets. They were loudly cheered by the assembled multitude."

Thus *The Times* in 1878, after the Australians had beaten Marylebone in a single day. I do not know who wrote the account, but it was very likely "Sporting Ward". Bernard Darwin has told us how the omniscient Ward used to cover practically all the games covered in the newspaper. Certainly he was an active veteran by 1896, and the report of Australians v MCC in that year (when the Australians were out for 18) seems to me to be much in the same style as the 1878 account. On the other hand, sports writers in those days were not encouraged to develop an individual style. Darwin himself, who began writing about golf for the paper soon after Sporting Ward finished, was the pioneer.

The first cricket correspondent *per se* that *The Times* possessed was Sidney Pardon. He was acquired from *The Daily Telegraph*, and was editor of *Wisden* for 34 years, until his death in 1925. He is reported to have suffered from bad eyesight and nervous irritability, despite which he built a weighty reputation.

When *Wisden* became too big a job to be combined with a correspondent's work, Pardon was succeeded on the paper by A.C.M. Croome. Croome was also an acerbic man, whose views became influential. An article he wrote in 1921, criticizing the play of Hubert Ashton, kept Ashton out of the England side that year, at a time when there was strong opinion for his inclusion. This is recounted by Sir Home Gordon, who adds: "Croome had called me into the writing-room of the pavilion to read that paragraph before he sent it to the printer, and he had made at least four drafts before it satisfied his cricket conscience." Leisurely days, when a correspondent could settle down to a succession of drafts in a pavilion writing-room!

Croome's life was saved once by W.G. Grace. He was playing for Gloucestershire, and in chasing a ball on the boundary injured himself in the throat on a spiked railing. W.G. held the edges of the wound together until a surgical needle could be fetched. Croome said the hand never shook, though W.G. had been fielding for over 400 runs. A twitch might have been fatal.

Both Croome and Pardon made their contributions anonymously, as did all other sports writers in the paper, with very occasional exceptions, until 1967. I have no doubt that the high standard of sports writing in the paper was connected with the anonymity rule. I think it was Delane who said that a name at the top of a report was merely a barrier between the news and the public. Nowadays I am afraid we grow too concerned with looking for a "style", instead of providing the information.

Anonymity did not prevent a variety of interesting people from writing about cricket for the paper, not all of them of course holding the rank of cricket correspondent. One who did was R.B. Vincent, in the thirties. He was known as "Beau" Vincent, and recalled the *Punch* cartoon of the Victorian servant: "Five reporters, ma'am, and a gentleman from *The Times*." But he had his oddities, such as carrying his dentures in his overcoat pocket. Robertson-Glasgow has written affectionately about Vincent. Once they were walking down a street in Manchester during a Test, and saw two posters: one said "Read R.C. Robertson-Glasgow in the *Morning Post*", and the other "Read *The Times* and see what really happened"; which, when you come to think of it, was another one up to anonymity.

The present Association Football correspondent was once also cricket correspondent. D.J. Insole, writing in 1960, thought Geoffrey Green the outstanding sports writer of the time. But Green's destiny was to write about soccer, and in any case the elongation of the soccer season made it increasingly difficult to combine the two jobs.

So in 1954 John Woodcock had taken over the cricket. The Sage of Longparish, as he is now affectionately known, was then a slip of a boy, 27 years old and looking about 10 years younger. A youthful appointment, a long and happy term of service – the pattern has recurred several times.

It is no business of mine to discuss the merits of a friend and colleague, but in one respect at least the Sage achieved something which none of his predecessors had done. For *The Times* decided, in 1967, that anonymity must depart. The date was to be January 23. John Woodcock was in South Africa, and January 23 fell in the middle of a Test match. I suppose it was thought incongruous that "Our Cricket Correspondent" should suddenly acquire an identity in the middle of a match. His preview, from Durban, on January 20, revealed all. It is not strictly true to say that it was the first by-line ever to appear on the sports page, but it heralded a new era, and caused sufficient of a stir for the Sage himself to hear the news in a South African bulletin.

They have been a rich assortment of characters, the people who have written about cricket for *The Times* – and I have not mentioned some of the richest: Denzil Batchelor, for instance, who in several ways resembled Falstaff, and who happily called his autobiography *Babbled of Green Fields*. Sports writing is no more than babbling of green fields, but it is also true that such men as these have, almost always, served both the game and the paper (and the English language) responsibly, even graciously. It is a tradition of which anyone who writes about cricket for *The Times* is conscious, and is proud.

Gloucester need some of that cream cheese

HOVE: Gloucestershire, with seven second innings wickets in hand, need 209 runs to avoid an innings defeat by Sussex

I gather that the pitch had been a little tricky on Saturday, when Gloucestershire were bowled out for 170, and Sussex scored a slow 63 for 1; but there was nothing wrong with it yesterday. Gloucestershire were without Procter, who had been injured on Sunday at Bristol, and who in any case has not been able to bowl lately. They must also have been taxed by their double journey. The computer which governs fixtures shares the belief of Londoners that the West Country begins where civilization ends, at Marble Arch, and it is all much the same place after that.

Two wickets fell quickly, but by lunch Prideaux and Greig had taken command, and there was not much Gloucestershire could do about it. Both batsmen moved on to centuries, which for some while had looked probable.

Greig's innings will have reassured him, and the England selectors. In its second half he played some superb strokes: lofted off drives, the square cut, and – even more impressively, though less dramatically – gentle pushes between cover and extra cover so well timed that you were waiting for one of the fieldsmen to lob the ball back, and then realized it had gone quietly between them for four. Greig also played with the edge of the bat occasionally: he often scored runs with a flick through slips. I am not sure all of these were intended, but he kept them on the ground.

Prideaux also played well. Sussex owed him much for keeping the innings together in the early stages. He was overhauled by Greig in the afternoon, but it was only sensible of him to leave most of the scoring to the other end, once the captain had found his form. No stroke of Greig's was better delivered than the off drive with which Prideaux reached his 100, half an hour later.

Greig was fourth out at 301, after a stand of 217. Because of the slow start, Sussex had only taken four batting points, but still led 9-1 on the first innings. It became a question of when they should declare, with a sunny afternoon yielding to a cloudy evening. "It's raining in London," said a local lady, surveying the sky: "You can bet your cream cheese, it's raining in London": a striking analogy I have not hitherto encountered.

Greig gave Gloucestershire nearly an hour and a half to bat, and bowled himself with Snow. Nicholls and Knight were soon out. The light was poor, causing the umpires to consult, and Snow went off for a while, returning to get Sadiq out, when it looked as if he was leading Gloucestershire out of immediate difficulty.

At a quarter past six, in came Milton. Snow called up an extra close fielder, and put a few yards on his run, but his first ball to Milton was rolled for a single to the covers – the way in which Milton has begun countless innings against all sorts of bowlers in all sorts of conditions all over the world. I am inclined to think it was the poet in Snow that prevented him from bowling a more ferocious ball, though a couple of overs later he duly delivered to Milton the bouncer necessary to the peasant in him.

Milton survived, but unless we are to have a surplus of cream cheese, Gloucestershire will not. By the end of the Sussex innings, even the juggernaut Jack Davey – though he was the best of the bowlers, and got Greig out – was looking weary to the bones; far indeed from jocund, like this silly joke which I now promise to abandon.

Milton gets impatient in his sunset hour

HOVE: Sussex (19 pts) beat Gloucestershire (1 pt) by an innings and 90 runs

Once Greig and Prideaux had found their stride on Monday afternoon, with Procter a casualty, it seemed that only the weather could stop Sussex winning this match. The last morning was sunny, and sure enough they had taken the remaining six Gloucestershire wickets by ten past one.

...

As usual on these occasions, the spectators were torn between anxiety that Sussex should wrap the match up, and the pleasure of sitting in the sun watching cricket. A long innings by Zaheer or Milton (well, fairly long, say 75 or so) would have been acceptable. But Zaheer was soon bowled by Greig, whose bowling was full of life and vigour. When he is in form, as he emphatically is at present in all three departments, there is no modern player who looks as if he is *enjoying* his cricket more than Greig.

Milton's innings was cool and rarely troubled, and had the special charm one always finds in an old favourite, in the serene evening of his cricketing life. Quietness and confidence have always been Milton's strength.

There was a burst of action round about 12 o'clock. Greig was hit for 11 runs in an over, mostly by Milton, and Swetman was dropped at short mid-wicket, an easy lobbed catch from a top-edge hook. Swetman nevertheless batted better than I remember seeing him for Gloucestershire before. Some of his legside strokes were hard and truly hit.

Milton was out with the total 127. Swetman, at 151, was caught at mid-wicket, second attempt, to the manifest relief of Griffith, the man who had missed him earlier. Snow was brought back to finish off the innings before lunch, and did.

Arthur Milton
'Quietness and confidence have always been his strength'

Sobers under pressure

WORCESTER: Worcestershire v Nottinghamshire (B&H Cup)

Nottingham, five for three wickets, and Sobers coming in.

In such moments of pressure Sobers is always even more languid than usual. He does not hurry between the wickets. "Plenty of time," his every gesture says. He engages in a little relaxed conversation. He gives himself a gentle, ruminative scratch. Then you look at the board, and think they must have got it wrong. The rifle fire is picking off the runs, with hardly a hint of the artillery in reserve.

Randall was out before tea, when the score was 38 for four off 15 overs, Sobers 23. It was going to be either a Sobers spectacular or a Worcestershire win. At 54, with Sobers playing ominously well, Gifford came on. Sobers tried to pull him over square leg, and got a top edge. The ball was in the air long enough for everyone in the ground to realize the significance of the moment. The catch was held: Othello's occupation gone. You could almost hear the knocking of the fieldsman's knees. Gifford ran to clasp Yardley. Sobers walked away, still languid, with a wry shrug.

An overheard conversation

BRISTOL: Gloucestershire v Kent

During one of the breaks in play, I heard the following conversation between a Gloucestershire official and a steward.

Gloucestershire official (wrathful): "And if she complains again you can tell her it's CLEAN!"

Steward (equally sympathetic): "I will, sir, I will, and what's more, I'll tell her to use it!"

I thought it must just go down as one of those baffling overheard snatches until it occurred to me that an office typewriter must have grown a bit grubby.

Somerset umpires

LEICESTER: Leicestershire v Hampshire

As the umpires led the way out for the last session, Alley was demonstrating strokes to his colleague Peter Wight, and I remembered how these two for the whole of one season had opened the innings for Somerset, an improbable but often successful and always diverting partnership. It occurred to me that there were no more than three, perhaps four batsmen of their quality in this match. Perhaps it is no more than early-season blues, but the cricket I have seen so far has been marked by a routine competence rather than true class: barring the occasional mastery of a Richards or a Davison, neither of whom are natives (but then nor were Alley and Wight).

Among Warwickshire folk

BIRMINGHAM: Warwickshire v Northamptonshire

Might Jameson play for England again? When he was chosen before, he did not have the best of luck. I have never doubted his spirit, only his technique, but there was not much technically wrong with this innings. I would pick him unhesitatingly if the tour this winter was to be to India.

And who, asked a gnarled pear tree of an old chap, did I think should be England's captain? He had no doubts. A.C. Smith was the only man. I countered with the name of Green. "Which Green?" "Why," I said, "either D.M. or T.H. would do. The one sure thing is that we shall need a philosopher."

Last overs of a drawn match

NOTTINGHAM: Nottinghamshire v Middlesex

There is a picture in the Long Room at Trent Bridge, cracked and forlorn, but a favourite of mine, called "Playing out time". It was exhibited at the Royal Academy in 1901. I spent most of the last hour looking at it, and then to the play again, and then back, until the two pictures seemed to mingle. For cricket in evening sunlight, however sterile the contest, can never be altogether without beauty.

Somerset in West Wales

NEATH: Glamorgan v Somerset

"In that misty country of the Celts all things are possible: for the stags hunt the dogs, and the muttons are friskier than the lambs." I was reminded of this familiar adage as I watched Brian Close remorselessly lead his assorted collection of ages, hairstyles and waistlines to a handsome win over a Glamorgan side full of talent, but short of experience.

J.M. Barrie

NOTTINGHAM: Nottinghamshire v Middlesex

Visiting a small bank in Nottingham yesterday morning, I discovered two handsome bronze plaques recording that John Drinkwater and J.M. Barrie had worked on the premises. I cannot remember whether Drinkwater was a cricketer, but Barrie was – with his own touring side, Allahakbarries – and a slow bowler, so slow that if he did not like the look of a ball he would run after it and catch it.

This was the only really cheerful cricketing thought which occurred to me all day.

Robin Jackman

THE OVAL: Surrey v Middlesex

Then Edmonds pulled Pocock to deep square leg. It was a fair run for Jackman, and he picked up the flight late, but he held the catch, falling and rolling over, then jumping up and punching the air like the Shoreditch Sparrow warming up at the Blackfriars Ring – one of his customs when pleased with himself.

GUILDFORD: Surrey v Northamptonshire

The Surrey hero was Jackman, who took six wickets in the first innings, the first two in the second, and came back to get another before the close. Arnold, at the other end, bowled just as well, but the wickets came Jackman's way. He was capering about, punching holes in the air, all day, tearing round the boundary for the exercise even when he had no chance of cutting off the ball.

I have been attributing Jackman's origins to Shoreditch, and now they tell me he was born in Simla, the son of a colonel in the Indian Army. This can only have been an aberration in the history of the Jackman family. There were Jackmans in Shoreditch in Chaucer's time. The original Feste in *Twelfth Night* was probably a Jackman. Any modern actor's interpretation of the part would benefit from watching Jackman playing cricket, whether he is singing high or low.

In the event of a tie

BASINGSTOKE: Hampshire v Middlesex

Early in the proceedings a lorry cut the press telephone lines. The hospitable sponsors were Berry Brothers and Rudd, who manufacture Cutty Sark whisky. In the circumstances it is a miracle you are reading these lines at all.

Cutty Sark whisky was christened 50 years ago by the water-colourist James McBey. He was consulted about a name for the product, picked up a copy of that morning's Times, and saw a picture of the famous clipper, just drydocked at Falmouth. His sketch and lettering still appear on the bottles. The name of the clipper itself, I learned, was taken from the poem by Burns, "Tam O' Shanter". "Cutty Sark" is Scots for short skirt, and I could not help thinking it a happy chance that the whisky was able to celebrate its jubilee at a time when the sarks had never been cuttier. A case of whisky will be presented to the side winning, or scoring most points. In the event of a tie both sides will have a case. It is the only match I remember in which both sides are playing for a tie.

The excitement of Sunday cricket

GLOUCESTER: Gloucestershire v Essex

Essex scored 193 for six in their 40 overs, a good and usually sufficient score in a John Player League match. They had scored 32 after 10 overs, and only 63 after 20, with three wickets down. At this point I heard a lady, not, I think, familiar with cricket, say to her escort, plaintively, "It's worse than going to church."

...

For the second time this month the tail was Gloucestershire's salvation. The wagging capacity of Graveney and Swetman ultimately brought them four points, with three balls and two wickets left. It was a capital Sunday finish, and the lady who had earlier been plaintive about the ecclesiastical overtones was inquiring of her escort: "Why do they keep all the excitement to the end?"

Tripe

BIRMINGHAM: Warwickshire v Essex

DAY TWO

"Where'er you walk cool gales shall fan the glade." I thought I had better begin with a quotation in deference to *The Spectator*, who last week in a pungent and partly laudable article concerning the place of sport in society, referred to cricket writing as "tripe masquerading as art". Fortunately he cannot have been thinking of this newspaper, for nobody on the staff of *The Spectator* is allowed to read red rags. ... An interesting finish is quite possible – depending upon the moods of the captains – but it had been mostly a dull day. Sometimes I think I shall abandon cricket and take up political journalism instead – only that must be so much more difficult. The tripe that conceals art is one thing: but few can achieve the subtlety of the tripe that conceals tripe.

DAY THREE

I have not seen Pont make many runs before, but I am sure that I shall again. At a time when the John Player League has lured so many young middle-order batsmen into heaves across the line, Pont has kept his cover drive and lofted straight drive. His off side play in front of the wicket was a delight and, though his bat was sometimes too far from the body when cutting, he scored runs in that direction, too.

Certainly he had some luck but, once Essex were over their first crisis, he scored his runs fast. The side's need for quick runs prevented him from worrying too much about his own score: until suddenly he was 99, when he looked at the scoreboard, started scratching himself and shuffling his feet, and peering nervously over his shoulder as if he expected to find the leader writer of *The Spectator* at leg slip.

What made the admiral hark back to school days

PORTSMOUTH: Hampshire, with all first innings wickets in hand, are 153 runs behind Derbyshire

Hampshire put Derbyshire in, perhaps feeling that in the uncertain weather they had a better chance of quick points for bowling than for batting. In the event they got three, frustrated of more by a Derbyshire batting performance that was dour – if you wish to be polite – and dismal – if you don't. Derbyshire took no points for batting. After 85 overs their score was 139.

The weather improved – most of the day was sunny, and in the evening, if I dare risk saying it, it had a settled look, the sky bright blue and the clouds high and flimsy. Quite a large crowd bore its tribulations serenely, fortified by the fairly regular fall of wickets. The pitch gave the spinners some help – they were on after nine overs – and O'Sullivan added to a steadily growing reputation.

Caution was understandable, and the Derbyshire batting is, some of it, inexperienced (but then so, some of it, is the Hampshire bowling). At any rate, Derbyshire scored enough to keep them in the match. We veterans could not be blamed for casting back a wistful look to the halcyon days of P.J.K. Gibbs and other carefree cavaliers of the past.

Michael Carey, who must know Derbyshire cricket as well as anyone, tells me that there is indeed a new and refreshing spirit in the county, since Bolus took over the captaincy, but it does not yet seem to have percolated from the dressing room to the field of play.

Borrington was out early, leg before, to Mottram. Hill was caught at the wicket when Richards came on, with his little off breaks. That was the twenty-third over and the score was 36. Harvey-Walker hit Richards for six, but was caught by him at slip off O'Sullivan. Bolus was caught at the wicket, Buxton bowled, playing defensively, Miller caught at slip – Richards again, and O'Sullivan's fourth consecutive wicket.

Page, however, had been holding an end, making few mistakes, though lucky that one edge off O'Sullivan just missed the clutches of both wicketkeeper and slip, and occasionally playing a stroke of quality. He and Taylor held on until the new ball was taken and the opportunity for more bowling points gone. Page was ultimately caught at the wicket after Herman had taken it: 140 for seven, and Hampshire eager to polish the innings off, but there was further frustration in an eighth wicket stand by Taylor and Venkataraghavan.

Some of the crowd did become a little cross at this stage. Perhaps the sundowners were getting to work on the retired admirals. "My old headmaster," I heard a voice say, "would have flogged me if I had batted like this. You didn't know my old headmaster, did you? You could smell the whisky on him as soon as you went into his study, even at seven in the morning. He'd say 'bend over, old chap,' and then you got it hot and strong. My word, how I --------" and I swear he was going to finish the sentence "how I enjoyed it" but he was interrupted by the fall of the last Derbyshire wicket. That was 176 all out, and Hampshire had 35 minutes to bat.

Derbyshire condemned by two stands

PORTSMOUTH: Derbyshire, with eight second innings wickets in hand, need 147 runs to avoid an innings defeat by Hampshire

On a day of lovely sunshine, even the Portsmouth ground, always rather drab and now with both its main stands condemned, looked well. So did the Hampshire batsmen. Vigorously chasing first innings points, they ultimately took eight for batting, 11 in all, against Derbyshire's three.

There was an early setback when Richards was caught at deep square leg, but Greenidge and Turner were soon pushing on merrily. There was even a prospect of a point in the first 25 overs, despite the relatively slow start the night before. The batsmen tried to hurry things with stolen runs, but their understanding was imperfect, and there were a couple of muddles before Greenidge was run out by almost the pitch's length.

So the first point was missed, but one was safely achieved when the 150 was reached well inside 50 overs. The only other wicket to fall had been that of Turner, caught at slip. Turner is in form at present and played technically the best innings, but it was Gilliat who caught the eye. He is fair, and well built, with three initials, eager to get on to the front foot and drive, and he looks the original boy's own paper picture of a dashing young captain determined to lead his side to the championship. He has had a good deal of luck, with some edges, and skied mis-hits which fell clear of the field. He was badly dropped in the morning at short fine leg. But it was that kind of innings, challenging rather than commanding and flowing with fine strokes, none better than the straight drive with which he reached his 100, the ball before he was out.

By then he had lost Sainsbury and Jesty. Sainsbury played a cover drive, something his square stance makes difficult. I was specially requested to mention this by the Hampshire secretary, who is considering putting up a plaque to mark the occasion, always assuming he can find a stand to put the plaque on. Sainsbury's part in the hour after lunch, when

100 runs really took Hampshire away, was important. Jesty needed more luck but banged cheerfully around. When the 85th over started, 12 runs were needed for the eighth batting point, and Stephenson and O'Sullivan got them amid much excitement. They subsequently took their partnership to 50. When the innings ended, at tea, Hampshire led by 202.

Meanwhile, what of Derbyshire? If not maidens all forlorn, they were certainly by the end cows with crumpled horns. They had a pitch to bowl on which was easier than it had been the day before, but still gave the spin bowlers some turn. They were without Harvey-Walker, who strained his back at fielding practice. This may not have made much difference to the quality of their bowling, but is always disheartening for a side.

Swindell was the steadiest bowler. He took six wickets for the second time in his career. It is good to see him taking his chances, despite Derbyshire's acquisition of Venkataraghavan. A number of chances went down, mostly awkward. The ground fielding was often untidy. On the other hand, throughout the long innings there were some excellent pieces of fielding, to which everyone contributed. Derbyshire did not wilt. Bolus and Taylor held them together. It was just not their day.

Nor did it grow any better when they batted. Borrington made a bold start, but he and Page were both out in the tenth over, bowled by Mottram. Hill and Miller clung to the crease. Forty overs were bowled while 55 runs were scored, although Gilliat set attacking fields.

Derbyshire will have a job to save the game. I expect O'Sullivan will take some playing today. "The best day's cricket I've ever seen," declared a gentleman who looked as if he had spent his life at sea. I would not go so far as that, but it was certainly a day to make any Hampshireman joyful.

Hampshire draw away as main challengers falter

PORTSMOUTH: Hampshire (21 pts) beat Derbyshire (3 pts) by 10 wickets

Derbyshire put up a stout rearguard action, but never quite looked like saving the match, and by a quarter to four the admirals were all standing by to reckon up their batting points and bragging about their cruisers like leviathans. It is too soon to be sure that Hampshire will be the leviathans this season, but this admirable win, at a time when their principal challengers were failing strongly improves their chances.

It was fine enough yesterday. The pitch gave the spinners some help. It looks like a bridle-track, and I can understand why there have been complaints about it, but the ball only turned slowly. I still felt that Hampshire ought to have won earlier, if they are really a championship side. O'Sullivan was uncertain in length and line, and sometimes turned the ball too much which, to be sure, is a good fault. Sainsbury, who spins less, but retains the sovereign bowling virtues, was much the better bowler on the day.

I understand that Hampshire have some anxiety about whether to keep O'Sullivan on their staff, or take on a fast bowler from Antigua. (They have to choose, because their quota of overseas registrations is full.) I have never seen the fast bowler, and would not presume to judge the question, but I would be sorry to see a spinner of such potential depart from the county scene.

Hill was soon caught at slip. There was a stand between Bolus and Miller. Bolus bore every mark of a man determined to be there at six o'clock. Had there been no tea interval, he would have left instructions that he was to be sent out a cup of tea at four, as Arthur Shrewsbury is said to have done. Miller played more venturesomely. He drove into the open spaces, especially on the leg side. He had been promoted to No 4 because of Harvey-Walker's back injury, and took his chance bravely, making his highest score in first-class cricket. But he hit the ball in the air a lot, and it was not really surprising when he was caught in the deep covers.

That was 138 for four, and Buxton was caught at the wicket in the first over after lunch: 159 for five. In came Harvey-Walker, a tall man clearly labouring a bit, like a sailing ship trying to wear about on a lee shore. He had a runner. They both did quite well, and there was just a hint of Hampshire nails being bitten until, at three o'clock, Bolus suddenly tried to strike Sainsbury straight over the rugby stand. He was marvellously caught by Greenidge, running a long way from mid-on.

That was the turning point. The rest of the Derbyshire side trooped politely in and out. There was another good catch by Greenidge, this time in the gully. Hampshire needed to bat for only one ball in their second innings.

DERBYSHIRE 176 (Page 65, O'Sullivan 4-60, Herman 3-23) & 203 (Miller 71, Bolus 50, Sainsbury 5-41)
HAMPSHIRE 378 (Gilliat 103, Sainsbury 45, Jesty 45, Turner 44, Stephenson 40*, Swindell 6-97) & 4 for no wicket

AUGUST: Surrey v Northamptonshire at Guildford 1973

Sense of anti-climax in a pallid day at Guildford

GUILDFORD: Surrey have scored 225 for six against Northamptonshire

It was rather a pallid day of cricket. This was chiefly, I suppose, because of a sense of anticlimax. Although the second place in the championship may depend upon this match, that is not quite a full inspiration to players whose thoughts have been set for weeks on a higher prize. Also, the weather was dismal, the air sour with the suburban smells of late August, which the rain (although it three times interrupted play) did not dispel.

There was, I must record, an attractive waitress in the refreshment tent, whose days are clearly spent in a battle between her conscience and her waistline. "It's the doughnuts that do it, Mrs Brown," I heard her say as she (sometimes) resisted temptation.

Edrich and Edwards scored 45 in 55 minutes in Surrey's opening partnership, and were both out at the same score, Edwards well taken by a running catch at point, Edrich leg before wicket. Younis and Roope put on 98 for the third wicket in 105 minutes. This was the nearest Surrey came to taking command.

...

I hoped for some liveliness when Jackman came in as early as No 7. He justified this optimism, but it took him a bit of time. For a while he batted as if overcome by his responsibilities, less like a Shoreditch sparrow than a pigeon newly promoted to Trafalgar Square. With assistance from Long, he led Surrey to their third point, in the 84th over. Shortly after 6 o'clock bad light stopped play. It had been, if Mrs Brown will forgive me, a doughnut of a day. But there was a suggestion in the evening that the clouds were lifting and moving, so let us hope that today is more of a soufflé. These are two good sides, and should be playing an entertaining match.

Howard Marshall

Had Howard Marshall, the radio commentator, died in 1938 instead of a few days ago there would have been a headline about him on the main page of every newspaper. At that time he was just about the best known voice in England. Where now does he rank among radio performers? Was he better than the best postwar cricket commentator, John Arlott? That is like asking whether Grace was better than Bradman. The conditions were so different that comparison is not valid. By any standard he must have been very good. He was also a useful player, and a more than useful rugby player. He won a rugby blue at Oxford, and wrote a history of the university rugby match, a fine book which somebody ought to bring up to date. He left broadcasting for other things fairly early in life, though he would sometimes return for a great occasion, such as the Coronation in 1953.

I remember a characteristic phrase from one of his postwar rugby commentaries. A Welshman had scored a try in an international, and Howard, after giving it a full and powerful description, added as the cheers died – "A Cardiff policeman I believe he is – and what a fine policeman he must be." This kind of background detail most of us would trot out to fill in a gap, irrespective of what was going on at the time: Howard Marshall would save such information in his mind until the moment came when it could be effectively used. John Arlott shares this gift with him, and perhaps one or two others, but not many.

I have been broadcasting and writing about cricket and rugby (among other things) for quite a long time, watching some famous occasions (Somerset v the Australians at Taunton in 1948 was the first) and many humdrum ones. I find, as I think most reporters find, that as time goes by it matters less and less who wins. Does England narrowly beat New Zealand in a remarkable match at Trent Bridge? I go to bed unconcerned, except for the muddle I have made in describing the Boycott/Amiss run-out. Does Yorkshire (whence I come) or Gloucestershire (where I live) win a championship, either cricket or rugby? Very good: but I am not stirred as I was when young, invigorated by victory, desolated by defeat.

Probably the most miserable day of my life was in 1938 when Huddersfield Town lost the Cup Final to Preston North End, by a penalty in the last minute of extra time. The referee's name (I have not looked this up, but I bet you) was Jimmy Jewell, and the unhappy man against whom the penalty was given was Alf Young, the Huddersfield captain and centre-half. I listened to the game on the radio. Tommy Woodroffe was the commentator. "If anyone scores a goal in this match," he had just said, "I'll eat my hat." And then, when Mutch was about to take the penalty, and the Huddersfield goalkeeper Hesford, was crouching there on his line: "I wouldn't be in his shoes for all the tea in China." After the goal, I ran from the sitting-room, where I had been listening, to the kitchen, where mother was preparing the tea. Tears of sorrow and wrath streamed down my face. "Alan," said mother very sharply, "what do you think you are doing – crying about a football match at your age?"

But only a few months later came what was probably the happiest day of my life, when Hutton, at the Oval, broke Bradman's record for the highest score in matches between England and Australia, and England declared at 903 for seven. There was some talk about slow batting. What did I care if England batted until Christmas, so long as they were grinding the Australians into the dust? As late as 1948, when Hutton was dropped from the England side and I a grown man, I wrote indignant letters to P.F. Warner and E.W. Swanton, the two men who instinctively I felt were to be blamed.

But then I began to be a reporter. Of all these sacred and profane passions nothing survives.

Whither is fled the visionary gleam?
Where is it now, the glory and the dream?

Well, almost nothing: there is just a twitch occasionally when Yorkshire win unexpectedly, and a general inclination to see the less favoured party succeed. There is also the university rugby match at Twickenham, when once a year the old atavism takes over.

When Howard Marshall began broadcasting about cricket, the commentator was "on his own". Perhaps there might be a producer with him, but quite likely not. A staff man, as Howard was, was usually expected to be his own producer. He had no colleague to relieve him for a spell, no expert summarizer to come in at the end of the over, no scorer. If the innings of a side ended while he was on the air, he could not give the bowling analysis, unless one of the engineers helpfully went to the scorebox to fetch it.

These conditions were just tolerable if there were no more than a few short broadcasts scattered throughout the day, but it soon became obvious that the listening public had an appetite for cricket, and objected strongly if they were whipped away from a Test match to chamber music at a critical moment. BBC schedules were more flexible in those days, and gradually Howard Marshall found himself doing more and more, several hours in a day, and still all by himself. The climax came in the Lord's Test of 1934. On the third day, Verity took 14 wickets, and England won by an innings. It was a day of tension: in the morning, Australia were struggling to save the follow-on, which they narrowly failed to do. The question was then whether England could bowl them out again before the close, because although there was a fourth day there was much rain about (hence Verity's performance), and England, one down in the rubber, had to be sure of winning. For hour after hour Howard went on, with hurried intermissions. "The engineers were very helpful," he said later. "They were always ready to fetch me a glass of beer or a cup of tea, or get the bowling figures from the scorers. They couldn't widdle for me, though."

So for the third test match at Old Trafford it was decided that Howard should have some assistance. There was a young man around Old Trafford at that time who had ambitions as a leg-break bowler and some knowledge of accountancy. He was the late Arthur Wrigley (upon whose account of these events I rely), and he was asked if he would score for Howard and otherwise act as general factotum, which he was very pleased to do for a pound a day. Arthur, as he would sorrowfully explain, could no more widdle for Howard than the engineers could, but he made sure that there was always someone at the end of the line when London called up, always an accurate and up-to-date score-sheet, always a helping hand. It was the combination of Howard Marshall and Arthur Wrigley which, even before the war, established the pattern of Test match commentary which has lasted ever since. Arthur soon found that the ordinary score-sheet was inadequate for his needs, and devised his own; that was the beginning of the modern system of scoring, Webber, Price, Rosenwater and Frindall, while all making their own special contributions to scoring techniques, had Wrigley's foundation on which to build.

Imagine though, the youthful Arthur (who had never scored before) and the harassed Howard at the Test match at Old Trafford in 1934. Compare it with a radio commentary box in a Test match today: bursting at the seams with commentators, summarizers, people who have just been interviewed, people who are just about to be interviewed, people who are hoping they might be interviewed, several producers, several producers' assistants, a couple of people from Radio Oswestry who have looked in to learn the job, and Bill Frindall, a host in himself. Tall oaks from little acorns grow.

Constant reporting of sport rubs the edge off a man's interest. I do not know but I believe that this was one reason why Howard Marshall left the sporting scene so soon. He was getting a little bored. He did not much care who won any more. And this is why, when he died, he had no headlines, but brief, though complimentary, notices in the obituary columns. That, too, is as he would have wished. It is a great man who can put fame behind him with a snap of the fingers.

A Season In Sinji by J.L. Carr

That Mr Carr is a writer of talent was recognised in the success of his second novel, *The Harpole Report. A Season In Sinji*, as he engagingly puts it himself, 'sank almost at once without trace.' I dive after it only to this extent, that nothing a good writer publishes is negligible, and that I would have enjoyed it if he had left out the cricket.

He forces his analogies, he strains his language, to show that life is just a game of cricket, which is neither more nor less true than that life is just a bowl of cherries, some of them going bad, or a sack of potatoes, or – well, whatever analogy comes to you.

Mr Carr is very strong on breasts and lavatories, which I suppose is mandatory in the modern novel. Just as I was beginning to get interested in the bosoms, there was a piece about cricket; and just as I was beginning to get interested in the cricket, back came the bosoms, and the dirt, and the violence. No doubt life is like that: but since we all have to experience it anyway, I doubt if we have any *obligation* to read about it as well.

The Hand That Bowled Bradman by Bill Andrews

What are the sporting books in the past year which deserve comment? The first that springs to the eye is *The Hand That Bowled Bradman*, by Bill Andrews, of Somerset and (well, nearly) England. I asked the editor of *The Cricketer* if I could review it: less, I think, for the fee (only very rich or very poor men write for *The Cricketer*) than because I wanted to give Andrews, from whom I have received many kindnesses, a leg up. For one way and another, he had been having rather a rough time. It was intended to be a sympathetic review, and it included this paragraph:

"Bill is an intensely genial, immensely kind, immensely voluble and immensely tactless man. The slight stammer from which he suffers, and of which he makes some play in his book, was surely a gift from an anxious guardian angel, a forlorn attempt to stop him from putting his foot in his mouth as soon as he opens it. He records, and frequently reminds us – with a mixture of injured innocence and delight – that he was sacked by Somerset four times, twice as player and twice as coach. There is no malice nor guile in him, though he is at times capable of a certain low cunning, of the kind which would not deceive an infant. Despite his ups and downs, he has far more friends than foes. Indeed, anyone who told me he did not like Bill would go down in my esteem – though someone who told me he had never been irritated by him would go down, too, for quite different reasons."

Well, that is what I wrote, and I find it hard to believe it did the sales any harm. A few weeks later, at the Weston Festival, I was in the commentary box and saw Andrews striding purposefully towards me. Eager for his meed of praise (for I held him in much awe as a boy), I hopped out of the box, hand outstretched. He shook it solemnly. "Did you, er, did you," I said bashfully, "happen to read the little piece I wrote in *The Cricketer*?" "Some liked it," said Andrews. "I'm told some liked it. Yes, some have told me that they liked it. I thought it b-bloody awful. It was the thing about being tactless that upset me."

Happy new year, Andrews (W.H.R.).

A Shropshire Lad by A.E. Housman

I am hard to pull away from poetry once I start, though not as bad as the philosopher Green (D.M., not T.H.). He is more of a menace than I, if only because he is bigger and stronger. "Earth hath not anything to show more fair," he will begin, casually clobbering some unpoetic comrade who has ventured no more than a gentle "Come on, Greenie, it's closing time." It is not so bad if it is a sonnet. It is when he starts on *Intimations of Immortality* that you know you are going to be in trouble with the landlord, and conceivably the landlord's wife. Ah well, happy new year, philosopher Green (D.M.).

The book of verse I enjoyed most in 1973, and for many years, was *A Shropshire Lad* by Housman (A.E.). I am not sure if I had ever read it straight through before. It is not, to be sure, exactly a sporting poem, but these lines are my justification for dragging it in:

> Twice a week the winter through
> Here stood I to keep the goal;
> Football then was fighting sorrow
> For the young man's soul.
>
> Now in Maytime to the wicket
> Out I march with bat and pad:
> See the son of grief at cricket,
> Trying to be glad.
>
> Try I will, no harm in trying,
> Wonder 'tis how little mirth
> Keeps the bones of man from lying
> On the bed of earth.

If we need an apologia for sport (there are times when I think we do) there it is: a little mirth, a little distraction in a drab scene. So a happy new year to you, too, wherever your bones are lying and your soul is flying, Housman (A.E.).

The best things first: Procter's hundred at Taunton, Close's hundred at Neath, Boycott's hundred against New Zealand at Headingley. Bedi's bowling anywhere. At a quick grab, those are the freshest recollections of the season. Procter's hundred at Taunton was, in terms of pure cricket, the best I have seen him make: it combined the classical and the casual. He was carefree in a lost cause, yet played – no, not flawlessly: for he deliberately flawed the innings occasionally, for instance tipping the ball through slips, like a poet risking a metrical lapse because he knows it will increase the ultimate effect. More than ever I did, I hope that Procter gives up bowling, except in emergencies and perhaps a fling at the start; that he bowls no more than Hammond bowled after his early years. Once he gives his batting full attention, I believe he will be recognised as the best batsman in English cricket and, for all I know, world cricket.

It was depressing, for a Yorkshireman, that Yorkshire only did well in the flimsiest of the competitions. I cannot help wondering whether Boycott will ever make a good captain. He does not seem able to capture and control the inward man. As a bit of a mental bungler myself, I can guess something of the strain. I see that *New Society* called Harvey Smith 'the Geoff Boycott of British riding'. If Boycott could win the battles with himself he would be a captain of more than Yorkshire, or England: the W.E. Henley of English cricket. In the meantime his head, while a touch bloody, is unbowed.

I have no doubt Yorkshire cricket will rise again, but it may take a little time. In the meantime, nothing would please me more than a Championship by Gloucestershire. I thought their captain, Tony Brown, was one of the outstanding cricketers of the season, not only for the Gillette Cup, nor even for his own performances, but for the way he has pulled the side together after a rather prolonged period of tetchiness. He has a varied bunch of players to handle, but has developed in character and technique, both on and off the field, while he has been mastering the job. Perhaps this success will give him the confidence, set free the imagination, the tactical flexibility, that is needed to win three-day matches. A drawback of one-day cricket which is commented on less than others (e.g. the handicaps to middle-order batsmen) is that, in captaincy, it encourages the negative virtues.

Whether Gloucestershire have the bowling to win the Championship, if Procter concentrates on batting, is doubtful – but that was what we all said about the Hampshire bowlers. However, towards the end of the season, Ken Graveney did say to me that he was beginning to think, for the first time, that his son David might turn out to be a better bowler than a bat.

I seem to have written a very parochial piece, but no doubt there will be plenty to take care of the others. One or two more stray memories: on a crowded train between Bristol and London, I was pleased but surprised to find myself adopted by one of the buffet attendants, who plied me with food and drink throughout my journey, when I never stirred a step from my seat. When I thanked him afterwards, he said, 'Always a pleasure for you, Mr Arlott.'

I greatly enjoyed the final of the *Church Times* Cricket Cup, played on the famous Walker ground at Southgate. The diocese of Gloucester beat the diocese of Liverpool by three wickets, and there were many palpitations before the match was over. Indeed, the representative of the BBC, next to whom I was sitting, knocked over his blackcurrant and lemon in the excitement. A popping sound as the players retired indicated that stronger stuff was at hand, and the Rural Dean of Northleach held the cup high and was numerously photographed: snaps which will be handed round at many a vicarage tea party. A happy day.

I was sent there to report by *The Times*, but not a word appeared in the paper. You might not think this matters much, but I had been warmly entertained by all the assembled clergy, and the following conversation took place, as nearly as I can remember:

AG: 'You remember it was always said that there were four things you could be sure of finding in an English vicarage: the Bible, the Prayer Book, a complete Shakespeare, and the current edition of *The Times*. Talking to all these parsons, I am perturbed to find that a lot of them don't take *The Times* at all!"

Bishop: 'Never mind, my dear fellow. You can be confident that every parson here will take *The Times* tomorrow.'

Crawling away from this debacle, I reached Lord's for the final of the Haig. This has been reported elsewhere, but allow me to say that it provided a fine example of Nemesis, the Goddess of Retribution, at work. Gowerton lost because they had to end their innings in very poor light. They ended their innings in very poor light because they had bowled their overs at such a dismal rate: 16 to the hour over 40 overs, and nine of them bowled by a slow left-hander who only walked four paces. This served them right. Mind you, the slow left-hander was a fine bowler. It was splendid to watch him, always on a length, though he is not very young, and his trousers seemed to hang some way above his ankles. His name was Thomas.

Thomas of Gowerton, the Rural Dean of Northleach, Brown of Gloucestershire, Procter of Gloucestershire, and the buffet car attendant would be my choice for the five cricketers of the year.

1974

Rarely can an English cricket season have been looked forward to more keenly than that of 1974. It had been a grim winter, of strikes, power cuts, snow, the oil crisis and the three-day week. Harold Wilson's Labour Party had won a General Election in February, but only by the narrowest of margins, promising more political instability to come. A drawn series in the Caribbean had helped to start to lift the gloom, but it was the arrival of the domestic season that, for a cricket-loving nation, would surely provide the longed-for relief from all the industrial unrest, political strife and economic uncertainty.

Great things were expected of the Indian tourists after their wins against England at home and away. But in the event, their batting proved brittle and their spinners much less of a threat than in 1971, especially in the Tests, where they were thoroughly mastered by the English batsmen, leading to three heavy defeats. They also had the worst of the weather, in what turned out to be an unsettled summer throughout. Their first eight matches were drawn, and most of them were badly affected by the weather. By the time they reached Northampton on May 23, disenchantment was setting in, and not just on the field of play. However, the Indians did give Alan his first sighting for the 1974 season of Robin Jackman, when they played (and beat) Surrey in early June, and the Shoreditch Sparrow did not disappoint.

A new system of points scoring was in place for the county championship, which Alan did his best to explain to his readers in his report on Middlesex v Hampshire, without attempting to conceal his exasperation at its complexities. But despite the machinations of the rule-makers, and the iffy weather, and the fact that he was working almost six days a week, he was at the very top of his game with his writing, bringing whimsy and wry humour to enliven otherwise dull and uneventful days. As when he arrived at Chesterfield on May 4, for the Benson and Hedges preliminary round match between Derbyshire and Yorkshire; or his report on the second day of Oxford University against Somerset on May 14, which gives such a delicious flavour of cricket in the Parks in May (and records how the great Brian Close was bowled by a future President of the Country Landowners' Association!); or his perfect pen portrait of Derek Randall in the field, from Middlesex v Notts on May 17.

After the excitements and triumphs of 1973, Gloucestershire were having a modest season, but Somerset were an improving side. Close led them with his characteristic mixture of cunning and belligerence and was hugely important in bringing on two outstanding young players who had joined Somerset that season: Vivian Richards, who was 22 and from Antigua, and Ian Botham, just 18, from Cheshire via Yeovil.

Not long afterwards, Alan was back on the Indian trail, for their match against Gloucestershire, at which he almost reverted to the running JJ? Davey joke that he had promised to abandon the previous summer. Quite what the 'unplanned' presentation involved, I am not now sure, but it no doubt involved at least one of those who would subsequently become pillars of the JJ?. Society.

Then, after all the high spirits, good humour and classic Gibson cricket reports, something happened. History does not record what it was; probably one of the furious rows that would erupt from time to time with his bosses at *The Times*, possibly over a last minute change in the reporting schedule. At any event, Alan was clearly in one of those bitter moods when he was determined to have his revenge and cause

Tests
England
beat India
3-0
England
drew with Pakistan
0-0, with three draws

Championship
1 Worcestershire
2 Hampshire
3 Northamptonshire
4 Leicestershire
5 Somerset
6 Middlesex

Sunday League
1 Leicestershire
2 Somerset
3 Kent
4 Northamptonshire
5 Hampshire
6 Sussex

Gillette Cup Final
Kent
beat Lancashire

Benson & Hedges Final
Surrey
beat Leicestershire

Most first-class runs
1 R.T. Virgin
2 J.A. Jameson
3 G. Boycott

Most first-class wickets
1 A.M.E. Roberts
2 B.S. Bedi
3 V.A. Holder

offence, and the more of it the better. That is the only explanation I can think of for the schoolboy offensiveness of the 'Scunthorpe' reference in his report of the Gillette Cup match between Middlesex and Lancashire at Lord's on July 10. The fact that he seems to have got into some sort of punch-up when trying to phone his copy through also suggests that he had been hitting the whisky.

What happened next I am not sure. He did receive a few letters, more in sorrow than anger, and no doubt a severe reprimand from *The Times*. Whatever was said, it had its effect. For the next several weeks, his writing entirely loses its humour and zest. It wasn't until July 31, when Somerset beat Surrey to reach their second one-day semi-final of the season, that the sparkle showed any signs of returning, and he remained relatively subdued for the rest of the season.

Meanwhile, the Pakistan tourists had arrived for their three-Test series. They were a talented, powerful side with both bat and ball, and they went through the tour unbeaten – the first tourists to do so since Bradman's Australians in 1948. Alan was in the BBC commentary box for the third and final Test of the series at the Oval, which, like the other two, ended in a draw. And, right at the season's end, it was Alan, rather than John Woodcock who was sent to the second of the two one-day internationals. His suggestion that this form of the game might not have much of a future was not to prove one of his more prophetic judgements!

So to the closing stages of the county championship, which had been dominated almost from the start by the reigning champions, Hampshire, now strengthened still further by the arrival from Antigua of the lightning fast Anderson Montgomery Everton Roberts. When Gilliatt's men thrashed their only serious rivals, Worcestershire, in two days on August 7 and 8 to establish a commanding lead, it looked all over bar the shouting, although Alan was careful to enter the caveat of unless "something very unexpected" were to happen.

And that, of course, was precisely what materialised. Hampshire threw away a winning position against Glamorgan, after Roberts had bowled them out for just 90 in their first innings, reaching his 100 wickets for the season in the process, and their last four days of the season were entirely washed out, leaving Worcestershire the winners almost by default, by a margin of just two points. Alan was at Bournemouth for what had seemed likely to be Hampshire's decisive victory, over Somerset, but the champagne would indeed remain unopened.

As if that wasn't cruel enough, a similar fate would befall Somerset, when they were on the very brink of finally winning something. Having lost two one-day semi-finals – to Leicestershire in the B&H and Kent in the Gillette – they now needed to beat Leicestershire in the final match of the John Player League to overtake them at the top. With Leicestershire making only 162 in their 40 overs, Somerset seemed to have every chance. But then the heavens opened, washing out the Somerset innings and washing away their hopes.

So 1974 ended on a disappointing note in several different respects, although by the time Alan came to look back for *The Cricketer*, the season was beginning to take on at least something of the rosy glow in retrospect that it had once had in prospect.

The new points system

LORD'S: Middlesex v Hampshire

Middlesex took eight points on the first innings to Hampshire's three. There is a new system for these first innings points, or bonus points as they are colloquially called. Four points are obtainable for batting, and four for bowling, over a span of 100 overs. The batting side gets a point for 150 runs, and another for every 50 runs thereafter. The bowling side gets a point for taking three wickets, and another for every two wickets thereafter. The first innings of each side is limited to 100 overs, though the side batting second may take up any spare overs if they have bowled their opponents out in less. The stupefyingly tedious and complicated nature of these changes, just as we were beginning to get to grips with the last lot, needs no emphasis from me.

We have, however, been given an extra half-hour's play on the first two days of championship games, in order to have sufficient time to work them out. I presume this is the reason for the extra half-hours, for I can see no other.

Woods and jacks

NORTHAMPTON: Northamptonshire v the Indians

There took place recently an important bowls match. It was on one of the crown greens of the north (by far the best form of bowls) and much money depended on the result. The last few critical woods seemed to be equidistant from the jack. Handkerchiefs, pieces of string, tape measures could not settle which was the nearest. Finally the contestants decided they must have an independent opinion, and called in a passer-by. The passer-by explained he knew nothing of bowls, but was assured that was of no importance: "Just tell us what tha' think, lad." He consulted the crucial cluster, and a light seemed to dawn. "Well, for a start," he said, "that little booger's got no chance", and kicked the jack away.

I tell you the story, first, because I heard it from Jack Mercer, the old Glamorgan player, who now scores for Northamptonshire and whose gifts as a raconteur are not always sufficiently credited; secondly, because that was the only really entertaining thing that happened to me all day; and thirdly, because this match has so far been very much a contest between the woods and the jacks, the big ones and the little ones. On Wednesday it was tiny Viswanath who led the Indians to a good score; yesterday it was the burly Willey who kept Northamptonshire in the game.

Queen's Park, Chesterfield

CHESTERFIELD: Derbyshire v Yorkshire (Sunday League)

The Queen's Park ground was like Andrew Marvell's coy mistress, "beautiful but cold". A little man marched enthusiastically round, crying out "Smartly drawn at teatime, smartly drawn at teatime." I wondered if he was an itinerant dentist, but he turned out to be selling raffle tickets.

Running between the wickets

CHESTERFIELD: Derbyshire v Yorkshire

Bolus knows a thing or two about setting a field for Boycott, but even his dispositions could not prevent the constant shrewd push to the gap for one, the occasional irresistible thrust for four.

We had a glimpse, however, of the flawed Achilles, when Yorkshire had scored 47. Boycott played a ball backward of square, on the leg side. Lumb called for a run, was sent back and had no chance of getting home. Under a normal system of calling Lumb was in the right, but, of course, Yorkshire's has not been a normal system for a long time, and it cannot be denied that if a wicket is at risk Boycott is worth a Lumb or two. Indeed, as subsequent events demonstrated, he is still worth nearly all the rest of the Yorkshire batsmen put together.

More running between the wickets

LORD'S: Middlesex v Nottinghamshire

Once Sobers had gone, the batsman who looked likeliest to play an innings was Bond. When he had scored eight, however, he struck a ball sharply towards mid-on, called and ran.

He ran down the pitch, past Latchman, who at the other end had not moved, and straight on towards the pavilion. I think it was a good run, and in any case Latchman should have had the wit to take a step outside his crease and surrender his own, the weaker, wicket. Bond turned round on his way back, and endeavoured to give a forbearing Methodist grin, but it was the kind of grimace with which John Wesley must have greeted a drunken tinker at five on a winter's morning.

There was another run-out soon afterwards, an entertaining one. Latchman was less to blame than Wilkinson, the sufferer; but the pair of them looked as if they were auditioning for "Dad's Army", or, of course, Yorkshire.

MAY: Oxford University v Somerset at The Parks (third day) 1974

Crowd pleasing frolic came too late

OXFORD: Oxford University drew with Somerset

At last it was good cricket weather, and there is nowhere I would rather have been than sitting in the sunshine in the Parks. This view was shared by quite a large number of others – well, large by current standards, perhaps a thousand drifted in and out during the day (you do not have to pay for admission to the Parks, though nowadays they make a small charge for a seat.) Many of them seemed to be American sociologists broadening their knowledge of the English scene or professors of philosophy. From a cricketing point of view, the philosophers had the best of it nearly all day: to watch the university's performance required a touch of stoicism.

Oxford resumed their first innings at 43 for four, and declared after 55 minutes at 84 for eight. Somerset scored 105 for one at a run a minute, and in turn declared at lunch.

The Oxford bowling was not too bad. Fursdon found a good one to bowl Close. The fielding was tidy, if lacking the bite one looks for in a good university side. It was the batting in the afternoon which was so depressing. Nobody looked a player of quality, or even imagination, except Imran Khan, and even he was not timing his strokes very well.

Parks, who was captaining Somerset after an injury to Close, gave the batsmen an assortment of bowling to try their hands on, but the batsmen grew more and more cautious and perplexed. Hardly a half volley was hit. Every grass snake was seen as a viper. The correspondent of *The Guardian* assured me that he would have hit numerous boundaries in the circumstances and I entirely believed him.

At one time it looked as if Oxford might be bowled out, but they struggled slowly to 90 for eight, and then, just before half past five, Imran declared for a second time. This left Somerset to score 70 in eight overs. They entered into the spirit of the thing, but apart from a few minutes when Denning was banging the ball in all directions, did not look like doing it, and ended at 50 for five. Oxford held some good catches in the deep, and their bowlers will have been glad to take a few wickets.

But Imran's chief intention in this frolic presumably was to please the crowd, which he undeniably did. Certainly it was good fun. But I, and I suspect the professors of philosophy, would have enjoyed it more if this spirit of bold gaiety had been evident somewhat earlier in the proceedings.

Gilbert Jessop

English cricket has had bigger hitters than Jessop. English cricket has had batsmen who scored more runs with a higher average. But there has never been an English batsman who hit so hard, and scored so fast, and yet still scored runs so consistently. In his career, which lasted from 1894 to 1914, Jessop scored 26,698 runs, at an average of 32.63, and if one believes all one hears – those in Gloucestershire who remember never tire of talking about him – hardly played a defensive stroke.

I felt I glimpsed a little of G.L. Jessop once, when I saw his son, the Rev G.L.O. Jessop, score a fast 80 or so for Dorset against Cornwall at Camborne. G.L.O. Jessop was then middle-aged himself, but a beautiful striker of the ball. He used the sweep a lot, as his father is said to have done, sometimes in the most daring circumstances, but he also had a splendid straight drive back over the bowler's head.

...

He was nicknamed "The Croucher". He bent low at the wicket, and sometimes would stoop down so far that his cap was on the level of the bails. He said that this helped him to judge the length of a ball early. It must have added significantly to the psychological and dramatic effects of his sudden spring, his pounce, his leap at the ball. But in later life, at least, he disliked the name.

About 1948, when I was a junior producer on the staff of the BBC, I was sent a capital script about Jessop, by Harold Gardiner, called "The Croucher". We put the programme into production, and billed it in the *Radio Times*. As a matter of courtesy, we sent a script to Jessop, though, as it was an almost entirely laudatory script, we hardly thought he would complain. But he did. He complained most sharply, particularly about the title: indeed, it took all the tact of Frank Gillard to calm him down, and the programme was postponed, to be broadcast at a later date under the less inflammatory title of "G.L. Jessop".

Well, most old men have cantankerous moments, but this incident has always baffled me. Did he resent the nickname because it was put upon him by the press? He did a good deal of journalism himself at one time and another. Did he resent it because the Gloucestershire public relished it? Amateurs in those days were inclined to disregard public esteem, but he must have been proud of the affection in which Gloucestershire held him (he was born and brought up at Cheltenham), and it is as "The Croucher" – the great cat about to jump – that he is still happily and proudly remembered.

Peter Denning
'He comes from Chewton Mendip, which has the best ring o' bells
in Somerset, unless you count the pub at Priston'

Brian Close in the West

BRISTOL: Gloucestershire v Somerset (Sunday League)

Somerset's innings built itself round a century by Close, his first in this competition. He had been out first ball in the championship match between these sides on Saturday, and took the opportunity to revenge himself. Somerset versus Gloucestershire is a bucolic version of Lancashire versus Yorkshire, and with the crowd, and the passion, it seemed that forgotten far-off things and battles long ago stirred the nostrils of the old warhorse. His strokes were a fair mixture of the classical and the baroque. That famous sweep, about which foes and friends have always had such varied feeling, was going well. Ultimately it got Close out, but by then he had scored 128, and Somerset were 223 for two in the 35th over.

Peter Denning on a Sunday

YEOVIL: Somerset v Kent (Sunday League)

The Somerset innings depended largely on Denning. He middled the ball remarkably surely, considering that he was nearly always hitting across the line. This is not a condemnation of his play. Hitting across the line is a useful and recognized way of getting runs on Sundays, especially for a left-hander.

I felt a little sad, because Denning, when he first came into county cricket, was a pleasing player with a notably correct method. Well, that is part of the price of the enterprise, and the size of the crowd quelled misgivings. This is not the kind of cricket to produce Test batsmen, but, on the other hand, there was more enthusiasm yesterday than I have often seen at Test matches.

Shepherd and Dunston

BRISTOL: Gloucestershire v Somerset

Gloucestershire ultimately managed a first innings lead of 22, batting to the one hundred and fifth over. For this they had largely (I think that would be the word) to thank Shepherd. A year or two ago Shepherd, by request, slimmed himself a bit, though it did not seem to improve his play much. The comforting folds are reappearing round his middle, but his brawny forearms still give the ball a fierce punch, and his equable ruddy Bideford face still confronts any situation with serenity.

Old Gloucestershire hands compare him with Dipper, a beloved, high-scoring, though not always agile, figure in the county's gallery, and Shepherd, in due time, will also have his niche. In spite of Gloucestershire's fragile situation, he let his bat go at the ball whenever he saw a fair chance. He reached his 50 with two bold, lofted boundaries in the same over from Moseley, and also gave some punishment to Jones, who was Somerset's most dangerous bowler. He reached his 100, scored out of 170 while he was in, when the total was 250, in the ninety-first over. He was leg-before to Richards, tempted unduly by an outfield invitingly left open.

Of the other Gloucestershire batsmen, Zaheer played some attractive strokes, and Dunstan, a young man from Redruth, worked hard for his 19. With Shepherd from Devon and Dunstan from Cornwall, it was a good day for the West Country. The West Country, I should explain, does not begin until you reach Taunton. This may surprise some Londoners, but is a good deal more logical than their own view, that civilization ends at the Marble Arch.

Jack Davey

GLOUCESTER: Gloucestershire v the Indians

The sponsors gave an award to the outstanding player of each side. Bedi, with nine wickets, none of them lower than No 8 in the order, did not have much competition. Stovold was given the Gloucestershire award. He scored well in both innings, and kept wicket capably on the whole, even though he faltered on the last morning. An additional, unplanned award was made to Davey. It was not that he took many wickets or saved many runs in the field, but he did score 37 not out in the first innings, and seven in the second, giving him a match average of 44. His three previous highest scores in first class cricket had been 17, 17 and 17 not out. The Gloucester crowd much appreciated this generous gesture to Tavistock-born, 29-year-old, left-hander, jovial Jessopian Jack.

Bob Clapp

TAUNTON: Somerset v Essex (Sunday League)

After 16 overs Clapp came on. This young schoolmaster, mostly a one-day player, needed only three more wickets to break the John Player record. He labours to the wicket as if he had learnt his trade on the sands of his native Weston-super-Mare, and for that matter he frequently looks as if he has rolled in them, but he is a useful medium-pacer.

Some sightings of the Shoreditch Sparrow

THE OVAL: Surrey v the Indians

It was the first time this season that I had seen Surrey, and I am pleased to report to regular readers that the Shoreditch sparrow, R.D. Jackman, is in chirpy form. Perhaps there is an inch or two more around his waist, but he still dashes about, waves his arms furiously, appeals loudly, scratches himself, occasionally delivers the ball backwards by mistake, and bends himself into knots to examine the soles of his boots, with as much zest as ever.

Suzanne Lenglen, I understand, used to examine her soles by flicking her leg backwards and resting her foot on her shoulder, and I hope to see Jackman emulate this one day. His bowling was full of life, and he earned his wickets.

...

Engineer went in with Naik, and scored all the first 21 runs, and by hitting the last ball to the boundary, took his own score to 32. Naik, when the score was 15 and he still on a stately nought, played and missed (I presume) at a ball from Jackman. The Shoreditch Sparrow jumped about two feet in the air when appealing and about a foot higher when it dawned upon him his appeal had not been granted.

"No sparrow he, for by his squawk
You'd take him for a sparrow hawk."

CHESTERFIELD: Derbyshire v Surrey

The morning was commandingly, but, as it turned out, delusively attractive, like a fairy woman of the Hebrides or a call by Boycott. Where better could one be, I thought, as I contemplated the pretty Chesterfield ground in the beaming sunshine? (How foolish I was not to take off my pullover.) ... When tea time came, however, the sun had vanished, a bitter wind was blowing, and it was raining. (Foolish I was not to have brought my overcoat.)

...

It was Jackman who did most work, with most reward. He took five wickets. He might, from the number of times he beat the bat, have taken 10, and from the number of times he clutched his head, 50. Of all current bowlers, Jackman most reminds me of the comment made of Maurice Tate, that he expected to take a wicket with every ball.

Throat infection

LEICESTER: Leicestershire v the Pakistanis

The Pakistanis were without Asif Masood, who had gone to London to have a throat infection treated. After the number of no balls by Asif which had to be called on the first evening, I would have thought it was George Pope who was the likelier to be suffering from a throat infection.

Sunday in Sunbury

SUNBURY-ON-THAMES: Surrey v Leicestershire

It was at Sunbury that Jerome K. Jerome, in the course of that famous journey up the river, rowed furiously up a backwater for five minutes, and looked up to see that he was under the same bridge from which he had started, much to the delight of the same colleagues who were steering for him. The Sunbury ground is near the river, though I was not able to identify the backwater; a small but pretty ground, despite an afternoon that was mostly cloudy and chilly.

...

Although the match was only won from the fourth ball of the last over, no other result had been likely for some time. It was an efficient all-round performance by Leicestershire, but I suppose that when they heard Kent had also won, they felt much as Jerome did when he looked up and saw that damned bridge still overhead.

Derek Randall

LORD'S: Middlesex v Nottinghamshire

Randall's fielding once again was outstanding. He does not *look* like a fielder. He seems to mooch about lopsidedly, his arms, which are rather too long for his body, hanging by his sides. Certainly his feet are always skipping, yet he does not produce an effect of athletic coordination. But just give him a smell of the ball, and you see the tiger.

Sent to Lord's

LORD'S: Middlesex v Lancashire (Gillette Cup)

First, I was going to Scunthorpe, where I have never been, and I looked forward to an enlivening experience, because anyone who served in the Army will tell you what you can be sure of finding in Scunthorpe. Then, because of a change of venue, I was going to Lincoln, and I have never seen the cathedral since I was a boy, so that was an interesting prospect too. But the Test match ended a day early, and schedules were changed, and I ended up at Lord's, happy enough to be there, except that it was raining earnestly.

...

At ten past six, it became too dark for play, and soon afterwards it started raining again. To add to the joys of the evening, I was assaulted in a telephone booth by a couple of drunken Australian yobs, one of them wearing an MCC tie. These little things are sent to try us.

Robin Jackman
'The Shoreditch Sparrow'

Balderstone's six with last hit keeps up Leicestershire's hopes

LEICESTER: Leicestershire (4 pts.) beat Yorkshire by four wickets

A six by Balderstone, from the last ball of the match (when four were needed for victory) kept Leicestershire riding high in the John Player League. The depth of their batting, the experience of their bowling, and their better ground fielding at moments of pressure, made them just too strong for a Yorkshire side who nevertheless played pluckily.

It was Birkenshaw's benefit match, and the day did not have an auspicious start for him. It rained heavily in the morning, and there was a smaller crowd than usual at Leicester on Sundays when play began. Furthermore, he was left out of the side. This has happened before – I mean, not Birkenshaw being left out of the side, an occurrence which he philosophically accepts, but a player being left out of his benefit match. But I cannot think it has happened before to a man currently of England standard, who had done such a lot for his county. It does not perhaps matter so much as it would in a three-day match, but I still thought it a shame.

However, Birkenshaw himself is not a man to complain. In the afternoon I happened to meet him; he was as polite, as pink and as ginger as ever. The weather had cleared and the crowd was improving – there must have been 4,000 by teatime. He was not cast down. I remember a story, which I hope I may use, told to me by Tony Lewis, England's captain in India. On the early part of that tour, Birkenshaw was not in the Test side, and had to do a lot of practice bowling. They moved to a new centre, sleeping under mosquito nets for the first time. Birkenshaw at breakfast addresses himself to Lewis: "Ee, skipper, tha's had me in nets all day and now tha' has me in nets all bluddy neet."

A lot of Yorkshiremen had come down to Leicester yesterday to give Birkenshaw a cheer, because, of course, he originally played for Yorkshire. He has always been, on and off the field, the best kind of county cricketer, and I hope his benefit (the fund is still open) is a great success.

Well, now, as to the match. It was like most other Sunday matches, often invigorating but infrequently classical. Yorkshire scored 187, losing their last wicket, run-out, to the last possible ball. Boycott and Hampshire gave them a fine start, Hampshire doing most of the striking. He was caught and bowled by Steele for 46 out of 81, off the first ball of the twentieth over. Boycott now took up the main running. Bairstow came in as number three and made several effective slogs.

After 30 overs Yorkshire were 144 for one, but in the next over, from McVicker, Bairstow was caught at long-off and Boycott bowled. After that the innings was a scramble. There was a vast cheer when Bill Alley confirmed an appeal by a Leicestershire bowler. He teased the crowd, waiting until the usual groan had begun, before suddenly putting up his finger.

The pitch was playing quite well, more truly than several Leicester pitches this summer, and with Leicestershire in such triumphant Sunday form I doubted if Yorkshire had scored enough.

After 20 overs Leicestershire were 77, Steele out, but Dudleston going well. The 100 came up in the twenty-fifth over, Dudleston out but the dreaded Davison established. Tolchard was caught at deep point, 102 for three. Yorkshire still had a chance if they could get Davison out, but this did not look likely to happen. With 10 overs left, Leicestershire needed 55. Then in the thirty-third over, at 142, Oldham bowled Davison. Yorkshiremen cheered as though the match was won (apart from that not inconsiderable portion who are on the Leicester staff). But there were still wickets in hand and good batsmen to use them.

Although the Leicestershire rate dragged perilously for a time, Balderstone, of Huddersfield, and Illingworth, of Pudsey, pulled them through with typical Midland grit. The crowd must have been more than 5,000 by the end, all day excited, and I daresay Birkenshaw of Rothwell, in his quiet way, was pleased too.

YORKSHIRE	187 (40 overs, Boycott 75, Hampshire 46, McVicker 2-25, Spencer 2-26)
LEICESTERSHIRE	190 for six (40 overs, Dudleston 56, Balderstone 42*, Davison 31, Oldham 2-31, Robinson 2-37)

Everybody burst out singing after Denning hit his six

TAUNTON: Somerset beat Surrey by five wickets

Somerset pulled off an exciting Gillette Cup quarter-final match at Taunton yesterday. Parks, formerly of Sussex, made the winning hit with 10 balls to spare, but it was a young man of true Somerset soil who emerged as the hero of the hour. He was Peter Denning, born at Chewton Mendip and schooled at Millfield – and you cannot get much more Somerset than that. Denning scored a century in 160 minutes and was everyone's choice as man of the match.

Close put Surrey in. It was a plumb pitch, a good three-day pitch, and it did not seem a rational move, but sudden inspirations have served him well before. Surrey, however, scored 254 for seven in their 60 overs. The highest score hitherto made by a winning side batting second in the Gillette Cup was 252, by Surrey themselves, at the Oval against Middlesex in 1965. So Somerset had to break that record if they were to win. I would have dismissed their chances had they been anyone but Somerset.

All nine Surrey men who batted reached double figures. Edrich and Younis both scored 50. If one man could have gone on to 100, or getting on for it, Somerset would have had no chance whatsoever. But nobody did, and for this some credit must go to persevering Somerset out-cricket.

Skinner was first out, at 66 in the nineteenth over. Howarth was run out at 109 in the twenty-fourth. Edrich was out at 140 in the forty-first. Surrey needed to press on, and did, but Roope was caught at midwicket in the forty-eighth. It was Younis and Storey, with some help from the lower order, who took Surrey to a commanding position. Younis scored his 53 in 55 balls.

There was a large crowd, perhaps 10,000, certainly too big for the ground. The gates were closed at 11 o'clock, and then opened again at the instance of the enthusiastic Somerset chairman. Few of the latecomers can have seen much, and none of them had seats, but nobody seemed to mind. Five thousand scorecards were sold, every one printed immaculately and up to the minute, as they always are in Somerset – and hardly anywhere else, with respect to Northampton.

Harold Gimblett told me that it was the largest crowd he had seen at Taunton since the Indians played here in 1946. I remember that match. I was travelling down to the west, from Oxford, and stopped to watch for an hour or two in the afternoon, on painful tiptoe. Somerset were going very slowly, I thought. At 3 o'clock Gimblett and Lee, the opening pair, had put on hardly 50. I think it was only the next day that I discovered that the Indians had already been bowled out for 69.

Well, the great crowd yesterday hung and throbbed upon every Somerset stroke. Kitchen, a key batsman, was out at 24. Tea was taken at 5.10, after 25 overs. Denning and Taylor, who is not really supposed to be a fast-scoring batsman, were going pretty well, but there was a long way to go.

Taylor was leg-before to Jackman soon after tea. Richards, on whom it seemed much depended, made 15 impressively, and then was run out off a no-ball, going for a single, an absurdity. At 156, in the forty-second over, Jackman bowled Close.

The light was becoming poor, and rain was falling, fitfully at first but then more steadily until the line of the Quantocks was blotted out. The umpires were frequently consulted. The weather improved, but the wet ball handicapped Surrey. Nevertheless, they seemed to share the general view that it might be as well to get the pain and the passion over.

With 15 overs left, Somerset needed 80, and Denning was playing so well that they were still hunting. Denning is a fair-haired, left-handed young man from Chewton Mendip, who is having his best season so far. The 200 came up in the fifty-first over. Denning reached his own 100 with a boundary in the fifty-fifth over, and then hit a six: never have I heard such cheering on the Taunton ground. In five overs, Somerset needed 25 runs.

The crowd, especially the cider lads, were singing an assortment of songs, hysterical and rude. The correspondent of *The Guardian* was so moved that he offered me a second glass of white wine. Parks was beginning to smack the ball away. Surrey began to look anxious. What, they seemed to be saying to one another, had gone wrong? At 241, in the fifty-seventh over, Denning lifted one too many, and was caught at midwicket. Denning and Parks put on 82 runs in 15 overs.

It was not now too difficult for Somerset: 11 runs required in three overs, six in two, and wickets in hand. A boundary by Parks in the fifty-ninth over gave them a gloriously improbable win. I do not envy any side who may be drawn at Taunton in the semi-final round.

SURREY	254 for seven (60 overs, Edrich 59, Younis Ahmed 53, Storey 33, Skinner 32, Moseley 4-31)
SOMERSET	257 for five (58.2 overs, Denning 112, Parks 42*, Taylor 36, Jackman 2-50)

Close throws his spanner into Hampshire's works

BOURNEMOUTH: Hampshire, with seven first innings wickets in hand, are 163 runs behind Somerset

After a stay in the beautiful village of Longparish with my colleague John Woodcock, the sage and (I have now discovered) the ecclesiastical patron of the place, I am feeling well disposed towards Hampshire. Yesterday, however, for most of the day they made only moderate progress toward their third championship, though I dare say they will still win this match.

Somerset won the toss, and after some early follies achieved quite a good score. Close, who enjoys nothing better than throwing a spanner into the works, was the man who kept Hampshire in check, after two wickets had fallen for 17 runs, and five for 118.

Taylor, who has by application become an admirable opening batsmen, was bowled by Roberts when the score was 17. From the next ball, delivered from the opposite end by Herman, Burgess was bowled. Denning was leg-before wicket, Richards caught at mid-on from a mis-hit. In the same over as Richards got out, Parks was bowled. These three wickets fell to Jesty who, with his medium pace, is no destroyer, but is too accurate and persistent to be played casually.

Close was not casual. He was erratic, certainly taking some chances, not least in his running between the wickets, but from the determined look of him I was sure he would make a long score. He had got 71 when he was caught at slip. The latter part of the innings was dominated by Breakwell, who has not fulfilled hopes as a slow left-arm bowler, but has shown before now that he might become a substantial middle-order batsman. In one over he hit Jesty for three fours – an on drive, an off drive, and a cover drive, all capital strokes. When Sainsbury came on instead of Jesty, Breakwell hit him for a straight six. The ball was caught by Herman, but beyond the boundary.

Breakwell scored 49 out of 74 in the seventh-wicket partnership. Botham had made a useful contribution, and Langford enjoyed his innings, but the end came quickly. Roberts, who had strained a leg muscle and left the field for part of the day, was too good for the tail.

Hampshire had nearly an hour and a half to bat. Close began with attacking fields. Jones bowled fast, his ferocious grunts resounding around Dean Park. Fast bowlers do sometimes grunt when delivering the ball, but I have not heard one with more timbre than Jones. Richards and Greenidge were not particularly perturbed, and built a solid platform for the Hampshire innings.

The last half hour, however, belonged to Somerset. Langford bowled both the openers, a useful performance for a veteran, and Burgess had Turner leg-before. The pitch was good, now and then giving a hint of eccentricity, like an ostensibly virtuous matron about whom you sometimes just wonder. So there may be fun and games yet. Each side has so far taken four points.

Hampshire must keep the champagne for little while longer

BOURNEMOUTH: Somerset, with six second innings wickets in hand, are 51 runs behind Hampshire

Hampshire, largely and enthusiastically supported on another fine day, made good progress towards maximum points, though the news from Worcester and the possibilities of the weather prevented any premature opening of champagne. In 1920, I believe that Lancashire held their celebration party for the championship a day too soon. Middlesex, in P.F. Warner's last match, made a remarkable recovery on the last day at Lord's against Surrey, and all that Lancashire champagne – was wasted. Well, not to say exactly wasted.

In the first over of the day, Langford turned a ball sharply, and I thought that Hampshire would be all out by lunch. In fact they batted until tea, with increasing ease. Their innings closed when they had scored 405 runs for nine wickets in the 113 overs which was all they were permitted under the current regulations: a lead of 141. I did wonder whether Gilliat might have declared the innings, once he had taken his eighth first innings point, even with a lead of 100 or so. This was not because I doubted Hampshire's capacity to win – there were some disturbing reports of weather prospects, not least from veteran local prophets.

The pitch continued to give a nod of encouragement to the Somerset spin bowlers from time to time, but they did not bowl very well. Langford was the best, but his arm does not move with quite the same relaxed swing as it did a few years ago. Breakwell has not the accuracy, nor perhaps the temperament, that a slow left-arm bowler needs. Close bowled himself, from each end in turn, but he is hardly in bowling practice.

In the latter part of the innings the most successful bowler was Jones the Grunt, who worked up a spirited, irritated pace. He bounced one ball so near his own feet that it soared over the batman's head. Sam Cook, with all the calm of a Tetbury plumber, correctly called a wide (you can have an upward wide as well as a sideways wide). The next ball was also short, though not as absurdly, and Cowley, going for the hook, pulled it to square leg who caught it.

Jones has presumably learnt his technique from an appeal from the Shoreditch Sparrow, and Breakwell is another always ready to make a confident proposition to the umpire. One improbable appeal by Breakwell stirred George Pope to raise his hand, but only to hold his nose.

Gilliat, Jesty and Sainsbury were the men who put Hampshire on top. When Stephenson, the night watchman, was caught out, the score was 129. When Jesty was sixth out, in the seventy-seventh over, it was 261. Sainsbury, beginning quietly as usual but later swinging the bat in a way he does not often let us see, commanded the rest of the innings (and incidentally had a raffle which produced £192 for his testimonial). Taylor and Cowley batted vigorously, and Roberts made two thumping drives which earned loud applause.

By the end of the innings, Somerset had wilted in the field. They are not a young side, even though they have some good young players. Nor had they recovered their balance when they batted. Burgess and Taylor were both caught at the wicket off Roberts. Denning and Richards were both leg before to Herman. At 22 for four, Hampshire were looking for a two-day win, but Close and Parks imposed a check.

If a fifth wicket had fallen Gilliat might have suggested the extra half hour (which can be taken on the second day, though in that case you forfeit the chance of it on the third). But Close was very sound, and Parks produced some of his most handsome strokes, so at the end Hampshire still had plenty to play for.

THIRD DAY: There was no play.

Hampshire v Somerset, Bournemouth, 28, 29 & 30 August 1974

Drawn

Somerset

+ D.J.S. Taylor	b Roberts	3	c Stephenson b Roberts	13
G.I. Burgess	b Herman	14	c Stephenson b Roberts	0
P.W. Denning	lbw b Jesty	43	lbw b Herman	4
I.V.A. Richards	c Gilliat b Jesty	45	lbw b Herman	4
* D.B. Close	c Greenidge b Roberts	71	*not out*	21
J.M. Parks	b Jesty	0	*not out*	46
I.T. Botham	c Richards b Jesty	20		
D. Breakwell	c Taylor b Cowley	49		
B.A. Langford	b Roberts	15		
A.A. Jones	*not out*	2		
R.J. Clapp	lbw b Roberts	0		
	lb 2	2	lb 1, w 1	2
		264	(4 wkts)	**90**

1/17, 2/17, 3/83, 4/118, 5/118, 6/154, 7/228, 8/261, 9/264, 10/264
1/4, 2/17, 3/17, 4/22

Roberts	14.5	2	40	4	11	3	20	2
Herman	11	3	43	1	9	2	14	2
Taylor	15	3	42	0				
Jesty	18	2	67	4	4	1	15	0
Sainsbury	21	7	46	0	10	3	32	0
Cowley	7	2	24	1	3	1	7	0

Hampshire

B.A. Richards	b Langford	51
C.G. Greenidge	b Langford	31
D.R. Turner	lbw b Burgess	1
* R.M.C. Gilliat	lbw b Jones	50
+ G.R. Stephenson	b Langford	13
T.E. Jesty	c Denning b Breakwell	73
P.J. Sainsbury	*not out*	88
N.G. Cowley	c Botham b Jones	20
M.N.S. Taylor	c Taylor b Langford	32
R.S. Herman	b Jones	8
A.M.E. Roberts	*not out*	9
	b 13, lb 11, w 1, nb 4	29
	(9 wkts, dec)	**405**

1/88, 2/89, 3/93, 4/129, 5/204, 6/261, 7/317, 8/368, 9/390

Jones	22	2	67	3
Botham	13	3	48	0
Clapp	7	1	24	0
Burgess	5	1	18	1
Langford	28	7	80	4
Breakwell	29	5	102	1
Close	9	0	37	0

Umpires: C. Cook and G.H. Pope

More regulations

BRISTOL: Gloucestershire v Hampshire

With 10 minutes to go, Gilliat attempted to declare, to end the match, but was not allowed to, under some regulation of which I am ignorant. It is absurd to try to prop up three-day cricket by devices such as playing on for a dead 10 minutes – or, for that matter, by starting half an hour earlier. It is like taking scissors to weeds. The roots of the disease lie deeper.

Journalese

WORCESTER: Worcestershire v Leicestershire

"That strengthens our championship bid," I heard one Leicestershire supporter say to another afterwards. I know we write like that, but did not think that people ever actually talked like it: a telling demonstration of the power of journalism, or journalese. Or, of course, you may take the lofty view that life imitates art.

...

So all goes well with Leicestershire's bid. I heard two disconsolate Worcestershire supporters discussing what had gone wrong. At any moment I thought they were going to demand a probe: but no. They expressed themselves more briefly and pungently. They cannot read the classics.

A century for a nightwatchman

WORCESTER: Worcestershire v Essex

There was a nightwatchman in residence, Inchmore, who was number eleven on the scorecard, assuming you could find a scorecard, which is hard work at Worcester nowadays. Inchmore is a burly moustached man of 25, who last year battled his way into the Worcestershire side as their third seam bowler. He has bowled well enough, but it had not occurred to me to consider him as a batsman. His highest previous first-class score was 30.

Inchmore's innings must be the most astonishing thing to happen in Worcester since the Parish Clerk of Ugborough was made Bishop. Inchmore likes to stand with his legs apart, fast-footed, and heave with shoulders and arms. So far, you might take him for another Jim Smith of Middlesex. But there is more to him than that. Sometimes he moves his feet, and cuts. He made one late cut which you would risk calling dainty, or delicate, if anyone else had made it. And as his confidence grew, he pushed the ball quite subtly into gaps on the leg side for ones and twos. Some of his drives echoed round the ground. It was, in the end, a proper innings, not a fluke – but that is not to say that Worcestershire have discovered a great new all-rounder.

Hampshire win in two days

PORTSMOUTH: Hampshire v Worcestershire

Something very unexpected will now have to happen for Hampshire not to win the championship. Yet although this was a memorable victory, I shall also remember the match for other reasons, not least the adventures of Mr Bill Shepheard, the genial Hampshire announcer.

At the end of the match, for instance, he set the stage for a presentation to the outstanding Hampshire cricketer of the festival, to be made by a Portsmouth garage which was celebrating its jubilee. But when we gathered round the pavilion, there was no presentation. It had not occurred to the innocent mechanics that play might end a day early, and they were far away changing tyres and looking forward to their day out. Mr Shepheard had earlier announced that a white boy's sweater had been found. Later, he announced that a wallet had been found. My colleague, Mr Rutnagur, who is an Indian, ventured to inquire whether it was a white man's wallet.

But Mr Shepheard's best moment came when he said: "Play has been resumed in the Test match – oh, and by the way, President Nixon has resigned." The cheer, a mixture of irony, relief and scorn, brought a man running out of the bar, thinking another wicket had gone. When he discovered it was nothing so important, he went back in again. Thus do the mighty fall.

Prudential Trophy

BIRMINGHAM: Pakistan beat England by eight wickets

I wonder whether these matches are worthwhile: not, indeed, because of England's defeat, which was justified by the play, nor even because of the weather, which cannot be helped. But there is something farcical about two sides of international players competing over 35 overs for £1,000, as well as large individual prizes. I wonder if, apart from the awkward aspect of the rules, they do not clutter up just a little too much of an already complicated season. They are a bonus for the players, certainly, and I imagine the sponsors were insured. But the Prudential cannot have had a great deal of value from this one, and if they feel that sponsoring cricket is a useful way of spending their money, conceivably they might find ways of doing it more helpfully to themselves and to the game.

Fidgety reflections 1974

As I threw away the little white booklet containing the regulations for the conduct of cricket in 1974, I wondered how many changes we should find when its successor makes its appearance next spring. Plenty, I expect. The end of the season has brought the usual crop of suggestions for improving the game, some of them sounding quite promising. But I would like it best if we were to declare a moratorium on all change for, say, three years. I found a pleasing parallel to my feelings in *C.S. Lewis: a biography*, by Roger Lancelyn Green and Walter Hooper, published during the summer. Lewis expressed himself strongly against priests who have what he calls the 'Liturgical Fidget', and attempt to lure people to church by 'incessant brightenings, lightenings, lengthenings, abridgements, simplifications and complications of the service'. 'My whole liturgiological position,' he says, 'really boils down to an entreaty for permanence and uniformity.' Well, cricket is a liturgical game, and that is *my* liturgiological position. Much the same was said many years ago by Alfred Shaw, the old Nottinghamshire bowler. He was asked what changes he would like to see in the game and replied that the best change would be to leave the rules alone for a bit. But I am afraid cricketing authorities have always been notorious liturgical fidgets. Come next May, and I shall be poring over the small print of that infernal booklet again.

Somehow I did not enjoy the season very much. I suppose it was mostly to do with the weather, especially the dreadful soakings we all had in September. A fine September, like a *deoch an doruis*, the glass of whisky at the door, always sends one away thinking kindly of one's host. But a cricket season nowadays is a scrappy affair, weather apart, even more I dare say if you watch the game regularly than if you only do so occasionally. This is not intended to be another knock at the one-day game: but the combination of two touring sides and four domestic competitions (to say nothing of odds and ends like the Prudential and the Fenner trophies) does mean that the old unity – one touring side, one Championship – has been destroyed. I saw a *bit* of the Indians, a *bit* of the Pakistanis, a *bit* of the Championship, a *bit* of the Benson & Hedges, and so on. The focus of attention was constantly shifting. There never seemed to be time to settle down and watch developments. I have much sympathy with those who feel that three one-day competitions are one too many. But no, I must not fidget. Let us leave things as they are for a few years, and no doubt the new pattern will become more easily comprehensible with familiarity. I am told a juggler finds it as easy to keep six balls in the air as three, once he has had the practice.

I shall, however, remember 1974 because I made two successful prophecies. I have never thought it part of a cricket-writer's duty to prophecy results, except now and then as a bit of fun, and when I have tried to do it I have been almost invariably wrong. However, in a radio programme at the start of the season I was pinned down to make a forecast as to who would win the Championship, and blurted out 'Worcestershire'. I had a letter at the end from someone who thanked me for the tip, and had made a bob or two – thought he had had doubts of my judgment in mid-August. He cannot have been a *Times* reader, or he would have seen that after Hampshire had beaten Worcestershire in two days at Portsmouth I had practically placed the crown on Gilliat's head.

The other prophecy was a sad one. During a break for rain in the Oval Test, we were discussing in the commentary box the outcome of the Gillette Cup final, and I suggested that anyone who wanted a good bet, as opposed to a good day's cricket, should put his money on a rainy day. After eleven consecutive fine September Saturdays it would hardly have been surprising, whatever the rest of the summer was like. I hope that one of those disappointed Lancastrians who travelled south took my advice and at least managed to pay the costs of his trip.

Down here in the west, Gloucestershire fell on hard times, but, of course, Somerset had a good season. And yet there was some despondency among Somerset supporters at the end: 'I'd swap any number of near misses for just one win' was one representative phrase I heard. Somerset have never won any of the competitions, and this year their hopes were raised, at one time and another, only to be dashed, in all of them. They would surely have won the Sunday League if Cartwright had been fit throughout: but he, and several other of their leading performers, cannot now have very long to go. However, they produced a most promising young player in Botham, who looked full of talent in everything he did. No doubt he will be put to a searching test next season as details of his strengths and weaknesses are passed round the circuit.

So far all I have against him is that he genteelly pronounces his name 'Boe-tham' instead of the fine old English 'Bottom' – independence, staying power, resolution, an excellent name for a cricketer. Still, I appreciate that misunderstandings may arise. Indeed, somewhat improbably, that takes me back to C.S. Lewis. He used to tell a story of a Bishop of Exeter who was giving prizes at a girls' school. 'They did a performance,' said Lewis, 'of *A Midsummer Night's Dream*, and the poor man stood up afterwards and made a speech and said (piping voice): "I was very interested in your delightful performance, and among other things I was very interested in seeing for the first time in my life a female Bottom."'

Winter well.

1975

1975 was the first of two golden summers, and the cricket was mostly as glorious as the weather. The first Prudential World Cup, in June, was a resounding success, thanks not least to what is arguably still the most memorable final that the competition has provided. That was followed by an exciting and closely contested series of four Test matches against the Australians, whilst all the time the county competitions were being lit up by the brilliance of batsmen like Clive Lloyd, Zaheer Abbas, Asif Iqbal, Alvin Kallicharran and Barry Richards. The season, suggested *Wisden*, would go down in the annals of English cricket 'as one of the best of all time'.

But for Alan Gibson, it was a bittersweet summer. He was writing as much as ever for *The Times*, and as well as ever, but he suffered in the heat, and the tensions with the BBC were growing ever more acute. There had been significant changes in the BBC's cricket set-up in the previous two or three years. Cliff Morgan was now in overall charge as head of outside broadcasts, Peter Baxter had taken over from Michael Tuke-Hastings as cricket producer, and Christopher Martin-Jenkins had succeeded Brian Johnston as the cricket correspondent. With Christopher, Brian and John Arlott being in the team for every Test, that left one space to be filled from the likes of Don Mosey, Neil Durden-Smith, a promising newcomer called Henry Blofeld and Alan himself.

At the top of his form, Alan was a match for any of them, with the possible exception of Arlott. But finding him at the top of his form was becoming increasingly difficult, especially after lunch, and the new BBC regime was much less tolerant of this amiable weakness, as Alan saw it, than their predecessors. In the end, Cliff Morgan put his foot down. Alcoholic drink was banned from the commentary box. Alan's response was to turn up for his next commentary session armed with a pint mug of whisky and water, which he proceeded to drink whilst on air.

The end came at the Headingley Test. According to Don Mosey, when Cliff Morgan heard Alan on the Monday evening, clearly the worse for drink, he swore there and then that he would never commentate for the BBC again. Fortunately, as it now seems, the fact that the 'George Davis is innocent' protestors dug up the pitch that night, and play had to be abandoned on the final day, avoided Alan being sacked in mid-Test match, and nothing official was ever actually said or written down. But he never did cricket commentary for the BBC again.

However, there was at least one occasion in 1975 – and a hugely important one at that – when Alan was most certainly *was* at the top of his form, and that was the Memorial Service for Sir Neville Cardus at St. Paul's, Covent Garden, on April 4. Over 700 people were packed into the church, including some of the greatest names in cricket, journalism and music, when Alan mounted the steps to the pulpit, in his Oxford MA hood and gown, to give the address. It was a daunting occasion, and he rose to it splendidly, the intellectual and the showman in him combining to produce a tribute that was as evocative in content as it was commanding in delivery.

After the blood and thunder of MCC's winter tour of Australia – where they lost the Test series 4-1, thanks largely to Lillee and Thomson – the new domestic season started gently. The Parks were looking at their springtime best for the visit of Sussex, and at this stage of the season, even routine one-day encounters, such as that between Nottinghamshire and Lancashire in the Benson and Hedges Cup on May 6, could be relished for their unexpected ironies.

Tests
Australia
beat England
1-0, with three draws

World Cup Final
West Indies
beat Australia

Championship
1 Leicestershire
2 Yorkshire
3 Hampshire
4 Lancashire
5 Kent
6 Surrey

Sunday League
1 Hampshire
2 Worcestershire
3 Kent
4 Essex
5 Nottinghamshire
6 Warwickshire

Gillette Cup Final
Lancashire
beat Middlesex

Benson & Hedges Final
Leicestershire
beat Middlesex

Most first-class runs
1 G. Boycott
2 D.S. Steele
3 A.W. Greig

Most first-class wickets
1 P. Lee
2 Sarfraz Nawaz
3 B.S. Bedi
J.K. Lever
M.A. Nash

Alan's adopted county of Gloucestershire were to have a difficult, injury-afflicted season. Procter had had an operation on his knee during the winter, which would keep him out until July, and the captain, Tony Brown, was also kept out of the side for the visit to Glamorgan in early May. That left David Shepherd, Gloucestershire's bucolic Devonian all-rounder, to take charge of the side, and it gave Alan Gibson every excuse for profiling one of his favourite cricketing characters for *The Times*.

Despite that promising start, May proved to be a cold and wet month, and play was stopped by snow at Buxton, early in June. But with the arrival of the eight international sides for the first Prudential Cup, the weather perked up, and it was sunshine all the way from then on. Alan's first world cup match for *The Times* was a one-sided encounter between New Zealand and East Africa, but it was evidently the match between Australia and Sri Lanka that brought out the romantic in him. In comparison with the protracted circuses of modern times, it seems extraordinary now how quickly it was all over: first-round matches on June 7; the final on June 21. Clive Lloyd's batting, Vivian Richards' fielding and Lillee and Thomson's fast bowling made for an epic contest, which stretched long into a warm, joyful summer's evening, still vivid in the memory.

No sooner was the World Cup over, than the Australian tour began. They were a strong side, confidently captained by Ian Chappell, and buoyed by their winter triumphs. Their first three day match was against Kent at Canterbury, and it turned out to be a memorable one, thanks largely to Colin Cowdrey.

As the summer drew on, so the sun continued to beat down from largely cloudless skies. In some of Alan's reports in July, one can sense a certain *ennui* beginning to creep in – often with amusing results, as in Hampshire match's with Glamorgan at Basingstoke starting on July 9. At Dover in the following week, it was the eccentricities of the scoreboard that caught Alan's attention on the second day. While at Weston-super-Mare, it was clearly just very, very hot.

But despite being in contention all season, and being by common consent, the strongest of the county sides, Hampshire didn't quite secure their second championship in three years. That honour went to Leicestershire, for the first time in their history and in their centenary year. Having earlier won the Benson and Hedges, it made for a triumphant season for a team who always seemed greater than the sum of their parts, and for the man who was largely responsible for that, their captain, the estimable Ray Illingworth.

That autumn, after some final, slightly weary-sounding reflections for *The Cricketer,* Alan and the family moved into a solid Edwardian house in Henleaze, a leafy Bristol enclave up by the Downs. Alan didn't much like it, saying that it reminded him of the manse in Leyton, but it seemed to mark another move forward, in a year in which, on balance, if only just, the good things had outnumbered the bad.

Born April 2, 1889

Died February 27, 1975

A tribute, spoken at his memorial service in St Paul's, Covent Garden

Since we are in a church, I thought it proper that we should have a text. Hear then these words from the prophet Blake (I am not sure if Blake was one of Sir Neville's favourites, though he has recalled how enthusiastically he would join in *Jerusalem* in his days with the Ancoats Brotherhood). Blake wrote, in *Auguries of Innocence*:

Joy and woe are woven fine,
A clothing for the soul divine;
Under every grief and pine
Runs a thread of silken twine.

On an occasion such as this, joy and woe are inseparable companions: thanksgiving for such a life, sadness that it has ended. But more than that: it was the mingling of joy and woe that made Sir Neville such a writer – the sensitivity to the human condition, not least his own; the ability to observe it, and to communicate what he saw, with detachment and yet with passion. His books are full of humour: rich comedy, sometimes almost slapstick, and yet he keeps us hovering between tears and laughter. For always he is conscious, and makes us conscious, of the fragility of happiness, of the passing of time. He loved the good moments all the more avidly because he knew they were fleeting.

There is no need to recite his achievement. His autobiographical books, the crown of his life's work, have done that already. His early cricket books gave him a reputation for "fancy" writing. The words "lyrical", "rhapsodical", were sometimes applied to him, usually by people who would not know a lyric from a rhapsody. These terms were still jostled about long after they had any possible justification, to Sir Neville's wry amusement. His mature prose was marked by clarity, balance, and indeed by restraint, though he never shrank from emotion or from beauty. Perhaps George Orwell was as good a writer of prose; or you may think of P.G. Wodehouse, or Bernard Darwin – everyone has his own favourites – but in this century it is not easy to think of many more in the same class.

I remember clearly how I was introduced to Cardus's writing. It was in August 1935. We were on holiday in Cornwall, at St. Ives, and my father was buying me a book because of some small family service I had done. I said I would like a cricket book, and the choice narrowed to two: a book of reminiscences attributed to Hendren, I think it was, and *Good Days*, by Neville Cardus. I doubt if I had heard of Cardus then, because it was difficult to get *The Manchester Guardian* in the south of England. I was inclined to Hendren, but father was inclined to Cardus. Father won. We bought *Good Days*. Father read it before I did, though I have more than made up for that since. Most of us, perhaps half a dozen times in our lives, read books – not always famous books – which change us, change our thinking, books which open doors, revelatory books. That was one of mine. It was the essay on Emmott Robinson that did it – do you remember it? – when Cardus imagined "that the Lord one day gathered together a heap of Yorkshire clay, and breathed into it, and said 'Emmott Robinson, go on and bowl at the pavilion end for Yorkshire'." And then the next bit, about how Emmott's trousers were always on the point of falling down, and he would remember to grab them just in time.

All cricket writers of the last half century have been influenced by Cardus, whether they admit it or not, whether they have wished to be or not, whether they have tried to copy him or tried to avoid copying him. He was not a model, any more than Macaulay, say, was a model for the aspiring historian. But just as Macaulay changed the course of the writing of history, Cardus changed the course of the writing of cricket. He showed what could be done. He dignified and illuminated the craft.

It was, it has occurred to me, fortunate for cricket that Bradman and Cardus existed at the same time: fortunate for them, too, since the best of batsmen was recorded by the best of critics. Each was worthy of the other.

In the music of Sir Neville's time, at least in English music, there was never one figure quite so dominant as Bradman. Elgar, Delius and Beecham were, he wrote, "the three most original spirits known in English music since Purcell, if we leave out Sullivan." He said it with a shadow of a wink, as if to say, "and take it out of that." You remember how he described Delius, when he met him in what now seem the improbable surroundings of the Langham Hotel: "His attendant carried him into the sitting-room of his suite and flopped him down on a couch, where he fell about like a rag doll until he was arranged into a semblance of human shape. There was nothing pitiable in him, nothing inviting sympathy in this wreck of a physique. He was wrapped in a monk-like gown, and his face was strong and disdainful, every line on it grown by intrepid living." There is a picture for you; there is a piece of prose for you.

As for Sir Thomas Beecham, he is always bursting out of Cardus's pages and making his own way. It was with some difficulty that Cardus stopped his splendid Aunt Beatrice from conquering his first autobiographical book. He never quite stopped Beecham, any more than Shakespeare ever quite stopped Falstaff taking charge of Henry the Fourth.

Perhaps the most remarkable episode in the life of Cardus, going by what he said himself, and one to which we should refer here, was his conversion. I think the word is properly used: I mean his conversion to music. It was achieved by one of the minor saints: Edward German. He was watching a production of a light opera, *Tom Jones*, at the Prince's Theatre, Manchester. He had gone there because he was reading Henry Fielding, but, he says, "the music of Edward German got past my ears and entered into my mind behind my back." Only twenty months after that first experience, he was listening to the first performance of Elgar's *Symphony in A Flat*, and wondering, with the other musicians in the audience, how Elgar was going to cope with such a long first subject.

He used to say that he was baffled that it should have been Edward German who had first revealed the light: yet he should not have been. It was all of a piece with the man and his thought. When Beecham and MacLaren, and Bradman and Ranjitsinhji, and Elgar came within the experience of Cardus, he rose to them and did them justice – but he was capable of being moved, such was his sense of humanity, by men who were not more than good county bowlers, Emmott Robinson or Edward German.

"Joy and woe are woven fine." They are not alien, they are complementary, "A clothing for the soul divine." And in another part of that poem, Blake says

It is right it should be so,
Man was made for joy and woe,
And when this we rightly know,
Safely through the world we go.

I am not sure whether Sir Neville Cardus would approve of that as an epitaph: but he is probably too busy to bother just now, arguing with Bernard Shaw.

Neville Cardus
'Joy and woe are woven fine'

The Parks, Oxford

It was pleasant to be in the Parks on such a sunny spring day, and no occupation could have been more pleasant than batting on a wicket like that, unless perhaps you were escorting a young lady around the scene. The young ladies in the Parks are less elegant than they were 25 years ago, but also less clad, and therefore equally nubile. The trees look much the same, the leaves a little late after the uncertain weather, but the blossoms on the fruit trees were gleaming pink and white and yellow, just like Keble College chapel, and there was an Oxford cricketing team taking a thrashing in a gentlemanly spirit: any of you who know the Parks will know what happiness it was to be there.

Northampton

Northampton is a town with many merits: a statue of Bradlaugh, defying God to strike him dead, an interesting boot and shoe museum, and a splendid assortment of dissenting chapels. It was the home of the cobbler, William Carey, who went to India, defying other gods to strike him dead, and founded the Baptist Missionary Society. Bradlaugh and Carey are both dead, though I would not make a theological point of it, and a few of us huddled upon the cricket ground yesterday wished at times that we too were dead, prepared to take a chance on the sequel. For whatever the other qualities of Northampton, its cricket ground is a miserable place to be when the wind howls in from the north-east, bringing with it flat scurries of cold rain.

Brighton and Hove

The observant will have noticed that this report is headed "Hove". I have suffered much in the past two days because I have been writing from "Brighton" and even quoted a rude sentence about Brighton. Hove, they persistently explain to me, is a different animal from Brighton.

I accept this up to a point, Lord Copper. But the same writer who was so rude about Brighton also said that Hove was "the genteelest town in the world" which, when one comes to think of it, even if still true, would be ruder. Hove is nothing but a developed smugglers' den. Morning service had to be cancelled here once, because the pulpit was full of tea, and the pews full of brandy.

Sunday at Cheltenham

There was another large and on the whole genial crowd here. Cobbett described the town as "the resort of the lame and the lazy, the gourmandising and the guzzling, the bilious and the nervous." This did not apply to most of those attending yesterday, though I did see a few aged colonels laying down the law about Gloucestershire's batting, and a few young men, looking hot in their beards and hairy necks, who had obviously been mainly attracted by the all-day licence. Nevertheles, it was a much better behaved crowd than the one at Weston a week ago.

Leicester

I arrived late at Leicester. After some misadventures with British Rail, and also with a number of Derby County supporters, who were working hard to counteract their hangovers, I reached the Midlands, like Wolsey, ready to lay my bones there.

Birmingham

"It is happily impossible," wrote a former cricket correspondent of this newspaper, "to libel a city", and went on to describe Birmingham as "this most offensive and intolerable of towns. It is astonishing that the place should have so strong and unpleasant an individuality and be so unlike any other decent Christian town."

A little hard he was, but it is a vigorous piece of polemic which goes on for more than a page. He was also writing before the new Edgbaston was built and before Leslie Deakins, the most welcoming and helpful of county secretaries (which is saying a good deal) was in office. Birmingham may not be a place easy to fall in love with, but I find it grows on one, or at least Edgbaston does, and the Snug Bar at long-off and the pork pies.

...

Some of Kanhai's drives rang the echoes, echoes of time, but also of the more commonplace sort, for the big Edgbaston stand contained only a scattering of spectators. This is the trouble, when you come to three-day cricket, with having so splendid a ground. The same number of people would have looked very well at Bournemouth, caused traffic jams at Yeovil, and arrived with all the force of a pop festival at Darley Dale.

Chelmsford

Chelmsford is not so pleasant as it was. It has been Basingstoked a bit, blocks and precincts and concrete squatting on the old country town, fast roads splitting it. But it has its good points: the cricket ground, in its wide park, is one; the old parish church, since 1914 raised to the status of a cathedral, is another. On one of its 13 bells is an inscription: "Too much against us may be said, to speak for ourselves we are not afraid." I suppose this might apply to the present erratic, enthusiastic, athletic, noisy Essex eleven. They are not likely to win the championship now, but they have contributed much to the summer's entertainment.

Lancashire's confidence flows like the tide

NOTTINGHAM: Lancashire (3 pts) beat Nottinghamshire by nine wickets

"We have seen a lot of exciting cricket in the Benson and Hedges Cup," said a representative from the firm (and no-one would dispute it), "and today's match," he went on, bravely, "has been no exception." It must be a tricky job to speak for Benson and Hedges in Nottingham, especially when Nottinghamshire have taken a trouncing, even more especially the day after Nottinghamshire have won a resounding victory in the competition organized by that other tobacco company

From the window of my hotel bedroom I can see Nottingham Castle, and in the dusk imagine I can see that old familiar bearded sailor in front of it. Last night he seemed to be giving a superior smile to the backs of the retreating Benson and Hedges cohorts, as an equable but hardened drinker might dismiss a mission from the Band of Hope.

The cricket was not without interest, but the match was one-sided. After the first few overs it was hard to doubt that Lancashire would win. Although Nottinghamshire won the toss and batted on a pitch with little harm in it, they were as diffident as Lancashire were confident. "Wedge 'em in," used to be Lancashire's motto in their run of successes in one-day cricket, and the way they played yesterday recalled that heroic time. They have now won their first two matches in their group of the competition.

Nottinghamshire, who had played so well on Sunday against lesser opposition, were never in this game. The bowling and fielding gripped them from the start. The first run did not come until the 17th ball. Harris then began to score a few, but Hassan had not scored at all when he was out in the sixth over. Smedley batted for seven overs and scored two. After 10 overs, Clive Lloyd and Wood came on instead of Lever and Lee, and Lloyd had Smedley caught at slip.

He was bowling large inswingers from the Radcliffe Road end, with the aid of a stiff wind blowing across to the Trent. He only needed to straighten one now and then to have the batsman in trouble. He nearly had Rice out twice, but it was at the other end that Rice fell, caught at mid-wicket off Wood, who had begun with three maidens and numerous passionate appeals. Rice played a couple of good strokes in his brief innings.

Harris continued to bat well, but when half the innings was gone and only 50 runs scored, Nottinghamshire were struggling, even more so when Randall and Johnson were stumped. Engineer was keeping wicket in one of his most efficient moods, taking an absurdly good diving catch to end the innings. Before then, Harris, stubborn as the Roseland peninsula whence he comes but no more able to push back the tide than Mrs Partington of Sidmouth, had been leg before to Lever, who bowled fast and accurately in both his spells - though still taking an inordinate time to bowl an over.

There is not much to say about the Lancashire innings. The only wicket to fall was that of David Lloyd, who was stumped off White in the 25th over, the score 69, the match nearly won. A young man called Hacker, left-arm medium to fast, bowled usefully as well as making an elegant two not out when he batted. He came into the Nottinghamshire side in place of Stead, who was unfit.

The only other Hacker I can remember is that bad-tempered master of the Shell at Greyfriars, know to his pupils as the Acid Drop. I thought this might be a relation, but I doubt it, for this Hacker is slightly built and mild in appearance, though zealous. The acid will creep in if he stays long enough in first class cricket, as it does with schoolmasters.

Donald Kenyon made Wood the man of the match. It was a reasonable decision, though I thought Harris, and Engineer, and even Hacker, may have contributed more to the prosperity of the Band of Hope.

NOTTINGHAMSHIRE	94 (52.4 overs, Harris 59, Lever 3-10, Wood 2-20)
LANCASHIRE	95 for one (38 overs, Wood 57*)

Brown, the Gloucestershire captain, is out of the side with a back strain; Procter, the vice-captain, is still some way from fitness, though the reports are encouraging: and therefore Shepherd, the newly-chosen senior professional, will lead the county in the match beginning today against Glamorgan. Pause here while all Gloucestershire cricketers say "Good Old Shep".

A pity the match is not at Bristol, for there he would have been given a special cheer: but the Cardiff people will probably do that anyway, for he is a popular as well as substantial figure in the county cricket scene ("Shep am byth, boyo").

Since the sad retirement of Milburn, David Shepherd has, so far as I can see, no challenger in one respect. Of all current English first-class cricketers he is the bulkiest, plumpest, amplest, tubbiest, best built, best rounded, most circumferous – let me cease weighing my words and make, er, no bones of it – he is the fattest.

He is not so fat as he was – he slimmed determinedly the winter before last – but he would still win by several inches any standing race for cricketers when the photo-finish was taken at the start. This is not meant to mock him. He keeps fit, in his own way and shape. He looks fatter than Milburn did, because he carries more weight to the front, but he has often said he would back himself against Milburn over a hundred yards, and after watching both field many times I have no doubt he is right.

I nearly said I would have a small bet on it, but I am suffering greatly from the supporters not to say relations, of this Wingfield-Digby of Keble, who I said would score 50 runs in the University Match. Their idea of a small bet is around £10, while mine is half a pint. Nor do any of them offer me odds, no doubt because these austere Keble men disapprove of gambling.

Shepherd comes from Devon, and looks as if he comes from Devon: any film producer making *The Farmer's Wife* or *Lorna Doone* on location would seize upon him as an extra, with double rate and free cider. His face is pink, tending to purple at strenuous times, like the sun seen from Dartmoor, making one of its spectaculars as it goes down across the Tamar. His hair is getting a little grey, like the clouds which hover above the sunset, thought he is only 34 and has a sunset or two to see yet.

Devon is a good cricketing county. With a few slightly different twists of luck, it might have been a first-class county, and would have borne the responsibility quite as well as several which are. In the match between Gloucestershire and Leicestershire last week there were four Devonians – the two Tolchards, from Torquay, Davey from Tavistock, and Shepherd from Bideford. He used to play rugby for Bideford, a well regarded club.

He played cricket for Devon from 1959 to 1964. He scored lots of runs in a boisterous style, and was chosen for the Minor Counties against the 1964 Australians. His first match for Gloucestershire was against Oxford University in 1965. The bowling was perhaps not very good and he scored a hundred, which was not altogether a fortunate thing to happen to him. It took him some time to adjust to the tighter, duller discipline of the three-day game. Indeed he has never quite done that: it is one of the reasons for his popularity, and also, I suppose we must admit, one of the reasons why, though he has scored 8,000 runs, his first-class average is only 24.

He had to wait until 1969 for his Gloucestershire cap. But he has developed into a good county cricketer. Twice he has scored a thousand runs in a season, not easy nowadays for a middle-order batsman. His sunny nature, hard to ruffle, though he is rather a shy man behind that apple face, has often been a virtue in moments of crisis, especially in one-day matches – not least in his famous 72 not out against Surrey at Bristol in 1973, the year Gloucestershire won the Gillette Cup. His fielding, if not speedy, is safe and zealous, and he has a good arm. He has taken two wickets at 34, a figure which occasional captaincy will not tempt him to try to improve.

"Good old Shep," they cry in Gloucestershire when he comes out to bat, one of the West's unmistakable own, usually following a series of much more talented chaps from places like Sialkot and Streatham. "Well done, Shep," they cry, as he chases unflaggingly round the boundary. When those powerful forearms make the ball hum over the bowler's head, how they chortle! When he gets out early through some optimistic bash on a turner, and comes in sorrowfully shaking his head, as if he could not imagine how he of all men could come to do such a thing, there is always a consolatory murmur. "Never mind! 'Ard luck. Good old Shep." Who cares what his average is? Doesn't he cheer us up!

David Shepherd
'Who cares what his average is? Doesn't he cheer us up?'

Last ball excitement

BRISTOL: Gloucestershire v Northamptonshire (Sunday League)

Gloucestershire would have won if their captain had hit the last ball of the match for six, and as the bowler was Bedi, presumably brought back for such an emergency, it was possible. Brown failed, but there was such dashing hither and thither by players and spectators, the fibrillations perhaps exaggerated by the players, but real and throbbing enough to most of the spectators, especially the small boys, who will grow up believing that this is what cricket is about. I suppose by the time they have grown up, it will be.

David Shepherd

BRISTOL: Gloucestershire v Glamorgan

Walking round the ground at this stage I met David Shepherd, who is out of this match because of an injury. He was wearing a sweater of violent purple, as though contemplating applying for a job on *The Guardian*. "The boys must think it's Sunday," he said as the boundaries flew about us.

The modern cricketer

BOURNEMOUTH: Hampshire v Nottinghamshire

Jesty was unable to bowl. He was, I heard him explain, suffering from "a strain on the inner wall of the lower abdomen". There is your modern professional cricketer. Tom Goddard would have said: "Oy dun me gut."

The view from the beer tent

DOVER: Kent v Nottinghamshire (Sunday League)

Cowdrey was caught at deep mid-wicket. It was an astonishing catch from a true hit which looked like six. Hassan leapt high, lost the ball, and recaptured it as he fell. By this time he had rolled over the line, but that does not matter under the present regulations if the catch was properly made. Hassan claimed a fair catch, the umpire agreed, and Cowdrey accepted the decision, even if some in the beer tent did not. They had a good view, certainly, for Hassan was diving among their feet, but beer is not the best medium for viewing events, even at close quarters, as many an unwilling recruit discovered when he found the king's shilling at the bottom of his tankard.

Whisky and champagne at Cheltenham

CHELTENHAM: Gloucestershire v Warwickshire

The weather was a little cooler at Cheltenham yesterday, which helped to make us all better-tempered; and crowds at Cheltenham (the ground nearly full again) need to be good tempered, because handsome though the setting may be, the facilities are on the primitive side. I have not visited the gentlemen's lavatory tent this year, but am assured, by many friends, and indeed by my own nose, that the Ladysmith tradition is preserved. When, in the members' bar, I asked for some water with my whisky, I was told: "There's a tap round the corner."

Still, Cheltenham is Cheltenham, and as one jolly round pink gentleman said to me, pressing a glass of champagne into my hand under the impression that I was his godson: "If you want real discomfort here you have to come to the Gold Cup."

Jack Birkenshaw

LEICESTER: Leicestershire v Essex (Sunday League)

The man who looked like he might turn the game for Essex was Gooch, who played both strokes and swipes, until he was caught and bowled by Birkenshaw. This was an exceptionally good catch. A man near to me in the crowd had just gloomily said (whether truthfully or not I do not know): "Birky dropped three yesterday," and it was as if Birky had heard him and was replying: "Ay, lad, these things happen to us all. Kindly watch this, if it's not trooblin' thi' too much." He then took another good return catch, which ended McEwan's innings, and five wickets altogether.

Beer glasses at Taunton

TAUNTON: Somerset v the Australians

The members' bar and the public bar were charging 10p deposit on their glasses. There is another bar, commonly known as the Stragglers' Bar, which comes under a different authority and makes no such charge. Posh people like the vice-presidents and the press congregate there, but admission is not strictly governed.

Throughout the match people have been unobtrusively dropping in to have a drink with the Stragglers and absent-mindedly walking away with their glasses, which they returned to one of the other bars, collecting their 10p. Yesterday morning the Stragglers were out of glasses, and much free beer had been consumed.

It reminded me of the man who lived on the border between America and Mexico. On the American side he would buy a drink, pay an American dollar for it and receive, as his correct change, a Mexican dollar. Then he would cross the bridge, buy a drink, pay a Mexican dollar for it and receive, as his correct change, an American dollar.

They say he had a beautiful look of contentment on his face the night they found him dead on the middle of the bridge. The question has always been, who paid for the drinks?

Cheltenham

Taunton

JUNE: Australia v Sri Lanka at The Oval (World Cup) 1975

Sri Lanka prospects please until Thomson injures two batsmen

THE OVAL: Australia beat Sri Lanka by 52 runs

I was having a drink with this beautiful girl from Ceylon. It was rather a lot of years ago, perhaps it would be unchivalrous to say how many. She is now a famous broadcaster in her country. I had just begun as a cricket commentator. "One day," she said, "you will broadcast upon England against Ceylon at Lord's." We had another beer on the prospect. It was an evening when every prospect pleased, and the spicy breezes blew soft o'er Ceylon's isle. "But," she went on to say, her golden eyes hardening, "when you do, you are to be kind to Ceylon."

Well, I have not yet seen Ceylon play England at Lord's, but I saw Sri Lanka – as they are now called – play Australia at the Oval yesterday, something which would have seemed even more improbable those years ago. As to being kind, there is no difficulty. They played extremely well, they batted better than they bowled, and their fielding varied between brilliance and wildness. Nevertheless, at one stage they had the mighty Australians worried, almost fumbling. Consider. Australia were 178 for no wicket in 34 overs at lunch, and went on to make 328 for five. All we expected of Sri Lanka was that they would do their best to bat it out and gain experience. But in the 32nd over they had scored 150, and lost only two wickets. Mendis and Wettimuny were going so well that anything seemed possible.

At this point Thomson laid Mendis out. It was not strictly a bouncer, but a short ball, aimed at the body. Thomson hit the batsman on several other occasions with similar balls. He was booed by the crowd, alike by those from the Indian subcontinent and those forthright souls from the Elephant and Castle. It will not, I am afraid, be a pleasant occasion when Australia meet West Indies.

Mendis was carried off, and in Thomson's next over so was Wettimuny, who had had several bangs on the legs and midriff. He limped most of the way, but had to be picked up before he reached the Pavilion. They were both taken to hospital for treatment. With two new batsmen needing to play themselves in, Sri Lanka could not keep up the scoring rate. Thus vanished their hopes, but not their bravery. They did not duck or dodge the fast bowling. They kept playing strokes: glances and cuts are what they do best. They will beat Australia one day.

Perhaps they were wrong to put Australia in, on a fast and true pitch. I suppose after their last experience they were afraid of an attack of early nerves, a sudden irretrievable breakdown. They certainly played better as the day went on. They were not helped in the morning by an invasion of the field by some young supporters who were, I understand, protesting against the selection of their side.

Sri Lanka's 276 for four was the highest score made in the second innings of a Prudential Cup match: not that it breaks any long-standing records, but it was done against Australia and their dreaded attack. Although Australia dropped some catches, they were not fooling about. The man of the match, Laurie Fishlock decided, was Turner, whose innings we had almost forgotten in the flux of events. Not that he did not deserve it. The woman of the match was a golden-eyed girl from Ceylon who prophesized long ago.

AUSTRALIA	328 for five (60 overs, Turner 101, McCosker 73, Walters 59, G.S. Chappell 50)
SRI LANKA	276 for four (60 overs, Wettimuny 53 rtd hurt, Tissera 52, Tennekoon 48, Mendis 32 rtd hurt)

Robin Jackman

I am pleased to report that the Shoreditch Sparrow, Jackman, was in lively spirits. He made by far the fiercest appeal of the day, and once ran a long way indeed to save a ball from reaching the boundary, flicking it back from the rope, and catapulting himself into the crowd as he did so, an heroic dash. They ran four. They even contemplated a fifth.

Robin Hobbs

It was a special occasion for Hobbs, who was bowling at his best, four for 21 in 15 overs. He took his 1,000th wicket in first class cricket. That takes some doing by anybody nowadays. For a true leg-spin bowler to do it, with such limited opportunities, sometimes even dropped by his own county, nears the miraculous. No other leg-spinner, I am afraid, will do it again.

Tony Greig

At 66 Greig came in. He looked as awe inspiring as Mr Justice Avory about to pass the death sentence. Even the large cheerful Southampton crowd trembled at the sight. He took his first ball, from Sainsbury, pushed down the pitch and ran. There may have been a slight confusion between the batsmen, but it was not a wise call. Richards came in from mid-on, threw down the wicket at the bowler's end, and back to the pavilion came Greig, looking – I was going to say, like Napoleon on his way to St Helena, but the physical analogy is not apt: more like Wellington coming back to Brussels if he had lost Waterloo.

Geoff Humpage

Humpage is the reserve wicketkeeper. It is the kind of name Bunyan might have given to a wicketkeeper (and Bunyan did play cricket, of a sort; indeed, had he not felt convicted of a sin while playing on a Sunday, we might never have had *Pilgrim's Progress*, which would have been almost as serious a deprivation as the loss of the John Player League).

Alvin Kallicharran

I went to Edgbaston with a friend from the BBC's natural history unit, who had rather lost touch with cricket lately, and had not seen Kallicharran bat before. When I asked him what he thought, he said of the little man: "Incredibly youthful, incredibly lithe." I asked him of which animal he had been most reminded. He pondered for a few moments over a kitten, but settled for an otter under water. "Something that is always chasing its tail and always catching it."

Barry Richards

96 not out v Glamorgan at Swansea

For all the cricketing talent that is assembling in Britain, it is unlikely that many better innings will be played this summer than that with which Richards carried Hampshire to victory yesterday. It was an innings which left one with a curious sense of peace, the kind of feeling that occurs after a long look at, say, a Titian or listening to the Ninth Symphony or finishing Pickwick. Even if we have no hope of doing it ourselves, we are consoled that others can.

112 v Leicestershire at Bournemouth (Sunday League)

An innings of the utmost splendour by Richards eclipsed everything and everyone else yesterday. Last year's champions put up a good fight for most of the match at Bournemouth yesterday, but once Richards was well into his stride, they must have felt like honest Trojan soldiers competing with Achilles, mortals struggling with the god-like. … He reached his hundred in 74 balls, with scarcely a mishit. He hit, all told, five sixes and 12 fours, and yet scarcely ever seemed to strike the ball hard. Illingworth used six bowlers, but it did not matter what they did, or where he placed his field: it was all one. He himself bowled accurately on the leg stump with a strong leg field, but Richards still found the gaps, or stepped away and hit him into the open spaces. He was out just before the end, possibly fearing an over-exuberant welcome from the crowd. There are occasions now and then when a Sunday League match produces an innings which transcends the usual slap dash slog, and this was one of them.

Jack Davey

Jack Davey, his shirt blowing open down his manly brown chest, looked as fast and as fierce as a 15th century janissary advancing on the gates of Constantinople, or possibly Painswick.

…

Surrey had not much to play for, and Gloucestershire were after them like the Beaufort hounds on a lame fox. The leading huntsman was Jack ("Jorrocks") Davey, who bowled first from the pavilion end, and after a brief rest came on again at the Orphanage end. He took three wickets yesterday, five in the innings.

Davey is 31, or will be on Thursday, and that is old for a fast bowler, but he looks to me to be bowling as well as he has ever done. If he was a spin bowler he would have his best years ahead of him. As it is, the wisdom which comes with experience, even if the muscles are less supple, will bring him many more wickets. That I sometimes joke about him does not mean I am blind to his talents.

Australians start their tour with confident and stylish authority

CANTERBURY: The Australians have scored 415 for eight wickets in their first innings against Kent

The Australians began their first class, or three-day, part of their tour with confidence and style. They scored their 415 in 120 overs. This is the kind of authority with which we expect a good Australian side to announce their presence. If the scene was not the traditional Worcester, but only Canterbury, which I have never thought a particularly attractive ground, there was still a cathedral ambiance and sunshine and a large crowd. You could find a seat in the sun if you walked round the ground in the afternoon, but you had to hunt for it.

Denness was unable to play for Kent because of a knee injury. This kind of accident may have large consequences, as two other England captains present would confirm. The principal batting success was Turner's. He opened the innings with McCosker; their partnership of 121 was well shared, both going along at a fair pace, but after McCosker had been caught at the wicket Turner took command.

His 156 came out of 273. In the meantime Laird had been out, smartly stumped by Nicholls, at 230. Turner was thought to be slightly fortunate to be chosen for this tour as an extra opening batsman without much of a record behind him; but he will take some keeping out of the Test match side the way he is playing.

The rest of the batsmen played their strokes and obviously enjoyed themselves. Ian Chappell was caught driving, Walters leg before just after reaching his 50, Gilmour well caught at long leg. He is going to be something of a character, this Gilmour. He struck a happy relationship with the crowd, who were sorry to see him out, it then being clear that it was only a question of how many the Australians would score.

Their first seven men all passed 25, before Lillee contributed a disdainful, Miller-like nought. Robinson, the reserve wicket keeper showed he could bat well, and although he was a little less zestful than the others, and even received a youthful slow handclap (after 400 runs in a day) I do not blame him.

Reserve wicket keepers on tour must make the most of what cricket they get. The most famous Australian reserve wicket keeper was K.E. Burn, in the 1880s. Only after the ship had left Fremantle beyond recall was it realized – perhaps only then did he reveal – that he had never kept wicket in his life. But he had to play in the big matches as a batsman, because there were some injuries, and he did not do so badly either.

The pitch at Canterbury yesterday was certainly a good one, but Kent did not bowl untidily, nor collapse in the field. They have four international bowlers and another who has sometimes been recommended, and they have been having a successful season, so it all adds up to an impressive Australian performance.

Higgs demonstrates art of leg spin

CANTERBURY: The Australians, with seven second innings wickets in hand, are 325 runs ahead of Kent

The Australians declared their overnight score, 415, bowled Kent out by 3.40 for 202, but did not make them follow on. Presumably Chappell weighed the advantages of three-day match practice against the stimulus of an early win. To have polished off a leading county in two days – which might well have been done – and have some extra free time, used to be the best of tonics for an Australian touring side, unused to the slog of the circuit six days a week. But then there are no precedents for the shape of the present tour, with a series of one-day matches succeeded in mid-season by a Test series.

Chappell's decision at least made sure of the third day's play, and although Kent are at the wrong end of the game there will probably be another substantial crowd today in the sunshine (touch wood, if this pagan ritual is permitted in so hallowed a city. I was once ticked off for using this phrase by a parson's wife in Glastonbury, but then Glastonbury was an abbey when Canterbury was a shed).

Luckhurst was caught at the wicket when the score was three. Johnson and Cowdrey put on 36 for the second wicket at about one a minute, which took some doing as the Australians bowled under 15 overs in the third hour. Cowdrey batted beautifully. He drove Lillee through extra cover and twice hooked him. He looked solidly in when he edged the ball from Gilmour and promptly walked away. A sigh went round the ground. Johnson was out soon afterwards.

Gilmour took the first three wickets. He looked as fast as Lillee, and more accurate. Hurst was also quick when he came on, and had Woolmer caught at the wicket, fourth out at 58. During the innings, Robinson took three catches and made three stumpings.

Ealham, Shepherd and Julien provided the bulk of the Kent runs. The over rate improved in the afternoon, and so did the scoring rate, and this was chiefly because we had a leg spinner bowling. Higgs could turn the ball a little, even on so true a pitch, and was not afraid to flight it. Shepherd hit him for two consecutive fours and was caught at third man next ball from a skier: a courageous ball.

I liked the look of Higgs. He has a nice sideways action, which at take-off rather comically resembled that of Thomson, showing the batsman the ball behind his bottom. Higgs is 25 next month, a good age at which to improve. Leg spinners are usually either finished at 19 (as a Venerable Personage will tell you) or beginning to get to work in their middle 20s.

I see that *The Spectator* has taken a whack this week at the "traditionalists" among cricket enthusiasts who do not altogether relish one-day cricket. Well, you would very rarely see a leg spinner flighting the ball in a limited over match, and yet leg spin is one of the most captivating arts in the game. "Change is unquestionably preferable to death," says *The Spectator*. Who can say? Change is sometimes for the better and sometimes for the worse, as we all know. Whether death is for the better or worse we are not in a position to say, but many men have thought there were circumstances when it might be preferable to a life faced with unacceptable change.

I am not an enemy of the one-day game, nor do I think cricket is dying. I enjoyed the play yesterday – the Australians ambled along in the evening against a depleted Kent attack – but the bowling of Higgs was not the least of the pleasures.

Memorable 151 not out by Cowdrey beats Australians

CANTERBURY: Kent beat the Australians by four wickets

Just after 6 o'clock yesterday with nine overs yet to play, Kent won the match, an unexpected but jubilated outcome. Cowdrey had won it for them. Plump, brown, benign, is the way we usually think of Cowdrey nowadays. It is reported that he cannot be sure of a regular place in the Kent XI and is thinking of going to Sussex for a year or ten. I suspect that his secret plan is to score another 100 centuries for Sussex. After all, Hobbs scored almost that many after he was 40, and Cowdrey is only 42, hardly more than a well developed boy really. As he came running triumphantly in after what must have been one of the most satisfying innings of his life, he looked less like the familiar archidiaconal personage than a skipping lamb finding another spring.

The Australians batted for another half hour in the morning, and declared with a lead of 353. Play was to continue until six, and so Kent had about 350 minutes to score the runs. This seemed only a theoretical consideration, especially as Julien has injured and unable to bat, and Elms was limping, and would need a runner, as he did in the first innings.

Luckhurst and Johnson made a useful start, but both were out before luncheon and soon afterwards Woolmer, going well, was hit painfully on the arm by Lillee. He made a plucky try to carry on, but had to retire. Ealham was out first ball. Kent were 116 for three, or 116 for five and a half, more probably. The Australians thought they had won, understandably. The pitch was still a good one but they were down to the middle of the order and grandpa was bound to make a mistake soon.

Chappell bowled his spinners for most of the afternoon, a sensible enough policy. Several times Higgs had Cowdrey in trouble and was always the likeliest man to get him out. But we began to notice that the runs were piling and Cowdrey had found a valuable partner in Nicholls. Cowdrey, 50, cheers. Hundred partnership, cheers. Kent 226 for three at tea, they ought to save it now – and then the dawning thought: goodness they might win.

The same thought had obviously reached the Australians. Lillee came on after tea with a fast spell, and two close short legs for Nicholls, the left-hander. He had Nicholls caught at the wicket at 242 and Shepherd leg before at 246.

There was an unexpectedly good innings by Rowe, and when he was out, caught at the wicket off Gilmour, Woolmer returned: more, louder cheers. His partnership with Cowdrey took Kent through with scarcely a tremor.

I don't know whether the Australians minded being beaten. Tests are the only matches that matter on tour, was the doctrine laid down by M.A. Noble in 1909. But the result cannot much have encouraged them, and correspondingly it will have encouraged English cricketers. The dreaded men are not unbeatable. The benefit of this match for the Australians was that several of their young men – Higgs, Robinson Hurst, Turner – had a chance to acclimatize themselves to the disciplines of the three-day game.

And what shall I say about Cowdrey? That he cut, that he drove, that he hooked, that he glanced? All these things he did. It was a memorable innings. But I shall reserve my full discussion of Cowdrey's batting until he retires, which is likely to be around 1984.

AUSTRALIANS	415 for eight declared (Turner 156, McCosker 58, Walters 50) & 140 for three declared (Laird 63*)
KENT	202 (Ealham 41, Julien 41, Higgs 4-49) & 354 for six (Cowdrey 151*, Woolmer 71*)

Colin Cowdrey
'He came running triumphantly in like a skipping lamb finding another spring'

Minor dramas take place over the hedge

BASINGSTOKE: Hampshire, with four first innings wickets in hand, are 131 runs behind Glamorgan

The turning point came just before half past three when a most dangerous batsman was beautifully caught at deep midwicket. It took some catching, high out of the sun, the fielder's arms stretched above the head. It deservedly won the loudest cheers of the day in all the neighbourhood, and soon afterwards, the match.

I could not identify the fielder, which I admit must be a failure in our modern ruthless journalism, but she was pretty, wearing a flowered frock, and about eight years old. Thus did the Blues beat the Greens in the Fairfields junior school inter-house rounders competition. There were other dramas. A large boy in a purple jumper, obviously with a formidable reputation, had the field scattered to its limits, yet never managed to connect with the ball, and was ignominiously run out. Poor lad, there is nothing left for him but to write for *The Guardian.*

The Blue bowler and captain was taken off, apparently at the insistence of the headmaster, who made a personal appearance on the field ("Life is more important than rounders, Vernon-Smith. My study in three minutes.") There were scenes of crowd hysteria at the crisis, drowning the polite clapping from the cricket ground. It even extended to the press hedge. The most hardened of reporters (well, me) found himself abusing a lineswoman. But in the end, corrupt decisions did not matter. The little girl in the flowered frock had done the trick.

Events were duller on the other side of the hedge. There was the Cutty Sark tent, which is becoming a Basingstoke tradition, and there was Bill Shepheard, whose prowess on the public address system would have been stretched had he been doing the rounders, and there was Glamorgan, batting uncertainly, and for the most part slowly, against Hampshire. ......

The Hampshire collapse in the evening was attributable to a vigorous spell by Nash and some casual batting. It was only when Richards was out, caught at the wicket at 63 for four, that Hampshire brows began to crease. Then there was a muddle of a run out and another wicket, but Gilliat is still in. He will need to play an innings today if Hampshire are not to lose a match they ought to be winning. Perhaps he should look over the hedge to pick up some flower power.

Nash could give England variation

BASINGSTOKE: Hampshire, with all second innings wickets in hand, need 297 runs to beat Glamorgan

... Nash took nine wickets for 56, all the wickets except for a run out. These were the best figures of his career, the best figures to any bowler this season. Nash is 30 years old and has always been an iffish player; but he seems to be getting a better, a sounder player, more secure in his mind, and a fast medium left hander would make a useful variation in the England attack.

By lunch, Glamorgan had lost four wickets. Majid, however, came in at No 7. He looked stiff and sneezy, but he played some of the best possible strokes, as he always does. It was said of Virgil, and later of Wodehouse, that he was incapable of composing a clumsy sentence, even if he was thinking of something else. Majid's batting often gives the same impression. ......

Basingstoke, the town, is now a concrete jungle, but you cannot see much of it from the cricket ground, which is surrounded by trees and has quite a festival air with its hospitable tents. Cutty Sark, no doubt fearing for their bank balance in such thirsty weather, had gone off duty, but Weller and Eggar, a firm of surveyors who might have been invented by Dickens, and *The Basingstoke Gazette* were doing their stuff.

The Basingstoke Gazette, which is only a year or two from its centenary, is enjoying the rapid expansion of the town, however much it may regret the destruction of that pleasant, homely place which Basingstoke used to be. I met the headmaster of Fairfields School, who asked me to explain that he had summoned that bowler from the rounders field yesterday nor for any lack of sportsmanship, but because he had an appointment with the dentist.

Comforting thoughts

BASINGSTOKE: Glamorgan (16 pts) beat Hampshire (4 pts) by 66 runs

.... So far as the future of first-class cricket at Basingstoke is concerned, there is no reason why the pitch should let them down, and neither did the public. It was a large crowd for a third day.

On the way back to the station I paused for a while in the old Church of St Michael, once the town's pride, now overshadowed, pushed into a corner, by the huge Ministry-of-Love-style shopping precinct. It is cool and peaceful. Indeed, I have written this report here, quietly, in a back pew. I daresay St Michael's will be here when the shopping precinct is gone, and I daresay that they will still be playing cricket up the road. Both of these are comforting thoughts.

A battle at Dover without the grim efficiency

DOVER: Nottinghamshire, with all second innings wickets in hand, lead Kent by 234 runs

"Perhaps the most famous of the gates of England, Dover has always worn a warlike mien. Less formidable than renowned Gibraltar, there is a look of grim efficiency about her heights, an air of masked authority about the windy galleries hung in her cold gray chalk, something of Roman competence about the proud old gatehouse on the Castle Hill…" Many readers will be familiar with this passage (if you are not, the characteristic spelling "gray" gives you a clue). Yes, I like Dover, the cliffs and the quays and the castle and the cricket ground, which has plenty of windy galleries, but the direction of the proceedings yesterday had an efficiency rather less than grim, and a competence rather less than Roman. At one point there was, as I heard a Very Senior Cricket Correspondent observe, a proper box-up.

Nottinghamshire began the day at 283 for six in 91 overs, and took their score to 328 for eight in 100. There had been a brief storm in the morning, before play, and later there was some light drizzle. Kent made a quiet, unbothered start: 27 for no wicket at lunch.

In the afternoon the sun came out, and the weather became quite hot. A couple of good spin bowlers, I thought, should run through a side in these conditions, and this White and Latchman started doing. At the beginning of the thirty-first over, Kent were 86 for two. At the end of the thirty-third, they were 88 for seven. The eighth wicket fell at 98, that of Asif, who had looked more at ease than anyone.

The pitch did not remain too difficult for long. I know there is a temptation to describe the hazards of a pitch in accord with the wickets which fall, yet it was only for about half an hour that the ball was really hopping. Ealham was seventh out to an excellent return catch, which might have been made on any pitch, and Asif to a careless drive.

Julien, though he had to use a runner, and Topley, were soon scoring freely. Latchman lost his control, and had to be replaced by Rice. White continued to bowl steadily, despite punishment, but had to move more to the defensive as the possibility increased that Kent would save the follow-on. At 159 Rice bowled Julien, which meant that the last Kent batsmen had to score – well, how many?

Here we come to the box-up bit. Only one scoreboard at Dover records the total of the previous innings, and even that does it with no indication to a stranger of its meaning. The numbers are simply propped up on an adjacent bit of cliff. They might just as well be a pile of spare numbers awaiting the attention of the enthusiastic but youthful operators.

I had noticed from the beginning of the Kent innings that this figure, if one can so call it, stood at 332. I knew, and the scorers and most of the crowd knew, that it should have been 328, but this hardly seemed to matter, until it became apparent that both teams were working by the scoreboard. Nottinghamshire thought they had to get Kent out for 182, whereas all Kent needed to score was 179. When Kent were 178, Topley played a ball down to third man for an easy single, but refused the run, because it would have given Jarvis the bowling.

There would have been some fun if Topley had got out next ball, but fortunately he scored a run. Shortly after this point, a voice floated across the ground "Oy, Bill, they've changed their bloody score." Sure enough, the jumble of figures now resembled 328. I understand this was done at the insistence of the correspondent of *The Guardian* who had even left his purple jumper behind in the excitement. Meyer, the umpire, ran from the field to consult the scorers. So, a minute or two later, did Smedley, the Nottinghamshire captain, with a war-like mien. No good. The follow-on was already saved, with nobody on the field knowing it.

Nottinghamshire were a little aggrieved, and might indeed have altered their tactics had they been better informed. But they have no grounds for complaint, any more than Kent would have had if Topley had got out after refusing that single. Cricketers, or at least their captains, should know the score. The public address announcer might also have troubled to advise spectators what was happening, though presumably they knew more about it than he did.

No, we did not have the Roman touch at Dover yesterday; they were more like Ancient Britons, the lot of them. Certainly a good deal of woad was flying about afterwards.

Dover

Basingstoke

Summer sun cannot shine all the time on Somerset

WESTON-SUPER-MARE: Hampshire, with six second innings wickets in hand, are 211 runs ahead of Somerset

It was a day of shining, sweating sun, one of those governed by the special clause which Ted Turner, once the public relations officer here, insisted upon in his negotiations with God. The principle on which this agreement was founded was that both parties accepted that the sun always shines upon Weston, even if the clouds sometimes get in the way; but Mr Turner put in this extra bit about a few entirely cloudless days while the angel of the south-west wind was not concentrating on the small print.

You could hardly move in the beer tent, or anywhere else, without bumping into an old Somerset cricketer, usually Bill Andrews. You could always tell when it was Andrews because your beer was spilt in the enthusiasm of the greeting. Gimblett was there, and Hazell, and Stephenson, and I am really better equipped to describe the Somerset-Gloucestershire match of 1938 than the Somerset-Hampshire match of yesterday.

Somerset won that famous match in 1938, when Jack Crapp dropped a hard catch in the outfield in the last over. They are not likely to win this one, though twice they have seemed to be on top of it. Hampshire were out on Saturday for 267. When Somerset were 146 for two, with Richards and Denning set and confident, they were looking for a substantial first innings lead.

This did not happen. Stephenson (the Hampshire one), who is a good multi-purpose wicket-keeper, caught Richards and stumped Denning. He had five wickets altogether. Roberts had six. He had Rose out early in the innings and came back in a spell of great speed to roll over the last five. Although Slocombe and Roebuck showed some form, from 234 for five it was 259 all out: Hampshire leading by eight runs on the first innings, their only advantage, since the points were level, seven each.

The crowd – it *was* a crowd, Clarence Park nearly full again – were cheering in every variety of Birmingham accent when Hampshire lost four wickets for 44. Jones had a fast and well-aimed spell, not grunting as much as usual, which, I have decided, is a good sign.

Greenidge was unwell and may not be able to bat. Jesty was rushed to hospital at lunchtime with suspected adhesions between the inner and outer walls of his lower abdomen, but was fit enough to bat well with his captain in a fifth-wicket partnership which gave Hampshire a formidable position by the end.

Gilliat's innings was one of the best I have seen him play. The pitch has played truly, if slowly, so far, but it will be dusty today, and perhaps Sainsbury will not mind bowling on it.

Sainsbury puts his wisdom to work

WESTON-SUPER-MARE: Hampshire (17 pts) beat Somerset (7 pts) by 101 runs

The Weston week has been an outstanding success, as it usually is when the sun is out: less in glory for Somerset, than in satisfaction for their treasurer, who happens not to be, you will be surprised to learn, Bill (hand that bowled Bradman) Andrews. This is about the only job in the county from which he has not been sacked, for the sound reason that he has yet to be appointed to it. He looked as happy as if he had sacked the Treasury himself yesterday, as he surveyed the crowded scene, splendid in vermilion trousers and pipe, his heart and voice so resounding that you would have thought someone was holding a choir practice in the neighbouring church.

Somerset were never really in the match yesterday, though they had one stroke of luck, for Roberts was not well – there were a lot of strains and sicknesses in this match – and not so much of a menace as usual. He did not field after lunch. However, this was hardly a crucial point, since it was the spin bowlers who were likely to win the game. The pitch was dusty, and turned sufficiently to make it tricky chasing runs.

The Hampshire innings ended at 256, which meant Somerset would have to score 265, with time enough if they kept moving. Rose and Taylor made a fair start, but Rose was stumped when Sainsbury came on. It was 52 for one at lunch, with three and a half hours to go.

It needed a big innings by one of the Somerset batsmen to get in range. Close might have provided it, and did indeed play well, but ran out of partners, in more than one sense. He was 61 not out at the end. His promising young middle order men, Slocombe, Roebuck and Marks, failed though Marks showed a sign or two of life. They all found the wisdom of Sainsbury too much for them. Southern supported Sainsbury well at the other end, and took the important wicket of Richards (this admirable wicketkeeper Stephenson again), but it was Sainsbury's afternoon. His flight and length were judged as you might expect from a man with 20 years of experience who still likes to learn, and regards every fresh batsman as a fresh problem. Even Bill Andrews spoke well of him, at least I think he did.

AUGUST: Northamptonshire v Essex at Northampton (3rd day) 1975

Night watchman is extra vigilant

NORTHAMPTON: Northamptonshire (8 pts) drew with Essex (7 pts)

Two heavy bursts of rain, one in the morning and one in the afternoon, put a stop to the game before it could approach a decision. Essex, starting at 74 for three, declared at 175 at lunch, which meant that Northamptonshire had to score 245 in three and a half hours. This was a more generous declaration than is common, but a sensible one, since an hour and a quarter had been lost in the morning, and there was always a likelihood that one of the circling storms would return.

The circumstances in which the players left the field in the morning were unusual. Lightning had been flickering and thunder rumbling, but not a drop of rain had fallen. The umpires, Palmer and Meyer, had just consulted one another and decided that the light was sufficient for play. Then there was a loud clap of thunder, which certainly seemed to come from over midwicket's head. It was enough to make Palmer grab the bails and join in the dash for the pavilion.

If you are killed by lightning you do not hear the thunder and although it was said later that the lightning had "come down" one of the football floodlighting pylons I doubt it. The interval between the lightning and the thunder was too long. Still, I ducked, irrationally, like everybody else. "Thunder stopped play" is a new experience to me.

McEwan and Smith batted well for Essex. McEwan began with a couple of his best cover drives, but after that it was Smith, the wicketkeeper, sent in as night watchman who did most of the scoring.

He will make many runs by the time he has done; and although he enjoys his leg-side swishes he will not make all of them in that style for he has an excellent, straight, lofted drive. He is not quite a youngster, this Smith – born in Dewsbury in 1949, played for Yorkshire in 1970. He has the cheerfully tough attitude to life you are led to expect from that part of the world.

I recall a story told by Fred Hoyle at a dinner of the Royal Astronomical Society (no, I am not lying). A young man from the south had taken his light opera company to the dark walls of Dewsbury, and as usual called on the local authority in the hope of some financial aid, or at least some free publicity. "Ay, lad," said the local authority. "So tha's what we might all an impresario, and tha wants a bit o' help. Now, what is entertainment tha's plannin' to provide?"

"Well, sir, we do 'Goodnight Vienna' very well." "Ee," said the local authority, shaking his head, "no more chance with 'Goodnight Vienna' in Dewsbury than you'd have with 'Goodnight Dewsbury' in Vienna."

There ought to have been some life in the pitch after the first storm, because the sun came out and shone quite strongly, and yet it continued to play fairly comfortably. It had been so dry that the rain went through it leaving it much as before, though the deep-lying worms were no doubt grateful for the drink.

Boyce bowled a long spell, always dangerous. He had Cook caught at long leg, and bowled Virgin, who had been batting soundly. That was 48 for two, in the 21st over. Soon afterwards, to nobody's surprise, came the second storm.

The passage of time before the abandonment was mitigated by the refreshment of the Pavilion bar, and its exceptionally pretty barmaid. "Looking at that girl," it was said to me by a local member, "is about the only thing you can be sure of getting for your subscription." And so goodnight Northampton.

Worcestershire v Glamorgan at Worcester (Sunday League)

A curious experience at Worcester

WORCESTER: Worcestershire (4 pts) beat Glamorgan by 49 runs

It was a curious experience to be watching this match. Here we were on a sunny Sunday afternoon at Worcester, with a partisan crowd, and hardly an empty seat, but the cricket proceeding in front of us, though as interesting as most Sunday League cricket is, was no more than a secondary conditional entertainment. Everyone was waiting for news from Darley Dale, which was somewhat sparsely provided by the public address system.

Announcers should not be shy of giving plenty of information to a Sunday crowd. A Sunday crowd is not like the aged members of the MCC who resent any interruption of the traditional hush. Surprising rumours circulated ("Richards and Greenidge both out in the third over") and on a stroll round the ground I was constantly accosted by friends who believed that anyone who has ever had anything to do with broadcasting can find any latest score by a quick manipulation of his navel.

Editor's note: Worcestershire, with a fixture the following Sunday, would retain a chance of winning the Sunday League if Hampshire lost to Derbyshire at Darley Dale. In the event, Hampshire's Richards and Greenidge both scored fifties, and they won comfortably.

AUGUST: Davison and Balderstone at Leicester 1975

One noble statistic remains unbroken

LEICESTER: Leicestershire v Nottinghamshire

The record stand for Leicestershire's third wicket is 316, by Watson and Wharton at Taunton in 1961. It was not broken yesterday, not quite: but it is a pity to waste such a noble statistic when you have conscientiously looked it up, and it is always a pleasure to remind yourself of batsmen so good as Watson and Wharton.

This is not a way of saying that Davison and Balderstone, who were only 12 runs from a record, are inferior players. If England were playing the Rest of the World this summer, Davison would probably be in the opposing side; and if Balderstone had played yesterday's innings – his highest score – last week, he might be on the brink of an England cap.

I have never seen Davison bat better. Some of his innings in limited over cricket have been more dramatic, but less evocative of his skills. As Sydney Smith said of the maturing Macaulay, his enemies might accuse him of talking too much, "but now he has occasional flashes of silence that make his conversation perfectly delightful."

Davison took a breather from time to time before renewing the power of his driving; I single out the drive, although he plays all round the wicket, because this is one stroke that demoralizes the opposition, especially on such a hot day, when 100 overs seem an aeon, and the next break for drinks at least a lustrum away.

Balderstone, patiently seeking his touch, was happy enough to follow Davison's path. After Davison was out, casually mis-hitting a drive, Balderstone took charge and batted well in the latter part of his innings. Davison would surely not have got out had he been aware of the desperate researches going on in the press box ("yes, operator, Frindall please, f, r and i for the iris that faded not, the light of thine eye, beg your pardon operator, nothing personal intended").

SEPTEMBER: The future of Brian Close at Taunton

Close is thwarted but still makes his point

TAUNTON: Somerset v Essex

DAY ONE

Close and Slocombe batted well. There is, I understand, some query about Close's future with Somerset. As far as cricketing merit goes, there need be none. He is supposed to be too hard on the young men: an ironic suggestion, if your memory goes back far enough. It was generally felt, after Close's unsuccessful tour of Australia in 1950-1, that what the boy needed was a bit of discipline.

Somerset were holding a committee meeting at 5 o'clock, a highly secret and important meeting, as Bill Andrews informed anyone within earshot, which means roughly Kingston St Mary to the north and Trull to the south. Close played as if he planned to reach his hundred at precisely 5 o'clock. In this he was thwarted, but chiefly by the weather. I thought he was sure to get it afterwards, but once the committee was in session he did not seem to bother too much, and was bowled by Lever, for 86, having made his point.

DAY TWO

What everybody is talking about here is the future of Brian Close. There was a meeting of the cricket committee on Wednesday night and their report is to be taken to the full county executive next Tuesday. It is rather like the Reg Prentice affair. "Secret Close verdict" was the headline in the local paper. Close himself wore a white, floppy hat, which he only took off to give himself a bowl (taking a wicket, of course) and wandered about rather ostentatiously from slip to slip. Who cares? He seemed to be saying. But he had an eye like a buzzard and an arm like a whip if any of his fieldsmen lost concentration or strayed a yard or two from their position.

Somerset will be silly if they do not come to terms with him. For one thing, they have no other adequate captain in sight, though several might be able to do the job in a few years. Equally, Close will be silly if he does not come to terms with Somerset. He has much cricket left in him. What does he want to be? Captain of Derbyshire, which most Yorkshiremen regard as the worst possible fate? Captain of Devon? Certainly, if Devon could manage to pay him for five years, they would be a first class county, as they have long wished to be, at the end of it.

The 1975 season was, we all know, great, unforgettable, scintillating, action-packed, sun-packed, scintillating, image-restoring, hope-restoring, and scintillating. Well, it certainly had many memorable moments: but it was also complicated and shapeless, and went on too long. I noticed, indeed shared in, an occasional weary tetchiness in the last week or two, both in the field and the Press box. This might have been worse had it not been that so many counties still had a chance of the Championship at a late stage. I am bound to say that by the middle of September I felt glad that I need not watch cricket again until the spring, except in the garden, where my son Adam is having trouble trying to decide whether he is a left-hand or right-hand batsman, and I feel it my duty to assist, less as a cricketer than a psychiatrist.

I shared in the general satisfaction at Leicestershire's success, partly because it made such a happy climax to Illingworth's career, and partly because they had never won before. I say the 'climax' to Illingworth's career, but he may surprise us yet. I find it encouraging that more players are prepared to stay in the game until they are 40. This was commonplace in pre-war days, but then there came a period when a man was considered a fogey or a freak if he went on after 35. Hobbs scored a hundred centuries after he was 40. Cowdrey, I dare say, does not forget this statistic. I enjoyed nothing all summer more than his match-winning hundred against the Australians at Canterbury, even though it missed me a connection and got me home at two in the morning – and in a game when we had been optimistically picking up timetables in the middle of the second afternoon! I am glad Close is to have another season with Somerset. The matter was not very well handled. It was said that he was too severe with some of the younger players, feeling that they did not take the game seriously enough. I cannot help being a little tickled by the emergence of Close as the stern patriarch, the dedicated professional. When he was a boy on F.R. Brown's tour of Australia, his play was not, apparently, marked by excessive dedication or readiness to learn. *Si jeunesse savait* ...

One reason why I found the summer more hectic than usual was none of my neighbouring sides did well. If you live in Bristol it makes a large difference to the amount of travelling you have to do if Somerset or Gloucestershire or Glamorgan are making a Championship run. Hampshire is not so far away if you are a crow or a motorist, but not so good if you travel by train. Sadly I miss the old Somerset and Dorset line, known to railwaymen as the 'Slow & Dirty', which used to take you direct from Bath to Bournemouth. There was a train called 'The Pines Express', a through train from the north. It made the oddest sight, with perhaps a dozen coaches up, shining nameboards and vast steaming engine, plodding down the single track through some of the loveliest and quietest countryside in the west. 'Pines Express!', the stationmaster/porter would cry out at the little stations. 'Next stop Evercreech Junction!' 'Next stop Blandford Forum!' It was a lovely way to go to Dean Park, and find at the end of the trip Bill Shepheard's beaming face, and Desmond Eagar wondering whether he might daringly make a bowling change (i.e switch Shackleton to the other end) and John Arlott murmuring that you'd arrived just at the right time, and there was a tent just along there ...

No, I am not wandering from my subject. Railway journeys are as much part of my summer as the cricket. I often recall a day not by a noble century from Boycott but a long wait at Didcot or, it may be, a lucky connection at York.

This year people in all counties were pleased that Yorkshire did well. What they really meant, when they said 'Good to see Yorkshire doing well', was that this was a county which, despite of all temptations, plays only Yorkshiremen-born. This has nothing to do with questions of colour, nor is it because of lack of enthusiasm for the overseas cricketers who have enriched the county scene. Procter went on to bowl for Gloucestershire in a Gillette Cup match and put himself out for the rest of the season, possibly permanently damaging his bowling career, simply because he was so keen for Gloucestershire to win. Down here in the West we regard 'Procky' as one of our own. But in the nature of things some of the overseas players are no more than highly-skilled hired servants. They are usually popular as persons as well as cricketers. But how can Wotton-under-Edge rejoice over a hundred by Sadiq as, say, Armley does when Carrick does well? Even the prisoners in Armley Gaol would have half-a-spoonful of sugar extra after Carrick had taken six wickets.

The people who did not share the pleasure of the Yorkshire revival were the Yorkshiremen, or some of them. At the Headingley Test I was surprised at the number of inhabitants who assured me this was the worst Yorkshire side they had ever seen. I hardly dared mention Yorkshire to my old friend Don Mosey, or he would spray his contempt all over the box – the commentary box I mean of course (his moustache acts as a distributor, like a nozzle at the end of a hose-pipe). 'He is playing for the same side as Leyland!' – thus a young Yorkshire batsman was condemned after playing what Don described as one of his 'more fluent' innings (he was out first ball). But when Leyland was a young man and getting noughts, they were saying 'He is playing for the same side as Denton!' and when Denton was playing ... why go on? I have explained before that nearly all Yorkshiremen possess the Latin American temperament.

1976

The year began for Alan Gibson on a high note. His autobiography, *A Mingled Yarn*, which had been several years in the writing, was finally published early in January and was well received. Reviewing it for *The Times*, the distinguished literary critic Ion Trewin observed that 'Gibson sees himself as a contemporary RC Robertson-Glasgow, without the tragedy.' That was presumably a reference to the fact that Alan had failed in his attempt to commit suicide back in 1963, whereas Robertson-Glasgow, whom Alan did indeed much admire, had sadly succeeded; although in the light of what was to follow, it has an ironic ring to it now. Nonetheless, the review concluded with a ringing endorsement: 'It makes a marvellous memoir with which to launch 1976.'

I was staying with Alan and the family at Henleaze at the time, and can remember feeling faintly disappointed when I read the book. I had expected there to be a lot more about cricket and rugby; that was, after all, what he was famous for. As it was, they had to share just a single a chapter between them. All the stuff about Dissenting preachers and his early life was interesting enough, but it certainly wasn't what fans of Alan Gibson – and I was unashamedly one of them – would have been looking forward to. But that, of course, was the point. This was a serious autobiography by a seriously well-read man who wanted above all to be taken seriously. It was his way of saying to the world: "There you are. Now you can see that there's a lot more to me than just being a jokey cricket-writer."

It had been a dry winter, in the course of which I had moved from London to Wiltshire and got married. The wedding was on a Saturday in Cambridgeshire. Alan failed to put in an appearance, leaving Rosie to come with Adam and Felicity, who was one of the bridesmaids. I did my best to persuade him to change his mind, for appearance's sake, but he would not be shifted. He had made up his mind that he was not going to attend what he no doubt regarded as a frightful middle-class bunfight with both of his wives in attendance and that was that. I do not recall feeling hugely put out, other than on behalf of my prospective in-laws. Had he turned up, he would undoubtedly have had too much to drink and there would inevitably have been a scene. We had long since given up expecting the normal family niceties from him. I think that the only parental guidance he ever offered me on the subject of relationships with the opposite sex was in the station buffet at Exeter after the break-up of a previous engagement: "Never mind, old chap. From now on, if I were you, I should just have a poke whenever you feel like it!"

By the time the cricket season arrived at the end of April, the effects of almost twelve months of drought were becoming apparent, even in the Oxford Parks, although the opening fixture of Alan's reporting season for *The Times* is perhaps more significant for the fact that Didcot makes its debut appearance as his *bête noire* of the railway network. A Jack Davey hat-trick for Gloucestershire was a bonus.

There could have been no more appropriate touring side that summer than Clive Lloyd's West Indies; pace like fire and blazing stroke play to go with the searing heat. Alan got his first sight of them when they played Somerset at Taunton on May 27, in a match that was to have momentous consequences. It would be going too far to claim that Brian Close's subsequent selection, at the age of 45, for the first three Tests was as a direct consequence of Alan Gibson's championing of his qualities in *The Times*, but it undoubtedly played a part. He would perform every bit as bravely as Alan had predicted, and with considerable skill as well.

Tests
West Indies
beat England
3-0, with two draws

Championship
1 Middlesex
2 Northamptonshire
3 Gloucestershire
4 Leicestershire
5 Warwickshire
6 Essex

Sunday League
1 Kent
2 Essex
3 Leicestershire
4 Somerset
5 Sussex
6 Nottinghamshire

Gillette Cup Final
Northamptonshire
beat Lancashire

Benson & Hedges Final
Kent
beat Worcestershire

Most first-class runs
1 Zaheer Abbas
2 D.L. Amiss
3 C.G. Greenidge

Most first-class wickets
1 G.A. Cope
2 M.W.W. Selvey
3 P.H. Edmonds

At this stage of the season, the weather was dry, but distinctly chilly. The heatwave didn't arrive until June. On 15 consecutive days, from June 23 to July 7, the temperature in the shade exceeded 90°F somewhere in Southern England.

And so to August, and the climax of the season. In the fifth Test, on a perfect wicket at a sun-baked Oval, Vivian Richards' 291 and Michael Holding's 14 wickets carried the West Indies to a resounding victory, to take the series 3-0. Alan, meanwhile, had been to Lord's to cover a very different international match, when England's women cricketers took on the Australians on August 5.

Middlesex, astutely captained by Mike Brearley, were by now in charge in the county championship. Alan watched the second and third days of their match against Glamorgan at Swansea on August 16 and 17, where the confidence of the visitors was in stark contrast to the trials and tribulations of the home county.

Alan found himself at Bristol for the traditional Bank Holiday match against Somerset. With the game finishing early, Alan repaired – as was often his wont – to the County Ground Hotel with a small group of friends and kindred spirits. There, in the bar, they founded the JJ? Society, its object being – according to the Rules, which were published in June of the following year – to express 'reverent admiration for JJ Davey and general affection for Gloucestershire cricket'. The 'duties' of members included wearing the society tie on specified days each season, to give JJ Davey a rousing cheer when he went out to bat and to present one penny to the funds of the Society for every run that JJ Davey scored above ten in an innings. Alan was the President, Arthur Anderson was (still is, in fact) the Secretary, and also present at that inaugural meeting were CC Buffrey and D Cook.

It was all good, cheerful, superannuated schoolboy fun, and Jack Davey himself took it in good part. Thereafter, respectable middle-aged gentlemen did indeed sometimes attract bemused looks at the County Ground and elsewhere by shouting out "Go berserk, Jack" (pronounced, of course, 'bearsark'), or "Cold steel, Jack", whenever their hero went out to bat. They still meet occasionally, the flame being kept alive by Arthur Anderson and Richard Walsh, who reports Somerset cricket for the *Somerset County Gazette* and *Western Morning News*.

The Gillette Cup having been won by Northamptonshire, that left just the John Player League to be decided among the major trophies. On the morning of the final round of matches, on September 5, five counties were still in contention: Somerset and Sussex, who were joint leaders with 40 points apiece, and Essex, Kent and Leicestershire all on 36. Sussex were always struggling against Warwickshire, which meant that if Somerset could tie or win against Glamorgan, the title – the first in their history – would be theirs. Alan was there for *The Times*.

How disappointed he really was about the outcome, I am not entirely sure. Had it been the championship, he would have been genuinely mortified. But, although he did his best to feign interest and excitement in the John Player League, he never much enjoyed it, still less the sort of supporters it tended to attract.

It was a sad note on which to conclude what had been a summer of memorable cricket as well as memorable weather. And that ended as well. All the prayers that had been offered up for a break in the relentless drought were finally answered in September, which – just to show that a climate of extremes is nothing new – produced some of the worst storms for a generation.

Davey strikes and Oxford surrender

OXFORD: Gloucestershire, with all their first innings wickets in hand, lead Oxford University by 23 runs

I usually begin my cricket season with a panegyric on the Parks – the trees, the blossoms and the boys and the girls. They were all there yesterday in quantity, as well as a shining sun, but I was not disposed to dwell on these matters. My mind was occupied, for a long time, with the public announcement system at Didcot railway station.

There I waited, in the morning, with several other hapless citizens while the Oxford train drew out in front of our noses. We had been warmly and confidently assured that the train in question was about to depart to Paddington. I quail at the thought of what lies before me this season if British Rail information conforms to the Didcot standard.

I arrived at the Parks soon after lunchtime, and when I saw the board saying 90 for three, I thought Gloucestershire must be batting. So little is my faith, I felt that if Oxford had batted first, they would have been out before now.

I gather that they had to this point batted soundly, if cautiously, on what was certainly a plum wicket. I saw Claughton complete his 50 with some useful strokes. I saw Wingfield-Digby make a majestic two. He has never come on as a batsman as I promised his relations a year ago. He was then leg-before to Davey, the first victim, as it proved, of a hat-trick.

As the next two wickets fell in Davey's next over, and there had been much action in between, hardly anybody realized it was a hat-trick, not even Demon Dave himself. It was the first of his career, he told me, when it had sunk in, if you do not count one in the East Cornwall League (I think I vaguely remember the match – Brown Willy v Roughtor in the skittle alley of the Butcher's Arms). The last six Oxford wickets fell for four runs.

It was a pity, but not surprising, that a fair start had vanished. Davey and Graveney pitched the ball well up and the batsmen were inclined to play them too much from the back foot. Procter bowled steadily at medium pace.

Sadiq and Cooper took Gloucestershire into the lead before the end without much trouble, though Sadiq was dropped at second slip early in his innings. The bowler was Gurr, who looked as if he might develop into something. He is also the first man I can remember in an Oxford cricket side from Regent's Park College, an establishment principally devoted to the training of young men for the Baptist ministry.

Sadiq played some happy strokes. The Oxford bowling was no more than tidy at its best, and often less than that. The fielding, however, was keen, athletic and occasionally brilliant. There is always hope for a university side if it fields well.

Apart from the hazards of the day, I now face the prospect of changing at Didcot again. After some of the expressions I used in the morning, I dare say I shall be remembered there.

An heroic effort by Wingfield-Digby

OXFORD: Oxford University, with eight second innings wickets in hand, need 297 runs to avoid an innings defeat by Gloucestershire

Never mock a Wingfield-Digby. I should have learned this lesson before. Gloucestershire, beginning the day at 150 for no wicket, declared at tea, 481 for five, a holocaust of an innings and only Wingfield-Digby had snatched any brands from the burning. He took all five wickets, for 122 runs, in 38 overs, eight of which were maidens. And I am bound to say it was an heroic effort.

I am told it was not, statistically, his best performance: once, about five years ago, in his early days as a student, he took five for 116 against somebody. I report this information as imparted. These theological students do seem to take a long time qualifying nowadays. But I will risk a small bet with the Wingfield-Digby clan: that he will captain his diocese, when he has acquired one, to victory in the *Church Times* Cup.

Sadiq was first out, caught and bowled, at 208. Cooper reached his first hundred, and gallantly thereafter did his best to get out, but by the time he was bowled, Zaheer was already catching him up: 305 for two, Zaheer and Procter batting. This would be a daunting situation for any side in the world, let alone students in the first match of the season, looking over their shoulders for their tutors (in the case of Wingfield-Digby, conceivably it is the tutors who are looking over their shoulders).

Zaheer played some dazzling shots, but was out before he had reached his 100. Much the same thing happened to Procter. Procter hit mostly from a fast-footed position, the weight on the back leg, He needed to do no more – he hit a six on to the pavilion roof with scarcely more than a twitch of the bat.

All the same, his movements were not always free of at least a suggestion of stress. He reminded me a little of Compton after his knee injury. But Compton scored many thousands of runs after his injury, and so will Procter, if he does not bowl too much. His zest for the game, his inclination to give his utmost effort in all circumstances, whoever he is playing for, could still be his undoing. I do hope he is careful. On the other hand, it is just this quality which has made him such a commanding player, and holds him higher in the affection of English cricketers than, I suppose, any other of the overseas players at present in the championship.

Oxford stuck to their task well, on the whole. The captain deserves credit for the way he kept them together. The coach, no spinner of honeyed words, was not altogether displeased with them. They also batted stoutly in the evening, making sure that there would be a chunk of play left for the third day. So in the morning I will arrive, and take a train, and get me to Didcot once again … though it would certainly take a team of Wingfield-Digbys, and all their friends and relations, to save Oxford this match.

Oxford lose but delay the obsequies

OXFORD: Gloucestershire beat Oxford University by 10 wickets

Well, well, wrong again. I caught an early train, which involved changing at Reading (keeping my head well down as we swept through Didcot) in order not to miss the obsequies, which I thought would be brief. Yet Oxford played uncommonly well, at one time it looked as if they might save the match, and though again their later batting faltered, kept the game going until after tea, making Gloucestershire bat a second time.

Last year, Oxford's highest score in a first-class match in the Parks was 211, so it was pleasing, at least for partisans, to see, at one stage, 300 for five on the scoreboard. Perhaps I exaggerate when I use the word "see", since the lads who operate the board, swiftly and efficiently, spoil the effect by standing squarely in front of the numbers they have just put up.

The best thing about the Oxford innings, the most encouraging for their captain (an extremely intelligent young man who was born in Middle Chinnock and is reading Greats in his spare time) was that the two major contributions came from freshmen, both playing in first-class cricket for the first time. But the pitch certainly remained slow and easy, but no more than is proper in a three-day match; nevertheless they were both memorable efforts.

Claughton, who had scored 50 in the first innings, showed again that he is a tidy, tenacious, cool player with a lot of runs in him. He built his score slowly, carefully but did not often look like getting out. Last season he was playing for King Edward's, Birmingham, where he was captain and head of the averages. He has had some games for Warwickshire second eleven.

He rarely failed to hit a bad ball. He kept his head admirably when he was, in the nineties, under pressure. The last Oxford man to score a hundred on his first appearance was W. Murray Wood, also in the Parks, and also against Gloucestershire, in 1936.

The other successful newcomer was Clements, who comes from Ipswich School, and has played with moderate success for Suffolk. He is a left-hander, who likes to go for his strokes, especially on the leg side. He has a cover drive, but is rather coy about letting on. Not a classical player, but just the kind of man a university side needs in the middle of the order. He is the sort of batsman who is likely to have a series of low scores from time to time, but his demeanour suggests that he will not allow these hazards to depress him unduly, nor to turn him from his natural game.

Neither of these innings, it must be said, might have been played, had not Pathmanathan, bold and cheeky, scored 44 at more than a run a minute in the morning, disturbing Gloucestershire's confident rhythm. Gloucestershire dropped some catches, looked a little slack at times, or irritated, or even worried – but after all they won by 10 wickets and had a health-giving run about, so their supporters have not much of which to complain. Brown used his slower and less orthodox bowlers skilfully when his main battery had been unsuccessful. Wingfield-Digby, fearlessly, pulled Procter for four to square leg, something his friends and relations will be glad to hear, though I should add that Procter was bowling slow off-breaks at the time.

OXFORD UNIVERSITY	127 (Claughton 51, Davey 5-32)
	355 (Claughton 112, Clements 91, Pathmanathan 44, Procter 4-73)
GLOUCESTERSHIRE	481 for five declared (Sadiq 123, Cooper 106, Zaheer 92, Procter 85, Wingfield Digby 5-122)
	4 for no wicket

King uses his captain on way to first century

TAUNTON: Somerset, with eight first innings wickets in hand, are 332 runs behind the West Indians

The West Indians are still full of runs and beans. They won the toss yesterday and had scored 389 for eight by five past five when they declared. Somerset are not a strong bowling side but did well within their limits. They also fielded keenly and Close, even when the batting was at its most ferocious, set sensible fields and kept his side together.

The pitch, while good, was not one of the Taunton classics of the Buttle era. Both Moseley and Burgess found some response in it. Though there was a large crowd, for Taunton on a Wednesday afternoon, the weather became chilly. However one considers it, this was another impressive West Indian performance.

The principal contributors were Richards, Lloyd and King. Greenidge gave the innings a lively start. Neither Rowe nor Kallicharran found their best touch. Richards, on a ground he knows well and before a crowd which admires him, produced some of his best strokes. When he was caught at the wicket (94 for two), the applause was half relief, half disappointment. Lloyd, in the afternoon, played even better.

There was a day years ago when he cracked a window, first bounce from a tombstone in St James's Church, which lies near the pavilion; and there were times yesterday when I thought he might bring a bell down from the tower. King's hundred was his first. He did not look a good player for 20 minutes or so. He might have been out several times and was lucky to have the settling influence of his captain at the other end. Later he hit the ball hard and far.

I must say a word for the catch at long leg made by Kitchen, no agile kitten now, which ended the innings of Kallicharran, for the reserve Somerset wicketkeeper, Gard, who survived an unfamiliar, taxing day with credit, and several words for the early Somerset batsmen.

They found the fast bowling, even though Holding was not present and Roberts below his fastest, hard enough to play, but never once did they move out of line. This said much for them and for their captain. Rose, in particular, though he might have been out a dozen times, will never play a better, braver, bad innings in his life.

If we really want to win Close is our man

TAUNTON: The West Indians, with all second innings wickets in hand, are 182 runs ahead of Somerset

What are we to make of this man Close? He stood there yesterday, not scoring quickly, though always ready to give the bad ball a bash, and the good ball a successful snick. He was the valiant warrior. He watched his young men, less capable than he, fight off the West Indian fast bowlers, and saw none of them flinch from a fast ball.

Rose must have as many bruises as he had runs. It was not particularly successful. Five wickets were down for 70, and to save the follow-on Somerset needed 239. It seemed a hard task, but Botham, Breakwell and Jennings all made brave scores, under the austere eye of the master at the other end. He gave them a good deal of the bowling, and let them get on with it, while still illustrating by example that a bald iron brow and a hairy iron will can cope with nearly every sort of bowling.

Not, mind you, that he played Padmore very well. He is not at his best against spinners. He only rises to his majesty when the bowlers are trying to kill him. When you think of the past few years, and the way that England's batsmen have ducked and dodged among the bouncers, it is absurd that we have deprived ourselves so often of the services of the Old Bald Blighter. He ought to be captaining England next week. Possibly he might do something outrageous, but then England's current imported captain has also been known to do outrageous things.

I was sad when Close failed to get his hundred. He was out just after tea, from a bad stroke to a bad ball. I suppose this, too, is part of his character. The pitch was slower than on the first day. When the West Indians went in again, they scored runs without difficulty. Bang-bang went Greenidge's sixes to long leg and fours to square leg. The Old Bald Blighter stood steadfastly at short leg, for as long as it was useful. Then, as evening clouds and shadows drew round the Taunton ground, he dropped back a little, ruminating like a Wharfedale bull who is trying to remember spring. He nevertheless made one marvellous, sudden, stooping stop.

Oh bring back yesterday, bid time return! What the very dickens and the devil of a cricketer Close ought to have been for England. The historians, in the future, will be puzzled about it all. Was it his own fault? Very possible, though others might also be to blame. Even now, from the shadows, if we really want to beat the West Indians next week, this dour, difficult and daring man might be recalled to the sunshine.

Rowe ends match on happier note

TAUNTON: The West Indians beat Somerset by 141 runs

I was not at my brightest yesterday. It was my birthday and I had had a late night in the company of such riotous characters as the Sage of Longparish, the philosopher Green (DM, not TH) and the Minister of Tyndale Baptist Church. Fortunately it was not a taxing day's cricket to watch. The West Indians declared their second innings at 261 for one, 343 ahead. Somerset never had any chance of getting the runs, but did not do too badly in scoring 192, and not losing their last wicket until just gone 10 to six.

In the West Indian innings Greenidge scored a good hundred, Rowe looked on happier terms with his bat when he ended the match than when he began it, and King again gave much pleasure to quite a large crowd with some heavy hitting. The pitch was dusty, giving some slow turn to the spinners and occasionally offering the faster bowlers an unpredictable bounce. Generally, though, it continued to be on the batsman's side.

The Somerset innings was dominated, morally even more than numerically, by the Old Bald Blighter. Several people who spoke to me appeared to think that in suggesting his recall to the England team, I was making one of my little jokes. Not so. If I may purloin a phrase from Sir Neville Cardus, I would never dream of making a little joke about a Test match. I think in the present circumstances Close would be a rational selection. He might not be a success, his reflexes are slower, but he would die in the breach against the fast bowlers rather than run away.

He had nearly reached 50 yesterday when he was out, as he was trying to play himself in again after tea.

The West Indians have one or two bowling problems. Holding has a strain and may not be fit for the Test. Daniel was warned twice for running on the pitch and did not bowl during most of the afternoon. He did not look comfortable in his action. This possible reduction in the strength of the main offensive arm of the foe might, I suppose, slightly diminish the case for bringing back the Wharfedale Bull.

Several of Somerset's younger men again batted well. It is too early for extravagances about Jennings, but he has a pleasing style, and looks about as good as Botham did a year ago. You only learn about the talents of a youngster in his second full season, when the old hands have given him a going-over. But there might be something here, and it is satisfactory that he is a local product, born up the road in Wellington (not the one in New Zealand, which constituted P.R. Johnson's qualification to play for Somerset).

Somerset v the West Indians, Taunton, 26, 27 & 28 May 1976

The West Indians won by 141 runs

West Indians

C.G. Greenidge	b Moseley	19	b Jennings	115
L.G. Rowe	c Gard b Botham	43	*not out*	70
I.V.A. Richards	c Gard b Botham	51		
A.I. Kallicharran	c Kitchen b Jennings	24		
* C.H. Lloyd	b Breakwell	70		
C.L. King	*not out*	105	*not out*	66
B.D. Julien	b Close	34		
+ T.M. Findlay	c Gard b Close	6		
A.M.E. Roberts	st Gard b Close	15		
W.W. Daniel				
A.L. Padmore				
	b 5, lb 15, w 1, nb 1	22	b 2, lb 3, w 4, nb 1	10
	(8 wkts, dec)	**389**	(1 wkt, dec)	**261**

1/28, 2/94, 3/132, 4/177, 5/276, 6/337, 7/359, 8/389
1/73

Moseley	13	2	44	1				
Botham	18	5	72	2	18	3	66	0
Burgess	21	4	68	0	17	6	45	0
Jennings	21	2	81	1	14	3	50	1
Breakwell	8	0	67	1	11	0	72	0
Close	6	1	35	3	6	2	18	0

Somerset

B.C.Rose	lbw b Roberts	21	b Julien	9
P.A. Slocombe	lbw b Daniel	2	c Findlay b Daniel	8
P.W. Denning	c Greenidge b Daniel	12	c Richards b Padmore	21
* D.B. Close	c Kallicharran b Padmore	88	c Findlay b Daniel	40
M.J. Kitchen	c Greenidge b Daniel	5	c Lloyd b King	7
G.I. Burgess	b Daniel	0	c Findlay b Julien	28
I.T. Botham	b Julien	56	c Findlay b Julien	0
D. Breakwell	c Padmore b Daniel	44	b Padmore	37
K.F. Jennings	b Roberts	49	b Julien	25
+ T. Gard	b King	7	*not out*	2
H.R. Moseley	*not out*	1	lbw b Roberts	1
	b 4, lb 11, w 4, nb 13	32	lb 10, w 1, nb 3	14
		317		**192**

1/5, 2/38, 3/64, 4/70, 5/70, 6/139, 7/217, 8/299, 9/316, 10/317
1/18, 2/18, 3/64, 4/74, 5/110, 6/110, 7/124, 8/184, 9/188, 10/192

Roberts	20	3	84	2	8.3	3	27	1
Daniel	20	3	77	5	13	3	29	2
Julien	18	2	47	1	11	4	22	4
King	6	0	34	1	11	3	22	1
Padmore	21	4	43	1	28	13	78	2

Umpires: H. Horton and A.E. Fagg

By Crumbs

TAUNTON: Somerset v Hampshire

It was a relief for me to get to the cricket, even though it was not very comfortable there, because once more a bitter wind belied the sunshine. During the night our small cat, Crumbs, had given birth to kittens. She took her time both about gestation and delivery. I had rung up friends in the Natural History unit of the BBC, seeking expert advice, but none of those highly-informed and highly-paid persons knew about small cats. The mating habits of Mexican spiders, yes; the battle-pattern of heated scorpions, yes; how to distinguish the song of a good thrush from a bad nightingale, yes; but domestic cats, er …

Well, at last Crumbs produced her kittens. They had taken so long to get out that we had already decided to call the first one Trevor and the second one Bailey. I invite suggestions for the name of the third, and any further kittens that may have arrived during my absence.

DAY TWO

Slocombe, less on his play than merely as a pun, has been nominated as the candidate for my nameless kitten. P.J.K. Gibbs and C.C.C. Case are currently the front runners. I shall report further when results are in from all precincts. I presented Crumbs and her family with a copy of yesterday's paper, because not every cat is put in the headlines. Trevor and Bailey were particularly swift off the mark and accurate in their aim.

Overheard at The Oval

THE OVAL: Surrey v Hampshire

The last wicket fell in the 107th over, from which it can be seen that the cricket was not compelling. In the Long Room people were beginning to talk of other matters, like horses and Stuart Surridge, and, for that matter, Hobbs and Hayward, and When We Were Very Young. I could not help overhearing this conversation between two senior Cambridge men.

First Cambridge man: "Do you know, there is a proposal to admit women to St Catherine's?" Second Cambridge man: "ah, well, cats to Cats, eh, ho, ho." *(they fall about)*. I pass this on as a sample of the wit bred in those East Anglian swamps.

An early finish at Lord's

LORD'S: Middlesex v Leicestershire

There was one chap who had a disappointing day. He had come down, with his wife, all the way from Silsden, which is close to Ilkley Moor. His wife had gone shopping, and he was relishing a day at Lord's. "Meet you at about six, dear." Clang, clang went the shutters on the bars almost as soon as the play was over. Well, there is always the zoo.

From Barrow-on-Soar

LORD'S: Middlesex v Leicestershire

There was a good, lively innings from Schepens, a young man who comes from Barrow-on-Soar. It sounds like a gardener's nightmare or an American space ship, but it turns out to be a Leicestershire village, a proper place to come from, and he looks a proper player.

Excitement in Hampshire

SOUTHAMPTON: Hampshire v Worcestershire

The Gillette semi-final has caught the imagination of the county, and presents the organizers with the largest attendance problem of their lives. Desmond Eagar is paling under his tan. Even Bill Shepheard's voice, as he announces all the complicated arrangements for getting tickets, quavers a little – though that did not stop a woman nearby from ringing to complain of the noise of the public address system. This was unfair to Shepheard, whose announcements are always witty, restrained and informative. Still, he rang the woman back, and looks forward to welcoming her to the next John Player League match. Now that he has lost so much weight, there is no telling what the good Shepheard will be up to next.

The pretty umpire's wife

BRISTOL: Gloucestershire v Hampshire

During the afternoon I was sitting with half a dozen friends, including the Purpureous Philosopher, a well-known Bristol character, and Jack Crapp, somewhat more widely known, the pride of St Columb Major, or, if it comes to that, St Columb Minor. We had a small bet whether, and when, play would start again: 5p a knob. The players came out just after five o'clock, as I had prophesised, and I had won 35p, and no, I had not been talking to the umpires, though I confess I passed the time of day with a pretty umpire's wife, severely knitting.

Sir, In the course of his report on the Gloucestershire v Hampshire match (July 20), Alan Gibson writes: "… I confess I passed the time of day with a pretty umpire's wife, severely knitting." Since when has it been the custom to comment on the umpire's looks? And what business has a Cricket Correspondent knitting, grimly or otherwise?
Yours sincerely,
STEPHEN CORRIN
10 Russell Gardens, London NW11

Fenner's, Cambridge

CAMBRIDGE: Combined University v the West Indians

DAY ONE

It was very hot. Towards the evening it became overcast, as if there might be storms about. At a quarter to six, it did rain, though not for long. For most of the day there was a large crowd enjoying the sun, varying in age and apparel. The very old were still talking about Sam Woods, and the very young were asking: "Who was Sobers, Daddy?"

The degree of clothing worn by all ages and sexes was minimal. I did not myself think this added to the aesthetic merits of the scene. Most human bodies are better left unexposed. The umpires discarded their jackets, and looked like Edwardian bank clerks taking their holidays at Great Yarmouth, or possibly Burra-Burra.

DAY TWO

It was a festive occasion again at Fenner's. The weather was not so hot as it had been on Wednesday, but the sun shone nearly all the time, and there was another large crowd, mostly youthful, cheering enthusiastically during play, and capering about during the intervals.

This match has been sponsored by Royal Insurance. It is a hazardous thing to sponsor university cricket in the 1970s, but they seem pleased with the arrangement. Certainly the sponsors's marquee brought a splash of Mays-week elegance to the scene. The clink of the glasses, the general aroma of salmon mayonnaise, the light, airy, stylish conversation ... that subdued guffaw in the corner means that Colin Cowdrey has made a little joke ... oh yes, it all took one back. It was like old times for the men of the 30s. Even Zuleika might have recognised the situation.

That other long-standing Fenner's institution, Tolly's beer tent, was also full of animation. The pints travelled through on time all day. That guffaw in the corner, unsubdued, hints that Tony Lewis has made a little joke ...

The cricket tended to be lost in the social hurly-burly.

DAY THREE

A train on the line from Cambridge to Liverpool Street caught fire and so no trains left Liverpool Street for Cambridge yesterday morning. You think I invent these things, do you not? Or that even the Royal Insurance (with whom, I am glad to say, I am still on cordial – that would be the word – terms) would rate me as accident-prone? I promise you that this is true.

Ultimately, I managed to catch a train from Kings Cross and arrived at Fenner's shortly after one o'clock, panting as the hart after the waterbrooks, and with a dreadful fear that I would have to report a day's cricket of which I had not seen a single ball bowled.

Yeovil

Yeovil is not one of the more attractive market towns of the West Country. It has lost much of its character beneath industrial development and suburban spread. But it has a long history, going back to Anglo-Saxon times, and some fine old buildings. It was a favourite tramping-ground of Bampfylde Moore Carew, who in the seventeenth century was known as "King of the Beggars", a man who must have been a strong candidate for the Somerset committee a few hundred years later.

By train to Westcliff

I enjoyed the trip out from Fenchurch Street, on the old London, Tilbury and Southend Railway. This was a line I once knew well (we had our Sunday School outings to Westcliff). Betjeman has described Fenchurch Street as "the only untouched Victorian railway terminus left in London". Perhaps that is why it seems to be the coolest. I thought of making a parallel with Illingworth, but he was not playing, and then with Titmus, but it turns out that he was born in St Pancras.

Worcester

They say of New York that it will be a fine city when they have finished building it. The same thought occurred to me about Worcester as, once more, I found myself locked in its traffic chaos. They are driving a new road through the centre. My taxi man assured me that the project was going well, "only two years behind schedule". In the meantime – and I suspect it will be a long, long meantime – what was once one of the fairest cities of England is reduced to a jumble of bulldozers.

It is full of one-way routes, down lanes so narrow that the Royalist cavalry could go down them only in single file at the risk of being picked off by Parliamentary citizens in the penthouses, of motorists who become so irritated by the delays that the sight of 50 clear yards ahead sends them into a frenzy of speed, of pedestrians so scared that they dart and flutter like hens in a farmyard when the fox is in. Even the calm cathedral is in bandages. Yes, it will be a lovely cathedral when it is finished. It was also a lovely city before they started mucking about with it.

...

The old scorecard man is famous for his unexpected prophesies, but not this time. Most of us who have watched cricket at Worcester will remember this man with his harrowed, crinkly face and his hoarse, cheerful voice. He seems to have been there longer than the cathedral, or D'Oliveira, or even (though this can hardly be possible) the road improvement schemes.

Tom Cartwright

TAUNTON: Somerset v Sussex (Sunday League)

One of the pleasures of this season has been to see Tom Cartwright bowling again. He lost nearly all the last one because of injury. He will be 41 in July, and there have been doubts whether he could make an effective return. But with the help of a captain who did not demand too much too soon, he has bowled beautifully, with the same high, easeful action as ever, the same thoughtful mind, the same accuracy.

It was therefore miserably disappointing when yesterday he tripped over a fieldsman while going for a quick run, fell awkwardly and heavily on the shoulder which has been the principal cause of his troubles, and had to leave the field in considerable pain. He sustained a cracked shoulder blade.

There was nothing sinister about the accident. Forty-nine times out of 50 it would have had no serious results. It was cruel luck. We shall have to wait to learn the consequences, and Cartwright is a man of much moral courage and physical resilience, but as he came wincing off I could not help wondering, along with many others, when and whether we should see him again.

John Snow

BASINGSTOKE: Hampshire v Sussex

Snow's innings was interesting. He played a cover drive for four, casually, elegantly, much as Hammond or Hutton might have played it. His batting has touches of bright light, even though, like his poetry, it lacks concentration. This is all very well if you are a genius: Coleridge hardly ever concentrated, but did produce occasionally marvellous works.

Snow is, or has it in him to be, cricket's Coleridge. Often boring, sometimes stupid, lazy or lively as the mood takes him, he nevertheless has the magic touch, as a batsman, a bowler, or even a poet. He has much more to produce yet within cricket, and even more to produce without it.

Colin Cowdrey

CANTERBURY: Kent v Surrey

Grandpa was playing again: not that one had ever doubted he would. He had been keeping his hand in, playing club cricket, waiting for the hard grounds, the August injuries and the Test calls to reduce the strength of Kent to the point when it would be absurd not to recall him. I have written a good deal about Cowdrey, and I am not going to start again now, but I can tell you it moved me, real lump-in-the-throat business, to see him fielding in the slips, like a discarded pillar of the Acropolis which the sculptors had not got quite right; or, a better analogy, an Archangel a little damaged, as Lamb said of the aging Coleridge.

Ian Botham

TAUNTON: Somerset v Warwickshire

If there had been any doubts about the result, Botham settled them, whirling his bat around his head. I am not so sure about Botham's technique, but as Robertson-Glasgow, who would have much enjoyed this match, once wrote: "Rushing fools have more fun than refraining angels."

David Gower

LORD'S: Middlesex v Leicestershire

Davison scored an admirable 100. Gower played almost as well. He is 20, born in Kent, a product of King's, Canterbury, and the English Schools XI, though with names like David Ivon he must have a trace of Welsh blood, and I think it was Tony Lewis who first told me what a good player he was.

Gower is a left-hander who likes to drive, fair-haired, strongly built, quick on his feet. It was the first time I had seen him make more than a few, but I doubt if it will be the last. He reached his 100, his first, just as the St John's Wood clocks were striking six. Illingworth at once declared.

Philip Sharpe

BRISTOL: Gloucestershire v Derbyshire

Ask a Yorkshireman who is the most unkindly treated Test cricketer of modern times and he will say John Hampshire, almost as certainly as in the 1920s he would have said Percy Holmes. Holmes was unlucky because he had to compete with Hobbs. In my view, as good a case can be made for Sharpe as for Hampshire.

Sharpe was originally chosen for England, chiefly because someone was needed to hold slip catches, an art in which he can seldom have been surpassed in the history of the game. Yet, as a batsman, in 13 Tests he has averaged almost 42, which compares well with Hampshire's average of 27 in eight. Their county records are about equal. Sharpe has the knack of playing better than usual on the big occasion, which is always the mark of a proper Test cricketer.

Sharpe has never looked the part. He is on the short side, a little plump. His strokes are efficient rather than stirring. He tends to hover between the forward stroke and the back, like a puppy wondering whether to chase a fierce, old tom cat. Nevertheless, by their fruits, ye shall know them.

Ian Botham
'Rushing fools have more fun than refraining angels'

Improbable agent of destruction

CHELMSFORD: Essex, with three first innings wickets in hand, are 12 runs ahead of the West Indians

Essex cricketers are thinking mostly of winning the championship, or at least the Sunday League. County matches against touring sides are not, generally, the occasions they once were. When, in 1899 and again in 1905, Essex beat the Australians, these were the great moments of their early history, still remembered by some of the small boys who were there. Nowadays nobody minds so much and leading players are often rested.

In these circumstances, it was good to see a full ground at Chelmsford, hardly a seat to spare. It was a tribute to the county's successful run, to the attractiveness of the tourists and to the weather. The crowd was rewarded by an invigorating day's cricket in which Essex were not outclassed, though they will have to bat last on a pitch of uncertain bounce.

The West Indians made a splendid start, chiefly through Greenidge, and at one point were 150 for three. But they were all out for 190 in the 49th over. Only Rowe made much of an innings after Greenidge's opening flourish. The agent of destruction was, improbably, Gooch, who I see Trevor Bailey has described as a "useful seamer" – but that was possibly Leytonstonian fellowship as much as dispassionate judgment.

I have much admiration for Gooch the batsman but Gooch the bowler was new to me, though I can believe anything of a product of Norlington School, against whom at the age of 10, I received the most unspeakable leg-before decision of my life. Gooch's medium-paced, right-arm seamers were certainly useful yesterday and he finished with five for 40, by some way the best figures of his career. Indeed, he had never taken more than two wickets in an innings before.

Essex lost the wickets of Edmeades, at nought, and Hardie, at 24, both bowled by Daniel, who then retired for a while, rubbing his back. He was off for only half an hour and seemed none the worse. McEwan and Gooch put on 100 for the third wicket at about five to the over. The slower West Indian bowlers were not accurate and nor was the fielding, though the outfield, badly needing a drop of rain, set problems. No strokes of the day, not even Greenidge's, were better than McEwan's cover drives.

In the 25th over Gooch was caught at backward square leg, in the 27th, McEwan at mid wicket. This set Essex back – 140 for four – but Pont and Fletcher seemed to be going well when Pont was caught at cover, at 170. These three wickets fell to King, all from aggressive strokes. After that it seemed that Fletcher decided to make sure of a first innings lead and the pace dropped, somewhat to the discontent of the crowd.

Nevertheless, taking the day as a whole, they had little about which to complain. The tactics were reasonable, but not, as it happened, successful. Turner and Fletcher were both out at 187. The lead, however, was achieved by East in the 56th over with a stroke which one might not call majestic, but it was majestically acknowledged by the crowd and, for that matter, by the batsman.

Essex awake to the possibilities

CHELMSFORD: The West Indians, with one second innings wicket in hand, are 184 runs ahead of Essex

Chelmsford is still beset by environmental problems, and I am not only referring to the drivers who seem to mow down the pedestrians, even if – indeed, especially if – they set foot on a crossing. There is trouble with a maggot-grinding factory which somebody is trying to set up in his garden, an area of outstanding natural beauty. His neighbours do not fancy the little fellows, either in their ground or unground state, getting inside the apples.

Unaware of the maggot menace, more that 6,000 people turned up yesterday and enjoyed the match. Empty seats were even harder to find than on Wednesday. The crowd saw some talented but, at times, curious cricket. Essex began 12 runs ahead with three first innings wickets in hand. They put on another 92 and lost only one more wicket.

East's innings was capital. He is an erratic batsman, a wasp rather than a maggot, but capable of doing much damage quickly when he has found an appropriate apple. The West Indians were 61 for one at lunch. The declaration was on, if Essex were set on winning the match. Perhaps they thought they were sufficiently on top already and the crowd might like to see the West Indians bat.

What would the crowd have liked? A display of West Indian batsmanship or an Essex win? From their reactions as the wickets began to fall, they obviously wanted a win, as soon as possible, though generous in applauding the good strokes. They would rather have lost a day's cricket on the morrow than miss a famous victory.

The Essex committee, seeing a third day crowd vanishing under their noses like a rail connexion from Didcot, could not be expected to share this view, and possibly communicated their attitude to the team. For a long time in the afternoon the bowling was left to Pont and Gooch and, with all respect to the Demon of Norlington and all remembrance of his first innings performance, these were hardly the most dangerous bowlers on an increasingly dusty pitch.

The West Indians on the other hand, with the rubber won, might not have minded losing a county match much if it meant a day off – so, at least, some of their strokes suggested. It is their custom to hit their way out of trouble but their batting in the afternoon was more careless than carefree. It seemed an unreal game for a time, as if neither side wanted to win.

At 141 for three the West Indians were doing well enough. Then Lloyd was caught at backward point after playing some handsome strokes. Essex awoke to the possibilities. Acfield came on, and then East. Acfield caught and bowled King and a fine throw from McEwan on the third man boundary ran out Julien – 182 for six.

Gomes played yet another sound innings. Both sides were trying in the evening. Even Jumadeen scored his first runs of the tour. Plenty of play should have been ensured today, which will please the financial authorities. I am not sure whether the maggots or the apples have had the best of it so far, but the grinders cannot be doing badly.

A mangled skein of a match that Essex could not avoid losing

CHELMSFORD: The West Indians beat Essex by 105 runs

The West Indians put on a few more runs in the morning, Findlay reaching his 50, and Essex had to score 203 to win. It was a cloudy morning, a few drops of rain falling, but there was another large crowd, the ground well over half full. The pitch was uncertain: the ball had occasionally kept low throughout the match, and now it was beginning to lift, sufficiently to give the batsmen an extra dimension of worry. When, later, the spinners came on it obligingly turned. Essex did not really have much chance, and the game was over soon after lunch.

I met a friendly parson (I meet them constantly in Essex). He told me how much he had enjoyed my book, *A Tangled Vein*. Endeavouring not to make my appreciative smile too varicose, I murmured: *"A Mingled Yarn."* (Substantial precedents have recently been set in this newspaper for plugging your own books.) We chatted on for a few minutes, pausing now and then to note the fall of another wicket, and he departed with the assurance that, to all his friends, without fail, he would recommend *A Mangled Skein*.

I recount this episode, not just because it happened, but because it was apt. It was rather a mangled skein of a match. Essex could hardly have avoided winning if they had pressed their advantage on Thursday afternoon. They could hardly avoid losing when the night brought the clouds; and after they had lost their first few wickets, they hardly, with the exception of their captain, seemed to care.

Edmeades and Hardie began the Essex batting, Daniel and Lloyd the West Indian bowling. Lloyd has bowled little his summer, but did not put himself on for a joke. He was setting his side an example: come along boys, no more nonsense, they have their third-day crowd, knock 'em off.

In the fifth over Edmeades was caught and bowled by Daniel, who was bowling fast. In the seventh over Daniel had McEwan caught at the wicket. In the eleventh over Hardie was out, also to Daniel. Lloyd took the next two wickets himself, those of Pont and Gooch. A good innings might have been a help to Gooch, so far as his Test prospects go, but he never looked in his best touch.

That was 37 for five, the spinners came on, took some time to find their length, and Fletcher and Turner made a stand for the sixth wicket. Fletcher is nine years older than Gooch, a severe handicap in the present climate, whether one considers it in meteorological or selectorial terms, but still a better batsman. He was out cutting at a short ball from Padmore. He spun his bat in the air, not an offensive gesture, simply an irritated, wry one. He had been playing so well that we had begun to remember that 203 was not, after all, such a large score.

But that was 68 for six, and the rest did not take long. Nearly all the batsmen were out to attacking strokes, even though Essex had heaps of time to make the runs. That was the kind of match it was: the blood occasionally ran red, or blue – whichever you think preferable – but the vein was tangled.

WEST INDIANS	190 (Greenidge 71, Rowe 47, Gooch 5-40)
	306 (Gomes 74, Findlay 51*, Fredericks 46, Acfield 3-41, Pont 3-81)
ESSEX	294 for eight declared (McEwan 76, East 49*, Gooch 43, Lever 31*, King 4-93)
	97 (Fletcher 26, Turner 23*, Padmore 3-15, Daniel 3-28)

AUGUST: England v Australia (women's one-day match) at Lord's 1976

England women dispel flippancy and the Australian challenge

LORD'S: England women beat Australia by eight wickets

The notices were still there on the pavilion doors: "The attention of all members of MCC, and Middlesex, their guests and visitors, is drawn to the conditions contained in regulation 3(v) of the regulations of MCC which require them to wear a necktie and jacket whilst in the pavilion."

Regulation 3(v) has never taken such a battering as it did yesterday. The doorkeepers turned their eyes away as the skirts whisked up to the dressing rooms. For this, as you will already know – it is not Rachael Flint's fault if you do not – was the first time the women had taken over Lord's. The editor of *The Cricketer* told me he had raced to the ground to be sure of seeing the first ball bowled.

Not many others had. Only a few hundred were there at the start, and when Australia lost a wicket to the second ball, the noise was rather less than it will be if the same thing happens in the men's match next year. But, as a sunny afternoon drew on, more and more people came along until there was a larger crowd than Middlesex often get.

They saw Australia all out, for 161. When nine wickets were down for 127, it looked as if they would score less, but a last wicket stand gave them something to bowl at, and prolonged the innings to the sixtieth, and in any case last, over. Marie Lutschini batted very well in this stand, as Sharon Tredrea had done earlier. It cannot have been often that players of Italian and Cornish extraction (as I presume these two to be) have made so big a contribution to an innings at Lord's.

I have never thought cricket a particularly suitable game for girls to play – I mean, I shall not grieve if my daughter Felicity does not take it up – but if they wish to, they should be encouraged by fellow-cricketers, not patronized or snubbed. I am glad Lord's has opened its door to them in the jubilee year of the Women's Cricket Association.

In my student days, I played often against and with women's teams. Some of these matches were quite serious. Westfield College, for instance, were not a side you could take chances with. The batting of the women then was much better than their bowling. They could catch, and field smartly on the ground, but their throwing was poor, and I do not mean just through lack of physique.

Watching the cream of the game yesterday (I use the metaphor advisedly: they were playing for the St Ivel Cream Jug) I thought that they still batted better than they bowled. They would score runs against a county, but it would take them a long time to get one out. The throwing, however, especially the Australian throwing, has improved vastly.

I dislike some of the WCA publicity, those giggly bits about leg-glances, etc. I was disappointed at some of the antics at the fall of a wicket, likes so many huge, hairy footballers (Australia were less emotional than England). They do not do themselves justice by these things. But I see their difficulties. They feel they must not spurn any chance of publicity.

Women's cricket, for all its well-established international pattern (England first toured Australia in 1934, and Australia returned the visit three years later) rests on a small numerical base. In 1970, Rowland Bowen estimated that one woman cricketer in a hundred plays for England, whereas the figure for men would be nearer one in a hundred thousand. Things have improved since then, but not by much.

Flippancy dropped away from the crowd, though, as England set out to get the runs. They were given a good start by two famous players, Enid Bakewell and Lynne Thomas. Thomas was caught at mid-on in the 38th over, Bakewell run out in the 41st. The score was then 93 for 2, with two new batswomen to play themselves in.

Chris Watnough, a Lancastrian, who now plays for Kent, and her captain, the pride of Wolverhampton, saw them through, amid genuine enthusiasm, with three overs to spare. Australia, however, took the St Ivel Jug, because they had won at Canterbury on Sunday, and had a faster scoring rate over the two matches combined. So everyone had something to celebrate.

AUSTRALIA	161 (59.4 overs, Tredrea 54)
ENGLAND	162 for two (56.2 overs, Watmough 50*, Bakewell 50)

John Jameson 1976

Jameson warms to the warmfulness

CARDIFF: Glamorgan v Warwickshire

"It was hot. Harry Wharton, Frank Nugent, Bob Cherry and Johnny Bull all agreed that it was hot. Even Hurree Jamset Ram Singh, the Nabob of Bhanipur, admitted that the warmfulness was terrific." These words, mystic to those bairns who knew not Frank Richards, Greyfriars School and the *Magnet*, may perhaps be recalled as the master approaches his centenary. In such weather, Hurree Singh could still be relied upon to bowl out St Jim's.

But the pattern was not quite fulfilled at Cardiff yesterday. It was one of the lighter-skinned men, Jameson, and a public school man, too, though he was born in Bombay, who, with a characteristically thumping innings, put Warwickshire on top, at least for a time. He was 98 not out at lunch, and 138 when he went, out for a total of 214 for three, in the 54th over.

Jameson is a batsman about whom I have never been able to make up my mind. Like most of the big hitters, he looks magnificent when he is going well, and if his touch is out he looks terrible. If he is to play Test cricket again, he should probably be picked for a whole series: either that or not at all. They used to do this with Jessop. Jessop had a low international average, but won a famous Test match. It is the kind of gamble that has to be taken, at heavy odds, or refused.

Yesterday Jameson bruised the balls, although he gave one of them a compensating cooling dip in the river. He was dropped several times, but when you have a batsman who so completely takes charge of the game, the old men do drop catches.

The Honourable Tim Lamb

Lamb makes most of sudden opportunity

LORD'S: Middlesex v Sussex

So many cricketers have been summoned to Old Trafford, just in case they are needed to play for England, that I was slightly surprised to see that Middlesex and Sussex found 11 men to play for them yesterday, none noticeably halt or lame. Sussex won the toss, and batted, and were all out for 90.

I must confess I did not see much of this innings, because I met an old friend who had been attending a meeting of the Lord's Taverners. He claims, almost certainly correctly, that he is the only man in the country who has never listened to a commentary on the Boat Race, nor even watched it on television. His countless friends, known and unknown, will be pleased to hear that John Snagge is in capital form, into his 70s and looking set for a hundred. We heartily agreed that the BBC isn't what it used to be.

Lamb took five wickets for Middlesex. He is an Oxford Blue, aged 23, who has not so far made the most of his talents, but perhaps was challenged by the sudden opportunity of Selvey's absence. He comes from a distinguished line. I do not know what his grandfather, Lord Rochester, with whom I once lunched at the Union in Oxford, would think of having a professional cricketer in the family, but I expect his uncle Kenneth, a useful player in his time, is quite pleased – if he has had an opportunity to notice, in the intervals of improving the BBC.

Glamorgan

A word about Glamorgan's problems. I say a word: I heard countless thousands of words about them in the course of the day. A special general meeting has been demanded. I doubt if Majid was a good choice for captain in the first place, but as he had been appointed, he deserved more faithful support. It is sad that they have parted company with Davis, who scored 1,000 runs last season for the first time, after arduous service, and whose best years should still have been ahead of him.

It would be wrong, though, to blame everything on the committee; it is certainly too large, but so are almost all county committees, and come to that almost all committees of any sort. They are not, as some of the public seem to think, dedicated to the destruction of their own organization.

I had a pleasant talk with the chairman, Judge Rowe Harding. He came into office half a generation ago as arbiter of another Glamorgan crisis, and takes a philosophical view of the present one. In this he is surely right. Someone has to be bottom of the championship, and this is always likely to produce a crisis of one sort or another, especially in a land where passions run high.

At the centre of the judge's first crisis, and not far from the centre of the latest, is the secretary, Wilfred Wooller. It is fair to say of Mr Wooller that he does not suffer fools gladly, and that his perception of folly is not always certain. But nobody who claims to be a Glamorgan supporter should ever forget his long, honourable and devoted services to the county.

Middlesex

Yesterday I dwelt upon Glamorgan's problems. I will say little more about them, except that the arguments still rage, much to the profit of the bar, and that according to one authority, whom I could not help overhearing, the national drought is all Wilfred Wooller's fault. The last words I heard, as I left St Helens, were, in sardonic west Welsh English, "Pity Barry Richards never joined us, so we'd never have the chance to sack him."

What about Middlesex? How is it that Middlesex, without Gomes, a fine middle-order batsman, without Selvey, their best seam bowler, for a couple of Tests, without their captain for a couple of Tests, which might well have been more, how is it that they have done so well?

Good spinners in a dusty season, yes. Good reserves, yes (few counties are in the position to bring in so able a bowler as Lamb as a deputy). Smith's capacity as a leader when Brearley is away, yes.

...

The man who has done it is Brearley. He is a highly intelligent man, who took a First, even if it was only at Cambridge. If he had played regularly since he came down – he is 34, and has captained Middlesex since 1971 – his place in the England side might have been long established, indeed, we should be crying out now for his retirement. I am not quite sure whether he is good enough to play for England now, but he is a natural leader, and since he has a philosophical turn of mind, he may take as much satisfaction from a championship for Middlesex as for any other honours of the game.

AUGUST: Gloucestershire v Somerset at Bristol (first day)

Day when Zaheer was outshone

BRISTOL: Gloucestershire, with seven first innings wickets in hand, lead Somerset by 26 runs

It was curious to be at a cricket match, especially one between Gloucestershire and Somerset on a Bank holiday when, apart from the small boys – and not even all of them, for some were sons of farmers – most were hoping for rain. These counties are still, principally, agricultural communities and know well that, at present, the price of a good downpour is beyond points.

There were storms in the night. Crumbs' kittens, Trevor and Bailey, kept us awake, in and out of the window all the time. It was their first smell of a seaming wicket. But the morning was dry, though the clouds loured, and it was possible to begin play, uncomfortably, at 10 to three. On Saturday, between showers, Somerset had scored 161 and Gloucestershire 55 for one.

On Sunday, in the League, Gloucestershire played when conditions did not justify it, partly because Somerset had the chance of the league title. Yesterday Somerset were the more ready to play because Gloucestershire had a chance of a high championship position. So, at least, I read the situation, though I am not suggesting any sinister collusion, merely an unspoken feeling, which does no discredit to the game, that one good turn deserves another.

The pitch was lively when Gloucestershire resumed their innings but that was not much help to the Somerset bowlers, as they could hardly keep their footing, and the fieldsmen were in an even worse pickle. No, pickle is not the right word, too sticky. It was more like trying to run on a floor of gherkins.

Brassington, sent in on Saturday evening, was soon out, but the old, nimble-footed partnership of Wotton-under-Edge and Charlton Abbas was soon warming Gloucestershire hearts. The likeliest way for it to be broken was always by a run out. And so it happened, but only when Zaheer – who, for once this season, was outshone – had scored 45 and the Somerset total had been overtaken.

By then the outfield was drying and the spinners were turning the ball. At tea, Gloucestershire were 187 for three in only 45 overs, Sadiq 95. Then it began to rain again and at least the Wotton-under-Edge farmers did not rejoice with the zest that they would have had in the morning. The Quantock farmers, however, agreed that 'twould be all for the best. The crowd crammed themselves into such bars as were open, remembering past Bank holidays.

I heard one grey-haired, respectable lady say: "Ah, if Wally Hammond was not out at lunchtime, I'd go and watch him. Yes, even if I had to give up my whatsit." There was much criticism of the omission of Discarded Davey, but I saw him hard at it in the kitchens, so possibly Gloucestershire are going to employ him in future as a cook.

Play was abandoned for the day at half past five, the Magic Dragon assuming his most sepulchral accents for the announcement. Gloucestershire have five first innings points so far and are well placed for eight if the rain, heaven forfend, should stop.

AUGUST: Glamorgan v Somerset at Cardiff (Sunday League)

When the cheering had to stop

CARDIFF: Glamorgan (4 pts) beat Somerset by one run

It was the most perplexing finish to a match I have ever seen. Nearly all afternoon, nearly all the crowd were under the impression that Somerset needed 191 to win. It turned out, late in the proceedings, and most of the crowd were unaware of it even then, that they needed 192. As it happened, Somerset scored 190, which meant (under the original impression) a tie, and also – because we knew by then the results from other grounds – the John Player title for Somerset. So they had at last won a major title after more than 100 years of county cricket! When the jubilant Somerset cheering had stopped, the announcer was heard, harassed and apologetic, confirming that it was Glamorgan, after all, who had won.

Sophia Gardens might have been Bridgwater Carnival. Hours before the start the crowds had been arriving from across the channel. By 12 o'clock well over a thousand were within the ground, not a Welsh accent within hearing, and not a gateman in sight to take the money. Plaintive invitations were made to the host who did not pay by men with buckets later, but I doubt if they had much success, since the crowd had not been able to get anything to eat or drink while they waited (mind, from the way some few of them behaved when the bars did open, this may have been just as well).

It was a good pitch and a fast outfield. Glamorgan were put in, and scored 190 in 39 overs, losing seven wickets. This gave Somerset plenty to think about. There was a critical moment at a fairly early stage of the Glamorgan innings. Ellis had been caught at the wicket at 31, and shortly afterwards Jones, who had made 21, clipped Burgess round the corner to backward short leg, a sharp but straight change, and Close put it down. I fear that on this occasion the great man was throwing up the ball before he had actually caught it.

Jones went on to make 70 and hold the innings together. After he was out, Nash beat about in his usual vigorous way. Somerset did not field very well, except in spasms. The tension showed. For the same reason, I thought much depended on their innings making a good start.

This they did not get. Denning was out quickly, Close was splendidly caught on the boundary – I know he is not subject to normal rules, but it seemed too ambitious a stroke at that time. Botham was caught and bowled. These wickets fell to Nash. He bowled a thoughtful, intelligent spell, but it lasted for five overs, and so did Cordle's at the other end. The Glamorgan second bowling line is less demanding, and Somerset have a reputation, not only in the Sunday League, for winning matches from improbable positions. Rose and Kitchen were soon going well. After 20 overs, Somerset were only 11 behind on the comparative rate. Rose was caught at the wicket at 97. Burgess, so often a shrewd player in moments of stress, began coolly. Kitchen was blazing away.

With nine overs left Somerset needed (so we thought) 64 and then Kitchen was out. As Breakwell came in, the crowd was quiet, even the boozers momentarily hushed.

Glamorgan, although, as their supporters kept reminding us, they had nothing to gain and nothing to lose, were obviously also feeling the strain of the occasion, and gave away overthrows, a sure sign. With six overs left, Somerset were still there with a chance, and had not lost another wicket. Nash came back, and 10 runs in the over with him. With three overs left, 21 were wanted – I beg your pardon, we now knew the proper figure, 22. A succession of run-outs as Somerset scrambled for the last few, ended on the last ball (the cricketers at least knew what they had to do) with an attempt at a hopeless third run.

It was enough to make a Somerset man weep: though mostly, as they departed from the ground, they just swore instead.

1977

1977 was a memorable year for English cricket. Geoffrey Boycott completed his 100th hundred on the perfect stage at Headingley; Ian Botham made his Test debut and celebrated it with his first five-wicket haul; Vivian Richards put bowlers to the sword, scoring almost 3,000 runs in all competitions, mostly at a furious rate; and Michael Procter's all-round heroics were not quite enough to take Gloucestershire to their first county championship for 100 years. But, as Alan Gibson concluded in his *Diary of the Season* for the *Cricketer* magazine, there could be only one candidate for man of the season, and that was Mike Brearley, whose intelligent and sometimes inspired captaincy played such a decisive part in Middlesex's share of the county championship and, even more so, in securing as resounding an Ashes victory as England has ever enjoyed. It was an achievement fit to lay before Her Majesty the Queen, in the year of her Silver Jubilee.

Off the field, and probably on it as well, all the talk was of the Australian media tycoon Kerry Packer and his World Series Cricket. It was in mid April that stories began to emerge that South African players were being signed up on lucrative contracts to play an eight week series of matches around the world. Over the weeks that followed, the list of the Packer rebels, as they were known, began to lengthen. In a scenario that now seems horribly familiar, the players would earn far more than they could ever hope to from 'official' Test matches sanctioned by the International Cricket Council by throwing in their lot with a man who, his enemies claimed, was out to destroy the game in its purest form.

Worse still for the establishment, it transpired that Packer's right-hand men were none other than the current captain of England, Tony Greig, and the immediate past captain of Australia, Ian Chappell. The plan was to stage a series of one-day internationals and Test matches between an Australian side, recruited by Ian Chappell, and a rest of the world XI, assembled by Tony Greig. The England Test players recruited included Alan Knott, John Snow, Derek Underwood and Denis Amiss. Virtually the entire Australian touring side were involved. All of this came to light on May 9. Alan Gibson, who was never much of a fan of 'the establishment', took what was, for the time, a relatively restrained, if distinctly cynical view of it all. Writing in his *Cricketer* Diary at the time, he risked two points:

> The first is that I expect the experiment to be a successful one, whatever attitude the cricketing authorities take. The second is that Greig's reputation, as a captain of England, has been destroyed.

He was right on both counts.

Alan saw a good deal of the Australians in the early part of the season. By the late 1970s, county matches for the tourists had begun to lose some of their former prestige but they were far from being the practice matches they have since become. So the celebrations when Somerset beat the Australians for the first time in their history, under sunny skies at Bath, were genuine and sustained. As for the Australians, although their form improved, they were clearly distracted by the Packer controversy, and were without two of their best players, in Lillee and Ian Chappell. In the Tests, they proved to be a pale shadow of the side that had carried all before it in the winter of 1974/75, and lost the series 3-0.

Tests
England
beat Australia
3-0, with two draws

Championship
1 Middlesex
Kent
3 Gloucestershire
4 Somerset
5 Leicestershire
6 Essex

Sunday League
1 Leicestershire
2 Essex
3 Middlesex
4 Sussex
Hampshire
6 Kent
Gloucestershire

Gillette Cup Final
Middlesex
beat Glamorgan

Benson & Hedges Final
Gloucestershire
beat Kent

Most first-class runs
1 I.V.A. Richards
2 C.G. Greenidge
3 K.S. McEwan

Most first-class wickets
1 M.J. Procter
2 I.T. Botham
3 G. Miller
J.N. Shepherd

There was to be no third long hot summer in a row. May was wet and so was the latter part of August. Gloucestershire had two championship matches washed out without a ball being bowled, which was to cost them dear in the final reckoning. It made for a slightly fractured, stuttering season for the cricket follower, and indeed for the cricket correspondent. Alan Gibson started the season with a heavy cold, then developed a mysterious eye infection, and it always seemed to be his misfortune to be sent to the matches where the excitement wasn't.

The county championship was close throughout, with Gloucestershire enjoying one of their best seasons despite the injuries which had deprived them of Tony Brown and Jack Davey, and left them dangerously reliant on the valiant Procter. He had taken over from Brown as captain, and was proving to be an inspiring leader who, when he wasn't changing the course of games by his own efforts, was bringing the very best out of his team – as in the Benson and Hedges Cup quarter final against Middlesex on June 8. Sadly, Alan would miss the semi-final at Southampton, when Procter took the first four Hampshire wickets in five balls, including a hat-trick, and the final at Lord's, where they overcame Kent with a fine all-round performance, and their supporters disgraced themselves by invading the pitch and fighting with the police.

Alan was having his problems at this stage of the season. Hardly a single train journey seems to have passed without untoward incident, and he was suffering with an eye infection, prompting one distinctly unsympathetic 'old friend' to suggest that it wouldn't make much difference if he couldn't see, since he never wrote about the cricket anyway!

For Alan, the season ended more than usually emotionally. At Taunton on August 31, he experienced the worst of both worlds: Gloucestershire beaten, but Brian Close – his much-loved Old Bald Blighter – missing out on the century that would have been such an appropriate adornment for his final home game for Somerset. Then at Bristol, a week or so later, with Gloucestershire still five points ahead of their two rivals, he watched while the home side's hopes ebbed, and finally flooded away as Hampshire's batsmen took control on the final day. Kent and Middlesex, meanwhile, both won, to share the championship, leaving Gloucestershire in third place.

It was a day of bitter gall and wormwood with which to end a season in which neither Alan, nor the county sides that he followed most closely, had enjoyed much luck. Brian Close always said that it was the toss of the coin that decided Somerset's truncated Gillette semi-final against Middlesex. Yorkshire began well, but were then riven by a furious internal row over Boycott's captaincy. Hampshire were dogged by injury problems, Essex were edged out in the John Player League by Leicestershire, and although Gloucestershire did make the most of their threadbare resources in winning the B&H, the denouement of the championship was a cruel disappointment.

Meanwhile, the Packer controversy continued to rage. Alan Gibson's last words on the subject in the summer of 1977 were these, in his *Cricketer* diary:

> I record my expectation that the outcome will be determined by two things: the courts, and money.

He was spot on again.

Rain at The Parks

Walking up Parks Road on a damp, gloomy morning, I was reminded of a similar morning in 1947 when I was accompanied by Edmund Dell. He was at that time a fervent communist, and explained to me that the only defect in the Russian system was that they had not yet appreciated the ameliorative effects of cricket upon the proletariat. He also bet me a pint that the Liberals would join the Conservatives within five years, and I have never had that pint.

**Edmund Dell was at Queen's with Alan and, like him, took a first in modern history. In 1977 he was President of the Board of Trade in Jim Callaghan's cabinet.*

DAY TWO

There was less than a quarter of an hour's play in the Parks yesterday. Soon after 11 a.m. the rains descended, and in the afternoon the floods came. The cricketers took an early lunch and called it off at 1.30.

Worcestershire had scored four more runs and lost a wicket. I must be honest and admit the only ball I saw bowled was the last one (more trouble at Didcot) and the weather was so conclusively glum that I retired to the pastures, the pastures of the Lamb and Flag, and then to the Randolph. I had some slight difficulty getting into the Randolph because "rent a picket" or some such organization made feeble moves to prevent me. There is some sort of strike going on. The hotel is functioning normally so far as I could see.

Oxford in pouring rain loses much of its beauty. Cambridge sometimes gains in looks by bad weather, but then it is more used to it, in that East Anglian swamp, and its stones are sounder.

Oxford in the rain. It is 30 years since I came down but I still love it.

Rain at The Oval

We spent the afternoon waiting for the umpires. Sam Cook and Peter Wight, clad in their saintly robes, are less enthusiastic about calling off play than when they were flannelled.

Yet it was not a wasted afternoon. I had a cheap and substantial portion of shepherd's pie which put the catering at Lord's to shame, and I met an underwriter from Lloyds, and a diplomatist from Burma, and a young man freshly back from a kibbutz. You do meet them, at the Oval.

Rain at Lord's

"Welcome to the Jubilee Monday high speed train, 125 miles an hour, to London," said the announcer. He tactfully did not mention that the previous train had been cancelled, nor that his high speed train would reach London in a longer time than most of the old slow speed trains.

He listed the places at which we should pause, five of them, six if you call Slough a place, and explained that in honour of the Jubilee there would be no refreshment facilities in the train. "But everyone's got a smile on their face today," he said.

Late, thirsty, unfed and observing the clouds sweeping down from the north-west, I could manage no more than a feeble grin. Still, I arrived at Lord's in the end, accompanied by a large family of Americans, whom I encountered and who were under the impression that they were going to see the Jubilee Test match.

I tried, unavailingly, to persuade them that their travel agents had got it wrong. They were perplexed that there should be nobody at Lord's, except a few members discussing Mr Packer, a few boozers outside the Tavern and many pigeons who had fled from the Oval.

Lord's even had to send its spare beer to the Oval yesterday, because they were almost dry at the Oval, and this was enough to make Sir Pelham Warner swivel on his plinth. I must also record, though, for nobody else ever will, the departing remark of the well-fitted American teenage daughter: 'Say, are all baseball reporters as cute as you?"

I cannot write much about the cricket because I did not see much of it. Rain and bad light kept interrupting play. … I took a taxi back to Paddington, and the driver explained to me that the fare was 30p more than usual, in honour of the Jubilee.

The lady of the bar

BIRMINGHAM: Warwickshire v Northamptonshire

I arrived at Edgbaston rather late (it was not one of British Rail's better days, even though I did not have to travel through Didcot) and made my way at once to the bar called "Long Off" – known more familiarly as "The Snug" – to see how Phyl was getting on. She had been poorly last summer, and distressed by the death of her husband. She was not there.

He first departed,
She a little tried
To live without him,
Liked it not, and died.

For countless years she served amiably and patiently in that bar. Among many other kindnesses, she cheered a nervous and harassed young commentator in his first Test match. Phyl was one of the great Edgbaston characters, and it is proper to salute her memory.

Bath enjoys return of Australian local boy

BATH: Somerset, with seven first innings wickets in hand, are 102 runs behind the Australians

The sun shone at last for the Australians at Bath, but they did not make the most of it, for they were all out, after winning the toss, by tea. This was greatly to the pleasure of the large Somerset crowd, and their equal pleasure was that Chappell – who as a young man used to play for Somerset, scored for them the very first century to be made in a John Player match, and whom they therefore regarded as a local boy – scored a splendid century.

…

Nor did the Australians shine when bowling, for Thomson was no balled 15 times by Bird, in seven overs. Not much significance, I think, should be attached to this. Thomson has been known to have such problems before, early in the season. "Come to Chew Magna; we need a new fast bowler," cried one gleeful Somerset optimist, but I did not share the glee. It was too much like baiting a tiger who is simply working out his strength and distance before breaking the bars of the cage.

Rose crowns Somerset's day with a century

BATH: The Australians, with six second innings wickets in hand, are 64 runs ahead of Somerset

Somerset began at 130 for three, 102 runs behind, and declared just before 3.45 – giving themselves both a break of innings and, in due course, a refreshing tea interval – with their score at 340 for five. This was possibly the most advantageous position they have ever occupied against an Australian side. I could imagine Close arguing with the committee about declarations, he principally concerned, as ever, with victory, they with the third day gate. Anyway, the declaration was made.

…

Towards the end of his long innings, Rose let his strokes flow, and duly reached his hundred, out of a total of 320.

Part of the reason for his relative slowness was the vigorous play of first Botham and then Slocombe, who were his partners. Botham scored his fifty at more than a run a minute. Slocombe, little less aggressive, was fifth out at 330. Somerset are fortunate to possess these two promising young men, among several others. In fact, I cannot think of any county with more potential talent than Somerset, and this has happened under the captaincy of Close, who, they frequently tell you in the cider tent, cannot be bothered with the youngsters.

Somerset have their first win over the Australians

BATH: Somerset beat the Australians by seven wickets

This was the first time Somerset have beaten a representative Australian team, and when you consider all the Australians who have played for Somerset, it is surprising it had not been done before: but it was a very satisfactory result, especially to the organizers of the Bath Festival, who have been having a struggle to maintain their city in the cricketing scene.

I felt that on Thursday evening Somerset had not been working quite so hard at winning as they should have been, the third day gate weighing upon their minds. There was never any doubt that they were in earnest yesterday. The Australians, beginning at 172 for four, 66 on, were bowled out before lunch for 289. This meant that Somerset had to score 182 to win, with adequate time – no more than three an over were required.

…

Their plan was that Rose should hold an end and Denning go for his strokes. A sound plan: 50 up in the 12th over, no wicket down. Chappell brought himself on to bowl, first change: an intelligent move, because he has bowled before on these early-season western pitches that give some help to those who seam the ball a little.

He bowled Denning, who had made 34 out of 50, in the 12th over. He had reasonable appeals for leg before against both Rose and Richards. These two ultimately went at the same total which made Somerset 129 for three. Richards did bat marvellously, though he was dropped twice. One straight drive reminded me irresistibly of Hammond. After the fourth wicket fell, there was just a chance that the Australians might break through, but Botham (attacking) and Slocombe (defending) made sure that they did not.

So Somerset who have never won any kind of competition in domestic cricket, have joined the counties (not so many, in this century) who have beaten the Australians. As the players walked up the steps of the little pavilion I thought I saw Sam Woods waiting to greet them at the top, with Bill Alley, Colin McCool, John McMahon, Tom Lowry and one or two others joining in the applause.

Oxford

It was my wife's birthday. I said to her, with clumsy gallantry, that she looked 25 years younger than I, and she responded briskly that she was well aware of it, and it was a pity I had aged before my time. Stung by this reverse, I caught a train to Oxford which immediately set off towards the depths of Wiltshire. I did not feel it was going to be a good day.

It is, incidentally, hard luck on British Rail that their new high speed trains (marvellous when they are working well) have again been flung into confusion by a track breakdown. Railwaymen are divided in opinion as to which is cause and which is effect. Myself, I put it down to the long claws of the Witch of Didcot.

However, I managed to arrive in the Parks just after lunch.

Ilford

Farewell for this season to Valentine's Park, a ground of which I am fond, except that you have to be a miniature mountaineer to walk round it; a ground on which I once saw, in about 1936, Watt, of Kent, score 28 runs in seven minutes, including a vast six; the nearest ground to the headquarters of the Poet's and Peasants' Cricket Club, an organization of which I am proud to be Poet. And also a ground where, if you find the cricket boring, you can go and watch the women playing bowls.

Bath

It was a beautifully warm day, the first day this season when I have watched cricket with my overcoat off. The Bath ground and its surroundings looked very well, despite the blank stare of the vast, ugly, although conceivably useful, "leisure centre" which defaces one end of it. The crowd was large and happy. The band of the Royal Marines played admirably (Crown Imperial and Cole Porter is a combination which can scarcely miss) and yesterday we could actually hear them, thanks to a fortunate change of wind.

This meant, of course, that we could no longer hear the public address system, but this exchange was no robbery. Besides, you would be rather disappointed to find an efficient public address system on a Somerset ground – it spoils the atmosphere.

The Oval

"Typical Surrey" was the comment of the man behind me, and he was not intending to be complimentary. "Yus," said his neighbour, "let 'em 'orf the 'ook." You could tell they were pedigree Elephant and Castle veterans because they said yus, not yuh. The fine old usage "yus" will soon, I feel, become as extinct as the wees on which Samivel's father insisted. Leaving this aside, you will gather that Surrey supporters are not pleased with their side at present.

Maidstone

Maidstone is a town I hardly know. It is many years since I last saw cricket here. Not that I have really seen much in the last couple of days, though conscientiously trying: the high pollen count, or something equally obscure, seems to have put what I can only call a mote in my eyes.

Nevertheless, I am able to report that Maidstone, while far from the little country town that Wat Tyler and Jack Cade knew, which Fairfax captured after five hours of hard fighting, is still a place of character, with many good buildings – though All Saints is boarded up and looking depressed – and does not seem to be in imminent danger of being Basingstoked. I can also say that the ground of the Mote club continues to be pretty – prettier than Canterbury, I think, though less striking than Dover; and that Surrey have the advantage of Kent in the present match.

Manchester

The barmaid had it right (I find barmaids more valuable sources of information, and inspiration, than the traditional taxi drivers). She said: "Well, we had had lovely weather for Test, and we expected we'd pay for it." This is the Manchester School of Thought, Cobden and Bright and Scott and Montague and Cardus, all that crowd, the natural free traders.

...

Lancashire were 70 for four when, after 70 minutes, the rains descended and the floods came. Clive Lloyd may be unable to bat, because of a strain, so Lancashire are in a good deal of bother. But the barmaid, still smiling, was joostified.

Birmingham

I was slighting recently about the conversational powers of taxi drivers, compared with those of barmaids. I must therefore record a remark made by the taxi driver who took me to Edgbaston yesterday. A spontaneous remark and so far as I know an original one: "I love cricket," he said, "always go there when I can. Chess on grass."

Procter strikes with thunderous spell

BRISTOL: Gloucestershire beat Middlesex by 18 runs

A thunderous last spell of bowling by Procter who was using his longest run, and at last approaching his old speed, won Gloucestershire a match which they had looked like losing. Graveney also bowled very well for them, and Shepherd played a match-saving innings, for which Richie Benaud gave him the man of the match award, but it was Procter who commanded the last tense minutes.

Gloucestershire, facing a hard task, even at home, against the only county who had won all their Benson and Hedges matches this season, won the toss, and batted, a decision which must have cost Procter a little thought, since there had been rain in the night, and although the pitch had been covered it did not follow that it was unaffected. It remained a lively pitch all day, giving the bowlers some hope, but when Gloucestershire had lost their first three wickets for 23, including the captain's, they might have thought it would be more comfortable to be in the field.

Stovold was bowled in Daniel's first bowl, Sadiq unbelievably run out, thinking there was a quick run, to Barlow, Procter himself leg before, first ball. After these shocks, Gloucestershire settled down, though the run rate was naturally slow for a while.

Ultimately, in their 55 overs, they reached 194 for seven wickets, which is a score that wins more often than not in a Benson and Hedges match: at least it was when I last consulted Bill Frindall and his computer on the subject.

Zaheer first moved the match Gloucestershire's way, and was beginning to make some of his more daring strokes, when he was out to an excellent, running catch by Barlow. Shepherd sustained the rest of the innings. Not that it was a characteristic innings by Shepherd. Most of his runs came in singles. With Gloucestershire forced to play several inexperienced men, he knew he had a heavy responsibility, and bore it as a heavy man should. He is putting on some weight again, as he nears the end of his career, but still is fit, sharp-eyed, and a proper rugged Devonian –

For I, when I undress me
Each night, upon my knees
Will ask the Lord to bless me
With apple pie and cheese.

I always associate, I am not sure why, these lines with David Shepherd. Foat was the only other batsman to make much of a contribution.

No bowler took more than one wicket, but Daniel was much the hardest from whom to score. Still, we thought – there was really quite a lot of us for Bristol in midweek on a not very warm day – that Middlesex, with a strong batting line, and Gloucestershire struggling to find five bowlers, would win.

They progressed steadily, usually up to the rate, and needed only 23 in the last six overs, with four wickets left, but were panicked a little, doubtless by the formidable sight of Procter, roaring in as if he had never heard of such a thing as a knee injury. The difference between Procter and most other overseas players who have come to play in the championship is that he attracts, and deserves, a deep loyalty.

Hampshire men are pleased when Richards scores a century for them. Nottinghamshire men were pleased when Sobers did. But none of them have ever quite won the affection of a provincial crowd in the way that Procter has in Gloucestershire. He so obviously cares about the county and its fortunes. "Mike, Mike," they were calling as he entered on his last few overs, and he responded to the call with all his heart and body.

GLOUCESTERSHIRE	194 for seven (55 overs, Zaheer 64, Shepherd 60*)
MIDDLESEX	176 (52.1 overs, Smith 41, Radley 40, Gatting 30, Procter 3-15, Graveney 3-32)

Mervyn Kitchen

TAUNTON: Somerset v Glamorgan

Kitchen has never been a cricketer quite of England standard, but he has been a thoroughly good county man for many years, and the way he bonks around, the stroke often bearing little relation to the nature of the ball, has heartened many Somerset sides and many Somerset crowds. It was a delight to see him still playing so well. I am afraid, though, that I got him out. I "put the mouth on him", as the West Indians say. I had just inquired when last he scored a first-class hundred – and it took some looking up – when he was caught at mid-on from a stupid mis-hit, for which he banged his pads all the way to the pavilion. He was loudly and properly cheered, by his own folk.

Why, I wonder, was he called Mervyn? It sounds more like the name of a Welsh tenor or a *New Statesman* columnist than a Somerset cricketer. But then Woods, whom Kitchen in some ways resembles, was prophetically and inappropriately christened with the names Samuel Moses Joshua.

Barry Richards

WORCESTER: Worcestershire v Hampshire (Sunday League)

It sounds easy: six wickets and an hour to spare. Yet Hampshire would probably have lost this match, except for an innings of restrained mastery from Richards; a better innings than many larger, and faster, and more dramatic ones that he has played. I remember a similar innings from him at Swansea a couple of years ago, when on an awkward pitch, with every kind of bowler clamouring to get on, he decided that it was his duty to win the match.

Once Richards had taken this decision, all the bowlers and fieldsmen can really do, is watch and pray. He may possibly have been moved by the anxiety that Hampshire have to beat Worcestershire, after Worcestershire sneaked a championship from them with major – no, Field Marshal – help from the weather.

On all the line a solemn vengeance waits,
And frequent hearses shall besiege your gates.

That is roughly what Hampshire think about Worcestershire.

...

Richards did not play a flawless innings. Gifford and Holder both troubled him, banging the ball on his pads, and sometimes finding the inside edge of his bat. If he had got out just after tea, Hampshire might still have collapsed. But he did not, I suppose because he had decided he would not. Ally the technique of Richards, and the concentration of Bradman, and the whole-hearted effort of Procter, and you would have a batsman as good as Hobbs, and nearly as good as Grace.

Zaheer Abbas

CHELTENHAM: Gloucestershire v Sussex

205 not out in the first innings

Shepherd played well, in his robust way, glowing in the afternoon sun, like Ugborough Beacon after the Armada.

But the Drake of the whole enterprise, the dominator of the innings, the pride of Sialkot and Charlton Abbas, was Zaheer. There were times in the morning when he seemed a little slow. He lingered in the 90s, as is not unknown. Sussex, moreover, with defensive field placings, fielded dauntingly well and gave very little away. But in the afternoon Zaheer played a series of resplendent strokes and reached his second hundred which most of the crowd justifiably expected from the moment he had reached his first.

108 not out in the second innings

Not even WG, whose statistics remain as impressive as his beard was, equalled the record set up by Zaheer yesterday. He followed his double century in the first innings with another century in the second. He had done this twice before. No other batsman has achieved this particular feat, 200 and 100 in the same match, three times.

Until yesterday, Zaheer shared the honour of doing it twice with an improbable companion, Maurice Hallam of Leicestershire. Two batsmen more different in style and circumstances would be hard to imagine. Hallam, though a pleasing stroke player, mostly had to grind out his runs, because Leicestershire had nobody else to score them.

Zaheer arrived in Gloucestershire already an international of renown, and has had his casual spells, but has always had formidable batsmen alongside him, and has always been capable of winning a match, as he did this one. His 100 in the second innings was an even better performance, related to the state of the game, than his double hundred in the first. It is interesting, and sheds a little light upon the man, that at the end of all six innings in this extraordinary series, he has been not out.

Barry Richards
'They must have felt like honest Trojan soldiers competing with Achilles, mortals struggling with the god-like'

AUGUST: Nottinghamshire v Gloucestershire at Trent Bridge 1977

Gloucestershire's turn to be driven into the ground

NOTTINGHAM: Nottinghamshire (6 pts) drew with Gloucestershire (8 pts)

It was a disappointing day for Gloucestershire. At the start, having batted once, they were 191 on, with nine second innings wickets to take, which should have been within their capacity. They were thwarted, in the first place, by Basharat Hassan, who batted long, never less than competently, and quite dashingly towards the end.

He is a Kenyan, in his thirties, whose career in English cricket has suffered from the inevitable abbreviation of his name into "Basher". He is a much better batsman when he does not try to bash, but just lets his strokes arrive, and has the responsibility of sustaining an innings, as he did yesterday.

That innings, though notable, was only one reason why Gloucestershire failed to win a match which would have been important to them. The pitch, slower and easier than it has been all week, was another. It was a kind of pitch that recalled the comment of Sir Neville Cardus, made more than half a century ago: "Trent Bridge, where it is always 4 o'clock in the afternoon, and 300 for two." At least, that is the remark as I remember it.

A third reason why Gloucestershire did not win was that they were not quite good enough. Ardently pursuing them around as they pursue what would be their first real championship, I, a local patriot, have not, I suppose, noticed sufficiently that they are an unimpressive bowling side when their captain is not taking wickets. Procter bowled Todd, the second wicket to fall, and Rice was also out in the morning, a catch via bat and pad from the bowling of Childs, who has a lot to learn about left arm spin, but is learning it.

Another wicket fell during the afternoon, but any more looked less and less likely, as Tunnicliffe settled in with Hassan. Procter accepted the reverse with smiles, and congratulations, especially to Hassan.

GLOUCESTERSHIRE	462 for seven declared (Stovold 196, Zaheer 83, Shepherd 52, Procter 42)
NOTTINGHAMSHIRE	265 (Johnson 78, Todd 62, Childs 5-54, Procter 3-73)
	339 for four (Hassan 182*, Tunnicliffe 64*, Smedley 39)

AUGUST: Somerset v Gloucestershire at Taunton (second & third days)

Close a great influence on the philosophy of Marks

TAUNTON: Gloucestershire, with four second innings wickets in hand are 104 runs ahead of Somerset

Somerset, who were 109 for three at the start, 127 behind, took their score to 349, a lead of 113. They also took eight points on the first innings, to Gloucestershire's six. Gloucestershire seemed to have fumbled their chance, after winning the toss, as they have been known to do before on an August Bank holiday at Taunton, one of the historic fixtures of the championship.

I beg your pardon, the Schweppes championship. Here in 1938, give or take a year, I saw Hammond score what must have been one of his best centuries, and then Jack Crapp could not quite hold a difficult catch in the outfield in the last over as Somerset won the match. That was a glorious one for the cider camp.

Yesterday Denning made his highest first-class score, while Kitchen and Close supported him, and so, later, did Marks, though he looked a little hesitant from time to time. Possibly he was under orders. It has always been part of the technique of the second, transformed version of Close to appear in trouble when you are really quite happy, and it may be that Marks has been picking this up. The earlier, unreformed version of Close always appeared cheerful, even when he was really in trouble.

Marks, if ever he should become captain of Somerset, will no doubt bear this in mind. An integrated personality is always needed to captain Somerset. I have read Brearley on Plato, Marks is reading Greats, philosophers all. I am talking just as much nonsense as they do: but I can see some force in the argument that a good captain needs a gift of command as much as his cricketing skill.

There was a good crowd, few seats empty, and the weather was fine, though deteriorating as the twilight advanced. Gloucestershire went for runs in their second innings, as they had to, and made a sound, speedy start: but they had lost two wickets by tea, those of Stovold and Zaheer; Hignell went soon afterwards.

Procter came in. He had Sadiq at the other end, not exactly set for the light was poor, and Burgess was making the ball hop from the seam now and then. Procter was soon after the runs. It was interesting to see how Close set his field to cope with him. In one over from Jennings, Procter hit five cover drives with such a smack that the crowd cheered every stroke as it left the bat.

The first three produced no runs, a fieldsman in the way every time. The last two produced four runs each, the fieldsmen left flat on their diving faces as the ball went through. I thought, after this, that Procter was going to score 100 and win the match.

Heigho! He was caught in the covers, a smart catch by Robinson, the Somerset coach, who is playing in this match because they could not find anyone else. I say "the coach" but Bill Andrews assures me that he is only the assistant groundsman, yet still "one of my boys". It was a good catch all the same and probably decided the match.

Sadiq, who had been going slowly in the early part of his innings, possibly overawed by the majesty of his captain, then began to score quickly but was caught at midwicket after he had lost his leader. Somebody, for Gloucestershire, will have to play an innings today. Might it be Shepherd? He was not out at the end and looking cheerful.

Close achieves object but misses objective

TAUNTON: Somerset (20 pts) beat Gloucestershire (6 pts) by five wickets

It must be 40 years since I shed tears, tears of disappointment at least, at and about a cricket match. I did so yesterday when Close, in what was presumably his last game at Taunton as the captain of Somerset, missed his 100.

Everyone on the ground, even the Gloucestershire fanatics, even, I suspect, the Gloucestershire team, were willing him to do it. He had been playing so well, so masterfully, and Somerset were winning the match with time to spare. But as he drew nearer to the century, cheered on by every run (Somerset have taken the Old Bald Blighter to their hearts), his strokes became rash, even foolish. He had three of those famously deplorable sweeps in an over, fortunately not making contact with any of them.

Then he went for an on-drive, which he did not quite time, and was caught, apologetically, by deep mid on. He walked slowly off, everyone standing and applauding. It seemed like an epitome, a school report, on his whole career: "Most brilliant boy we have, but loses concentration at critical moments." Nevertheless, Close had the satisfaction of giving Gloucestershire a licking, and this match is a kind of West Country Roses contest.

I said yesterday that there would have to be a major innings by one of their remaining batsmen if Gloucestershire were to stay in the game. Shepherd duly provided it. His score was only 11 short of his highest in first class cricket. Now, Gloucestershire are eight points behind Middlesex in the county championship, with Kent having only one point in hand at the top.

Somerset did not bowl, perhaps, too hard, once Shepherd had settled in. They were waiting for the declaration. Procter left them 272 in three hours, which was, I thought, generous; for though Gloucestershire needed to win the match more, the pitch was playing slowly and fitfully. Also, Somerset have many left handers, which diminishes the threat of the most dangerous balls which Procter and Brain can bowl. There was never much doubt that Somerset would win, though Burgess was out early, a fine diving catch to his left by Stovold. Stovold is an excellent batsman and an excellent wicket-keeper when he stands back.

Denning, from Chewton Mendip, rang an attractive peal, and reached his century. It was an excellent innings, but all our thoughts were on Close at the other end. Richards, who had been announced as going to bat only in an emergency, came in at No 5, and scored a few without much apparent discomfort.

But all out thoughts were on the Old Bald Blighter, and all Somerset's delight in winning was slightly destroyed by the sight of him, head bowed, walking back to that grubby, pleasant, tiny Taunton pavilion. That will be the sight of the day which will stay longest in my memory. Just missed it again.

GLOUCESTERSHIRE	236 (Sadiq 88, Bainbridge 39, Dredge 3-63, Burgess 3-67)
	384 for seven declared (Shepherd 142*, Sadiq 88, Procter 46, Stovold 40, Burgess 3-87)
SOMERSET	349 (Denning 122, Richards 70, Taylor 40, Kitchen 32, Procter 4-100)
	272 for five (Denning 107, Close 87, Kitchen 36)

Awesome innings for young and old

BRISTOL: Hampshire, with all their first innings wickets in hand, are 115 runs behind Gloucestershire

I had the pleasure yesterday of watching one of the best innings I have ever seen. It was played by Procter in such circumstances as would have taxed the ingenuity of Hylton Cleaver, Talbot Baines Reed or R.A.H. Goodyear, whose stories entertained my youth so vividly. I still read them to my youngest son, who seems to enjoy them, and was also present to see Procter's century.

My son was not exactly delighted, though he is a Gloucestershire boy. Awe-stricken, rather, to see the great man laying about himself with such command. It was a sunny morning. There would be play. Sighs of relief all over Bristol for were not Gloucestershire, with luck, about to win their first championship for 100 years? There was a large crowd, even at 11 o'clock.

Procter won the toss and decided to bat, which might have been arguable, and was indeed sharply argued by senior Gloucestershire members in the bar when wickets began to fall. I can not recall a moment on the Bristol ground when feelings of the populace have been more involved, carefully and thoughtfully, not like a Sunday match. The pitch was damp and helped the spinners. Goddard and Parker would have taken one look at it and booked their seats for the races on Friday.

Hampshire had no spinners of comparable quality, although Cowley, with off-spin, and Southern, slow left-arm (you can see the valuable influence Sainsbury has had on his method), bowled well enough. Sadiq and Stovold came out to ringing cheers. Sadiq was caught at square leg before a run had been scored. Stovold and Zaheer anxiously prodded on their way.

At 28, Zaheer, who was limping badly – he ought not to have been playing with his injured thigh, he could hardly run, but it was an understandable temptation – played on. Still at 28, Stovold was caught at slip. And oh, agony, still at 28, so was Hignell. Disaster. Why doesn't it rain now? Not a cloud in the sky.

Procter, who had come in at the fall of the third wicket, observed the fourth fall at once and contemplated the scene sombrely but serenely. He took a long time to score a run, which obviously worried him less than it did the Hampshire bowlers. Slowly, we noticed that he was making a nudge here and flick there and his runs were accumulating.

Procter played through the pitch at its worst, gently increased the pace and ultimately brought in all his strokes. His drives seemed to stride between the off side fieldsmen, almost casually. He reached his 100 with a six. It was impossibly heroic because he is not supposed to be a batsman this season and it might be his last match for Gloucestershire.

It was, in any case, an unforgettable innings by a man who has given all his heart and every muscle to the county he is proud to lead. The Gloucestershire innings ended in the 100th over, the tail having given Procter tolerably good support. I wish, as an adopted Gloucestershire man, that I could report more happily of the last hour.

But Richards and Greenidge scored much as they pleased, the pitch smiling in the evening sunshine or dead as a bone, according to which metaphor you prefer or which county you support. Whether Gloucestershire win the match and the championship or not, I shall never forget the way Procter batted yesterday.

Gloucestershire look at the sky and hope

BRISTOL: Gloucestershire, with seven second innings wickets in hand, lead Hampshire by 188 runs

The thunderstorms, in the early autumn, roll up the Bristol Channel, usually brief but occasionally devastating. We had one shortly after six o'clock yesterday, which ended play for the day, and the sky bore with it all the hopes and fears of Gloucestershire, so near to their first championship for 100 years. As I write it has stopped raining, but looks gloomy in the west. We can (I write, by this stage of the season, as a strong partisan) only hope that the storms choose their moments well and descend also on Edgbaston and Blackpool.

Gloucestershire badly needed to break the Hampshire opening partnership, which stood at 118 when play started, only 115 behind. They did not look at all likely to do this for half an hour. Richards was obviously intent on playing an innings. I feared this after Procter's century on Wednesday. Richards and Procter, who began their English careers together, the merest boys, playing for Gloucestershire Second XI, have always had a rivalry at once fierce and amiable.

Procter began by bowling fast. In the 51st over, the score 128, he had Greenidge caught at the wicket. He then switched to off breaks and soon had Turner leg-before-wicket. He then had Jesty caught at short leg, first ball. Childs, the left-arm spin bowler, another of the Gloucestershire Devonians, who at 26 is not quite a youngster but improving steadily – he was given his county cap on Wednesday – bowled responsibly at the other end. It was he who took the wicket of Richards, who lobbed the ball up rather vaguely as if wondering why Procter was not bowling at him. Full marks to Childs, though, for keeping his length and aim when Richards was getting after him, especially after one big six to the pavilion, which nearly laid a lady out, even on the bounce.

Hampshire were 166 for four, and once Richards had gone the innings dissolved. They had a lead of only six runs. Procter bowled them out for the most part with his innocent-looking spinners, cunning changes of pace and flight concealed among them.

What, in all the Cotswolds and the Vale of Severn, or the Forest of Dean, where Puff the Magic Dragon dwells, what in all Gloucestershire am I to say new about Procter? Six wickets in two styles, and another commanding innings in the evening. Was Hammond a greater all-rounder? In a week at Cheltenham in 1928, Hammond took nine wickets in an innings, for 23 runs, and in the next match scored two centuries and made 10 catches. But Hammond, possibly because he was not given the chance early enough, was not comparable with Procter as a captain.

Will Procter's enormous efforts this season be crowned with the championship? We look at the sky and wait in hope.

A hundred years of waiting unrewarded

BRISTOL: Hampshire (18 pts) beat Gloucestershire (6 pts) by six wickets

So it was not to be. A hundred years of waiting for the championship, which would have been the crown of Procter's career, possibly his last match for the county to which he has given such valiant service, were not to be honoured in the successful way even Hampshiremen had hoped. Not a partisan, not a crying man, I found the drops stealing down my cheeks as Hampshire made their way steadily throughout the afternoon. I realized Hampshire's victory was growing inevitable, and the news from the other places, confirmed that Gloucestershire would not be champions. Procter, after playing a great match and a marvellous season, could not, in the end, quite carry them on his back.

Bristol awoke to a sky of flawless blue. At least there was going to be no anti-climax because of the weather. Hignell and Shackleton resumed their fifth wicket partnership, 188 runs on. In 40 minutes, they put on 44, before Hignell was caught at slip. It was a pity that he missed his 100. He had batted extremely well, coming in at a moment of concern, on Thursday, and hitting the ball hard and cleanly. It crossed my mind that we might have been watching a man who could in the future lead Gloucestershire to the championship. He was given his county cap, after the lunch interval.

After that the wickets fell frequently, and at 12.20 the innings was over. Gloucestershire let the bat fly towards the end of it, and scored 276 which meant that Hampshire had to score 271 in 270 minutes. I felt Gloucestershire could have done with 10 minutes more of batting, because the pitch was playing, probably, better than it had done in the match, and Richards, to say nothing of Greenidge, are just about the most dangerous opponents, as an opening pair, in the world, in a situation of this kind.

Procter and Brain bowled three overs each at speed, providing few problems. Then Graveney came on, an indication of the route Procter hoped to take to victory, and in his first over he had Richards caught at slip by Zaheer, a remarkably agile catch for a limping man. In the last over before lunch, Greenidge was dropped at mid-on off Graveney, a hard but straight chance. This diminished the pleasure of the crowd – the largest I have seen on the Bristol ground since Walter Hammond's last match – as they turned eagerly to their lunchtime bread and cheese (double Gloucester, of course). At lunch, 58 for one, Hampshire were going comfortably, and Greenidge and Turner continued to knock the bowling about afterwards.

A hush fell upon the hitherto exuberant crowd. They still cheered when they had the least excuse, but their excuses were fewer. Hope revived when Greenidge was out, caught at mid-on, and Turner was caught at cover soon afterwards. But at 156 for three, in only 28 overs, Hampshire were still able to take their time. Cowley and Jesty made a fairly gentle, but confident way through the rest of the afternoon, or almost all of it.

GLOUCESTERSHIRE	223 (Procter 115, Bainbridge 43, Cowley 5-94, Southern 3-86)
	276 (Hignell 92, Procter 57, Zaheer 56, Southern 6-81)
HAMPSHIRE	229 (Richards 94, Greenidge 52, Cowley 30, Procter 6-68)
	271 for four wickets (Greenidge 94, Jesty 58, Cowley 43*, Brain 3-54)

Week ended April 29
I have a heavy cold. I always start the cricket season with a cold. Is it the weather, or is it all in the mind? I must remember the precept of P.J.K. Gibbs: 'Ne'er chance a clout till June be out, and even then not before lunch.'

Incidentally, returning from Oxford to Didcot on Tuesday afternoon, I caught a train which started on time and arrived 2¾ hours late, which is my personal record for a scheduled 15-minute journey.

Week ended May 6
Another dismal week, sniffing and sneezing in the rain. I saw two notable innings at Taunton by Vivian Richards, one in the Sunday League, and one in the Championship match against Glamorgan. He was out in the second to a memorable catch by Llewellyn at backward square leg, one that Milton (Arthur, I mean, not the poet John) would have been proud to hold. There were those who felt that Richards had thrown his wicket away, at a time when Somerset still needed some runs, by taking an unnecessary risk, but catches like that are acts of God rather than man. Besides, it is the way he takes the occasional risk which makes Richards so compelling to watch. And additionally and alternatively, as the lawyers say, he does not take so many risks as a casual glance might suggest. His bat sometimes wanders from the classical line, but not his eyes. Maurice Tate thought that Bradman would never score many runs in England unless he kept his bat straighter. Hm.

Week ended May 13
At Bournemouth, where I went for the Benson and Hedges match against Somerset, I was saddened to hear of the death of Bill Shepheard. He was not so young, and he had been ill, but it came as a shock, for he was never a man to give in. I was told that only a few days before his death he had struggled to get up the steps to the announcer's box, just to see if he could do it, but found that he could not. Bill was, in many different capacities, a strength and stay of cricket, especially Hampshire cricket, and the kindest of friends. He was buried last week, with his MCC tie, his Hampshire tie, and his Hampshire membership card. If you think this funny or sentimental, by all means laugh about it. Bill would not mind. I used to tease him sometimes in my reports, especially about the time at Portsmouth when he triumphantly announced, after a Hampshire victory in two days, that the sponsors were about to present the Man of the Match award, and it transpired the sponsors, a local garage, were not present, being under the impression that their match would last three days, and still looking forward to their party on the third one. Ah, happy days, and how I shall miss you at the Hampshire grounds, dear Bill.

Week ended July 8
I watched cricket during the week at Taunton, Lord's, and Maidstone. I say 'watched', but there were times when I saw precious little of it, because of this eye trouble. The high pollen count? New glasses needed? Or something nasty in the woodshed? The medical men do not seem quite sure. The prospects for a blind cricket-writer must be limited. One old friend kindly said that it could hardly make much difference, since I never wrote about the cricket anyway. Another, a player, suggested I took up umpiring.

Week ended July 22
Scotland beat Denmark by 158 runs, at Broughty Ferry. This is about all I can tell you of the three-day contest between the old Scandinavian rivals, because newspapers consider that Scottish cricket is of no interest to English readers, and possibly not even to Scottish ones. But you could pick a strong all-time Scotland XI: reasonable qualifications have been held by Jardine, Peebles, Greig, Denness, P.A. Gibb, Robertson-Glasgow, to name a few; and of course there is Aitchison, a Presbyterian minister of dour mien upon whom I once strove to commentate as he scored a hundred against the Australians at Glasgow. It was an innings so austere and leisurely that I have never been tempted to go and hear him preach.

Week ended July 29
Every week I intend to have a good look at the averages. This week I remembered. The man with more wickets than anybody, though well down the list, is young Botham, of Somerset, with 75 (and five more in Australia's first innings in the current Test, in which England appear to be doing rather well). Several people and places claim a share in Botham. There is Cheshire, where he was born in 1975. There is Bill Andrews ('one of my boys'). There is Lord's where he spent two years on the staff. There is Bill Andrews ('spotted him at once, natural genius'). There is Yeovil, where he lives and where his interest in the game developed. Down in Somerset they have been saying for some time that he is the best all-rounder they have had (not counting importations) since Arthur Wellard. Some reservations on the last point from Bill Andrews ('course Arthur did play for England, but I wasn't very fit at the time').

Boycott is in the England side again, to universal interest, though not universal approval. After making some favourable reference to him recently, I received a stern letter from a lady in the Isle of Wight, accusing me of succumbing to 'boycottitis'. (She had already stopped reading the Sage of Longparish, 'because he always brings Boycott in', and I fear that between us we have lost a reader.)

The Packer ramifications mount, and are getting very boring, quite spoiling the season. He is reported to be having trouble with one or two of his signatories, notably Thomson, whom I heard described as 'the nigger in the woodpile', not the most felicitous of analogies. The Test and County Cricket Board, photographed in all their panoply, and looking rather less impressive than the executive committee of the Bristol West Liberal Association, have threatened a ban, on county cricket as well as Test cricket, for those who join the enemy. I do not propose to write about this again, until something amusing happens, like Mr Packer entering a round-the-world yacht race with Rachel Heyhoe Flint as crew. I record my expectations that the outcome will be determined by two things: the courts, and money.

Week ended August 26

The delayed Gillette Cup semi-final between Middlesex and Somerset was a sad farce. After two blank days it had been decided, if necessary, to settle it by spinning a coin, but in fact a 15-over game was possible on the last (sixth) day. Close said wryly afterwards that they should have made Smith man of the match for winning the toss.

Close also said, it is reported, 'The whole thing typifies my life. It was a complete farce.' If he meant that his life has been a farce, he was wrong. If he meant that his life has been a failure, he was wrong. If he meant that things have often gone badly for him just when they seemed propitious, he was right; but he is not singular in such misfortunes. However, a man cannot be expected to weigh every word in a moment of acute disappointment, and he is not the only one disappointed that he will not end his career in a Gillette Cup final. (I say 'end his career', but one cannot be sure: he keeps bobbing up like the cork of a bottle of Irish whiskey in the roaring forties).

In the Schweppes Championship, Kent lead Middlesex by four points, Gloucestershire nine points behind Middlesex. All three have played 19 matches. I spent the week endeavouring to watch Gloucestershire. They had play on the second and third days against Warwickshire. Both sides tried for a finish, but Gloucestershire could not quite manage a stiff, though in the circumstances justifiable, goal set by Kanhai. Against Yorkshire, they had no play at all. This was less frustrating for me than usual. Since I do not live far from the Bristol ground, I was able to spend some time at home, and make desperate, unco-ordinated attacks on my in-tray. By this time of the season I am always so far behind with my correspondence that I have lost friends, and contracts, and every time the doorbell rings I expect it to be the bailiffs. So I was glad of the chance, though sorry not to have seen Yorkshire.

A man from Worcestershire writes to me: 'Would you settle an argument and place these batsmen in an order of (*sic*) precedence, D'Oliveira, Gibbons, Graveney, Kenyon, Turner, Walters, Wyatt.' It would make an interesting morning, and I am tempted to reply simply 'R.E. Foster', but no stamped, addressed envelope is enclosed, so I throw it away, and turn to the next. It is an ominous buff, with something about Inland Revenue on the envelope. I look out of the window, hopefully ... no good, it is still raining.

Week ended September 2

I saw Gloucestershire lose at Taunton. The disappointment was that Close was out for 87 after looking as if he was going to get a hundred in his last innings there. He let the thought bother him too much. There was no special need to hurry, but he was swinging the bat wildly towards the end, as if he was back at Old Trafford in 1961. We all stood up and cheered him in.

Week ended September 9

Kent and Middlesex have tied for the Schweppes County Championship. It is no use pretending I am pleased about it. I wanted Gloucestershire to win, less for any reasons of local patriotism than because such a pleasing historical symmetry (1877 and all that) would have been worthy of Procter's farewell to Gloucestershire – if such it should prove to be. I wept for Gloucestershire's failure, as I had wept when Close was out at Taunton last week. I was, on reflection, puzzled that I should start crying over cricket matches at my time of life. Then I remembered that the drops they have given me for my eyes, among their other qualities, are supposed to stimulate the tear-ducts, so I have an excuse (not counting the whisky).

Week ended September 16

I wonder how Schweppes are feeling about their first County Championship. They do not seem to me to have got a great deal out of it. It is easy to think of 'The Gillette', 'The Benson and Hedges' and so on, because the names arrived at the same times as the competitions, and are in a sense definitions. But the Championship is just the Championship, and has been going on so long that it is very difficult to get into the habit of thinking of it as 'The Schweppes'. And then there are so many supplementary sponsors also bidding for attention. At one match at Hove, vast imitation eggs – not the happiest of cricketing symbols – were mounted round the ground in the interest of a firm called Stonegates; and then there was Rediffusion who gave away scorecards in handsome brochures, and announced that the match was being played for the Rediffusion Trophy; and the Sussex Building Society came into it somewhere; and poor Schweppes hardly seemed to get a look-in. If I were them, I should be more assertive.

1978

In October 1977, Alan Gibson and the family had moved to High Littleton, the North Somerset village that he was to make famous in the columns of *The Times* over the ensuing years. Rosie's mother Margaret had died that summer, and whilst this was obviously very sad, it did give the family the opportunity to move out of the Bristol inner suburbs so that the children could grow up in the countryside. Not that High Littleton conforms to the stereotype of a Somerset village, by any means. It had developed in the nineteenth century as a small mining community in the North Somerset coalfield, and is plain, not fancy: solid, stone-built, terraced houses, running along either side of the main Bath–Wells road, and not a thatched roof in sight. Rather like the sort of Durham mining villages in which Alan's father had been brought up around the turn of the century, in fact. But there is handsome countryside on every side and Alan could be at Bath or Bristol and their respective railway stations in less than half an hour. It was the perfect place for him to live: in the country, but not of it; slightly scruffy, but proud with it; middle-class, but with working class origins. And to cap it all, the house that they bought, the Old Market Tavern, had once been a pub!

Developments in the world of cricket were not so cheerful. Although the first World Series matches that winter had attracted small crowds and disappointing television ratings, Kerry Packer was a determined man and, as Alan had observed the previous summer, in the final analysis, his money would be the decisive factor. Feelings ran high, the players' union, the Cricketers' Association, got involved, there were tales of dressing room arguments and even fights, and negotiations seemed to be getting nowhere. It all added up to one of the most unhappy periods in the history of English cricket.

The weather that May was foul. In the week ending May 5, Alan saw just two and a half hours of cricket. 'The whole of England and Wales is one vast puddle,' he wrote in his *Cricketer* diary.

Alan saw a lot of Somerset that season. This was partly a matter of convenience and partly, no doubt, down to sheer chance. But mainly it was a reflection of how well Somerset played in all competitions that year. Brian Rose's style of captaincy might have been very different from that of his authoritarian predecessor, but he was equally successful in bringing out the best from his mixture of established stars, stalwart journeymen and bright young prospects. The latter included a certain fast-medium bowler called Colin Dredge, from Frome, where he had opened the batting as well as the bowling, and clearly had the reputation locally of being something of a demon cricketer. That, at any rate, was the soubriquet that Alan Gibson famously chose for him, and which makes its first appearance in his report of the match against Kent at Taunton, starting on May 24.

Even at this early stage of the season, Kent were looking a good bet for the county championship. On the day that John Woodcock was deploring the way in which Bob Willis had felled the Pakistan night watchman, Iqbal Qasim, in the Edgbaston Test, Alan was watching Kent beat the previous year's champions, Middlesex, at Lord's. He concluded: 'Although it is too early to form opinions about this year's championship, it is quite likely that this match will, in retrospect, appear one of the most important.' So it would transpire.

Somerset too had their chances in the championship. They were in the top half

Tests
England
beat Pakistan
2-0, with one draw
England
beat New Zealand
3-0

Championship
1 Kent
2 Essex
3 Middlesex
4 Yorkshire
5 Somerset
6 Leicestershire

Sunday League
1 Hampshire
2 Somerset
3 Leicestershire
4 Worcestershire
5 Lancashire
6 Essex

Gillette Cup Final
Sussex
beat Somerset

Benson & Hedges Final
Kent
beat Derbyshire

Most first-class runs
1 D.L. Amiss
2 C.E.B. Rice
3 C.G. Greenidge

Most first-class wickets
1 D.L. Underwood
2 J.K. Lever
3 M.W.W. Selvey

dozen all season and only just missed equalling their best ever position, of third. But it was in the one-day competitions that Somerset really excelled that summer.

Kent continued to make the running in the county championship, and Alan was sent to cover their away game against Leicestershire at the end of July. Ray Illingworth set Kent the distinctly ungenerous target of scoring 286 in 165 minutes, but they got there with just five wickets down. 'It was,' wrote Alan, 'the kind of victory of which championships are made.'

So to perhaps the best day of the entire summer: Somerset's Gillette Cup semi-final against Essex at Taunton on August 17. For once at a one-day game, Alan sounds genuinely excited and enthused by Somerset's dramatic, last-ball victory – but the story was not to have a happy ending. In the final, Sussex's relatively unsung bowling attack restricted Somerset to just 211 in their 60 overs, and Paul Parker saw the underdogs home with a stylish 62. Alan wasn't there, but, writing in the *Cricketer*, he doesn't sound as if he was so much disappointed in Somerset's defeat as pleased by Sussex's victory – not least because they had sacked Tony Greig, whom he never liked, and replaced him with the very antithesis of 'Packerman' in Arnold Long, their wicket-keeper, of whom – or perhaps it would be more accurate to say, of whose type – he so much approved.

There was no time for Somerset to lick their wounds. The very next day, they were back in action at Taunton, seeking the win or tie that would give them the John Player League. As in 1976, they were to fall at the final hurdle, leaving Alan to express something that sounds suspiciously like *schadenfreude* at the discomfiture of Somerset's one-day followers, whose antics he never much enjoyed.

Kent, in the meantime, had secured the championship, not with a dramatic, clinching victory, but because their only rivals, Essex, failed by a whisker to overcome Derbyshire in what was a close and exciting match throughout, this time to Alan's undoubted disappointment.

Towards the end of October, Alan profiled Viv Richards, for whom 1978 had been such a bittersweet season, for *The Times*. He didn't know it at the time, but it was to be the last piece about cricket that he would write for the newspaper for over a year. On November 30, the management of Times Newspapers, led by two of Alan's near neighbours in North Somerset, the Chief Executive Duke Hussey and Editor William Rees-Mogg, carried out their threat to suspend publication if agreement was not reached with the print unions on the introduction of new working practices. There were warnings in the House of Commons that the dispute could stretch on for 'many weeks'. It turned out to be many months. Not until November 13 1979, did *The Times* reappear, with the *Sunday Times* following on November 18.

At the time, I was in the process of moving from Wiltshire to Devon. We had sold our bungalow in Sherston, but couldn't take possession of the barn conversion we were buying at Clayhidon in the Blackdown Hills, until February. So Alan and Rosie once again stepped into the breach and very kindly put me up for a few weeks before Christmas at the Old Market Tavern. Considering that one of his greatest friends and political heroes, Jeremy Thorpe, was on trial for conspiracy to murder, and that his main source of income had disappeared virtually overnight, Alan managed to remain remarkably good-humoured. But it was a difficult time for him nonetheless, which became more difficult as time went on.

Raymond Illingworth
'An odd chain of circumstances brought him to the captaincy of his country'

Raymond Illingworth 1978

Several times an odd chain of circumstances has brought a cricketer to the captaincy of his country. Would Lord Hawke have led England if his uncle had not died without an heir, thus putting the son of a Lincolnshire parson in the direct line for a peerage? Would A.P.F. Chapman if A.W. Carr had not dropped a catch in the first over after putting the Australians in (Macartney, who escaped, scored a hundred before lunch)? Would Walter Read had it not been for the argument and muddle which resulted in two England sides touring Australia at the same time? (He was captain of neither, but when they combined forces for a Test match he was felt to be a diplomatic choice.) Would C. Aubrey Smith if he had not looked like a youthful Duke of Wellington? So we could go on.

The way in which Raymond Illingworth became England's captain was as odd as any of these, as we are reminded in an interesting biography of him by Michael Stevenson, just published (*Illy*: Midas Books, £3.95). The only thing I dislike about the book is the title, illustrating as it does the curious infertility of the modern cricketer in nicknames.

From what I know of Illingworth, I like him very much, and I have always admired him as a cricketer, rather more than the England selectors did for a long time. But it was only by a succession of improbable chances that he became England's captain.

...

Even then, though this can hardly be called luck, Illingworth had to show not only shrewdness in captaincy (few doubted he possessed it) but talent as a player, which he had not consistently demonstrated at Test level before. There were those who thought that Pocock in 1969 was as good an off-spin bowler and a better prospect. One of the reasons it is difficult to have a regular bowler as captain is that he seals off a place, unless the attack is to be unbalanced.

Illingworth's response to this was to score a great many runs, in the middle of the order, often when the side were in trouble. It was this, I imagine, as much as anything, which caused the selectors to choose him before Cowdrey for the leadership in Australia in 1970. As a captain he was inclined not to bowl himself enough, but with his skills in other departments this hardly mattered (except no doubt to poor Pocock) and he was always worth his place in the side.

He took quantities of wickets, and scored quantities of runs, for Yorkshire; but when he left for Leicestershire (perhaps Brian Sellers, who was mainly responsible for his going, did Illingworth the best turn of his life) his standing was still that of a fine county cricketer who had not quite made it in the highest grade, in spite of many Test appearances. Of course, he had to face stiff opposition as an off-spinner: Titmus, Allen, Mortimore were all around, apart from the rising Pocock. As Stevenson says, "He rarely seemed able to play as well for his country as he regularly did for Yorkshire." Stevenson attributes this not just to bad luck, but to a "natural tendency towards insecurity which was accentuated by the belief that he was only a stop-gap selection."

Nevertheless, when his late and unexpected promotion came he did so well that he ensured his place among the successful England captains. After all, since the 1914-18 War, only three other Englishmen have won the Ashes in Australia: Chapman, Jardine and Hutton. All these men – even Chapman, who became such a hero with his youthful, beatific looks – were at times the subject of controversy and criticism. So it was with Illingworth. Most of the arguments have centred on his tour of Australia, which suffered many troubles, the walk-off at Sydney only the most dramatic.

Stevenson puts Illingworth's side of the case sympathetically, as befits a biographer, but is not unduly partisan, and sometimes is sharp in his criticism. Indeed, I doubt whether he emphasizes sufficiently the exceptionally heavy burden which Illingworth must have carried on that tour. For one reason and another, relations with the manager and the vice-captain were not happy, and though the bulk of the team were as loyal as could be wished, the senior man had not quite the character to give him the support he needed. No wonder the strain told.

Stevenson also accepts criticisms of Illingworth to the effect that, at least in his early days, he could be "a moaner" or "a barrack-room lawyer". But again the biographer is rarely harsh, and appreciates the problems of a young man with a thrifty disposition struggling to make his way in a toughly competitive and uncertain profession. I use the word "thrifty" carefully, rather than a more disparaging one such as "mean". After his return from Australia, Illingworth naturally was interviewed on television. Another England cricketer told me of the fee reputed to have been paid which was substantial but not, in the circumstances, excessive. "Why," this other English cricketer said, "they *had* to have him. He could have asked *anything*." I think a good day's work for a good day's pay is the Illingworth policy, rather than aspirations towards millions.

I put the book down feeling that I had a greater understanding of Raymond Illingworth than before, and with my liking and admiration for him confirmed. This is, alas, more than I could feel after reading the recent autobiography of his most famous Yorkshire contemporary, Brian Close.

MAY: Oxford University v Yorkshire at The Parks 1978

DAY ONE

Boycott won the toss and led his side in to bat. Now I confess that, owing to some trifling delay at Didcot, I did not see the incident, but when I arrived at the ground, about half an hour later, everybody was still laughing, and there was a large 0 on the board below "Last Man", so I guessed directly, that Boycott was out. I did not know, of course, that he had been caught and bowled by Wookey, in the first over. Wookey is already a Blue, a Cambridge one, and a theologian, so he has numerous years in front of him as a student. He is at Wycliffe Hall, which is, or used to be, an Evangelical place, and countless hours of extemporary prayer from the community were doubtless the power responsible for getting Boycott out. It comforts me to see Wookey in an Oxford side: a natural successor to Wingfield-Digby.

Boycott's mortification cannot have been allayed when the next partnership, between Love and Lumb – who sound, if you say with a Yorkshire accent, rather like a J.B. Priestley play – put on 217.

DAY TWO

Oxford were all out for 125. Now, it was not so sunny a day as Wednesday had been, and the cloud could have been expected to help the ball to swing. Also, the pitch was taking some spin. But it must be said that these things were only noticeable when Oxford were batting, and when I suggested them as excuses to the Oxford coach, Arthur Milton, I got a dusty answer. Perhaps I chose the wrong moment to ask him, for he had just been going round the ground with the "Voluntary Contributions" box, doing his best to muster an uncharacteristically baleful stare for the recalcitrant.

"I don't think it's fair," he said, "to have to preach the sermon and take the collection."

Yorkshire chose to bat again. Presumably they were in search of further practice, and it is not inconceivable that their captain had the first innings on his mind. Boldly he faced the dreaded Wookey, who bowled him two maiden overs. Then, with a bit of a scramble he was off the mark, but he had scored only three when, cutting at Marie, he was caught in the covers. Never have I heard such hearty laughter, no, not in Wombwell. To my surprise, he did not immediately declare.

DAY THREE

Yorkshire batted on until their lead was about 500. Their declaration left them four hours and a half to bowl Oxford out, and I rejoice to say they failed to do it. My sympathies, except in the Parks, are always with Yorkshire, but I did not feel much affection for them in this match. The way they played it was an insult to their young opponents, and to the spectators, of whom again there was quite a number. Boycott, however, had his second bowl of the match, and must have enjoyed it. At least I think it was Boycott, because somebody was bowling in a cap, and badly.

...

When the third wicket fell, Claughton's, I feared a collapse, especially with the alarming Boycott on again. I have seen Oxford sides collapse ridiculously in just such circumstances. Claughton, who certainly played a splendid innings, was unnecessarily caught at long leg. The next pair, like startled rabbits, at once tried to run each other out, just as if they were young Boycotts. But sanity prevailed, and Boycott, who bowled the last over, returned to the pavilion with, as I heard an undergraduate say, a good deal of egg on his box.

Although I love the Parks as dearly as a man can, I must report that their catering is inferior to Fenner's. On the first day they ran out of whisky, and on the second they ran out of water. Why cannot Oxford provide comparable facilities with that other place which, apart from its nice clubhouse, has, for a long time, had Tolly's Tent? We shall never achieve a winning margin in the cricket matches until we do.

Cambridge

CAMBRIDGE: Cambridge University v Essex

The four members of the Cambridge side who suffered stomach upsets, and were unable to field in the second innings, no doubt were wise in their generation, and I trust wrote worthy essays as they relaxed with their bicarbonate of soda in their warm bedrooms. I do not know what Cambridge stomachs are coming to.

Once upon a time Sam Woods and Gregor MacGregor, who shared rooms in Jesus, asked all the amateurs of a visiting side to breakfast, providing nine hot lobsters and a pin of ale. Their visitors clamoured for coffee and bacon and eggs, which were provided, while Woods and MacGregor ate the lobsters and drank the beer ("they were prime birds, those lobsters," Woods said reflectively, many years later). Then they started cricket, and Woods took all ten wickets in an innings.

Boycott, they say (chiefly) in the south, let England down by leaving the Test team at the time he was most needed, because he was scared of the fast bowlers. The first part of this accusation may be true. As for the second part, I do not profess to understand Boycott's motives for withdrawing, and I doubt very much whether he does himself, but they were certainly more complex than fear.

Brearley, they say (chiefly) in the north, would never have been in the England side at all, had it not been that Lord's wanted an 'establishment' captain in the old tradition. He was only a second-bester to start with. All right, he hasn't done so badly, but they would never have thought of him if he hadn't been a fancy-cap. As against this, Brearley, though he certainly had the misfortune to be educated at Cambridge, is not at all the kind of man whom Yorkshiremen identify with the establishment. His views might be described in many ways as leftish. He markedly did not join in the Packer hunt last summer, keeping a cool, impartial attitude, one fitting to an England captain – and much needed, after the contortions of Greig.

I suppose it would be cowardly not to declare my preference, though it is early days and much may happen. I am a Yorkshireman, but I am on Brearley's side. Maybe if winning, or at least avoiding defeat, is all that matters, he would not be the best choice. But it is not. After all, we sometimes beat Australia, and they sometimes beat us, and the operation would be pointless were it not so. A happy tour next winter, a popular touring side, is, in the present state of international cricket, more important than who holds the Ashes. Brearley is of course not nearly so good a batsman as Boycott, nor quite so utterly dedicated to the game. Boycott might be the harder man to beat, but I have never known it suggested that anyone on his own side has deliberately run Brearley out.

Geoffrey Boycott
'I received a stern letter from a lady in the Isle of Wight, accusing me of succumbing to "boycottitis"'

Johnson sets Tavaré an example

TAUNTON: Somerset, with five first innings wickets in hand, are 236 runs behind Kent

It was a sunny day, especially in the evening, though not always warm. The pitch was a good one, as we expect at Taunton, with just a touch of help for the quicker bowlers in the morning, and a touch for the spinners in the afternoon.

Somerset had done well to take four Kent wickets, for 161, by the sixty-second over. Effectively, they had taken four and a half, because Clinton had to retire with a damaged hand, struck by a lifting ball from the Demon of Frome, Dredge. Dredge, though his run-up is still that of a country boy, is becoming a bowler. He looked, at times, as dangerous and almost as fast as Garner, and much more interested.

It was Garner, however, who took the first two wickets, Woolmer leg-before and Asif caught by the wicketkeeper. Kent had then scored 87 for two. Neither side, of course, were at full strength, for one reason or another, and Somerset had an additional handicap because Breakwell, who has done very well lately, was not fit to play.

The third wicket for Kent put on 43, and then Ealham, their captain, was out and Shepherd, who looked powerful but, for him, a little clumsy, as if he was not going at his best, was the fourth to be out. It was at this point that the innings turned.

Tavaré, who had been playing soundly if a little unambitiously, was encouraged by the example of Johnson at the other end. Somerset, who depend more on Botham's bowling than they would like to admit, wavered in the late afternoon, although not in their fielding. Tavaré proceeded to his century and Johnson to his fifty.

Kent, with their fourth batting point smiling ahead, lost a few wickets through undue haste (and also through Garner, returning refreshed, one presumes, from a 20-minute visit to the pavilion).

However, Kent did manage to get their fourth point in the 100th over and, instead of declaring at once, batted pointlessly on for a ball or two, and lost another wicket, thus ensuring that Somerset took the same number of points on the first innings.

However, at present Kent will not be worrying about stray points, because although Somerset made a confident beginning, possibly too obviously confident; suddenly wickets fell. Shepherd was chiefly responsible, aided by some casual batting. Yet Richards did not get out and his was the wicket which Kent wanted above all.

Sun grows steadily along with Kent's lead

TAUNTON: Kent, with three second innings wickets in hand, are 264 runs ahead of Somerset

On the train down, as we were passing through Backwell, a lady came marching through the buffet car, where we were taking a sedate coffee, declaring "a gentleman has dropped his trousers in the corridor." She had her evidence, too, quite a nice dark blue pin-stripe pair. She presumably found the gentleman in the end because she returned at Creech St Michael, without the trousers.

I felt, after this, that it was going to be a good day and so on the whole it was. The sun grew steadily. Somerset began at 67 for five, 236 behind, Richards and Rose together. Richards played several strokes of the kind which would make us marvel if anyone else played them and Kent were looking a little fretted, when, hooking at Woolmer, Richards mis-hit the ball to mid-on.

Still, that was 125 for six, much better, and Rose, who had suffered some early difficulties, especially against Shepherd, played admirably. Henry Blofeld rightly warned me not to call it a "captain's innings", but it was the kind of innings of which any captain should be proud. I am not quite sure whether Rose is a good enough batsman to become a stay of England, but he certainly has the character for it.

The Somerset innings ended soon after lunch, in the sixty-first over, 89 runs behind. The pitch was playing well and, though the occasional spurt of dust arose as the day wore on, nobody takes too much notice of that at Taunton. Somerset, with their batting strength, could still hope for a chance on the last day, provided they did not let Kent get too many. Kent led by eight points to six on the first innings.

However, Somerset were deprived for most of the innings of the bowling of Garner and Burgess, both unfit, though Garner had a brief try. The burden, therefore, fell principally upon Jennings, Richards – who was bowling seamers – and Dredge. The Demon of Frome bowled long, painstakingly, and successfully. I have never seen him bowl better. He has, whether consciously or not, adjusted his action since I first saw him: although still prone to no-balls, he has cut out the shuffles and strides out well. His action reminds me very much of that of the present rural Dean of Northleach, whom I saw take many wickets on grounds around Taunton, including this one and whose action was always regarded as a model – just as his sermons still are.

Kent ought to have done better in their second innings and, indeed, looked as if they would once Woolmer had settled in. But somehow the innings fell apart and, though Shepherd was going well at the end, they are not quite secure yet. If they were to lose this match, after so much of the luck has gone their way, they would feel like a man who has lost his trousers: but that, too, can happen.

Kent made to work for victory

TAUNTON: Kent (20 pts) beat Somerset (6 pts) by 66 runs

The match ended in the way that always seemed probable, from the time Somerset had lost five wickets quickly on Wednesday evening. There was a moment in the afternoon when it seemed that Somerset might win, and though the moment swiftly vanished, for a couple of hours more they made Kent work for it.

The Kent innings ended for 191. There was little hope of many more runs for them once Shepherd was out, hooking at Garner, and snicking the ball into his stumps. Asif was unable to bat, and had returned to Kent, nursing pain in the lower quarters of his back. Somerset had to score 281 in 320 minutes and it was not impossible.

Somerset began as if they intended to get the runs. At 26, Denning was caught at second slip, attempting to drive, an excellent catch. Richards came in with the match in his delicate, muscular hands, and was bowled by the first ball he received. I understand that it was not such a devastating ball as all that: just the odd first one which can overthrow the best.

At 44, Kitchen was caught at long leg by Cowdrey, substituting for Asif, another good catch. Roebuck was run out at the same score, Cowdrey again chiefly responsible. It was 55 for four at lunch, and soon, with Slocombe caught in the gully, it was 60 for five. Somerset could not now expect to win the match, indeed hope must have faded when Richards was out, but set themselves to save it.

Rose and Taylor played soundly for the sixth wicket. Kent seemed for a time uncertain of their policy whether to attack or to tempt. Underwood, I felt, did not go on early enough. However, he had a good long spell later, and duly won the match. Taylor was out at 144. At tea, 77 overs bowled, Somerset were 155 for six, with Burgess accompanying his captain.

Soon after tea, Rose was out, bowled by a ball from Underwood which kept low. With 88 overs bowled and the last hour upon us, Somerset were 177 for seven. Burgess and Dredge put on 50 which was somewhat surprising. Burgess played, and continued to play, until he was the last man out.

Dredge batted like a man thoroughly accustomed to opening the innings for Frome against Midsomer Norton.

Somerset v Kent, Taunton, 24, 25 & 26 May 1978

Somerset won by 66 runs

Kent

R.A. Woolmer	lbw b Garner	25	c Taylor b Dredge	54
G.S. Clinton	*not out*	4	*not out*	8
C.J. Tavaré	b Jennings	105	b Dredge	21
Asif Iqbal	c Taylor b Garner	41	*absent hurt*	
* A.G.E. Ealham	b Dredge	32	b Dredge	13
J.N. Shepherd	c & b Jennings	12	b Garner	37
G.W. Johnson	c Taylor b Garner	62	c Richards b Garner	12
R.W. Hills	c Jennings b Garner	3	b Dredge	16
+ P.R. Downton	c Taylor b Garner	0	c Taylor b Richards	4
D.L. Underwood	c Burgess b Jennings	14	run out	2
K.B.S. Jarvis			b Dredge	0
	lb 2, nb 3	5	b 2, lb 10, w 1, nb 11	24
	(9 wkts)	**303**		**191**

1/30, 2/87, 3/130, 4/161, 5/284, 6/288, 7/288, 8/295, 9/303
1/39, 2/99, 3/114, 4/129, 5/146, 6/159, 7/169, 8/183, 9/191, 10/191

Garner	27	6	65	5	16	7	38	2
Dredge	20	4	71	1	30.3	6	53	5
Jennings	26	7	68	3	18	7	45	0
Burgess	18	7	57	0				
Roebuck	8	0	33	0				
Richards	1	0	4	0	14	3	31	1

Somerset

P.W. Denning	c Downton b Jarvis	20	c Tavaré b Jarvis	19
M.J. Kitchen	c Asif b Shepherd	13	c sub b Shepherd	21
I.V.A. Richards	c Jarvis b Woolmer	60	b Shepherd	0
P.A. Slocombe	c Tavaré b Shepherd	1	c Ealham b Underwood	13
+ D.J.S. Taylor	c Tavaré b Shepherd	0	c Tavaré b Underwood	46
P.M. Roebuck	c Johnson b Shepherd	0	run out	0
* B.C. Rose	*not out*	89	b Underwood	35
G.I. Burgess	c Downton b Hills	15	c Tavaré b Underwood	55
C.H. Dredge	b Jarvis	1	b Underwood	12
K.F. Jennings	c Woolmer b Shepherd	8	lbw b Johnson	0
J. Garner	c Johnson b Underwood	1	*not out*	2
	lb 2, w 1, nb 3	6	b 5, lb 2, nb 4	11
		214		**214**

1/34, 2/34, 3/36, 4/38, 5/58, 6/125, 7/168, 8/181, 9/213, 10/214
1/26, 2/29, 3/44, 4/44, 5/60, 6/144, 7/155, 8/207, 9/208, 10/214

Jarvis	19	1	101	2	8	2	13	1
Shepherd	24	8	70	5	20	5	39	2
Woolmer	8	3	12	1	3	1	7	0
Hills	6	0	18	1	6	3	6	0
Underwood	3.1	1	7	1	31.3	13	74	5
Johnson					27	9	64	1

Umpires: W.E. Alley and R. Julian

Bath

BATH: Somerset v Lancashire

It was a chilly morning, which became slightly warmer in the afternoon. The pitch helped the faster bowlers. There was a good crowd, for a cool Monday. Brian Close was among those present, signing copies of his book, but did not need to stay long. John Arlott made his presence felt in the press box. "I am very well," he said to his editor on the telephone, "but fat and unfit and yes, I love Hampshire dearly; I am even prepared to go north of the Trent to watch them."

Outside the box, a putative, or possibly reflexive, commentator droned on all day; to judge from his accent, he was practising for an audition for the High Littleton Hospitals Broadcasting Service. It reminded me of the days when I was a disc jockey, and whenever I entered a pub, the barmaid would burst into song, hoping she might be discovered.

Colin Dredge

BATH: Somerset v Sussex

The man who denied Sussex such hopes as they might have had of recovery was Dredge, the Demon of Frome. He is becoming quite a bowler, this young man. His pace, and his length, were more suited to the pitch than were Garner's.

The authors of Methuen's *Little Guide to Somerset* once wrote that "Frome has never helped to make history" and that "the visitor would do well to make his way at once to the church, which is practically the only thing in Frome worth seeing." The next edition will have to have a footnote for our lanky and enthusiastic Demon.

Glimpsing the future

TAUNTON: Somerset v Kent (Benson & Hedges)

At the start of play Somerset needed 172 to win with nine wickets in hand and 42 overs to go. It was not too difficult on the face of it, but much depended on how the pitch would play. Until we reach the stage of sliding roofs, which I suppose will ultimately be introduced at Lord's (you think I am joking? You would have thought I was joking if five years ago I had told you that England would be led out at Lord's by a man in a crash helmet), cricket is going to be affected by the weather.

Eight wickets down

TAUNTON: Somerset v Yorkshire

At 6.15, with 19 overs and five balls of the last permitted 20 bowled and Moseley prepared to go in, Yorkshire came off the field. I am not sure why Boycott, however irritated he might be because Yorkshire's winning run has ended with his return, forewent the last ball. There are such things as no-balls and run outs. Never neglect the least opportunity, however improbable, as the philosopher Lecocq would say, with the merest lift of an eyebrow at the plainer girls in the old garret in Limehouse.

Peter Denning

CARDIFF: Glamorgan v Somerset (Gillette Cup)

Denning made his highest score in any sort of county cricket. He is not quite a boy, 28 years old, Millfield and St Luke's, born at Chewton Mendip, which is just down the road from High Littleton, and has the best ring o' bells in Somerset, unless you count the pub at Priston. I have always liked Denning since he told a fatuous television interviewer that no, he did not expect to play for England, and when pressed for a reason, said amiably: "Because I am not good enough."

But he was good enough for Glamorgan yesterday and, though his first-class average is only about 26, he has a gift for limited-over cricket. Yesterday provided his fourth man of the match award. He used to be a front foot player, and still is chiefly, but he scores runs nowadays off the back foot as well.

Boycott and Hampshire

HEADINGLEY: Yorkshire v the New Zealanders

Yorkshire cricket, not for the first time, is a house divided – you had only to sit among the crowd here yesterday to realize it – and it is high time Raymond Illingworth arrived to call "Order! Order!" The division concerns whether the county should be led by Boycott or Hampshire; or, to be more accurate, whether it should be led in the *style* of Boycott or Hampshire.

I must not make too much of the little local rumpuses, but it is possible that Yorkshire cricket has come to a parting of the ways.

Yesterday's play illustrated the difference in the style. When Boycott and Hampshire were brought together, what happened in the partnership was predictable, except that there was no run out. Hampshire, batting as if he was interested in winning the match, scored a fast 90. Boycott, batting as if he was interested in scoring a century, slowly and duly scored it.

Top Marks for all-round display

LORD'S: Cambridge University, with all second-innings wickets in hand, are 100 runs behind Oxford University

It was a long time since I had seen the University cricket match. I knew it had gone down in the world but it was still a shock to see only four people, in the morning, scattered around the top tier of what used to be called "the free seats". I thought there were five for a while but, at a closer look, the fifth turned out to be a dustbin. It may, I suppose, have had an occupant waiting for Sam Woods to return.

It was on this stand that I used to consort and cavort with hundreds of Oxonians and Cantabs and thousands of Cockneys, who are so keen on watching the cricket, that we young men were put firmly in our place by them if so much as a bread roll was lobbed in the direction of the opposing party. There were more spectators at the pavilion end of the ground, though perhaps in this case I misuse the word "spectators" (I am nervous about my prose at the present after doing a radio programme with Philip Howard). Most of them were not watching the cricket. They sang of old, forgotten, far off things and battles long ago.

It was not a sunny day, for the most part, but it was never a cold one, or a wet one, so the weather was not to blame for the attendance. I think it is time the University match left Lord's. The players are keen enough, keen to the point of embracement when a wicket falls, and the standard of cricket is still high.

The Combined Universities have done much better than the Minor Counties in the one-day competitions. There are half a dozen players in this match who will play Test cricket and half a dozen more, at least, who would establish their places in county sides, should they be induced to make cricket their profession.

Why, then, has the match lost the support? Why do the undergraduates no longer come? Why do the country parsons no longer come? I only saw one clerical collar yesterday and its owner confided to me that he was an incomer from Belfast and found Lord's so convenient because he had not got used to the English licensing laws yet. Where would they play it then, now we have decided that it is to be taken away from Lord's? Or if, wisely, the Universities decide to abandon it before they are shown the door? Well, Bletchley used to be the place where we paused for a few minutes, or a few hours, when passing from one University city to the other. Hitchin, where I once saw Hertfordshire beat Essex, is another possibility. They would get much better gates at Hitchin, and have more fun, and need not forfeit their first class status. The pitches of Bletchley and Hitchin would, I am confident, be no worse than some of those I have seen lately at Lord's, including yesterday's.

Cambridge, winning the toss, were all out for 92 by a quarter to three. They batted for 41.3 overs to score their laborious runs. The Oxford bowling was tidy and their fielding better than that but it was still not good batting. If they decided to bat in the first place, and it was an arguable point, Cambridge should have had a go at it. Parker, who can be a lovely player, hardly ever risked a stroke.

To be sure, a lot depended upon him and when he was sixth out, just after lunch with the score 77, Cambridge's hopes of a revival swiftly vanished. Wookey did not manage to take a wicket against his old University, though he bowled soundly. Ross took three wickets and did the early damage. Marks, who is not nearly as innocuous a bowler as he contrives to look, cut away the tail.

Indeed, it turned out to be Marks's day. After Oxford had lost their first two wickets at 27 – Claughton, caught at the wicket, and Pathmanathan, who played on when going nicely – Marks attacked. He had some luck. He was in some peril from his first ball. He was dropped at mid-on, not a difficult chance except that the ball was hit hard, when he was 24. He could have been stumped when he was 40.

But he kept hitting, which was exactly the right game in the circumstances, and Cambridge grew bothered. Apart from the missed chances, they did not field as well on the ground as a University side should. By tea, Oxford had reached 100, at almost five runs to the over, and Marks his 50. When Marks was caught, where he should have been caught before, Oxford's batting immediately looked frail.

Their seventh wicket fell at 134, which was not a substantial lead, given that they had to bat last. Nevertheless, they sensibly kept on the attack against the Cambridge spin bowlers, Orders batting vigorously and successfully, and they have much more reason to look back on the day with satisfaction. It would all have been so much more exciting if only we had been at Hitchin.

CAMBRIDGE UNIVERSITY	92 (Marks 3-4, Savage 3-21, Ross 3-26) & 118 for two (Parker 61)
OXFORD UNIVERSITY	192 (Marks 60, Orders 32, Allbrook 6-81, Gardiner 4-52)

Essex claim some bowling points after failing to get any with bat

SOUTHEND-ON-SEA: Derbyshire, with four first innings wickets in hand, are 39 runs behind Essex

I had a bad trip from High Littleton to Southend. Even the memory of Sunday school outings in my youth did not console me. Our marvellous high-speed train from the west was stopped outside Didcot because a herd of cows was on the line. Then, when I had reached Southend, and it was a cold, windy, though dry day, I had to pick up a driver who had never heard about the cricket ground, and only vaguely of cricket. He was enthusiastic.

He made strenuous effots to drive me to Chalkwell, Shoeburyness, and even Chelmsford, where he thought there were some games going on, but I arrived at Southchurch Park at about 3pm, glanced at the scoreboard, which displayed 141 for nine, assumed Derbyshire were batting, and then perceived they were in the field. The tenth wicket fell almost immediately.

This has significance, for it meant that Essex had no batting points, and correspondingly that Kent could win the championship in their last match, with first innings points (bonus points, as they are commonly, although not very appropriately known). I had a good informant on the morning's play, none less than the Intrepid Trevor, who I gather is not yet mayor of Southend, nor president of the MCC, but will doubtless be both, given a few more years, and if he bothers. He told me that Gooch had batted particularly well, McEwan and Fletcher fairly well and that Hendrick had bowled well.

He also told me that Derbyshire would be out for 120, and the subsequent events have so far justified him.

Essex had been 90 for two at lunch and lost wickets which they would otherwise not have lost because they felt they had to go for the maximum points. They also lost wickets because it was not an easy pitch. Southend pitches seldom are nowadays, thought it was on this ground that the Australians in 1948 scored 700 runs in a day, an occasion which the Intrepid Trevor remembers well.

Derbyshire, sure enough, lost some quick wickets. Lever was in excellent form, looking forward to a winter in less chilly weather. In a fiery spell he dismissed Miller and Hill, which made him the second bowler to pass 100 wickets this season. East and Acfield showed that the pitch would be helpful to spin, something Essex must be wary of in the last innings.

At the close, Derbyshire had scored 102 for six. Essex had therefore taken two points for bowling. They are still not entirely without hope for the championship. The weather, bitterly cold though it became, looks the kind of weather which could change its mind. Kent cannot relax just yet. Kent ought to be steaming home to the championship, but there are stubborn cows on the line.

Icicles on the sight screen as Essex climb higher than ever before

SOUTHEND-ON-SEA: Essex, with eight second innings wickets in hand, lead Derbyshire by seven runs

The news is encouraging for Derbyshire, but we were not interested in Derbyshire when Essex still had a flicker of hope for the championship. At the start of play, Derbyshire had scored 102 for six, 39 runs behind. They reached 146, which put them five runs ahead. By taking four points for bowling, Essex had at least made sure of finishing second, which is higher than they have ever been before.

They were third, I am informed, in 1897, though I have not been able to check it and it may be that the guileful *Daily Telegraph* correspondent, with all the inscrutability of the East, has misled me. Still, Essex were a good side at about that time. I remembered by myself, though I did not witness it, that they had beaten one of the strongest Australian teams in 1899.

It was a morning with a little sunshine. At one point, strolling around the ornamental gardens which adjoin the ground, watching the children sailing their yachts and motor boats on the lake, the fathers struggling to repress the temptation to take over and show them how to do it, I almost forgot that I left my pullover at High Littleton.

But it grew colder and colder, quickly. My grave Oriental friend pointed out to me the icicles on the sightscreen. It began to drizzle before lunch and rained in quantity in the afternoon. There was no more play, except for a few forlorn minutes after six o'clock. Taylor and Walters continued their seventh-wicket stand, not looking in much difficulty, though Essex, in their enthusiasm, made frequent improbable appeals.

At 130, Taylor was caught at the wicket, a catch which was not obvious to onlookers, from a bad ball by Lever, a long hop, and had begun walking away before the Essex chorus had assembled its lungs. This was not, I think, consciously intended as a reproof to Essex. I mention it as an illustration of Taylor's natural sportsmanship. If England are to have a vice-captain in Australia, he would be the best choice for the job, though I doubt whether he would welcome it.

Tunnicliffe was caught and bowled by Lever at 136. In the same over, Lever bowled Mellor with something approaching a yorker. Walters and Hendrick did enough for the last wicket to give Derbyshire their narrow lead. Lever, with six wickets, bowled well. We know he can do it but this, without much support except from East, who took the last wicket when it looked as if it might be getting awkward, was an exceptionally stout-hearted performance. The pitch gave Lever some help but no more than it has given to the others.

When Essex went in before lunch, they lost Denness, caught and bowled by Tunnicliffe, and McEwan, caught at square leg off Hendrick, each having only just managed to pierce the dreaded doughnbut. In the last few minutes of play, in a light which was soon recognized to be impossibly bad, nothing of moment happened, which was just as well.

Essex see title pulled out of their reach off final ball of the day

SOUTHEND-ON-SEA: Essex (4 pts) drew with Derbyshire (4 pts)

Kent are the winners of the county championship this year and Essex are the runners-up. Narrowly Essex failed to beat Derbyshire yesterday. The last ball of the last 20 overs might still have kept us waiting until the end of next week, to be sure. At that point, Derbyshire needed five to win and Essex needed one more wicket. The philosopher, East, bowled it with due philosophy, Mellor pulled it round the corner, they ran three, but reluctantly recognized there was no chance of running five, or even four.

I am not prone to eulogies of cricket matches, especially at the end of the season on cold days (though I must record my gratitude to an old friend who lent me a pullover), but I am bound to say that the cricket yesterday, all day, was bold and sportsmanlike, if that is not now considered too much of an establishmentarianism word. Essex made a declaration which gave Derbyshire a fair chance and Derbyshire responded by going for the runs, and continuing to go for them until the end, even though they lost wickets.

Perhaps they should have stopped whacking in the last over, at the beginning of which they still neeeded 13. A Kent supporter near me emphatically thought so, but as they did not lose another wicket, nobody can say their tactics were unjustified. It was an occasion when both sides, though denied success, could be solaced by the satisfaction of doing their best and demonstrating it.

The question in the morning was when Essex would declare. They began six runs ahead with eight wickets in hand. The pitch was slow, after Thursday's rain, and not too easy. They were kept in check for a while. The 50 was not reached until the 25th over but no further wicket had fallen. Then Fletcher and Gooch began to move the score along. Fletcher was caught at slip at 83 in the 35th over. Gooch was now well in and using his strokes. He was caught from a strong hit on the leg side, at 137, for 84. This was the innings which gave Essex a chance. At lunch the score was 159 for four after 49 overs.

Essex batted on for a quarter of an hour afterwards and the declaration asked Derbyshire to score 186 in about the same number of minutes. It was, I thought, about the right time and the right score. It was certainly a generous declaration if you viewed the match as an end in itself. But, since Essex had to win if they were to retain a hope of catching Kent and Derbyshire, though they naturally like winning, could always choose to settle for a draw, Fletcher judged it well enough.

Derbyshire lost their first wicket at six when Hill was caught at short leg by Fletcher, whose catching, though they will not believe me in Headingly, was one of the most skilful achievements of the match. Derbyshire then began to prosper. Lister and Kirsten were well up with the required rate, which was about three and a half runs to the over. Suddenly before tea Kirsten and then Borrington were out.

The score then was 83 for three, the game open again. Lister, a boy from Durham who looks as if he may become a good one, was out soon afterwards at 91. In the last 20 overs, assuming Essex did not bowl more — they would have done except that they took wickets — 73 were needed. But the pitch was taking spin, East and Acfield were the bowlers for it and, though the Derbyshire batsmen kept seeking valiantly to recover the advantage, nobody, not even the determined Taylor — who batted much better than his average and was not out until the last over but one — could do it.

Without, in the excitement of the moment, seeking to make a mature judgement, it is obvioulsy fitting to congratulate Kent on another win and congratulate Essex on their narrow failure with a touch of sympathy. And also to congratulate Derbyshire, who, after a bright start, have not had much luck this season but still showed that they have spirited cricketers.

ESSEX	141 (Gooch 60, Hendrick 5-32)
	190 for five declared (Gooch 84, Fletcher 34, Hardie 32, Tunnicliffe 3-80)
DERBYSHIRE	146 (Hill 43, Walters 36, Miller 34, Lever 6-55)
	184 for nine (Lister 41, Kirsten 34, East 5-70, Acfield 3-65)

Somerset fail off the last ball

TAUNTON: Essex (4 pts) beat Somerset by two runs

I suppose we should not have been surprised. All through their talented but eccentric history, Somerset have been winning the matches they were bound to lose and losing the matches they were bound to win. So they still remain one of the two counties (Essex is the other) who have never won anything, though on Saturday morning they had bright prospects of winning both the Gillette Cup and the John Player League.

After the Gillette Cup failure, only the most sophisticated Somerset supporters would have found the League full compensation. But compensation in some measure it would have been, and it looked as if it was to be theirs when they pinned the Essex batsmen down for a long time and even when they set out to score 191 to win, or 190 to tie, which would have been as good.

The gates at Taunton were closed. The crowd was prospectively jubilant and remained so until the very last ball. From this, Somerset needed four runs with nine wickets down. They could score only two before the inevitable run out. We had heard by then that Hampshire had beaten Middlesex and were therefore the John Player champions.

Twelve were wanted from the last over, Taylor and Jennings were batting with all the top men out. They were running for everything and the Essex fielding, amid all the excitement – though there was no reason why *they* should have become particularly excited – was becoming erratic. Three was taken from the first ball of the over, helped by an overthrow, a single from the second and another from the third.

There was another single from the fourth but Taylor was run out, going for a forlorn second. In came Moseley, with five wanted in two balls, a position not hopeless for Somerset because he can hit the ball hard a long way from time to time.

But all the fifth ball produced was a leg-bye. It left the unfortunate Jennings, who had batted pluckily and run fast between the wickets, to face the last ball from Phillip. No six-hitter he, but he gave the ball a good tuck and they ran like the devil, but it was a scramble before Essex managed to put the wicket down on the third run.

The match bore a resemblance to the semi-final of the Gillette Cup, on the same ground between the same sides, a few weeks ago, except that then it was Essex who were chasing the runs and needed three off the last ball. I suppose their anxiety yesterday was partly due to the need for revenge. It would have been an oddity if the scores had tied again, as they nearly did.

Essex, put in to bat, lost three wickets for 29, reached 50 only in the nineteenth over but were saved by a stout innings from Fletcher, who did not look in touch when he began. Pont and Hardie were his principal supporters, although Rose again held Dredge back for his eight overs, after giving Moseley all his eight at the beginning – which, given the appropriate circumstances, seems to me a good tactic. Essex were scoring freely towards the end. Yet 190 for the League did not seem a particularly formidable job for Somerset. There was nothing wrong with the pitch, nor the weather.

Rose was out to the last ball of the fifth over, Denning to the first of the sixth, but this hardly seemed to matter when Richards began with four smooth, almost silent boundaries. After 14 overs the score was 69 for two, well up with the rate, and Richards looking as if he could never mishit a ball in his life. But he did all the same, to midwicket, off Gooch, who bowled what was from a Somerset point an irritatingly steady spell. Then East bowled beautifully, bothering all the batsmen. He bowled Roebuck, at 85 in the 20th over, and had Botham dropped.

In Botham rested Somerset's main hope but he was not at his best. When he was caught at 157, going for a big hit to square leg, he was seventh out. Somerset needed 34 runs in the last four overs and could only make a brave try. So we are saying, as we have said at the end of so many seasons, "well tried Somerset", and no more than that.

As a matter of fact, the section of rowdies in the crowd who sang irrelevant and untuneful songs, presumably in support of Somerset, made me momentarily glad that Somerset had lost, although I imagine the rowdies, who certainly had not come for the cricket, did not notice the result.

ESSEX	190 for five (40 overs, Fletcher 76*, Hardie 38, Pont 35)
SOMERSET	188 (40 overs, Botham 45, Roebuck 30, Lever 3-38)

Chris Tavaré

LEICESTER: Leicestershire v Kent

Tavaré, after settling in with deliberate caution, began to play the best strokes the match had seen so far. He really did very well. If you had never seen him bat before, and had no idea who he was, you would have known he was a player of high class. Some of his drives reminded me of Beldam's pictures of Victor Trumper. He should surely be chosen for the Australian tour, unless Mr Packer snaps him up. He is a sideways batsman, always ready to go forward, quick on his feet.

Whether he has the temperament for the tough stuff we do not yet know. But the Tavarés, I am told, though long established as a family of Kent, were originally Huguenots, driven from France after the Revocation of the Edict of Nantes: and the Huguenots had a habit of riding to a critical battle. "Kill yourselves, brave Crillon! We fought at Arques, and you were not there."

An Old Trafford crowd

MANCHESTER: Lancashire v Middlesex (Gillette Cup)

Play started on time, although the skies were grey, and there was always a threat of the interruptions which subsequently came. There was a crowd of about 20,000, a bubbling, boisterous Lancashire crowd, who cheered everything possible. What they enjoyed most, to go by the noise, was any misfield by Brearley, the news that there was no play in the other matches, and an announcement that four cars were causing obstruction, having parked (one presumes inadvertently) in the neighbouring police station.

I was surprised at the hostile attitude to Brearley. Some of it was good natured ribbing, but some of it was not. The general view in these parts seems to be that David Lloyd should take the England side to Australia.

Somerset win – on fewer wickets lost

TAUNTON: Somerset v Essex (Gillette Cup semi-final)

Eighteen were wanted off the last two overs, 12 off the last. It was to be bowled by Dredge. With his third ball, he bowled East and then, which seemed to everybody but his faithful eleven brothers and sisters (all, I understand, present) the culminating horror, bowled a no-ball.

They took three from it and needed four from the last two balls. There was a single and then the tying, but not winning, hit. Dredge had, after all, done enough in his last over to send palpitating Somerset hearts home happy.

The Folkestone pitch

FOLKESTONE: Kent v Gloucestershire

The Folkestone pitch is no longer quite the blessing to batsmen it was in the brave, if sometimes slightly bogus, old days of the Festival, when bowlers, if offered the choice, would go to Scarborough, and batsmen, even including Walter Hammond, would settle for Folkestone "with a couple of centuries thrown in". No centuries were thrown in yesterday.

FOLKESTONE: Kent v Essex

DAY ONE

It is a dangerous thing, I have found, to make the least criticism of the Folkestone pitch. Cricketers here are as proud of it as if it had been laid by the Roman legions which once marched past the ground. All the same, the pitch was lifting rather more yesterday, especially in the morning, than a three-day pitch should.

DAY TWO

At the beginning Kent were in the better position. They had scored 61 for two after Essex, who won the toss, had scored 226 on the usual beautiful, perfect, flawless and glorious Folkestone pitch (these are my last words on the subject, at least until tomorrow when I shall be safely out of Roman territory and back among the Ancient Britons).

Season's end

WORCESTER: Worcestershire v Somerset

I always associate Worcester with the beginning of the season, not its close. I suppose its most memorable starts to a season have been in the Bradman years (three double centuries and a century in four matches).

Nevertheless, Worcester makes as gracious a setting in autumn as in spring, even on a grey evening when the light was hardly fit for cricket. The umpires offered the Somerset batsmen the chance of withdrawal after tea, but they decided to stay on and try their luck.

...

With 65 wanted in 10 overs and 33 in five, Somerset still had a hope, which looks better in figures than it did in reality. Breakwell was the man who might possibly have done it. Denning, coming in late with a damaged ankle and a runner, was run out, as chaps with runners so often are. Marks, playing some elegant strokes, and Gifford, bowling thoughtfully and accurately, were for me the end of the season, and not a bad one, either.

Vivian Richards
Man of the Match, Gillette Cup semi-final, v Essex, Taunton

Richards is again the architect

TAUNTON: Somerset v Essex (Gillette Cup semi-final)

Richards did not go until he had made 116. His end was worthy of his life, a magnificent falling catch by Denness at mid-wicket. Once he had settled in, there was not much Essex could do about him, hard though Fletcher tried. He switched his bowlers around, using six, but terrific assaults by Richards knocked first Pont and then Turner off. Fletcher placed his field as cannily as might be, but how can you set a field for such a man?

He will make a late cut off a fast bowler like Frank Worrell, an orthodox drive as surely and elegantly as Hammond or Hutton, and step back outside his leg stump to clout a ball into the covers, choosing his spot, time after time, everyone knowing what was to come and powerless to avert it, like – well, like Vivian Richards, I suppose.

For one reason and another, I saw a lot of Somerset during the past cricket season: an exhilarating, if sometimes maddening, experience. Thus I saw a lot of batting by Vivian Richards.

There is always a temptation to call the hero-batsman of the moment "the best I have ever seen", or some such extravagant phrase. I would make no such claim for Vivian Richards. It is enough to say that he is the best on the English county scene at present. Barry Richards has left us – I was saddened but not surprised by his departure – and deeply though I admire Boycott's play, he is not to be compared in the most exciting attributes of batsmanship, nor the ability to dominate a fielding side.

The question to be asked of overseas cricketers in the English game is, can they identify themselves with their adopted counties? Some of the most famous ones though providing plenty of runs and wickets have failed to do so. For them, county cricket has been a pleasant exhibition game. They were the mercenary troops and ready to move to the highest bidder. I do not use the word "mercenary" disparagingly. In, for instance, the Thirty Years' War, the mercenaries were often more "civilized" in battle than the patriotic armies, carried away by zeal for their country or their religion. But the patriots won most of the battles.

I shall think of Michael Procter as the best example of a mercenary who also became a patriot. If there was such a thing as the freedom of Gloucestershire, he would be awarded it. But Vivian Richards had not done so badly. I wonder if he knew where Somerset was when in 1974 he was asked to join. How readily could you put St John's, Antigua, on the map? That was where Richards was born, in 1952. He made his opening first-class appearance for the Leeward Islands against the Windwards in 1971 and then played for the Combined Islands in the Shell Shield. He did not play for the West Indies until after his first season for Somerset, for whom he had scored 1,200 runs at an average slightly above 30.

He looked pretty good, but it would be wrong of me to say of that season: "I never doubted…." There were a lot of good young overseas players coming into English cricket at about that time. This was another hawkeyed West Indian who hit the ball hard but we could not be sure that he would settle to the county game.

But in the past few seasons we have seen him do it. I am judging not by the number of runs which he has scored, nor how he made them, though that has been memorable, but by the way he has fitted into the Somerset scene. He has acquired a popularity, one might almost say, independent of the runs he scores. Somerset supporters know that he is as concerned with the county's success as they are themselves.

This can, just occasionally, have its drawbacks. Consider the end of last season. Somerset, you will remember, had never won any of the county competitions and on the morning of Saturday September 2 they were favourites to win both the Gillette Cup and the John Player League. On the Sunday evening, they had lost both. A big innings by Richards would have won either.

He did not bat badly or foolishly, but he did not produce the match-winner, and I felt that part of the reason was that he cared too much. Perhaps I can make my meaning clearer by saying that if Barry Richards had been in a comparable position, he would have knocked one of them off, simply because he would not have felt the same burden of responsibility.

On the Saturday at Lord's Vivian Richards played, for him, cautiously. If after his cautious beginning he had scored another fast fifty, this would have been approved as sound tactics (Procter, for instance, had played some of his best one-day innings in that way) but he did not. The critics, which meant most of the population of Somerset, were unanimous on the Sunday that Richards must "play his natural game".

This he played, indeed over-played. He began with some of the best boundaries imaginable: five in a couple of overs, something like that. Somerset did not need many and he put them ahead of the required run-rate. All that was needed, now, was that Richards should not get out. It was a time to relax a little. He was too tense to relax and this was not because of any lack of quality in his batting. He was going to lead his side, his county, to a victory, and a glorious victory too. He got out.

Many great athletes have said, more or less, that when they look most relaxed they are most worried. Barry Richards, I expect, would have been truly relaxed and taken the rest in singles and the odd four. After all, what did it matter to him?

Yet Vivian has this deep affection for and from the people of Somerset, which Barry has never had with the people of Hampshire. I do not know what conclusion to draw from this: perhaps that both mercenaries and patriots have their points.

Many an *enfant terrible* has finished his career as an elder statesman. Close is as extreme an example as Disraeli, though I do not suggest that otherwise the two men had much in common. I use the past tense about Close, because although he is still very much with us, his first-class cricket is supposedly ended – not that it should surprise anybody if he pops up again somewhere next year, or next decade, or next century, or in eternity. A fast bowler, in the after-life, finding himself facing Close, would deduce that he was in for a long spell of purgatory. A leg-spinner, on the other hand, could reflect that his punishment, thought it might not be light, would be brief, and that soon he would be transferred to a better place.

It is sometimes forgotten especially by younger people, that the venerable, stern Close of recent years, the Old Bald Blighter, was once considered an irresponsible, rather wild boy, who would never do justice to his talents unless he took the game more seriously. He did not play like a Yorkshireman – not at least as Yorkshiremen were supposed to play in those days: more like somebody from a fancy-cap county such as Somerset. It is tempting to say that he only began to play like a Yorkshireman when he joined Somerset, but that would be to overstate it. The turning-point in his career, psychologically, had come before that, when he was appointed captain of Yorkshire.

If there had been those early doubts about his character, there was none about his talent. The first time I saw him was, curiously enough, at Wells, on that pretty ground where Somerset no longer play. It is my recollection that it was one of his very early matches (I am sorry not to be able to give the details, but all my books are packed away at present in the course of a complicated move). At any rate I knew nothing of him, and I used to follow Yorkshire cricket enthusiastically then. I had to leave at about tea-time on the third day when Yorkshire, after collapsing in their second innings, looked like losing. I travelled from one of Wells's then numerous railway stations, and later on, at Yatton, heard a distressed porter explaining to the guard that Somerset had been beaten after all, because of some spin bowling by a big, young (well he did not quite say blighter) name o' Clorse.

There is no need, for *Cricketer* readers, to retrace the details of his career. How he scored a thousand runs and took a hundred wickets in his first full season (never to do so again); how he went to Australia under F.R. Brown in 1950, scored a century in his first match, and then flopped; how he made his way back into the England side, and then out of it again, several times; how he was out sweeping at Benaud in the crisis of the 1961 series to almost universal condemnation (I read about it in the Central Library in Moscow, the only place you could find a copy of *The Times*; but I heard all about it afterwards, and so far as I can remember the only person to say a word in his favour was Tom Graveney); how in 1963 he went down the pitch to Wesley Hall at Lord's, and nearly won one of the most famous of Tests; how he gained and lost the England captaincy; how he was recalled to the side in 1976, to set younger men an example in playing fast bowling, and did not fail – all of this, making up an extraordinary tale, has often been told, and will often be told again.

I would just comment on a couple of points. The first concerns his dismissal from the England captaincy. You will remember that he had been given the job for the last Test against West Indies, winning the match by an innings, although the rubber had already been lost – heavily. He was captain again the following summer, successful, though not against very demanding opposition. He was the first choice of the selectors for the following tour of West Indies, but the appointment was not confirmed at Lord's, after he had been censured for alleged deliberate time-wasting in a match between Yorkshire and Warwickshire.

That is commonly said, but not quite the whole picture. Time-wasting was not new. Close had certainly provided a flagrant example, but many captains have been guilty of it, before and since. WG would spend a long time ruminating into his beard. Tony Lock, simultaneously with Close, put up some shrewd performances when he was captain of Leicestershire.

If Close, when summoned to Lord's, had said something like: 'Look, I'm sorry, I know I overdid it, but it was a very tight match and I got a bit carried away,' would he have lost the captaincy? I very much doubt it. Instead he put out, or allowed to be put out in his name, a preposterous statement saying that the reason for the delay was that the crowd were making so much noise that he could not make his instructions known to his fielders. This produced the proper retort that if he found it difficult to make himself heard at Edgbaston on the third day of a county match, what on earth would he do at Kingston, Jamaica? A touch more humility would have served him well at this time.

On the other hand, valour does not often march with humility, and that he was a valorous cricketer there is no doubt at all. He has had the defects of his qualities. I remember writing, after he had been chosen again for England in 1976, that I was not sure whether he would score many runs, but that he would die in the breach before he ran away. This was not just a convenient phrase. He would have done.

Brian Close
'The old bald blighter'

Week ended April 29
You may remember that, when I left you at the end of last season, I was bothered about my eyesight, and I was deploring the weather. I am relieved to say that the eyesight, thanks to some new pills and new glasses, is greatly improved. The weather seems to be carrying on just where it left off.

Week ended May 5
There has been very little cricket to write about. On Saturday, in the Parks, Kent batted for two and a half hours, but that was all for the whole match. Since play did not begin on the Saturday until half-past three, I naturally missed the late night final edition of the *Sunday Times*, who like their cricket reports best during the interval between the toss and the beginning of play. Woolmer seemed to enjoy his innings. I suppose after some of the stuff he had been playing in, during the winter, even a match against a University has the tang of true competition. But I am thoroughly bored by the Packer business and, since a writer always becomes a bore himself when he writes about the subjects that bore him, I propose to say as little as possible about it.

Week ended May 12
On Monday, Gloucestershire had to bat in a light as bad as I can recall in a county match. Well, umpires are born blind or learn it, as Bill Andrews likes to say, so I suppose they just had not noticed that the people who walked in light had seen a great darkness. I sometimes think that it is a pity that the appeal against the light is abolished, but no doubt a snort from David Shepherd, worthy of a Wessex Saddleback, drew the weather to their attention.

I shall remember a diversion at the end when Davey batted. He and Shepherd are the two Devonians, who have a joint benefit this year. Gloucestershire's hopes had gone by the time Davey arrived, but he is in my view – not widely shared – an elegant and correct batsman, and has been sponsored for 50p a run. Shepherd, of course, since it is a joint fund, will have his share of the wealth from any innings played by Davey. His comments as Davey played two noble strokes, both of which the umpires remorselessly ruled to be leg-byes, were anguished, and must have done much to disturb The Society for the Confidence of Cricketers in Fair Umpiring. However, Jack did get a run, indeed two; and stood there like Casabianca playing the ukulele on the burning deck, as the ship went down about him.

Week ended May 19
My wife is not very well, and *The Times*, gratefully do I record it, are generously sending me to matches which enable me to get home at nights, and keep an eye on the children and animals. Crumbs conscientiously contributes to supper by bringing in a couple of extra shrews.

Week ended June 2
A rather dismal week for me. I should have been at Swansea, but was abruptly copped by one of those internal bugs which make it necessary to have plumbing facilities within easy reach. I did manage Lord's, for Middlesex and Northamptonshire.

Lord's is usually one of the easiest journeys for me, but I had a bad trip back. Because of some sort of strike, the Welsh trains were not running, and hundreds of weary Welsh families had to come with us. They were not, many of them, very experienced travellers, and there was a panic at every stop. I tried to play some games with the children, and we had quite a tolerable session of 'My Aunt Went to Llandudno', but they were really past everything poor bairns, even lollies and coke. I missed the bus connection at Bath, had difficulty in raising a taxi; it was late by the time I was back on the old familiar bathroom patrol.

Not that the week was totally in vain. I became a grandfather. They have called the child Joanna, against my advice. Her destiny will obviously be to marry Henry Blofeld, who falls in love with every woman he meets, as long as she is called Joanna.

Week ended June 16
It ought to have been a lovely week, because it was the Bath Festival, which I always enjoy. Because of my wife's illness (she is in hospital in Bath, but the operation is over, and she seems to be well) I was allowed to do it all. Somerset won both matches: against Lancashire, by four wickets, and then against Sussex, easily, by an innings.

Two championship wins for Somerset in a week, and they up at the top already! ''Tes unbloodyblevable,' I heard it said, countless husky voices clamouring for their close-of-play cider. I met lots of old friends, and received warm hospitality, as you always do at Bath, whether the game be cricket or rugby. But I was fretting all the time, not so much about Rosemary, whom I knew was in good hands, but about the children's supper. The worst day was Thursday, when Adam said that he thought that he was going off chips, and Felicity said that she thought that she was going off baked beans. Fortunately I produced a bag of peaches, bought from that splendid fruiterer's on the Bath Bus Station (heartily commended to you all), so they did not quite starve.

Week ended June 23
Rosemary was restored to me, on Father's Day, and not before time. Felicity was just about to go off peaches.

Week ended June 30

One of the interesting things about the averages used to be the proportion of amateurs to professionals. For many years most of the leading batsmen were amateurs, most of the leading bowlers professionals. Nowadays the comparison we make is between home and overseas players. I notice that in the current batting list the only Englishmen are Randall, Ormrod, Roope and J.F. Steele, of whom only Roope is in the Test side. The first three bowlers, however, are Hendrick, Underwood and Willis, with Lever at 6, Edmonds 7, Ratcliffe 9, Pocock 10 – and Old and Botham nearby. One of the reasons the Pakistanis have looked a bad side is the strength of English bowling at present.

Week ended July 7

In the first round of the Gillette Cup, I saw an astonishing match between Somerset and Warwickshire. Warwickshire scored 292 for five, which meant that Somerset had to score more runs than any side batting second had ever done in the competition. This they did, with two overs and five balls to spare, and also with five runs to spare, since Richards (139 not out) hit the last ball for six.

I thought that Whitehouse, whose sturdy (and in its later stages dashing) innings had done much for his side, made a mistake in taking off Willis after only five overs of his allotment. When he first faced Richards, Willis bowled him three very fast balls – not bouncers – any of which might have had him out. Two more overs of Willis, or even seven, would have been a good swap for Richards' wicket. But I do not suppose that Whitehouse, any more than I, really contemplated Somerset getting the runs. After Richards had reached his hundred, in the 42nd over, Somerset could take it by singles and the odd four, and duly did so. I am glad to have seen this match, and will – do not think I am suffering from Somerset bias: I am past partisanship at cricket – think of it as an outstanding memory. I was given a black eye by a drunken lout, for no reason at all that I could understand. I just managed to keep the eye open long enough to finish my report.

Week ended July 14

Why is it that black eyes are considered funny, and not, say, broken noses? (Why is it that lumbago is considered funny, and the merest mention of arthritis brings murmurs of sympathy?) I am determined to wear my rue with an indifference, and on Saturday set forth for Cardiff, where I was greeted with loud mirth by my friends, and solicitous enquiries (much worse) by everybody else. We had much interesting conversation, chiefly about my black eye, but some of it about the Cardiff weather-vane. Swansea people say it points in the wrong direction anyway. Even Cardiff people are puzzled as to what it represents. It has a fishlike shape, and I suggested that it is a replica, or possibly the fossilized original, of a kipper which Wilfred Wooller once disdained at breakfast on the Brighton Belle. It is to be known henceforth as Wooller's kipper.

I moved back to Bristol, for Lancashire against Gloucestershire, where there was a good moment at the beginning. The lady in the secretary's office, carrying the stencil from which the scorecards were to be printed, had it blown from her tray by an unexpected draught, and it swept gracefully into the shredder.

Lancashire won by lunchtime on the third day. Fortunately there was no shortage of major sporting activities in the neighbourhood for the disappointed spectators. I repaired to the High Littleton School Sports. Adam came second in the 70 metres sprint, and second in the sack race, which he was expected to win. He maintains that the chap who beat him had a hole in his sack, and could slip out a crafty foot, but I am afraid Adam has learnt to think the worst of everybody after the World Cup. Felicity came third in the under-seven sprint, but failed to live up to training form in the blue bean race. Rosemary valiantly entered for the mothers' race, and came 'about third' (the worst position you can get in a mother's race is 'about third'; it's like a Bonny Baby competition). They were too young for her, she said (another thing about mothers' races – they are the only time when women, at least the 'about thirds', add years to their age rather than subtract them). Still, the family had two silvers and an about-bronze, a respectable result.

Week ended September 8

I spent the last few days at Worcester. I always associate Worcester with the beginning of the season, not its close – I suppose because of the Bradman years, and also because of a more recent occasion when the lady behind the bar, surveying the pelting rain on a Monday morning, declared 'The weather's a disgroice', looking as if she was about to go over to the cathedral to have a sharp word with God about it.

The match was drawn, in bad weather. Neale, who will be a sound county player, to say no more, scored a century. It was a nice innings but not a significant one, as a girl called Veronica Walewska ('I have not yet met my Napoleon') once said to me in Moscow. I mention this because Neale took his degree in Russian.

Worcester makes as gracious a setting in autumn as in spring. I visited the cathedral. I did not have the nerve to reprove God for the weather, though I had framed a prayer ('Two shocking summers running, Lord, gets a bit much'). There, in the silence, and with more thanksgiving than sorrow in my heart, I said farewell to the season.

1979

1979 was the 'lost year' in Alan Gibson's cricket writing for *The Times*, for there was no *Times* to write for. A dispute with the print unions had led Times Newspapers to suspend publication from the end of November. As the months went by, hopes of a settlement appeared and then disappeared like trees in a swirling fog, but as the cricket season got under way in April, there was still no end in sight. Fortunately for Alan, he by now had an agreement with *The Times* that they would pay him a retainer, covering a certain number of days' cricket or rugby each year, with the facility of additional payments if he did more than that. And, as he acknowledged in his *Cricketer* Journal in early May, the retainer was continuing to be paid, despite the absence of the newspaper.

But it was still a difficult year financially. There were no expenses to help defray the cost of day-to-day survival, and he still had to watch some cricket, in order to be able to produce his diary for the *Cricketer*. He did the occasional television commentary for HTV, and wrote periodically for the *Spectator* – sometimes, but not always, about cricket – but his accounts for that year show that his gross earnings from *The Times* and *Sunday Times* were £6,500 less than in the following year, of which over £2,000 was represented by expenses. Considering that his net income even in a normal year was no more than around £8,500, it represented a huge financial blow, from which he never really recovered.

In the world of cricket, the Packer controversy continued to bubble and seethe. England's winter tour to Australia might have been a resounding success on the field – Brearley's men winning the series 5-1 – but it had been a disaster for the cricketing authorities, as the Australian public deserted the 'official' matches in their droves, for the razzmatazz – and Australian victories – of the World Series version. As the crowds grew, so did the prospect of a Packer victory.

The West Indies Board was the first to come to terms with WSC. Then, at the end of April, the Australian Board of Control announced that it had granted exclusive television rights to Packer's Channel 9 – which is what the dispute had really been about all along – and that the planned programme of incoming tours was being scrapped, to be replaced by two shortened Test series each season, supplemented by a triangular one-day international tournament. This was desperately hard on Pakistan and New Zealand, who were the next scheduled tourists, but the ICC had no choice but to go along with it. The future of Test cricket had been assured, and if the traditionalists baulked at some of the concessions that had had to be made to secure it – floodlit cricket, more one-day games, white cricket balls and so on – hindsight would suggest that there were as many gains as losses.

On the field, as well as off it, the season improved as it went on. May was – yet again – horribly wet. The early rounds of the Benson and Hedges Cup were badly affected, but by the time they arrived at Worcester on May 23 for their final group game, a strong Somerset side knew that, win or lose, they would qualify safely, as long as *both* Worcestershire and Glamorgan did not overtake them on wickets taken per 100 balls. And after he had won the toss, Brian Rose, the Somerset captain, knew that there was one way that he could make absolutely certain that didn't happen, which was to declare with one run on the board, leaving Worcestershire with no chance of improving their strike rate. The condemnation was instant and universal, and it most certainly included Alan Gibson.

Tests
England
beat India
1-0, with three draws

World Cup Final
West Indies
beat England

Championship
1 Essex
2 Worcestershire
3 Surrey
4 Sussex
5 Kent
6 Leicestershire

Sunday League
1 Somerset
2 Kent
3 Worcestershire
4 Middlesex
Yorkshire
6 Essex
Leicestershire

Gillette Cup Final
Somerset
beat Northamptonshire

Benson & Hedges Final
Essex
beat Surrey

Most first-class runs
1 K.C. Wessels
2 A.J. Lamb
3 D.L. Amiss

Most first-class wickets
1 J.K. Lever
D.L. Underwood
3 R.D. Jackman

I am not sure how much Alan saw of the second Prudential World Cup, which was played in June, either in person or on the television. He could hardly afford to travel to matches with no-one paying his travel expenses and he had always hated the television, cricket or no cricket. So I suspect that the experience which he relates in his *Cricketer* Journal of watching England play Australia at Lord's "on the bloody box", as he called it, was very much the exception that proved the rule!

West Indies, with their hard-hitting batsmen and battery of fast bowlers, did not disappoint, Vivian Richards scoring 138 not out and Garner taking five for 38 to overpower England's gallant but unavailing efforts in the final. In Alan's assessment, the novelty of the competition was beginning to wear off. I am not sure it was a view that was widely shared at the time.

Essex, meanwhile, were enjoying a tremendous season. They had the best of the early weather and made the most of it, getting off to a flying start in the championship and reaching the final of the B&H, in which they defeated Surrey. At long last, they had won something, and Alan was as pleased about it as anyone. They went on to take the county championship, wrapping things up as early as August 21 and finishing with six wins more than any other side. It was a truly commanding performance, in which Fletcher's captaincy was a major factor.

If Essex were one of the teams of the season, Somerset were the other. The uproar over the 'thrown' game at Worcester turned out to be the darkest hour before dawn. Botham was in his pomp, Richards had learned to season brilliance with circumspection, especially on the big occasions, and Garner – now available for the full season – was miserly at worst, unplayable at his best. With talented youngsters like Marks, Slocombe and Roebuck in the ranks, and unsung heroes like Dredge, Denning, Taylor and Burgess always ready to step into the breach, Brian Rose had probably the strongest Somerset side ever at his command, and rarely did he fail to bring out the best in them.

Once again, in early September, they faced the prospect of one weekend which could make or break their season: the Gillette final on the Saturday, and the last match of the John Player League season on Sunday. I suspect that Alan watched both matches on the dreaded television, but that doesn't seem to have dampened his enjoyment of their outcomes.

The fact of the *Times* dispute, and of watching vastly less cricket than usual in the season of 1979, did have one very substantial consolation. It enabled Alan, finally, to complete his *Cricket Captains of England*, on which he had been at work – to the increasing frustration of his publishers – for several years. It was worth the wait. When it was published shortly before Christmas in 1979 it was warmly received on all sides and was short-listed for that year's Cricket Society Literary Award. The Chairman of the Judges was Jim Swanton to whom – entirely by coincidence, I should stress – the book is dedicated. It was typically generous of him to write Alan a '**strictly confidential!!**' personal note, saying that, in the final judging, *Cricket Captains* had been edged out 'by the narrowest possible margin' by Geoffrey Moorhouse's *The Best Loved Game*.

I doubt if Alan was too distressed. *The Times* had returned to the news stands on November 30, he was rightly proud of his book and the critical acclaim provided a welcome glow of seasonal warmth, as the old decade gave way to the new.

Week ended May 4

It looks like being a tricky season. The outlook is gloomy, not only here in High Littleton, where the south-westerly is pouring rain on the windows, but at New Printing House Square. *The Times* is looking after me generously, and I used to complain when they swished me around the country so much but, like the aged African Emperor, crowned triumphantly at the end of *Black Mischief*, after countless years in prison, I keep fumbling at my ankle, because I miss my chain.

So far, nothing much has happened, except the rain. Even the Village Championship, where they take a pride in playing in the rain, did not do too well last Saturday. About a third of the matches were rained off. This competition is organised by *The Cricketer*, and sponsored by Samuel Whitbread. When it began, in 1972, it was sponsored by John Haig, but Haig have now transferred their sponsorship to the 'club' championship, presumably on the grounds that the taste for whisky is urban rather than bucolic. Whitbread, primarily a beer firm, as it has been since the eighteenth century (producing one of the most famous radicals who followed Fox), feel that their association with village cricket is a natural one. The present director (another Samuel) writes: 'The village green and the local pub: could any two institutions be more delightfully representative of the British summer tradition?' Well, I see his point, even if the beer is fizzy keg and the cricket limited-over, but no British summer institution is more representative (even if not delightfully) than the weather. I contemplated watching Bathford playing Coalpit Heath, or Cranmore playing Evercreech, or Queen Camel playing South Petherton. I wished I could travel so far as to see Easton and Martyr Worthy playing Longparish. ('A commodity of good names.') But one look at the sky, and it was back to the typewriter and the telly.

Week ended May 18

When Gloucestershire made the arrangement with an insurance company which guaranteed the continuance of county cricket at Bristol, not all their members were happy about it – some saw it as an erosion of their rights – but it is certainly making them more comfortable. The newly panelled members' lounge and dining-room is handsome. The old Bristol pavilion used to be something of a joke. I wrote of it, about 10 years ago:

> 'If you want to go to the room next door, you are likely to have to find a flight of stairs, which takes you down and round to the back, and then find another flight of stairs. The door you think you want will be jammed. You try another: it opens, but it is the wrong one. Suddenly you are lost. You catch a glimpse of the cricket, unattainably distant, through a high attic window. You grow desperate, try any door you can see, burst in on aged members and wake them up, flush a committee or two, and thankfully emerge where you started. At least, you usually do. There may be a few heroes still trudging round.'

Much exaggerated, but if you knew the old pavilion you would find it pardonable. Now, though it looks much the same from the outside, with the cock-eyed clock two-thirds of the way along the roof, it is transformed within.

Week ended June 1

Somerset are out of the Benson and Hedges Cup, and Glamorgan take their place. The melancholy events at Worcester on May 24 will have been well chewed over in *The Cricketer* by the time you read this, so I will not recount them, just add a couple of points. I strongly disapproved of Somerset's action, and wrote to that effect in *The Spectator* before the TCCB decision was announced. I wrote that I hoped they would win nothing this season, and that they would immediately be knocked out of the Benson and Hedges. Since they have been knocked out even more immediately than immediately, and accepted the decision so gracefully, it is now happily possible to forgive them. All the same, I am not sure that exactly the right decision was reached. Whatever reserve powers the Test and County Cricket Board possesses, Somerset were essentially suspended by retrospective legislation. However unwise Rose may have been in his action, it was within the law. It would have been better if the Board had simply expressed censure, and invited Somerset to consider their position. They could then have withdrawn voluntarily. Still I suppose that is a pettifogging point, and the important thing is that justice (not always quite the same thing as law) has been done – and tempers restored.

The other good news of the week – or relatively good news – was the agreement between Mr Packer and the Australian Cricket Board. It is much too early to say how it will work out. The postponement of India's tour to Australia is a breach of faith, and an alarming indication of the extent of Mr Packer's victory. The long battle has left many victims by the wayside, not least the Australian Broadcasting Commission. But almost any sort of agreement is better than none. Since nearly all the prophecies I make have the permanency of bubbles perhaps I may say that when the troubles began I wrote an article for *The Times* (which was not published) saying that I thought Mr Packer's activities were deplorable, but would be successful.

It was just as well that these events occurred to give cricketers something to talk about, because they have had precious little cricket. All I saw myself, not for want of good intentions, was a truncated John Player match on television. I studied the scores in *The Guardian* on the Glorious First of June, to find that on the previous day not a ball had been bowled in all six matches in the Schweppes championship. We also read, unsurprised, that it had been the wettest recorded May. So far 37 championship matches have been played, and 31 drawn or abandoned.

But English cricketers are, more or less, used to these hazards. What was sadder was the way the weather has mucked up the ICC Trophy. From all over the world these little (in a cricketing sense) countries have sent their teams, often with much difficulty. For some, such as Papua-New Guinea, it seemed doubtful whether they could raise the money to come. To make that great effort, and to be rewarded with a weeping Wolverhampton.

Week ended June 15

The first day of the Prudential Cup proper was much as expected. Canada did not disgrace themselves, but duly lost; so did Sri Lanka; so did India, who have never come to terms with the limited-over game. England beat Australia without, in the end, much difficulty, after the Australian batting had failed on a Lord's green-top. The most remarkable aspect of the match was that Boycott took more wickets than he scored runs.

I doubted whether I should be able to get in at Lord's, still passless, so I decided to watch at home on television, something I have not in the past had much occasion to do. Watching cricket on television is not very satisfactory for, though you have an amplitude of information, there is a lack of atmosphere and contact. This is no criticism of the producers, commentators and engineers (though for myself I could do with fewer slow-motion replays): it is simply the nature of the medium. I did my best to create the right atmosphere. I took up my position in the best seat in the playroom, the children bravely accepting the decision that they would have nothing to watch all day unless they wanted cricket (I am pleased to say that Adam did, for a while, but Felicity's attitude was aloof: no Heyhoe-Flint, she.) I had, by my side, a bottle of hock on ice, and at lunch Rosemary was to bring me salmon and cucumber sandwiches (I cannot stand cucumber, and would have to remove it, carefully, from the sandwich, as I have done countless times before on cricket grounds: what could be more evocative than that?) But it did not work. I was bored, without the wander round the ground, the old pals in the press-box, the gossip. I left after lunch and took the dog for a walk.

Bristol is a city which used to be (and still is, so far as cricketing qualifications go) partly in Gloucestershire and partly in Somerset, so there is an argument for playing the John Player match between the counties there at the Imperial Ground, where there was a large, if distastefully rowdy, crowd. All the same, I doubt if it is a good practice to take these Sunday matches away from the main grounds, which have the facilities to cater for large crowds. Nearly all the crowd seemed to have come from Taunton anyway – though this may be a false impression, since Somerset won so easily that the Gloucestershire supporters never had anything to cheer about.

Not that I would wish to see the lesser grounds removed from the schedule. A season would be the poorer without the possibility of a visit to Glastonbury, or Darley Dale, or Long Eaton, or even Basingstoke. But not on a Sunday, with queues for everything when it is fine, and no shelter when it is wet. I know that an occasional county visit is a pleasing tribute to local clubs, who do much to keep the game going, but it was once forcefully put to me by a senior member at Kettering – on a packed Sunday when everyone was more interested in their chances of getting a cup of tea, a pint of beer, or some personal relief, than the score – that for Kettering cricketers it was all a bit grooby (I think that was the word he used: it suggested a combination of grubby and groovy) after their old, leisurely, conversational three-day match.

Week ended June 22

The drama this week has been near home. For the first time in my life, I saw a side bowled out for four. It was High Littleton Primary School. It is plucky of them to play matches, since they have no ground, no facilities for practice, and their numbers are few. They went to a large, impressive school near Midsomer Norton, with acres and acres of playing fields, and a sports master as enthusiastic as he is vocal (and, I should think, a good coach). It was a 20-over match. The others scored 60-something. Then our brave lads met their fate, stoically on the whole. I suppose I ought not to mention it, but Adam carried his bat through the innings, for two. There cannot have been many instances of this in cricket history. Several of them got out – remember they were playing on a proper pitch for the first time – by attempting impossible runs. Adam, securely, stayed within his crease while his partners were charging about. I can see him developing into a sound opening batsman, on the lines of Jim Swanton.

Extracts from: Journal of the Season – July and August 1979

Week ended July 6

Reflecting on the second World Cup, I feel that though it could not be called a failure – it is reported that attendances were higher than in 1975 – it was less gripping than the first. The weather did not help, though in such a summer as this it could have been much worse, and we could hardly expect a repetition of the 1975 heat wave. It was always fairly obvious that the West Indies would win. There was just a chance, some thought (indeed I was one of them) that, on an inspired day, the Pakistani batsmen might do enough to beat them: but this view did not sufficiently take into account the depth of the West Indies fast bowling. It is hard to score quickly when, having battled through the opening spells of Roberts and Holding, you are faced with Croft and Garner. The only real chance of the West Indies losing would have been in a series of drastic interventions from the rain. None of these things quite made for the drama of 1975, but the competition had to prove itself in less favourable conditions than it had then, and this it has done.

Week ended July 20

Good news: High Littleton School, after their disastrous start to the season, and still without proper facilities, won their last two matches, in two days. If you had seen the faces of the lads when they returned, you would have realised that there was still something precious in cricket. And all done without sponsorship (well, almost: I did give Adam a bar of chocolate).

Week ended July 27

Essex won the Benson and Hedges, without too much trouble, so the only county now which has never won anything is Somerset. They must fancy their chances both in the Gillette Cup and the John Player League, but they can hardly hope to catch Essex in the championship, nor can anyone else. Essex now lead the Schweppes table by 69 points, with eight matches to go. It would take a series of disasters even more cataclysmic than those which overtook Hampshire in 1974 (so feelingly recalled to this day by John Arlott) to thwart them. I saw part of the Essex match at Bournemouth. They won by an innings, and I was impressed not only by their abilities, which were known, but by their confidence, which has not always been apparent at critical moments in the past. They played as though the thought of defeat did not enter their heads, so much so that I was occasionally reminded of Yorkshire in the 'thirties and Surrey in the 'fifties. (East, of course, has always had touches of Queen Victoria about him: "There is NO depression in this house, &c'). I wish I could still go to Bournemouth by the *Pines Express*, a marvellous, luxurious, though not exactly speedy train which used to run there from the north, through Somerset, not a couple of miles from High Littleton. It used to stop at places like Midsomer Norton and Evercreech Junction. Now I have to take a bus to Bristol for the train, change at Reading and then Southampton, all round the houses. Still, I recognize that the message from society to those of us who prefer not to drive is a straightforward one – **die as soon as possible**.

Week ended August 3

Yorkshire have had their second win in a week, after bowling Warwickshire out for 35 on a wet pitch. Whitehouse, the Warwickshire captain, had some sharp things to say about uncovered pitches. He was not taking the defeat unsportingly: he just takes the view that pitches should be covered at all times. There have, of course, been arguments about this for a long time, and various attempts at compromise. I am inclined to think it would be better to cover them completely, or not at all. My own preference would be for the latter, though I do not suppose I should have many county treasurers on my side. The majority of cricketers have to do without covers, and the fewer barriers there are between the first-class game and the rest of it the better. If you play a game like ours in a climate like ours, you must expect the weather to take a hand in it, as it has done since cricket began. It is a complicated game, and we seem to spend a great deal of time making it more complicated, and more artificial. There was an old definition of it: "an assault with a ball on three straight sticks, and the defence of the same with a fourth". We have come a long way from that.

Week ended August 27

The Weston and Cheltenham festivals have both suffered severely. At Weston, over 22 hours were lost during the week. Cheltenham still has four days to run but as I write, after an abortive day there, the skies do not suggest that their luck is going to improve. For many years I have tried to make sure of a visit to both – along with the Bath festival, these are my favourite cricketing occasions – and my memories of them are mostly sunny. Whatever the miseries of May, you say to yourself, as you sit freezing and beerless in the Parks, "Roll on Cheltenham and Weston." But when it does rain, they are even more desolate places than most, lacking the shelter and facilities of regular grounds. I took a walk to Cheltenham to visit one of my favourite epitaphs:

> *Here I lies with my two daughters,*
> *All along of drinking Cheltenham waters*
> *If only we'd stuck to Epsom salts*
> *We shouldn't be lying here in these vaults.*

Week ended September 8/9

No, it was not a replica of the end of last season: more a reversal. Somerset, you recall, then lost two titles in two days, and now they have won two in two. At the beginning of the season, Essex and Somerset were the only two counties which had never won anything. Now they have each won twice. The final Test also had an exhilarating ending. Brearley made a declaration which required India to score 438 in the last innings. Nobody has ever made so many runs to win a match, in the fourth innings of a Test, but I was inclined at the time to think that the declaration was a little too generous, given that England needed only to draw to win the rubber; and the Indians again showed their capacity for second-innings recoveries. They were only nine runs short, with two wickets left, at the end and, if Gavaskar had managed to continue his marvellous innings a little longer (and Botham had not made a characteristic intervention, with two catches and three wickets) they must have won.

So the Indians ended their tour not, I imagine, dissatisfied. They won only one county match, and that was against Glamorgan (whose dismal season has continued) but they did have poor luck with the weather. The famous spinners are not, on this evidence, the force that they were – though it would be unwise to write off a man of such classical method as Bedi. The batsmen took some time to run into form. Given their temperament, the Prudential Cup was not a happy preparation for them. They still look as if they will take some beating on their own pitches. It is sad that they will not be touring Australia, and that we are lumbered with this bastard tour instead, at the behest of Mr Packer. But I am glad that Brearley has accepted the captaincy, bravely when you consider that he has so much to lose and so little (barring the shekels) to gain.

Essex's championship win gave pleasure far beyond the boundaries of the county, not just because it was unprecedented. They are a popular side with a popular captain. Although Fletcher has scored more than 3,000 runs in Tests, at an average of over 40, he never quite became the dominant force in English cricket he once suggested. There was rarely anything violent about his methods. His off-drive would be made quietly, almost gently, and then you looked again, and the men in the covers were not bothering to chase it. Yet not many of his admirers thought that he had in him the makings of a captain. A shrewd adviser, yes, but hardly a captain. That is what we used to say of Fletcher. It is also what we used to say of Illingworth. He has succeeded where men with more obvious talents for the job – Douglas, Wilcox, Pearce, Insole, Bailey – have failed. Naturally he could not have done it without the players – though he had no miracle-workers, every man doing his stuff when it was most needed. They were lucky with the weather, and also that Lever was not called away more often for England, but they have still been substantially the best side of the year. Their fielding had a lot to do with it. Under Fletcher, they have developed a central restraint to cover their centrifugal abandon. For years they have been "athletic" in the field, but they used to fling themselves around needlessly, as though the thud of a soaring body on the ground was more important than the saving of a run. Fletcher dislikes waste. I had a special personal pleasure in the success of Essex, because they were the first county I watched regularly, in the old days at Leyton.

I also had a special personal pleasure in the success of Somerset, the second county which I watched regularly, and the one where I live (we will have no nonsense, please, about "Avon", which may be a useful Administrative district, but is not a county). They beat Northamptonshire with only the occasional tremor. Richards played the innings he did not manage last year – not too restrained, not too aggressive. Garner took most of the Northamptonshire wickets. That the two West Indians were dominant on the day should not distract us from the thought that this had been a side constructed mainly from born-and-bred talent. Once the Gillette Cup was won, I thought it probable that the John Player League would be too, and sure enough a relaxed Somerset won at Trent Bridge, while Kent nervously lost at Canterbury.

It has been a frustrating season for me. It was the third wet summer running, and there has been no *Times*. But at the end of it we have some interesting and (again, for me) enjoyable results. I wish Yorkshire had done a little better. They did show their possibilities at times. The closing stages of the season were much cheered by a visit of the Poet's and Peasants' CC (please get the apostrophes right, editor). You will remember that I am the Poet of this excellent club. They were touring in the west, and their first match was washed out, and their second (at Newton Abbot, against South Devon), had to be abandoned because a water main had burst under the pitch. These disasters had the advantage that they were able to call on their Poet at High Littleton. It was a genial session at The Star, but they refuse to give me the statutory bottle of whisky until I write the statutory ode. It seemed an appropriate conclusion. Here were the Peasants, who mostly come from Essex, and they were visiting the Poet in Somerset. We were all happy.

David Green
'The philosopher Green (D.M., not T.H.)'

Jack Davey
'As fast and as fierce as a 15th century janissary advancing on the gates of Constantinople, or possibly Painswick'

1980

After the excitements of 1979, with the World Cup and Somerset and Essex sharing the county competitions, 1980 was frankly a bit of a let-down. It was the wettest summer since 1958, Alan's counties of Somerset, Gloucestershire, Yorkshire and Essex won nothing, the Test series against the West Indies was a bad-tempered, attritional affair and the Centenary Test was spoilt by the rain. The fact that by now Mrs Thatcher was firmly ensconced in Downing Street will have done nothing to lift the Gibson spirits!

But it wasn't all bad news. Times Newspapers had emerged victorious from the long battle with the print unions and Alan was by now writing regular features for them as well as his cricket and rugby reports.

His season opened, as so often, with a bleak day in the Parks. It was a poor Oxford side this year, but at least Gloucestershire were the visitors, which made for some amusement; although, surprisingly, we have to wait until he travels to Cambridge, for the University's match against Essex, for Didcot's first appearance of the season.

Alan got his first sight of the touring West Indians at Leicester on May 15. He should have been there on May 14 as well, but the TUC's 'Day of Action' accounted for the trains from Bristol to the Midlands, and, having long since given up driving, he was stuck. Had he been there on the first day, he would have seen Garner bowl Leicestershire out for less than 100 and Greenidge crash a rapid century. It was a commanding performance by the touring side which continued into the second day, when much interest was also focused on how the golden boy of English batsmanship, David Gower, would fare against the West Indies quicks.

June was a busy month. Alan found himself at various times at Worcester, Gloucester, Northampton (where he saw the eventual winners of the Benson and Hedges beat Nottinghamshire in the quarter-final) and Lord's, as well as what should have been a full week's cricket at the Bath Festival. In the event, the first three-day game, against Lancashire, was entirely washed out, but he enjoyed what turned out to be a close match against Hampshire, and was evidently much taken by one of the barmaids during the Sunday League encounter with Glamorgan! However, the trip that evoked the happiest memories was, of all places, to the unlovely Racecourse ground at Derby; the home county's drawn game with Glamorgan also providing him with the opportunity of re-telling a favourite cricketing story.

For the first round of the Gillette Cup on July 2, you might have expected to find Alan at Taunton, where Somerset were playing Worcestershire. Instead, he was even further west, having evidently persuaded the Sports Editor that the prospect of Devon playing Cornwall at Exeter was too mouth-watering a local derby to be ignored.

The 1980s was the decade of the great all-rounders: Botham, Imran, Kapil Dev and Richard Hadlee. Mike Procter was by now nearing the end of his career, but there were still plenty of people in Gloucestershire prepared to argue that he was twice the cricketer of Somerset's upstart Botham. So, in what had once been one of the great cricketing traditions, they organised a single wicket contest to settle the argument once and for all. Alan was sent along to cover it for *The Times*.

Middlesex were unquestionably the team of the season. Their batting was consistent; their bowling attack, which included Edmunds, Emburey and the West

Tests
West Indies
beat England
1-0, with four draws

Championship
1 Middlesex
2 Surrey
3 Nottinghamshire
4 Sussex
5 Somerset
6 Yorkshire

Sunday League
1 Warwickshire
2 Somerset
3 Middlesex
4 Leicestershire
5 Surrey
6 Derbyshire
Northamptonshire
Worcestershire

Gillette Cup Final
Middlesex
beat Surrey

Benson & Hedges Final
Northamptonshire
beat Essex

Most first-class runs
1 P.N. Kirsten
2 G.M. Turner
3 A.J. Lamb

Most first-class wickets
1 R.D. Jackman
2 D.R. Doshi
3 V.A.P. van der Bijl

Indian Wayne Daniel, frequently irresistible. However, the real surprise packet, and the man whom captain Mike Brearley described as 'the biggest single factor behind our success' was Vintcent van der Bijl, a tall, strong South African fast bowler, who took no fewer than 85 first-class wickets during the season, as well as hitting powerfully down the order.

In the championship, Middlesex had hit the front in early June and never looked like being headed. Their only challengers were Surrey, but Middlesex needed only 10 points from their last two fixtures to establish an unassailable lead. Alan was there for the first of them, at Cardiff against Glamorgan, starting on August 30.

This year, there was to be no dramatic climax to the John Player League. The reigning champions, Somerset, did come with a late run to finish second, but never seemed to be in with a serious chance of over-taking the long time leaders, Warwickshire.

The highlight of the closing weeks of the 1980 season should have been the Centenary Test against Australia at Lord's, starting on August 28, which was previewed by Alan for *The Times*. In the event, the match was marred first by the weather, which accounted for more than ten hours' play over the first three days, and an incident on the Saturday afternoon, when the frustration of some of the MCC members at the reluctance of umpires Dickie Bird and David Constant to re-start play boiled over into an unseemly fracas, for which the MCC was forced subsequently to apologise. The game itself petered out into a disappointing draw, after England had declined to chase the 370 in 350 minutes that they had been set by Greg Chappell's declaration.

The Centenary Test was a sad occasion in one other respect: it was John Arlott's last match as a BBC commentator. *The Times* asked Alan to write the valediction, which – such was the affection in which Arlott was held – was carried on the front page.

After that, and with Middlesex already anointed champions, the rest of the season was something of an anti-climax, as one can gather from Alan's final match report, on Somerset's match with Warwickshire, on September 4. Happily, his mourning of the passing of the Stragglers Bar proved to be premature. It survived that and several subsequent ground re-developments, and would provide shelter and refreshment for Alan for a good many seasons to come.

There remained just one further cricket-reporting commission – to cover the experimental floodlit game that was played at Ashton Gate, the home of Bristol City FC, on September 17. One can be fairly sure that Alan had made up his mind weeks before the event that this would be a hateful occasion, and the reality did not disappoint!

However, he was soon back on more familiar territory, with a series of features on 'Great Teams' which *The Times* ran to keep its cricketing readers happy through the gloomy watches of November and December. Alan contributed several pieces, including an assessment of the Lancashire side of 1926-28. This was the sort of sporting journalism in which his heart lay – reflective, rooted in the past and above all literate. And it was with a quiz for 'literate sportsmen' (like himself) that he rounded off his year for *The Times*; and I would venture to suggest that you would need to be very literate indeed to answer all of the questions correctly!

Gloucestershire's outlook is Broad

OXFORD: The University, with three wickets down, are 292 runs behind Gloucestershire

Once more on the bat's back I do fly, after summer merrily (I must not forget the Bard on his birthday); and once more summer missed its cue, for it was grey and chilly in the Parks. However, we had some liveliness on the field, for after Gloucestershire had won the toss, Broad scored a century before lunch.

Broad is 22, tall, left-handed, a local product, who has played for Long Ashton, on the outskirts of Bristol (where he was born), and St Paul's College, Cheltenham. I thought how much Arthur Russell, who died recently, would have enjoyed reporting the innings, for he was a St Paul's man.

Not that we should make too much of the innings. David Graveney suggested whimsically that the Oxford bowlers had a theory that Broad was vulnerable to half-volleys. Twenty-two boundaries in his innings of 120, mostly driven, indicates they were mistaken. Broad made a few appearances for the county last year and will no doubt make many more, but he will hardly again make a century before lunch on the first day of the season. I cannot recall an instance of it happening before.

Gloucester find time for batting practice

OXFORD: Oxford University need 501 runs in their second innings to beat Gloucestershire

When an Oxford University side has lost the toss, especially early in the season, the important thing to remember on the second day is the number they need to save the follow on. This rule, laid down by one of the senior inhabitants of the Parks press box, seemed very likely to apply yesterday, but, as it happened, did not, partly because Oxford never looked remotely like saving the follow on and partly because Brain (who is captaining Gloucestershire in this match) did not enforce it. He decided to give his side batting practice, which was a reasonable choice, and opened the second innings with Bainbridge and Graveney. These improbable successors to Hobbs and Sutcliffe put on 100 in 24 overs, so easily that it was almost embarrassing.

Graveney scored a century, his first. Very pleasingly he batted for it, though I think he would agree that, like Broad the day before, he had a few half-volleys to help. I remember quite a long time ago, an argument between his father Ken and his uncle Tom. Ken thought he would be a batsman. Tom thought he would be a bowler. He has turned out more bowler than batsman, but I bet his father was pleased last night.

Oxford's fall is no joke

OXFORD: Gloucestershire beat Oxford University by 342 runs

I had hopes for the day when I experienced an old Oxford joke. I was approached by the leader of a party of tourists. He was puzzled. They had seen Christ Church, New College, Balliol, and a good many other things, but they had not found the University itself. Flinching from an explanation of the collegiate system, I directed them to the Roman Emperors.

But despite this happy omen, the Oxford second innings, for a while, bore a depressing resemblance to the first: a bad start, a bit of a recovery, a dismal collapse in the middle.

...

Orders was joined at the fall of the seventh wicket by an effective partner, Mallett. Orders is a left-hander, with an elegant cover drive, as befits a Wykehamist. He has been around for a year or two, indeed his 70, not out, was not quite his highest score, but I do not remember seeing him make runs before, and was impressed.

Mallett bats much as his father did, mostly off the back foot, strong on the cut, perky, a valuable man to have in the lower-middle order. The partnership more than doubled the score, which was 145 when Mallett was caught at the wicket.

Brain took the ninth wicket, and then removed himself to give Hignell the chance of the tenth. If Brain takes 99 wickets this season, he will regret this act of generosity. So the game did not end until 4 o'clock, by which time I trust the tourists had identified the Emperors.

GLOUCESTERSHIRE	319 for three declared (Broad 120, Stovold 75*, Hignell 63*)
	260 for four declared (Graveney 119, Bainbridge 49, Windybank 43, Sutcliffe 3-92)
OXFORD UNIVERSITY	79 (Wilkins 4-12, Partridge 3-18, Surridge 3-24)
	158 (Orders 70*, Mallett 38, Graveney 6-49)

Cambridge

It rained only briefly, but it was grey and bitterly cold. I was relieved to discover that the windows for the press box had at last arrived. I was late arriving myself, after some misadventures at Paddington, when a hitch on the Underground caused an enormous taxi queue. The man standing next to me was dolefully whistling an old song from operetta, and I found myself fitting revised words to it: "Rose of Didcot, thou shalt not fade here."

Southampton

During the afternoon I sat on the seat inscribed: "In Happy Memory of Bill Shepheard", and Southampton has never seemed the same place without that genial man. I tried to consult his shade at tea-time, and possibly did, because Bill was always an optimist. I heard a voice say: "Oh, we'll bat this out all right, and even if we don't that's another half-hour in the bar." It turned out to be 90 minutes in the bar. Graf, who had hit Doshi for two whacking sixes, was clearly not in a mood for dour defence; Stephenson batted more responsibly but could not prevent a peaceful, if early, death. On a day which had had its warm spells, but was bitter again by the end, few complained.

Briefly to The Oval

I knew it was going to be an interesting day when I entered the press box at the Oval, and saw our Cricket Correspondent, sagely installed. I am grateful for the clerical error which enabled me to meet him, a rare event in the season. It was decided, after a couple of quick snorts, that it would be best if I returned to the West, to pick up what was left of the Gloucestershire match.

Gloucester

I have never been very fond of the Wagon Works ground (the Winget ground, as it is now known, after a takeover). Its beauties and facilities are few. It has seen great performances. Charlie Parker took 17 wickets here (against Essex) in 1925, and Walter Hammond scored many runs, including a partnership of 321 in 1937 which is still Gloucestershire's fourth-wicket record. His lesser partner was his friend, Billy Neale, a farmer. England's sides, it was said, were often chosen when they were walking round Neale's orchard.

I put in these reminiscences because there was not much to remember yesterday. And the Wagon Works ground looks no prettier. The players did their best in miserable conditions. There had been no play on Saturday; and yesterday was cold and drizzly, with never a glimpse of sunshine.

Derby

It must be about five years since I have been to Derby for cricket, partly because first-class cricket matches here were suspended for a time. I was in one way not sorry to hear the news of the suspension, because the facilities were so poor: but I regretted it in another way for personal reasons. It was here that in 1966 Sobers bowled out Derbyshire before lunch on the third day, thus giving me the time to spare to go back to the west via London and take out a young lady to dinner, and (successfully) propose to her. I am glad to see that since the ground has been restored to county cricket, improvements are being made, though I do not include among the improvements the cinema organ in the clubhouse.

Cardiff

There was no play of significance at Cardiff yesterday. A great yellowish pall of cloud overhung the ground in the morning. It did not yield much rain, but the light was impossible for cricket. In the afternoon the light became no better and even more inspissated. Glamorgan formally declared, and at 3.15 the players went out. After three overs, the last two of which you could scarcely see from the ring, they came in again and I wondered that they could find their way to the pavilion.

I am only really writing this piece to tell you about the station announcer at Bristol Temple Meads, who produced the remarkable request: "Will the person who has the key to the cash box attend platform six immediately?" What was wrong? It was repeated several times, in tones of increasing desperation.

Were the staff being deprived of their coffee money, or was an American millionaire raging because he could not pass a cheque? Might it have been the Chancellor of the Exchequer, or the chairman of the NUR, travelling incognito? I shall never know.

Wet July

Flanders and Swann, in a memorable ballad, sang "June it rains and never stops, 30 days and spoils the crops." Apt enough it has been this year. I have almost given up going into my local because of their tales of woe about the hay harvest, and when I point out that it has not been much fun for a cricket correspondent either, the farmers sniff scornfully and say "Some be lucky."

Well, in the light of events elsewhere, I suppose we were lucky to have some play at Southampton. … The extra half hour was not taken, and we were glad to get away from the lowering clouds. Let us return to Flanders and Swann: "In July the sun is hot. Is it shining? No, it's not."

A memory of Warsaw

It was a more interesting day than had seemed likely on a cloudy morning. A strong wind kept the clouds moving over, but also kept us chilly. The best place to sit was in front of the vast, blind face of the leisure centre. This has the additional advantage that you cannot see the thing. I remember that once in Warsaw it was explained to me, on the same grounds, that the only good view of the city was from the top of the Palace of Science and Culture.

A sweatered bosom

There was a girl behind the bar whose delicate bosom was covered by a sweater declaring: "Bath University: M.A.U.S." I took this to be a protest against the low standard of degree, or graduate unemployment, or something of the kind. But no, it was a plug for "Management Association University Studies", whatever they may mean. I reported this to my friend Eric Hill, a sombre and conservative man, and he said that it did not surprise him because he understood that degrees were shortly to be awarded in bingo-calling.

Water may yet be best at the portly woman's Bath

BATH: Hampshire, with nine first innings wickets in hand, have scored 191 runs against Somerset

Outside Bath Abbey there is a statue of a portly and dignified woman rather like Queen Victoria. She presides over a fountain, and the inscription on the pediment is "Water is Best". You would not have found many Bath cricketers to agree with her this week. The first match of the festival was washed out, though oddly the weather relented to allow the Sunday match to be played. On this evidence, God is on the side of temperance, but not sabbatarianism.

Yesterday a fine morning dried the pitch sufficiently for the start to be made at 2.40. Hampshire won the toss and batted. Presumably the idea was to get quick runs while the pitch was easy, and then get at Somerset as the sun warmed it up. Unfortunately, the sun did not co-operate. It went in, and the afternoon was cloudy, and later chilly.

The pitch was slow, not difficult, but not one for stroke-making. The outfield was like one of my daughter Felicity's treacle tarts (she is improving, but they still come out a bit funny). Tremlett and Smith for a long time could hardly score at more than a run an over against accurate bowling and tight fielding. At tea, after 34 overs, they had reached 71.

Timothy Tremlett is the son of a much-loved captain of Somerset, Maurice. He was born at Wellington (but I will not tell that story again). It was his first game for Hampshire this season, and he made his highest score in first-class cricket. He does not have the majesty of his father's drive, but he probably has a sounder defence. Smith is a South African who was with Glamorgan last year and has a one-year contract with Hampshire. It is the second time this season that I have seen him look as if he might become a formidable batsman, wanderer though he is.

The stand prospered after tea. The umpires offered the batsmen a chance to go off because of bad light, but the batsmen were now full of confidence and declined it. The first wicket did not fall until the seventieth over, the score 174, when Tremlett, rightly trying to push on, was caught from a hoick which I can only call hereditary. He was warmly applauded by the Somerset crowd, quite a large one, who, loyal as they are, would have enjoyed seeing him make a hundred. Smith was nearly at his when play ended, and Hampshire nearly had their second batting point. The skies were so threatening that I feel the portly woman outside the abbey is the likeliest winner of this match.

Tremlett father and son

SOUTHAMPTON: Hampshire v Yorkshire

Tremlett is not very much like his father photographically, but the style is there. It could have been Maurice who hit that long pull to mid-wicket, and even more it was irresistibly Maurice when Timothy walked in, bowled by Cope. Clearly finding the whole thing inexplicable, he removed his cap in response to the applause, and rubbed the nape of his neck with the back of his hand. I have seen Maurice do this hundreds of times. Whether this is an argument for environment or heredity, I am not sure.

David Gower

LEICESTER: Leicestershire v West Indians

Balderstone and Gower came together. Balderstone has always been a fighter who does not believe in surrender, and Gower has been, so the theory grows, sent home to Leicester to tighten his game. It was an important innings for Gower. He had to prove himself, especially against the fast bowlers. Did he, or did he not? He took time to play himself in, then gradually began to make his strokes. Some of his drives raised cheers from the West Indian portion of the crowd, as well as the Leicestershire men. There was quite a large crowd, and I think that Holts Products must be encouraged in their efforts to revive interest in matches between the tourists and the counties.

Balderstone absurdly pulled a long hop on to his stumps – Kallicharran's first ball – at 111. It is not often that you see a batsman so disgusted with himself, and it made quite a cheerful sight, because he was not seeking to blame the umpire, or the pitch, or the bowler, or the crowd, or the flashing sun from the windscreens, or anything at all but Balderstone.

Now attention was concentrated on Gower. He continued to play handsomely for a while, but was caught in the slips, soon after reaching his 50, just the time when – as all the pundits have so often said – he *ought not* to get out. It was a good ball from Holding, which might have got a good batsman out at any time, but there was a sufficiently unwise and unnecessary element in the stroke to give Gower's critics a little more ammunition.

Sussex cricket

HOVE: Sussex v Kent

Dudley Carew, once cricket correspondent for this newspaper, wrote that "There is about the game whenever Sussex play it, the faint suggestion of sand-shoe, of a breeze off the sea, and of people inordinately enjoying themselves." There was a breeze off the sea yesterday, but no inordinate enjoyment. Sussex cricket, one way and another, has got itself into a proper muddle in recent years. There have been more heavy clogs about than sand-shoes.

Bob Woolmer

HOVE: Sussex v Kent

It was Woolmer's day. He made 171, his highest score in first-class cricket. It was not too taxing an occasion for him, because it was a strokeful pitch for batting, not too fast and not too slow; but the bowlers against him included Imran, who worked up a smart pace coming down the hill, and Arnold, who swung the ball about in a gusty, chilly wind. Woolmer was aided, as all batsmen in the match have been, or should have been, by the short pavilion boundary. Most of his fours were made on that side.

Nevertheless, it was a notable innings. I used to think of Woolmer as a workmanlike cricketer, certainly a good one, but without the delicate touches of Cowdrey senior, or even Denness. The passing years (not so many, for he is only 32) have brought the elegance but do not seem to have damaged the determination. His late cuts were a delight. I shall be surprised if he is not chosen for England this summer.

A Warwickshire collapse

BIRMINGHAM: Warwickshire v Worcestershire

It was the sixteenth over of the last twenty when Worcestershire took the last wicket, a somewhat unexpected win. I must say I thought Warwickshire had no business losing the match, but some of their ancestral voices had been prophesying woe. They have been getting accustomed to batting collapses. "Croomble," an old man in the pavilion kept muttering. "That's what they'll do. Croomble." And he was dead right.

At tea, after forty-five overs, it was 188 for three. Soon afterwards, Whitehouse was out. It was at this point I felt Warwickshire, having made a brave effort, should have turned their minds to saving the game.

But the croombling began. Ferreira was run out. It was a fine throw by Turner from square leg, but a pointless run. Amiss was leg before to Alleyne when he was 99. Hopkins lobbed a catch to mid-wicket. Oliver batted with a limp and a runner, quite well, but was bowled by Gifford in the eleventh over of the last twenty. The rest did not take long, and what there was of it was chiefly occupied by Small's reluctance to depart from the wicket when he had been given out leg before.

I have not done sufficient justice to Amiss. It was a pleasure to see him in the runs again.

Man of the Match

THE OVAL: Surrey v Yorkshire (Gillette Cup)

Knight was made man of the match – at least I think he was, because I saw him step forward to collect something, although a defect in the public address system caused Bill Edrich to howl and shriek like a nightingale that had got at the vodka.

How England and Australia put their friendship to the test

The Centenary Test at Lord's is in one respect a more significant anniversary than its predecessor at Melbourne, three years ago. It is true that, for statistical purposes, Test matches are now reckoned to have begun in 1877, and that is a rational starting point, since it was the first time a Combined Australian team had met English tourists on level terms – that is to say, 11-a-side.

The match caused much excitement in Australia but very little in England. Alfred Shaw, in his reminiscences, called the England side "Lillywhite's 11 x 1". Readers of *The Times* had to wait two months for their report, which came in their usual "Melbourne Letter". It appeared immediately after a description of a rumpus in the Victorian Parliament, and just before the latest population statistics. For Englishmen Test cricket began in 1880, at the Oval.

In the meantime an Australian side had toured here, in 1878. They did not play England, but they met MCC at Lord's and the MCC 11 x 1 was stronger – or so it was thought at Lord's, though possibly not in the provinces – than Lillywhite's had been. On a bad pitch the Australians won in a day by nine wickets. W.G. Grace scored four and nought. *Punch* wrote *"Our Grace before dinner was very soon done, and Grace after dinner did not get a run."*

So there should have been high interest when the next Australians arrived in 1880, but there was not.

There were several reasons for this. The 1878 side had employed James Lillywhite as a match-maker, very successfully, but the 1880 Australians seem to have trusted to luck. It was only in the spring that we knew for certain they were coming, and by then the home fixture list had largely been made up.

The list was much less crowded then than now, and doubtless accommodations could have been made, given good will; but there was not much good will towards Australian cricketers at the time. In the winter of 1878-9, Lord Harris had taken a side to Australia (losing the only Test played), and the second match against New South Wales had been marked by one of cricket's early riots. An umpiring decision was disputed by the Australian captain, and also by the crowd, who invaded the field. Harris was struck by a stick. A.N. Hornby, a tough Lancastrian, seized the offender and dragged him to the pavilion, losing most of his own shirt in the process. Ulyett and Emmett, two hardened Yorkshire professionals, plucked a stump each and escorted their captain safely from the field. Harris sent an account of the affair to the English press.

So when the 1880 Australians did arrive, they were like the young lady who took her harp to the party: nobody asked them to play. Yorkshire gave them a couple of matches which were called "unofficial". W.G. Grace tried to raise a side against them which would have had some sort of representative character, but did not succeed. The Australians offered to play a match for the benefit of the cricketers' fund: it was declined. They had to spend most of their time playing minor matches against odds. They were reduced to advertising for opposition.

However, public interest grew, and hostility lessened, partly because it became clear that W.L. Murdoch, the Australian captain, was a much less abrasive man than his forerunner, D.W. Gregory, had been. Later in the season, it was arranged that they should meet England, at the Oval. It is a pity that the Centenary Match is not also being played at the Oval. Lord's cold-shouldered the 1880 Australians and it was the Surrey secretary, C.W. Alcock, who came to their rescue.

Alcock was one of the great sporting figures of his era, not only in cricket but association football. He had initiated the England-Scotland match and the FA Cup, the final of which was for many years played at the Oval. The success of his plan for the match against Australia was assured once he had persuaded Lord Harris to collect and captain the English team.

This was a far-reaching and generous decision by Harris, who is not always thought of as a generous man. Not all Englishmen were so forgiving, it seems. Hornby, Emmett and Ulyett all declined invitations to play. But Alcock and Harris are, above all, the names that should be toasted this week.

The loss of the northern men to England was balanced by the loss to Australia, through injury of Spofforth, their best bowler, probably the best bowler cricket had seen until then. The match itself was rather disappointing, apart from an unexpected English collapse which raised interest in the last innings, and set many an unhappy precedent. England won the toss and scored 420, W.G. 152.

W.G. does not figure largely in the history of Test cricket. Although he went on playing for England until 1899, when he was 51, he was just passing his peak as it began. Still, it was appropriate that he should score a century. Two of his brothers were playing in the match, E.M. and G.F.. G.F. scored a pair, took a magnificent catch in the deep, off the Australian giant, Bonnor, and either the occasion was too much for him or some damp sheets at Basingstoke were, for he died soon afterwards.

Australia were out for 149, and followed on. Murdoch bet W.G. that he would pass his score, and did, 153 not out, the total 327. England needed only 57, but had to scramble for them, losing five wickets in the last innings. W.G., who had not bothered to open, had to go in after all. The only other batsman in the match to pass 50 was Harris. The most successful bowlers were Morley, of Nottinghamshire, who was fast and A.G. Steel, a Lancastrian, a leg-spinner. They opened the bowling, because they were the best bowlers: a practice with a lot to be said for it.

I have never shared the more romanticised views of Test cricket: that it was an empire-builder, or once the word empire fell into disuse, an agent of international harmony; that it was a moral pattern for life, and so on. But matches between England and Australia, though marred by numerous controversies (bodyline, throwing, Mr Packer, to take three that have occurred in the latter half of the century), have given a lot of fun to a lot of people.

And if we had not had Test cricket, we would be sure to have had something a great deal worse. In the past two years, we very nearly did.

The retirement of John Arlott

The voice of cricket declares

When the Centenary Test match came to its end yesterday, there also came to an end, at least as far as Test matches were concerned, the most famous of cricketing voices.

Broadcast cricket commentary began soon after broadcasting itself, but for a long time it was rather amateurishly done. The usual practice was to find some distinguished old cricketer, such as Pelham Warner, prop a microphone in front of him, and leave him to get on with it.

In the 1930s, Howard Marshall appeared, and after him E.W. Swanton (and we must not forget Arthur Wrigley, who founded the technique of modern scoring).

But it was only after the war that we heard the voice of them all, John Arlott.

He came from Basingstoke, and his Hampshire accent in those days was sharp. The Hampshire accent is not naturally a mellow one, such as that of Dorset, which helped to make Ralph Wightman such a broadcasting success.

It took a year or two for the public, brought up on Marshall and Swanton, to grow accustomed to Arlott. He did not sound like a member of MCC. But by 1948 he was established, and ever since has remained, for every Test in England, a necessary part of the scene.

He did that because he was a cricketer and a poet. He was never, I think, expected to be an outstanding cricketer, though he had a passion for the game, and when he abandoned his first-class ambitions he was determined to stay in touch with it somehow.

He became very knowledgeable, partly because he pestered cricketers for information: not the dressing-room gossip, but technical stuff. "What does he *do*? What's his dangerous ball?" he would demand if a new bowler appeared.

"We all loved and admired John in the Hampshire dressing room," said his old friend Desmond Eagar, then the Hampshire captain, "but we did sometimes wish he would stop asking questions."

The greatest honour that he feels he has been paid is to have been invited to be Chairman of the Professional Cricketers' Association, a post he will retain in retirement. Not that he really retired: he is going to live in his beloved Alderney, but he will speak and write as long as he lives. He has immense industry, a constant urge to work, more than any man I have known.

But he would not have become so famous had he not been a poet. He was considered one of the most promising post-war poets. He gave that up too ("The words don't come any more"), but his adventures in poetry gave him a command of words, a gift of phrase such as no other cricket commentator has possessed.

He also had an unforced sense of humour. When he used phrases such as "the fieldsmen are scattered in the wilderness, like missionaries", people used to think he had thought them up beforehand. Sometimes, I suppose, he may have done, but he never needed to.

I remember one Test morning at Trent Bridge when I was in the commentary box with him and Trevor Bailey. Trevor began, as usual, with his introduction about the state of the game, finishing with "and now come the umpires in their new-style short coats, looking like dentists. Over to John Arlott."

John immediately said: "It occurs to me, Trevor, that it is rather suitable for the umpires to look like dentists, since one of their duties is to draw stumps."

A single-wicket competition 1980

Procter takes the prize again but Doshi is man of the odd match

Single-wicket cricket has a long history. Indeed, it was the first aspect of the game to command large-scale popular support. In the second quarter of the last century there was an attempt to establish something like a cricketing equivalent of the championship belt for prize fighting, and crowds of many thousands attended such famous matches as those between Pilch and Marsden and Mynn and Dearman.

There were set laws, which for many years were published in *Wisden*. The boundary was 22 yards. No scoring behind the wicket was allowed. To make one run the batsman had to cover the length of the pitch twice. When the striker hit the ball, one foot had to be on the ground behind the popping crease, otherwise it was adjudged "no hit". From this it will be seen that it was not exactly a speedy game, which probably accounted for its decline.

A drawback to various modern attempts to provide a pepped-up version of single-wicket cricket is the absence of standard rules. Procter and Botham were meeting under the same ones last year, when Procter narrowly won. Each had 20 overs. Ten runs were deducted every time the batsman was out. Each bowled 10 overs, and the remaining overs were the duty of an agreed choice, in this case Doshi, of Warwickshire.

There was a full fielding side, provided by Bristol Cricket Association. They had the assistance of Brassington as wicket keeper and of David Shepherd and Mervyn Kitchen, both aspiring to the first-class list, as umpires.

There was a prize of £1,000 and a crowd of about 4,000. Procter was bowled first ball, so his score was minus 10, which baffled the scoreboard. By the third over he had gone into credit. He was bowled again, this time by Doshi, in the seventh over, which reduced his score to six.

He then got going, but was caught at deep square leg off Doshi, which reduced him to 80. In the eighteenth over he was stumped twice off Doshi, the Gloucestershire supporters feeling that Brassington was a touch disloyal, and then ran himself out. His final score was 112, 70 deducted.

It was not a very good score, and it had been an odd innings. Doshi conceded nearly all the runs and took nearly all the wickets. A resilient character, there was always the chance that he might bowl as well again. Once I saw him bowl out Essex in even more improbable circumstances, for Hertfordshire at Hitchin.

Botham was leg-before to Procter in the fifth over and caught in the deep off Doshi in the eighth. In the same over he was caught at the wicket. Then he was bowled, by Doshi. Procter chipped in again himself and bowled him in the eleventh over, which reduced the score to 29. He began to move and had reached 95 when he was caught twice on the square-leg boundary, good catches by Ian Crawford, of Stapleton. He was then run out, and caught in the deep, by Tucker, and ended 27 runs behind.

So Procter won the prize, thought had there been a man of the match award it should surely have gone to Doshi. It was a comical and cheerful occasion, which did not much resemble cricket; but the spectators, and possibly even the players, enjoyed it. The fieldsmen of the Bristol clubs showed that they were not much below county standard.

Brief memories

Harold Larwood at Leyton

I have a clear memory of Larwood: and not just the Larwood of the later years of his career, when the injury he suffered had taken the fine edge off his speed.

It must have been 1932, conceivably 1931, when I first saw him at Leyton. He was not a big man, though he had solid shoulders and bottom. His run-up was not long, by today's standards, but fast, and quiet. It was often referred to as a 'carpet-slippered' run. Perhaps it was this that made him awesome, in a way which Bowes and Farnes, both of whom I also saw at about that time, were not, though they were much taller, took longer runs, and looked much more like a small boy's idea of what a fast bowler ought to be.

Martin Donnelly at Oxford

I saw, I think, at least part of every innings he played in the Parks in 1946. Town and gown crowded to the Parks when he batted.

His batting had one quirk. He did not bother about the quick single. He would take a leisurely single, but scored most in boundaries. His belief was that if he hit a ball it should go for four and, if it did not go for four, one would do. He had some embarrassment when he had to bat with H.A. Pawson, who was just about the fastest man between wickets I have seen. It delighted the Parks to see Pawson halfway down his third run while Donnelly was deciding it was not worth embarking on a second.

Cakes are more digestible than Somerset's play

TAUNTON: Warwickshire (20 pts) beat Somerset (8 pts) by ten wickets

Since Surrey had polished off Lancashire in two days, I went to Taunton, my favourite ground, for the last day of the first-class season. The season ended as it had begun, with clouds scudding across the sky, and wind howling in the eaves of the press box. It was the last time I shall ever have a drink in the little side pavilion, wood and corrugated iron, which has latterly been the clubhouse of the Taunton Cricket Club, doubling as the vice-presidents' bar on county occasions, but which has always been known, to those familiar with Taunton, as "the stragglers' pavilion". The Somerset Stragglers were a great force in the development of the county's cricket. It is to be demolished in the course of renovations. I trust that the ladies of Taunton CC will be provided with somewhere else to sell their home-made cakes. Not even the ladies of Worcester approach the ladies of Taunton in this respect.

It rained in the morning, but play started at two o'clock.

...

The rather dismal collapse at the end of Somerset's innings meant that Warwickshire had only to score 104 in 135 minutes. Somerset bowled their spinners, even to the point of ridicule when Botham came on, and bowled laboured off spin from round the wicket. He did not seem very interested in the proceedings. Amiss and Smith knocked off the runs without difficulty, in fact with a careless mocking ease. It did not make, for Somerset, a happy climax to the season.

Everything but the real thing at Bristol

ASHTON GATE, BRISTOL: The Rest of the World beat England by eight wickets

England played the Rest of the World at a game purporting to be cricket last night, on the Bristol City ground at Ashton Gate. I had been warned that I would find it a repellent spectacle, but the half had not been told me. I felt bitterly towards our cricket correspondent who had been unavoidably prevented from attending by a previous sporting engagement (boating on the Thames with Brian Johnston). Not since I played for Yorkshire against the Rest of the World on a rough common outside Smolyensk have I seen a more gross caricature of the game, but the competitors at Smolyensk were a coach party of tourists, and at Ashton Gate they were some of the best cricketers in the world. In this was the tragedy.

No doubt floodlit cricket has a future, for this is the age of the sporting stunt, and it is only fuddy-duddies who remember that it was once the meadow game with the beautiful name. I did meet one or two regular cricket followers among the crowd – about 9,000 it was estimated – and they muttered shamefacedly things like "a bit of fun" and "does no harm".

I suppose the harm has already been irredeemably done. But how any cricketer with any feeling for the game at all can regard the sight of the best players in the world bashing monotonously into the stands on a narrow football field as fun passes my comprehension. Never mind. In 10 years' time, mark my words, we shall have the pylons up at Lord's and the riots to go with them. They have had a promising trial run for rioting already.

The emetic-yellow pads, the umpires dressed in red nightgowns like Chinese mandarins, the white ball, the black sight screens, the indiscriminately yelling crowd (I imagine the things they like most about soccer are sudden death penalties), the artificial pitch, combined to make it all a hideous nightmare.

England were sent in to bat, and lost four wickets for 31, but Boycott and Botham put a stop to these brief hopes of an early finish. It was just the game for Botham, able to mis-hit as much as he liked, and still score sixes. Boycott, whose inner soul must have shrunk from what was going on around him, could not resist the temptation to play a proper cricketing stroke now and then. Doshi showed that even in such conditions bowling a length could bring a reward. The fielding was of high quality, even in the difficult period when daylight gave way to floodlight. These are the only polite things I can think of to say.

The English innings ended for 214 in the 38th over. The Rest of the World scored 220 for two. The players and Bristol City both made some money, and Bristol City, at any rate, need it. But the end does not always justify the means, and I would have thought it much better to see Bristol City in the third division than survive by such tales told by an idiot, full of sound and fury, signifying nothing.

ENGLAND	214 (Botham 84, Boycott 68, Doshi 6-48)
SOMERSET	220 for two (Gavaskar 68, Sadiq 64)

Week ended May 9

We are on the captaincy arguments again. Brearley has said he will not tour again. The name most frequently mentioned as his successor is that of Botham. Botham, at 24, would be the youngest captain since Ivo Bligh (discounting M.P. Bowden, who was deputy for C. Aubrey Smith in one match – subsequently granted Test status – in South Africa in 1889). But Chapman and May were not much older when appointed. They were both, on balance, successful captains, and their principal successes came in the early part of their careers. So youth is not a barrier in itself. Another argument is that Botham has no experience of captaincy. This is not conclusive, either. Three Yorkshiremen, Jackson, Hutton and Illingworth, all of whom beat Australia, were never (except for the odd match) captains of Yorkshire. Chapman had been sacked from the England captaincy before he captained Kent. May had not reached the Surrey captaincy when he first led England.

There remains a further query: are we asking too much of Botham, with such heavy responsibilities as he already has? This was an argument used against Hutton, and it is true that, by his last season, Australia 1954-55, the strain had told upon his batting. There is a real risk that Botham might burn himself up too soon, especially because of an exceptionally demanding, and absurdly crowded, Test programme in the next couple of years.

Botham has the physique for it. Has he the character? 'A couple o' year, and he'll be a great captain. Pitch him in now and he could ruin. Still a touch too hot in the head.' I will not give the source of this quotation, since I have not obtained permission, but it came in an authoritative, experienced and friendly Somerset voice. Yet we have to consider: who else? Bailey thinks that Fletcher would be the short-term man: an excellent tactician, who has made many runs in Tests. But he has often failed against fast bowling, which is going to be the problem this summer and next winter. Gower had his supporters a year ago, but the Australian tour showed his immaturity. The choice of Boycott would be hardly practical: there is too much bitterness in the background. Willis has the character for the job, but there are doubts about his form and fitness. Hampshire might come into consideration if he scores a lot of runs early in the season. Knight has been mentioned, but for all his agreeable qualities and talents he has never been near the England side.

There are several things to be said for Rose. He has played for England, and, though he was not very successful, he is as likely – in the present state of our batting – to score runs in a Test as most. His declaration at Worcester last year will count against him, and should. We now hear it said that it was not really his fault, that he was under pressure from his team, and so on. That simply makes him a weak captain, instead of a rogue. Still, he has otherwise led Somerset very capably, and is the kind of man who will have learnt from his lesson. If it is thought that Botham is not ready for the job just yet, and that Fletcher is a little beyond it when the bowling is so fast, there is a case for Rose.

Week ended May 30

This has been a Benson and Hedges week, with matches, now restricted to an allocation of two days, beginning on Saturday, Tuesday and Thursday. I think, on the whole, this is a good idea, though it removes interest from the championship before it has properly begun. On Saturday I was at Taunton. It was a warm day for a change, with a large crowd, and Middlesex won by a run. Taunton, for so long one of the quieter, remoter county grounds, where you could enjoy the prospect of the Quantocks (and of empty seats in the foreground) now hums with enthusiasm. The skeleton of the new pavilion is built. I am afraid it is going to do nothing for the view, but it is needed.

I was there again on Sunday, and this time Somerset won, easily, against Yorkshire. There was passion in the air, but very little misbehaviour (it is a good idea closing the bars on Sunday afternoons). The only really nasty bunch of yobbos, at least in my proximity, were – and as one of the tribe I write it with regret – Yorkshiremen. Hampshire and Boycott opened Yorkshire's innings, and each was run out for 0. There ought to be a good tale here, but it was no more than a couple of exceptionally good throws by Slocombe.

Yet again I was at Taunton on Tuesday, for the Surrey match. It was good to see the old Shoreditch Sparrow, now more of a Starling, or even a Thrush, the wise thrush 'who sings each song twice over, least you should think he never could recapture the first fine careless rapture.'

Week ended May 30

I was pleased to see that Marks was chosen for the second Prudential Trophy match, and played acceptably. I make very few correct prophecies about cricketers, but I did say, years ago, that Marks would play for England, and was mocked for it by a purple-sweatered *Guardian* man.

I spent half the week at Swansea, and half at Hove. Swansea is, as Dylan Thomas said, a lovely ugly town, and St Helen's is a lovely ugly sports ground. It was a long time since I had been there, at least for cricket. It provided some sunny days, many happily renewed acquaintances, and a ferocious number of steps. I have a game leg just now, and notice the steps at St Helen's much more than I did. (And there are no handrails.) The press box might as well be an isolation hospital, though I suppose that was intended when it was built. It also has, or had, a large number of defective chairs. I collapsed on one and, amid hearty Welsh laughter and a *penillion* or two, was assured that I was the third man to collapse on that chair this season. But, at lunchtime on Saturday, Wilfred Wooller, in one of his masterful moods, smashed up the duds and flung them out. I have never felt fonder of him. There were a few more reliable chairs by Monday.

On the first day, Glamorgan let a good batting position crumble, though there was an admirable innings by Alan Jones, an underestimated cricketer. I see that *Wisden*, ridiculously, has just deprived him of his only Test cap, against the Rest of the World in 1970. Among the other week-end delights of Swansea were a barman who looks like Don Mosey, a senior member who looks like Jim Swanton, and a commentator who actually turned out to be Alun Williams. Nottinghamshire won comfortably in the end, and I was struck by an innings from a young man called Curzon, played primarily for his wicket-keeping. He showed a sound technique and a sound temperament, until he was caught at deep square leg, off Hobbs. It was a pleasure to see Hobbs bowling again, the last of the Mohicans (though, as I remember, a central character in the book was called Natty Bumpo, more a name for a fast bowler than a leg spinner). On the last day of the match I decided, rashly, to get as far as Cardiff before telephoning my copy, as there seemed to be plenty of time. I left my notepad on the train, which was late, and had to do my report 'off the top of my head', in a hurry. It was garbage, but nobody seems to have noticed yet. This gives me a nasty feeling that I always write garbage.

Week ended June 13

At Derby, on the last day, there might have been a good moment when Kirsten was batting. He mishit a steepler, and every Jones in the Glamorgan side circled underneath it. Nash, the captain, kept his head, and called 'Eifion!', and Eifion duly caught it. Supposing, I thought, he had called 'Jones', or even 'Alan' (for there are two Alans among the Joneses, and a third in reserve). That's captaincy. While the ball was in the air, I thought of the story of Sir John Squire, who had drummed into his touring side the necessity of listening, in such circumstances, to the captain's call. Sure enough, up went a skier. Jack Squire's voice rang out like a clarion: 'Thompson! Thompson!' The fieldsmen obediently stepped back, the ball fell to earth, and the captain remembered that Thompson was not playing that day.

Week ended July 4

The most interesting experience of my week was a visit to Exeter to see Devon play Cornwall in the Gillette Cup. I have spent much of my life in the two counties. Often I have reported their contests at rugby, some of which have been epic. Correspondence afterwards could be neatly divided into two piles, one saying, more or less, 'you Cornish basket' and the other 'you Devon clod'. But this was likely to be the only one chance I shall have of seeing them in a quasi-first-class cricket match. The Exeter ground was a pleasant place to be, with the Haldon Hills and Dunchideock Castle, and a pitch that was good enough for any county ground in the country – I have this on the authority of Bert Flack, who has retired to Devon from Old Trafford.

I am not sure that all the Cornishmen would agree with him, for they had a disappointing day. … So as a cricketing occasion it was not a great success, though it was for meeting old friends, among them Jack Davey, now retired from Gloucestershire to the Devil's Elbow at Princeton. (I have received a disturbing report from D.M. Green that he is not always as prompt as desirable at opening time.) I am sure he would have loved to have been playing, but Devon did not need him.

Week ended August 22

On Saturday at Taunton there was a beautiful innings by Gower. After his first few strokes a staunch Somerset supporter, a man who hates his side to lose, said 'D'you know, I'd like to see him make 50.' Gower quickly did, and I said 'Well, you can start cheering for Somerset again', and he replied 'No, I'd like to see him make a hundred.' I was on the point of asking him whether he would settle for 150, and I am sure he would have said 'yes', when Gower was caught at the wicket for 94. His dismissal was greeted by the crowd with as much a sigh as a cheer. Brightness fell from the air. Such is the compelling effect which Gower has upon cricketers when he is going well.

Week ended September 5

Middlesex have won the championship. What an acquisition van der Bijl has been to them! They call him Bidgie on the Tavern side (not because they are ignorant, you understand, just their little joke.) I had my doubts whether, not young and unaccustomed to the championship grind, he would last till the end of the season, but he has confounded them. He has not only taken a lot of wickets, but often been a scourge to the opposition in the later batting, especially when runs were needed. Of course he is a strong, big man. Wilfred Wooller says he is considering an appeal under Law 42 – 'to have a man that size *must* be unfair play'. 'Bidgie' and Daniel have been the foundation of the Middlesex success, although it has also made a big difference that they have had Brearley available regularly.

Arthur Wellard (Somerset)

In 1936, I was sent to school at Taunton, which gradually gave me an introduction to Somerset cricket. We did not see the county play very much, because of limits of 'down town' leave, but we caught glimpses of them now and then, and heard tall stories about them from the Day Boys. Sometimes, on half-holidays, if we had saved up sufficient of our pocket-money, we could watch them for several hours.

Somerset were not then a very good side – they could not afford sufficient professionals – but they were popular, popular with more crowds than their own, because they were genial and unpredictable. They would beat the best and lose to the worst: that was the Somerset pattern for more than a hundred years – until, of course, last season, when they began to win things.

The man upon whom all boys' eyes were fixed was Arthur Wellard. In the following few years, we began to turn to Gimblett, who had begun his first-class career dramatically with the fastest century of the season in his maiden match; but Gimblett's glories were mostly to come. Wellard was our hero.

Wellard was our hero because (a bad reason) he was the most regular hitter of sixes the game has ever known. Ron Roberts says that Wellard scored more than 12,000 runs in first-class cricket and that about a quarter of them were hit in sixes. This would not be an easy thing to check, if only because scoring was erratic in the 1930s, but does not seem improbable. I remember him coming out to bat, dark, tall, weighty, a cheerful grin on his face which must, to the opposing bowlers, have looked Mephistophelian, and then knocking one after the other into the River Tone. He usually hit straight to long-on, from the pavilion end, because he liked the splash when the ball hit the river. But I remember a time when he landed one on the bridge, whence it bounced, and alarmed several negotiating farmers in the cattle market.

Tommy Mitchell (Derbyshire)

I only saw Mitchell a few times, but enough to remember him, a busy, enthusiastic figure, rather oddly shaped with a trunk which seemed too long for his legs: enough to recognize the wit of Robertson-Glasgow's description of him as a kind of Donald Duck. 'No cricketer so conveys to the spectators the perplexities and frustration of man at the mercy of malignant fate. He has much in common with that golfer who missed short putts because of the uproar of the butterflies in the adjoining meadow.'

I rather doubt, though, Robertson-Glasgow's judgement that the fluctuations of Mitchell's form were because 'he only does it when he feels like it.' It seems more possible that he failed to do it when he felt the need too much. He reminds me of Hamlet as much as Donald Duck. Hamlet, as some critic has somewhere said, lacked the big-match temperament – all right on a little affair against pirates, but too worried about his responsibilities when the state of the kingdom was his concern.

'Stan' Nichols (Essex)

When I was seven years old, we left Ilkley, and moved to Leyton, in East London. I did not much like the change, but there was one major compensation. Leyton was the home of the Essex County Cricket Club. What was more, our house overlooked the ground.

Essex in those days were a pleasing, eccentric, not very successful side. I supported them faithfully, except when they were playing Yorkshire. They had two England players, a batsman, Jack O'Connor, and an all-rounder, Morris Nichols. Nichols was often called "Stan", an abbreviation of his second name. He used to open the bowling, and bat at No. 5.

He was a fast bowler, not one of the fastest of his era – when there were many about – but would have ranked as fast at any time. In, say, 1919-24, or 1946-53, he would have been the fastest in the country. He had a curious, slightly splay-footed action, which probably deprived him of the last few inches of speed. Sir Neville Cardus compared his gait to that of a sailor, accustomed to spreading his feet on a rolling deck. His batting style, as I remember, was also unusual. He did not use his feet much. His forward stroke, even if defensive, was a ferocious fast-footed jab. Yet, if he was not graceful, he was effective. He took more than 100 wickets in a season 11 times, and in eight of those seasons he scored more than 1,000 runs. In those days the press would make much of what they called "the race to the double" (how times have changed) and Nichols won it, year after year.

When he was asked about the hardest batsmen to get out, Morris Nichols thought first of George Gunn, who was a well-known master of fast bowling, but into his forties when Nichols first bowled at him. "He used to walk down the pitch to me. I always felt a fool trying to bowl him out." According to an ancient scorecard, I must have seen Nichols bowling to George Gunn: but the treacherous mind carries no recollection of it.

'Endren, 'Earne and 'Aig (Middlesex)

It is an odd thing, but I cannot remember much about my first visit to Lord's. I know I was staying with Uncle Dick and Auntie Mollie at Hendon. I often would spend short holidays with them – special treats – in the early thirties. They were both cricket enthusiasts, and would take me with them to Lord's on a Saturday, the *specialest* treat of all. I was already watching first-class cricket regularly at Leyton, and can remember a good deal about many of the matches I saw there. But the pictures of Lord's are vaguer. I would have guessed that my first match was Middlesex *v* Nottinghamshire – I can see Uncle Dick scanning his scorecard with a professional air, and saying disappointedly, 'Oh, Sam Staples isn't playing'; or it might have been Middlesex *v* Lancashire, a match in which a Lancastrian called Hodgson (a fast bowler) took a splendid catch in the deep, only a few yards away from us. We usually arrived early, and took seats in front of the Tavern, though on one occasion at least – perhaps there was an especially large crowd, or Uncle Dick had had a rise in pay – we ascended to the Mound Stand. Yet I have studied the scores in *Wisden* for the conceivable season, and no detailed memories are stirred.

But I retain a strong impression of some of the Middlesex players of those years. The strongest – very properly, for a small boy – is of Hendren. He was small, he was nimble, he could catch in the deep as well as the slips, he could hit the ball like a thunderbolt: everyone knew him as Patsy ('He was baptised Elias and the crowds would have none of it,' wrote Cardus, 'for he is Patsy not only by name but by nature'). Once the Middlesex players were throwing catches to one another, at the fall of a wicket. They were fairly languid catches, for it was a hot day. Hendren caught a gentle one near the ground, and in the same movement flicked it smartly backwards to his captain, Haig, who was standing, arms folded, a few yards behind him. It took Haig in the tummy. How we laughed!

Hendren was not one of those cricketers whose apparently brimming good humour on the field was matched by moroseness off it (we can all think of one or two of those). He was a man of wisdom as well as gaiety, what our ancestors used to call a 'thorough' man, the same wherever you sliced him

Uncle Dick and Auntie Mollie were both northerners, as I was myself, but like everyone else they yielded to Hendren, and cheered when he made a big score, even if it was against Yorkshire or Lancashire. They had plenty to cheer. I know that a comparison of the statistics of different periods is a vague guide, but he scored over 57,000 runs, average nearly 51, in a career lasting from 1907 to 1938, with 170 centuries. Only Hobbs and Woolley have scored more runs, and only Hobbs has scored more centuries. It is true that Hendren took some time to get going in Test cricket. This was partly because he was hesitant early in his innings, not a good quality against Gregory and McDonald. But he would hook the fast bowlers fearlessly when his eye was in, and had the footwork to run down the pitch to the spinners. At the end of his 51 Tests he had scored 3,500 runs, average 48.

We did not – Auntie Mollie and Uncle Dick and I – think so much of Haig, or even Hearne, who after Hendren was the best Middlesex batsman. In the case of Hearne, this was understandable. He was near the end of a long and distinguished career, which had been much handicapped by ill health. He had become a slow, and even dull, batsman at least to small boys. I have a recollection of even the Lord's boys urging him to get out, so that Hendren could come in. We were unjust to the elegant Hearne, but even Robertson-Glasgow was constrained to write of him, 'So smooth and contained was his method that few spectators, with all respect to them and their shillings, could know how wonderful was the art presented to them.' I was not one of the few, though Uncle Dick, anxious to be knowledgeable, made explanatory comments. Hearne scored 37,000 runs, average nearly 40, so he could not have been too bad; and also took 1,800 wickets, mostly with leg-breaks, though we did not think of him as a bowler by the time I saw him.

The joke has often been repeated that the Lord was being mischievous when, in the 1900s, he granted Surrey a succession of cricketers whose name began with the letter H. All the talk at The Oval was of 'Ayward, 'Obbs, 'Ayes, 'Olland and 'Itch. But Middlesex (where the aitches are not, apart from the pavilion, much more common than at the Elephant and Castle) were doing well in the early thirties with 'Endren, 'Earne, 'Ulme, 'Art and 'Aig. Auntie Mollie, who was careful to pronounce her aitches, did not like Haig much. 'Too much of a toff,' she said, and certainly he looked one as he strode down the pavilion steps (the professionals used to come out from their own dressing-room, tucked away to the side, a comfortable distance from the pavilion. They need not have done so, but they thought it was not worth the bother of walking round).

Haig was captain of Middlesex from 1929 to 1932, in which years they came nearer to the bottom than the top. He was in one respect a good captain, fond of a chancy declaration. Sussex felt that one season he deprived them of the championship when he made a rash one against Lancashire. In another respect he was a bad one, because once he had started bowling (fast-medium with the occasional out-swinger) he could not bear to take himself off. He played for England against Australia in 1921 – but many great cricketers played for England in that series. I think Hendren did quite right to smack him in the tummy.

Lancashire have won the championship eight times, and shared it four times (according to the customarily accepted records) which is not really very many, considering all the talent they have had at their disposal. Their best run was from 1926 to 1928, when they won three in a row. They were then the most unpopular side in the country because they were supposed, with some justification, to be slow in their batting and cautious in their tactics. Cardus (and in writing of Lancashire in the '20s there can be no getting away from Cardus) described how he arrived one morning at Lord's and heard one purpureous old gentleman say to another, "Those Lancashire cads are batting."

Another cause of Lancashire's unpopularity was that they had been early investors in the overseas market. The existence of the Lancashire Leagues meant that players could earn a living, while acquiring a residential qualification. It was thus that McDonald came to play for them. McDonald had been, with Gregory, the scourge of English batsmen during the Australian tour of 1921. Yorkshiremen, sticking firmly to their birth-only qualification, were sarcastic. Emmott Robinson always called McDonald "that Tasmanian", as if he were some kind of aboriginal. (But it must be pointed out that Yorkshire, too, were an unpopular side in the '20s, chiefly because of their field manners.)

McDonald could usually be relied on to take a few wickets quickly (he bowled best against the best), and to come back in the middle of the innings, if it seemed necessary, and to knock off the tail. Lancashire only needed a good spinner at the other end, and they had one in Richard Tyldesley, a tubby leg-spinner who played seven times for England between 1924 and 1930. In Lancashire's run of three championships, McDonald took 484 wickets, and Tyldesley 303. There were other useful bowlers developing: Iddon, Hopwood (both slow left-handers, who could bat, and played occasionally for England) and Sibbles, who was what we would call, nowadays, an off-cutter. Cardus wrote of Sibbles that there was "nothing cheap or spectacular about him. I doubt if I have ever heard him appeal; he even asks the umpire, puts a question to him, instead of stating a fact. A nicer mannered cricketer never wore flannels. He has the gift of modesty and his upright way of carrying himself and his crinkled hair (they called him 'Top' in the Lancashire side) seem entirely in keeping with the style of his play." But Sibbles, despite his modesty, and despite a career shortened by illness, took 932 wickets, at an average of 22.

So the bowling was good enough. The fielding, though not athletic by modern standards, was sound. Few catches went down, and in Duckworth they had the best wicket-keeper in the country – equally good at standing back to McDonald as he was standing up to Richard Tyldesley. The batting was the query. It was not that there was likely to be a shortage of runs, but could they be scored at a championship-winning rate? The only batsman who seemed able to score fast, against good bowling, was Ernest Tyldesley. He was no relation to Richard, but a much younger brother of J.T., who had been England's leading professional batsman in the early 1900s. Lancashire men grieve to this day that Ernest Tyldesley was not given a proper chance in Test cricket. He played in only 14 Test matches, the first in 1921 and the last in 1929, and only five of them were against Australia. But he scored nearly 1,000 runs, average 55, with three centuries. He had to fight his way into the side against extremely tough opposition, because Hobbs, Sutcliffe, Woolley, Hendren, Hammond and Jardine were among his competitors. He scored nearly 40,000 runs in his career, average 45, a higher aggregate and average than his famous brother.

But Tyldesley was the only naturally quick seamer. The other pillars were Makepeace, Hallows and Watson, who were the kind of people the purpureous gentleman at Lord's had in mind when he spoke of "those Lancashire cads". Makepeace played four times for England, on the 1920-21 tour of Australia, averaged 35, and made a century. In his career, which began in 1906 and ended in 1930, he scored 26,000 runs, average 36. Cardus tells us that McDonald once, in late-night conversation, chose Makepeace to open with Trumper in a Word XI. "Best on a sticky," explained McDonald. Everyone present was staggered, though Makepeace himself kept calm. "Nay, nay, Mac," he said. "A few years ago, perhaps, but not now."

Hallows played from 1914 to 1932, and scored 21,000 runs at an average of 40. He played for England in 1921 against Australia (when about half the cricketers in the country did), and against the West Indies in 1928, when Hobbs stood down for a Test. His Test average was 42, but he only batted twice and was only once out. His choice for England that year was due to an astonishing 1,000 runs in May, something he had never looked the kind of man to achieve, either before or after. He began batting on May 5, and ended with an innings of 232 on May 31 (perhaps he was helped a bit in the latter stages of the last day). The only other batsmen to have scored a thousand in May (as opposed to before the end of May) were then, and are now, Grace and Hammond. He lived until he was 77, continued to be active and fit, doing a lot of coaching, until one day he walked briskly back from the library, sat down, said he felt "a little short of breath", and died. David Green wrote recently of Hallows (Hallows was then Lancashire coach and Green on the staff) that he "never approved of my slightly frantic method as an opening batsman. While reasonably effective when all my cylinders were firing, on bad days I looked like an out-of-control threshing machine, which caused the dour Charlie much pain."

The dourest of the lot, however, was Frank Watson, who played from 1920 to 1937, and scored 26,000 runs, average 37. He never played for England, though he was close to it, and was chosen for the Players, and in Test trials. When he died in 1976, *Wisden* wrote of him that he "was a batsman whom spectators of fifty years ago will, unless they were fervent Lancashire supporters, remember as one of whom they wished to see as little as possible." No dasher, he: but apart from the three successive championship wins he stayed in the side for two more, in 1930 and 1934. Apart from his rocklike batting, he took over 400 wickets with little inswingers.

The Lancashire side of the late '20s makes an interesting contrast with the Middlesex side of 1947. Middlesex had an inadequate attack, but scored their runs so fast and copiously that their bowlers had sufficient time to take their wickets. Lancashire could rarely score fast, but McDonald and Tyldesley were so effective that they gave their batsmen sufficient time to make their runs.

And who, in these their days of glory, was the Lancashire captain? You may well ask. He was captain all three years, not before or afterwards, so he never led a losing side in the championship. He was Colonel Leonard Green. He did not say much about himself, and not much has been written about him, but he skilfully handled a bunch of men who had much turbulence in them, and I expect would be content with the tribute of P.F. Warner, someone who knew the difficulties: "an admirable leader, as one would expect from so good a soldier."

A Christmas quiz for literate sportsmen: five cricket questions

Answers on page 245

Some 10 years ago, I wrote a piece for this newspaper, a kind of quiz for literate sportsmen (of whom there are many). It led to some interesting correspondence, and I am tempted to try again. Please consider the following extracts, and answer the appended questions. There are no prizes, though if anyone conscientiously claims he has got them all right, there will always be a glass for him at The Star, High Littleton, at my expense (mornings only to avoid the juke-box).

1. *Mrs ________ was a very good woman, and wished to see her children everything they ought to be: but her time was so much occupied in lying-in and teaching the little ones, that her elder daughters were inevitably left to shift for themselves; and it was not very wonderful that _____, who had, by nature nothing heroic about her, should prefer cricket, baseball, riding on horseback, and running about the country, at the age of 14, to books."* Fill in the gaps, and provide the name of the author and the title of the book. That was a comfortable one to start with. This might be harder.

2. *Mostly, though – about 55 minutes in each hour I was with him – I had to talk cricket. It was his only solace. I had to pretend a devotion to the game which I no longer felt, which in fact had been lukewarm in the thirties except for the pleasure of his company. Now I had to study the scores as intently as when I was a schoolboy. He couldn't read for himself, but would have known if I was bluffing. Sometimes, for a few minutes, his old vivacity would light up. But if I couldn't think of another question or piece of news, he would lie there, in the kind of dark loneliness that comes to some people before they die.* Who is writing of whom?

3. *No apology is needed for telling again the story of Stott's career. Certain details will still be familiar, it is true, the historic details which can never be forgotten while cricket holds place as our national game.... There are many people alive in Ailesworth today who can remember the sturdy, freckled, sandy-haired boy who used to go round with the morning and evening papers; the boy who was to change the fortunes of a county. Ginger was phenomenally thorough in all he undertook.* Author and book, please. For which county did Ginger Stott play? On which cricketer is he supposed to have been modelled, and on which remarkable person the subject of the book, his son?

4. *It was not a time for half-measures. He could not go home. He must carry the thing through, now that he had begun, and find something definite to do, now that he had to support himself. There seemed to be only one opening for him. What could he do, he asked himself. Just one thing. He would have to become a professional. Could he get taken on? That was the question. It was impossible that he should play for his own county on his residential qualification. He could not appear as a professional in the same team in which his brothers were playing as amateurs. He must stake all on his birth qualification for Surrey.* Who was he? and the author and the book?

5. Finally, rather a cheeky one, and I take refuge in the usual excuse that it is Christmas. This letter appeared in *The Times* on August 19 this year, in the course of a correspondence about what batsmen talk about when they have a chat in the middle of the pitch.

Sir. Not all mid-wicket conferences concern matters of import. Last season, I once came to the wicket when the score was 12 for 5. The other batsman, who had been there from the outset, solemnly beckoned me to mid-wicket to give, I assumed, some useful advice as to what I should do. "I'm sorry to trouble you," he said, "but I've just lost a fly-button. Would you mind keeping a look-out for it?" Unfortunately, I did not remain long enough to assist him in the search.

Yours faithfully,

DAVID A. PEARL

Captain, Poet's and Peasants' Cricket Club, Lincoln's Inn

As you will see from Mr Pearl's careful punctuation, which this newspaper carefully reproduced, this admirable club has many Peasants, but only one Poet. Who is the Poet?

1981

1981 was a great year for English cricket; rather less so for Alan Gibson. It had begun unpromisingly, with death, controversy and defeat in the West Indies. Ken Barrington, England's hugely popular tour manager was struck down by a heart attack during the Barbados Test, the Test in Guyana had to be called off, because of the host government's refusal to accept Robin Jackman, with his strong South African connections, as a member of the England team, and the series was lost by two matches to nil, albeit against a vastly stronger side. Under the circumstances, it is hardly surprising that in his regular features for *The Times*, Alan chose to dwell on happier times in the past, as with his comparison between the two greatest county sides – Surrey in the 50s and Yorkshire in the 30s – and in recalling his own salad days, as a member of the Oxford Crocodiles touring side.

The year saw the introduction of some important changes in domestic cricket. The 100-over restriction on first innings in championship matches was scrapped, and not before time; NatWest took over the sponsorship of the senior one-day competition from Gillette; pitches were fully covered, in county as well as Test matches; and there was Sunday play in the Tests for the first time. However, some things were just the same – including the spring weather, the train service via Didcot and the Oxford Parks in early season!

Alan had never much enjoyed the Sunday afternoon 'thrash and bash', as he called it, and by this stage in his career had reached an accommodation with *The Times* that he should not be expected to cover more than two or three 40-over matches per season. His first of 1981 took him to the County Ground, Taunton, for Somerset against Essex. It also provided him with his first sight of the County Ground's new pavilion, which had been completed during the winter. You will not be surprised to discover that he hated it!

The Times was also accommodating in the matter of his schedule. He was nearly 58 now, and increasingly lame. He disliked long train journeys and didn't much enjoy staying away from home. So his cricket itinerary was mainly restricted to south of Birmingham. Only once during 1981 did he venture any further north – to Derbyshire, for the county's Benson and Hedges preliminary round match against Scotland – and with the championship front-runners mostly playing their home games beyond what had become his normal compass, he often found himself covering relatively inconsequential matches, simply because they were close to home. However, it was the rain, rather than any intrinsic lack of interest, that reduced so many of the early season championship matches of 1981 almost to the level of farce.

From the beginning of June onwards, the weather improved and with it, the quality and interest of the cricket. The Australian tourists had arrived by now. Alan had seen them briefly on the one day's play that was possible in their match against Somerset at Taunton:

'Hughes made a big hit into St. James' churchyard, without cracking a stained glass window on the bounce as Clive Lloyd once did,' he wrote in his *Cricketer* Diary. 'Botham bowled an impressive spell during the afternoon, encouraging to his supporters, who down here are numerous, though a touch anxious.'

The reason for their anxiety was their hero's dramatic loss of form since taking over the England captaincy from Brearley, the previous season. Not only that, but his captaincy had won few plaudits, and the newspapers were full of speculation as

Tests
England
beat Australia
3-1, with two draws

Championship
1 Nottinghamshire
2 Sussex
3 Somerset
4 Middlesex
5 Essex
6 Surrey

Sunday League
1 Essex
2 Somerset
3 Warwickshire
4 Derbyshire
5 Sussex
6 Hampshire

NatWest Final
Derbyshire
beat Northamptonshire

Benson & Hedges Final
Somerset
beat Surrey

Most first-class runs
1 Zaheer Abbas
2 G.M. Turner
3 Javed Miandad

Most first-class wickets
1 R.J. Hadlee
2 E.E. Hemmings
3 J. Garner

to whether he should step down, and by whom be replaced. Alan was firmly in the Brearley camp, although whether comparing him to a mahogany dining table will actually have advanced his captaincy cause, I am not entirely sure. But it was at least a sign that Alan's spirits were reviving, as was his description of Surrey's Pat Pocock, taking the opportunity for some serious batting, after being sent in as nightwatchman in Surrey's game with Worcestershire.

The first Test of what was to be a six-match Ashes series was played at Trent Bridge, staring on June 18 and was won, slightly unexpectedly, by Australia. Alan had previewed the series for *The Times* the previous Saturday, although neither he nor anyone else could have possibly have imagined the dramas that would unfold, not least at Headingley in July. That, of course, was Botham's match, and it was no coincidence at all that Brearley – who somehow always managed to bring the best out of this remarkable cricketer – had taken over as captain by then.

While Australia were winning the first Test, Alan was at Bristol, for Gloucestershire against Sri Lanka, the match in which Jack Russell made his first-class debut and an immediate impression. Somerset against Surrey at Taunton was another happy occasion, with both the Demon of Frome and the Shoreditch Sparrow in fine mid-season fettle, and then, on July 8, really the only 'big cricket' that Alan saw the entire season: Somerset's Benson and Hedges semi-final against Kent. Somerset would, of course, go on to win the final; Garner's five for 14 and Richards' 132 not out proving far too much for Surrey.

From then to the end of the season, Alan's cricketing itinerary proved to be interesting, rather than spectacular. He noted the potential of a young Gladstone Small, in Warwickshire's game with Surrey; and rain on the second day of Gloucestershire against Essex provided the opportunity to catch up on Jack Davey's progress in retirement. A week in bed with a tummy bug at the end of July was a low point, although he seems to have appreciated the cricket all the more once he had recovered and was heading for the Oval. Then, with the championship building to a climax, Alan somehow persuaded the *Times* sports editor to let him cover a Minor Counties match – Devon against Cornwall at Exeter – in the expectation that Jack Davey would be playing.

Somerset had a good campaign in the championship, as well as winning the B&H. They never quite looked like winning it, but victory against Yorkshire at Bramall Lane on August 4 – their first on Yorkshire soil since 1902 – marked the start of a run which saw them win seven of their last nine matches, and equal their best ever championship placing of third. Victory against Warwickshire in the last match of the season, after a full day had been lost to rain, provided an appropriate finale for a team that was, under Brian Rose's leadership, at last playing to its full potential.

But the championship had gone to Nottinghamshire. Sussex put up a gallant fight, but the combination of Richard Hadlee, Clive Rice and the Trent Bridge wicket proved, in the end, irresistible. When Glamorgan were seen off by ten wickets inside two days on September 14, it was all over. Even though Sussex also won their final game, against Yorkshire, they still came up two points short. Alan Gibson had a soft spot for Sussex, and would have liked them to have won.

The best ever county team 1981

On the morning that my colleague, John Woodcock, quoted *Wisden* as saying that Surrey in the 1950s were probably the best ever county cricket team, I was rung up from Yorkshire and instructed in irate tones to write a piece explaining that they could not compare with Yorkshire of the 1930s.

I was born in Yorkshire, and the county's team of those years were my boyhood heroes. So I set out on the task enthusiastically, and knowing that the records would provide strong evidence.

Yorkshire never equalled Surrey's seven consecutive championships, but from 1931 to 1939 they won seven out of nine. If you include 1946, when the side were inevitably much changed, they won eight out of 10. The breaks in the run were made by Lancashire in 1934 (when Yorkshire were much disturbed by Test match calls) and Derbyshire in 1936.

The opening batsmen in the early 1930s were Holmes and Sutcliffe. Holmes was succeeded by Mitchell for a season or two, then the young Hutton took over as Sutcliffe's partner, with Mitchell at No 3. Leyland would usually come next, followed by Barber.

Every one of these men played for England as a batsman. The wicketkeeper, Arthur Wood, played for England in the last two seasons before the war. He was a handy man to have in the lower-middle order.

The captain, effectively from 1932, though he was not officially appointed until the following year, was A.B. Sellers. He had never played for Yorkshire until he was considered as captain. This was the custom in those days, when an amateur captain was thought necessary.

Sellers proved an acquisition as a player as well as a dashing captain. In his one season after the war, when Yorkshire's batting was wobbly, he moved up to No 3 to show the youngsters how it should be done and was very successful. He would have scored many more runs had he batted higher throughout his career, but his value was probably greater at No 7, where he could apply his mind to attack or defence as seemed appropriate.

Sellers was one of the great captains, though he could upset his professionals occasionally by his sheer driving ruthlessness. He once made Verity and Bowes bowl in a Lancashire match when neither was fit; not with happy results. He was one of the best and bravest of close fieldsmen.

Surrey and Yorkshire may be given equal marks for captaincy; but Yorkshire must have been much stronger in batting. Take away May (a substantial subtraction) and the Surrey batsmen of the 1950s had nothing comparable to offer. I think we may give equal marks for fielding as well, with a possible bias in wicket-keeping to Yorkshire because of Wood.

Where Surrey score is in bowling. They had Bedser (two Bedsers, though Eric was as valuable for his batting as his bowling), Laker, Lock, Loader and Surridge. On the Oval pitches of the time they were overwhelming. Yorkshiremen (and Australians) will tell you that the Oval was rigged for Surrey's bowlers. It was very different from the Oval pitches before the war, when in good weather a side winning the toss felt ashamed if they did not score 400. But those bowlers took large numbers of wickets on every sort of pitch all over the world. What had Yorkshire of the 1930s to match them?

There was Verity, who was at least as good a slow left-hander as Lock. I would say rather better, but that may be prejudice. There was Bowes, who was a better fast bowler (more successful in his later seasons as a fast-medium seamer) than Loader. But Bowes could not, in either capacity, do for Yorkshire what Alec Bedser did for Surrey.

Yorkshire never had an equivalent to Alec Bedser. Bowes was a fine player, and his record against Bradman bears examination, but Bedser has to come first. Nor can Yorkshire really match Laker: their off-spin early in the 1930s depended on Macaulay; when Macaulay retired, Ellis Robinson came along.

Macaulay was a fighter. In 1926 Macartney thought him the most dangerous bowler in England and scored a hundred against him before lunch to make sure that England did not pick him again. Macaulay bowled variations between slow off-spin and what we would now call off-cutters.

He had a quick temper, was engaging, irritating at times and he was a good man to have on your side when things were bad. He played only once against Australia, at Leeds in 1926, and took one for 123 in 32 overs (the wicket was Macartney's). He saved the match for England with an innings of 76 – he went in at No 10 – and had a partnership of 108 with George Geary (who had taken two for 130).

He was unlucky, or possibly silly, not to have played for England more. But you could not put him in the same class as Laker. His successor, Ellis Robinson (no relation to Emmott Robinson, who retired in the early 1930s), was a sound county off-spinner who never played for England, though many thought him unlucky not to be chosen for the tour of Australia in 1946.

Yorkshire's other principal bowler in those years was Frank Smailes, another who mixed off-cutters with spin, and a useful batsman. He was selected against Australia at Old Trafford in 1938, when there was no play because of four days' rain. The final England side had not been picked, so he never won a cap, except for one against India after the war.

Another Yorkshireman chosen for that Old Trafford Test (and bound to be picked because he was the wicketkeeper) was P.A. Gibb, who was a great success as a batsman in South Africa that winter, but had to wait until after the war for his solitary Australian cap. Norman Yardley, a Cambridge contemporary of Gibb's, was twice twelfth man for England in 1938 and an England captain afterwards.

In 1938-9 Yorkshire were choosing from 14 when all were available, as they usually were after the university term was over: Sellers, Sutcliffe, Hutton, Mitchell, Leyland, Barber, Yardley, Gibb, Verity, Bowes, Smailes, Wood, Robinson and Turner. All of these except Robinson, Turner and Sellers were or became Test players. Sellers had to make do with being a selector.

I remember a broadcast by C.B. Fry at about that time in which he said that Turner was just the kind of tidy all-rounder needed to tighten up England. There were five Yorkshiremen in the England side at the Oval in 1938, the side who won by an innings and 579 and, as Cardus observed, if Sutcliffe had been playing instead of Edrich the chances were that England would not have been less fortunately placed.

It was a staggering richness. And yet – I hope I shall not be drummed out of Sheffield for ever – I think I would just give the palm to Surrey because of the bowling. Or perhaps I could take refuge in the compromise which a friend of Ian Peebles once suggested: Yorkshire under the old l-b-w law, Surrey under the new.

Laker would have had much difficulty in getting Sutcliffe out under the old law, but the new one (new then) gave Herbert some trouble. And even Hutton was never at his happiest against off-spin. Yes, after much travail and pointless reflection, I think Surrey have it.

Jack Crapp – an obituary

The death of Jack Crapp – while not unexpected, for he had been in uncertain health for some time – will grieve a great many cricketers not only in Gloucestershire, for whom he played, nor Cornwall, where he was born. He is, so far, the only Cornishman to have played for England – though he had some hopes that there might soon be another, Richards, the young Surrey wicket-keeper. He also recollected that Harris, of Middlesex and Nottinghamshire, did not miss by much.

Crapp was born at St Columb Major (he always stressed that it was St Columb *Major*, not St Columb *Minor*) in 1912. He came into the Gloucestershire side in the mid-thirties and in all scored over 23,000 runs, with 38 centuries, and played seven times for England. He later became an umpire and reached the Test match panel. He was a left-hander, and his natural style was aggressive, but in his early years he had a reputation for being a slow batsman.

This was undeserved. He *looked* slow, and the clock seemed sometimes to confirm the judgment, but you must remember that the leading Gloucestershire batsmen of those years were Hammond and Barnett. Barnett was always a dasher and Hammond, even if he did not happen to be scoring particularly quickly, liked to keep the bowling. The job of a young Gloucestershire batsman, if he was partnering Hammond (which Crapp constantly did), was chiefly to be alert at the bowler's end, waiting for the call on the fifth or sixth ball of the over.

After the war, we saw a different man. The war robbed him, as it did so many others, of his best years, but he was still good enough to be chosen for England in 1948. That was against Bradman's mighty Australians, not the best moment to win your first cap; but he would not flinch from Lindwall and Miller and did enough to be chosen for the successful tour to South Africa the following winter. His Test batting average was 29, respectable for the circumstances.

Crapp was a quiet man, which is not to say he was withdrawn; he never married, which I always felt was a pity, because he would have made such a good father. He could face a party when necessary, but I think what he most enjoyed, latterly, was a few pints in a pub, with two or three old friends, sharing memories. He did more listening than talking, though when moved he could talk well, with the Cornish burr which he never lost.

I was present at a small dinner, not long before his death, at which he was the guest of honour. He came on the strict understanding that he was not to be asked to speak, but after his health had been drunk he did, compellingly.

He was not envious of modern cricketers, but thought that since the top ones were being paid all this money, they should mind their manners a bit more. The only other thing I can recall him being cross about was the way in which people would make jokes about his name.

In 1953 he became Gloucestershire's first professional captain. This was not a role that suited him, though he was proud of the honour. He was not ruthless enough: the worrying made him ill and brought out a skin disease, which I am sure was psychomatic. He was happy enough, after a couple of seasons, to hand over to George Emmett, whom he loyally supported.

To Oxford in April

I made my way to Oxford from High Littleton yesterday with some slight difficulty, leaving a cottage without electricity behind me. On the train I was reading the current copy of *The Cricketer*, and found myself described as "a fearless meanderer". Almost at once we drew into Didcot.

I doubted if these were fortunate omens of a new season. However, the delay did not matter, as there was no play until after tea. The weather at Oxford itself was not unpleasant, but there had been so much snow and rain on Sunday that the ground was too wet to begin sooner.

NEXT DAY

There were two brief spells of cricket in the morning, before the rain, always threatening, closed in. It abated in the afternoon, and the umpires conscientiously waited until 4 o'clock before they abandoned the match. They might well have done so earlier. Nobody wanted to play, and there were no spectators.

I can foresee many more wasted hours, should the summer turn out to be a bad one, sacrificed to the belief that pointless and uncomfortable cricket is better than no cricket at all.

The new Taunton pavilion

It is well equipped internally, but ugly. It looks like an executive annexe to a gasworks. Quite apart from spoiling the view of the Quantocks, it has no architectural distinction and shows no feeling for the tradition and character of Somerset cricket. A great chance has been missed.

Bristol in the rains of May

Gloucestershire will have neither bowled nor received a ball in the County Championship until June is in.

I had spent two wet days at Worcester, and thought that I might as well stand the third watching the rain fall nearer home. As a matter of fact, there was just a chance of play in the morning. For several hours the weather had been dry, and the umpires were encouraged to announce an inspection at 12 o'clock, with hopes of a start after an early lunch. No good. It rained again just before the inspection. "Hath the rain a father? Or who have begotten the drops of dew?"

Gloucestershire are due to play the Australians today, and as I write, surveying the sodden ground, it does not seem probable that they will. However, Gloucestershire keeps its spirits up, and if I may continue quoting from the Book of Job: "He sayeth among the trumpets, Ha, ha; and he smelleth the battle afar off, the thunder of the captains and the shouting."

To Gloucester in late June

It was a lovely morning, a real haymaking morning. The country lanes were full of haywains, all looking as if they were about to topple over, and I think there must have been one on the railway line to Gloucester, because the train stopped dead for half an hour about a couple of miles outside the city. All the birds started singing in the sudden silence, just like Adlestrop.

NEXT DAY

There was once a Baptist minister in the Isle of Wight who was invited to return for a visit to his former flock. He began his sermon by saying how pleasant it was to see the old Cowes faces again. I always feel a little like that at the Gloucester Festival. The same kittle-kattle turn up year by year, with the same broad smiles, the same red faces and the same fearful boring jokes. Cricket at Gloucester has clumsy and inadequate facilities, but nowhere is there more sustained loyalty to the county and the game.

Zaheer needed only 35 runs to reach his thousand in June, and duly got them. This is rightly considered a less memorable feat than a thousand in May, but Zaheer, because of the weather, did not have the opportunity to play a single first-class innings in May. Furthermore, so far as the records can tell us, only Grace and Hammond among Gloucestershire batsmen have scored a thousand runs in a month before.

Bristol in the rains of July

Although we had very little cricket, the day was not wasted altogether – few are, for me, at the Bristol ground. I saw Grahame Parker, once revered on all Gloucestershire grounds as Puff the Magic Dragon, looking very fit and not at all puffy, and several members of the JJ? Society who reported that Jack Davey was taking wickets for Tavistock and might be in the Devon side this year.

Plans have provisionally been made for an expedition to watch him, so that the old cry – when he goes in to bat – "Put them to the sword, Jack" will ring out again over the green fields of the West.

To Lord's in August sunshine

The weather was lovely. I was glad to be back on the trail after a week in sick bay, if that is not a mixed metaphor. On the train up from Bath, I put aside *The Times*, yes, in the middle of the second leader, and lifted up my head to see the countryside, where the valleys laughed and sang. You could see the barley rippling, as all properly brought up barley should. Lord's itself looked at its best, and quite a lot of people – enough to make a substantial crowd at, say, Taunton – had come to enjoy it.

Philip Mead (Hampshire)

An unceasing complaint today is the slow rate at which overs are bowled. In Mead's case, the problem was the slow rate at which overs were *batted.* Before every ball, he went through a careful routine, involving tugs at his cap and pads, and a series of little steps from outside the leg-stump to his guard. This was often called a 'shuffle' of his feet, but 'shuffle' implies something random, and Mead's inch-worm movements were deliberate and constant. I doubt if Lance Gibbs, in however much of a hurry, could have bowled an over to Mead in less than three minutes.

I saw Mead but a few times, towards the end of his career, and certainly the thing I most remember about him is his slowness. Trying to refresh my memory from *Wisden*, I must have seen him score, in 1933, 70 at Lord's and 61 at Leyton. *Wisden* says, on both occasions, that he batted 'steadily'. But my recollections are not really evidence, partly because small boys like hitters best – unless they have personal affiliations, and I had none with Hampshire – and partly because he had the *reputation* of being a slow player. Thus everyone was ready to point this out when the reputation was justified, and on occasions – not so frequent – when he scored quickly, the comment was: 'Fancy Mead batting like that!'

He must have felt it was a hard life, though he was an equable man. He was not Hampshire-born (Surrey, his native county, let him go) but there was an air of the traditional Hampshireman about him: something like one of those country characters around White Ladies in the novels of Dornford Yates. Solid – unhurried – resolute – loyal. These are the kind of words that come to mind. But he could always contentedly shrug off disappointment with the thought of all those runs.

His later years were marred by the loss of his sight, an affliction which he accepted with his usual dour – and yet not graceless – courage.

Eric Hollies (Warwickshire)

Hollies was a leg-spinner, though younger readers of *The Cricketer* will scarcely remember what that is. He did not, in his approach to the wicket, a few ambling strides, *look* like a leg-spinner. Slow left-armers, yes, they were expected to amble, but leg-spinners were expected to look menacing. O'Reilly bowled with a run-up and an expression on his face which caused him to be nicknamed 'Tiger'. Grimmett, less extravagantly, always had a subtle menace, and the hint of a shadowed scowl about him. Douglas Wright, with his various and complicated run-ups, always looked as if he was taking the business very seriously. Hollies just ambled, with the air of a man who hopes for the best, and would not place a bet on it. He was of average build, an amiable-looking fair-haired man. He did not give the impression of youth when young, nor of age when he was old.

R.J. Hayter, writing of him as one of *Wisden*'s Five Cricketers of the Year in 1955, said, 'He persuades his opponents out with an almost apologetic air.'

Colin McCool (Somerset)

I do not know who was responsible for fetching him from his Queensland milk-round to Somerset. (In case this should meet his eye, I must explain that a milk-roundsman in the remoter parts of Queensland is a very posh chap, selling a great many things besides milk: more like a bloated capitalist than your friendly morning milkman in Somerset.)

But he still liked playing cricket, and was tempted back to England to play in the Lancashire League, and qualify for Somerset. While he was qualifying, the regulations were changed, so that he had to wait an extra year before he could play in championship matches. It was then 1955, when he was 40 years old. There was much gloomy talk in the bars of Taunton and Bath about investing in an old man. Nevertheless, he gave Somerset five years of splendid service. He bore the burden of a frail batting side, and scored about 1,500 runs a year for them, taking nearly 50 wickets as well, and holding about 140 catches, almost always in the slips.

Colin McCool, I am proud to say, became a warm friend of mine during his years in Somerset (and Devon, I must add, not forgetting the Torquay Festival, and some evenings at the Cott Inn, Dartington). He did not quite come to terms with the West Country, as Sammy Woods had done, long before, or Bill Alley did, soon afterwards. Woods and Alley settled here. McCool, his five years up, went back to Australia. He missed the sunshine. 'There's no winter,' he said, 'and the beer's better; and the b… off-spinners don't turn.'

I think an additional reason was that he found some difficulty in accepting the conventions of English cricket, as it was then. There was a Somerset committee-member, who liked and admired him, and would greet him in the morning with 'Morning, McCool'. The committee-member was seeking to be courteous. He would have thought it pompous to say 'Mr McCool', and impertinent to say Colin. But it infuriated Colin. He thought it was a reflection on his status. He would have preferred something like 'Hi, Col, you old bastard'. The worlds were too far apart.

Younis directs morning rush hour

THE OVAL: Surrey, with seven first innings wickets in hand, are 245 runs behind Worcestershire

The pavilion at the Oval is often more stimulating conversationally than at Lord's. The topics are more varied. "You must understand," I heard it firmly said, "that the Swedish are tomtits." I could not help wondering about the context but thought it impolite to stay and concluded that it must bear some reference to the Shoreditch sparrow, whom it was a pleasure to see playing again.

However, it was Clarke who took the first two wickets, bowling both Turner and Neale with swinging yorkers when the score was 22. Ever since he and Surrey parted, not on entirely amicable terms, Younis, who came in next, has relished scoring runs against them. He made 85 by lunch, out of a total of 138 for two, and reached his 100 soon afterwards. He played his best strokes and there was not much Surrey could do about it. At the other end, Scott was staunch.

After his 100, Younis became a little casual and was smartly caught at midwicket off the persevering Jackman. That was in the 46th over, 175 for three. Once he was out, the innings faltered. Hemsley was bowled by Thomas and Scott was neither nimble nor experienced enough to cope with Intikhab. When Patel was caught at the wicket, in the 62nd over, the score was 212 for six, disappointing for Worcestershire after the morning splendour.

Younis was a little lucky with several airy hits to the legside and might have been caught at the wicket had Richards been playing. Richards had a damaged toe, which is not expected to keep him out for long, and Roope was keeping wicket, which, as a natural fielder anywhere, he did well.

Scott, a Londoner aged 22, was making his first appearance and it is one he will remember happily. He played exactly the right game while Younis was in, calm and deferential. It would have been too much to expect that he could have taken charge after Younis was out. Worcestershire needed somebody to do so but nobody did.

The pitch was not difficult, though the ball swung occasionally under the fluctuating clouds. The spin bowlers found a little turn and I daresay Gifford will get something out of it before the end. It was good to see Intikhab bowling again, the last of the Mohicans. I do not think the Mohicans had mastered the art of leg spin but I seem to remember they were a subtle and twisty lot.

Intikhab had Gifford leg-before after tea, when Worcestershire were beginning to make progress again, and then dismissed Alleyne, a splendid catch just inside the boundary by Pocock. That was 255 for eight. The innings ended at 273 in the 88th over. Surrey were pleased to have made such a good recovery but Worcestershire have the runs on the board and the clouds were threatening again in the evening.

Furthermore, Surrey lost three wickets in the last 45 minutes. The light was not good and Alleyne bowled fast. Somebody will have to play an innings tomorrow, and no tomtit either.

Pocock has another of his proper innings

THE OVAL: Worcestershire, with all their second innings wickets in hand, lead Surrey by 130 runs

Despite all the regulations for covering, and the new devices which are employed to dry the ground, the rain will have an irresistible say. There had been a lot of it in the night, and no play was possible until 2.30. Surrey began at 28 for three, 245 behind. The pitch, to begin with, played straightforwardly, though it became a little trickier later on. The outfield was slow and slippery.

Roope and Pocock were batting. Roope was, theoretically, Surrey's principal hopeful. He played some good strokes, and looked to be settling in, but was the next out, bowled by Cumbes, four for 85 in the 30th over. It was a poor stroke. Meanwhile, Pocock was proceeding with an assured majesty, rather like Peter May out of form. I have known Pocock several times before enjoy the luxury of playing a proper innings after being sent in as nightguard.

At tea, 37 overs bowled, Surrey were 115 for four, Pocock still austerely in command, with Smith going vigorously at the other end. Smith was caught in the slips soon afterwards. The question now was whether anyone could stay with Pocock. He tapped the pitch thoughtfully, walked along it to give paternal advice to young Lynch, drew his head loftily away from a bouncer by Alleyne. Alleyne was getting irritated and hit Pocock in the box. He picked himself up in the slow and dignified way so characteristic of Hobbs, and, after another tap or two on the pitch, was ready to resume. Pridgeon also bowled him a nasty one, but when nightwatchmen have advanced so far they cannot expect immunity.

I thought Gifford was the likeliest bowler to get him out, and so he did, in his first over, Pocock making a hasty swing towards long-on in the hope of reaching his 50 in style. It was not Pocock's largest innings, but I bet it was one he will remember with satisfaction. The Oval crowd, though tiny, roused itself to an appreciation which was, *pro rata*, as warm as anything ever given to Barrington.

At 150, Thomas was splendidly caught from a skier which went behind the bowler. Lynch batted well, and the Shoreditch Sparrow made a delicate cut, worthy of Pocock, but the innings was over at 5.50, Surrey 103 behind.

Declaration revives a dying duck

THE OVAL: Surrey (17 pts) beat Worcestershire (7 pts) by four wickets

A match which had looked a dying duck in the middle of the afternoon had an exciting finish, Surrey winning with a couple of overs to spare after it had seemed beyond them, and thereby going to the top of the championship. Worcestershire, 130 runs ahead overnight, with all their second innings wickets in hand, declared at two o'clock, the score 168 for two, setting Surrey to make 272 in three and a half hours. This was about four and a half runs to the over.

Since the pitch had been playing easily, this was a generous declaration by Turner. No doubt he had in mind the weather. It did not rain, but the light was often poor.

Butcher was caught in the slips in the fifth over. Knight was in next, much depending upon him. He had some anxious moments to begin with, but settled in and played well. All the same, at tea the score was only 79 for one, after 31 overs.

Afterwards, Knight made a brave effort to get things going. The 100 came up in the twenty-sixth over, and his own 50 in the twenty-eighth. Worcestershire bowled their spinners in the hope of picking up a wicket or two, and Gifford got Knight's, caught at long leg in the thirty-fifth over, with the score at 134. Knight was not the first man to misjudge one of those innocent-looking near half-volleys from Gifford.

Clinton's innings had been developing nicely, and he reached his 50 in the thirty-seventh over. With 20 overs left, the score was 145 for two, with 127 needed. Lynch batted in a vigorous manner from the start, but was bowled by Gifford at 173. Clarke now came in and hit Gifford for four and six from the first two balls he received. Looking back, I am inclined to think these were the decisive moments of the match. Clinton was caught at midwicket at 183. Surrey needed 59 in 10 overs. Clarke was caught at the wicket, off Alleyne, at 219. Intikhab was caught at cover almost at once. That was 220 for six.

Thirty-seven were needed in six overs, 22 in four. The target was coming in sight again. Worcestershire became a little rattled in their bowling and fielding. Smith batted very well, hardly making a false stroke, despite the stress, and with Thomas saw it through.

Surrey v Worcestershire, The Oval, 10, 11 & 12 June 1981

Surrey won by four wickets

Worcestershire

* G.M. Turner	b Clarke	21	run out	73
M.S. Scott	b Intikhab	46	c Smith b Intikhab	52
P.A. Neale	b Clarke	0	*not out*	12
Younis Ahmed	c Thomas b Jackman	116	*not out*	24
E.J.O. Hemsley	b Thomas	5		
D.N. Patel	c Roope b Intikhab	13		
N. Gifford	c Roope b Intikhab	17		
+ P.B. Fisher	*not out*	28		
H.L. Alleyne	c Pocock b Intikhab	10		
A.P. Pridgeon	b Intikhab	3		
J. Cumbes	c Roope b Jackman	4		
	b 2, lb 4, w 1, nb 3	10	lb 5, nb 2	7
		273	(2 wkts, dec)	**168**

1/21, 2/22, 3/175, 4/188, 5/199, 6/212, 7/245, 8/255, 9/258, 10/273
1/125, 2/130

Clarke	21	3	44	2	11	4	15	0
Jackman	19.2	4	74	2	4	0	17	0
Thomas	17	5	51	1	7	0	35	0
Knight	11	4	28	0	7	1	21	0
Intikhab	19	3	66	5	14	1	49	1
Pocock					8	2	24	0

Surrey

A.R. Butcher	c Scott b alleyne	3	c Scott b Alleyne	7
G.S. Clinton	lbw b Pridgeon	1	c Hemsley b Alleyne	69
* R.D.V. Knight	lbw b Alleyne	3	c Pridgeon b Gifford	62
+ G.R.J. Roope	b Cumbes	38		
P.I. Pocock	b Gifford	46		
D.M. Smith	c Turner b Pridgeon	23	*not out*	42
M.A. Lynch	b Pridgeon	33	b Gifford	16
D.J. Thomas	c Cumbes b Pridgeon	5	*not out*	29
Intikhab Alam	run out	1	c Pridgeon b Gifford	0
S.T. Clarke	c Cumbes b Gifford	6	b Alleyne	24
R.D. Jackman	*not out*	2		
	lb 1, w 1, nb 7	9	lb 13, w 3, nb 9	25
		170	(6 wkts)	**274**

1/3, 2/5, 3/17, 4/85, 5/115, 6/131, 7/150, 8/154, 9/166, 10/170
1/15, 2/134, 3/173, 4/183, 5/219, 6/220

Alleyne	17	5	46	2	18	4	64	3
Pridgeon	22.3	6	49	4	12	0	61	0
Cumbes	9	0	40	1	4	1	10	0
Patel	1	0	5	0	6	0	31	0
Gifford	6	1	21	2	16.4	1	83	3

Umpires: W.L. Budd and P.J. Eele

Gladstone Small

THE OVAL: Surrey v Warwickshire

I have written about this young Barbadian before. He is a fastish bowler, who will become faster as he develops, and he is not as yet very accurate. But it is a comforting thought, if you approve of the regulations, that in a few years' time he will be qualified to play for England. His first name is Gladstone. The early editions of the London evening paper had a headline "Gladstone bags five". This must have been the biggest publicity for the Grand Old Man since, in 1880, he was elected for three parliamentary seats simultaneously.

Jack Russell

BRISTOL: Gloucestershire v Sri Lankans

There was another Gloucestershire debutant, Russell, who is 17 years old and comes from Stroud. With both Brassington and Stovold unfit, Gloucestershire badly needed a wicket-keeper, so out went the emergency call to Stroud. Russell was due to take an A-level examination yesterday, but the spirit of W.G., who never cared much for book-learning, commanded him (he will be allowed to take the examination later).

After an understandably nervous start, Russell kept very well later in the day, and made a smart stumping.

THIRD DAY

The boy Russell again kept wicket well. I am sure he has a distinguished future if he cares about the game, though it may not be with Gloucestershire, since Brassington, one of the best in the country, is not yet 27. Brassington's Achilles tendon injury is likely to keep him out for another fortnight, but Stovold is fit again, so Russell can return to Stroud, with justifiable pride, and concentrate on stumping the A-level examiners.

The value of the championship

TAUNTON: Somerset v Hampshire

Some destructive bowling by Garner in the afternoon and early evening gave Somerset their conclusive win before six o'clock. This match was important to both sides, since both still have a chance of the championship: it was especially important for Somerset, who have never won it.

One championship is still worth more than all the one-day competitions put together. I speak in cricketing terms, though it perhaps might apply also to the sponsorship: nobody has suggested that Schweppes does anything to damage your health, though cigarettes and even your friendly neighbourhood bank manager easily might.

Phil Edmonds

LORD'S: Middlesex v Yorkshire

Edmonds bowled long and persistently. I have always admired his cricket, though I think his field manners are deteriorating. If you ever hear a furious instruction to "Catch him!" when the ball has been near neither bat nor fieldsman, you can bet Edmonds is bowling. Brian Close only used to do this when he had headed the ball on from short leg.

Hartley and Bairstow provided a valuable partnership, secured the second batting point, in the 86th over, and set out in pursuit of the third. It seemed rather a forlorn chase, but Bairstow is in splendid form at present, and after he had hit a six into the pavilion in the 99th over, only one was needed from the last. Edmonds bowled it. He appealed, solitarily, for leg before from the first two balls. "Now for the hat trick!" cried a voice full of Sheffield sarcasm.

It was an ill-omened remark. Hartley was bowled by the third, Carrick stumped off the fourth. Stevenson was nearly bowled by the fifth, and run out off the last.

A covered pitch

TAUNTON: Somerset v Essex

Somerset's chances of winning the championship, something they have never done and would like to do more than anything else, have not arithmetically vanished, but are now remote. They failed to bowl Essex out yesterday, and the match ended quietly with six of the last twenty overs left to play.

We did not begin until 1.45. There had been heavy rain in the night, and again in the morning, but by then the sun was shining, which it continued to do, quite warmly, for most of the afternoon. It was an interesting example of the pros and cons of covering pitches.

Uncovered, the pitch would have provided one of the traditional "stickies" of years ago, and Essex might have been bowled out in an hour. Covered, it enabled play to start at least an hour earlier. This gave Somerset more time to bowl Essex out, but less help.

My old friend, Bill Andrews, as voluble and cheerful as ever, told me at tea, in between reminiscences of Bradman, that the key to Essex's survival was their refusal to use the heavy roller, at the start of the innings. The Essex score then was 142 for three. Well, Bill is a man who knows his Taunton cricket, but the principal reason why Essex were surviving was an even heavier roller, Gooch. It was encouraging for England to see him in such masterful form.

David Gower, Swansea
'His dismissal was greeted by the crowd with as much
a sigh as a cheer. Brightness fell from the air.'

Demon of Frome excels at his ease

TAUNTON: Somerset, all wickets in hand, are 246 runs behind Surrey

Surrey came to Taunton as the championship leaders. Not that the leadership means very much at this stage of the season, after so drenched a May, and so chilly a June. I return to my old friends, Flanders and Swann: "In July the sun is hot. Is it shining? No it's not."

The sun did not shine yesterday, except sparsely, and a drizzle sometimes interrupted play. Somerset, who also have championship aspirations, put Surrey in, with a damp pitch and a heavy cloud.

However, Clinton and Butcher made a good start. Clinton is an improving batsman. He is beginning to play his strokes with more confidence, even against Garner, who ought to have been suited by the pitch, but whose first eleven overs cost 40 runs. The score was 83 when the first wicket fell, Butcher leg before to Dredge. The demon of Frome bowled very well, perhaps because he did not try to do too much. He took the next two wickets, Clinton caught in the slips, as was Knight, who did not look in any sort of form, all edge.

Garner took the fourth wicket, bowling Smith. At 118 for four, the word "collapse" was on our lips. But Roope and Lynch played very well, riskily at times, but not suggesting there were many tremors in the pitch. Lynch, after hitting a four over midwicket, was caught there next ball, the score then 172. Roope, nearing his fifty, was caught at the wicket. That was 184 for six. At tea, after 56 overs, Surrey were 193 for six.

They must have been quite pleased with this, in the circumstances. Eric Hill, who knows the Taunton pitch as well as anyone, had said at the beginning that he thought 150 would be a good score, but after tea Intikhab and Thomas went on cheerfully. The pitch really did not, by now, look difficult, but the clouds from the south-west were steadily mounting, and nobody can tell what the weather may yet have to say in this match.

The innings ended at 275, which left Somerset 25 minutes to bat. They had taken some good catches, made some good stops, but had not generally shown quite the elan in the field which championship contenders should possess. Their bowlers were not consistent, and provided too many no balls.

Somerset did not lose a wicket, although Rose might have been out from a skier towards the covers, which none of the fielders picked up against the dark sky.

Day of the Sparrow leaves Surrey in a good position

TAUNTON: Surrey, with eight second innings wickets in hand, lead Surrey by 168 runs

It was the day of the Sparrow and Shoreditch should be proud. Jackman took six wickets for 70 in 27 overs, and made, I estimate, 63 enthusiastic appeals. I knew he was in good form when I heard him roar in the last over on Wednesday. In his first spell yesterday he took three wickets for 10 runs.

Somerset had been 29 for no wickets overnight, 246 behind, but were soon 66 for three, including the vital wicket of Richards. There followed a stand by Denning and Roebuck. Denning held the innings together, although he batted for as many as 46 overs for his 65. Roebuck was out just before lunch: a good ball, but a bad time to get out. The score at lunch was 144 for four, in 43 overs.

Afterwards, Jackman resumed his destructive course, Popplewell and Marks were out to good catches. Intikhab, demonstrating that leg spin still has its uses, had Taylor leg-before. He also bowled Denning, and in the meantime Jackman had taken another wicket. When Jackman took his sweater, after his second long spell, and retreated to the deep field, still instinctively appealing for anything that he thought conceivable, the Somerset crowd applauded him warmly. It was just as if he came from West Bagborough, a Quantock village which in my youth had a notable reputation for chirpiness.

They also, of course, warmly applauded Denning, of Chewton Mendip, who has always been one of their favourites. It was not one of the Dasher's more dashing innings, but it served his side well in a time of need. Moseley hit a couple of good smacks through the covers, but the innings ended in the 72nd over, Somerset 85 behind.

The pitch was not really all that difficult. Perhaps the word for it would be "uneasy". The bounce of the ball varied. The weather was cloudy. There was a threat of a heavy rainstorm in the afternoon, but it passed us by, though it looked as if it was giving West Bagborough a dousing.

I must record that I watched much of the day's play from the new Taunton pavilion. It is now by far the best place from which to watch, because it is the only one from which you cannot see the confounded thing. This is not a new joke.

Surrey, batting again in poor light, lost two wickets, but are healthily placed.

Somerset's hopes depart with Richards

TAUNTON: Somerset (5 pts) drew with Surrey (7 pts)

Before the Crystal Palace was officially opened for the Great Exhibition of 1851, there was trouble with the droppings of the sparrows, dwelling in the trees within the vast building. Queen Victoria consulted the aged Duke. "Try sparrow-hawks, Ma'am." It was Wellington's last victory.

I wrote that Thursday was the day of the Sparrow, and there was a time yesterday when it seemed as if it might be the day of the Sparrow-hawk, for Richards was clobbering Jackman all over the place. Surrey had made a generous declaration at lunch, setting Somerset 305 to win, in four hours – at least, it was generous considering Richards. The pitch played pretty well, but the weather was doubtful and 20 minutes was lost in two breaks soon afterwards. Lynch had played a good innings in the morning.

Rose was leg before to Jackman in the seventh over. The imponderable Richards came next. He hit Jackman for four boundaries in swift succession. Olive played some good strokes, for himself, and sensibly gave Richards as much of the bowling as he could. The score was 51 when Olive was caught at long leg, a low one which Intikhab judged admirably.

In the last over before tea, Richards hit Thomas for three consecutive boundaries. At the interval, Somerset needed 205 in two hours, and all was possible while Richards remained. He was bowled playing onto his stumps when trying to pull Intikhab. Knight, I thought, brought on his Sparrows rather late, though they had a good bowl in the evening, because the light was usually too bad to risk the quick ones.

With Richards gone departed any hope of a Somerset victory, but Surrey still had a chance, and Roebuck and Popplewell were out soon afterwards. Marks and Denning, however, wearing helmets against the fearsome bouncers of Intikhab, Pocock and Lynch, survived until the match was safe.

Somerset v Surrey, Taunton, 1, 2 & 3 July 1981

Match drawn

Surrey

G.S. Clinton	c Richards b Dredge	66	b Garner	4
A.R. Butcher	lbw b Dredge	22	c Denning b Moseley	3
* R.D.V. Knight	c Denning b Dredge	18	c Taylor b Marks	57
G.R.J. Roope	c Taylor b Moseley	46	c Richards b Popplewell	18
D.M. Smith	b Garner	0	run out	34
M.A. Lynch	c Rosebuck b Moseley	19	*not out*	66
Intikhab Alam	b Marks	31	lbw b Dredge	0
D.J. Thomas	c Denning b Garner	26	lbw b Moseley	2
+ C.J. Richards	*not out*	5	*not out*	18
R.D. Jackman	c Roebuck b Garner	0		
P.I. Pocock	b Marks	21		
	lb 7, w 1, nb 13	21	b 5, lb 8, nb 4	17
		275	(7 wkts, dec)	**219**

1/83, 2/104, 3/117, 4/118, 5/172, 6/184, 7/248, 8/248, 9/248, 10/275
1/7, 2/18, 3/83, 4/96, 5/176, 6/176, 7/183

Garner	23	4	73	3	15	2	40	1
Moseley	18	2	69	2	15	3	47	2
Dredge	22	6	60	3	13	0	45	1
Popplewell	11	4	32	0	9	1	32	1
Marks	3.4	2	20	2	14	5	38	1

Umpires: B.J. Meyer and D.R. Shepherd

Somerset

* B.C. Rose	lbw b Jackman	35	lbw b Jackman	3
M. Olive	lbw b Jackman	19	c Intikhab b Knight	19
I.V.A. Richards	b Jackman	4	b Intikhab	68
P.M. Roebuck	c Roope b Thomas	31	c Roope b Intikhab	27
P.W. Denning	b Intikhab	65	*not out*	50
N.F.M. Popplewell	c Roope b Jackman	2	b Intikhab	5
V.J. Marks	c Smith b Jackman	1	*not out*	16
+ D.J.S. Taylor	lbw b Intikhab	4		
J. Garner	c Richards b Jackman	3		
H.R. Moseley	c Richards b Thomas	14		
C.H. Dredge	*not out*	4		
	b 5, lb 2, nb 1	8	b 5, lb 5, nb 2	12
		190	(5 wkts)	**200**

1/49, 2/59, 3/66, 4/143, 5/147, 6/153, 7/158, 8/163, 9/171, 10/190
1/18, 2/51, 3/107, 4/155, 5/165

Jackman	27	6	70	6	12	3	37	1
Thomas	16.4	5	38	2	12	0	50	0
Knight	5	0	22	0	5	1	8	1
Roope	3	0	18	0				
Pocock	6	2	13	0	12	1	29	0
Intikhab	14	6	21	2	20	4	55	3
Lynch					3	1	9	0

Jumping Jack takes leave

EXETER: Devon v Cornwall

I went down to Exeter partly because I like going there, and it is a lovely ground on a sunny day, and I have lived most of my adult life in Devon and Cornwall: but principally because I had heard that Jumping Jack Davey would be playing, and as president of the JJ? Society, I felt that it was a moment to send out the old rallying cry when he goes in to bat: "Put them to the sword, Jack!"

Alas! Though his name was there on the card, he was not present. The reasons given for this varied: he had not been picked, he was stocktaking in the Devil's Elbow at Princetown, he felt old age coming upon him, it was a misprint in the scorecard.

I favour the last explanation, because the card contained very little but misprints. Furthermore, the scoreboard was working to a different set of numbers from the card. Our only tolerably reliable source of information was Gregory Evans, a 12-year-old who handled the public address system.

Hence I submit this report with caution. Cornwall, who had just had an excellent win over Somerset II, won the toss and batted. Devon, who have not done as well as they had hoped this season, had four of them out for 39.

Cornwall made a brave but slow recovery. The fifth wicket held out until 86, a solid partnership between Bryant and Meneer, before Bryant was caught in the covers.

Meneer went on, not very excitingly, and reached his 50 in 170 minutes. He was caught and bowled for 58. At tea, when they declared, Cornwall were 163 for seven in 84 overs.

It was a pleasant, friendly, slightly disorganized occasion, as Minor Counties' matches frequently are, but the cricket was not compelling. I decided to try my luck with evensong in the cathedral, only to learn that the choir were on holiday.

Sadiq and Hignell turn it Gloucestershire's way

CHELTENHAM: Hampshire, with all first innings wickets in hand, are 368 runs behind Gloucestershire

Many have rhapsodised about the Cheltenham Cricket Festival. Cyril Holinshed, in *A hundred years of Gloucestershire cricket*, wrote of "the flurry of flannels in the sunshine, and the gay arcs of tents, glasses clinking … and, of course, the backcloth of College buildings, Gothic and gracious."

But it does all depend on the weather. I have known many Cheltenham days like that, and yesterday was another, though I have also known some grim and chilly ones, as lately as last Saturday. It was not reassuring that the clouds were coming over again in the evening.

There is a belief among Gloucestershire supporters that their side always does well at Cheltenham. It dates back to the time W.G. scored 300 here in 1876. Last year they won all three matches, which took them from almost bottom of the table to the upper middle. This year they have won their first match, and made a good start in their second.

They lost two early wickets in a good spell by Stevenson, Stovold caught in the slips, Broad leg before. The third wicket did not fall until 129, when Zaheer, looking full of belligerence, was unexpectedly bowled by Cowley. Bainbridge was caught at short mid-on when Bailey came back for his second spell, at 188. So far, Hampshire could feel reasonably satisfied with themselves, especially as they were below full strength.

But Hignell and Sadiq then took the game away from them. Sadiq had strictly no business to be playing at all. He was not among those originally chosen. However, Whitney, the young fast bowler, was summoned to join the Australians for the Test, and with Hampshire's agreement, Sadiq replaced him, even though the match had already begun.

Whitney had of course taken no active part in it. Had he bowled or fielded, I doubt if a replacement would have been justified, though Whitney would still have been entitled to answer his country's call. I was reminded of the incident long ago, when W.G. Grace hauled Midwinter away from Lord's, where he was about to open the innings for the Australians, to the Oval, to play for Gloucestershire. International matches were less important then.

Sadiq certainly enjoyed his unexpected outing, but the best batting came from Hignell, with many powerful drives. It was a pity that he missed his century. Windaybank had also played a valuable innings before the declaration came, just before six o'clock.

Dismissal of Zaheer ends Gloucestershire's hopes

BRISTOL: Somerset (20 pts) beat Gloucestershire (4 pts) by 58 runs

At the beginning of yesterday's play Gloucestershire needed 144 to beat Somerset with seven second innings wickets in hand. The weather stayed dry and even sometimes sunny. The pitch was tricky, with an uneven bounce, though not much more so than it had been throughout the match. Zaheer and Hignell were together and it did not seem impossible; but it all ended rather dismally, from a Gloucestershire point of view, soon after lunch.

Hignell was the first to go. I did not see him given out leg-before because my taxi had been trapped in some furious traffic in Bristol city centre, but as soon as I reached the ground a gateman shouted out to me, "Shameful decision!" He had not seen it himself but the word had gone around.

From better informed sources, I learnt that Hignell had been playing a long way forward to Dredge, but if a man cannot be leg-before just because he plays forward, nobody would ever be leg-before.

In any case this did not matter too much, so long as Zaheer was there. He had scored 72 when he was bowled by Dredge. He had batted better than when he has made many higher scores: it was a graceful, restrained, responsible innings. He held the key.

Once he was gone, both sides knew in their hearts who was going to win. That was 145 for five and soon, with Garner getting among the later batsmen, it was 173 for nine. Doughty hit a couple of good strokes. Graveney made a proper resistance and Childs and Wilkins made stout attempts to support him, but they could do no more than prolong the match into the afternoon – for which the caterers, I am sure, were grateful.

It had been an interesting match. I would say that it had been won by the toss, except that Graveney told me that if he had won the toss he would have put Somerset in. There was a telling innings by Lloyds on the first morning, excellent bowling by Garner, Dredge, Childs and Graveney himself, and of course there was Zaheer, keeping Gloucestershire hopes alive until the moment he was out. It looked a pretty good ball by Dredge: one up for Frome against Sialkot.

I heard one remark made by a disappointed Gloucestershire supporter, who has seen many matches against Somerset: "Well, s'pose we should ha' been cheerin' them, 'cos they've still a chance, see, and we'm none, and 'tis all in West like." And then he took out his pipe, lit it ruminatively and added: "Still, I do like beating the ..." I did not catch his last word: but it was plural and I am fairly sure it began with a B.

Asif and Knott open door

THE OVAL: Surrey, with seven first innings wickets in hand, are 215 runs behind Kent

I know that journalists are regarded as pariah-dogs, likely to communicate rabies, by most of the county cricket authorities and that the rain falleth alike upon the just and the unjust, but I was unprepared for the sign on the entrance to the press box: "This Door To Be Kept Locked At All Times".

I wondered how many starving colleagues were in there and which would be the last survivor, after they had resorted to cannibalism. If a betting shop had been handy, I would have had a fiver on the Sage of Longparish, who has a fisherman's patience.

Well, I managed to find it, aided by a kind lady who took me through the office to get in and a genial West Indian gentleman who offered me a key to get out.

Kent had lost four wickets by lunch: Johnson, Tavaré and Woolmer all caught in the slips, and Aslett at the wicket. The innings was redeemed by Asif and Knott, with assistance from Cowdrey. Cowdrey was caught at 122, another at slip, in the forty-fourth over. When Asif was out, in the fifty-fifth, the score was 192; he was leg-before to Payne, which made a change from the edged catches

Asif had some luck. Surrey fielded well on the whole, but one or two chances went down during the innings and the ball kept dropping just short, or wide, of grasping hands. Nevertheless Asif's was an innings of quality.

Knott's innings was more of character than quality. He was warmly welcomed and even his callisthenics were approved. He began quietly, venturing a stroke just now and then, but became more ambitious, and yet at the same time, in his curious way, more responsible, after Asif was out.

There was a break for bad light in the afternoon, mitigated by the tea interval. Afterwards Knott carried on and was having a swing when Monkhouse bowled him.

The Kent innings ended at 257 and they must have been pleased with it, especially as they had gone at well over three runs to the over.

They must have been more pleased in the last hour, when they took three Surrey wickets and might easily have taken more.

Colin Dredge, bowler and batsman
'The Demon of Frome'

Cheltenham

Southampton

Week ended May 22

The Australians are here, and have begun in miserable weather. There is not quite the excitement about an Australian tour that there used to be; Test matches are played too often. It will be the fifth time in seven years that we have seen them. The magic of my youth – when Australia came once every four years, and as soon as a tour was over we began discussing prospects for the next – has gone. In the Star at High Littleton, I was asked, 'Who's coming over this year, then?' and when I said 'Australia', the response was a bored 'Oh, them again'. This proliferation of Test matches (we are to have six this summer) is done in the sacred name of money; but it will get its come-uppance in another decade or two. There is such a thing as the doctrine of diminishing returns.

Week ended May 29

To Cardiff. I was astonished, after two blank days, to find that there was any play on the third, so drenched was the land as I travelled up. However, there was a bit, and Kent lost five wickets for 44. The cricket might be described as good though gargly. The details were provided for me by my friend the correspondent of the *Alexandria Advertiser* ('I write about cricket all over the world,' he threw off casually in a press-box earlier this season). Nash bowled well, or so the correspondent of the *Baltimore Bulletin* assured me. It rained in the afternoon. I had a word with Tom Cartwright, still looking remarkably fit though doleful. He asked me, 'Have you ever known a worse May?' and I had to agree – though I know it is the kind of question we have often asked before – that I had not. I was grateful to the correspondent of the *Canberra Chronicle* for a lift to the station; thence homeward, hoping that the builders had coped with the leak in my roof.

Week ended June 5

At Taunton Somerset beat Glamorgan to make sure of a place in the quarter finals of the Benson and Hedges. There was a useful innings by Denning. It is his benefit year, and in honour of the occasion he has improved his hair style. He no longer looks like a man who has been dragged through a Chewton Mendip hedge backwards; only forwards. Botham looked fit though burly.

The match between Gloucestershire and the Australians was ruined by rain, though it was agreed to give an extra day to it, but my wife and I had the pleasure of entertaining for the weekend the correspondents of the *Delhi Diurnal*, the *Ecuador Echo* and the *'Frisco Folly*. We taught them how to play the noble game of 'Donkey' with the full rigour of the game applied, and they promised to become 'Donkey' champions of Boodle's as soon as they have the time.

I usually enjoy myself at Basingstoke, and the bright sunshine helped to make the first day a happy one, though there was no rounders match to look at, over the wall, when the cricket grew dull. There was a splendid innings by Greenidge, who just failed to make his hundred. How glad Hampshire must be to have him back with them! The second day was miserable, although the players did their best. The main trouble was the bitter wind, although I suppose it did us a service by keeping the clouds rolling over for most of the day. The press tent was nearly torn away by the gale. It was a toucher who would be the first reporter manfully to say, 'I am just going outside and may be some time', for the Cutty Sark tent (a Basingstoke tradition) was only a hundred yards away, and though just as cold and windy, had its in-built protection. There was a century from Brearley. He has never quite been an elegant batsman, but has become a polished one, rather like a Victorian mahogany table, of little intrinsic beauty but shining from many years of assiduous toil. Hampshire saved the match on the third day, despite some wobbling in the afternoon. I was deeply impressed by the way David Shepherd gives batsmen out; his finger points to the heavens, unmistakably, his circumference swells nobly. He looks like Ajax defying the lightning. When he becomes a Test match umpire, as I have no doubt he will in time, and especially against the Australians, he may find (as Ajax did) that the lightning sometimes strikes back.

The Prudential one-day Tests have begun. I can't remember what has happened so far, but if I need the information I know I can rely upon the correspondent of the *Gunglywallah Gazette*.

Week ended July 3

I was pleased to see Gladstone Small do well. It reminded me that I had forgotten to send my entry to the *Times Diary*, who are running a competition for flattering remarks. I would have quoted to them Disraeli's customary reaction to strangers: 'How is the old trouble?' I shall suggest to the *Diary* a new competition, for the best remark which, while intending to be flattering, produces maximum irritation. I encountered a good one lately: 'Mr Gibson, I do want to say how much I enjoy your flowery prose.' The correspondent of the *Hobart Herald* was there with me to say if I lie. I suppose there might be better: say, a Yorkshire batsman of a few years ago greeting his captain, returning sweating after an immaculate century, 'My word, your running has improved, Geoff.'

Week ended July 10

The second Test was a disappointing draw, especially from England's point of view. Botham has been dropped as captain, and Brearley recalled in his place. The appointment of Brearley was made on the basis that he was the likeliest man to save the series against Australia. This was, in principle, a correct decision, because beating Australia should be regarded as an end in itself, not a preparation for anything else. Even if none of your best 11 is going to make the following tour, they should still be chosen. Still, it does make you wonder who is going to captain in India next winter. Brearley has repeated that he will not be available. I suppose Botham might be reappointed, if he recovers his form, though that cuts both ways for the poor chap. For if he does, there will be plenty to say, 'Just shows how much better he is when he's not captain.'

Week ended July 17

I began the week with a visit to Oxford, where the county played respectably against Glamorgan in the knock-out competition, which we are in future to know by this cacophonous name of the NatWest Trophy. There is nothing smooth and soothing about it, as there is with the name Gillette. NatWest suggests more to me the irritant midges which cop you when you are walking your dog on a summer evening in Somerset. The match was played on the Christ Church ground, partly because in the Parks no charge can be made.

The best cricket I saw in the day was played by Hobbs and Cartwright, bowling in a net, both England bowlers, both masters of their different crafts, both looking fit and happy. Tom Cartwright was typical of his time, with his accurate swing and seam. Some think Shackleton was better, but myself I would place them about level. Robin Hobbs was typical of an earlier age and a lost art: the last, and not the worst, of the English leg-spinners.

Week ended August 14

It is a pity that the Weston and Cheltenham Festivals so often coincide. I would enjoy attending both, but I have to dodge between them. The first Saturday at Cheltenham only provided a little play in the evening, far too late for *The Sunday Times*, whose idea of the best copy is 'a full, rounded report' before the captains have tossed for innings.

On Monday and Tuesday I was at Weston. It is, now that first-class cricket has been abandoned at Wells, Glastonbury, Frome, Yeovil, and the Imperial Ground at Bristol, the only place for Somerset supporters to go, between Taunton (which is nearly in Devon) and Bath (which is nearly in Wiltshire). The claim is that it is not economic, and that more people come up to Taunton from Devon and Cornwall. But it is, after all, the *Somerset* CCC.

Week ended August 21

Well, there it is. The rubber won, the Ashes retained. It has been a joint triumph for Brearley and Botham. I have never been sure of the theory that it is dangerous to give your best player the captaincy, lest the extra responsibility will cause him to lose his form (there are too many examples to the contrary) but Botham's case will certainly be quoted every time the question arises in future. But then he is an exceptionally temperamental cricketer, and Brearley an exceptionally calm and wise captain.

Week ended September 18

Nottinghamshire are champions. Sussex are second, maddeningly close. Sussex have never won the Championship, despite many marvellous players and several near-run things, especially in the early 'thirties when they made repeated challenges to Yorkshire. Somerset have never won the Championship either. I hope Somerset win it next year, and Sussex the year after. No, I don't really. At heart I always have the hope that Yorkshire will win, but there is a double-devil of a row going on up there at the moment. I have suggested in print before that Yorkshiremen have much the same temperament as Latin Americans. No banana republic could do better than the latest efforts of the county broad as ten thousand beeves.

This is the fifth, and possibly final, season that I have written this journal. At first I strained too much, trying to make sure that I had recorded every major cricketing event, whether I had seen it or not. This became very boring to me, and no doubt boring to you. Once I realised I was writing a journal, not a book of reference, it became easier to write, and I hope easier to read. You have favoured me with a considerable and kind correspondence, and it is interesting that your letters have mostly concerned, not Boycott and Brearley and Botham, but Didcot, the Shoreditch Sparrow, the demon of Frome, Adam and Felicity and sundry other characters and places I have encountered.

I still enjoy cricket, though there are things in the game I would wish to see ordered differently. The major sadness of the last five years has been the decline, almost to extinction, of the leg-spinner. My thoughts have recurred to the words Dicky Rutnagur said at The Oval when Intikhab came on: 'I suppose this may be the last time we shall see him bowl.' He might also have been the last regular leg-spinner we shall see in county cricket. Cricket in England is in an euphoric state at present: but hard hits, fast bowling and frantic finishes should not be its only quality. The subtleties are slipping away. On the evening of that day at The Oval, I met Colin Cowdrey. He fully agreed with my view, though now I come to think of it, he gave up leg-spin as soon as he left Tonbridge.

After this unexpectedly prolonged stint in these pages, I lay down my pen with much gratitude, both to readers and editors; and some relief. Do not be concerned about my future. I have an influential contact, in someone who writes about cricket all over the world, the correspondent of the *Zimbabwe Zealot*.

One of the qualities of cricket is its casual, or fun, sides. They are not incapable of taking a game seriously, but their purpose is to enjoy it, irrespective of the result. Most cricketers have been associated with such a club, and everybody thinks his own the best, so I have no hesitation in claiming the Oxford Crocodiles as a great side.

The genesis of the Crocodiles was a more long-standing institution, Queen's College (Oxford) Imperial Quondams CC. I knew them, indeed captained them, in the years after the war. The Quondams, who played the villages around Oxford, consisted mostly of men in their finals year, who could not give time to the serious business of the college first XI, and of those not good enough even for the college second XI but who could not resist the game.

Sometimes an aging don might play, sometimes a man who had scarcely played cricket but had social merits. It meant that we usually had three or four pretty good cricketers, the rest being cheerful rabbits.

The Quondams had been founded, as my memory goes, in the early 1930s. The first president was D.G. Bradman who, when invited, wrote a polite letter of acceptance. Later it was proposed, for reasons now obscure, that Emperor Hirohito should be made president. A compromise was reached, Bradman and Hirohito holding the office jointly. The Emperor also wrote a polite letter of acceptance, and the word "Imperial" was included in the club's title.

After the war it was suggested that the Emperor should be struck from the roll. This was rejected on the ground that the joint president had suffered much and needed no further public humiliation. Indeed, we passed a resolution condoling with him on the loss of his godhead. A polite note of gratitude was received from Tokyo.

The Crocodiles (so called because they always had a long tail) were a touring side. They worked on much the same principles as the Quondams – several men were members of both – though the general standard of play was higher, and we drew on other colleges besides Queen's.

For several years we did much to improve the profits of West Country inns. M.P. Donnelly was our president and once, in a warming-up match at Oxford, he played, though he did not bat because it rained. My most vivid memories are of our two opening games.

We began with an evening at Buckfastleigh in Devon. I greeted the Crocodiles (for I lived at nearby Taunton), off a series of afternoon trains. Many of them had come from far. It was a hot day and all were perspiring and thirsty. The beautiful Buckfastleigh ground is on a plateau and at the bottom of the hill which approaches it is (or was) a pub. The pub opened at five and the match not until 6.30.

They decided with one accord, since they were in Devon, that the correct drink was cider. I did my best to warn them that scrumpy had demonic properties, but many of these young men from Oxford had served in the war and were confident that they could handle any drink.

At about 6 o'clock I led my more-than-cheerful side up the hill. The average consumption had been four pints and a half. My hopes were not improved when I saw that the match had been advertised as "Buckfastleigh v Oxford University", with extra prices charged, and that it was expected that Donnelly (whose name was on our notepaper) would be playing.

We were also two men short and had to recruit local help. None of this perturbed my happy band of brothers. The only thing to do was to win the toss, put the others in and give the scrumpy a chance to wear off. I lost the toss and we were put in.

Laughing and smiling, the Crocodiles approached the wicket swiftly and departed from it, all out for 26, and though we took a few wickets, it was an ignominious defeat. The local paper reported: "Oxford cracks shattered".

The next day we had to play a full-scale match at Torquay. Blimey, they had scorecards at Torquay and C.V.G. Haines was their captain. He had been playing a good deal for Glamorgan that season, and was head of the first-class batting averages with about 80. This was such an alarming prospect that I wondered if I could get the side there at all, and I believe that M.J. Kalysunderam lost the rest of us and (though he denied it) paid to get in.

There was nobody better than Kalysunderam with an Indian song after dinner, but he was not much of a batsman. In this match he scored a four to long leg, driving towards mid-off (his most prolific stroke) and I heard a Torquay colonel say, in all seriousness: "Marvellous eye these Eastern fellows have."

We had lost the toss. After Torquay had scored about 40 we took a wicket and Haines came in. I decided then on a bit of dashing captaincy and brought on Bill Howarth (now professor of French at Bristol). We had only two chaps who could bowl and they had done their best. Howarth announced that he was an off-spinner and he looked impressive with a green cap, the Australian sort that bulges over the ears. He insisted on a deep square leg.

That duty fell on Jimmy Craig, who is now high up in diplomatic law. Craig was really our wicketkeeper and it was a long time since he had fielded anywhere else, but though we had increased our numbers to 10, and Torquay had generously lent us a player who would play only if he kept wicket, Craig had been dispatched to pastures new.

Haines had scored 1 and Howarth began to bowl at him. His first ball was a long-hop, but it turned, yes, it turned and Haines, hitting a little too early, sent it soaring. Howarth insists to this day that he deceived him by flight. How high it went! We imagined it would clear the ground, but then we realized that it was going to drop within the boundary, and that Craig was standing underneath it.

As it went going up and up I would not have blamed him if he had quietly turned his back and walked away to look up some intricate legal point in the public library. But he stood there like a man and caught it. From that point the Crocodiles became a cricket team. We lost but we got them out for about 180 and were not far behind at the end.

Gone are the Crocodiles, or rather now they are the Quondam Crocodiles, and it is some time since any of us put a bat to ball. But, lord, we did have some fun in our time.

Dennis Lillee

NOVEMBER: In Perth Dennis Lillee had obstructed and kicked out at the Pakistani batsman Javed Miandad

Dennis Lillee is a stormy petrel, as the phrase goes. The stormy petrel is a bird which flies close to the ocean when the weather is at its worst, seeming to pat it with each foot alternately, as though walking on it, as St Peter did. According to Brewer's *Dictionary of Phrase and Fable*, the term became figuratively used for one whose coming always portends trouble and can be expected to "raise Cain" wherever he goes or whatever he does.

Well, that is Lillee, and he is raising Cain again. He will so long as he lives, in whatever capacity. It is his nature. He can be a genial man, even a gentle man, but when his temper is suddenly sparked he cannot control it, and when he thinks he has a point to prove (as with the episode of the aluminium bat) or a challenge to meet, or a bet to win (as when asking the queen for her autograph), he will never flinch, however unwisely.

He does not much like Poms, or anyone except Australians, and not many Australians either. This aggression, this ferocity, is said to be a characteristic of great fast bowlers. It is not always true. Think of Brian Statham. More recently think of Michael Procter who might have had as good a record as Lillee, given the same opportunities. Procter has bowled many a bouncer, but would never have got deliberately into a batsman's way and then kicked him.

I remember an incident at Lord's involving Snow, and a bouncer bowled (most would have said thrown) by Griffith at Trent Bridge against Underwood, a tail-ender. Neither are pleasant recollections. But Lillee just goes on raising Cain, time after time, for the hell of it. No doubt part of his problem is that he is now expected by his supporters, particularly at home, to do it.

He no longer has the excuse of youth, as McEnroe in tennis does. In fact, when Lillee was younger – he first played against England in 1970, when he was 21 – his behaviour, although impulsive, was better than it is now. He has always been recognized as a tough customer and one of the best fast bowlers of his time: but he does not appreciate (as Trueman did, or for that matter Lindwall and Miller) the difference between the tough customer and an ugly one.

He is a courageous man, as he showed in persisting with the game at the top level after a great deal of injury trouble, particularly to his back, a vulnerable point for a fast bowler. His return to England last summer was warmly welcomed by everyone here, except the English batsmen. There is a fund of affection and admiration for him among cricketers all over the world. But it is diminishing.

Answers to the Christmas Quiz (page 225)

1. Mrs Morland, Catherine, Jane Austen, *Northanger Abbey.*
2. C.P. Snow of G.H. Hardy.
3. J.D. Beresford, *The Hampdenshire Wonder*, Hampdenshire, J. Wells of Kent, the father of H.G. Wells.
4. Mike Jackson, P.G. Wodehouse, *Psmith in the City.*
5. Alan Gibson. Happy New Year to all Peasants.

1982

John Woodcock, the Sage of Longparish, who was now Editor of *Wisden* as well as Cricket Correspondent of *The Times*, described 1982 as a 'disturbing' year, citing politics off the field and bad behaviour on it. Certainly, there was no shortage of material for the tabloid headline writers, what with Gooch and Boycott leading a rebel tour to South Africa that threatened to split the cricket world in two, and Pakistan's captain, Imran Khan, making his feelings at the standard of English umpiring all too clear during the Test series that summer.

These were not the sort of events that Alan Gibson enjoyed writing about. His ideal cricketing occasion would consist of two county sides with plenty of local 'characters' in their ranks, engaging in hard-fought but sportsmanlike competition, in front of a small and knowledgeable crowd at somewhere like Bath, over three fine but not sweltering days, before settling for an honourable draw. Increasingly, as the years went by, he disliked big crowds, hot days, controversial incidents, big names from overseas and almost anything that might pass for excitement. There was more than a hint of snobbishness about all this. One of the sporting journalists whom he most admired was *The Times*' legendary golf correspondent, Bernard Darwin. In the following passage, from Darwin's chapter on the Ryder Cup in *Golf Between Two Wars*, if you were to substitute 'cricket' for 'golf' you would have a perfect summary of Alan Gibson's views on the big one-day occasions and Test matches:

> The crowd is enormous and it would be unmeaning flattery to suggest that the majority know anything about golf; their emotions do not as a rule go much beyond making pyrotechnic noises over a big drive or frenzied clapping over a long putt. The accompaniments to the match in the shape of booths and side-shows and itinerant vendors are rather too much like those of Derby Day. The golf is too essentially 'popular' to give much pleasure in the watching.

But there were still some cricket matches that could by no stretch of the imagination be described as 'popular' – like the early season encounters between the Universities and the counties at Fenner's and the Parks which, in 1982, seem to have been blessed with unusually fine spring weather. The Gibson spirits were lifted on both accounts. Nor is it any coincidence that one of his favourite cricketers of this era was the cerebral Mike Brearley – a connoisseur's cricketer if ever there was one – who had already announced that this would be his last season as captain of Middlesex, and whom Alan saw make a century against Northamptonshire on May 12.

Cricket did not rank high in the scale of national priorities in the early summer of 1982. Britain was at war with Argentina in the Falkland Islands, putting the triumphs and tragedies, victories and defeats, of the summer game for once in their proper perspective. Alan was no admirer of Mrs. Thatcher, and probably didn't approve of going to war in order to recapture a remnant of Britain's imperial past, but he was sensitive enough to the prevailing mood to avoid anything that might be construed as flippant, especially when he went to Southampton in early June, on the day after the RFA Sir Galahad had been blown up off Fitzroy.

India and Pakistan were the summer's tourists. Alan marked the arrival of the Indians with a look back to the original 'All India' side, whom he had seen taking the field at Leyton 50 years previously. He saw the Pakistanis at Taunton, where his

Tests
England
beat India
1-0, with two draws
England
beat Pakistan
2-1

Championship
1 Middlesex
2 Leicestershire
3 Hampshire
4 Nottinghamshire
5 Surrey
6 Somerset

Sunday League
1 Sussex
2 Middlesex
3 Leicestershire
4 Kent
5 Essex
Hampshire
Nottinghamshire

NatWest Final
Surrey
beat Warwickshire

Benson & Hedges Final
Somerset
beat Nottinghamshire

Most first-class runs
1 A.I. Kallicharran
2 P.N. Kirsten
3 G. Boycott

Most first-class wickets
1 M.D. Marshall
2 N.G.B. Cook
3 S.T. Clarke

second-day report, praising Dredge's batting to the skies and mentioning Richards' 181 almost in passing, is still fondly recalled by the Somerset faithful.

Earlier in the year, Alan had been accorded the considerable honour of being appointed the first President of the Cricket Writers' Club. His duties were largely ceremonial, but did include attending the Annual Meeting, which the Secretary, Robin Marlar, had decided should be held immediately before the start of play on the first morning of the Lord's Test against Pakistan. For Alan, it meant a trip to Lord's, rather than to Weston-super-Mare. *The Times* – really rather generously under the circumstances – made his journey worthwhile by asking him to write a 'colour piece', describing the occasion, which he seems thoroughly to have enjoyed.

In the meantime, the county season was building towards its climax. For once, Alan seems to have been genuinely impressed by the efforts of an overseas mercenary, when he watched the fearsome Sylvester Clarke blitz the Middlesex batting in the NatWest semi-final. In the final, on September 5, they overwhelmed Warwickshire, winning even more comfortably than Somerset had in the B&H. Once again, Alan was asked to write a 'colour piece'; something which – curiously, given his tendency to write about almost anything *except* the cricket in his day-to-day reports – he never much enjoyed or found particularly easy. Whether that, plus the prospect of a packed Lord's, had anything to do with the mysterious failure of his press pass to materialise, we will never know. But at any rate, he decided to stay at home and watch it on the television, and ended up writing, not about the atmosphere at Lord's, but about the mood in the Star at High Littleton, to which he appears to have retreated, shortly before lunch!

By this time, he was in dispute with *The Times* over his expenses. They were complaining of the shambolic way in which his claims were (belatedly) presented; he was convinced that he was being underpaid. In early October, he wrote a long letter to Norman Fox, his sports editor, in which, amongst much else, he reminded him that he had an agreement with his predecessors that he could travel up to London and back in a day, claiming the taxi fares from High Littleton to Bristol and back, rather than staying overnight:

> I detest staying overnight in London unless it is necessary, and the rail fare with taxis costs *The Times* rather less than staying in, say, the Great Western Hotel would. This is another thing which I have agreed with previous editors. But again, if you wish to change the arrangement, let me know, and I will go and sleep Underneath the Arches.

It was a typical thrust, but in a losing and, ultimately, deeply counter-productive cause. He may by now have built up a large and loyal following among *Times* readers, but no cricket writer is indispensable, especially cricket writers who fail to make it to one-day finals, or decide upon last-minute changes of plan for their own convenience and who threaten to sue their employers over their expenses claims. For all his reputation as 'by far the most amusing sports writer of the present day', as John Arlott described him, Alan was running the risk of coming to be regarded as being more trouble than he was worth.

When I say, in print, that a young cricketer is promising, it is usually the kiss of death for the lad. So I apologize in advance to those I am going to mention in this article. The trouble is that to form a judgment on a player you need to see him more than a few times, and this is not easy for one who travels from ground to ground. There is not much point in guessing on a brief performance.

It is a common ploy among cricket enthusiasts, especially writers, to use such phrases as "Spotted him in the nets one morning at Kidderminster, always knew he was a good 'un!" In safe retrospect, remembering their successful diagnosis, they forget the dozens of failures for whom they also prophesied triumph.

When I first saw Alan Ward, of Derbyshire, taking wickets against Glamorgan, I was sure that he was the coming England bowler. So, I may say, was Tony Lewis, who had been one of his victims. When I first saw Bob Willis, playing for Surrey, he seemed uncoordinated, all over the place. No doubt if I had chanced to see them on different occasions, my opinion of their merits might have been reversed.

I remember Brian Johnston, who had been luckier with Willis, maintaining that he would be the better England prospect, and I did not believe it, though he has been amply justified.

With these reservations, and rather reluctantly, at the Sports Editor's request, I suggest one or two players whom I expect to improve this season. Cautiously, I begin near home, in Somerset.

Nigel Popplewell did not develop so swiftly as had been hoped last season, but then I was lucky with him. I saw him make some good-looking runs, take useful wickets when they were needed, and hold some marvellous catches. There are more high-class fieldsmen in county cricket today than ever before, but Popplewell is still outstanding among them. There was a time when I thought he was a possibility for India, but he did not quite keep it up, partly because, in a strong side, his chances were limited. I am sure we have still to see the best of him.

The same thing is true of Vic Marks, though he is older (26 to 24). I thought from his Oxford days that Marks would be an England cricketer. So he has been, just, in a one-day match. Marks, like Popplewell, has to go in relatively late in the order, almost always either to make a quick dash for runs, or hold the fort in times of difficulty.

These alternating circumstances do not help his average. His bowling has always looked more innocuous than it is. Every selector and every journalist, sitting comfortably round the ring, feels instinctively that he could hit him for six every other ball. Perhaps Marks should cultivate a more menacing air.

I was impressed, on the few occasions I happened to see him, by Neil Mallender, of Northamptonshire, a view shared by many who watched him more intensively. I see he headed the Northamptonshire bowling averages (if we discount the four adventitious wickets of Larkins) with 46 at 22.3. That may not sound startling, but he had a high striking rate for a seamer. He is only 21, and a Yorkshireman. As a Yorkshireman myself, I entirely agree with Yorkshire's refusal to play overseas men, but they do seem to let too many of their own get away.

John Childs, of Gloucestershire, is 30. Nevertheless, slow left-arm spinners have come into their own in middle cricketing age. Charlie Parker, who, many still insist, was the best of them all, played for England at 39, and was summoned to a Test by aeroplane – though he did not play – nine years later. Charlie used to describe his flight, which was then considered rather a dramatic thing: "As soon as it got near Leeds, there was a signal that it wasn't a wet wicket, so we turned round and came home."

Hedley Verity did not establish his place in the Yorkshire side until he was 25, and the England side until he was 27. Childs is not, as yet, quite so good a bowler as Derek Underwood, chiefly because he lacks Underwood's vast experience. Underwood, who is 37, probably still has some years to go.

Perhaps by the time Childs takes over from him, there will be no place for a slow left-arm bowler in a modern Test side, but he is the likeliest prospect I have seen of maintaining a great tradition, with no disrespect to his captain, David Graveney, an admirable all-round cricketer from whom Childs has learnt much.

Well, these are the names that occur to me, as some worth watching. I shall be keeping a close eye myself on Adam Gibson, of Wellington School Under-14s. Last year he did win a house match with a sudden six, which so astonished everyone present that it was mentioned in his house report. I have advised him to concentrate on defence for this season. Probably I am wrong, because I am afraid that is what every county captain is advising every promising lad to do.

Sunshine in The Parks

OXFORD: Oxford University v Worcestershire

For most of the last 40 years, my cricket season has begun at The Parks, usually in wet or bitterly cold weather. Yesterday was as pleasant as I can recall, the sun shining almost all the time, with just a touch of cool wind blowing from Northam Gardens, where the philosophers and the feminists now, I am told, live.

I had left High Littleton with some sadness. The landlord of The Star, contemplating the reduction of his lunchtime profits in the next few months, had a tear in his eye. However, I was soon reminded of Somerset.

I arrived only a few minutes late, having subtly changed at Reading instead of Didcot, and when about 100 yards away heard a strong cry of "Ovurr", from which I deduced, correctly, that Mervyn Kitchen was umpiring. He has had to wait a while to get on the list but I am sure he will do well at the job.

Half a day's play at Taunton

TAUNTON: Somerset v Leicestershire

It was so wet a morning at Taunton that I doubted whether there would be any play at all. However, it cleared up sufficiently for a slippery start to be made at three o'clock, and in the evening, with the wind moving round, unusually, to the south-east for a time, there were glimpses of the sun, and patches of blue sky.

Leicestershire put Somerset in and two wickets quickly fell: Roebuck, run out, and Richards, bowled by Taylor. This was an encouraging beginning for Leicestershire and for a while they kept up their aggressive spirit, and the crowd (a large one, given the weather) was broody, like Somerset farmers contemplating the hay harvest once the Ring O'Bells is shut.

Yet it was gradually demonstrated by Denning and Rose, two fair-haired left-handers, neither born in the West Indies, that there was little wrong with the pitch, although the run rate, after the early shocks, was rather slow.

Denning reached his 50 out of 95 in the 36th over. In the same over Rose put the hundred up with a handsome cover drive. Neither batsman looked in much trouble, though there was one confident appeal for a catch at the wicket against Rose, austerely declined by David Shepherd. Shepherd is popular in Somerset, now that he has stopped batting for Gloucestershire. "Lovely decision, sound of snick, yurs, but no deviation, see it from 'ere," said a farming type in the Stragglers' Enclosure, which stands at about 45 degrees from the pitch.

Several days in Cardiff

CARDIFF: Glamorgan v Leicestershire

It had rained heavily overnight as the puddles around Sophia Gardens proclaimed. Play started nearly an hour late.

The press box, the possibilities of rugby conversation exhausted, talked about soccer. Cricket is not a popular subject in Wales just now, although Wilfred Wooller, with whom I had the pleasure of a drink, uttered a few mordant words about it. He is not altogether favourable to the present Glamorgan regime. I also enjoyed meeting Wilf's brother, a tennis international who has come down from North Wales, and seems to have stood up with remarkable resilience to all those years of fraternity with the great man.

NEXT DAY

The trains in these parts, incidentally, are in some chaos; or at least the passengers are. The summer timetable has just been introduced, but you cannot get a copy of it because, I am told, it contains so many mistakes that it has had to be reprinted. The guessing game seems to have extended to drivers and other railway staff. I pray that my forthcoming travels do not include Didcot.

CARDIFF: Glamorgan v Warwickshire

My daughter Felicity, in knapsack and jeans, all too near to being a teenager, went off proudly with the High Littleton School camp party to investigate Roman ruins at Cirencester. I went to Cardiff to investigate some Welsh ruins. But the ruins at Sophia Gardens are not irreparable. Glamorgan have not been playing very well this season and are likely to lose this match, but they batted pluckily.

That the fierce spirit of Welsh cricket is still alive I was reminded by meeting Wilfred Wooller, full of beans and improbable recollections, and also Willie Jones, whom I had not seen for years. He made many runs and took quite a lot of wickets for Glamorgan, apart from being one of the best fly halves of his day. With these two survivors of the famous 1948 championship side present it was impossible to despair of Glamorgan cricket.

NEXT DAY

It was another enjoyable Cardiff day. I met Wilfred Wooller almost at once, left him to bump into Ossie Wheatley, and caught a glimpse of Carwyn James, sombrely retreating.

As I was settling down to write, my shoulders were seized by Robin Marlar, who had no business to be in Wales, but declared he had been searching Europe for me to discuss some matters concerning the Cricket Writers' Club. Still, I saw some cricket, and that was all right too, so far as it went.

Letter from Somerset 1982

Somerset is divided into three parts, if we forget the recent invasion of Avon, which all Somerset people do, until it comes to paying the rates. There is west Somerset, the most beautiful and remote part, surrounding the Brendon Hills. That is where "the green hills of Somerset go sliding to the sea". There is the plain, more commonly called the Levels, stretching from Wells to Taunton, give or take a hummock, always the first to be flooded. And there is north Somerset, up towards Bristol and Bath, which used to be considered the industrial part of the country, because it held the coalfield.

Although the last mine was closed nearly 10 years ago, you can still detect the difference between the agricultural background. High Littleton, where I happily live, still has the tang of a mining village, not the cosiness of a chocolate-box cover.

The accents are sharper, the cottages grimmer, built for business, not for decoration. Old Mr Hathway died last year, a veteran miner, a tough, genial old bird. His son is the village book-maker. One of his grandsons is an admirable local preacher. Now my own father began as a miner, up in Durham, and became a parson, so I can sense something of the tradition.

Father would have been shocked at the idea of "making a book", yet he would look after his brothers' whippets when asked. Whippets were the favourite wherever miners dwelt, and much money passed on their races. They were responsible for the tales, haughtily told at garden parties in the 20s, that the miners were claiming public assistance, starving their families, and buying steaks for their dogs.

Our dog Dusky is mostly whippet, and can beat any dog in the village across the field in front of our cottage.

When we first came to High Littleton, more than four years ago, we were warned in The Star (our one public house) that we would miss the floods, but cop the snow. So it has been this winter. We were hemmed in for a few days, but the electricity did not go, thought from all around us we heard horror stories. My eldest son, who lives at Clayhidon, high on a hill near the Devon border, is something to do with the National Farmers' Union, and was frequently to be heard on local radio stations. "Don't panic," was his ringingly confident message to the farmers of the West. He was broadcasting by telephone from his home, by candlelight.

I like the picture of the new technology rescued by the old ("The spirit of Man is the candle of the Lord") though I was disappointed not to hear an intervention by my granddaughter Joanna, who, when she seeks to raise her voice, can interrupt the bell ringers at Taunton.

It is a fair view from my study window. Downside Abbey is to the right, and to the left is Cranmore Tower, a skinny folly seen close up, but a dignity to the landscape in the distance. In the middle is a big black slagheap, the last relic of the Midsomer Norton mines. My daughter Felicity, when she first saw it, cried: "Look! A volcano!" and ever since it has been known as "Fluffy's Volcano".

Suddenly it became a white volcano. There was much beauty in that countryside, spread with snow, though I was glad I did not have to go out in it. How pleased I was when at last the weather improved, and Fluffy's Volcano, not the least of the black hills of north Somerset, came peering again through its white blanket.

All-India 1932

Fifty years ago I saw the Indians play at Leyton. I can tell you the date: it was May 28, my ninth birthday – no, I tell a lie, because there was no play on the Saturday, but I had a chance of watching them on the Monday and Tuesday.

Our house overlooked the Leyton ground and on the Saturday, as a birthday treat, I had been allowed to go in, paying sixpence, to watch from closer quarters. It was a disappointment that there was no play, after numerous consultations, but I can remember several things about the rest of the match, though by then I was only surveying it from the balcony at home.

I had bought a scorecard (twopence, a stiff price we thought) and conned it eagerly. No. 1 in the Indian side was described as H.H. Porbandar, with an asterisk to show he was captain. When India went in, after bowling Essex out of 169, their No 1 played some handsome strokes.

We had some romantic ideas about Indian cricket at that time, because of Duleepsinhji, and the Nawab of Pataudi, and vague folk memories of Duleep's uncle, Ranji. So, although neither Duleep nor the Nawab were available for the Indian party, we expected magic. When the Indian No 1 was so dashing, I thought that this Porbandar was going to be another oriental star.

"Cor, old Porbs looked good," I said to my friends. I wondered what the H.H. stood for. 'Arry? My friends suggested, or 'Erbert? I cannot swear to this, but I do believe I suggested 'Orace, because I knew he was something foreign.

Alas! I discovered later that though Porbandar had played in that match, he had not batted and that the No 1 who had played the strokes was Naoomal Jeeoomal – or words to that effect (even *Wisden* was uncertain in its transliteration of Indian names in those days). Naoomal played three times against England and averaged 27, so he cannot have been too bad. He made 1,300 runs in that 1932 season, 1,500 in all matches. So I had seen a pretty good innings; but it was a disappointment that he had not been Porbandar.

H.H., I also discovered, stood for his "His Highness", and the full title was "The Maharajah of Porbandar". *Wisden* of 1933 described his appointment as captain of the Indian side (there had been touring sides from India before, but this was the first to be granted a Test match) in these terms:

"Some little difficulty was experienced with regard to the captaincy, and after one or two disappointments the choice fell upon the Maharajah of Porbandar ... For reasons apart from cricket, the necessity existed of having a person of distinction and importance in India at the head of affairs, and it was almost entirely because of this that Porbandar led the team."

(Did anyone murmur anything about sport and politics?).

Wisden continues: "No injustice is being done to him, therefore, by saying that admirably fitted as he was in many respects for the task, his abilities as a cricketer were not commensurate with the position he occupied."

I checked Porbandar's figures for the tour:

At Pelsham, v Mr T Gilbert Scott's XI (not first-class):
b R.S.G. Scott 0: b Owen-Smith 2.
At Hove, v Sussex: b Tate 0.
At Maidenhead, v Mr H M Martineaus's XI (not first-class): b Lowndes 2.
At Cardiff, v Glamorgan: b Jones 2.
At Cambridge, v the University: c Titley, b Rought-Rought 0.

He did not play again after the Cambridge match in the second week of June: at least, I can find no trace of it in *Wisden*, which nevertheless attributes 8 runs to him in all matches (average 1.14). Where are the missing runs? I can agree with their verdict on first-class matches (2 runs, average 0.66), but there is a problem here which I feel the Society of Cricket Statisticians should immediately investigate. There is no record of his bowling or taking a catch.

That is not all there is to say about the Maharajah. The tour was difficult, experimental, and it passed off happily. India ("All-India" as the team was then called) did well and though they had given England a shock or two, E.W. Swanton wrote that Porbandar "made a creditable success of keeping his men a happy and united party." It was also graceful, if inevitable, for him to step out of the side.

That it was not so easy to captain an Indian side in England was shown on the next tour, in 1936, when the amiable Vizianagram ("call me Vizzy," he used to say in the commentary box) struck trouble, and Amarnath, the best all-rounder, was sent home. In a later book Swanton refers, rather unkindly, to Porbandar's "fleet of white Rolls-Royces", but also states that he had made only two runs on the tour – "from a leg-glance at Cardiff, I seem to recall."

Fifty years later, with cricket between England and India still going on, I think we owe a salute to him. Porbandar – the state – produces limestone, which, according to the *Encylopaedia Britannica*, "is used for buildings in Porbandar without mortar, and is said to coalesce into a solid block under the influence of moisture." Well, the limestone still holds, and he applied his touches of moisture in those early days.

Porbander mystery solved

BIRMINGHAM: Sussex v Warwickshire

It was a pleasure at Edgbaston to meet Robert Brooke, the editor of *The Cricket Statistician*, who has solved the Porbander mystery, of which I wrote in these columns some weeks ago, and which has perplexed a number of correspondents. Brooke has confounded *Wisden* and demonstrated that the Maharajah did make two more runs, equalling his highest score, in a match, twelve a side, against Blackheath in 1932. This confirms his tour average, for all matches, at 1.14. He still holds the record for a tour captain.

This was such gripping news that I am afraid Mr Brooke and I missed one or two statistics after lunch. By the end I was practically calling him "Rajah". However, I can inform you that Sussex, who were 302 for 9 at the start, did not lose their last until the score was 343.

The rumpus about the South African tour, and the continuing, boring row in Yorkshire, have been occupying most of such headlines as cricket can command at this time of year. Neither is a particularly attractive topic, and both involve Boycott, of whom I am weary of writing. It is a relief to turn to Lord Harris, a formidable figure of a previous generation, who died 50 years ago, March 24, 1932, 81 years old.

Harris is not a character to whom it is easy, in retrospect, to warm. I once called him, in print, an antediluvian old tyrant, and though it was a phrase lured by the false enthusiasms of youth, I can see what I meant. He was one of the major figures in the administration of cricket, in this country, for half a century.

Most of his decisions were probably for the good of the game: all of them were for what he *considered* to be the good of the game. He remained firmly Victorian in his outlook. He did not court popularity, and did not win it (Pelham Warner, for instance, was a more popular public figure, but the weaker character, at least off the field).

Many humbler cricketers of his time thought of Harris as "the old bastard", half affectionately, as a private might think of his sergeant. None would have described him, even if the word was familiar to them, as "duplicitous".

Harris was a pretty good player, though not one of the great ones. He played for England in four Tests, once in Australia and three times at home, in the years 1879-84. He was captain in all of them, which was then natural if you had a peer of the realm in the side, and justified his place with a batting average of 29 for six innings, once not out.

He had many good performances for Kent, and captained Oxford in a win against Cambridge in 1874. He first practised at Lord's in 1862, and was still playing at Eton, in a second XI match, on the Fourth of June, 1930. A year before that, he had played at Lord's for the last time, for MCC *v* Indian Gymkhana.

The young Bill Bowes was also playing in this match, and has given us an account of it in *Express Deliveries* (one of the best books by a professional cricketer, and all his own work: it should be reprinted.) Bowes writes of how Harris, his captain, "dressed in the style of all the cricketers of his day. He had a white shirt with starched collar and white bow tie, an old tie to hold up his narrow trousers, and a sweater which buttoned up the front."

Harris fielded in the gully, after leaving the final disposition of the field to Bowes, and after a couple of balls noticed that third man was directly behind him. He called imperiously "Bowes! You should never have two men in a line." Bowes said "Sorry, sir, I thought you would prefer that." "I shall stop them," said Harris. "Move the fieldsman to which side of me you prefer."

The name of Harris is still remembered with some wrath in Gloucestershire, because it is part of the county tradition that "'twas 'Arris tried to keep Walter out." So, at one time, he did. Harris was proud of his Kentish ancestry and allegiance, though as it happened he was born in Trinidad.

Hammond, though nurtured in Gloucestershire cricket, as it happened was born in Kent. He had already started playing for Gloucestershire when Harris, a stickler for qualifications, intervened. This held up the career of Hammond for two years, and I dare say had a considerable, and unhappy influence on a complicated character.

Harris was technically correct. He always was. But many great men have sensed that there are moments to turn a blind eye. And yet there were occasions when cricket could be grateful for his clear sight. The most famous was the throwing controversy in the 1880s and '90s.

Throwing was a problem then as it was not to be again until the 1950s. Crossland and Nash, the Lancashire fast bowlers, were thought to have especially doubtful actions. Kent, on Harris's initiative, cancelled fixtures. Crossland and Nash were dropped, and fixtures were resumed.

Test cricket between England and Australia might never have developed, at least at the time and in the way it did, had it not been for Harris. In 1879, he was captain in Australia. There was a riot in a game against New South Wales, after an umpire's decision of which the Australians disapproved. The details do not, in the present context, much matter, and are in any case confused. Harris, who had to be escorted from the field by his team, was stern, unyielding, and sent home an account to the English press.

As a result of this, and other factors, including bad organisation, the Australian side which toured Britain in 1880 found it very difficult to get fixtures. No Tests had been arranged, and it seemed improbable that any would be played, but near the end of the season C.W. Alcock, the Surrey secretary, persuaded Harris to lead a more or less representative side against them at the Oval. This was a generous action on Harris's part. His presence (he was also responsible for raising the side) gave the stamp of authority to the occasion. Its centenary was duly celebrated in 1980.

For many years Harris was Treasurer of MCC, but showed a talent for negotiation, and reaching the nub of an argument, which approached that later achieved by H.S. Altham: though Harris could be as gruff as Altham was gracious. When Lord Harris died, Lord Hawke wrote in *Wisden* that "he was just one great Sahib." It is a phrase prompted no doubt by Harris's service as Governor in Bombay, but still makes us laugh a little today. Nevertheless, it says much about the man, his attitudes, and his time.

There were those who thought, just before the second world war, that Desmond Eagar would make an England player, and possibly an England captain. He had had a successful school career at Cheltenham, whom he captained for two years, won a Blue at Oxford, and made a promising beginning with Gloucestershire. As it turned out, after the long break, he never surpassed a fair county standard – a stylish batsman, an outstanding close fieldsman – yet his services to cricket, especially Hampshire cricket, amounted to more than many Test caps.

He joined Hampshire as secretary-captain in 1946. For more than 30 years, until his sad, sudden death in 1977, he was their guide, philosopher and friend. No man ever worked harder for his county, and much of the work was of a routine kind, you would think boring even to such an effervescent spirit. He never wilted under any number of club dinner speeches. If a few more Hampshire memberships could be coaxed from his audience, he counted the long hours (many clubs confuse the annual dinner with the annual general meeting) well spent.

He was a good speaker, a good broadcaster, a good writer. He was hockey correspondent of *The Sunday Telegraph* for many years, reporting from some bleak expanse with the nearest telephone about three miles away. He had been a fine hockey player himself, but only took on the job because it was a way in which Hampshire need pay him less money. (They declined his suggestion.) Much of his writing time was devoted to *The Hampshire Handbook*, which soon became the best in the country, to the history of Hampshire cricket, and to collecting and annotating its library and museum. He could have had a choice of several careers, had he wished, but he decided that cricket was the thing for him, and the rest would have to be peripheral. (In a slightly different way, his son Patrick made the same decision: discovering he had a gift for photography, he concentrated on *cricket* photography, in which he rapidly reached the top of his profession.)

Desmond took Hampshire to third place in the Championship, the highest position they had then achieved. This was in 1955, and the team was given dinner at the House of Lords. In 1975, when they also came third the result was described as 'disappointing'. He used to relish this contrast, rightly seeing it as a reward for many years of hard labour. The first Hampshire side to win the Championship, in 1961, was captained by Colin Ingleby-Mackenzie. Desmond had steadily built up the side (though I think it is fair to say that Ingleby-Mackenzie, a touch rasher and more of a dasher, deserved to crown the edifice). I remember some people saying what a pity it was that Desmond had retired before Hampshire won the Championship, which had become his heart's desire. Desmond was not among them.

Here let me interpose a lesson in the difficult Christian virtue of humility. If you can create, say, the best symphony in the world, or write the best novel in the world, or sing the best song in the world – if you can do any such thing: and know it to be the best, and rejoice because it is the best, *but rejoice no more and no less than if anyone else had done it* ... Well, then you are a truly humble man. Desmond rejoiced in Ingleby-Mackenzie's success, I do believe, every bit as much as if it was his own.

I have been writing with some emotion of my old friend, so I must appease the statisticians, standing over us like mathematical Molochs, with a few figures: Desmond scored 12,178 runs, average 21.86, according to *Wisden*, and took 367 catches. He also took 31 wickets, with left-arm spin. He was no bowler, and I expect he only bowled left-arm in the first place because of a joke or a bet.

He was one of the best old-style county captains. He did good by stealth, and would have blushed to find it fame. His professionals pulled his leg, but did not make jokes about him behind his back that they would have been ashamed to make to his face. They knew how much they owed him in those hard years of Hampshire's recovery, and that he had worked as hard as anyone. 'Skipper says we make one change a day. That's middle of afternoon when he switches me to t'other end and lets Vic swan around in't field for half an hour.' No prizes for placing this quotation. But they were very fond of him, and he got the best out of them. I saw his last match, when Shackleton and Cannings had bowled Gloucestershire out on the second evening, and the team stood back, almost reverently, and his cheeks were wet as he came up the steps.

He could be tough, at times, as Ingleby-Mackenzie, still young, discovered as he took an early evening shower, when due to bat. So did his beloved wife Marjorie, discover, when they had a row one morning over the breakfast washing-up. He made her so cross that she threw a cup at him. 'What made her even crosser', he said later in the day, 'was that I caught it.'

Brearley's century makes him a contented cat

LORD'S: Northamptonshire, with all first innings wickets in hand, are 339 runs behind Middlesex

Brearley made a century at Lord's yesterday, indeed it was nearly his highest score in this country, and it seemed to me, on my first visit this season, just what was needed. I have always admired him, not just as a captain, but as a batsman. If the strains of captaincy have affected the batting of such mighty men as Hammond, Hutton and Botham, the same has been true at a lower level of Brearley.

Here he is in his last season, the struggles and triumphs of the field mostly behind him, and there was an air of contentment about his batting which we have not often seen. He was rarely in trouble and remained unbothered when he was. Yet for much of his innings he was under pressure. From the time he lost his opening partner, Slack, at 112, until Emburey came in at No 6, runs were not coming easily at the other end.

Griffiths, who was steady for a long time, was the best of the bowlers. He had Slack leg-before, Barlow caught at short leg, Gatting at slip and Radley at the wicket. Gatting looked good while he was there. Emburey, who is making strides as a batsman, soon began to hit the ball about confidently and when he reached his 50 had scored nearly half the fifth-wicket partnership.

But it was Brearley who commanded the scene. He reached his 100 out of 181, and after a breather accelerated. At tea, with 80 overs bowled, the score was 250 for four and Brearley was 140. The 300 came up in the ninetieth over. At 312 Brearley, with a carefree pull, was caught at square leg (Griffiths again). He retired to the pavilion looking like my cat Crumbs when she has demolished a colony of shrews: still a touch wary, and wishing there had been more, but contented. And crumbs! he had batted well.

However, the sunshine of the evening went to Emburey who carried on to his first first-class hundred. It is true that in its latter part it was mostly a matter of swatting weary bluebottles but Northamptonshire made him work for the last few runs. Brearley declared as soon as the deed was done, giving Northamptonshire 25 minutes to bat. Despite a succession of lusty Middlesex appeals, they did not lose a wicket.

Exercising mind over matter

LORD'S: Northamptonshire, with six second innings wickets standing, need 52 to make Middlesex bat again

It was another day for Magisterial Michael. Long has he been accustomed to say to a man "go", and he goeth, and "come", and he cometh, but in his golden gloaming he even seems able to say to a pitch "spin", and it spinneth. Perhaps Wilfred Rhodes, though not a professional psychologist, used the same method when he said: "If batsman thinks she's spinnin', she's spinnin'."

Northamptonshire began 365 runs behind, with all wickets in hand. Their only chance was to make a good score, declare behind, and hope that Brearley would leave their powerful batsmen something within range on the last afternoon. This was presumably their strategy when they had put Middlesex in. However, it did not work out. By a quarter to four, they were following on.

They made an uncertain start against the quicker bowlers. Cook, Larkins and Williams were out by the time the score was 59. But Lamb settled in, and had reached an impressive 50 when, at 124, he was caught at the wicket. At lunch, after 52 overs, the score was 153 for four. That still did not seem much cause for Northamptonshire alarm, for Steele was solid and Yardley confident, quite dashingly so at times.

Then, at 170, Steele was bowled and the rest went for 50 runs to Emburey and Edmonds. Brearley crowded the bat. It was certainly a good spell by Emburey. I was watching from behind the arm at this stage, and saw only the occasional ball turn, not very quickly. Probably more did later on, but by then I had retreated to the distant cross-eyed view from the press box. The only other Northamptonshire batsman to show intelligent resistance was Carter.

When Northamptonshire went in again, Brearley made a further contribution, an excellent catch at slip, which had Cook out at 14. Larkins was belligerent, but at 47 he lost Williams, bowled by Edmonds, from the pavilion end. Brearley was constantly switching his bowlers. The classical wisdom is that you do not bowl slow left-handers from the pavilion end at Lord's because they have to turn the ball uphill, but there have been exceptions (notably Verity against Australia in 1934) and this was another useful one for Middlesex. At 70 Larkins was caught at the wicket, also off Edmonds.

Emburey then came on, Edmonds moving to the Nursery end. Emburey had Lamb leg before. By the close of play, Northamptonshire had not lost another wicket, but had not much left to play for. The weather remained clear after a sunny day. The Magisterial One, in current form, has only to say to the sun "shine", and lo! it shineth!

Michael Brearley
'The Magisterial One'

Hampshire finessed by a pair of jacks

SOUTHAMPTON: Hampshire, with six first innings wickets in hand, are 112 runs behind Lancashire

Lancashire won the toss, and, with it, for a while, trouble. It was a day of hot sun and blue sky, with a relieving breeze; as pleasant a day for cricket as you could wish. There were many old friends and acquaintances at Southampton. "Why Mr Gibson!" said one, affectionately, "how nice to see you about still." This took some pondering.

The pitch had some early life, but the chief reason for the fall of wickets was the Hampshire bowling, especially that of Marshall, who is – and I heard a Lancashire supporter offer the explanation – a kind of black Brian Statham. He was well supported by Emery, and his fieldsmen. Tremlett also was steady. At present, it looks as if Tremlett's career will develop from batting to bowling: his father, you will remember, did it the other way around.

The first two wickets fell with the score at 23, and Clive Lloyd was in the undignified position of having to avoid a hat-trick; he went out at 40, and two more were out in the 70s. Cockbain was the only batsman to come out of the morning with much credit. At lunch, after 35 overs, Lancashire were 88 for five.

However, the afternoon provided a stubborn Lancashire recovery. Several times previously this season Hampshire have made an early breakthrough, and then found themselves in difficulty against 8, 9, 10 and jack. In this case if was particularly Jack, for Simmons and Hughes are old hands at rescuing an innings from the rocks. Hughes had made 40 before he was seventh out at 128, and Simmons reached a solid, and not ungraceful, 50 before the innings ended at 210.

We had just decided that the pitch was now easy, and would become easier, in the tradition of Southampton pitches, when Hampshire wickets were flying about us: Greenidge bowled, Rice caught at short leg, Jesty at slip. Lancashire bowled fast, and crowded the bat. For a time, every other ball seemed to produce an edge.

Pocock cools the hot pot

SOUTHAMPTON: Lancashire, with eight second innings wickets in hand, are 191 runs behind Hampshire

A splendid innings by the Hampshire captain, Pocock, the highest of his career, transformed this match yesterday. Hampshire had begun at 98-4 (and had at one point been 32-3) with Pocock 51 and Cowley 0. The fifth wicket, Cowley's, fell at 261. By then Lancashire had gone off the hot pot.

Pocock's bat had had some edges on Wednesday evening, but yesterday morning had nothing but a broad middle. I have never seen him bat better, or, come to that, anything like so well. The foundation of his score was the off-drive, but as his confidence grew he played a variety of strokes, including a kind of delicate steer with an upright bat, to find third man. It looked perfectly secure, but did not give much pleasure to Croft, who was bowling. His more orthodox cuts were also working well. It was an innings which will have done him, and his side, a lot of good.

The Southampton pitch, after its eccentricities on Wednesday, returned to its customary emollience like a middle-aged Edwardian governess ashamed of casting an appreciative eye on the handsome young chauffeur. The weather was dry, sunny till the evening, when the light became poor. There was not much help for any kind of bowler though Lancashire tried seven.

If Pocock's was the decisive effort, he could not have done it without Cowley and it was a century from Marshall – his highest score, as well – that put Hampshire into a position to declare about 5 pm. Cowley batted diligently, as was required, though he managed to play some strokes before he was caught at slip – a high, leaping catch.

After Pocock had lifted a ball to cover, and retired full of glory, Marshall took over, hitting sixes and fours in all directions. One, to judge by the alarming clang, must have left a large dent in a car outside the ground. Another was skilfully caught by Simmons, on the rebound from the broadcasting box. Another set back the building of Hampshire's new cricket school.

Pocock decided to bat on for a big lead, rather than declare when he had garnered the batting points, hoping Lancashire might offer him something in the fourth innings. He was probably right. Lancashire, looking weary, worn and sad, did not bat well in the evening.

Lancashire save game, only to throw it away

SOUTHAMPTON: Hampshire (20 pts) beat Lancashire (5 pts) by 10 wickets

Southampton's mind was on other things yesterday, and despite the sunny, if sometimes cool weather, there were not many people at the cricket. This was a pity, because the play was interesting, and Hampshire had a notable and unexpected win in the last few minutes.

Lancashire began at 57 for two, needing another 191 to save an innings defeat. Abrahams was soon out, caught at the wicket off Marshall, who throughout the day looked by far the most dangerous bowler. He did not, however, get much help from a placid pitch. The two Lloyds settled in. They did not hurry, nor had they any reason to do so.

At lunch, the score was 149 for three. At 185, when we were all inclining our minds to a peaceful draw, Clive Lloyd was leg before to Marshall, who had just returned to the attack. This gave life to Hampshire and anxiety to Lancashire. David Lloyd gave a hard chance to slip, also off Marshall. Had he gone then, Hampshire would have been on top.

But he stayed, ultimately reaching a valuable if unspectacular hundred, and at the other end Hughes, always one for the aggressive option, banged the ball about. The Hampshire fielding was enthusiastic, but sometimes untidy.

Hampshire hopes rose again when Lloyd and Hughes were out just before tea, and Maynard just afterwards (301 for seven). But Reidy played capably, and Simmons, that admirable cricketer, who always looks as if he is enjoying himself whatever the state of the game, helped him – we thought – to take victory beyond Hampshire's reach.

We were wrong. Lancashire, having valiantly saved the game, chucked it away. Their last wickets were dribbled away quite unnecessarily, and suddenly Hampshire had 18 overs to score 112. Greenidge took two boundaries in the first from Croft, and thereafter he and Rice were never in trouble.

Hampshire v Lancashire, Southampton, 9, 10 & 11 June 1982

Hampshire won by ten wickets

Lancashire

I. Cockbain	c Parks b Tremlett	31	c Parks b Emery	15
G. Fowler	c Pocock b Marshall	2	c Tremlett b Marshall	6
D. Lloyd	c Rice b Marshall	0	b Jesty	112
* C.H. Lloyd	c Southern b Marshall	11	lbw b Marshall	60
D.P. Hughes	c Rice b Jesty	40	b Cowley	65
J. Abrahams	b Marshall	0	b Marshall	17
B.W. Reidy	c Parks b Emery	15	*not out*	33
+ C. Maynard	b Jesty	20	c Parks b Emery	1
J. Simmons	c Rice b Marshall	50	run out	27
C.E.H. Croft	c Parks b Emery	18	run out	1
L.L. McFarlane	*not out*	4	lbw b Jesty	0
	lb 5, nb 14	19	b 7, lb 8, w 2, nb 5	22
		210		**359**

1/23, 2/23, 3/40, 4/70, 5/77, 6/103, 7/128, 8/145, 9/190, 10/210
1/24, 2/28, 3/67, 4/185, 5/292, 6/296, 7/301, 8/347, 9/358, 10/359

Marshall	18.1	7	48	5	32	9	108	3
Emery	20	5	55	2	26	7	71	3
Tremlett	15	8	22	1				
Jesty	18	5	56	2	16.3	5	42	2
Southern	2	0	10	0	17	4	62	0
Cowley					26	11	54	1

Hampshire

C.G. Greenidge	b McFarlane	9	*not out*	62
J.M. Rice	c Abrahams b Croft	4	*not out*	50
M.C.J. Nicholas	lbw b Simmons	31		
T.E. Jesty	c Hughes b Croft	2		
* N.E.J. Pocock	c Reidy b Hughes	164		
N.G. Cowley	c C.H. Lloyd b Hughes	71		
M.D. Marshall	*not out*	116		
T.M. Tremlett	c Abrahams b Hughes	2		
+ R.J. Parks	run out	28		
J.W. Southern	*not out*	16		
K. St J. D. Emery				
	b 3, lb 6, w 1, nb 5	15	lb 2, w 1	3
	(8 wkts, dec)	**458**	(no wkt)	**115**

1/11, 2/17, 3/21, 4/90, 5/261, 6/312, 7/334, 8/438

Croft	27	3	102	2	8.4	0	62	0
McFarlane	23	3	102	1	5	0	36	0
Reidy	18	6	58	0				
Simmons	22	6	53	1	3	0	14	0
D. Lloyd	8	1	36	0				
Abrahams	7	0	29	0				
Hughes	14	0	63	3				

Umpires: C. Cook and A.G.T. Whitehead

Vic Marks

TAUNTON: Somerset v Leicestershire (NatWest Trophy)

Philip Sharpe made Marks the man of the match, a shrewd decision since Marks had much to do, with bat and ball, at the critical moments of the game. Sharpe might have some natural sympathy with Marks. He was often neglected by the England selectors, though always doing what was required of him when he was called on. I have a gloomy feeling, in view of the latest selections, that the same thing may happen to Marks.

Shrub Hill Station, Worcester

WORCESTER: Worcestershire v Glamorgan

We go to Worcester partly because of the beauty of the ground, thinking of the cathedral, the Glover's Needle and the Severn getting into its stride. A less obvious attraction is Shrub Hill Station, a handsome building of purplish stone.

Few trains go there now (at least from Bristol, where in the morning you have a choice between the 7.45 and 11.25); but it was once a notable station (indeed, only a few years ago, it still ran its own cricket team). And it is faithfully maintained by a loyal staff who remember better days. In the little buffet, for instance, you will find fresh flowers on the table.

The Cricket Writers' Club again

WESTON-SUPER-MARE: Somerset v Yorkshire

I missed some portions of the day's play, chiefly because of attempts to get in touch with the secretary of the Cricket Writers' Club, who always seems to be in Paris or Auckland when you want him. I inform all members, because this is the only notification they are likely to get, that the annual general meeting will take place on Friday in the press box at Lord's at 10 in the morning.

The timing was a cunning idea of Robin Marlar, ensuring a quorum, since many members will be stuck there anyway, and also (since the match starts at 11) limiting the length of the speeches which are inclined to overflow on such occasions.

Soporific cricket at Weston

WESTON-SUPER-MARE: Somerset v Yorkshire

As my old friend and schoolmate Eric Hill (the most dreaded outside right I ever faced on the soccer field) commented in the middle of the afternoon, the groundsman must have been the happiest chap.

After all the fuss about the previous match, this Weston pitch was not playing at all badly. I still would not have vouched for its future behaviour, because a good deal of dust was rising from it, which is usually a sign of forthcoming trouble. But Boycott's mastery was sufficient to suppress any deficiencies and as the day went on, Lumb also batted increasingly well.

The afternoon and evening did become drowsy in the sunshine: in the press box a yawning colleague said "I am soporific" to which Eric Hill replied, "Church of England myself."

A sign of the times at Bristol

BRISTOL: Gloucestershire v Somerset

It was a shock to me that my old friend The Purpureous Basil was missing from his usual seat. It was also an ill omen for Gloucestershire. I assumed that Basil had been summoned to the Cathedral to sing a Requiem, his only valid excuse for absence. Imagine my horror when I was told he was watching the Test on telly. The condition of county cricket grows increasingly grave.

Derek Randall at Worcester

WORCESTER: Worcestershire v Nottinghamshire

The Worcester ground has its own beauty, even in the gloom. There was a time, about four o'clock in the afternoon, when the cathedral, drizzle swirling about it, looked more like the church of Widecombe when a Dartmoor mist is closing in. Do not misunderstand me: Widecombe is also a noble building, but such weather can play curious optical tricks with scale.

I doubt whether Randall was consoled by such reflections, for he was 99 not out, when rain stopped play at half past three. The players took an early tea, and were out again, though only briefly, at 20 to five. A young lady sitting next to me in the press box was making assiduous notes from Mill's *Utilitarianism*.

Randall's innings was interesting and, considering the imminent selection for Australia, timely. I have often seen him more commanding, but he dug his side out of a hole, and showed as he progressed that he still has the strokes. One drive through extra cover was as good as anything of the kind I have seen all season. He is still a fidgeter, though I understand he is making efforts to control it. I am not quite sure if he is wise in this. I am inclined to think that the more he fidgets, the better he bats.

When play was resumed it lasted for only an over, enough for Randall to complete his 100, his first of the season. Before the vital ball, he tapped the pitch twice, scratched his box twice, waggled his knees three times, and tugged his helmet five times. I counted.

Richards finds unlikely partner

TAUNTON: The Pakistanis, with all second innings wickets in hand, are 111 runs ahead of Somerset

Somerset, beginning at 39 for one, 305 behind, did not do very well in the earlier part of the day, and when their seventh wicket fell at 147, it was possible that they might have to follow on. However, the pitch was giving no trouble to batsmen, and Richards was still in. Somebody had said in the morning (inaccurately) what a poor season he had been having. Perhaps he overheard. When Somerset declared, at five o'clock, they were only 44 behind, and Richards had scored 181.

He had hardly ever looked in difficulties. The question was, could he find an adequate partner? Roebuck played on to Abdul Qadir at 58, and in the same over Popplewell was caught at slip, an odd catch which had travelled via gully. I am told, by those in a better position to view, that both balls were googlies. Certainly Qadir seemed the only bowler who found movement from the pitch. It was a hot day, and after a testing opening spell from Imran, the fast bowlers lost some of their zest.

Slocombe is too good a cricketer to have so few chances, and I thought he was going to take advantage of this one, but he was caught at mid-wicket at 117. Rose was caught at the wicket from the last ball before lunch. Two more wickets fell soon afterwards. Richards was nearing his 100, but where would he find his strength and stay?

There came now, down the pavilion steps with scarcely a stumble, the commanding figure of Colin Dredge of Frome. Often though I have commended his demonic qualities as a bowler, his batting, in my experience, has been no more than gnomic. But he played as if this was his day.

It is true that he was dropped early on, and again near the end of his epic, although all faithful Somerset supporters agreed that they "didnree" carry. He bats left handed, and signalled his promotion to No 9 by wearing a helmet, just as if he was opening the innings in a needle match against Midsomer Norton. He leant into an on-drive, which sped to the boundary, like another Woolley. He defended, in dourer moments, like John Edrich; occasionally he drove like Bob Barber, and usually got four, sometimes from the edge rather than the face of the bat.

When the declaration came, Dredge, with some assistance from Richards, had put on 153, a Somerset record for the eighth wicket, surpassing the 143 of E.F. Longrigg and C.J.P. Barnwell, both masters of the unpredictable in their time, in 1938. Oh, yes, Richards played quite well too. But it was the Demon's day.

SOMERSET 300 for seven declared (Richards 181*, Dredge 34*)

Demon of Frome raises the Somerset spirits

THE OVAL: Somerset beat Surrey by two wickets

The standard of cricket in this match was not high, considering that the teams included so many good players, but it was to some extent redeemed by its closeness, especially on the last afternoon.

Somerset's win, which had several times been in doubt, came off the fifth over of the last possible 20. Neither Richards nor Botham played a big innings, and I had thought that at least one of them must. It was Roebuck, Popplewell, Marks, those university types, who held the innings together, though at the last crisis it was the Demon of Frome who struck out for the country bumpkins.

Dredge must (and should) be really thinking of himself as a batsman by now, and I do not fancy Nottinghamshire's chances if he goes in with an hour to play and a blinding light today.

...

Rose was seventh out, caught at the wicket off Knight, at 153. The match was going Surrey's way, but Dredge came in to join Marks. He looked austere, even severe, as if he could not imagine what all these supposed batsmen had been doing.

Marks was out at 190 (another for Mackintosh), but Dredge, with an unusually restrained Garner at the other end, safely steered the ship to Watchet Harbour.

SOMERSET 204 for eight (Roebuck 51, Popplewell 48, Marks 44, Dredge 34*)

The next day, in the Benson & Hedges final at Lord's, Somerset beat Nottinghamshire by nine wickets. Dredge did not bat.

Jones still one of the best

WORCESTER: Worcestershire, with nine second innings wickets in hand, are 91 runs ahead of Glamorgan

Glamorgan began at 24 for two, 343 behind. Daniels, the night-watchman, was soon out. The first question was whether the follow-on could be saved. It was not exactly tricky, but it was hard to score runs quickly. Glamorgan sensibly took their time.

I thought it would need a big innings by someone if they were to stay in the match. By far the likeliest person to make it was good old Alan Jones, and so, bless him, he did.

Jones has been one of the best county cricketers of my time. Not one of the great international stars, but as sound and as faithful a player as any captain could wish to have in his side. He can go fast when it is needed. I remember him winning a match at Cardiff after a Lancashire declaration which seemed to offer Glamorgan no hope – and he can, when necessary, be cautious, as he was yesterday, at least in the earlier part of his innings, before he reached 100, out of 201, in the 83rd over.

Yet he is never strokeless. A half-volley is still a half-volley, and he will dance down the pitch to kill the spin even if only planning a defensive stroke. He is 43 years old. Another lesson he gives to his young men about him is his nimbleness and swift judgment in running between wickets.

Before lunch, he was partnered by Ontong, who also batted well, though restlessly. Ontong kept changing his bat, and lost patience with the accurate, economical bowling of Patel, by whom he was caught and bowled. In the afternoon, Hopkins shared the burden and the follow-on had been saved when, at 218, he was caught and bowled by Gifford.

Gifford, who is only a year and a bit younger than Jones, was another who demonstrated that skills can survive into (in terms of cricketing careers) old age. But Jones knew all about him. "Ah, boyo, I remember that one from Pontypridd about 1965," he seemed to be saying as he made quick, late adjustments to an awkward ball.

The declaration came, none too soon, at half past five, after Glamorgan had missed their third batting point by one run. Jones was applauded warmly by a Worcestershire crowd which has an inherited respect for these stubborn fighters from the Marches.

Hampshire come from gloom to shining win

BOURNEMOUTH: Hampshire (20 pts) beat Somerset (5 pts) by 10 runs

Hampshire had one of the wins they will treasure at Bournemouth for a long time when they came from the darkness into the beaming light and beat Somerset by 10 runs.

On Saturday, Hampshire, put in, had been bowled out for 119, chiefly by the Long Black Telegraph Pole, if I may borrow Peter Roebuck's description of Garner. Somerset had not done too well either, with 130 for seven.

However, yesterday morning their last three wickets put on 64. The man concerned was again Garner, who scored 40 not out, with two straight sixes, the second of which Tremlett caught: unfortunately he had one foot over the boundary at the time.

When Hampshire went in again, Greenidge began with a dash, but was caught at the wicket after a quick 20. Rice, who had been painstaking, to seek a kind word, was caught at short leg, from bat and pad, soon afterwards. Both these wickets fell to Garner. At lunch, the score was 37 for two. At 49, Nicholas, who had batted for 87 minutes for his two (so I was reliably informed, though it seemed longer) was out. Turner was caught at the wicket, off Garner, a run later.

Pocock began with an elegant late cut, Jesty was going well and there was a hint of Hampshire recovery. The pitch was dusty, the seamers found movement from it and a variable bounce, but the outfield was fast and the edges sometimes baffled the fielders too. It was also hot work for them, as the sun beat down.

...

Somerset had to score 83. They batted rather casually, and Marshall took the opportunity to demonstrate that Garner is not the only West Indian fast bowler.

The second wicket fell at 13. The third and fourth wickets fell, both at 38, one of them that of the captain who had looked in form. Marks was fifth out at 39. Taylor attempted an irresponsible hook and was sixth out at 44. The innings had been overcome by panic. The seventh wicket fell at 55, the eighth at 58, the ninth that of Garner at 60. The extra half hour was taken, and an extra quarter of an hour after that, under what regulation I know not, but the last wicket fell and Hampshire had achieved what, in the circumstances, was a remarkable win, though Somerset had also achieved what must only be considered a remarkable defeat.

HAMPSHIRE	119 (Garner 6-23) & 157 (Jesty 50, Garner 5-57)
SOMERSET	194 (Garner 40*, Jesty 4-31) & 72 (Marshall 5-37, Jesty 4-8)

Speed of Clarke too much for Brearley's army

THE OVAL: Surrey beat Middlesex by 125 runs

O brother Sylvester! (I remember a song which went something like that from my University days). After the opening words the chorus would inquire: "What has he got?" "He's got a row of medals on his chest! (Big chest!") It would take all the Army and Navy, we gathered, to put the wind up Sylvest. Well, Sylvest and his mighty chest put the wind up Middlesex all right, and decided this NatWest Bank Trophy semi-final.

With Middlesex needing 206 runs to win, he had Brearley caught at the wicket, in the fifth over. Brearley had faced him much as a brave Christian, sword in hand, must have faced a lion; the last spring was too much for him. Tomlins was leg-before first ball. Gatting very nearly made the hat-trick, saved by a touch of bat before the ball hit his pad. Slack was caught at the wicket, a fine edge, though it could have been a thick one for all he knew about it. Clarke had now taken three for six in four overs.

At about this time, a Middlesex supporter said to me: "Always a chance so long as Gatting's there." Two minutes later a Surrey supporter, of quite a different conversational group, said that he would "not breathe happily until Gatting's gone." This struck me as an impressive tribute to Gatting from both friend and foe. But a moment after the words were spoken, Gatting went, caught off bat and pad, another to Clarke.

Clarke had bowled seven overs, and taken four for 10, when Knight reluctantly took him off (he was not so reluctant to make the change as Clarke was). The Surrey supporting bowling was more than equal to the task. It was some time before Middlesex lost another wicket, but the run rate required grew ominously higher. Monkhouse bowled Radley in the 24th over, Emburey was well caught at deep point by Clarke in the 31st – 54 for six. Jackman took this wicket, and a couple more later.

It was, as it happened, Clarke's last contribution to the match; he was not needed to bowl his dreaded last five overs. Monkhouse was quite good enough in his place. His was useful bowling in its own right. He is a fair-haired Cumbrian, who looks like every romantic's idea of a young man from the Fells. Roland Butcher put up a fight for Middlesex, but they were never in serious contention.

It had been a sunny, fresh morning, with the breeze from the Vauxhall End, when Surrey began at 40 for one in the 14th over. Smith and Butcher, both left-handed, pushed confidently on. There was nothing much wrong with the pitch: it was on the slow and low side, with gentle turn for the spinners. The size of the crowd was rather disappointing, but no doubt many, having taken one day off, were unable to take another.

Surrey laid the basis of a big score, but when they sought to make the necessary acceleration they ran into trouble. Brearley is a difficult captain against whom to score quick runs, and Middlesex gave little away in either bowling or fielding. At 90, in the 28th over, Smith went down the pitch to Edmonds, missed and was bowled. Edmonds had seen or sensed him coming. Knight, another left-hander, began quietly but confidently. It was a surprise when, trying to drive Emburey, he was caught and bowled – a good catch, Emburey diving to his right. Emburey bowled an accurate, searching spell.

Lynch might have been run out before he had scored – would have been if the throw had hit – and seemed to be chiefly responsible when Butcher was run out, at 121. Butcher had reached a sound 50, and was beginning to find his strokes. At 135 Richards, after a couple of boundaries, was caught at the wicket off Gatting. Gatting was brought on as Middlesex's sixth bowler, and found some movement in the air, sufficient to encourage Brearley to bowl him through his full 12 overs.

With two thirds of their overs gone, and half their wickets, Surrey were in trouble. Lynch could not get the bowling away for a long time. It was Thomas who, if he did not break the chains, stretched them. He scored 27, including five fours, in 28 balls. He is also left-handed – with ball as well as bat, and he bowled a lively spell in the afternoon.

Daniel took three quick tail wickets and the score of 205 did not seem enough. The Middlesex innings was delayed by bad light, but the sun soon came out again. Neither the weather nor the pitch could be blamed for Clarke's devastating burst. It was mostly sheer speed that did it, with a touch of devilry. You could see the lightning flashing from his shoulders as he ran in.

SURREY	205 for nine (60 overs, Butcher 55, Smith 43, Lynch 29*, Thomas 27, Daniel 4-24)
MIDDLESEX	80 all out (41.5 overs, Butcher 21, Clarke 4-10, Jackman 3-20, Monkhouse 3-27)

Titmus taking coffee at the Lord's table

LORD'S: Middlesex have scored 273 runs for the loss of eight wickets against Surrey

Middlesex will be champions again, in all probability, this season, but need to win this match. It would make a fitting end to Brearley's career if he was to win it, his last home match at Lord's, against Surrey, as P.F. Warner did in 1920.

He therefore decided to win the toss, and to ask Titmus to call in for coffee. Such decisions as these are taken only in his higher moods. Titmus, aged 49, had to borrow kit before he was able to assume his duty as replacement for Hughes, who is injured.

This added a further romantic touch to the proceedings, but he was also a practical choice, since the pitch is likely to take spin before the match is over. …

Time for a tot when hope is abandoned

LORD'S: Surrey, with all first innings wickets in hand, are 96 runs behind Middlesex

Soon after lunch it started to rain, which had seemed likely for some time. "Looks a bit grim at the back," everyone was saying. This was one of the three most used phrases at the pavilion end, the others being "Do you remember when Denis…?" and "Care for another tincture?"

However, the rain, though heavy, did not last long, and the players were back by a quarter to three. … At tea, the score was 180 for no wicket after 77 overs, Howarth 87, Butcher 78.

Then it rained again, another severe shower. Its severity abated in hardly more than the interval's allotted span, but was followed by a persistent drizzle, which seemed to make an extra effort every time the ground staff began to remove the covers. Then we had another real storm, with a great clap of thunder which seemed to emanate from Father Time, and at half past five hope was abandoned.

Most of the crowd, never a large one, had already gone home. There did not seem to be much in the match, and it is hard to see how there ever will be, especially as Denis isn't playing, and it looks a bit grim at the back. I consoled myself, along with most of the survivors, with another tincture.

A good day for the Middlesex old warriors

LORD'S: Middlesex (22 pts) beat Surrey (5 pts) by 58 runs

In 1920, in Warner's last match as the Middlesex captain, at Lord's, Middlesex won the championship, beating Surrey, who kept going for the runs in the last innings although hope grew remote. Yesterday, in Brearley's last match as Middlesex captain at Lord's, something of the same kind happened. For though Middlesex are not yet sure of the championship, it will be very surprising if they lose it.

Once again there was a generous Middlesex declaration, and once again a brave effort by Surrey that was possibly pursued beyond reason. Brearley, who was applauded off the field after his last innings, an entirely admirable one, also had the satisfaction of seeing his belief that this would become a spinners' pitch and his choice of Titmus triumphantly vindicated. There is no foxing the old master of hounds.

In the morning the sun shone, from a mostly blue sky, and with two captains with reputations for enterprise, and much at stake, there seemed a chance that two dull, damp days might be redeemed.

Surrey declared at lunch … Middlesex had a scramble for a while, Slack and Tomlins both going well after Brearley had given his lively lead. …

The declaration set Surrey 161 to win in 125 minutes. Edmonds came on in the second over, and had Butcher out, a good catch by Brearley at mid-on. The Middlesex catching was a considerable factor in their victory.

Emburey came on in the fifth over, and soon had Howarth out, driving. Lynch was caught and bowled, at 24, in the tenth, by Edmonds. At 40 Knight was caught at mid-wicket, driving at Edmonds, and had I been a stern Surrey supporter I would have thought it was about time they settled for a draw. However, after Richards had gone to Emburey at 49, Clarke came in and had numerous big swings. He lost Smith at 70, and was himself caught in the deep at 84.

This was off Titmus, who proceeded to make hay among the tail before learning he is in the Middlesex party again for today's match at Hove. At least eight overs were left when the match ended. It was a good day for Middlesex, especially the old warriors.

MIDDLESEX	276 (Slack 79, Brearley 43, Radley 40, Butcher 36, Mackintosh 6-61)
	157 for two declared (Slack 71*, Tomlins 51, Brearley 27)
SURREY	273 for four declared (Howarth 112, Butcher 82)
	102 (Clarke 35, Emburey 4-24, Edmonds 3-24, Titmus 3-43)

Old friends and hot supper

It had been several years since I had seen a Test match at Lord's, and I was pleased to be there again. Most things were much the same. The gate men were that little more fussy and pompous, with a proper pride of occasion; the man behind the press bar who remembers every one's name, though I can never remember his (I have an idea it is either Adolphus or Bert, and have decided to call him Bardolph in future); the faces and handshakes of old friends, though not so many from the West Country as can usually be found outside the Tavern.

The rain was – no, I will not say "usual", because on the whole I have been lucky with the weather at Lord's – but not exactly unfamiliar. The public address system still rivals London Airport's for inaudibility.

One thing, however, *has* changed. This is a *Cornhill* Test. I beg your pardon, I have got it wrong. It is a Test sponsored by Cornhill. Our Sports Editor, who was among those present in the morning, is insistent on the precise terminology.

I am inclined to think that sponsors sometimes protest too much about these things: one of the reasons Gillette gave it up was that they found their name was becoming associated with cricket more than razor blades.

The light was poor from the start, and we had a shower in the morning and prolonged rain in the afternoon. This was not altogether a grief to me, since there were so many old friends with Bardolph zealously to attend to us and the details of the match sponsored by Cornhill could safely be left to our cricket correspondent, the Sage of Longparish (sponsored by the Sports Editor). When the afternoon rain came Mohsin was 199 not out. This set off much speculation in box and bar about previous double hundreds scored in Tests at Lord's.

Mohsin must have had an anxious wait. I was reminded of Chipperfield, an Australian who, in his first Test (not sponsored by Cornhill) at Trent Bridge in 1938, was 99 not out at lunch, and was out in the first over afterwards. Cardus consoled him by saying, "A number of cricketers have scored centuries in their first Test. You are the first to score 99."

The rain became so heavy after tea that I decided to go back to Cornhill – I mean High Littleton, sponsored by the thought of a hot supper.

A wailful Warwickshire choir

I had been looking forward to going to Lord's for the NatWest final. I do dislike that abbreviation, while casting no aspersion upon their banking. It reminds me of the line of Keats. 'When in a wailful choir the small gnats mourn...'

The small gnats mourning on Saturday evening were the Warwickshire supporters. It was an acute disappointment for them. They should take comfort that their side redeemed an unsuccessful season by reaching a Lord's final, even though they lost it.

However, I must tell you how I watched the match. You need special passes for these great occasions, and mine, by Saturday morning had not arrived. By the last time we could hope that the post would come, the match had started. I therefore felt I could best fulfil my duties to you and my editor by watching the match on television.

When the seventh Warwickshire wicket fell, I felt this was a wise choice, because even if I had taken a fast train from Bath, and taken my luck in arguing with the Lord's gatekeepers, I would not have seen much of the match. It is very difficult arguing with Lord's gatekeepers, as I have discovered before, because somehow I never *look* like a *Times* reporter. I have not the soothing smile of the Sage of Longparish, not the august ways of Jim Swanton.

Watching cricket on the telly is something that I have not often done, except for the evening matches, or "highlights" as they are called, and a painting made up entirely of highlights does not resemble a painting at all.

I found the commentators and the camera work admirable. What did depress and confuse me were the constant replays, often entirely unnecessary. Cricket is a game with a rhythm, a rhythm which the watcher does not like disturbed. After a ball has been bowled you like to think about it for half a minute or so, have a word with your neighbour about it, and settle down to the next ball.

I did miss the Lord's conversation, especially because at this time of the year everyone is choosing his own side for Australia. However, we have some *cognoscenti* in High Littleton too, and at my lunchtime visit to *The Star* I found unanimous approval for the choice of Marks.

Marks has two outstanding qualities for a long tour. He is an exceptionally pleasant man and will make a good tourist. He has mental toughness for a crisis as he has shown countless times for Oxford and Somerset – and in the latest Test match such qualities often outweighed technical weaknesses. Character tells.

Edmonds, Gatting exchange roles

WORCESTER: Worcestershire, with one second innings wicket standing, are 40 runs ahead

On Saturday, Middlesex made sure of the championship. Yesterday they confirmed their authority.

An interesting thing about the day's play was that it produced splendid performances by two of England's rejects, Edmonds and Gatting, though they got them, so to speak, the wrong way round – Edmonds did the batting and Gatting the bowling.

Middlesex began the day at 221 for five, 53 on. They went on to 382. Edmonds banged about vigorously, every ball played as though it was a punch at the selectors.

The selectors would have been comforted, though, by the performance of Cowans when Worcestershire went in again. He took the first two wickets, and looked very fast indeed, with eight close catchers to encourage him.

You could see what they mean when they talk about another Tyson, though he has not got the Tyson physique: more like Marshall, of Hampshire, but I suppose that would not do too badly either. I bet he will surprise the Australians now and then.

Middlesex were held up for a bit after Cowans went off, but Brearley, who has a good line to the Holy Ghost, or possibly the Holy Doust, brought on Gatting. Gatting took the next four wickets, bowling every ball as if he was aiming at the bridge of the nose or the private parts of an England selector.

It was a sunny, peaceful day, the cathedral sharp against the deep blue sky, down to the smallest pinnacle. Brearley, one of the great cricketers of his generation, and I would say the best county captain since Sellers (with full respect to Surridge), has chalked another one up, looking as usual amiable, intelligent and innocent. But beneath the benignity you must never forget he is as tough as teak.

Brearley claimed an extra half-hour in an attempt to complete the victory, but hopes of this had died before bad light ended play 15 minutes early.

WORCESTERSHIRE	168 (Humphries 56) & 263 (Weston 64, Neale 50, Gatting 4-43)
MIDDLESEX	382 (Butcher 94, Edmonds 92, Gatting 61) & 50 for no wicket

Fittingly, on the final day, in his last act as Middlesex captain, Brearley scored the winning runs.

Somerset have a silly day

TAUNTON: Lancashire (21 pts) beat Somerset (8 pts) by 14 runs

Since the match at Worcester clearly did not have long to go, I spent the last hours of the season at Taunton, less in expectation of an exciting finish than to bid a seasonal farewell to old friends. When I left in the morning from Bath's high and draughty station, the weather was misty, and there was an autumnal tang in the air. I felt as if I was going to a rugby match. By the afternoon, the sun was beating down from a blue sky, and it seemed ridiculous to be thinking of anything else than cricket.

Overnight, Lancashire were 86 for four in their second innings, still 56 behind. They reached 275, chiefly because Clive Lloyd played very well. But the innings was over by 2.10 and Somerset had plenty of time to make the 134 they needed to win.

The pitch was up to no more tricks than might be expected on a third afternoon – a little help for the spinners, certainly. Marks was the most successful bowler. Lancashire, especially Lloyd and O'Shaughnessy, accepted his invitations to have a slog and he was expensive, but he kept inducing the occasional mistake. It was odd that Garner did not bowl. He looked nimble enough in the field. It was almost as if Somerset were, subconsciously no doubt, not in too much of a hurry to end it, unwilling to deprive their faithful supporters (there were many present) of a last spell in the sunshine.

If that was so, they had a sharp lesson. Allott bowled a testing opening spell which showed that that there was something in the pitch for fast bowlers after all. David Lloyd and Hughes, when they came on, made the ball turn, no more I think than Marks had done, but once they had lost their first three wickets for 15 runs, the Somerset batsmen developed into a curious mixture of bafflement and frenzy.

The tail put up a fight, but Lancashire had won by 5.45. How like Somerset! I say this affectionately. We would never like them as much as we do if there were not a few days in each season when they make such silly asses of themselves!

LANCASHIRE	165 (O'Shaughnessy 55, Botham 4-44) & 275 (C. Lloyd 79, O'Shaughnessy 62, Marks 6-128)
SOMERSET	307 (Richards 178, Hughes 4-22, O'Shaughnessy 4-72) & 119 (D. Lloyd 4-36)

The Gravities 1982

There was once a Mayor of Cheltenham who, though by definition a worthy gentleman, did not include among his attributes a deep knowledge of cricket. When it came to doing the civic honours at the cricket festival, he was prudently equipped with notes, which he tried, manfully, to look as if he was not reading. He welcomed to his fair town Emmett, Crapp, Cook, and the rest of the Gloucestershire heroes, concluding with '... and, of course, the brothers Gravity.' It said much for Ken and Tom that they kept their gravity on that occasion, for they are not naturally grave men.

Tom Graveney began his career for Gloucestershire, and soon for England, at about the same time that I was beginning my humble career as a writer and broadcaster about cricket. Because we both lived in the west, and because we were both inclined to a pint at the end of the day, we became friends. I may say, with a clear conscience, that the first time I saw Tom play a long innings, I knew he was a master. He was also, I soon knew, an exceptionally *nice* man (I use that awkward word in the best of its many senses). He was a touch impatient, prone to take sudden decisions, which might concern whether he should try to hit a slow spinner off his length, or whether he should resign the captaincy of Gloucestershire, or whether he should play for England if it conflicted with a promise to play in a benefit match. His judgements on these occasions were not always, in retrospect, wise, but were taken courageously and honestly at the time.

His batting from the first had a bloom which no post-war batsman has equalled (counting Hutton and Compton as pre-war). It withered a little, under the influence of cautious advice and the slow Bristol pitch, and then blossomed again on the freer pastures of Worcester. He never batted better than in his last years, during which he made a triumphant return to the England team. We have had no more handsome batsman since he appeared, except May and, from time to time, Cowdrey and Dexter; and these came from a different tradition. Boycott and Barrington were more prolific and I suppose they had sounder methods, but they never looked so well, even when they were in the runs. The trouble with Tom Graveney was expressed in the words of Oliver Edwards to Dr Johnson: 'I have tried, too, in my time to be a philosopher; but I don't know how, cheerfulness was always breaking in.'

So it was with Ken, who is the elder brother by two-and-a-half-years; and he had less to be cheerful about, for his cricket career ended through a back injury when full of promise. In 1949, he had taken all 10 Derbyshire wickets, at Chesterfield, for 66 runs in 18.4 overs. He managed to return to cricket for a few seasons, when Gloucestershire were in need of a steadying captain, and he did that job satisfactorily, as he did his subsequent job as chairman. Brown's happy and successful run for Gloucestershire owed, I am sure he will not mind my saying, much to the benign influence of Ken Graveney (not forgetting Grahame Parker: now there is a grave man, if you want an example – when his solemn and massive face breaks into a smile, it is like a great rock tumbling down all the way from St Briavel's into the River Wye). Ken was a fast-medium bowler, who could also bat. He was less a seamer than a cutter, so far as I understand these terms – all the experts had, and have, slightly contradictory explanations of the difference. We shall never know just how good a cricketer Ken Graveney might have been.

And then there was David, born to Ken and his beautiful, lamented wife (she died tragically young) in 1953. He is now Gloucestershire's captain, with a notable record behind him as a slow left-arm spinner, and, I would expect, a useful 10 years or so ahead of him. There have been, from time to time, stern arguments between father and Uncle Tom as to whether David would make a better batsman or bowler. I can't remember now who said what, partly because they kept changing sides on the subject, but they would no doubt agree he is a good cricketer. His bowling has been his principal contribution if you look at the figures, but his batting at number seven or thereabouts has been frequently of high value in moments of crisis. I am inclined to think he has the best temperament of the three and will make the best county captain.

I was in such awe of the Graveney brothers, in my early days, that I still feel I have a bit of a nerve to write about them. David used to call me 'Mr Gibson' and even 'Sir', when he was young. Yet he is now the most awesome of the lot. For when he finishes cricket he plans to become a full-time accountant. In the meantime he puts in a fierce winter's practice at accountancy and I have been among his victims, I mean clients. As the Duke of Wellington said of his accountants, 'I don't know what the tax inspectors think of them, but by god they scare me.' Well, I've got it more or less right, as the Mayor of Cheltenham said as he sniffed his celebratory champagne.

Test Decade 1972-82 by Patrick Eagar

Books, at least cricket books, are for me a matter of words, not pictures. I suppose this is because, when I was young, the standard of cricket photography was not high. There were exceptions, going back to G.W. Beldam early in the century, but most illustrations were blurred and unrevealing, or posed.

Nothing was more absurd than to see a famous bowler, supposedly about to deliver, with both feet planted firmly on the ground, and one arm held up in the air. It told you nothing about his bowling action. I began to notice that when there did happen to be a good action picture, it had little to do with the text and had simply been stuck in on its merits as a picture.

So I used to skip the pictures, feeling cross that they had taken up space which could have been much more profitably occupied with words.

To this day, I always treat the news on sound radio as more reliable than the news on television. The news on television is governed by the film available. I worked for the BBC for many years and grew accustomed to hearing television news editors who began their conference by saying not "What's the news today?" but "What film have we got in?"

But I must not be distracted from my central message, which is to say how vastly cricket photography has advanced (not altogether because of technical improvements) and that I know of no better exponent of it than Patrick Eagar.

Test Decade 1972-82 (World's Work, £12.95) is quite frankly a picture book, the best pictures Patrick has taken of Test matches in those years. The covering narrative is cursory, which was wise. It is, however, worth reading Patrick's introduction about the development of cricket photography, and also his careful captions to the pictures.

Every picture tells a story, my mother used to say, and these pictures will tell many stories, not always happy ones; stories of declining manners, of heightened physical aggression, but also brilliant fielding and bold stroke-play. The ferocity has increased, but the skills are still high.

Harold Gimblett: Tormented Genius of Cricket by David Foot

The author of this biography has always been capable of high-class writing but, as an old friend, I have always felt he left himself too little time for it. Now, in *Harold Gimblett: Tormented Genius of Cricket* (Heinemann, £7.95), David Foot has given us one of the best cricket books I have read for a long time.

It was Gimblett's idea in the first place. He had asked Foot to collaborate in his autobiography, and made some tape recordings to that end. His efforts were fitful and when he died, by his own hand, in 1978, Foot was not sure how much of them existed. There turned out to be quite a lot and, with the cooperation of the Gimblett family, he has been able to use them as the basis of the book. He has backed them up with careful research and clothed his findings, even if they are occasionally cruel, with the respectful devotion due to a hero of his boyhood.

John Arlott says in his foreword that "It is not a biography, nor an autobiography, nor the data for a psychological study, but something of all three." I would not quite agree with this statement. I think the book's lasting importance, for which it will be read when cricket is only a game to interest social historians, is a case history of depression.

Without intruding too far into the terminology of psychiatry, I would say Harold Gimblett was "manic depressive", a man of intense ups and downs. So was R.C. Robertson-Glasgow, another Somerset cricketer: so, not that it matters much, am I. Gimblett used to throw his bat around the dressing room when he got out, whether he had scored 0 or 100, whether he was out to a good stroke or bad. He was surly when, after a great innings, compliments were paid him. He was often surly in any circumstances, and yet, instinctively, a kind man, capable of acts of generosity which were not only spontaneous but sustained. In his last days, in acute pain from arthritis, he spent much time driving round Verwood, taking old people to their free lunches. This probably gave him as much satisfaction as any century; he did not spurn their thanks.

He was a very good cricketer, an attacking opening batsman, who scored 23,000 runs with 50 centuries, but only played for England three times. In Somerset it was thought that this was because he played for an unfashionable county. Foot suggests that it was because he did not, in his heart, *want* to play for England; and even that, at the beginning of his career, he did not want to play for Somerset. Would he have been happier as a Somerset farmer? I doubt if he would have been a happy man, however the lot had fallen to him.

He was unlucky on his cricketing debut in 1935. Called from the family farm at Watchet, in an emergency, with very little time to spare, he went in at No 8 for Somerset against Essex at Frome, the score 107 for six. He made a century in 63 minutes, which proved to be the fastest of the season. He immediately became the wonder boy of the moment: one London newspaper chartered an aeroplane to photograph him on the farm. A more difficult start, for a man of his temperament, cannot be imagined.

In a cricketing sense, Gimblett was also unlucky in that, for most of the time he was in contention for an England place, his potential captain was Hammond, a depressive of quite a different sort. Had Brearley been captain, who knows?

In one respect Foot is rather like his hero. He has been reluctant to work seriously at his writing, and I suspect would have been just as pleased knocking off his regular quota for the *East Coker Mercury & Advertiser* as he suspects Gimblett would have been just as pleased to hit his sixes for Watchet as England. But he has played a notable innings, as Harold did so often, and we should be grateful to them both.

The History of I Zingari by R.L. Arrowsmith and B.J.W. Hill

I Zingari (Italian for "The Gypsies", or so at least its founders believed) is the oldest of the "wandering" cricket clubs, that is to say those with no ground of their own. Since 1845 it has serenely gone on its various ways, its collective nose firmly stuck in the air. It is very Victorian, very aristocratic (the team lists over the years sparkle with peers, baronets, and double-barrelled names), very amateur – from the start professionals were barred, even for bowling, a pursuit not then usually thought to be fit for a gentleman. It is also very endearing, like great-grandmother's sampler. I put down this book, the official history of IZ, with an affectionate smile. This was partly, no doubt, because it is so well written.

In the early years the club claimed that their purpose was to spread cricket to backward parts of the land. At their jubilee, they pointed out how successful they had been, since cricket has undoubtedly spread. This was a bad case of *post hoc ergo propter hoc*. Cricket had spread because of the efforts of the professional touring teams, the All-England XI and its successors. IZ played on posh grounds against largely patrician sides. The privilege of the plebs was to watch. W.G. Bolland, who held the office of "Perpetual President", invited his members to:

> *Hear again that happy laugh ringing from yonder group of peasants, in triumph of the downfall of the wicket of some opponent of their lord … the genuine offspring of esteem and affection begotten in the service of a master who sympathizes with his lowly brethren, softens their trials, and welcomes them to a share in his pleasures and amusements. Oh! that such sympathy were more universal!*

The history wonders whether this might have been satirical, but I bet it was not.

G.J.V. Weigall, of whom there is a delightful character sketch in the book, thought that IZ should have closed down after the first war, because there would be no more country house cricket. The club persevered, although there was a time in the Twenties, as the members grew older, when it "became a byword for producing sides of elderly non-benders". That has been put right, and matches still take place on country house grounds; and though without the lavish hospitality of Victorian days, there are still good parties. IZ was founded as a party, and will last, I expect, as long as parties do. When Lord Cobham (another man of whom there is an entertaining and affectionate portrait) was Governor-General of New Zealand, he suggested an IZ tour there, and Rothmans were prepared to help, but "it was felt that IZ of all clubs ought not to accept sponsorship for playing cricket." The authors go on to explain that "to accept the very generous sponsorship of Hambros in the production of this book is a different matter." Er, up to a point, Lord Copper.

IZ has always insisted on proper cricketing manners. It is a point of honour not to show irritation when an appeal is declined. They are not even allowed to rub their heads, or their black, gold and red caps. In an age of diminishing sportsmanship, this is certainly a tradition to be cherished, even if they do still have names with handles. After all, "It is wonderful how much you can conceal between the touch of the handle and the opening of the door if your heart is in it."

1983

The summer of 1983 was one of contrasts. One of the wettest Mays in living memory was followed by weeks of scorching sunshine from June to the middle of August. New Zealand were the touring side, and the third Prudential World Cup would occupy most of June, just as Mrs Thatcher was winning a landslide election victory over Michael Foot.

For Alan Gibson, the most striking – and ironic – contrast was that between his continually growing reputation as a witty and original writer about cricket and the mounting problems in his personal life, which included ill-health and chronic financial difficulties. On May 28, his 60th birthday, he was due to report on Middlesex against Sussex at Lord's. It was somehow cruelly appropriate that the day's play was washed out.

It was all so very painfully different from those happy, carefree, sunlit days of long ago. Days like those spent at the long departed Torquay Cricket Festival, for example, which he recalled with wistful affection, in a feature for the January edition of *The Cricketer*.

When the first-class season began towards the end of April, Alan headed for the Parks, via Didcot of course, to watch Oxford University play Lancashire. In what was to become very much the pattern for the next five weeks or so, the match was badly disrupted by frequent heavy showers, and dribbled away into a tame draw. For Alan, what followed was '*a frustrating week of attempting to watch cricket, and staring mindlessly at the rain*'.

The opening round of the Benson and Hedges Cup was seriously disrupted, to the point where the entire season was acquiring an air of unreality, as with the match between Glamorgan and Surrey at Cardiff on May 20.

As May drew to a close, so at last the weather began to improve. The county championship match between Somerset and Sussex provided three days of uninterrupted cricket, and the opportunity to take a pop at one of his favourite targets, the British Rail buffet

1983 was World Cup year. The West Indies, with Greenidge, Haynes, Richards and Lloyd among their batsmen, and, in Roberts, Holding, Marshall and Garner, possibly the most formidable battery of fast bowlers that even they have ever fielded, were hot favourites. India and Zimbabwe were among the outsiders, but both produced tournament-shaking shocks in a protracted preliminary round: Zimbabwe beating Australia at Trent Bridge and, in what no-one at the time suggested might be taste of things to come, India getting the better of the West Indies at Old Trafford.

This was the third Prudential World Cup, and the first in which some of the non-Test grounds were used as venues. Thus, Alan found himself at Taunton's first international match, England v Sri Lanka on June 11, where Gower's 130 reminded him of one of his boyhood heroes, the great Frank Woolley.

But it was a week later, at Tunbridge Wells, that he was able to witness a genuinely remarkable innings. Kapil Dev's 175 not out against Zimbabwe was a record in all forms of one day competitions at the time; it announced the arrival on the world stage of one of the greatest all-rounders; and it changed the course of the tournament.

Alan's assessment that 'with such a player in such form, India are a difficult side for anyone to beat' proved prescient, although it was the unlikely figure of Roger

Tests
England
beat New Zealand
3-1

World Cup Final
India
beat West Indies

Championship
1 Essex
2 Middlesex
3 Hampshire
4 Leicestershire
5 Warwickshire
6 Northamptonshire

Sunday League
1 Yorkshire
2 Somerset
3 Kent
4 Sussex
5 Hampshire
6 Derbyshire
Essex

NatWest Final
Somerset
beat Kent

Benson & Hedges Final
Middlesex
beat Essex

Most first-class runs
1 K.S. McEwan
2 G. Boycott
3 C.L. Smith

Most first-class wickets
1 J.K. Lever
D.L. Underwood
3 N. Gifford

Binny, with his gentle medium pace, who proved the undoing of the mighty West Indies, on a scorching day at Lord's in the final.

Two days later, it was a very different scene across the city at The Oval, where Surrey, after a dismal start to the season, were playing Northamptonshire, and Alan – not for the first or last time in his career – encountered trouble with officialdom.

That chilly day at the Oval proved very much the exception, as flaming June turned to baking July. Alan hated the heat. Particularly in later years, he liked to watch the cricket from the comfort of a bar, huddled in his overcoat, large scotch to hand, wearing gym shoes to ease the pain from the neuritis in his feet. So I doubt if he was in the best of humour when he set off on July 6 to travel to the County Ground Bristol to watch a below strength Gloucestershire side take on the touring New Zealanders on the first of three sweltering days:

The Test series in 1983 was memorable mainly for New Zealand's first victory, after 52 years and in 29 attempts, against England in England. That was achieved in the second Test at Headingley, with Richard Hadlee and Jeremy Coney strongly to the fore. Alan was asked by *The Times* to write a "colour piece" to preview the next Test, at Lord's.

Meanwhile, in the one-day competitions, a Somerset side featuring Botham, Richards and Garner was carrying all before it: top of the John Player League and in the final of the NatWest Bank Trophy, thanks to a last ball victory against Middlesex in the semi-final at Lord's. The match report for the final, against Kent on September 4, would naturally be written by John Woodcock, as Cricket Correspondent. But Alan was asked to be there as well, to offer some thoughts – as an adopted West Countryman – on the atmosphere of the day. He did actually make it to Lord's this time but, as with most big one-day cricket occasions, it was not to his liking.

Somerset won comfortably enough, although the Sunday League escaped them, Alan making no pretence of shedding any tears when Yorkshire's win at Chelmsford relegated Roebuck and his less than merry men to second place.

In those days, the county championship finished in early September, in Alan's case, at Bristol, in what sounds as if it was very much his sort of match.

It was the prelude to a miserable autumn. Alan was in dispute with *The Times* over his expenses, and his creditors – headed by the Inland Revenue – were growing ever more impatient. In despair, he wrote to the Official Receiver in October, asking to be made bankrupt. Thanks mainly to the intervention of his son Andrew, who was a partner in the Plymouth firm of solicitors, Foot and Bowden, this drastic remedy was narrowly avoided, but it was still a grim time.

Meanwhile, as always, there was comfort to be found in the past and in old friends, and he rounded off the year with a typically generous tribute in *The Cricketer* to the doyen of the Taunton press box, Eric Hill.

The Scarborough of the West

I wrote last month about Jack Walsh and, in the course of the piece, mentioned the Torquay Cricket Festival. As I was writing it, in the refreshment room at Taunton station, while waiting for a train (I know you will find it hard to believe me, but the refreshment room was actually *open* at a useful time) I met an old friend from Devon and we fell to memories of Devon cricket. He told me that I ought to write something 'proper' about the Festival.

I cannot do that. The memories are too dim, at least of the cricket itself, but I can pay the occasion a belated salute. Devon has seen very little first-class cricket, though it has produced a lot of first-class cricketers and from time to time has sought first-class county status. It was partly in order to demonstrate that such an ambition was feasible that the Torquay Festival was begun in 1954. It lasted for only five years and failed to make its point: but it provided some happy times.

First-class cricket was a dubious financial proposition anywhere then, before sponsorship and the one-day game had made an appearance. It needed courage to start it at Torquay. Six days in September was the plan: 'the Scarborough of the West'. I believe it was Harold Gimblett who had the idea. Ben Brockman, a local enthusiast, took it up, and David Haines became the secretary. My old friend David was a pretty good slow left-arm bowler, who played a lot for Devon. In a county match I once saw him have three chances dropped off his bowling, from three consecutive balls, by the same fieldsman at long-off. That was at Torquay, and no doubt gave him an appetite for punishment there, which his work for the festival gave him every opportunity to gratify.

At first, it went well. In the second year, there was a small profit, which was adequate, since it was intended to be an advertisement for Torquay as much as a money-maker. But the weather turned unkind, and in 1957, five and a half days of play were lost. The only action was on the first morning, in bitter cold and drizzle. This was not altogether wasted, since it gave D.F. Cole his only opportunity to play in first-class cricket. Cole was the Devon captain, and a highly successful all-rounder in Minor Counties cricket – the first man to win the award for the Minor Counties player of the year.

The setbacks from the weather were accepted by the corporation and ratepayers of Torquay. But in 1958 there was another severe financial loss, even though the weather had been reasonably good. One morning, in bright sunshine, Worrell and Sobers were batting, two of the most attractive stroke-makers in the world. Lock was bowling to them, and Lock never enjoyed being hit, festival or no festival. Yet the ground was less than half full. George Emmett, who was playing in the match and had been professional at Torquay in his time, turned to David Haines and said, ruefully, 'What *do* they want? Good heavens, what *do* they want, if this doesn't please them?' What they wanted, though we did not know it then, was limited-over cricket. Somerset have drawn big gates at Torquay for John Player games.

I still have the Torquay Festival tie, which must be becoming something of a rarity of cricketana. I remember some of the midnight bathes. Maurice Tremlett majestically led one, looking even more than usually like Apollo, but when we got to the brink (it was chilly) he did no more than dip in a disdainful toe. On another occasion, the party was led by A.C.D. Ingleby-Mackenzie. We had four cars and the car park at Babbacombe, which could take about 400, was totally empty when we arrived. Nevertheless, an attendant emerged from his sentry box, and not only charged us but insisted on the cars being meticulously lined up in the corner. I think I have written before about the famous bet between Willie Jones (cricket for Glamorgan, rugby for Gloucestershire) and Ted Dickinson (amply built member of the local committee). Willie maintained, upon a glass or two, that he could throw a rugby ball further than Ted could kick it. Spurred on, he declared that he could throw a *reverse* pass further than Ted could kick. We all trooped out to the field to watch. Willie lost – by a foot.

There was the furious series of Test matches at table football played one night at the Cott Inn, Dartington. Sam Mearing, the landlord, and his barmaid were nearly invincible on their own table. They represented England against C.L. McCool and V.E. Jackson for Australia. The Australians lost 14 times running. The night was well advanced, but they were not departing until they had won. They won next time and we were all just going when they became suspicious that their victory had been a fix, and it started all over again.

It was great fun, but it does seem a long time ago. *Eheu fugaces* ... the fleeting years are slipping by.

Surrey's sleepwalkers

CARDIFF: Match abandoned: Glamorgan (1 pt), Surrey (1 pt)

I believe it was Lord Hartington, in the 1880s, who dreamt he was speaking in the House of Lords, and woke up to find he was. I was reminded of this by the early Surrey batting yesterday.

They still seemed unsure whether they were awake, or in a morphean twilight. This is not a criticism of the batsmen, just an explanation. So rarely have they had a bat in their hands in real contest this season that they could be forgiven for thinking it was all a dream.

It must be said for Glamorgan, however, that they had woken to the alarm clock, sounded by their new captain, Selvey. He and Nash made the ball swing, under the heavy skies, and Surrey, after winning the toss, batted languidly.

Clinton was leg-before in the first over, Butcher and Smith progressed uncertainly on a pitch which was slow but of doubtful bounce. Smith, trying to shake off caution, had a heave at Nash and was leg-before at 25. After 16 overs, the score was only 36.

Selvey brought on Lloyd, of whom one still thinks as "the young off-spinner", although he has taken more than 200 wickets for Glamorgan, and was born at Neath 30 years ago. They grow their plants to last at Neath: more stubborn leeks than lovely, ephemeral daffodils.

Lloyd bowled well, but it was Nash who got the next wicket, Butcher leg-before at 49. Nash bowled his quota through, and finished with 2 for 21. Neither Knight nor Howarth looked at ease. Knight was caught at the wicket off Rowe, who also bowled off-breaks, at 68.

Then it rained, but only for 10 minutes. All morning the clouds had lain ominously about, and the ground was already so soaked that it only needed another storm to send us home. We dodged it that time. Lynch and Howarth began to put the Surrey innings together, and played some brave stokes. At 133, Wilkins, fielding from his own bowling, ran out Lynch with a splendid throw after Howarth had sent Lynch back.

The score had reached 142 in the 45th over when Wilfred Wooller appeared on the pavilion balcony. I have told you of the Cardiff balcony before. It has a large sign saying that you may not sit or stand on it and there is a terrible Welsh curse upon anyone who transgresses. I cannot remember the precise words, but an approximate translation would be "gorsedd off". Wilfred, never a superstitious man, hauled a chair out of the bar, and plumped himself in it, facing the sign.

Disaster immediately followed. The rains descended and the floods came. There was no possibility of any more play. Wilfred, unperturbed, announced that he was going off for a game of bowls, which I expect was much what Hartington said when he woke up to find himself speaking in the House of Lords.

Wilfred Wooller
'It is fair to say of Mr Wooller that he does not suffer fools gladly, and that his perception of folly is not always certain.'

Somerset ravaged in the sun

TAUNTON: Sussex have scored 408 for six against Somerset

Yes, the sun shone, though the evening grew a little cloudy. The Somerset crowd did not really mind watching their bowlers being bashed around, because at least they were able to watch in warmth. The Somerset countryside looked lovely as I travelled down from Bath, and I thought the bright yellow splotches of oil-seed rape enhanced it scenically, though this does not mean I commit myself to any of its political or bacterial implications.

Sussex won the toss and batted on a slow, easy pitch. The outfield, however, was surprisingly dry and fast. Possibly the pitch may help the spinners later; Somerset gave Marks, Lloyds and Richards a lot of bowling. But it was a day for batting, and Sussex enjoyed it. One of their strengths is that they bat a long way down the order. When Imran rejoins them, they will present a grim aspect to any bowling side on a good pitch.

Mendis played handsomely in the morning. He had reached his fifty by lunch, when the score was 112 for two, Green and Barclay out. When Mendis was caught at the wicket off Garner, who made a ball lift by reason of his physique and pace rather than any touch of venom in the pitch, the score was 132 in the forty-eighth over.

Somerset were not too doing too badly at this point, but were destroyed by a stand between Parker and Wells, who put on a hundred in an hour, much as they pleased. Parker's, I thought, was the best batting of the day. It was splendid to see him in such good form. He will be a force in England cricket yet.

C.M. Wells, who had gone in before him, batted admirably, though Parker was soon catching him up. His younger brother, A.P. Wells, also scored fifty. Sussex reached their fourth batting point in the ninety-second over, but decided to bat on, presumably seeking an innings win. The Somerset bowlers must have felt, towards the end, like a field of raped oil-seed, if I may put it that way.

It occurs to me that this is quite a year for the Wellses. Here we have C.M. and A.P. both in form; I understand that there is a new biography coming out of H.G., whose father was a professional cricketer; and what is more T. Wells has a World Cup match.

Going off the rails in a BR buffet

TAUNTON: Somerset, with nine wickets in hand, need 129 runs to avoid an innings defeat by Sussex

One of the sponsors for this match, according to the card, was British Rail (Western), and I looked forward to an interesting discussion with them, though for one reason and another this did not take place. The point I wished to make is that buffet rooms on railway stations are convenient refuges for travellers waiting for trains, which are sometimes late, but that is their primary function: they are not intended to be discos.

We who wait need to hear the station announcer. Twice this year I have missed trains because of the inaudibility of the announcer against the thundering fury of the juke box, operated by people who clearly have no intention of catching a train at all. I exempt from this general criticism the refreshment room in Didcot, in which you could always hear the announcer clearly, if there happened to be one.

However, I was safely at Taunton before lunch, and though the sunshine mixed with patches of clouds, and a wind which sometimes became chilly, it was another pleasant day for watching cricket.

Sussex declared at their overnight score. The questions were how the pitch would behave, and whether Somerset could save the follow on. The pitch did give the bowlers some help, especially the spinners in the afternoon. All those inches of rain, subjected suddenly to sunshine, made it dusty. But Somerset's disappointment, I think, was largely because the bowling and fielding were better than the batting.

Lloyds was caught by Pigott at 16, and Richards caught at the wicket off le Roux at 19. From these early blows, Somerset never recovered. Roebuck was stumped at 61, an uncharacteristic stroke.

At lunch, the score was 82, after 38 overs. Rose played a capital innings, seeking to pull his side together as a captain should, and had reached his 50 when he was caught in the gully.

Denning, in his first match of the season, looked as if he was getting into form, but was caught and bowled when deciding, too late, not to go through with a drive. He had possibly been shaken by the fact that Botham had failed. Barclay and Waller bowled accurately and teasingly.

It was time, I felt, for Marks to play an innings, though number eight in the order is hardly the place to encourage his batting. He did, and Dredge played some classical forward strokes at the other end, concluding one of them by falling gracefully upon his correctly stooping nose. I wish Patrick Eagar had been there to catch him.

Garner gave us some fun, hitting Waller for three consecutive sixes, but Somerset were batting again by half past five, and soon lost a wicket.

Laughter on way to Tyburn

TAUNTON: Sussex (24 pts) beat Somerset (4 pts) by 10 wickets

Overnight, Somerset, following on, were 129 behind, with nine second-innings wickets in hand, though Lloyds and Richards had been going so comfortably on Thursday evening that the game seemed still to hold possibilities for them. But both were out quickly, Richards to a vague stroke from the first ball of the second over. This seemed to demoralize the side and it is the inevitable result of having a great batsman that gloom sets in if he fails at a critical time. It looked as if the match would be over before lunch.

Botham, coming in at 72 for five, seemed at first to take the same view. He hit Barclay, who had bowled very well, for three sixes in an over. Give the lads a laugh on the way to the Tyburn. But then he settled down and began to play cautiously.

At lunch the score was 122 for seven, in 46 overs. Botham found a partner in the new Somerset wicketkeeper, who looks quite a useful batsman. In the first innings he had been run out before he had even taken Gard (I owe this witticism to a senior Somerset committee man who had kindly been saving it up for me).

Gard had helped to put on 56 when he was splendidly caught low down at cover. He had been missed, at mid-on, when only five, but the Sussex fielding had much more pluses than minuses.

Botham continued to vary his mood. Two successful reverse sweeps off Barclay were followed by more caution: three drives off le Roux, all for four and more caution. He had, I hoped, a promising partner in Dredge, but the Demon of Frome abandoned his classical forward defensive stroke, possibly because his nose is still a little sore. He made a violent hook, an elegant leg cut, and then a shot which I have never seen before, a squarish cut which dropped beautifully over the head of third man (about halfway out) and went for four.

Botham was last out and Sussex needed only seven runs, which they obtained in two balls, Gard bowling, Botham keeping wicket. Somerset are not playing well at present. Sussex are.

Somerset v Sussex, Taunton, 25, 26 & 27 May 1983

Sussex won by 10 wickets

Sussex

G.D. Mendis	b Garner	65	*not out*	8
A.M. Green	c Marks b Garner	12	*not out*	0
* J.R.T. Barclay	c Botham b Marks	26		
C.M. Wells	b Lloyds	63		
P.W.G. Parker	lbw b Marks	79		
A.P. Wells	*not out*	61		
I.A. Greig	c Popplewell b Marks	59		
† I.J. Gould	*not out*	33		
G.S. le Roux				
A.C.S. Pigott				
C.E. Waller				
	b 1, lb 2, w 2, nb 5	10		
	(6 wkts, dec)	**408**	(no wkts)	**8**

1/28, 2/96, 3/132, 4/235, 5/261, 6/343

Garner	20	4	49	2				
Dredge	11	1	44	0				
Botham	6	0	25	0				
Marks	37	9	112	3				
Lloyds	27	6	108	1				
Richards	12	4	32	0				
Roebuck	2	0	15	0				
Popplewell	6	0	13	0				
Gard					0.2	0	8	0

Somerset

J.W. Lloyds	b Pigott	12	c sub b le Roux	31
P.M. Roebuck	st Gould b Barclay	19	b Pigott	0
I.V.A. Richards	c Gould b le Roux	2	b Barclay	30
* B.C. Rose	c Barclay b Pigott	52	b Barclay	5
P.W. Denning	c and b Waller	36	c sub b Barclay	4
I.T. Botham	c Pigott b Waller	27	c A.Wells b Pigott	81
N.F.M. Popplewell	c and b Barclay	9	c Mendis b le Roux	3
V.J. Marks	st Gould b Waller	26	c Barclay b Pigott	3
† T. Gard	run out	0	c A.Wells b Greig	22
C.H. Dredge	c A.Wells b le Roux	6	c sub b Pigott	6
J. Garner	*not out*	23	*not out*	2
	b 4, lb 3, w 1, nb 4	12	lb 2, nb 1	3
		224		**190**

1/16, 2/19, 3/61, 4/121, 5/159, 6/160, 7/187, 8/187, 9/196, 10/224.
1/2, 2/62, 3/62, 4/67, 5/72, 6/95, 7/100, 8/156, 9/173, 10/190.

le Roux	16	3	44	2	22	5	80	2
Pigott	20	3	55	2	13.4	1	44	4
Greig	5	0	15	0	15	2	33	1
Barclay	26	10	54	2	14	8	30	3
Waller	22	10	44	3				

Umpires: D.G.L. Evans and A.G.T. Whitehead

Gower a memory of Woolley

TAUNTON: England beat Sri Lanka by 47 runs

There was nearly a full house on Saturday for Taunton's first international match. The ground looked very well. The pitch was a beauty for batting; with the collaboration of the short boundaries, heavy scoring was certain. England won the toss, but the start was no more than adequate, with the opening pair out for 78. However, Lamb and Gower put on 96 at high speed, and Gower went on to a century, for which he was made man of the match.

There were a couple of slightly disconcerting runs out in the middle of the innings, but Gould joined Gower in a stand of 98, and Dilley again played with a quality far above that of your knockabout tail ender. The second run out was that of Botham, for nought, to the acute disappointment of the crowd. A good long throw from Ratnayake just beat him on the second run. Sri Lanka fielded well for a long time, though inevitably they fell into some flusterment during the final assault.

What makes a Gower innings so enjoyable is his combination of delicacy and power. I have only a vague memory of Woolley, but he must have batted in such a way. Some of Gower's drives were so strongly hit that they would have been sixes at the Oval. But the wristwork, the late cutting, and glancing, suddenly flashed out. And the rashness, the lapses of concentration which once cost him his place in the England side, has gone (touch wood, if one may invoke an ancient Pagan ritual in favour of a man brought up in Canterbury).

Sri Lanka batted much better than they bowled. The bowlers pitched too short under pressure. This is an instinctive thing to do when the batsmen are going for their drives, but not always the wisest policy, as the bowling of Marks later demonstrated. Marks keeps the ball well up on principle, with cunning variation of flight and pace. He took five wickets, all of them those of major batsmen, and was never collared. Had it not been for the marvellous innings by Gower, Marks must have been made the man of the match.

Sri Lanka batted well enough and the England faster bowlers did not look very impressive. Allott, in his later spells, was expensive, Willis sound, Botham erratic. Dilley took four wickets, two at the beginning and two at the end.

There was only a minimal chance of scoring 334 and Sri Lanka never looked like doing it. They needed someone to play an innings the size of Gower's. Mendis was the only one who suggested he might.

ENGLAND	333 for nine (60 overs, Gower 130, Lamb 53, Gould 35, Tavare 32, Dilley 29)
SRI LANKA	286 (58 overs, de Alwis 58, Mendis 56, Ranatunga 34, Wettimuny 33, Marks 5-39, Dilley 4-45)

Zimbabwe pluck is not enough to cause another upset

WORCESTER: West Indies beat Zimbabwe by eight wickets

The day was dry, but cloudy. I was sorry that the Zimbabweans did not have the chance to see this loveliest of our country grounds in sunshine. I was sorry for them, too, when, after being put it, they had struggled through 33 overs to be 70 for four at lunch.

It was not the pitch that was responsible. It was not the atmosphere, for the clouds were too high to cause excessive swing. It was the unaccustomed pace of Roberts and Holding that made the early breaks, and then Pycroft was run out, a fine throw by Richards.

Just before lunch, with Gomes bowling, Heron, who had batted more than 100 minutes for 12, got himself stumped. This was odd, like a clock which chimes 13; not only absurd in itself, but making nonsense of all that had gone before.

Houghton had made a steady start, but there had not been much to enthuse the crowd, which about half filled the ground. Worcestershire had made some special preparation, including a baked potato stall, of which we were frequently reminded on the loud-speaker, in thunderous tones. At least it is a better system than they have at Taunton, where you can often not hear it at all.

However, this Zimbabwe team have resilience and pluck, and the afternoon went much better for them. There was an excellent partnership between Houghton and Fletcher. The score had reached 157, in the fiftieth over, when Houghton was caught at slip. He reached his own 50 in 95 balls.

Fletcher reached his in 45, a capital innings bursting with strokes which kept finding the gaps. He is left-handed with strong yet supple wrists, and of course a player of some stature, who has captained his country since 1979, and had English experience in the Lancashire League and with Cambridgeshire. He carried boldly on after Houghton went, and was well supported. The final score of 218 for seven was a considerable recovery.

When West Indies went in, the sky was darkening. They lost Haynes early, and then bad light stopped play. Tea was taken early, but nearly half an hour was lost. When they came back, only a couple of overs were possible. They tried again, about half past five, and Richards was soon out.

This was rather an alarming position for the West Indies. It was the nineteenth over before the 50 was up. Gomes played and missed several times outside the off stump, but gradually he and Greenidge got on top, and the hundred was reached, fairly confidently, in the twenty-eighth over.

The Zimbabwe second line bowling was not strong enough, and though their keenness in the field never diminished, their very zeal caused them to make a few mistakes. Greenidge reached a solemn but necessary 50, and then accelerated. With the light holding well, West Indies were safely coasting home.

ZIMBABWE	217 for seven (60 overs, Fletcher 71*, Houghton 54, Roberts 3-36)
WEST INDIES	218 for two (48.3 overs, Greenidge 105*, Gomes 75*)

Kapil Dev blooms at rhododendron time

TUNBRIDGE WELLS: India beat Zimbabwe by 31 runs

It was a day to remember, sunshine, an astonishing change of fortune and an innings of great skill and power by the Indian captain, the highest ever made in the Prudential World Cup. The ground looked handsome, all tents, clinking glasses and rhododendrons. Hearts beat and bosoms swell proudly at Tunbridge Wells, as the poet has it.

Amid the excitement, I felt sorry for the Zimbabweans, who played bravely and sportingly, but must have felt as if they were overwhelmed by an elemental force of nature, like someone tossed over the Victoria Falls in a barrel.

India won the toss and batted. The pitch had some early life, Rawson and Curran bowled well, and five wickets were down for 17. I thought it was a mistake to take them both off so soon. They only needed to get Kapil Dev out – one sensed this, even at the time – and they were home. The prize was worth the risk. Even more, I felt they should have brought Rawson back straight after lunch.

The score then was 106 for seven, with Kapil Dev 51. By the time he did come back, things were beyond mending. The weakness of this Zimbabwean side is their second-line bowling.

Kapil Dev came in when the score was nine for four. When the innings ended, he had made 175, out of a total of 266 for eight. I must emphasize that this was not a slogger's innings, apart from a few sketchy shots near the end.

Its foundations were classical. It reminded me of a Cardus phrase, I think originally written of harps: "He put a bloom on the orthodox." He did hit the ball very hard (16 fours and six sixes), but they were rhododendron-size blooms. The strokes were correctly conceived and executed. He gave no chance. He played so well that, on reflection, I doubt if anything Fletcher could have done with his bowling would have made much difference.

It was an innings stamped with the sovereign mark. Binny, Madan Lal and most of all Kirmani, who shared in a record ninth-wicket partnership for the competition, provided the necessary support, but we hardly noticed them.

Zimbabwe, given their shaken condition, batted well. At tea, after 25 overs, they were 86 for three and an innings from the formidable Houghton was in prospect. But Houghton was leg-before to Madan Lal soon afterwards, Brown was run out, and Fletcher was caught splendidly in the deep by Kapil Dev, the ball coming to him awkwardly over his shoulder.

That was 113 for six, and very little hope for Zimbabwe. Yet they produced another flourish, Curran hitting the ball erratically but vigorously all over the place, and were only 31 runs short at the end.

Kapil Dev, not otherwise a major force with his bowling, took the last wicket. He gave a salutary reminder that, with such a player in such form, India are a difficult side for anyone to beat.

A summary of the match might lie in the answer to the old child's riddle which Billy Bunter was prone to use when perplexed: "One rode a horse and the other rhododendron!"

INDIA	266 for eight (60 overs, Kapil Dev 175*, Rawson 3-47, Curran 3-65)
ZIMBABWE	235 (57 overs, Curran 73, Brown 35, Madan Lal 3-42)

The Taunton ground staff in action

TAUNTON: Somerset v Sussex (Benson & Hedges Cup)

In the afternoon, the luck with the weather did not hold. Twice there were interruptions, though they were minimised by the zeal of the ground staff, who handled their clumsy covers with speed and skill. At one point Eric Hill, dour as ever, announced that the Taunton ground staff had reached a record, the first to make 100 coverings and uncoverings in May. I asked my old friend and schoolfellow if I might quote this statistic, but he glared at me and said, "No, I'm not having you pinching me bonn-motts."

Vic Marks

TAUNTON: Somerset v Sussex (Benson & Hedges Cup)

Marks once again showed how oddly good he is at this limited-over game. I say "oddly" because he does not bowl with a flat trajectory and more than normal speed, which is the supposed recipe of spinners in these circumstances.

He gives the ball air. It is accuracy that does it, accuracy plus temptation, because every vigorous young batsman feels he ought to be hitting him for a boundary every ball. His innocent face, though he has unsuccessfully attempted to disguise it with a beard, increases the illusion.

Batsmen will continue to get out against Marks until they realise he is not so green as cabbage looking.

TAUNTON: Somerset v Hampshire (Benson & Hedges Cup)

Smith was out, caught at mid-off when Wilson came on. The catcher was Marks, who then proceeded to get out Jesty and Turner and bowl his full overs for 22 runs. Both were caught attempting big hits. At present Marks seems to be able to get good batsmen into trouble merely by alternating long-hops and half-volleys; they suspect depth of cunning in both. He has shaved his beard, and has now less the look of the wizard than the imp. But he does keep getting them out.

Dredge, bowled Marshall, 0

TAUNTON: Somerset v Hampshire (Benson & Hedges Cup)

Dredge, looking every inch a Frome opening batsman, was bowled, although he had played one stylish stroke which staggered the infield and produced four byes.

Lacking the Blake spirit

TAUNTON: Somerset v Essex

As Botham had come down the steps, fire engines and ambulances charged, roaring round the ground, and he did play pretty well for a while. He was warming up, they said in the Stragglers' Bar: "We shall see something soon." We did: a whacking six off Acfield and then an attempted reverse sweep which had him leg before. Well, he had tried. Once he was gone, Somerset could still have saved the match, with sufficient application, but did not seem to bother.

Acfield certainly bowled well, but the surrender was too easy. When Blake, the defender of Taunton in the Civil War, was asked if the starving town would yield, he replied to the Royalist summons that he still had three pairs of boots and would eat two of them first. I think Somerset need a touch more of the Blake spirit at present.

A Sunday century by Peter Roebuck

BATH: Somerset v Gloucestershire (Sunday League)

Roebuck batted from the first ball of the 40 overs to the last and reached his first hundred in the John Player League. He did not quite receive the full applause he deserved. "What came ye out for to see?" In this case, I fear it was a mighty prophet, Botham, and Roebuck in public comparison ranks only as a good preacher.

Late arrival at Bournemouth

BOURNEMOUTH: Hampshire v Somerset

I am afraid I did not arrive at the ground until just about one o'clock, after some travelling misadventures (which had nothing to do with Didcot). I noticed at once that there was a large crowd enjoying the sunshine, and thought how pleasant was the scene. Then I glanced at the board: Somerset were 68 for eight. "What on earth has been going on?" I asked a Somerset man. His answer was succinct: "Green seamer. Put us in. Marshall." Further investigation confirmed that this was an accurate summary.

A memory of Reading

READING: Berkshire v Yorkshire (NatWest Trophy)

The last time I was present at a cricket match in Reading was on D-Day, 1944. The Queen's College, Oxford had a fixture with Reading School that day, and as we were not on the beaches we saw no reason not to play. But transport was difficult, and only eight of us arrived. Bold as brass, I asked the opposing captain for three substitutes ("things a bit chaotic today, you understand, old man"), and he provided them. And all of them took marvellous catches, and we won, theoretically by four wickets, factually by one.

Surrey's tailenders make a fight of it

THE OVAL: Northamptonshire, with seven second innings wickets in hand, lead Surrey by 151 runs

I did not enjoy my visit to The Oval as much as I usually do. It was very chilly, and most of the few present flocked to the pavilion, where the commissionaire, feeling the cold himself, kept the doors closed, and delayed matters further by a zeal for checking passes and addressing the shivering ones waiting on the steps as though they were a public meeting. However, the cricket was interesting, once you had got inside near the Scotch.

Surrey began the day at 16 for nought, 264 behind, and lost wickets steadily. There was no obvious reason for such a collapse: the day was overcast, so the ball was moving occasionally, the bounce of the pitch varied, and Surrey did not bat as well as Northamptonshire bowled. Griffiths, Walker and Mallender shared the wickets, Griffiths removing the opening pair. Walker looked promising, a quickish bowler who, like Mallender, was born in Yorkshire. He comes from Doncaster. Griffiths comes from Wellingborough, one of the homes of Northamptonshire cricket, where the doorstep of W.G. Grace is preserved, and a square of turf from his Downend orchard used to be, until some unwarned workmen dug it up by mistake.

Between them, these three bowlers had Surrey at 77 for seven just before lunch, and we began to think in terms of a follow-on, even a two-day finish. Thomas was dropped before he had scored, and decided to die boldly. He began to bang the ball round the vast, empty expanses. There were nine fours in his 50. Monkhouse followed his example. The next wicket did not fall until 164, when Thomas encountered a ball which kept low. Monkhouse, soon afterwards, played on, trying a hit against the same bowler, Griffiths. Clarke was, however, in an agreeably thumping mood, and the last wicket did not fall until 217. Both Monkhouse and Clarke made their highest scores of the season. Surrey could feel pleased with their recovery. Griffiths had the best bowling figures, and deserved them.

Because Larkins has damaged a hand, Bamber opened the Northamptonshire second innings with Cook. Bamber was much the livelier of the two. Of the first 50, he scored 27, Cook 10 – the rest were extras.

Gateman serves double fault

THE OVAL: Surrey (5 pts) drew with Northamptonshire (7 pts)

I rejoice to inform you that Henry Blofeld, representing on this occasion *The Guardian*, had his car denied entrance for a while at the Oval yesterday because the gateman thought he (Henry) had been rude about him (the gateman) in the morning paper.

This was a double fault. Mr Blofeld had not written about the gateman. Mine was the offending article, and it was about the pavilion commissionaire, not the gateman. The commissionaire, Mr Macleod, who is obviously a sportsman, later asked me for my autograph. He clearly believes, with the late Lord Beaverbrook, that there is no such thing as bad publicity.

Northamptonshire declared at 203 for seven, shortly after lunch. They must have hoped for more, but Surrey bowled better, more accurately, and with more spirit than they had done on Monday. It was warmer than then, though we had no real sunshine. The pitch, never certain, grew dustier as the day went on. Steele and Lamb played the best innings.

Surrey had to score 267 in 210 minutes to win; but, at 33, in the tenth over, Butcher was caught at backward short leg. It was a powerful hit, and it was brave of Cook not to try to get out of the way. In the next over, Clinton was caught at second slip. At 51, Lynch was caught at mid-on and, at 68, from the last ball before tea, Stewart was caught at the wicket. With 23 overs bowled – Northamptonshire were bowling them slowly – Surrey were in trouble.

Knight and Richards renewed hope. At one stage, they scored 27 in two overs and Northamptonshire began to look a little flustered. But Knight, when going really well, was bowled by Walker at 120 and, in the next over, the thirty-second, Thomas was leg-before to Griffiths. This was Griffiths' sixteenth consecutive over.

The match was now beyond Surrey. Richards, a product of the Humphry Davy Grammar School, Penzance, ceased to be piratical and began to display his safety lamp. With the last 20 overs to go, Surrey needed 143. Griffiths came off, looking weary and worn, but not sad, after his nineteenth over.

Richards and Needham batted out the last hour, without too much trouble, though Griffiths came back for a last fling. It had been a well contested day and I hope Henry Blofeld managed to get his car out of the ground.

NORTHAMPTONSHIRE	280 for eight declared (Lamb 108, Willey 52) & 203 for seven declared
SURREY	217 (Thomas 52, Clarke 43, Monkhouse 41, Griffiths 4-66) & 163 for six (Richards 44*)

Gloucestershire off the rails

BRISTOL: The New Zealanders, with all first innings wickets in hand, are 105 runs behind Gloucestershire

I thought I had put the Witch of Didcot behind me for this season. But waiting at Bath for one of our treasured high-speed trains to take me to Bristol I learnt that all trains from London were delayed because of – if I heard the announcement correctly – "a broken rail at Didcot". This sounded alarming, but I managed to get to Bristol by a train which had come from Portsmouth. It is a depressing thought that in future I must travel to London via Portsmouth to avoid the Didcot curse.

I arrived at the ground just as Hignell was walking off it, third out at 79. Fortunately I have my sources of information at Bristol, notably Purpureous Basil and GRIP (you remember her, the Glorious Red-headed Imperturbable Pamela, who presides over the Hammond Room).

I can therefore inform you, through their urbane illumination, that the New Zealanders won the toss and put Gloucestershire in. Romaines was leg-before to Hadlee, Bainbridge caught bat and pad off Chatfield, and Hignell trod on his wicket.

Wright was out soon after I arrived, and then Stovold, who had batted with authority and vigour, went in the last over before lunch. He had scored 58 out of 99, but tried a hook at that stage, mishitting it to mid-on. What an irresponsible end to what had been a responsible innings.

Shortly after lunch, Graveney was caught at slip. At 2.40 bad light stopped play. Some rain followed, the drops heavy but not sustained. A thunderstorm would have cleared the air, but it refused to come. I felt that play might have been resumed before 4.30. The light then was no better than it had been during the afternoon when Gloucestershire had lost their last four wickets in a quarter of an hour – 120 all out in the forty-fourth over. I was astonished when, at the fall of the last Gloucestershire wicket, the umpires called for the covers to be put on. It was not raining, no more than it had been earlier, and the light seemed much the same.

Chatfield was the best bowler, and deserved his figures. The pitch played acceptably, but the high humidity made the ball swing. Gloucestershire, below full strength, did not bat well, Stovold excepted, while the New Zealanders' bowling and fielding was tight and keen.

For no obvious reason, except the irritation of the crowd, who had been sitting patiently without retreating to shelter, it was decided that play was possible at 6 o'clock, with 12 overs scheduled. However after 6.30 the light became really impossible, and that was that. The New Zealanders had not lost a wicket. Let us hope that a consoling and refreshing thunderstorm arrives in the night.

Poor response to touring side

BRISTOL: The New Zealanders, with four first innings wickets standing, are 218 runs ahead of Gloucestershire

Not for the first time, I mourn that county matches against touring sides have fallen from their high estate. Upon the ground where, perhaps, the most famous of them all was played (Gloucestershire's tie with the Australians in 1930, gates closed) there cannot have been much more than a thousand present yesterday.

Holt's Products tried for some years, in one of the braver and more imaginative efforts of sponsorship, to revive them, but the counties did not respond.

Gloucestershire fielded a weak side in this match. I do not doubt that the injuries which kept various senior players out were genuine, but had it been, say a NatWest Cup match, one or two would, I think, have struggled into their flannels. No, the counties have ceased to take these matches seriously, and so the public has too.

It was another sultry day, though the clouds were higher than on Wednesday, and the ball did not swing about so much. There was also the factor that the quicker Gloucestershire bowlers are no Chatfields or Hadlees.

We had some sunshine in the afternoon. The New Zealanders, beginning at 15 for 0 wicket, after bowling Gloucestershire out for 120, took the opportunity for some congenial batting practice.

Wright and Edgar did not hurry, and had some luck in the field. Wright was missed at slip early on, and then gave, when he was 31, an easy catch to the bowler, Doughty. Wright was trying to pull, but lobbed the ball back from a top edge.

Wright was walking away, yards down the pitch, when, after a fumble or two, Doughty saw the ball on the ground at his feet.

If he had picked it up he could still have run Wright out: but he stood there a stricken man.

His only comfort can be that such things happen to all good cricketers once in their lives and he has had his bad moment.

In the last over before lunch, Edgar, who has also played some edgy strokes which could have led to slip catches, was bowled by Tracy. This was Tracy's first-class debut. He is a

New Zealander, 20 years-old, over here for a season on a cricket scholarship, whatever that may be.

He was obviously anxious to do well against his countrymen, and fairly hurled himself at them. His run-up was fuller of action and speed than the ball after it had left his hand. But the lad did not bowl badly.

In the afternoon, Wright proceeded to a century, which in its later stages approached majesty. There are not, in the current game, many better drivers of the ball.

J. Crowe was second out, at 136, also off Tracey, a legside catch by the admirable wicket keeper, Russell. Wright went at 218, very well caught by Hignell at deep mid-wicket. Hignell later took another good catch, at extra-cover, which got Howarth out, but only when Howarth had scored 60. The New Zealanders swished the evening casually away, M. Crowe enjoying himself, and did not bother to declare.

It was, as so often in such hot weather, what my mother used to call a crotchety day. The players stood the heat pretty well, less so than some who were watching. I lost my temper, quite superfluously, with several telephone operators and Barry Dudleston. Even GRIP, the supposedly imperturbable one, admitted she had had an altercation.

The GRIP can squash reformed character next time

BRISTOL: Gloucestershire drew with the New Zealanders

My wife has been telling that, when I go to Bristol, I drink too much: though what she really meant was something slightly different, that I spend too much money on drink. My explanations about old friends have been coldly received. When I went to a bar for my first one yesterday, with the sun well over the yardarm, the man by my side had just purchased a pint of grapefruit squash and was putting in plenty of ice, and I decided that was just what I wanted. It was a very hot day. As I opened my mouth to give the order, however, I found that the Glorious Red-headed Imperturbable Pamela had already placed a whisky before me. So much for the path of reform.

The cricket was only mildly interesting, except for the most intense Gloucestershire partisan, who could take satisfaction from his side's stubborn batting, and particularly an admirable hundred by Bainbridge. At the start, they were 218 behind, with their second innings to come. They had nothing to hope for but a draw.

At lunch, at 100 for three, it looked as if New Zealand would bowl them out. There was not much batting to come. Stovold had been caught at slip and Romaines was run out, or rather ran himself out, for he hesitated in response to the striker's call for a feasible single. Hignell was bowled, beaten for pace, I thought, by Snedden.

The pitch was easy; the kind of pitch where it is not too difficult to stay in, if you make up your mind not to get out. This is what Bainbridge basically did, though he revealed from time to time his pleasing cover drives. It was his highest score in first-class cricket. He lost Wright, caught at short leg, at 133, and Doughty, caught at silly point, at 141. Both these wickets fell to Bracewell, who bowled steadily without getting much turn.

Still, Gloucestershire could lose, but Bainbridge found the partner he needed in Russell, who had made a solid 30 by the time he was out to a skier at extra cover at 225. By then, Gloucestershire were ahead, and time was growing short. Although Bainbridge was out, more from exhaustion than anything else, Graveney saw to it that there was no nonsense.

New Zealand's out-cricket was efficient, but perhaps unimaginative. When they found themselves stuck, they might have experimented a bit more. They had nothing to lose. A barmy bowler in these circumstances often helps, as A.R. Lewis used to say when he put himself on for a leg break or two. I can also inform you that, when next in the Hammond Rooms, I shall be presented automatically before I can open my mouth, with a pint of grapefruit squash and ample quantities of ice.

GLOUCESTERSHIRE	120 (Stovold 58, Chatfield 6-40, Hadlee 3-25)
	305 for eight (Bainbridge 146, Romaines 30, Russell 30, Graveney 27*, Bracewell 3-87)
NEW ZEALANDERS	338 for six declared (Wright 136, Crowe 61*, Howarth 60, Edgar 39)

In front of the selectors

LORD'S: Middlesex v Sussex

Sussex were thwarted by Gatting, who played one of the best innings I have seen from him.

He had certain advantages. The Tavern boundary was short, so that even a mishit might carry for six, but he did not make many mishits. The Sussex bowling, faced with a double onslaught when Butcher got going, wavered. Barclay hardly knew where best to place his field, for which he could not be blamed.

Gatting reached his hundred with a second consecutive six off Jones. This innings will have improved his chances of selection for England, especially as it was played at Lord's, where everyone is a selector, or has a pal whose brother is a second cousin of Peter May.

An unrewarding journey to Birmingham

BIRMINGHAM: Warwickshire v Middlesex

Overnight Middlesex were 49 for four, needing 193 more to win on a difficult pitch. I wondered whether the journey to Birmingham would be worthwhile, with the infernal cacophony of New Street station to be undergone. However, there was a chance that Gatting or Butcher might play an innings, and I knew that the Sage of Longparish would never forgive me if Gatting did, and it was not fully reported.

Vain hope. Warwickshire swept Middlesex away before lunch. It was their sixth consecutive victory, something they had not achieved for a quarter of a century, and kept them near the top of the championship.

...

I travelled back, thinking how well Warwickshire are playing, but also how much they owed in this match to their old men, Gifford, Amiss and Willis. I had to wait in the New Street abomination of desolation for more than an hour, but ultimately caught a train which had come from Dundee, where I met an injured singer who had fallen from the stage at Pitlochry the night before. Well, that was what the man said, and it was, when you come to think of it, no more improbable than Gatting's decision to ask Warwickshire to bat.

Middlesex beat Gloucestershire

BRISTOL: Gloucestershire v Middlesex

Yesterday was the feast of St Bonaventura. He was the chap, I think, who maintained that heart and will had more to do with the destiny of man than intellect, contrary to Aquinas. I am afraid it was Aquinas who added to his record yesterday. Gloucestershire tried very hard, but Middlesex had so much more talent than the effort was vain.

NEXT DAY

The legend of Swithun, Bishop of Winchester, who lived in the ninth century, originated because "he was an humble man": he did direct that he should be buried outside the walls of the cathedral, "so that the raindrops from the eaves might fall upon his grave."

His faithful followers soon decided to haul him back inside, but, because it kept raining, had to wait 40 days before they could do it. You will see, therefore, that the St Swithun's tale applies principally to rain, not sunshine. And this is just as well because I could not stand another 40 days of the heatwave. Nor did Gloucestershire and Middlesex enjoy the weather very much yesterday, because they had finished their match by lunchtime.

Middlesex look a formidable team at present. The general county standard has become so even that rarely do you see a side which dominates, and knows it is going to dominate, from the first ball until the last. Yorkshire under Sellers and Close, Surrey under Surridge, yes. Middlesex under Gatting bear that stamp. If they think the sun will shine on them for 40 days more, they may well be right.

Not much of a crowd at Lord's

LORD'S: Middlesex v Warwickshire

The weather was cooler, but still clammy. The size of the crowd was disappointing. There cannot have been many more than 1,000 present, all told, in the prime of the day, and though many dropped in, as usual, in the evening when the offices were closing, it was a poor turn-out for an important championship match.

Much depended on Gatting. For a time the play seemed to condense into a match between Gifford and Gatting, the old warrior of many battles and the young one with most of his to come. Gatting had his tentative moments, but had won the initial contest by tea.

It was a significant moment when he hit Gifford for six over long-on. After the break he began to lay about him generally. He went on to a noble hundred, with the satisfaction of seeing his side well in command. He is becoming a hero of the Middlesex crowd, in the same line as Hendren and Compton – at least, he would be, if there had been a crowd.

Mark Nicholas has a bowl

WORCESTER: Worcestershire v Hampshire

Three wickets went to Nicholas, whom I do not remember seeing bowl before. At the beginning of this season he had taken one wicket for 13 runs in three overs. He bowls with his right arm, at medium pace. I fancy that he gave a speculative look at himself before beginning his run-up, as if deciding which arm to bowl with.

Still, they were good wickets to take, even though the batsmen, giving the occasional anxious glances over their shoulders to see if Marshall was warming up, must have been following the principle.

Always keep a hold on nurse
For fear of finding something worse.

Zaheer and Stovold at Cheltenham

CHELTENHAM: Gloucestershire v Warwickshire

Again the sound of carnival, again we swarm, a badly ventilated crew … I cannot remember how it goes on, but it was the ballad of the Eton and Harrow match, by R.A. Knox, long ago, and the Cheltenham festival carries echoes of those distant days. A large crowd attended in warm weather, but the only things that swarmed were the wasps, especially around the press tent, all looking eagerly for their 100 stings in August.

Gloucestershire lost two quick wickets, Broad caught in the slips and Bainbridge leg before. Stovold and Zaheer then scored centuries. The third wicket did not fall until 264, when Zaheer was caught at mid-off. He had batted beautifully, but then we expect that. It was his fiftieth century for Gloucestershire, something of which most of us were unaware until, over a large ice cream, he informed the correspondent of the Bristol and West News Agency, who I suspect paid for the ice cream. There is no end to this cheque book journalism. Still, Zaheer is one of those cricketers, like Fred Trueman, who would always pass a quiz on his own statistics.

Stovold's innings was less beautiful, yet in a way more interesting. When he scored a lot of runs earlier in the season, I thought he was a sound professional having a good run. When he wilted a little, I was not surprised. Now he is batting like a combination of the Inchcape Rock and the storms that attack it. Although he is 30 years old, should he ever be summoned to higher duties, I do not think he would let England down.

Horace Hazell

Horace Hazell was successor in the Somerset side to J.C. White as slow left-arm spinner. He took 950 or so wickets from the years 1929 to 1952. He was a tubby man, on the short side; not flabby, you understand – he could bowl long spells in the heat on plumb pitches without wilting – but plumpish.

Near the end of his career, I was broadcasting commentary on a Gloucestershire/Somerset match at Bristol. (It was Hammond's last match, but that aspect of it is another story.) Gloucestershire were nearly 200 for 0, Milton and Emmett; I and my No 2, Michael Bowen, agreed that Somerset's only hope lay in the new ball, in those days due after 200 had been scored. To our astonishment, the Somerset captain, a cheerful fair-haired Cambridge basher called Rogers, did not take it, but kept Hazell on. Well, I was a young man, as commentators then went, and thought I knew more about the game than I did. I declared myself baffled by the decision. Michael Bowen, who was also young though less dogmatic than I, concurred. Hazell then bowled Gloucestershire out for a total of about 300. Collapse of commentators. Michael and I did not drink on the ground that evening (you must remember that even in 1951, radio was still a kind of miracle, and the players used to listen to us in their dressing-rooms, chiefly in order to catch us out). We crept away to a nearby pub to share our consolatory pints.

I made another mistake in this match. Attempting to describe Hazell's approach to the wicket, I said that he 'waddled' up to the crease. I am not so sure, looking back, that the word was all that inappropriate.

Like bias to the bowl,
Which, as more pond'rous, made its aim more true,
Obliquely waddling to the mark in view

Pope, who wrote the lines, had not of course seen Hazell bowl, but it is not a bad description. I cannot claim, however, that I had Pope consciously in mind when I used the term in that commentary.

And now, young commentators, mark this. If you have used the wrong word or even a word which you are inclined to regret, forget it immediately and press on. Instead of forgetting 'waddled', I went back to it, saying, 'No that's too unkind a word', thus drawing everyone's attention to the fact that I had used it and provoking some irate correspondence from Somerset. I think, though I cannot be sure, that while I was making this embarrassed and superfluous apology, Horace took another wicket.

St Aidan comes to aid of Romaines

BRISTOL: Worcestershire, with eight first innings wickets in hand, are 311 runs behind Gloucestershire

It was the feast of St Aidan, the apostle of Northumbria, who came from the monastic community of Iona and whose ministry extended from Edinburgh to Hull, via Lindisfarne. I was sure Romaines would score some runs since he comes from Bishop Auckland; and so he did, after Gloucestershire had won the toss on another slow, easy Bristol pitch.

... Romaines reached his century out of 230, in the seventy-second over. He has gained assurance and, now that Broad has gone, can settle down to opening the innings regularly. I am sure this is his best position. He has some attractive strokes, and risks showing them when well set, but his principal virtues are solidity and perseverance.

Little to disturb the peace

BRISTOL: Gloucestershire, with seven second innings wickets in hand, are 170 runs ahead of Worcestershire

There once was a steeplejack working at the top of a high factory chimney. He called down to his mate at the bottom: "Come on up 'ere, Bill." So Bill toiled up, and was told, "Listen!"

"Can't 'ear nuffink."

"No. Ain't it quiet?"

This story, illustrated by Lee in his *London Laughs* cartoon in the *Evening News* in the early Thirties, convulsed the small boys, of whom I was one. It came back to me yesterday afternoon as I sat, alone with the purpureous Basil, in the Grace Room at Bristol. Golly, it *was* quiet. Not a sound was heard, not a funeral note, although Basil did, to enliven things, tell me an improbable tale about how, when a squaddie in the Sappers, he happened to dine out with the Attorney-General of South Africa.

There were very few – at the match, I mean, not at the dinner – and they had very little to cheer. ... The question was whether Worcestershire could save the follow-on.

The eighth wicket fell at 199, and there was a brief air of interest. Someone clapped near the scoreboard, and Basil paused in his contemplation of another story. Then Humphries, in the most vigorous innings of the day, saw them safely past the danger.

Damp and gloomy end to the Bristol season

BRISTOL: Gloucestershire (8 pts) drew with Worcestershire (3 pts)

It was a dismal end to the Bristol season. GRIP has been away all week. I inquired whether she was on holiday and was told, "Not exactly. She's entertaining visitors," which sounded rather sinister. The purpureous Basil had no further stories of attorney-generals and left early. But the weather, as I warned it might be, was chiefly to blame.

A quarter of an hour was lost at the start, and the afternoon was punctuated by frequent semi-colons for rain and bad light. Graveney did not declare until he was 302 ahead, leaving Worcestershire three hours and a half to get the runs.

Gloucestershire nevertheless looked as if they might snatch a win when the first three wickets fell, all at 14. Weston was caught at slip, off Shepherd, Neale – who has not had a lucky match – was leg-before in the same over, and McEvoy was caught at the wicket off Sainsbury in the next.

Patel and Curtis held the innings together, which was to their credit, since they suffered so many interruptions, and by the time the covers had been laboriously taken on and off (twice they had not been fully installed before the umpires reappeared at the pavilion gate) the showers had given the pitch a touch of whip.

On the other hand, a bitter wind came to supplement the damp and gloom and fielding must have been very uncomfortable. At one time the middle canvas section of the sight screen at the Orphanage end kept blowing up and down, to and fro, "like Fred trying to leave the rugby club," observed one of the JJ? Society of its most venerable member.

A long break, causing an early and extended tea interval, made a full colon: and shortly before half past five everybody settled for a full stop.

GLOUCESTERSHIRE	351 for four declared (Romaines 121, Bainbridge 56, Wright 56, Stovold 43, Doughty 32*)
	204 for five declared (Russell 64*, Bainbridge 50, Stovold 38, Doughty 31*, Newport 3-40)
WORCESTERSHIRE	253 (Humphries 53*, Curtis 50, D'Oliveira 42, Patel 38, Shepherd 4-76)
	81 for three (Patel 53*)

Didcot Station
'I quail at the thought of what lies before me this season
if British Rail information conforms to the Didcot standard.'

The Star, High Littleton
'Mornings only to avoid the juke box'

At The Oval for the First Test

I cannot become accustomed to the Oval Test being anything but the last. The Lord's Test should come early, while the series is going and tempers have not risen too high. The Oval should be the climax, hot and noisy, like the trams rumbling down Harleyford Road. The trams have long gone, but I always feel they are spiritually present at the Oval.

The difference between Lord's and the Oval was once described by, I think, Herbert Farjeon, in some such terms as these (it was in the days when men wore hats, even in warm weather):

At Lord's: "Oh, er, do please excuse me, sir, it's just that, er, your hat if you wouldn't mind, er, the view ..."

"I do beg your pardon, sir, my foolish, er, thoughtlessness, so sorry."

At the Oval: "Oy!"

"Yus?"

"'ats orf."

Silence.

We have had the heat in this match, not so much in the temper of the players, who have been on their best behaviour most of the time, nor the crowd, most of whom seemed more interested in the golf championship to judge by their transistors, but in the weather itself. I cannot abide London when it is so hot.

A curious business that was on Saturday morning, when Fowler scored a five – a single plus a boundary overthrow – and, since the batsmen had run through twice, was about to resume batting from the wrong end. There was quite a long delay before they sorted things out.

Something even odder happened earlier this season, in the Prudential World Cup match at Worcester between West Indies and Zimbabwe. In the evening, with West Indies batting, there was an interruption for bad light and afterwards Richards returned to the wrong end. What is more, he was out second ball. The only person to notice this at the time was the BBC scorer, Anthony Gibson, who uses the Frindall system with its double-checks. It made no difference to the result because West Indies won easily, but consider if it had happened in a tight match.

Theoretically, I suppose, such a happening should invalidate all subsequent proceedings. But cricket observes the tradition *de minimis non curat lex*. When Warwick Armstrong bowled two consecutive overs in a Test match in 1921 and nobody realized it until some time later, it was not suggested the match should be null and void. Similarly, many seven-ball and five-ball overs have been bowled, when concentration wanders, but once the moment has passed there is no question of revision.

At Lord's for the NatWest Trophy final

My pleasure in Somerset's win was marred by the behaviour of the Somerset crowd, with their incessant, boring chanting. I know we always say, on these occasions, that it is "only a minority" of supporters who are responsible, but it was a substantial minority.

I should think every non-partisan on the ground was wishing by the middle of the afternoon that Kent would pull it off. When Tavaré and Johnson were making the second-wicket stand, I even found myself half-hoping it would continue, because it diminished the cacophony for a while.

Why is it that Somerset followers have won themselves such an unenviable reputation? It does not fit the county's public reputation, which is one of bucolic calm. This is not quite true, but after an adult lifetime spent in the West of England, I would think it as acceptable as such generalizations ever are. Life is fairly peaceful down here.

We used to say that it was partly due to their being starved of success for so long; but they have had a good deal of it in recent years, so the novelty should be wearing off. I thought it might be partly due to a provincial anxiety to cock a snook at Lord's, a defensive assertion that "We'm just as good as you be."

But they also behave badly at Sunday League matches at Taunton (though there has been some improvement recently thanks to stricter licensing hours). Part of the trouble, I am sure, is that there is no League football in Somerset. There is no other focus for county sporting interest than the cricket side.

There has always been an excitable streak in Somerset's cricket supporters. In their first season in the championship in the 1890s, they had an unexpected win at Taunton against the giants of Surrey. Sam Woods, who had taken the last Surrey wicket with the last possible ball of the match, wrote that: "This match made Somerset cricket. Our supporters went barmy, threw their hats in the air and hit each other about." The trouble is that nowadays they tend to hit the other side about.

No, I am baffled. I am also baffled by the way that *You'll never walk alone* has become the Somerset song (as well, of course, as that of a hundred other clubs). It is totally inappropriate for community singing. It has no beat, it has a high note near the end which is beyond the range of the would-be singers, and results in an acutely painful whine. It has nothing to do with Somerset and can only encourage those members of their side who are tone deaf.

I once took part in a television programme with Lord Constantine and Harold Pinter. We were asked to play the old game of choosing an all-time cricket XI: an odd selection committee, you will agree, but we enjoyed ourselves, whatever the viewers thought. We settled on Hobbs and Trumper for the opening pair, and then considered batsmen to follow.

"Headley, said Learie, at once.

"Bradman?" suggested someone.

"Yes," agreed Learie. "We will have Bradman as well because, after all, he was the white Headley."

This was a reference to the constant description of Headley by English and Australian journalists as "the black Bradman", a description which did not altogether please Headley or his fellow West Indians.

George Headley, whose recent death we mourn, was not perhaps quite so good as Bradman, but had to bear heavier burdens. He was probably the best West Indian batsman there has ever been, despite the magnificence of Worrell, Weekes, Walcott, Sobers and Richards. None of the others was so unsupported as Headley.

When he began, shortly after West Indies cricket began, it was usually a case of "Headley out, all out". He had no comparatively easy Tests to boost his figures: his opponents were England and Australia. Nevertheless, he scored 10 centuries in 40 innings in 22 Tests. His Test average was 60.83; in all first-class matches, from 1927 to 1954, it was 69.86.

He played his first Test in 1930, when he was 20. England sent a side to the West Indies. It was not a full Test side (another "England" team was playing in New Zealand at the same time), but a strong one, including Hendren, Ames, Wyatt, Sandham, Voce, Gunn (aged 49) and Rhodes (aged 52). Rhodes took Headley's wicket in the second innings of the first Test, but only when he had scored 176, one of four centuries in the four-match series. Rhodes played his first Test in 1899, Headley his last in 1954; it must have been an interesting confrontation.

In 1930-31 West Indies made their first tour of Australia. Headley was then almost entirely an off-side player and the Australians tied him down for a while, as they did Hammond, by attacking his leg stump. He realized an extra dimension was needed, with the result that Grimmett, who had been causing him problems, later said that he was the greatest master of on-side play whom he had ever met.

Headley toured England twice and was particularly effective on wet pitches. His record in such conditions was, as C.L.R. James points out in his remarkable book *Beyond a Boundary*, much better than Btradman's. He had a successful series at home in 1934-35, ending with 270 not out in a Test which West Indies won by an innings. After the war he was not quite the same force again. He mostly lived in England. He was the first black man to captain West Indies, when England toured in 1947-48, but had to retire after the first Test because of a back injury. In 1953 the Jamaican public subscribed to bring him home for the next England series, but he played only in the first Test and Lock got him twice, for 16 and 1.

I saw Headley bat before the war. I have quite a clear recollection of his innings at The Oval in 1939. He scored 65 and a century seemed sure, when he was run out. The culprit was Victor Stollmeyer, and it must have been a horrifying moment for him in his first and, as it proved, only Test, although he made amends with a brave 96. What impressed me about Headley was his litheness. You would have to say that he was primarily a back-foot player, as Bradman was, but he always seemed to be dancing.

I saw him again after the war. Indeed I saw what must have been his last first-class match, in 1954, when he played in the Torquay Festival, batted beautifully for an hour or so for 64, and capered happily around the field. He seemed as nimble, as lithe, as ever. The circumstances were not, of course, testing, but I remember I was sitting next to Jack Walsh, one of the best Australian leg spinners of the day, and Jack said: "I'd love to be bowling at that blighter, just for the pleasure of watching him carve me about."

Sports writers have always rather liked finding nicknames for their characters, not always to the characters' pleasure. John Gully, for instance, who held the heavyweight belt early in the nineteenth century, did not much approve of being known as the Game Chicken, especially when he because a Member of Parliament after the Reform Act of 1832. G.L. Jessop intensely disliked being known as 'The Croucher', and once wrecked a radio programme, of which I was the young and unfortunate producer, because we had given it that title. Brian Close never quite appreciated being the Old Bald Blighter. Even the kind and gentle John Woodcock, I think, had some mild doubts when he began to be known as the Sage of Longparish.

I cannot remember when I first was moved to call Robin Jackman the Shoreditch Sparrow, but it was some years ago, and the name was picked up by others (indignantly by Brian Chapman, who insisted that an eagle would be a better analogy). The original Shoreditch Sparrow was, I believe, a lightweight Regency boxer, and Jackman, when he had taken a wicket – even more, when he had just failed to – used to punch the air, in delight or fury. In either case he was anxious to get on with the next ball. I suppose this was the reason why the name occurred to me. The reason it stayed was because he was in every way such a chirpy chappie.

I am very sorry to hear that he is retiring: indeed, I do not quite believe it. I would take a modest bet that I will see him playing first-class cricket again, even if not for a year or two. It would not surprise me if he were to do another Illingworth, and turn up captaining Surrey, or somebody in 10 years' time.

Although when I first used this description of him, it was not meant unkindly, I was a little concerned lest he take offence. He did not come from Shoreditch or anywhere near it. He was born in Simla in 1945, a member of a distinguished military family. He learnt much of his early cricket at St Edmund's, Canterbury. He only became a son of the Elephant & Castle by adoption. So I was relieved to have a card, next Christmas, from 'The Father and Mother of the Shoreditch Sparrow'.

Jackman has been one of the unluckiest cricketers of his time, so far as Test cricket has gone. It was extraordinary that he was not chosen, in the first place, for the West Indies tour of 1980-81. He had just had the two most successful seasons of his career: 93 wickets in 1980, 121 in 1981. Had he been chosen in the first selection, I doubt if there would have been much trouble. By the time he went out as a replacement, attention had been drawn to his South African associations, and feeling had risen, or perhaps it would be more accurate to say had been roused.

I was glad he was chosen for Australia last winter, though again he was unlucky in the timing of his choice. With the captain a fast bowler, there was one position sewn up already (his old friend Pocock had a similar experience when Illingworth became captain). With the preliminaries to the Test series so brief, a man swiftly had to be in form and in luck. When he did have his chance, in the one-days, he did well enough, and must have been pleased with his Man of the Match award; but it cannot have been quite the climax to his career for which he had hoped (one of the reasons why I suspect we may yet see him play again. He has an instinct for drama.)

I must tell you a couple of other things about him. When he was granted a benefit, he asked me to contribute an article for his brochure. This is a commonplace thing for any cricket writer, however humble, to be asked to do. We usually do our best, though there is of course no payment. I have done a good many over the years. Robin Jackman is the only one, so far as I remember, to write a personal letter of thanks and, come to that, buy me a drink.

The other is an incident in a match at The Oval, only a year or two ago. Nothing much was at stake. Surrey were playing Lancashire. Surrey were already sure of the second place in the Championship, but nothing better. Lancashire were thinking of getting back to Blackpool for the illuminations and were beaten in two days. On the second evening, with the match almost settled, Jackman bowled Fowler. He bounced up the pitch, gathered the ball as it rebounded from the stumps, rolling over and appealing loudly for a catch, and then, just to make sure, threw the remnants of the wicket down and appealed for a run out. This exuberance epitomised the man, his zeal, his determination, his chirpiness, the fun in him.

He has been an unlucky cricketer, yes, in some ways; but those who have watched him have almost always reckoned that their luck was in.

The Lord of the Taunton press box

Eric Hill was a disappointment as a cricketer. He played for Somerset for several seasons after the War and scored a couple of thousand runs, so you could not call him a failure. But he was still a disappointment because he had looked so good. The first cricket match on which I ever broadcast was Somerset v the Australians in 1948, in a very junior capacity to John Arlott. Eric had been made twelfth man. I remember John saying 'Somerset have left out, unwisely in my opinion, their most promising young batsman.' That was the general feeling: that Somerset had a good one here, the kind who would make a thousand a season for the next 15 years.

It was a feeling I heartily shared, but then I was prejudiced. I had been at school with Eric. The first time I became conscious of him was when I met him on the soccer field in a junior house match. He was playing outside-right for Day Boys 'A', and I was playing outside-left for Winterstoke East. Although we were much of an age, he was about twice my size at that stage and I spent the afternoon dodging him as discreetly as possible. Not long afterwards I saw him playing cricket for the First XI, while still a Colt, and we became friends.

I came to know him well in those odd early weeks of the Second World War. Some boarders who lived in supposedly dangerous areas had been sent back to school before time, much against our will. There were not many of us, and we became friends with the Day Boys, of whom we did not see much in term-time. Eric was very popular, because his father ran an admirable sweetshop in Taunton, and he could sometimes wangle us bargains from Dad. 'This Week's Special' was one of Mr Hill's best lines, and I can still remember a whacking bag of toffees for a shilling, which must have been worth twice the price. Looking back on those strange weeks, I did pretty well out of them because I also made another lasting friendship, with Morris West, who was President of the Baptist Union recently and introduced me to my first pub: only for lemonade and bread and cheese, but it seemed a very daring thing to do. I cannot remember the name of the pub, but it was at West Bagborough, after a stiff walk along the top of the Quantocks.

Eric had a passion for cricket, a quiet but deep passion, and his ambition was to play for Somerset. This had to be delayed, however, because he went into the RAF, where he served with much distinction (D.F.C., D.F.M.). He began his career with Somerset as an amateur in 1947 and became a professional in the following year.

He had a graceful, classical style. The leg glance was one of his most attractive strokes. He was not very forceful in front of the wicket, but he was strong, and the power would no doubt have come with more experience. His defence was well organised. He was a good deep fieldsman. All the ingredients seemed to be there. Yet his contract was not renewed after the 1951 season. So what went wrong?

I don't know. Even Ron Roberts, an historian of Somerset cricket, a close student of it, and an admirer of Eric, was puzzled. All he could say was that he was 'inconsistent'. So he was, but that does not really take us much further.

Perhaps he was handicapped because he usually opened the innings with Gimblett. Gimblett was still one of the leading batsmen in the county, a dominant figure in the Somerset side, and not always an easy companion. Such a personality can be a stimulus to a young man at the other end, but also sometimes a depressant, as several of Boycott's partners will tell you. And Eric is a sensitive man, though like many sensitive people he strives to conceal it with an air of gruffness.

Despite his early retirement, Eric and cricket were not to be separated. He joined the *Somerset County Gazette* before becoming a freelance journalist and over the years has become recognised as among the soundest of cricket reporters. Besides, he can write very well when the mood is on him, and grumble with the rest of us about what the subs do to his stylish bits. He has toured both South Africa and Australia. He rules over the tatty old press-box at Taunton with what purports to be an iron glove, though there is a velvet hand within it. He will growl about 'you cowboys' to visitors, especially when they arrive late and want to borrow his scorecard, but having been suitably humbled they get their information, and their telephone calls, in the end.

He is not now an ambitious man. He is content to be a steady professional, and live in Somerset, and watch Somerset (he can have missed very few of their home matches in the last 30 years). He keeps his home telephone number ex-directory, an odd thing for a freelance to do ('I don't want these cowboy editors ringing up in the middle of the night'). He rightly dislikes a stream of dirty stories in a press-box (I am afraid this is all too common) but I have noticed he is becoming increasingly voluble himself. Last season I heard him mutter 'Good shot' twice in one over. He has given much to cricket. Long may he flourish to keep us cowboys in our place.

1984

The winter was survived and bankruptcy avoided. My late brother, Andrew, who was a partner alongside Alan's great friend John (by then Lord) Foot in the Plymouth firm of solicitors, Foot and Bowden, reached an accommodation with Alan's various creditors for payment by instalments. Principal amongst them was the Inland Revenue, to whom he owed – at least according to *their* calculations – something over £2,000. This was to be paid off at the rate of £100 per month, although the payments don't seem actually to have started until 1985, and didn't last very long even then. In the meantime, the interest was accumulating. I think the last tax demand I saw – received long after he had finished working – was for something of the order of £24,000. I suspect it was of some comfort to my father in his declining years to know that the Revenue would never see a penny of it!

But the threat of court action, the prospect of bankruptcy and the general unpleasantness of being pursued by creditors had taken its toll, on Alan's output as well as on his health. He was struggling to complete his 'cricketing autobiography', *Growing up with Cricket*, and wrote comparatively few features for *The Times* during the winter months. He was drinking more heavily than ever, and becoming ever more impossible to live with.

He was also suffering from what he described, with unconscious humour in a letter to his accountants, as 'considerable problems with my balance'. This further restricted his travelling, to the extent that he hardly ever ventured much further than Taunton or Bristol. But he did at least make it to The Parks for his traditional start to the season – even though that meant braving the dreaded change at Didcot!

The summer of 1984 developed into another hot one. This served only to compound Alan's problems with his mobility, and it sounds as if he endured a distinctly uncomfortable afternoon when he made a rare visit to a Sunday League match at Bath on June 10, although whether the bars were really as short of ice, orange squash and whisky as he claimed must be open to some doubt.

One of the more unlikely results of the season was the defeat of Yorkshire – Boycott and all – by Shropshire in the first round of the NatWest. I suspect that for Alan, proud Yorkshireman that he was, the sting of defeat was drawn by the fact that it was only a one-day game, as well as being symptomatic of the turmoil which continued to swirl around Boycott. Alan seemed more inclined to mock than to mourn when he went down to Taunton for the Hampshire match, mainly at the expense of Sam, the Yorkshireman who presided in the Stragglers Bar.

For Alan, the season came to an abrupt and premature end. He was at Weston for the Festival in early August. And then nothing. His next contribution to *The Times* didn't appear until December. The letters which might have explained what happened have not survived, but Rosie suspects that it was the *Times* sports editor finally losing patience with Alan's increasing tendency to arrive at matches late or not at all, and to phone his copy through when half-cut, and frequently in a filthy mood. To make matters worse, the dispute over his expenses rumbled on.

His contract was terminated. The one surviving letter from the affair was written by the *Times*' Deputy Editor, Colin Webb, in October. In it, he rejects what sounds as if it may have been a suggestion from Alan to let bygones be bygones, with the words: 'To have tried to stagger on would have imposed an unfair burden on you, and in those circumstances we did not think we could provide our readers with a

Tests
West Indies
beat England
5-0
England
drew with Sri Lanka
0-0, with 1 draw

Championship
1 Essex
2 Nottinghamshire
3 Middlesex
4 Leicestershire
5 Kent
6 Sussex

Sunday League
1 Essex
2 Nottinghamshire
3 Sussex
4 Lancashire
5 Middlesex
Worcestershire

NatWest Final
Middlesex
beat Kent

Benson & Hedges Final
Lancashire
beat Warwickshire

Most first-class runs
1 G.A. Gooch
2 A.I. Kallicharran
3 M.W. Gatting

Most first-class wickets
1 R.J. Hadlee
2 J.K. Lever
3 E.E. Hemmings

proper service.' This didn't mean, he continued, that Alan would not be considered for 'occasional freelance work' but there would be no contract or retainer. The letter concludes: 'This wipes the slate clean, allows us all to forget what has happened and offers the possibility of future earnings. They cannot be guaranteed, of course, but in all the circumstances, I do not think you could ask for that.'

On top of everything else, it must have come as a hammer blow. And yet it did have its consolations. Crucially, it gave Alan the time to finish the long-delayed *Growing up with Cricket*. Judging from his notebooks at the time, he seems to have taken himself off to The Star every lunchtime and early evening to write the concluding chapter, which he titled *Envoi*. Much of it consists of a slightly rambling discussion of whether cricket is a fit subject for prayer. But it opens with what is as clear an expression of what might be termed his 'cricket-writing philosophy' as he ever made, and that is certainly worth repeating.

> The Sage of Longparish says of our reports in *The Times*, 'I write about the cricket, and Alan writes about "A Day at the Cricket"', and this is a perceptive remark. I hope to write about a few more days at the cricket before it is time to draw stumps: but my own day has at best reached a late tea interval. Indeed, most of this book is about the play before lunch, rather like a *Sunday Times* report. I am not very optimistic about the evening session. There are too many things I dislike about modern cricket – the excess of bouncers, the disappearance of leg-spin, the commercialism, the Sunday bashes, the plague of hysterical appeals. I do not expect to enjoy the game as I have done in the past. I do not mind so much when it rains. Sometimes I am glad of the chance to escape from a dull match to the bar, especially at Bristol where the Glorious Redheaded Imperturbable Pamela (known by the acronym of GRIP) is presiding. But the game still has its moments, and I look forward to a few more yet.
>
> How important is cricket? It has been important to me because it has helped me to earn a living. But how seriously should we care about it? The best of games, yes, it is still that, at least for those who have taken to it and respect it (not 'love' it. I distrust anyone who says he 'loves' cricket). The best sports writers, and not only about cricket, are those who have interests in other areas, and can therefore keep a sense of proportion.

He did, of course, miss the climax of the season, which featured one of the most exciting finishes to the county championship in its entire history. It came down to the last two balls of the final over of Nottinghamshire's match at Taunton, where I was scoring for Henry Blofeld, who was commentating for the BBC. If Mike Bore could score the remaining four runs that Notts, with nine wickets down, needed, then they would be champions. If not, then the title would go to Keith Fletcher's Essex. Booth bowled, Bore drove, and down below us on the long-on boundary, out of view from the commentary box, Richard Ollis, fielding as a substitute, took the catch. Had Alan been at Taunton, he would no doubt have been pleased, for Essex were one of 'his' counties, and Fletcher one of his favourite cricketers.

To Oxford via Didcot

OXFORD: Oxford University v Nottinghamshire

Our sports editor, generous man, in sending me notes about plans for the season, said: "I will do all in my power to keep you away from Didcot." He then sent me to Oxford, and it is very difficult to get to Oxford from the south except via Didcot. However, I examined the timetable, and found that by leaving Bath at 1.26 a.m., and changing at Bristol, Cheltenham and Worcester, with peaceful halts in Moreton-in-Marsh and Ashcott-under-Wychwood, I could arrive at Oxford at 1.02 p.m. If I cheated a bit and left early, catching the 7.03, I would arrive back at Bath at 6.40 a.m.

Still, we respect our sports editors; but unfortunately I had not noticed that the initial 1.26 from Bath was marked MX–Monday excepted. So it had to be Didcot after all, and though there were some trifling difficulties, I reached the Parks well before lunch.

NEXT DAY

It was foolish of me to tempt the Witch of Didcot so early in the season. She struck back swiftly. On Monday evening, the 9.00 p.m. for Didcot broke down irretrievably at Oxford. By the time it had been lugged away, manually, by the pace of it, and a substitute found, even the patience of my companion, the philosopher Green (DM, not TH), was wearing out. When I arrived at Bath, my wife announced that she was charging a pound a minute for waiting time throughout the season, and there was £87 on the clock already. I am wondering whether the editor will permit an expenses claim or the Revenue a tax allowance.

An unlucky day at Bristol

BRISTOL: Gloucestershire v Kent

It was not a happy day, either for Gloucestershire or for me. My wife kindly drove me to the ground, stopped to get petrol at Keynsham, ran up £15.50 on the clock and then innocently discovered that she had somehow left her purse at home. That cleaned me out pretty well, and the first thing I had to do was cash a cheque from the always helpful Gloucestershire office.

I feel I should mark this report "E and OE" because my notes and scorecard were swept away in the early evening by a zealous waitress tidying up my table while I was away on the telephone. I did tell you it had not been a lucky day.

Unwillingly to Oxford

OXFORD: Oxford University v Middlesex

Although Oxford is my Mecca, I left High Littleton with some reluctance, for The Star were due to play The Butcher's Arms in the final of the Chew Valley shove-halfpenny competition. I will report the result tomorrow. I think it may turn out to be more exciting than the cricket in The Parks.

NEXT DAY

At tea it began to rain. It had been a pleasant sunny morning, and we did not take the light drizzle too seriously, but it grew heavy and relentless. It was a depressing end to the day, and it had been a depressing beginning too, for The Star had been beaten by The Butcher's Arm in the Chew Valley shove-halfpenny cup. My informants tell me we had shocking luck, and were dead out of form.

A slow train journey to Taunton

TAUNTON: Somerset v the West Indians

I managed to catch a train successfully at Bristol yesterday morning. The trouble was that it did not start. The guard, after some time, explained that this was because we were about to have "the controlled explosion of a wartime bomb" at Parson Street, a couple of miles down the line. Whether it ever went off, I did not discover, but ultimately we passed the spot in safety, thanks I am sure to a venerable clergyman whom I besought to pray. After all, I pointed out to him, it was his street.

Wanting a drink at Bath

BATH: Somerset v Middlesex (Sunday League)

The only spare seats at Bath were in the west wing of the rugby stand, where you need binoculars or very keen eyesight to detect what is going on. This shows that the Bath festival is still going strong, though I agree with those who say that if it is to continue on this scale, it must be better organised, notably in the catering department. I approve of closing the bars on Sunday afternoon, because there are too many louts about, but it is absurd that, when on one of the hottest days of the summer, they run out of ice at noon, and orange squash at three o'clock in the afternoon. At six o'clock they even ran out of whisky.

NEXT DAY

BATH: Somerset v Middlesex

I got a fearful walloping, to use a polite version of the phrase, from the catering manager, because of some comments I had made on Monday. Since he was an old friend, I was sorry to have distressed him, and am pleased to report that ice, orange squash and whisky were all available yesterday in ample quantities at appropriate times. I understand that he had been teased by some Somerset players, led by the mischievous Popplewell.

Wilf Barber (Yorkshire)

Wilfred Barber was becoming a pillar of the Yorkshire side in the days when I first used to watch them. He was born in 1902, first played for the county in 1926, but only established himself in the early '30s.

He was a shortish man, quick on his feet, strong on the leg side. One of his hundreds I remembered quite clearly, at Taunton in 1946. Somerset scored over 500, and there had been an extraordinary innings by G.R. Langdale. Langdale, a left-hander who played in spectacles, an amateur who batted in the old amateur style, never had much time to play cricket. He had had some previous experience with Derbyshire, but this, though not his first game for Somerset, was his first at Taunton. He was only in the side because Wellard was injured, and batted at number eight. The small boys called him "Gogs". Soon, it was "Shot, Gogs!" and at the end of his innings there was a great cheer of "Good Old Gogs!" R.A. Roberts compared Langdale's batting, on this occasion, more romantically, with that of Woolley. Yorkshire, understandably shaken, lost five wickets quickly. Barber, however, stayed calmly there, collected a hundred, and saved the match. Every stroke seemed to be saying to his colleagues "There, there; never bother, lads: settle down." I enjoyed (partisanship again partly, no doubt) every gentle run of it, and Barber, you could see, enjoyed it too. He could be an aggressive batsman, and even a graceful one, especially in those leg-side strokes, but orthodox defence was his *forte*. Bill Bowes wrote of him in a memorial notice that perhaps even more than Hutton, "He was a textbook player."

His nickname among his fellows was "Tiddley-Push", but it would be a mistake to think of this as an appellation of contempt or derision. Tiddleywinks is a very good game, and was taken seriously in Yorkshire in the '30s, and Barber had a great talent for persistently nudging them in. Like many north-country professionals, he could be an argumentative man but had a sense of humour. When E.R.T. Holmes's side was in the field once in New Zealand, they were perplexed by some raucous cries from the crowd, in strong Antipodean accents: "Git a bag!", "'Ave a go!" etc. Barracking of this kind was almost unknown in New Zealand then. After some raised eyebrows, it was discovered that the ringleader was Wilfred Barber, who had the match off, and had enlisted the support of two other resting team-mates, Denis Smith of Derbyshire and (save the mark) Billy Griffith. Rather more than a tiddley push there.

Willie Watson (Yorkshire and Leicestershire)

The first time I saw Willie Watson bat in a Test match was against South Africa at Lord's in 1951. It was the match in which Tattersall took 12 wickets and England won by ten. But they had been in some trouble at 103 for three on the first day, when Watson came in to join Compton. They put on 122, Watson 79. He played in all five Tests that year and scored useful runs in each of them, several times at awkward moments. Temperament was clearly one of his assets.

I remember I was struck that day by the easefulness of his play. He was occasionally in difficulty, but never looked worried. His strokes were graceful rather than forceful. Only when you noticed how fast the ball was travelling did you realise how much power lay behind them. By the end of the season it was the unanimous view that he would be a fixture in the England side for some time, the eagerly awaited left-hander in the tradition of Leyland and Paynter, the "concrete in the middle" as Jardine used to say.

Although he scored more than 25,000 runs, he did not achieve all expected from that lean, fair, graceful figure whom I had seen stroking the South African bowlers around Lord's in 1951. I shall never think the England selectors made the best use of him. But then it may just be, as I said at the beginning, that I was lucky with him. I saw one of his last innings, at Leicester. It had been a dull match in damp weather, but for an hour or so on the last day he illumined it. I was sitting with Michael Melford on the bleak benches opposite to the Grace Road pavilion. When Watson was out, caught in the deep, Michael and I, with no more than a glance at each other, moved to the bar and had some champagne. I do not much like champagne, and I am not sure whether Michael does either, but it seemed the appropriate tribute. "The trouble is," he said after a sip or two, "there are so few like that left."

The Magic Dragon nearly runs out of puff

BRISTOL: Gloucestershire (5 pts) drew with Hampshire (5 pts)

It was a pleasant occasion: three fine days, many old friends. There, bonny as ever, was the cheerful commander of the bar in the Hammond Room. She had needed a handkerchief at one point, and I lent her a clean one "I always carry a spare," in Lord Peter Wimsey's words), and she returned it to me washed and anointed with her perfume. I was getting some vicious glances from sniffy neighbours all day. Grahame Parker, looking very fit, was there. He was once known as Puff the Magic Dragon, from his heavy breathing on the public address system; but it was better than the present Gloucestershire system, which has settled for inaudibility. The purpureous Basil was there, though he has spoiled the shining beacon of his bald patch by wearing a peculiar yellow cap, which he picked up, he thinks, in Shanklin, or possibly Antibes.

Only the cricket had been dull, though it livened a little on the third day. At the beginning Hampshire, one second innings wicket down, were 100 on. The pitch was still slow, and that they lost wickets was due more to a creditable impetuosity than any natural problems.

They had reached 165 for five at lunch, after 58 overs, and declared at 214, setting Gloucestershire to score 266 in three and a quarter hours: say about four and a half to the over, so far as one can judge from these complicated rules.

The pitch was turning, but still slowly. It was, in the circumstances, a generous declaration. Gloucestershire had a go. Romaines was caught at slip at 37. At tea, 72 for one in 24, they were still in with a chance. Stovold was leg-before at 113. Zaheer was caught at square leg, Shepherd at deep mid-off. Athey was run out after a silly muddle: 175 for six, eleven overs to go. Russell was out, leg-before, at 203 in the 14th. It was now just a question of whether Gloucestershire could save the match. This they manfully did, though not without a few alarmed squeaks from behind the Hammond Room bar, and a few puffs from the Magic Dragon.

JULY: Somerset v Hampshire at Taunton

Yorkshire's defeat is noticed at Taunton

TAUNTON: Hampshire, with all first wickets standing, are 396 runs behind Somerset

It was another lovely day at Taunton, the blue sky dappled with high flakes of cloud. Somerset won the toss, and made a confident beginning. By lunch, Felton and Roebuck had scored 108 in 39 overs, without much excitement but without much concern.

There were two interesting things. On the top of the sponsors' flagstaff hung the trousers of Sam, a Yorkshireman who commands the Stragglers' Bar, and who had rashly said that they could debag him if Yorkshire lost to Shropshire. The other was that the scoreboard was only half-working, because it had been vandalized during the night. I felt nothing but contempt for these inefficient vandals. If they had made a proper job of it and burnt the wretched thing down – because it is the worst scoreboard on any regular county ground – I would, lame as I am, have struggled along with a can of paraffin to assist.

Soon after lunch, Felton was caught at the wicket. Popplewell, after a few good strokes, was caught at square cover. Roebuck was accelerating mildly. Crowe came in and when he had reached 9, passed his thousand runs for the season.

There was another strangeness in the afternoon, when senior Somerset supporters went round the ground, rather shamefacedly holding out begging bowls for the poverty-stricken Botham. The current benefit system has become absurd and should be abolished. But all went well for Somerset on the field, for Crowe is in the kind of form where the ball goes wherever he advises it to and Roebuck was steadfast.

Crowe had to retire, suffering from the heat, after getting his admirable 50, but Roebuck carried on like an unimmolitable iceberg.

Gloucestershire at Bath

Wisden Cricketers' Almanack

I am sorry that this review of *Wisden* is rather late. The reason is that when the publishers eventually sent me a copy, it turned out to be last year's. I did not notice this at first. I settled down to read "Notes to the Editor", with which I always start, and began to feel a little puzzled. I scribbled down an irreverent note, "Johnny getting a little repetitive." I had wasted quite a lot of time before I realized that in the circumstances this was not surprising.

However, the editor was coming to stay at High Littleton the next weekend, and when he heard of my predicament generously brought down his own copy. We shall cherish it as a holy relic. Perhaps we shall use it as the pediment of the bust of Spurgeon, which stands on the mantelpiece: preachers of the Word, both.

It is not difficult, of course, at a casual glance, to mistake one *Wisden* for another. The immediately interesting bits, after the editor's notes, are the feature articles, especially the "Five Cricketers of the Year" – an honour cricketers value next only to a Test cap – the obituaries, and John Arlott's review of cricket books.

I will take these, so to speak, backwards. I have some reservations about the last two. John Arlott, following the *Wisden* tradition, can never bring himself to be severe about a cricket book. He never says, for instance, "this is a superfluous book" (and there are many), nor, of a ghosted book, "I doubt if the supposed author ever read a word of it." This says much for the kindness of the man and the tradition, but it does diminish the effect of the comments on the really good ones. A critic who is never condemnatory carries no weight with his praise. I wonder if the policy of reviewing every cricket book that is published is the right one. A good many of these could have been, not condemned, but quietly omitted.

It is another *Wisden* tradition that every cricketer who has achieved even minor eminence in the game has to be given his obituary. You will probably remember the most famous one:

> **Sub-Lieutenant Rupert Brooke (Royal Naval Division)** died at Lemmos of sunstroke on April 23. In 1906 he was in the Rugby Eleven, and although he was unsuccessful in the Marlborough match he headed the school's bowling averages with a record of nineteen wickets for 14.05 runs each. He had gained considerable reputation as a poet.

This was a happy stroke in retrospect, but it does seem to me a great deal of space is wasted on brief obituaries of cricketers who would, surely, have been more suitably, and adequately recalled in school magazines or county handbooks.

Some very distinguished cricketers died in 1983, who deserved more than the stiff, statistical style of the obituary columns. George Headley should have been honoured in the features pages. I suppose it saved space to tuck him away in the small print, accurately but briefly, shoved in between Harper ("who made one appearance for Worcestershire without success") and Hill, who played once for Ireland against Scotland, and scored five.

Seriously, I think the obituaries policy of *Wisden* need revision. Half of them could be cut out, that would give space (for I know the editor is always bothered by his space problem), and then we could have proper articles on Headley, and (to take another couple of current examples) such splendid cricketers as Melville and Valentine.

However, the early sections still provide some interesting features. David Green writes well on Zaheer. Matthew Engel writes a balanced article on the proposed tour of an MCC side to South Africa. It was a good idea to get R.J. Parish to write about the Australian Board of Control's reaction to the Packer affair.

The Five Cricketers of the Year are Gatting, Smith of Hampshire, Emburey, Amarnath and Coney. An odd selection, you may think, but as the editor explains, this is an honour for which nobody may be chosen twice. And several more obvious competitors had been chosen already. I think this is a sound principle. How boring it would have been to have the same name recurring year after year in the days of Bradman, Grace, Hobbs, Sobers and so on. How difficult it would have been for the wretched sports reporters who would have had to write the repeated articles.

And so I came back to the "Notes by the Editor". He is not very controversial this year: indeed, to readers of this newspaper, who are familiar with his views, he may almost seem repetitive. He dislikes bouncers, and hints that he may even be coming over to the "white line" theory. He gives consideration to Bradman's idea on electronic umpiring. He approves of the insistence of minimum over-rates per day in county cricket, and so, I suppose, do I, though I am miserable at the prospect of all those missed editions and trains, and endless waits at Didcot.

Still, it is an exceptionally good edition, coping with its increasing problems of compressing even more quarts of peas into a pint pot. But that is too large a question for me to tackle just now.

On Reflection by Richie Benaud

Richie Benaud has been one of the best all-rounders, one of the most successful captains, and one of the most influential commentators, that cricket has had since the second war. This hardly needs repeating. He is also a very pleasant man, as I can aver from working with him on a number of occasions; and a capable, fluent writer, as you can discover for yourselves by reading this book. It contains some errors and solecisms, but I have only been given the opportunity of reading an uncorrected proof – a mangy habit of some publishers, probably to frustrate the mangy reviewers who delight to make lists of errors – and they will no doubt have been put right in the final version.

What I can say, however, is that it makes compelling reading, a welcome relief in the present glut of superfluous cricket books; and yet I disagree with much of the author's philosophy.

He has the nerve to claim that cricket is a game, and yet his whole approach shows that, at least in recent years, it has become for him a business, and the only important thing is whether it can be made to pay. If this can only be done by pink pyjamas in floodlight, so be it.

For a game, so far as it is to remain a game, depends basically for its health not on how much money can be made out of it, but how many people wish to play it. Nine men's morris must have been a good game, which gave pleasure to a lot of people over hundreds of years. Then fewer people wanted to play it and it died. Well, hard luck on nine men's morris, but it had served its purpose. Its time was up, and no real harm done. No doubt sponsorship might have saved it. World Series Nine Men's Morris could have stepped in. Pall Mall is no longer with us, and Benson & Hedges might surely have made something out of a name like that, but the same logic applied, just as it will to cricket, one day. Life is valueless if it has become dependent on a life support apparatus and it is better to let nature take its course than give the appearance of preserving what is in fact dead. I am not suggesting that cricket is anywhere near that condition yet, but it is heading in that direction with its commercial obsession.

However, Benaud's views on these matters, if controversial, are vigorously put, and in any case only part of the book. Much of it is autobiographical. I particularly enjoyed the account of his early days at home. There is a deeply interesting chapter on captaincy with appraisals of four great captains – Miller, Illingworth, Ian Chappell and Brearley in particular. He discusses, too, four great all-rounders – Botham, Hadlee, Imran, Kapil Dev. And there are many light-hearted touches and not too many technicalities. Also, it is always satisfying to know that every word of the book has been written by the man whose name appears on the cover, though I dare say his wife Daphne interpolated a paragraph or two, and a large number of exclamation marks. I used to have some correspondence with Daphne, long ago, when she was E.W. Swanton's secretary, and I have never known a girl who was so profuse in her exclamation marks. She would end a letter, "Well, that's all for now!! Thanks for the information!!! Must go!! His lordship calls !!!!" So perhaps I should end this review by saying I think you're wrong, Richie! But thank you for the book all the same!!

At The Rendezvous of Victory by C.L.R. James

John Arlott maintains that the best cricket book he has ever read is *Beyond a Boundary* by C.L.R. James, and I am inclined to agree, at least among books of the last half century or so. James is a Trinidadian, and not primarily known as a cricket writer. Most of his books have concerned political matters, especially those of the West Indies. He has been one of their leading thinkers along their struggling, sometimes straggling paths to independence.

This collection of his writings would be hard going to anyone not interested in political science or West Indian problems, but it is no surprise to find such names as Headley and Constantine in the index (Constantine was responsible for James first coming to England, to Nelson, where Constantine was professional in the 1930s). Kanhai gets a whole chapter to himself, and a remarkable chapter it is. It describes an innings he played at Edgbaston in 1964 against An England XI. Kanhai scored 170 in three hours, and James writes: "At that moment … the West Indian could strike from his feet the dust of centuries. The match did not impose any burdensome weight of responsibility. He was free as few West Indians have been free." It must certainly have been a notable innings, but James describes it *sub specie aeternitatis*, almost as a turning-point in West Indian history. To realize the force of his argument, you should read the whole article, and possibly the whole book.

1985

The summer of 1985 was a wet one, but with more than its share of cricketing consolations. For Alan Gibson, it was a difficult one, but he had at least settled his differences with *The Times* to the extent that he covered matches for them most weeks, right through to the end of the season.

By this stage in his career, he was cutting an increasingly eccentric figure, shuffling along, in his overcoat, corduroys and black gym pumps, usually in the direction of his chosen bar, there to cradle a half pint glass of whisky and water and stare glassy-eyed out towards the middle. If there was still a touch of humour in his writing, there was precious little of it in his manner. For much of the time, he appeared sunk in unutterable gloom.

His 'lameness', as he called it, was largely to blame. Quite what was causing the pain in his feet – sometimes it was one foot, at other times both – we never really knew, but it was probably neuritis, brought on by his drinking, and as that got worse, so did the pain. In his health as in his life, he was locked into a vicious downward spiral, the primary cause of which he refused to accept, and the consequences of which – despite all the misery and pain they caused him – he lacked the willpower to escape.

Nor – despite a £1,500 advance from the publishers of *Growing Up With Cricket* – had his financial worries gone away. In January, he was writing to his Tax Inspector, the long-suffering Mrs Provis, who was threatening legal action, to explain why he still hadn't started paying the £100 a month that had been agreed over a year previously, and signed off as follows: 'Isn't the weather beastly? With my bad leg, I have not been able to get out of the house this week. I suppose a snowstorm a day keeps the bailiffs away.'

If that suggests that he was still capable of at least some gallows humour, the final paragraph of a feature he wrote for *The Times* that month, recalling Ashes series of the past, provides a much sadder indication of his mood. He concluded:

> Despite the differences between England and Australia, I believe that Test matches between them, taken over a century, have done more good than harm. Even today I gladly go to one, *as long as I am paid.*

That may, of course, have been a dig at *The Times*, which he was still accusing of failing to pay him what he was due. But I am afraid it also provided further confirmation that watching cricket was no longer a pleasure, and had become an increasingly painful chore.

That was in the depressing depths of winter. By the time the season got under way at the end of April, he seems to have recovered his spirits.

It was at about this time that *Growing Up With Cricket* was finally published. It is by no means Alan's best book and he had struggled to complete it. Even so, the review in *The Times* by John Graham was quite startlingly harsh.

> This is really not a very good book. There are far too many minor characters, of little interest to anyone at the time, and none at all now. Gibson's whimsical style and oblique approach to the rituals of our national game are perfectly suited to a short match report on page 27, but they won't do for a whole book. He is too intelligent, his interests too wide-ranging and his understanding too deep to have buried his talents beneath such mounds of eminently forgettable trivia.

Tests
England
beat Australia
3-1, with two draws

Championship
1 Middlesex
2 Hampshire
3 Gloucestershire
4 Essex
5 Worcestershire
6 Surrey

Sunday League
1 Essex
2 Sussex
3 Hampshire
4 Derbyshire
5 Northamptonshire
6 Gloucestershire
Warwickshire
Yorkshire
Leicestershire

NatWest Final
Essex
beat Nottinghamshire

Benson & Hedges Final
Leicestershire
beat Essex

Most first-class runs
1 G.A. Gooch
2 D.W. Randall
3 C.L. Smith

Most first-class wickets
1 N.V. Radford
2 M.D. Marshall
3 D.V. Lawrence
C.A. Walsh

Whether Alan ever read that, I am not sure. Had he done so, he would have been hurt, but would also probably have found himself at least half in agreement with the critic. Much as he enjoyed the game and much as it had given him, I am sure that in his heart of hearts he did indeed regard cricket as a trivial subject for someone with his depth of intellect and breadth of knowledge to have wasted so much time upon. As FE Smith, Lord Birkenhead, had said to CB Fry, when the great man was Captain of the Training Ship *Mercury*: "This is a lovely place and a fine show, CB. But for you it has been a backwater." Alan by this stage did not even have the consolation of being particularly happy in his chosen backwater.

Yet all in all, in 1985, Alan seems mostly to have got to wherever he was supposed to be going, to have filed his reports on time and to have maintained a high standard of writing. If his fortunes had not been transformed, they had at least recovered.

But not for long. Disaster was lurking just around the corner. His cricket-writing may have recovered, but his behaviour at home most certainly had not. Rosie had had enough; of his drinking, his foul moods; his erratic behaviour; and his never-ending financial crises. She warned him that if he didn't mend his ways she would divorce him, but he took no notice. When the blow fell, in November, and she told him to leave, he took to his bed with a bottle of sleeping pills. It was thus that I found him when I drove up to High Littleton to try to persuade him to see sense. Fortunately, it was more an expression of self-pity than a serious attempt at suicide. He was taken by ambulance to the Bristol Royal Infirmary to be pumped out, and thence to an alcohol and drug rehabilitation centre near Weston to be dried out. But Alan was never an easy man to confine. No sooner was he up and about again, than he summoned a taxi, arriving back at High Littleton at Sunday lunchtime, and expecting Rosie to pay the fare!

There was to be no reprieve. The next time I went to see him it was to collect him and take him to a flat in Queen's Court in Clifton, where he had lived when he and Rosie were first married. Very little money had been spent on the building in the interim. Alan's flat was cold and tatty. He made no attempt to make it any more comfortable, existing on whisky and tins of corned beef or baked beans, surrounded by piles of books and other belongings: the wreckage of his married life, as it must have seemed to him. It couldn't continue. This time, he would have killed himself, not from sleeping pills, but from neglect. Fortunately, he was found in time and, for the second time, he was taken by ambulance to the BRI, for subsequent transfer to the hospital at Ham Green, which specialised in treating alcoholics on their last legs, as Alan was presumed to be.

Yet he proved himself remarkably resilient. I remember talking to the ward sister, just after a series of his blood samples had been analysed. Considering the amount that he had obviously been drinking – at least a bottle of whisky a day – and the state he had been in when he had arrived, she was amazed that his liver was not more damaged. Soon, he was on the road to recovery and spent Christmas there, not happily by any means, but in sufficient health and spirits to record some impressions of the experience, in an article that I don't think was ever published. But it was an encouraging sign.

A Bristol reunion

BRISTOL: Gloucestershire v Lancashire

"And are we yet alive, to see each other's face?" These lines by Wesley, which I trust are still heartily sung at the beginning of every Methodist Conference, apply with equal fervour to the meeting of familiar friends at the first home match of the season.

Everyone was full of beans at Bristol, though the last time these two sides had met, in a desperate finish, Lancashire had batted out the last 11 overs for a draw, keeping themselves just above Gloucestershire at the bottom of the table.

The Glorious Red-Headed Imperturbable Pamela (GRIP) was presiding behind the bar again, and she was wearing a fetching outfit in pale pink, which made her, a friend suggested, more a QUOM (Queen of the May). Purpureous Basil was late on parade, but looking even more joyful than ever when he glanced at the lunchtime scoreboard, which showed Lancashire, after 32 overs, 76 for four.

A candle but no match

BRISTOL: Gloucestershire v Somerset

It was a disappointing day, with no play. It was my birthday, and the sun was shining from a blue sky, decorating the light, white clouds, when I woke up. The prospect of watching two of my favourite counties playing at Bristol lifted my heart, even though a result to the match, after a day and a third lost to the weather, seemed improbable without fiddling.

The pitch and square and outfield were so wet, after the sobbing, sogging weekend's rain, that play could not begin on time, and, as it proved, never began at all. The match was abandoned before 2 o'clock. I am inclined to think that this was a proper decision.

I must tell you, however, in consolation, that I had an unexpected birthday present. I was given a small pink cake with a lighted candle. It was one of those joke candles that re-lights as soon as they are blown out, and when you actually extinguish it, your age is known according to the number of blows. I did it in a perspiring 11, but I am afraid I am older than that.

Stragglers talk

TAUNTON: Somerset v Warwickshire

It was one of the most beautiful mornings imaginable, and the western countryside glowed handsomely as we basked through it. One woman, serving in the Stragglers' Bar, said, "Now tell me, who'd want to live in one of the cities?"

Another said, "Very boring today, 'tis." The first was thinking of the scenery, the second of the cricket.

Both were right, but only partly. The weather lost its morning glory, becoming increasingly overcast, and so did the match. It had contained some good cricket, nearly all of it by the batsmen, but in the end died less with a whimper than a snuffle.

Poor light at Worcester

WORCESTER: Worcestershire v Lancashire

Play began in a dim, religious light. If the organist in the cathedral had bowled a bouncer with an apple down the aisle to a recalcitrant choirboy, one felt that the vergers would have immediately made an offer to the batting side.

> Sir, Mr Alan Gibson's intriguing image of a cathedral organist bowling apples down the aisle is not entirely whimsical. It is certainly not unknown for cricket-minded organists to feature cricketing conundrums on a cathedral service sheet or signal the test score to understanding lay clerks.
>
> But organists are not alone in getting their priorities right. When Dr Cyril Allington was Dean of Durham, he was sometimes invited to preach at other cathedrals. On his own admission, his thoughts as he processed up the nave were not on things heavenly, nor even on the architecture, but on whether the nave would take spin.
>
> Yours faithfully,
> RICHARD LLOYD
> (Organist, Durham Cathedral),
> 6 The College, Durham

Phil Neale

WORCESTER: Worcestershire v Essex

I have had rotten luck with the weather this season, and not much better with the trains, though I know some readers think that the iron horse is my hobby horse. However, yesterday we had sunshine between the showers, and I even spotted a greater crested guard or two, a species still known in the remoter parts of the West.

Neale, who grows in poise and assurance year by year, was Worcestershire's most successful batsman. He has a reputation for being a bit of a toff, a scholarly type ("Speaks the Russian," they tell you in slightly awe-stricken Archer accents beneath the horse chestnuts) and possibly as a result has been regarded rather suspiciously as both captain and batsman. But he is now establishing himself well in both capacities, and his innings was full of careful, effective strokes.

An alternative to the Bath festival

BATH: Hampshire v Lancashire

I am running, or rather limping lame this season, and had very much looked forward to the Bath festival because it was the shortest distance I could hope to travel. So far, the weather has rather spoiled it. In a summer such as this, I feel there should be a Didcot festival, because the atmosphere there seems so much more suited to hanging about.

No refreshments

TAUNTON: Somerset v Leicestershire

I am sympathetic towards British Rail though the staff at Didcot would not agree with me. But I was really startled passing through Temple Meads station at Bristol yesterday, to hear that the train from Penzance to Aberdeen had no refreshments upon it throughout its journey. Not even with a word of apology was this information offered. Presumably, passengers require the line or it would not be provided, but it is hard on them to be required to starve. Possibly it is useful as a training course for monks getting themselves into shape for Lent.

No man goeth forth from this place except by prayer and fasting, might have been the appropriate comment.

The Gloucester festival

GLOUCESTER: Gloucestershire v Worcestershire

I suppose there was a special reason for preserving the Gloucester festival this year, since one of the heroes of Gloucestershire's unexpected renaissance has been a Gloucester boy, Lawrence. I was not, however, prepared for the fact that the main bar was not to open until seven in the evening.

There was a poky little tent, from which you could see no cricket, and for the high and mighty, there was the civic marquee, to which I was graciously admitted, possibly because it was the 200th anniversary of *The Times*, or possibly because they thought I was John Woodcock.

JUNE: Somerset v Warwickshire at Taunton

Richards scores 322 in a day

Editor's note: While Alan was in the Stragglers Bar, I was up in the commentary box, for my first stint as a BBC commentator for Saturday afternoon's Sport on Two. Cricket commentary was something I had dreamed of doing since I was a small boy, and I was as nervous as a kitten, hoping slightly shamefully for an uneventful day, which would get me off to a gentle start. In the event, Vivian Richards scored 322 in just under five hours of the most commanding batting you are ever likely to witness, and I found myself broadcasting around the world, unsure whether to laugh or cry. I seem to remember describing some of his strokes as "sumptuous", a level of hyperbole to which Alan notably failed to sink in his strikingly matter of fact report for the Sunday Times.

Somerset have had a disappointing season so far, but yesterday, a sunny day, not a cloud to be seen from the Quantocks to the Blagdons, they shewed signs of pulling themselves together. They won the toss, batted, and found Richards in form.

Bail, an odd name for a batsman, was hit on the behind when he had scored 8 and had to retire. Felton came in and was caught at second slip first ball. That was 28 for one.

The next wicket to fall was Popplewell's, but by then the score had reached 150. Popplewell played an innings of which his father would have been judicially proud. Ollis then came in and played an innings which made us forgive his father for the vast trucks which lumber around Keynsham. But the truth was we had no eyes for Popplewell or Ollis. We were impatient whenever Richards did not have the bowling.

He has taken a little time to settle down into this English season, but he left no doubt yesterday that he is still, when he decides to be, the master. At lunch, Somerset 145 for one, he was 71 not out.. He reached his hundred (103 out of 185) in the 41st over. He lost Ollis, caught from a careless off-side slash, at 324, but Marks made an adequate replacement and at tea, after 72 overs, Somerset were 376 for three, Richards 219 not out.

The pitch was placid enough, and the Warwickshire bowling, though they tried, not very testing, but the latter must have been partly due to the discouraging sight of Richards carving the ball away in any direction that occurred to him. At twenty past five, Richards passed his three hundred and soon afterwards the highest score ever made by a Somerset player.

Australians get a taste of Curran as their just deserts

BRISTOL: Gloucestershire, with four first innings wickets in hand, are 24 runs behind the Australians

It was a surprising day's cricket. The weather, though not often sunny, was warm and dry. The pitch, though it had a greenish look, might be expected to be lively for not more than an hour or so. When Australia decided to bat, it seemed the natural thing to do.

Yet shortly after lunch, they were out for 146. Wessels was bowled by Lawrence with his third ball, which the kind might call a yorker, and the unkind a full toss. Wellham was second out, at 28, caught at the wicket, also off Lawrence. Then Border went, leg before to Walsh. The Australians looked no happier than they had done many years ago when two other big black men, Hall and Griffith, thundered away at them.

W.B. Phillips was next to go, caught at square leg off Curran, and when Walsh bowled O'Donnell, it was 40 for five. Here, at last, came the steadying stand, between R. Phillips and Matthew. At lunch the score was 105 for five, and we suspected a lot of Australian runs to come.

There was a big crowd, though a high proportion of it consisted of occupants of sponsors' tents, whose interest, I dare say, was devoted less to the cricket than the browsing and sluicing. They must have had quite a shock as, reluctantly digesting the last mouthful of *anchovie suprême* and the last sip of Cointreau, they turned round to find Australia all out.

It was Curran who did the later damage. He is in thumping good form just now with both bat and ball. I still could not see anything much wrong with the pitch, though when Gloucestershire had lost four for 34, mostly to Lawson at the Orphanage End, every Gloucestershire man was saying the pitch was unworthy of such a match.

Gloucestershire also had their mid-innings revival, through Bainbridge and Curran, but at 79 for six, were scarcely in a better position. Graveney and Lloyds perseveringly improved the situation, until play ended early, so that the Australians could go and meet the Princess of Wales, or Mr Geldof, or Jimmy Young, I can't remember which.

Still, there have been some interesting matches between Gloucestershire and Australia in the past, and this could easily turn out to be another.

Rich fare from Border

BRISTOL: The Australians, with seven second innings wickets in hand, are 375 runs ahead of Gloucestershire

It was Australia's day. In the morning, Gloucestershire were 24 behind with four first-innings wickets left (effectively three, since Russell had damaged a finger). Lloyds and Graveney continued their partnership sufficiently long to show that the pitch was playing presentably, Wednesday's touches of venom gone. But once they had parted, the rest did not last long, and Australia began again, 35 behind.

It was not an optimistic lunchtime for Gloucestershire, though the inhabitants of the sponsors' tent seemed happy enough as they waltzed through from their turtle soup to their angels on horseback. I regret that a noble rich claret, Basilica Purpurea, in which I have made a mild investment, did not seem to be selling so well. I wish GRIP had been there to supervise the publicity, but she is far away at St Brelades, no doubt teaching the Channel Islanders the way to drink wine, and bowl inswingers, and possibly other things.

Anyway, when the last angel had been plucked from the saddle and those from the tent emerged to watch the cricket again, they found the Australians in command. So too did the back seats on the popular side, who had been enjoying their pork pies and canned ale. The crowd was larger than on Wednesday, when it had been reduced by some absurd publicity warning spectators to arrive early. Your Vale of Severn man does not much care for getting up at seven in the morning on the off chance of a seat four hours later. But yesterday, the publicists having dropped their silly stunt, the ground was full and comfortable.

To spend a day watching the Australians bat is not the usual Gloucestrian idea of a blissful cricket match, but I think we all enjoyed the centuries. Border looked the very picture of a main Australian batsman warming up for a Test match. Wellham, first to his fifty but second to his hundred, looked just a little more concerned with reassuring himself about his form.

Border, his hundred passed, did his best to get himself out as quickly as possible and ultimately succeeded, though the Gloucestershire fielders did their best to prevent him. Apart from this sudden spasm of lapses, Gloucestershire fielded competently and did not bowl badly. Lawrence will, I think, turn out to be a pretty good bowler, worth an England place, if only he is saved from too much publicity.

The Australians, even after their centurions were out, charged cheerfully on. Wessels, who had had to retire after a nasty knock from Walsh, returned when Wellham was out, and O'Donnell decided to play one of his more graceful than bashful innings. The crowd kept applauding with appreciation, but with perhaps a little less affection towards the end. After all, Gloucestershire had seemed to be doing so well on Wednesday. The Australian is a naughty animal. When he is attacked he defends himself.

Athey and Curran put off last rites

BRISTOL: The Australians beat Gloucestershire by 170 runs

The Australians declared at their overnight score, 375 ahead, and had bowled Gloucestershire out by 3.30. The contest was more interesting than that brief statistic suggests. Gloucestershire collapsed early against Thomson, made a brave recovery, chiefly through Athey and Curran, and fell apart again at the end. The weather, grey, sometimes nearly dark, with hints of showers, always contained the possibilities of an interrupting demolition.

Lawson, who has ricked his neck, possibly, it was suggested, by bowling to the Princess of Wales in a net – it is never wise to try to bow when bowling a bouncer – was unable to bowl. Russell, with a damaged finger, was unable to bat, so the luck in that respect was even. Thomson began the bowling, and at once nearly had Romaines caught at the wicket. Stovold was soon caught at short leg, a dolly catch, and Wright was bowled. That was 23 for three, and Thomson was looking quite pleased with life.

Athey and Bainbridge defended stoutly for a while, but at 70 O'Donnell bowled Bainbridge, and at lunch, 78 for four, there seemed nothing to wait for but the obsequies. Not so. Athey and Curran put on 108 in a vigorous partnership. They were, in a way, assisted by the bad light, since the Australians were hesitant to use their quicker bowlers. But they both batted well.

At the beginning of this match, the arguments here in Gloucestershire were whether Lawrence was too inexperienced to play for England. He almost certainly is, and the example cited against him that of Athey, who was flung into it far too soon. But at the end of the match Athey, with a few more years behind him, and away from the constant Yorkshire thunderstorms, is looking very much like an England player.

Once these two were gone, Athey to Holland, Curran to Gilbert, the proceedings drew to a swift and decorous close. Even the bars closed, for no discernible reason, though the public address system, which is not one of Bristol's blessings, kept roaring on with quantities of inaudible and probably pointless information.

Gloucestershire v Australians, 24, 25 & 26 June 1985

Australians won by 170 runs

Australians

Batsman	1st innings		2nd innings	
K.C. Wessels	b Lawrence	0	*not out*	61
W.B. Phillips	c Bainbridge b Curran	22	b Walsh	48
D.M. Wellham	c Russell b Lawrence	10	b Graveney	105
* A.R. Border	c Russell b Walsh	5	c Stovold b Graveney	130
S.P. O'Donnell	b Walsh	3	*not out*	31
G.R.J. Matthews	*not out*	41		
+ R.B. Phillips	c Russell b Curran	23		
G.F. Lawson	b Lawrence	0		
R.G. Holland	b Curran	0		
J.R. Thomson	b Curran	10		
D.R. Gilbert	b Curran	10		
	b 4, lb 5, nb 11	20	b 15, lb 9, w 1, nb 10	35
		146	(3 wkts, dec)	**410**

1/0, 2/28, 3/42, 4/44, 5/48, 6/110, 7/111, 8/112, 9/123, 10/146
1/98, 2/334, 3/339 *(Wessels retired hurt at 44 and resumed at 339)*

Bowler	O	M	R	W	O	M	R	W
Lawrence	12	1	52	3	16	0	89	0
Walsh	11	2	33	2	9	0	37	1
Curran	12	4	35	5	12	0	43	0
Bainbridge	3	0	17	0	8	0	34	0
Lloyds					13	0	83	0
Graveney					20	1	100	2

Gloucestershire

Batsman	1st innings		2nd innings	
A.W. Stovold	lbw Lawson	16	c Holland b Thomson	8
P.W. Romaines	c RB Phillips b Thomson	6	c RB Phillips b Thomson	0
A.J. Wright	lbw b Lawson	4	b Thomson	9
C.W.J. Athey	lbw b Lawson	0	b Holland	83
P. Bainbridge	c Border b Gilbert	23	b O'Donnell	25
K.M. Curran	c Wessels b Thomson	25	lbw b Gilbert	58
J.W. Lloyds	c sub b Holland	71	c Wessels b Holland	0
* D.A. Graveney	lbw b O'Donnell	23	*not out*	4
D.V. Lawrence	b O'Donnell	1	b Gilbert	0
C.A. Walsh	*not out*	2	b Holland	4
+ R.C. Russell	*absent injured*		*absent injured*	
	lb 2, nb 8	10	b 5, lb 6, w 2, nb 1	14
		181		**205**

1/22, 2/29, 3/29, 4/32, 5/73, 6/79, 7/167, 8/177, 9/181
1/1, 2/12, 3/23, 4/70, 5/178, 6/178, 7/200, 8/200, 9/205

Bowler	O	M	R	W	O	M	R	W
Lawson	10	0	42	3				
Thomson	10	1	36	2	9	2	38	3
Gilbert	16	1	63	1	13	1	55	2
Holland	8	2	26	1	13.2	2	56	3
O'Donnell	8	1	12	2	10	5	13	1
Mathews					10	2	32	0

Umpires: B.J. Meyer and D.R. Shepherd

Gloucestershire's championship challenge 1985

BRISTOL: Gloucestershire v Essex

Strictly speaking, Gloucestershire have never won the County Championship. *Wisden* records them as victors several times in the earlier years, but the championship then was a muddled, informal affair, run by the Press who often interpreted the rules of scoring according to their local affiliations.

Still, Gloucestershire were generally recognised to be the best county in 1877 and, 100 years later, were within a finger-stretch of it when, in a more formal age, and in the last game, they seemed to have Hampshire down; but Greenidge was dropped on the third morning, and went on to score a century. There was also 1930, when Gloucestershire won, if I remember rightly, four more matches than any other county, but still were deprived, because of the curious system of scoring points which prevailed at the time.

So you can see why we are getting a little excited about things down in Gloucestershire. The 1930 side had two masterful spin bowlers, Parker and Goddard. That of 1977 depended greatly upon Procter and Brain, two quick men. This year's team, which has made such a surprising leap to the heights after such a dismal season last year, has also owed much to two fast bowlers, Lawrence and Walsh, both of them as black as your grandfather's top hat at a Cheltenham funeral. Lawrence, it is constantly pointed out, is a local lad, born not only in the county, but the city of Gloucester.

BRISTOL: Gloucestershire v Northamptonshire

It was, mostly, a day of blue skies and sunshine, but so sodden had the field become through previous drenchings that play was not possible until a quarter past four. This was irritating for the crowd, some of whom were venturing to sunbathe, but there was no doubt, in my mind, that the delay was justified.

There is no more maddening game than cricket at such times. Even GRIP behind the Hammond Bar was not quite her usual, imperturbable self.

The morning was enlivened, however, by the presentation of five new Gloucestershire caps, to Lawrence, Walsh, Davison, Curran and Lloyds, all truly earned in the course of a successful season.

When play at last started, Northamptonshire put Gloucestershire in. The pitch was not too difficult, but sufficiently so to give the fast bowlers encouragement. Edges, and narrowly missed edges, were frequent. Despite this, Gloucestershire went after the runs bravely. This is in accordance with the way they have played this season, and one of the reasons for their improvement. "He either fears his fate too much, or his deserts are small, that puts it not unto the touch, to win or lose it all."

NEXT DAY

Still, Gloucestershire, looking back on their season – not that it is quite over yet, but this was their last game at Bristol – can take a good deal of happiness from it, especially when compared with last year's disasters.

Book review

Gubby Allen: Man of Cricket by E.W. Swanton

First three paragraphs of review in The Cricketer

Old Man River, he still keeps rolling along. I refer not to the subject of this book, but to its author, though it is a phrase which could apply to either (or would 'Old Father Thames' be more appropriate in the case of G.O.B. Allen?). E.W. Swanton continues to bless us with his broad, smooth, massive flow of words, like the Mississippi brimming its banks as it nears the sea.

Cricket writers are often said, with some justification, to be back-scratchers, when it comes to reviewing one another's books, so, endeavouring to put myself into an implacable mood, I dare suggest that this river has sometimes overflowed its banks. As a general rule, most books are too long. You would certainly include in that category the Bible, and the Complete Works of Shakespeare, if you had actually read them, cover to cover. (Hands up, those who have! Oh, sorry, Bishop Sheppard, I should have remembered. After all, you did once declare that you read *The Cricketer* cover to cover, which I would have thought a much tougher task than *Leviticus* or *Titus Andronicus*.)

But I digress, just as, I am afraid, E.W.S. sometimes does in this book, letting his thoughts attract his discourse, until the reader finds himself led a long way from the theme. Never mind. If the book is too long for the biography of any cricketer, even such a distinguished one, and if some of it is a touch repetitious to those familiar with the earlier works of E.W.S., nobody was better equipped to write it, and it needed writing (for Allen has been shy of words himself) and the fluent prose keeps the reader contentedly rolling along.

Christmas in hospital (this was my fourth) is always a bit of a struggle. Everyone tries too hard. Even at Ham Green, Bristol, a singularly friendly place, it was a strain to maintain the bonhomie. The most relaxed of my four Christmases was in a mental home: a case, I suppose, of *sancta simplicitas*.

The first proper hospital I was ever in (not at Christmas) was in my first term at school – not generally a happy time. There was nothing much wrong with me, but I stayed in for a longish convalescence. This was enlivened for me by a cricketing game called "OWZTHAT?" It came in a little tin, smaller than a matchbox, and could be played on a plate. It consisted of two hexagonal cylinders, which you rolled. The first bore the legends 6-4-3-2-1-OWZTHAT? If OWZTHAT? turned up you rolled the second, which gave you the choice BOWLED – CAUGHT – LBW – STUMPED – NO BALL – NOT OUT. I added some refinements to the rules to make it a shade more realistic and kept a careful score of all my matches (I always played by myself).

Before long I decided that random matches were not enough and planned something more elaborate. This took the form of a competition between the four Home Counties, each playing the other. It seemed an odd choice, because all my sympathies were with Yorkshire. But I suppose in my delicate condition I felt that the passions involved in a Yorkshire match would be too severe – and OWZTHAT? was not a game in which it was easy to cheat. It did not, after all, matter much which of the Home Counties won.

I recall that it was Kent who were successful. Woolley was still playing for them, but he was not their outstanding performer. This turned out to be Tom Spencer, who was just establishing himself in the side. He hardly failed. Often when watching him umpire in more recent years, I have reflected that in his valuable career he never quite equalled the form he had shown in Taunton School Hospital in the late 30s.

I believe that OWZTHAT? is still available. I saw one, or something very like it, in the corner of a shop window only a few years ago. At least two of my sons have played it in their time. If I had had a Christmas stocking this year, I would have been pleased to find one tucked away in the toe. I wonder what competition I would have chosen now. Something nostalgic, I think. I have recently been refreshing myself with another boyhood companion, Frank Richards, and a triangular tournament between Greyfriars, St Jim's and Rookswood has its appeal. The choice of the teams would have presented some difficulty because Richards tended to vary his teams according to the necessities of his plot. (Thus Cardew of St Jim's who was not even a regular member of Junior XI once made a dramatic appearance for the school First XI taking a lot of wickets including the hat-trick: but never seems to have been asked again.)

But no OWZTHAT? this Christmas. There was, however, some cricketing talk. Although I did not meet many actual cricketers, once it was known that I had a connection with the game, everyone asked me about Botham. Ham Green is in what used to be (and still is for cricketing purposes) the Somerset part of Bristol. The ground of the excellent Portway Club, where I first played with a touring side nearly 40 years ago, is nearby. So is the pub run for years by Roy Jennings, a considerable Cornish cricketer and an even better rugby-footballer, who toured South Africa with what we would now call a British Lions side. I wish Roy had been still around and could have paid me a visit. As it was, the sporting talk was mis-informed, and I soon began to run out of things to say about Botham. The most persistent enquirers were the nurses, and they were not interested in a technical description of his reverse sweep. That reminds me. Our ward was beautifully decorated but there was no mistletoe, and we had some very mistletoe-worthy nurses.

Perhaps it was as well, for I had whiled away the time growing a beard and it might not have exhilarated them. It is a long time since I have tried a beard, it did not look too bad then, when trimmed, coming out a decent brown. This one is grey and straggly, far from trim but lacking the majestic luxuriance of Grace or, come to that, of Vladimir Brusiloff, the great Russian novelist who "permitted his face to become almost entirely concealed behind a dense zareba of hair" (you will remember from *The Clicking of Cuthbert* that Brusiloff turned out also to be a golf enthusiast). I doubt if I dare retain it in the Hammond Rooms at Bristol, or the Glorious Redheaded Pamela would cease to be the Imperturbable.

For I am confident of being at the Bristol ground next summer and probably even more at Taunton and an assortment of other places as well. When I came into hospital, I was quite unable to walk, even to rise from a chair. But you should have seen me, after a week or two, dashing down the ward on my trusty zimmer. On Christmas Eve I graduated to a stick; muttering proudly to myself, OWZTHAT?

1986

It would be foolish to pretend that the process of rehabilitation after Alan's physical and mental breakdown in the autumn of 1985 was anything other than painful and difficult for all concerned. He had recovered sufficiently to be allowed to leave Ham Green by the end of January, and spent a fairly fraught couple of weeks convalescing with my family and me in our farmhouse in the Blackdown Hills. Loudly though he protested otherwise, there was never any question of him going back to High Littleton and Rosie. Divorce proceedings were already at an advanced stage. But we managed to find a comfortable little flat for him at Highlands, just off the Trull Road, on the outskirts of Taunton. Viv Richards had lived in the same small complex when he had first come to Taunton, and it was just up the road from my office.

He had been thoroughly dried out in hospital, and I was determined to do what I could to prevent him falling back into his old, whisky-fuelled ways. That didn't mean keeping him off the booze altogether. That would have been entirely futile and, besides, going to the pub (or the bars at cricket matches) was half his life. It was where – when not completely sozzled – he did most of his work and obtained much of his inspiration. But it did mean attempting to control what he drank, and where, and that was made easier by the fact that Highlands was a good half mile from the nearest pub, and that he lacked both the mobility and the funds to get there without my assistance.

So, almost every day, I would collect him from the flat and take him down to the Westgate Inn, at the Taunton end of Trull Road, for a couple of pints of Whitbread's West Country PA. The pub was run by Roy Marshall, the Barbadian who had opened the batting for Hampshire so thrillingly back in the 50s and 60s, his wife Shirley and their three daughters. They knew Alan – and his tendencies – of old and were only too happy to be partners in the process of getting him back on the cricketing trail. No whisky was the rule, and it was strictly enforced.

For that was very definitely the aspiration – to get him fit enough, mobile enough and sober enough to be able to report cricket for *The Times* when the season opened in April. Fortunately, it was an aspiration that he himself shared, even if it did spring from a delusion: which was, I am sure, that if he showed himself capable of working again; of earning a living; of becoming once again the Alan Gibson whom his friends and family so loved and admired, Rosie would have him back. I knew, of course, that this would never happen; that the marriage was irretrievably broken, and I gave him no encouragement at all to think otherwise. But that small glimmer of hope was vital in persuading him to summon the willpower to get back on the cricketing treadmill, and when it was finally extinguished, then so was his career.

Through all the vicissitudes of the preceding months, Alan had kept his type-writer with him. And he was still using it to good effect, writing articles on spec for *The Times* and a variety of other publications, such as his thoughts on the bicentenary of the MCC, which was written for *The Spectator* and which concluded: 'There are some who do not bother to join the massive waiting list for membership because they feel that £50 a year is more than they can afford, even for the privilege of wearing ostentatiously (and it is impossible to wear it otherwise) what must be the ugliest tie in the world.'

When it came to the season itself, *The Times* took some persuading that Alan was well enough and would be reliable enough to resume writing for them. But eventually the call came, and he was asked to cover the Combined Universities against the Indian touring side at Oxford, starting on June 12. It seemed a good omen that his

Tests
India
beat England
2-0, with one draw
New Zealand
beat England
1-0, with two draws

Championship
1 Essex
2 Gloucestershire
3 Surrey
4 Nottinghamshire
5 Worcestershire
6 Hampshire

Sunday League
1 Hampshire
2 Essex
3 Nottinghamshire
4 Sussex
5 Northamptonshire
6 Somerset
Kent

NatWest Final
Sussex
beat Lancashire

Benson & Hedges Final
Middlesex
beat Kent

Most first-class runs
1 C.G. Greenidge
2 G.A. Hick
3 R.J. Bailey

Most first-class wickets
1 C.A. Walsh
2 N.A. Foster
3 M.D. Marshall

season would, as so often in the past, start at the Parks, even if it was a month or so later than usual. It was a big day: the resumption of a career that had appeared to be completely shattered: Alan Gibson's come-back as one of the nation's best-loved cricket writers. I didn't want to risk him missing the train, so collected him from the flat and delivered him to Taunton station in good time. "Now remember," I said to him, as I helped him onto the train. "No whisky." He said nothing until the train door was safely shut. Then he called to the guard, who was passing. "Which way's the buffet car? I need a scotch."

I knew then that my labours had been in vain. I couldn't possibly control what he drank when he was away at cricket matches, and if he was determined to drink himself to the destruction of his life, there was nothing whatever I could do to stop him. I sometimes think that I may have been too severe and impatient of his self-pity; that if I'd gone a bit easier on him, he might not have rebelled quite so pointedly against the regime I had imposed. But I don't really think it would have made any difference. He was not the sort of alcoholic who was ever going to recover. And the remission which I had helped to provide him with did at least give him one last productive season.

He was certainly busy during June, covering eight matches. He seemed genuinely happy to be back at his old haunts: the Parks, the County Ground at Bristol, and – the easiest to get to of all – the County Ground at Taunton. This was to be a disappointing and, ultimately, deeply traumatic season for Alan's adopted county. Roebuck had taken over the captaincy from Botham, and although he was popular with the younger players, he really had nothing in common with the stars of the team and singularly failed to bring out the best in them.

Alan twice went to matches at Lord's: all three days of the Varsity Match and also a Sunday League match, at which he arrived in a state of some disarray. It will be gathered from this that the battle with the bottle had now been lost, if it had ever seriously been joined. The handwriting in his notebooks, which had always been so well defined, was beginning to tail off into scratchy illegibility as the end of each day neared. As the season went on, so his commitments became increasingly sporadic and confined to Taunton. His final championship game was on August 20th, when Somerset played Sussex. The fact that his last match should have been cut short by the rain, still with more than a day to play, provides a sadly appropriate metaphor for a prematurely curtailed career.

The news had broken that the contracts of neither Richards nor Garner would be renewed, and that Botham was threatening to leave in protest. I was due to cover their next home game for *Sport on Two* and was asked to get an interview with Botham. Being anxious to do the right thing, I approached the cricket manager, Tony Brown, who said that it was no good asking him; he was only the manager. So I duly asked the man himself, who promptly told me to fuck off. It seemed to me to be symptomatic of the complete lack of management and leadership which had been evident throughout this sorry affair. I wasn't the only commentator to think that, if Vic Marks had been made captain instead of Roebuck, Somerset would never have got themselves into this awful mess.

A hot Sunday

BATH: Somerset v Kent (Sunday League)

It was a hot day, with the Bath ground packed, as it usually is for these Sunday capers when it does not rain. Never have I seen so many half-naked, pot-bellied, middle-aged men within so small a compass. The cricket was also much as usual, a cheerful bash which nobody but small boys and some of their seniors took very seriously.

Kent won the toss, or possibly Somerset did. (Opinions varied, and the public address system, true to Somerset form, was inaudible.)

A hot Monday

BATH: Somerset v Kent

It was another day of intense heat, from which the Bath ground provides almost no shelter. I hesitate to criticize the cricketers, seeing them coming off streaming with sweat, for any failings. Yes, yes, I know they have to play at places like Bangalore and Barbados, burning with heat, but they naturally do not expect it at Bath, with the Molly Gerrard rugby stand presiding distantly over the proceedings, a safeguard to chilly autumn evenings. But it was not built as a summer bakehouse.

Getting to the ground

BATH: Somerset v Northamptonshire

I do like the Bath Festival, though I may tell you that getting to the largest city in Somerset from the county town is hard work for a lame man. You have to change at Bristol and cross about six platforms, and nobody can ever tell you which you should be aiming for. Also, and this really surprised me, yesterday I met a damnedly rude Bath taxi-driver, something that has never happened to me before.

Somerset v Northamptonshire at Bath (third day)

Roebuck and his men hold the fort

BATH: Somerset (4 pts) drew with Northamptonshire (8 pts)

Northamptonshire, who in the morning were 99 for three, were all out after a cheerful swing for 195. Cook kept his end going while the others risked their lives against Marks and Palmer. Somerset were left to score 323 in 74 overs, or whatever the regulations might ultimately dictate.

I did not think they had a chance but *they* did and they made a brilliant start. Felton was out early, a good catch at the wicket on the leg-side, but Hardy was soon going well and Roebuck the Restrained was relaxing his austerity from time to time. Hardy hit Griffiths for a fine six over mid-wicket, and Somerset hearts began to lift.

The pitch never became really difficult, but the bounce of the ball varied and wickets fell steadily throughout the afternoon. When Roebuck, who had played one of his best innings this season, passed Marks at the pavilion gates I think the word was "hold the something fort". Richards, who might have led the victorious sally, had been caught at mid-wicket almost as soon as he went in.

The weather, warm in the morning, grew cooler and windier. The handsome sponsors' tents were deserted after the lunchtime celebrations. The crowd had dwindled in the chill. My whisky, in its plastic container, was blown over. Still, it has been a good week, and Marks and Davis duly held the fort.

NORTHAMPTONSHIRE	355 for six declared (Capel 103*, Wild 85, Bailey 69)
	195 (Cook 70, Boyd-Moss 37, Palmer 4-77, Marks 3-28)
SOMERSET	228 (Richards 59, Hardy 50)
	241 for eight (Roebuck 62, Hardy 50, Marks 35*, Rose 34)

A Christian lionized

TAUNTON: Somerset beat Dorset by eight wickets

I have long been fond of Dorset and Dorset cricket, for which I have seen many fine players perform. There were Michael Walford, Cuan McCarthy and – best memory of all – the Rev GLO Jessop, whom I once saw, though he was approaching the venerable stage, batting much as his father must have done in a match against Cornwall at Camborne.

Another reverend gentleman, now playing for Dorset and from an old Dorset family, drew me to Taunton yesterday. There he was, Andrew Wingfield Digby, who qualified for the ministry after innumerable years at Oxford. He won four Blues over a period of seven years.

Whether his absences were due to periods of meditation or rustication, I have never been sure. He is now director of an organization called "Christians in Sport" and took a cricket team under their name to India last winter. It was in aid of Indian spastics and cannot have done them much harm, since 35,000 people attended their match at Coimbatore.

His captain on the tour was Vic Marks. Marks, Roebuck and Wingfield Digby all played for Combined Universities when they had their famous win over Yorkshire in, I think, 1977. So there was some friendly rivalry going on beneath the surface of the match.

Wingfield Digby looked much the same, with those long legs consorting so oddly with his short strides in the run-up, like an evangelical curate approaching a session with the Bishop of London. He must have been delighted to get Roebuck out and sorry he did not have the chance to get to grips with Marks, either with ball or bat.

There was not much of the cricket itself. Dorset were put in and bowled out for 132. Kennedy (formerly the Lancashire Kennedy) held the first part of the innings, and Stone put some strength into the tail, but Garner was too much for the middle order.

Roebuck and Felton got Somerset away to a comfortable start and there was little excitement, apart from Wingfield Digby's moment, doubtless the product of much prayer, as they proceeded to victory by eight wickets in the 34th over. Felton was made man of the match, though I thought there was just as good a case for Kennedy or Garner.

Dorset fielded well. They were outclassed but not disgraced, and I expect they will have a good season. It was a lovely, sunny day, and a pity that the match could not have lasted longer.

Last days at Lord's

A Sunday League match

LORD'S: Middlesex v Essex (Sunday League)

"Mr Gibson," said a considerate person following me up the steps, "I am not sure if you are aware of it, but your braces are falling down." I looked down, and there they were, ankle-trailing. A moment of inattention in the train, no doubt. He held my blazer while I hauled them and restored respectability to myself. A fine way to start my season at Lord's, and the university match coming up next week.

The first day of the Varsity match

LORD'S: Oxford University v Cambridge University

Cambridge won the toss and put Oxford in. It is never a bad tactic in a modern university match, with young batsmen nervously trying to make an impression at Lord's, but the pitch was dry and played well, and Oxford intended to bat all day and score 350.

They made a tolerable start, and at lunch were 87 for two, in 31 overs. In the afternoon, the innings fell away, and at tea, after 65 overs, they were 165 for seven. The only man who had been able to stem the Cambridge tide was Thorne, the Oxford captain, and when he was bowled just after tea the Oxford hopes of an even moderately impressive total vanished swiftly.

I have known for some years that Lord's was no longer a suitable place for the University match to be played (urging the claims of Bletchley, Torquay or Scarborough). The paying gate yesterday may have been about 80, which was certainly more than one some years ago when I was able to count precisely four people in the public stand. At least, this was what I faithfully reported, but on later investigation one of them turned out to be a dustbin. No, it is no use hanging on to the tattered and faded flag at headquarters. Put them in the church and salute them as you pass. Then go and have a game at the seaside.

Frank Woolley: Gallant ghost of a bygone summer 1986

Frank Woolley played 64 times for England, a high figure for his time. (Hobbs, roughly his contemporary, played 61). Woolley's first Test was in 1909. This is the sad tale of his last, in 1934.

Woolley was less admired than adored. His attributes, especially in Kent, were considered godlike. In a famous sentence, Cardus wrote: "There is all summer in a stroke by Woolley." His achievements were vast. He scored almost 59,000 runs, more than anyone except Hobbs, with 145 centuries; and took more than 2,000 wickets. He was left-handed with both bat and ball.

In Tests, it was true, he was not quite so dominant. His dashing grace did not take easily to the time-unlimited game which then ruled in Australia. He scored only two centuries against them over there, and in England none, though he had 95 and 93 in the Lord's Test of 1921, which he considered the best two innings of his life.

He had not played, nor, one imagines, been seriously considered, in the first four Tests of 1934. Before the fifth Hendren, who had been doing pretty well, was injured, and Woolley, in his 48th year, was recalled (Hendren was in his 46th). He had been making runs for Kent, and it was thought that his left-handedness would be an asset against the leg-spin of O'Reilly and Grimmett. Leyland, another left-hander, had been England's most successful batsman.

Woolley's return was greeted with surprise. England had made a successful recall of a veteran at the Oval with Rhodes, eight years before. In the first innings, going in after an opening partnership of 104, Woolley had only scored four when he nudged O'Reilly to short-leg.

This was sad, but as Australia had already scored 701 (during which Woolley was said to have dropped two very difficult catches), was hardly critical to the destiny of the match. Worse was to come. England were all out for 321.

Since the rubber stood at one-all, the match was to be played to a finish, and it was a reasonable decision for Australia to bat again. Ames had a bad back. Who was to keep wicket? A tall, straight figure stepped forward to the table and picked up the wicket-keeping gloves. Guardsman Frank was answering the call of duty.

England had to bat again. When Woolley came in, McCabe was bowling, having disposed of C.F. Walters. Cardus wrote: "Woolley's second failure in the match broke the hearts of his adorers. First of all he was nearly run out. Then he drove at McCabe with an energy quite unlike him: he is never obviously violent at his best. The ball lifted a little, and Woolley's drive was transformed into a terribly weak catch to mid-off."

The selectors had taken a risk, and lost. A hallow'n summer would have been a delight, but none thought the worse of Woolley, even if it was only his gallant ghost that they had been watching.

Albert Craig: The McGonagall of The Oval

A familiar and affectionately-held character at Kennington Oval – and other London cricket grounds, but especially the Oval – at the beginning of this century was Albert Craig, the "Surrey Poet". You may still see his photograph, looking rather like a Methodist local preacher, in the Oval pavilion.

Craig was a Yorkshireman, born in 1850, but he tired of his life as a Post Office clerk, came south at the age of about thirty, and discovered an unusual, indeed unique way of earning a living. He wrote topical verses about the events at cricket matches, printed them on his own small press, and hawked them round the ground, with considerable success. By the time anyone wondered whether he had any authority to do it, he had become an institution, and was allowed to carry on, a friend of the players as well as the public, until his death in 1909.

His poetry was execrable – about the standard of an English McGonagall – but it had immediacy. Thus when Hobbs scored a century in his first championship match, and was rewarded with his county cap, Craig was first to praise him, with:

Joy reigned in the Pavilion
And gladness 'mongst his clan
While thousands breathed good wishes round the ring;
Admirers dubbed the youngster
As Surrey's coming man;
In Jack Hobbs' play they saw the genuine ring.
'Twas well worth going to see
Illustrious Hayward's smile,
While Razor Smith and Walter Lees
Cheered with the rank and file.

This I consider one of Craig's better efforts, and many a supporter contributed his coppers and carried a smudgy copy home as a memento, cherished as a scorecard might be, of the great occasion.

Generally speaking, we must agree with Ronald Mason, who says that most of Craig's verses were "of paralysing badness, for his literary style tempered a cursive facility of cliché with a dire metrical uncertainty". But Craig himself made no claims for their artistic merits. Once on his peregrinations a spectator called out, "Call yourself a poet? Why, I could write better poems myself!" to which Craig courteously replied,

"Doubtless, sir, oh doubtless – but could you sell 'em?" And such was the rapport with his customers, and his cheerful badinage, that sell them he did, his pockets visibly weighted down with the returns as he completed his circuit.

He came to be quite an influential figure among the crowd, proudly calling himself "Captain of the Spectators". In 1906 there was a rough match against Yorkshire at the Oval. Surrey won, but for some reason the crowd was displeased, and there was hooting of the Yorkshire players afterwards. Craig raised his arms and his voice: "Three cheers for Lord Hawke and Yorkshire!" The cheers were given, and the malcontents shuffled away.

This may have been an instance of Craig remembering his Yorkshire origins, but in his writing he was often generous to counties other than Surrey. He wrote a stirring tribute to G.L. Jessop, which certainly had a memorable opening line:

Hail! Prince among smiters, all hail!
Whose fame spreads o'er mountain and dale
What a chorus of cheers
When our favourite appears,
When bowlers and fielders turn pale.

In the third verse, his metrical weakness trips him, but he makes a brave recovery:

You may perhaps get a "duck" now and then,
Like Tom Hayward and other good men;
But the foe is in doubt
Till the umpire says "Out",
And the enemy whispers "Amen".

The last verse suggests that on this occasion Craig may have been paying a visit to the west.

Yes, Cheltenham delights in her son
In the glorious achievements he's won,
"Here's your health", I'll be brief,
You're a practical chief,
As you stand undismayed at your gun!

Towards the end of his life, Craig perhaps became a little overbearing, as such people do when they come to think of themselves as "characters". Jack Hobbs tells us that "in course of time, his scope of action became subject to certain limitations", which may mean no more than that he did not have casual entry to the professionals' dressing-room. But he never really lost his status.

He was a pleasing, baroque ornament to the game in a decorative period. And it should comfort literary aspirants that if he had been a better writer, he would long since have been forgotten.

Hugo Yarnold: Little man with a big heart

There was a match between Somerset and Gloucestershire, at Bath 20 years or so ago, when Gloucestershire were making quiet, steady progress on a peaceful Saturday afternoon. Somerset made a bowling change. Bryant was brought on to bowl to Milton. Yarnold was moving to the umpiring position at square-leg.

I was broadcasting radio commentary. We were not getting very much commentary time in those days, and Robert Hudson, then Director of Outside Broadcasts, had devised a scheme by which we might get a little more of the action. This required commentators to record passages of exciting play, in advance of the next scheduled transmission, so that even if the play then proved to be dull we would have some moments of drama on which to fall back. The difficulty was, of course, that you can never tell when, in cricket, the exciting moments are going to occur and much effort was abortively expended by commentators and engineers on wrong guesses. However, I felt that I was on a good bet that day at Bath. There had been much controversy about 'throwing'. Bryant was already a suspect thrower, and Yarnold known to be a stern judge. So we switched the machine on.

Bryant was a slow left-armer, who meant no physical harm to any batsman, and did none. But he did have an odd action. The arm was bent, in a kind of upward jerk, especially when he tried to flight the ball. Yarnold watched him from square-leg, for the second ball crossed over to deep point, went back to square-leg and no-balled the third. He went on no-balling him. His calls were resonant and picked up clearly by the effects microphone. It gave me good marks with Robert Hudson when it was broadcast a little later on.

I cannot now remember how many balls that over took to complete, but it must have been nearly a dozen. I do remember the gentle refusal of Arthur Milton to try to hit them. He sensed the distress of a fellow professional. I do not think that Bryant ever bowled in first-class cricket again.

Yes, Yarnold was a stern man, when he was umpiring. He was reluctant to approve appeals. I remember Eric Hill, one afternoon when the Somerset bowlers had been flailing their arms and voices about in vain, pronouncing judgment: 'This man Yarnold,' he said in his dark brown voice, 'is a Notter.'

He was a good umpire, all the same, and before that a good cricketer. … His health was a bother and he had to have a severe operation, both kneecaps removed, during his active career. It was courageous of him to continue and courageous too to take up umpiring, with its nagging, prolonged strains on the legs. He umpired in three Tests.

A flying visit

There had been heavy rain overnight and no play was possible before lunch. However, the morning was not devoid of incident, since Botham arrived on the ground in his helicopter, and subsequently took off again, it seemed to me a little erratically. He was not spurned. The small boys cheered him. But it would be an exaggeration to say his reception was rapturous.

Grumpy reflections

All reports from Taunton should carry the comment "E and OE". The scorecards, lavishly presented in a new, dull and expensive magazine, are always inaccurate. So is the scoreboard, which appears to follow a different system of numeration: whether more accurate or less it is hard to say, because half the figures are too small to be perceived by an ageing eye.

The public address system has always been a Taunton joke, and a much-hailed revision of its mechanism has reduced its quality dramatically. (And the batsmen wear helmets, which often make them indistinguishable, not that that is a particular fault of Taunton.) These are rather grumpy reflections on what was not, on the whole, an unpleasant day.

Even if he is Boycott

Roebuck finally declared at 279, short of the Somerset first-wicket record of 346, set up by Hewett and Palairet in 1892. I am sure that with a little more time Roebuck would have gone for it. He likes batting, which is always a good quality in a cricketer, yes, even if he is Boycott or PJK Gibbs.

JULY: Gloucestershire v Sussex at Bristol (last day)

Breathless hush in the gloaming as Sussex fall to narrow defeat

BRISTOL: Gloucestershire (22 pts) beat Sussex (2 pts) by one wicket

There's a breathless hush in the Close tonight –
Ten to make and the match to win –
A bumping pitch and a blinding light,
An hour to play and the last man in.

I could not help being reminded of these lines written by Sir Henry Newbolt of a match on a ground less than a couple of miles away from this one, as the Gloucestershire last pair, Lawrence and Russell, stood with 10 runs to make in the gloaming last night. It had been a close, fluctuating game all through, and it seemed a shame that anyone should lose it.

Sussex began at 186 for three, still 62 runs behind in their second innings. They batted usefully, and so long as Parker was there, had a chance of setting Gloucestershire a target. He batted until the score was 290, and his own 120. I happened to meet him at lunchtime, and he said he thought his form was improving, and that Sussex would win the match.

They certainly batted on bravely to 341, a total which left Gloucestershire 94 to win, in 55 overs. They lost Wright and Stovold for nine runs. When the score was 17, Babington took a hat-trick. The batsmen were Bainbridge, Curran and Lloyds. A useful trio at any time.

The score then ascended with hops to 82, when Graveney was the ninth man out. Then in came Lawrence. Imran was bowling. Lawrence hit him for a massive six over square leg, and somehow or other the rest of the runs were scrambled.

And it's not for the sake of a ribbon'd coat
Or the selfish hope of a season's fame
But his Captain's hand on his shoulder smote –
'Play up! Play up! And play the game!'

It was really, I suppose, a bit too much of me to unload Newbolt on a county cricket match. But that was the impression I did bring from it, although I still feel it might have been better had the match been a tie.

GLOUCESTERSHIRE	350 for six declared (Alleyne 116*, Stovold 62, Tomlins 51, Wright 46, Russell 45*)
	94 for nine (Russell 23*, Babington 4-18, Imran 4-42)
SUSSEX	102 (Reeve 27, Graveney 4-17, Lawrence 4-34)
	341 (Parker 120, CM Wells 50, Imran 47, Green 35, Reeve 31, Lloyds 5-111, Walsh 4-95)

Harden and Marks set about Sussex

TAUNTON: Somerset have scored 315 for eight against Sussex

Rain was spreading from the west, in the phrase often used in the morning weather forecast, but it was not actually falling in the west and we got up to a sunny day. Because so much rain had previously fallen, play was delayed for a few minutes at the start. Roebuck, perhaps discouraged by some recent experiments in captaincy, decided to bat, and was, in the end, justified.

There were damp patches at both ends of the pitch, which the batsmen spent much time patting smooth, and the bowlers perhaps seeking to stir up. They always had looks of the utmost innocence when the umpires, as they occasionally did, investigated.

Two wickets fell quickly, those of Wyatt and Felton. However, the pitch grew easier, Roebuck began to settle down and Richards, who has had several disappointing performances lately, seemed as if he was determined to play an innings.

Just before lunch, Richards was caught at the wicket, trying to glance to leg. He looked cross, but I do not think it was more than crossness with himself.

Just after lunch, Roebuck was out, leg-before, a decision he accepted with his customary stoicism. That was 108 for four, the game evenly balanced, but during the afternoon Harden and Marks batted equably in continuing sunshine. They had 200 up by tea. Harden scored most of the runs to begin with, but Marks had caught up with him by the time they were both in the seventies.

Marks progressed mainly by his drives through what is called the V triangle. He has always been good at these. Harden's strokes were rather more varied. They both became more sparing in attacking shots as they neared their hundreds. Marks was the first to reach his, just. It was, I think, his first hundred in a county championship match, though he has scored profusely elsewhere.

I remember Marks being dropped from the England side after scoring three consecutive Test fifties, something which can hardly have happened to anyone else. Harden followed him to the honour of a century in the following over. Both had done exceptionally well, and the Somerset crowd – and I have no doubt their captain – had every reason to be proud of them.

Cheers for man at The Oval

TAUNTON: Sussex, with nine first innings wickets in hand, are 267 runs behind Somerset

Again, I was greeted in the morning by the familiar BBC announcement, that rain was spreading from the West, but again some sun was shining through my lonely Taunton room. Again, the weather took some time to catch up with its forecast.

We had no rain until nearly lunch time. By then, against Somerset's 333, Sussex had scored 66 for 1. It was not, however, altogether a dull morning. From time to time a cheer, assisted by transistors, reminded us of the progress of Botham at The Oval.

During the afternoon the umpires stole chances between prolonged showers to go out and inspect the wicket. But at four o'clock, when it was drizzling again, admitted there was no more chance of play. So again, today, it will be up to the ingenuity of the captains if they are to contrive a finish. Fortunately, we have two ingenious men available. But no amount of ingenuity, not even from the habitat of Rutherford and Leavis, or to name another respectable Cambridge man, Bernard Manning, can prevent rain from spreading from or, more importantly, staying in the West.

Manning was author of 'The Hymns of Wesley and Watts'

There was no play on the third day.

SOMERSET *captain: P.M. Roebuck (Millfield and Emmanuel College, Cambridge)*
333 (Marks 110, Harden 108, Richards 41, Roebuck 39, Pigott 5-81, CM Wells 3-77)

SUSSEX *captain: P.W.G. Parker (Collyer's and St Catharine's College, Cambridge)*
66 for one

The last years

By the time 1987 came around, Alan Gibson was in no state even to contemplate going back on the circuit. It wasn't quite the end of his writing. In the following year, I persuaded him to edit a selection of the huge number of surviving radio scripts that he possessed from his time with the BBC, for publication as what we called *A West Country Treasury*. But his efforts were half-hearted, and never amounted to much more than substituting 'we' for 'I' in the text, in recognition that this was supposed to be a collaborative effort by the two of us.

For the rest, it was a sad and seemingly inevitable decline. He moved from his flat to sheltered housing and then to a succession of nursing homes, never with happy results. If he ever got even half a chance, he would take himself off to the nearest pub, get roaring drunk and make a scene. Then he had a series of minor strokes, which confined him to a wheelchair, and in his final years – the crowning irony – this man who had such a gift for words, and such a breadth of knowledge to underpin it, had once been so fluent, who could charm the birds out of the trees with his eloquence and wit, was reduced to mumbling incoherence. His disintegration was no less tragic for the fact that it was largely self-inflicted.

There were some happy moments on the way down. He would sometimes be taken by kind people to the County Ground, where he would sit with his back to the play in the Stragglers, reading a favourite old book and nursing the inevitable whisky. I shall always be grateful to Richard Walsh, who now reports Somerset cricket for the local papers, for regularly taking Alan out to the White Hart at Corfe in his final years, and arranging one or two reunions of the JJ? Society, which gave him much pleasure. And there was a final interview on BBC Radio Bristol, after the publication of *A West Country Treasury*, when the late and much lamented Roger Bennett recalled the great days of *Good Morning*. For a few short minutes, the glazed eyes brightened and the ashes of his talent glowed briefly red.

Alan was seven weeks short of his 74th birthday when he died in a nursing home in Taunton of a chest infection on April 10, 1997. David Foot provided an eloquent and honest tribute at the funeral, in Silver Street Baptist Church, which Alan had often visited as a boy at Taunton School, and I was pleased that Peter Baxter, the producer of *Test Match Special*, had travelled down from London to represent the BBC. After the service and committal, a small group of family and friends adjourned to the Old Pavilion at the County Ground to share reminiscences, to drink to Alan's memory and to reflect, not so much on what he had achieved in his life – although that was considerable – but on the pleasure which he had brought to countless people through his writing and broadcasting.

Alan Gibson may not have been in the very first rank of cricket writers as analyst, critic and reporter of the game itself, but no-one – not even the great RC Robertson-Glasgow – has captured the atmosphere of a day's county cricket, and the characters, on and off the field, who make it what it is, quite so evocatively and amusingly. If it was an uneventful day on the field of play, then so much the better, for it gave him more scope for the weather, his running jokes, literary allusions, hobby horses and adventures in getting to the ground. What we are left with is not a photograph in words of the day's play, so much as a painting of it: usually an impressionist painting, occasionally something distinctly more abstract. It was the way in which he offered his readers so much more than the mere facts which sets him apart from his contemporaries, and which makes his writings about the game as rich and enjoyable now as they were at the time.

Alan Gibson's last contribution to The Cricketer 1992

Remembering John Arlott

Alan Gibson wrote fitfully for The Cricketer through 1987 and 1988, mostly in his series Cricketers Remembered. *Then, for the issue of February 1992, he submitted one last piece: in memory of John Arlott, who had died.*

I first met John Arlott at The County Ground in Taunton, where I was in the late summer of 1948 – the occasion being my first cricket broadcast. John had begun cricket broadcasting before me and had done it extremely well, under the guidance of Nicky Crocker who was Head of Outside Broadcasting for the West of England Region at that time.

The Australians were in Taunton to play one of their final tour matches against Somerset. They scored a lot of runs as they normally did. Hamence had made a lot of runs that season but not made the Test team nor had he made a century. He'd got to 99, when the dreaded leg-spinner Miles Coope got him out.

I was in the commentary box – well, actually in front of the box, high above the compact County Ground – for much of the time whilst John was doing his commentary. He was already well known as a commentator and a man of great distinction.

When the time came for me to make my broadcasting debut that day he asked me if I wanted him to stay in the box or to clear out. That was typical of John, showing kindness and understanding to a youngster learning the trade. Even though you knew you weren't going to be as good, he gave you a sense of importance. His most endearing qualities were his kindness and his generosity in word and deed. He would never speak badly of anyone.

That match in Taunton was after the fifth Test match, and during the day John asked to broadcast a fifteen-minute review of the first-class counties for the BBC Overseas Service. He made a flawless broadcast, dealing with each county in turn with only the County Championship table as his prompt.

In his review he mentioned, of course, Len Hutton who had already scored eight centuries that season and was to

end up with ten, more than anyone else in the country. Len Hutton was, of course, the greatest English batsman since Hobbs. Since the war, during which he was injured, he had re-established himself as the batting primate of all England – a fact that the Yorkshire contingency, which includes myself, delighted in.

The careers of John Arlott and Len Hutton are for me very closely linked. During the 1948 season Len Hutton was approaching his peak in the same way that John was. Whenever I think of John, I think of the Hutton period – as do many others. People used to mimic him, 'Aar'rgh, and Hutton has got another hundred.'

John did, of course, do some television commentary later on, but I don't think he liked it very much. It wasn't his style. He had a gift for matching cricket to sound commentary in a way that nobody else has since, nor has anyone achieved with television. He was always very proud of his mastery of sound radio broadcasting.

With his granddaughter Joanna

I remember a day at The Oval when an English batsman was injured, and the physiotherapist rushed out to attend him. It seemed to me that he was administering a pain-killing injection. Trevor Bailey by my side said, 'No, I think it's a spray.' John Arlott, standing behind us for he had just vacated the commentator's seat, leant forward and said, 'No, not too bad, I think. Not past spraying for.'

Cricket is still worth a spray of hope, and even a prayer. I think I shall risk a private petition to the Lord, not for a hundred runs, not for a Yorkshire championship, for my native county, though still dear to me, seems determined to make its land (I write in 1984) 'desolate, and an hissing; every one that passeth thereby shall be astonished and hiss because of all the plagues thereof.' Yea, they will even wag their heads at the county which men once called the perfection of beauty. I am afraid I am a Jeremiah now as far as Yorkshire cricket is concerned.

But, I repeat, cricket is worth a prayer. I call upon Jim Swanton and John Woodcock to join in. Jim is a High Churchman, so high that he reminded me of the slight transliteration of Montgomery's hymn, 'For ever with the Lord', which ends, you remember, very nearly

And nightly pitch my moving tent
A day's march nearer Rome

though he still clings to the Pusey bank. Johnny is patron of the church of Longparish, where he valiantly clings to the 1662 liturgy, and has promised that one day I may preach, miserable Baptist though I am. So between us we will make quite an ecumenical trio of petitioners, and my suggestion is that we don't worry the Lord with everything at once, but just put in a word for fewer bouncers and more leg-spinners. There is a lot more to say, of course, but Cardus was sensible in concentrating on the middle stump in the middle of the over.

Whether the prayer is answered or not, I will still give thanks to the Giver of all Good for countless happy days at cricket, the game with which I grew up.

Growing Up with Cricket

INDEX OF CRICKET GROUNDS

INDEX OF PEOPLE

(Alan Gibson and his family are not included)

Fairfield Books

Full list of publications

(currently out of print)*

Stephen Chalke, **Runs in the Memory – County Cricket in the 1950s**

Stephen Chalke, **Caught in the Memory – County Cricket in the 1960s** *

Stephen Chalke, with Bryan 'Bomber' Wells, **One More Run** *

Wombwell Cricket Lovers' Society Book of the Year for 2000

David Foot, **Fragments of Idolatry – From 'Crusoe' to Kid Berg**

Stephen Chalke, **At the Heart of English Cricket – The Life and Memories of Geoffrey Howard** *

Cricket Society Book of the Year for 2001

John Barclay, **The Appeal of the Championship – Sussex in the Summer of 1981** *

David Foot, **Harold Gimblett, Tormented Genius of Cricket** *

Stephen Chalke, **Guess My Story – The Life and Opinions of Keith Andrew, Cricketer**

Stephen Chalke & Derek Hodgson, **No Coward Soul – The Remarkable Story of Bob Appleyard**

Wisden Cricketers' Almanack Book of the Year for 2003

Wombwell Cricket Lovers' Society Book of the Year for 2003

Douglas Miller, **Born to Bowl – The Life and Times of Don Shepherd** *

Stephen Chalke, **A Sporting Scrapbook – The Wimbledon Club 1854-2004**

Douglas Miller, **Charles Palmer – More than just a Gentleman**

Stephen Chalke, **Ken Taylor – Drawn to Sport**

David Foot & Ivan Ponting, **Sixty Summers – Somerset Cricket since the War** *

National Sporting Club / Cricket Writers' Club Book of the Year for 2006

Peter Walker, **It's Not Just Cricket** *Wombwell Cricket Lovers' Society Book of the Year for 2006*

Stephen Chalke, **A Summer of Plenty – George Herbert Hirst in 1906** *

Stephen Chalke, **Tom Cartwright – The Flame Still Burns**

Wisden Cricketers' Almanack Book of the Year for 2007

Simon Lister, **Supercat – The Authorised Biography of Clive Lloyd**

Stephen Chalke, **Five Five Five – Holmes and Sutcliffe in 1932**

John Barclay, **Life Beyond the Airing Cupboard** *MCC / Cricket Society Book of the Year for 2008*

Stephen Chalke, **The Way It Was – Glimpses of English Cricket's Past**

National Sporting Club / Cricket Writers' Club Book of the Year for 2008

Mark Wagh, **Pavilion to Crease ... and Back**

Patrick Murphy, **The Centurions – From Grace to Ramprakash**

Dudley Doust, **Bradley Brook – An American Walks Down An English Stream**

Anthony Gibson, **Of Didcot and the Demon – The Cricketing Times of Alan Gibson**

If you would like more details of any of these,
or would like to placed on the mailing list for future publications, please contact:
Fairfield Books 17 George's Road, Bath BA1 6EY telephone 01225-335813